Microsoft Word for Windows: The Complete Reference

Mary Campbell

Osborne **McGraw-Hill**

Berkeley New York St. Louis San Francisco
Auckland Bogotá Hamburg London Madrid
Mexico City Milan Montreal New Delhi Panama City
Paris São Paulo Singapore Sydney
Tokyo Toronto

Osborne **McGraw-Hill**
2600 Tenth Street
Berkeley, California 94710
U.S.A.

For information on software, translations, or book distributors outside of the
U.S.A., please write to Osborne McGraw-Hill at the above address.

Microsoft Word for Windows: The Complete Reference

1234567890 DOC 9987654

ISBN 0-07-881948-2

Contents

PART III

Special Features

5

Exchanging Data with Other Applications 651

6

Desktop Publishing in Word 673

Acknowledgments

The efforts of many individuals played an important part in completing this book. Without the team of experts who lent their assistance with this book, it would not have been possible. I would like to offer my special thanks to the following individuals:

Gabrielle Lawrence and Elizabeth Reinhardt for all of their hard work in helping to meet a schedule that was almost impossible. Their knowledge of Word for Windows 2 and 6 were an invaluable help with this project.

Bob Kermish, who did a fantastic job of reviewing the manuscript. Bob's suggestions helped to insure that the book met the needs of users at all levels.

Scott Rogers, Acquisitions Editor, for his help on all phases of the project from lining up beta software to reading over chapters to insure that they were clear.

Edith Rex, Project Editor, for an incredible job of keeping all the pieces of this project together and moving it through the system despite almost impossible time schedules. Special thanks to Carol Henry, Janice Paris, Wendy Rinaldi, Claire Splan, Carl Wikander, and Judy Ziajka who did a wonderful job of copy editing. Vanessa Miller and Kayla Sussell did a great job proofreading.

Tracy Van Hoof at Microsoft continually provided everything we needed to complete this project.

The graphics you see in the book came from several sources. Jim Anderton at A. J. Graphics (800/782-7321) provided the samples of Yesterday's Art. Jim markets an interesting collection of clip art and provided some of the clip art for this book. His graphics are the ones that look like sketches. Jim Haney at New Vision Technologies Inc. (617/727-8184) provided Presentation Task Force that has 3,500 pieces of CGM clipart to add to Word documents. Another source of graphics was CorelDRAW! that this book used for graphics editing features that go beyond the capabilities of Word's drawing features. Julia Galla and Micheal Bellefeuille at CorelDRAW! were particularly helpful. CorelDRAW! 4.0 also includes 750 additional TrueType fonts that Windows applications such as Word can use and 18,000 pieces of clipart.

Introduction

This book is for all Word for Windows users. If you have been using an earlier version of Word for Windows you will find that it will help you make a quick transition to the new release. Chapter 4 includes coverage of all of the new features as well as existing features that have new options or procedures for completing them. As you are ready to look at more advanced applications you will find more ideas in Chapter 5 through 8 on how to get more benefit from desktop publishing, file transfer, macros, mail merge, and workgroup options.

If you are new to Word for Windows you will find the help you need in the first three chapters to get you up and running quickly. You will then be ready to access any of the commands and features in Chapter 4.

How This Book Is Organized

The information in this book is organized into eight chapters. The first three provide the basics to get you started with Word. You will learn how to create, save, and print a Word document with the instructions provided. You will even learn some of the formatting basics needed to tailor the appearance of your document to meet your exact needs.

Chapter 4 is the next chapter and largest section of the book. It is a comprehensive command reference. It is organized alphabetically making it easy to look up any specific topic or feature. Cross-referenced entries are amply provided throughout Chapter 4 to make it easy to find related topics.

There are consistent sections that can be used within each topic although many of them are optional. The sections you will find throughout the command reference are

- *Procedures* to guide you through the steps you will use to perform the features

- *Options* that describe how you can change the many options for a Word feature

- *Hints* that point out interesting points about the feature

- *Related Topics* to find out more information on similar Word features

The last four chapters provide more detail on some specialized topics. They cover desktop publishing, sharing data with other applications, macros and mail merge, and workgroups and networking. These chapters have more of an application perspective and provide specific examples in each area. The appendices cover installation and provide reference information on templates, icons, and Word commands for WordPerfect users.

Conventions Used

For features available in both Word for Windows 2 and Word for Windows 6, the instructions provided will work for both releases. If there are differences in the procedures for utilizing a specific feature, the difference will be provided for Word for Windows 2 to make it easy to use this reference if you are a Word for Windows 2 user.

If you prefer to use the keyboard to make menu selections, you will find the mnemonic that can be used for menu selection underlined. The underlining matches the underlining for Word for Windows 6. In most cases, this is the same underlining used in Word for Windows 2.

All function keys and other keyboard selections are shown in small capital letters. For example, you will see F1 and ENTER when you need to press a specific key. If you need to press two keys at the same time, they will be joined with a plus symbol (+) as in SHIFT+ENTER. If two keys must be pressed sequentially, a comma (,) is used to separate them as in HOME, LEFT ARROW.

Any data preceded by the word "enter" or "type" is shown in boldface. This will clarify exactly how much data you are expected to type.

About the Rules Boxes

Over the years I have taught thousands of people how to use word processing programs. I have listened to the requests of many students in writing this book by incorporating some of the information they indicated they wanted close at hand such as state code abbreviations and rules for capitalization. Although I couldn't answer all of the requests and still cover the needed Word features, I did try to include the things that were requested most frequently. All of the additional information has been placed in rules boxes scattered throughout the text:

Rule Box	Page
Rules for Entering Numbers	29
Rules for Comma Placement	45
Common Abbreviations	68-69
Rules for Creating Correctly Spelled Plurals	87
Rules for Using the Correct Date Format	146
State Code Abbreviations	185
Rules for Correcting Wordiness and Redundancy	255
Problem Homonyms to Watch For	256
Footnote Forms	268
Rules for Adjectives and Adverbs	306-307
Rules for Using Pronouns Correctly	309-310
Rules for Hyphenation	342
Forms of Address	407
Rules for Abbreviating Degrees and Professional Associations	408
Rules for Quotes	568
Aligning Entries in Tables	603

Rule Box	Page
Problem Verbs	613
Embedding and Linking Data	659-660
Rules for Using Specialized Characters	680-681
Things to Watch Out for When Writing Macros	715
Adding Emotional Impact to Your E-mail Messages	759

These rules boxes present information relating to grammar and punctuation to conform with commonly accepted business standards. Sometimes this information might conform to *The Chicago Manual of Style,* 14th Edition (The University of Chicago Press, 1993), *Webster's Secretarial Handbook* (Merriam-Webster), *The Gregg Reference Manual,* 7th Edition (Glencoe, 1992), and *Webster's Guide to Business Correspondence Handbook* (Merriam-Webster, 1988). Where all of the sources agree, common business practice would dictate the use of the common suggestion. In other cases, there is a discrepancy in the advice presented by the various sources. Since the *Chicago Manual of Style* is oriented toward the publishing industry and the Webster's references are oriented toward business correspondence it is no surprise that they might differ. The information presented might conform to some of the rules from each or a common business practice may suggest yet another solution.

What's New in Word for Windows 6

Microsoft Word for Windows has many new features as well as retooled features. These new features make the leading Windows word processing program even better. Some of the most important new features are

Feature	Function
AutoCaption	Creates captions and cross-references.
AutoCorrect	Fixes your spelling mistakes automatically after you teach it how. Can also expand abbreviations to their full form.
AutoFormat	Applies formatting to styles and other text once you tell it the kind of text you entered.
AutoText	Functions as a glossary to add boilerplate text.
Bulleted and Numbered Lists	Lists are easier than ever to create.

Feature	Function
Copying Formats	The Format Painter button can copy formats.
Drag and Drop	Text and graphics can be dragged from one location and dropped in place in another location.
Drop Caps	Dropped capital letters or words as well as graphics can be added to a paragraph for visual interest.
Find	You can search for non-printing characters such as page breaks and tabs.
Forms	You can create forms for completion on the screen.
Mail Merge	Simplified creation of form letters, additional features that let you create envelopes or catalogs. Bar codes can be added to envelopes to show the ZIP code with a POSTNET bar code for U.S. destinations.
Newspaper Columns	Columns can be unequal width.
Numbered Headings	Numbers can be placed automatically when you add or delete a heading.
Page Layout Options	Improved header and footer options.
Print Preview	Thumbnail sketches provide an overview look at the document.
Options	The Tools	Options command has tabbed selections that make it easy to customize how Word works.
Shortcut Menus	The right mouse button accesses frequently used commands.
Status Bar	You can change views or switch between insert and overstrike by clicking the status bar buttons.
Styles	New character style options let you alter individual characters easily. You can copy styles, macros, and toolbars with the Organizer.
Templates	Many new pre-defined documents to give you instant letters, fax cover sheets, and other forms.

Feature	Function
Toolbars	New toolbars offer support for specialized features. You can display or hide these toolbars to customize your screen display.
Undo	Select one or more items to undo from a list.
Wizards	Wizards lead you through the paces for the completion of tables and some templates.
Workgroup features	Include several features including electronic mail support, master documents, forms for onscreen completion, annotation, and comparing versions.

THE
COMPLETE

REFERENCE

PART ONE
Word Basics

CHAPTER 1

The Word Window

Before you create your first document in Word for Windows, you need to know some fundamental information about both the Word and Windows programs. This chapter covers the basics about Windows applications; windows, menus, and dialog boxes; mouse and keyboard techniques; and how to use on-line help. If you have used other Windows applications, you will be familiar with some of the information presented in this chapter, and can skim through it quickly to look for items that may not be familiar. If you are new to Windows and Windows applications, you will want to take your time and read through the chapter slowly—preferably with

Word for Windows on the screen in front of you—to familiarize yourself with the tools that you will need to use Word productively. Learning these basics will make you more comfortable as you begin learning how to create a Word letter or report.

In Chapter 1, you will learn how to start and end a Word for Windows session. You will find out what the various screen elements will do for you, and explore fundamental techniques for using the mouse and keyboard. You will also learn about common screen elements such as the status bar, the toolbars, the ruler, and dialog boxes. To complete your introduction to the basic building blocks, you will learn about Word's on-line Help features. After reading this chapter you will be ready to complete your first document by following the directions in Chapter 2.

TIP: Most features described in this book apply to both Word for Windows 2 and Word for Windows 6. Only when a specific version is mentioned does a feature apply to only that version. Word does not have a version 3, 4, or 5 for Windows, so the newest version of the Word programs for DOS, Windows, and the Macintosh all have the same version number: 6.

Throughout the first three chapters you will see the icon that appears at the left of this paragraph. The text accompanying this icon will always refer you to Word features that are more advanced than the basics offered in the chapter.

Starting and Ending a Word for Windows Session

To use Word for Windows, you must have three programs loaded into the memory of your system: DOS, Windows, and Word for Windows. DOS must be started first and is automatically loaded when you turn on your computer. Depending on how your system is set up, Windows may load automatically, too. It is possible that you may have to enter one or more commands to start Windows. You may need to type **WIN** at the DOS prompt and press ENTER to start it, or you may need to precede the WIN command with **CD \WINDOWS** and press ENTER to first activate the Windows directory. Try the simplest approach first.

Starting a Word for Windows Session

Once Windows is up and running, opening Word for Windows to start a Word for Windows session is easy. First, in the Windows Program Manager, open the program group window that contains the Word for Windows program item. This is most likely the group named Microsoft Office, Applications, or Windows Applications. You can do this by clicking the program group's icon, or by selecting the group from the Window menu. The underlined letter represents the letter that you can use in Word for Windows 6 along with the ALT key to make your selection. This underlined letter is called a mnemonic and is used for menus, pull-down menu options, and dialog box options when the keyboard is used. In many instances, Word for Windows 2 will use the same mnemonic, but in a few cases it is different. After selecting the program group, select the Word for Windows program item, labeled "Microsoft Word," either by double-clicking it with the mouse or by moving the highlight to it with the keyboard arrow keys and then pressing ENTER.

NOTE: Unless specifically noted that Word for DOS is the intended reference, you can assume that Word always refers to Word for Windows.

When Word has finished loading, you may see a Tip of the Day (explained later, in "Accessing Help"); you can remove this by pressing ENTER or clicking OK.

NOTE: It is recommended that you have 2MB of memory to run Word by itself, plus an additional 2MB (total 4MB) if you want to run Word along with other Windows applications.

Ending a Word for Windows Session

To end a Word for Windows session, choose Exit from the File menu. Ending the session closes all open document windows (you'll learn about these shortly) and the Word application window. If you have not saved the current document or any document you have open, Word prompts you about saving it, to prevent your losing unsaved work as you exit Word. At this point you can save the document, using the Save dialog box.

The Word Application Window

Once you start Word, your first screen will look like Figure 1-1; this is the Word application window. This window is normally *maximized,* which means it fills your entire screen—you do not see the windows of other open Windows applications, or the Program Manager.

The Word window contains a document window (described just below), which is also maximized. When a document window is maximized, that document takes up the entire space of the Word window. If you want to see more than one document at a time, you can make the current document window smaller. Most of the time, however, you will find that you work with both the Word window and the document window maximized, because you are usually only working on one document at a time and you can see more of it this way.

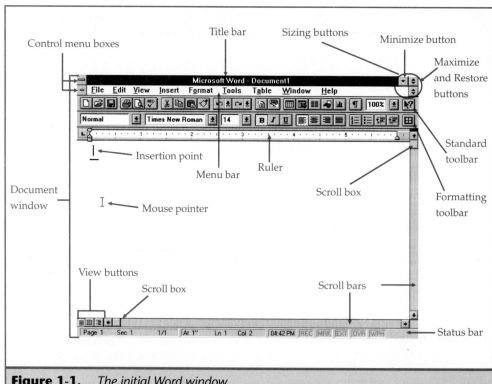

Figure 1-1.   *The initial Word window*

Document Windows

A *document window* contains all of your text for a memo, report, or chapter. Word for Windows lets you have many documents open at one time, each one in its own document window. You can quickly switch and transfer data among multiple open documents, or compare one document to another. The document window that is at the top of the stack that you are working on is called the *active window.* It is the one that contains the insertion point (or cursor), and its title bar has a different color or intensity than the other title bars.

Elements of the Word Window

The Word window has many different elements. At first it might seem a bit cluttered, but each element is an important tool that is ready when you need it. The elements of the screen are organized to make them easy to use—just as you might organize the objects on your desk. Figure 1-1 shows the Word window with the following items labeled: title bar, control menu boxes, menu bar, scroll bars, ruler, standard and formatting toolbars, status bar, insertion point, and mouse pointer.

   The window for Word for Windows 2 is similar to what you see in Figure 1-1 and has most of the same components.

   In the sections that follow, you will take a closer look at how each of these tools can make your Word for Windows sessions productive and efficient.

The Title Bar

The title bar appears at the top of the window, and describes the window's contents. With a document window maximized in the Word window, as it is in Figure 1-1, Word's title bar shows the contents of both the program window, "Microsoft Word," and the name of the maximized document, "Document1." If the document window were not maximized, the document window would have a separate title bar, containing the name of the document.

   Besides describing the window's contents, the title bar contains the program window's *control menu box* on the left end and one or two *sizing buttons* on the right end. In a maximized document window, the document window's control menu box appears on the left end of Word's menu bar (described in a later section). When the document window is not maximized, the document window's control menu box appears at the left end of the title bar. Either control menu box can display a menu of options or close the window.

Later in this chapter you will learn how the sizing buttons let you change the size of a window (maximizing, minimizing, and restoring it). A title bar will show one or two of these buttons, but not all three.

The Menu Bar

The menu bar offers a horizontal list of menus; these menus are the primary method of accessing Word commands. Most Word features are available through the menus. You can access the menus with either the keyboard or the mouse. Figure 1-2 shows what the Help menu looks like when it is "pulled down" from the menu bar.

To pull down a menu with the mouse, click the menu title in the menu bar. Then click the desired menu command or option to select it from the pull-down menu.

Using the keyboard, you press ALT to first activate the menu bar. To pull down one of the menus, press the letter that is underlined in the menu title, such as H for Help. Once the pull-down menu is open, press the underlined letter of the menu command or option you wish to use. You can also press the arrow keys

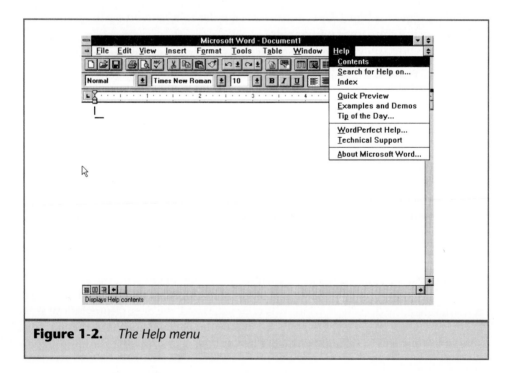

Figure 1-2.   *The Help menu*

to move horizontally among menus in the menu bar or vertically among the commands in a pulled-down menu. As you move from menu to menu or command to command, the status bar will display a description of the highlighted item. To select the highlighted menu or command, press ENTER.

NOTE: *All of the menu items in this book show the underlined letter that Word for Windows 6 uses. In Word for Windows 2 many of the same letters are underlined, although some are different. In this book, Word commands are expressed as the series of selections from the menus; for example, File | Save means selecting File from the menu bar and then choosing Save.*

The Standard Toolbar

Word has several toolbars. The *Standard toolbar* displays buttons representing the most popular Word features. By clicking one of these buttons with the mouse, you can quickly access the feature. Although you can also select these features from menus, using either the keyboard or mouse, clicking the button in the Standard toolbar is quicker. You must have a mouse to use any toolbar.

In Figure 1-1 the toolbar appears at the top of the window, under the menu bar. Word for Windows 6 lets you move it, however, to another location. You can also remove the toolbar altogether if you are not using it or if you wish to display more of the document in the window. In Word for Windows 2, you can toggle between showing and hiding the Standard toolbar by using the View | Toolbars command. When you use this command in Word for Windows 6, you must select the Standard toolbar as one of the toolbars to display before you select OK to complete the command.

TIP: *The status bar will display a description of a particular button on the toolbar. In Word for Windows 2, to display the purpose of a toolbar button, move the mouse pointer to the button, then press and hold down the mouse button. If you move the pointer off the button before releasing the mouse button, the button is not selected. In Word for Windows 6, when you move the mouse pointer to a toolbar button, a description appears in the status bar. When you move the mouse pointer to a button for more than a second or two, the name of the button is displayed next to the button in addition to the status bar entry.*

The features invoked when you click toolbar buttons are introduced in Chapter 4. Word for Windows 6 has seven toolbars that you can display by right-clicking the standard toolbar and then selecting from the shortcut menu. Several of Word's features, such as View | Outline and View | Headers/Footers, also display specialized toolbars. Also, Word for Windows 6 lets you create your own custom toolbars. The "Toolbars" section in Chapter 4 explains how to switch to other toolbars, how to reposition or remove the Word for Windows 6 toolbars, and how to change the items available on a toolbar.

The Formatting Toolbar or Ribbon

Underneath the Standard toolbar is the *Formatting toolbar* (in Word for Windows 6) or *ribbon* (in Word for Windows 2). The Formatting toolbar and the ribbon provide many of the features needed to format text in a document.

You can use the toolbar/ribbon to make characters and paragraphs look different. You can apply styles to your text, change the typeface or size of selected text, change the alignment of paragraphs, or apply boldface, italic, or underlining to text. The Formatting toolbar or ribbon is designed to be used with a mouse, but you can also use keyboard shortcuts to access these features.

The Ruler

The *ruler* tells you how your document is laid out on the page, showing you where the margins of a paragraph are, any paragraph indentation settings, and tab stops that you can quickly move to by pressing the TAB key. The ruler appears horizontally beneath the ribbon or Formatting toolbar when the document is maximized. When the document window is not maximized, the ruler appears at the top of the document window. In Word for Windows 6, you can also set a document to display a vertical ruler.

To learn about how to change ruler settings with the mouse, look under "Ruler" in Chapter 4. To learn about the tab stops that a ruler displays, see "Tabs" in Chapter 4.

The Scroll Bars

Scroll bars, which appear at the bottom and right of the window shown in Figure 1-1, let you to move through large documents quickly. With a mouse, you can click the arrow buttons on these scroll bars to change the part of the document currently displayed in the window. The small box that appears within the scroll bars is the *scroll box*; it indicates the relative position in the document of the section you are viewing. Chapter 2 explains how to use the scroll bars to change the section of the document that appears in the window.

The three buttons to the left of the horizontal scroll bar are the View buttons; they allow you to change the way you view the document.

The vertical scroll bar contains, in addition to the arrow buttons and scroll box, a splitter box that you can use to divide a document window into two parts, or panes, as described in Chapter 4. "Viewing Documents" in Chapter 4 also tells you how to use the View buttons to change the view of a document.

The Status Bar

The status bar at the bottom of the window displays information about what is going on in Word. This bar is divided into sections for different kinds of information. The far left end of the status bar tells you what page you are on, which section of the document you are in, and how many pages there are in the whole document. The next section tells you the distance between the top of the page and the current position of your insertion point (cursor), the number of that line, and how many characters there are between the left margin and the current position of your insertion point. Next, Word for Windows 2's status bar tells you the percentage of reduction or magnification of your document on the screen, as compared to its actual size; Word for Windows 6's status bar contains the current time. The sections on the right end of the bar are indicators that show when various features are turned on, such as bold or italic text.

The information in the status bar depends on your current activity. For instance, when you highlight a menu command or point with the mouse to screen elements such as the toolbar buttons, the status bar tells you what task that command or button will perform. When you use certain keyboard shortcuts for commands, such as F2 or SHIFT+F2, the status bar displays a message asking for more information about that command and lets you enter your response. The status bar can also tell you the status of a command as Word is performing it—for example, how much of the document has been saved.

The Insertion Point

The *insertion point* is a marker on the screen that indicates where you are in a document. Another term frequently used for the insertion point is the cursor although Microsoft Word documentation always calls it the insertion point. When you type, the characters you type appear at the insertion point. In addition to this marker, information on the left side of the status bar tells you where the insertion point is in the document (as described earlier). Before entering text, editing text, or doing anything else with your documents, you will want to know exactly where the insertion point is.

Using the Mouse

Using the mouse is the simplest way to get around in Word for Windows. The mouse controls a mouse pointer that moves across the screen as you move the mouse around your desktop. A mouse lets you point to and select objects on the screen to perform actions rather than using the keyboard. This is often called *pointing and clicking*. For example, by pointing and clicking on the scroll bar arrows, you can move through a document quickly. A few actions, such as a SHIFT+click, require the use of the mouse and keyboard at the same time.

Other pointing devices, such as a trackball or stylus, can be used in a similar way.

Mouse Actions

To use the mouse in Word for Windows, you have to master a few basic techniques: *drag, click, right-click,* and *double-click.*

All of these techniques require you to press the mouse button and release it. For dragging, clicking, and double-clicking, you use the left button on the mouse. Only for right-clicking do you use the right mouse button. You will never need the center button of a three-button mouse with Word for Windows.

For clicking, right-clicking, and double-clicking, you *press and quickly release* the mouse button; for dragging (or moving) an object with the mouse, however, you have to *press and hold* the mouse button. Place the mouse pointer on the object you wish to drag. Then press the left mouse button and hold it down. *Without releasing the button,* drag the mouse pointer to where you want the object to appear, and then release the mouse button. In Chapter 2 you will learn how to use dragging to select text in a document.

You can click with the mouse to highlight objects or to select something. Point to the object you want to select, and press the left mouse button once and quickly release it.

Right-clicking is used to open Word for Windows 6's Shortcut menus. You point to an object or location on the screen, and press the *right* mouse button once.

Double-clicking usually selects an object or carries out an action. To double-click an object, point to that object and press the left mouse button twice in quick succession. You may have already used a double-click, on the Microsoft Word icon to start the Word for Windows application.

TIP: You can change the clicking speed required for recognition of a double-click, as well as which mouse button is designated as the primary mouse button (left or right). These changes are made through the Windows Control Panel. If you find that your double-clicks are frequently interpreted by Word as a single click, you can change the double-click speed setting to a lower number to allow more time between clicks. Left-handed people often swap the left/right button setting to make the mouse easier to use with their left hand.

In Chapter 2, you will learn about selecting and rearranging text. In Chapter 3, you will learn about how to change the appearance of selected text. These options will use the mouse actions you have just learned.

Mouse Pointer Shapes

The *mouse pointer* marks the location of the mouse on the screen and shows you which object will be affected by your next mouse action. The mouse pointer changes its shape frequently as you use it. These shapes indicate that certain options are available and tell you various things about what is occurring at the moment. When you know the shapes of the mouse pointer, you can use Word and other Windows applications more efficiently. Table 1-1 shows you some of the mouse pointer shapes and their meanings.

Using the Keyboard

Indeed, your mouse lets you do some things on the screen more easily, but you will also use the keyboard frequently in Word for Windows. As you are typing, you may find it easier to enter a command using a keyboard technique rather than the mouse. Anything that you can do with the mouse can also be done with the keyboard. Word also has many valuable command shortcuts that are

Mouse Pointer	Purpose
▶	Selects the item you are pointing to
I	Moves the insertion point to the text you are pointing to
⧗	Tells you to wait while Windows or the application is busy
⟷	Sizes the window or other object you are pointing to
🖑	Provides more information on the Help topic the hand is pointing to

Table 1-1.   *Mouse pointers and their roles*

accomplished from the keyboard. In addition to using the keyboard to enter text and commands, you use it to move the insertion point in a document to where you want to add or remove text.

There are several available layouts for keyboards. One of the most common is the IBM Enhanced keyboard, shown in Figure 1-3. If you are using another keyboard, you will find the same keys, just in different positions.

Figure 1-3.   *The IBM Enhanced keyboard*

In the next chapter, you will learn about using the keyboard and mouse to move through a document you are creating. Keyboard or mouse: The choice is yours since the results are the same. Use whichever technique you find most convenient.

The Function Keys

The *function keys* are the keys labeled F1 through F10 or F12; on most keyboards these keys are usually positioned along the top. By pressing the function keys, you can quickly perform tasks in Word. Function keys combined with the CTRL, ALT or SHIFT keys provide *keyboard shortcuts* for the most popular features.

Word has assigned tasks to the function keys. An important function key that you will use from the beginning is F1. This key accesses the on-line Help that you will learn more about later in this chapter. The other function keys will be explained when their features are introduced.

TIP: Word assumes that you have 12 function keys. If you have only 10, you can press ALT+F1 in place of F11 and ALT+F2 in place of F12.

Working in Dialog Boxes

Dialog boxes are small windows that appear on your screen when Word needs information from you in order to carry out a command. They contain some objects you have not yet encountered in this introduction to the Word window: command buttons, text boxes, list boxes, option buttons, and check boxes. These objects are identified in Figure 1-4.

The contents of a dialog box will depend on what command or feature you have selected. However, all dialog boxes behave the same—whether you are describing how you want text to appear, the document you want to see on the screen, or the graphic image you want to add, you will do similar things in every dialog box. To make dialog boxes easier to use, Word may even change the display in a dialog box as you make selections, removing components that are no longer appropriate. Once you are familiar with the process of making selections in dialog boxes, you are ready to use the dialog boxes as you employ Word's features. The prompts that appear in a dialog box will clearly identify the information a command or feature is prompting for.

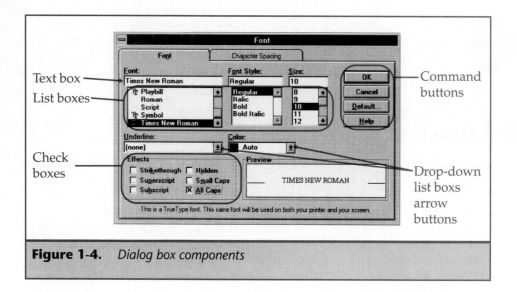

Figure 1-4.   *Dialog box components*

To make a selection within a dialog box, you first move to an element of the
dialog box by clicking it. If you want to use your keyboard, all elements in the
dialog box have an underlined letter. You can move to an element in the dialog
box by pressing ALT and the underlined letter, or by pressing TAB until the
element is highlighted.

Command Buttons

Command buttons appear in every dialog box. When you select one of these
buttons, an action is carried out. If the text on the button displays an ellipsis,
selecting the button opens another dialog box. To select a command button, you
can click it, or you can press ALT and the underlined letter on the button (or press
TAB until the button is highlighted) and then press ENTER.

Two command buttons appear in nearly every dialog box—the OK button
and the Cancel button (see Figure 1-4):

■ Clicking the OK button starts the action for which you opened the dialog
box, using the information you provided in the dialog box. The OK button
has no underlined letter, but you can select it from the keyboard by
pressing ENTER when the button has an extra outline around it, as it does
in Figure 1-4.

■ Clicking the Cancel button closes the dialog box without carrying out any action. You can also select Cancel from the keyboard by pressing ESC.

Text Boxes

Another important element of dialog boxes is the *text box*, into which you can type information. For example, when you use the File | Open command to access existing files, the dialog box that appears will contain a text box for the filename.

Text boxes can occur independently, or can be attached to a list box (explained just below). If a text box is independent, you can type the required information into it. If the text box is attached to a list box, you have a choice: You can either type information directly into the text box, or you can choose an option from the list box, and Word will put that option into the text box.

Sometimes a text box calls for a number to be entered. When a text box has a set of up- and down-arrow buttons on the right side, you can increase or decrease the number in the text box by clicking the appropriate arrow button, as well as by simply typing a new number. This special type of text box is sometimes referred to as a spin box. It is used for setting page margins, for example.

List Boxes

In dialog boxes, you frequently need to make selections from lists. Lists can be in either list boxes or drop-down list boxes (you can see examples of both in Figure 1-4). A list box, such as the Font list box in Figure 1-4, displays a number of choices. When the list is longer than the box, a scroll bar appears at the side of the box, and you can use it to move through the list to find the selection you need. You select an item on the list by clicking it or highlighting it with the arrow keys and pressing ENTER.

The list boxes in Figure 1-4 have attached text boxes. Only some list boxes have text boxes attached. The adjoining text boxes show the item that is currently selected in the list. You can also type an entry in the text box, rather than selecting it from the list.

The Underline box in Figure 1-4 is a drop-down list box. The selection that appears in the box before you select the arrow button to drop down the list is the current selection for that list. To view the entire list, as shown here, you must click the arrow button or press DOWN ARROW:

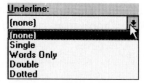

Most drop-down lists require that you select one of the items listed rather than type it in. Select the item with the usual mouse or keyboard method; or, if you press a letter key, Word will select the next item in the list that starts with that letter.

Option Buttons and Check Boxes

Option buttons (also called *radio buttons*) and check boxes are two more ways to specify settings for Word to use. Option buttons allow you to select from a set of mutually exclusive options. Check boxes toggle a specific feature on and off.

Option buttons appear in sets, like these:

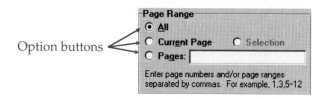

You can select one and only one option button from a set. When you select one, the others in the set are deselected (turned off). The selected option button has the dark circle in the middle; the unselected ones are clear.

Check boxes turn features on or off. The All Caps check box in Figure 1-4 is currently turned on. You can tell this because it is filled with an X. If All Caps were turned off, the check box would be empty, and this character formatting option would not be added.

Tabbed Sections

Word for Windows has divided some of its dialog boxes into *tabbed sections*; in Figure 1-4 you can see the tabs for Font and Character Spacing at the top of the dialog box. To select the tab of dialog box options you want to use, click the desired tab, or press CTRL+TAB or CTRL+SHIFT+TAB until the tab you want is on top of the "stack."

TIP: You can use either a mouse or the keyboard to make dialog box selections. It is the final selection in a dialog box that accepts your changes or cancels the request so you will have some time to make a correction if you select the wrong option before you process your entries.

Sizing Windows

You may need to change the size of document windows within the Word application window, and you can also size the Word application window itself. Sizing lets you display several applications or documents on the screen at the same time. You can allocate how much of the screen Word uses versus other applications. And when Word is the active application, you can decide how much space each document uses within the Word window. The directions for sizing both types of window are the same, except that documents in Word for Windows 2 cannot be minimized. A document window cannot appear outside the Word window.

In Windows applications there are three techniques for sizing windows: you can maximize, minimize, and restore. When you maximize a window, it takes up all the available space, and you can see the maximum amount of text and data. In Figure 1-1, both the program window and a document window are maximized.

To maximize a window, you can either click the Maximize button on the right end of the title bar, or open the window's control menu and select Maximize. (To open the Word window control menu, press ALT+SPACEBAR. To open a document window's control menu, press ALT+- (hyphen).)

When you minimize a window in Word for Windows 6, it is reduced to an icon. You may want to minimize the Word window when you want to make room on your screen to work with another application window. To minimize a window, click the Minimize button in the title bar, or open the control menu and then select Minimize (as described just above for maximizing).

The third sizing technique is the Restore option. When you click the Restore button or select the Restore command from the window's control menu, the window is changed to an intermediate size; it's not maximized, but it's not an icon, either. A window at this intermediate size has window borders that are lines surrounding the entire window. In this state, you can change the size of the window to any size you want.

Using the mouse to size a window is easy once you have practiced a few times. Point the mouse at the window's border. When the mouse is correctly positioned, the mouse pointer turns into a double-headed arrow. Then drag the border to where you want that side of the window to be. The double-headed arrow points in the two directions in which you can move the border. For example, when you point to the lower-right window corner, the mouse pointer changes to a double-diagonal arrow, telling you that you can move that corner in or out diagonally, to shrink or enlarge the window size.

Sizing a window with the keyboard is almost as easy. After restoring the window, select Size from the window's control menu. A four-headed arrow will appear. Press an arrow key to move to one of the window borders, and the pointer will move to that border and become a double-headed arrow. Then use the arrow keys to move the border; when the window is correctly sized, press ENTER.

TIP: Word has several function key-combinations that you can use to size a window. CTRL+F10 maximizes a document window, and ALT+F10 maximizes an application window. CTRL+F5 restores a document window's size, and ALT+F5 restores an application window's size. CTRL+F8 lets you size a document window using the arrow keys.

Moving Windows

After you have sized the windows on your screen, you may want to arrange them in some fashion by moving them. You use the same methods for moving document and application windows, using either the mouse or the keyboard. (Maximized windows cannot be moved since they occupy all the available space.)

Moving a window with the mouse is a one-step operation. Simply point the mouse at the title bar and drag it to a new location. This moves the window to that location.

To move a window using the keyboard, select Move from the window's control menu. Then use the arrow keys to move the title bar to a new location. Press ENTER when the window is correctly located, and the window will be redrawn in the new location.

TIP: When moving a document window, you can press CTRL+F7 instead of selecting Move from the window's control menu.

Accessing Help

Word's on-line Help feature is the perfect way to answer a quick question about any of the program's features. Word for Windows Help is a separate application and appears in its own window. When you open Word for Windows Help, it replaces any other help window you have open at the time. Word has multiple types of help to answer your questions.

You already have seen several examples of help that Word has to guide you through using its features. When you start Word for Windows 6, you may see the Tip of the Day that offers pointers about Word features you may want to use. Also, Word for Windows 6 will display toolbar button names when you point to them for a couple of seconds. And in the status bar you can see help about where you are in a document, the command you are pointing to, or the dialog box you are working with.

Showing a Help Window

Help is always easy to access: Just press F1. When you press F1, Word guesses about what topic you want to know about; this is called *context sensitive help*, because it is based on what you are doing when you press F1. For example, if you press F1 in the middle of selecting a command from a menu, the Help window displays information about the command you have highlighted before pressing F1.

The Help application window opens with Word's best guess. Word also has a help index or Word Contents that appears when Word cannot tell what specific task you want information about. Figure 1-5 shows the Word for Windows 6 Help Contents window.

You can also access help by opening the Help menu, and selecting one of the options there. If you select Index, the Help window opens with Word's help index. The Getting Started and Learning Word commands in Word for Windows 2 start lessons about the fundamentals of using Word and various Word features. In Word for Windows 6, the Quick Preview and Examples and Demos commands provide guidance through Word's basic operations and show off some of the features you may want to know more about.

If you have previously used the WordPerfect program, look into WordPerfect Help. The help supplied by this command will assist you in translating your WordPerfect skills into fluency with Word for Windows.

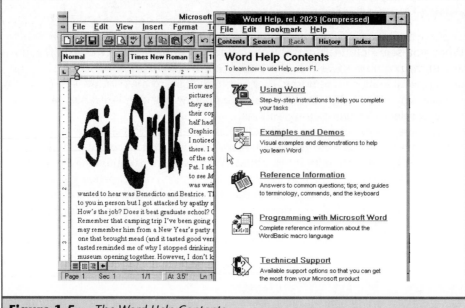

Figure 1-5.   *The Word Help Contents*

Moving Among Help Topics

Once you see the Help window, you can read the information displayed there, and you can also move from that topic to explore other information. The easiest way to switch to different information is to select one of the topics displayed. The names of Help topics appear in green or are underlined. When you point to a topic, the mouse pointer changes to a hand. When the topic has a dotted underline, the information will appear in a pop-up box to show a definition or quick description. When the topic is underlined with a solid line, selecting it will change the information shown in the Help window. To choose a topic with the mouse, click it; with the keyboard, press TAB until the topic is highlighted and then press ENTER.

Word for Windows 6 Help sometimes opens a How To window. This window has numbered steps to guide you through execution of one of Word's features. If you need to, you can keep a How To window on the screen by selecting On Top. This selection keeps the help window on top of your current document. When you are finished with Help, close the other help window, and the How To window will remain displayed to guide you through the task.

Search

The Search feature can also help you find the topic that answers your questions. When you select the Search button in the Help window (by clicking it or pressing ALT+S), you open the Search dialog box. There, in the top text box type the word or phrase you are curious about. The list box just below will shift to display the subjects that match what you type. You can always press TAB to move into the list box and select the subject you want. Then press ENTER or select the Show Topics button. The list box at the bottom will then show a list of available Help topic windows related to the subject you selected. Highlight the topic you want and press ENTER, or double-click it. The Help window will then change to show the topic you selected.

CHAPTER 2

Creating and Editing a Document

When you write a letter, you start with a clean sheet of paper. When you create a document with Word, you start with a new document, which is just like a clean sheet of paper. With it, you can get started creating your letter, report, or other text. In this chapter, you will learn how to create a document, edit it, save it, print it, and check its spelling—in other words, all the basics of document creation. When you finish, you will be ready to try other Word features.

The documents you will work with in this chapter use some of the formatting described in Chapters 3 and 4. As you learn more about Word, you will be able to incorporate more of these formatting features in your own documents.

Creating a Document

When you start a new Word session, Word always provides a new document, called Document1. This document is in a document window that is maximized, so it occupies as much of the Word window as possible. Document1 appears in the Word title bar; but later, when you save your document, the Document1 will be replaced by the file name you use for the document.

Once you have a blank document displayed, you are ready to start typing the text you want it to contain.

Creating Additional New Documents

Whenever you want to create a new letter, memo, or report, you will need a new document. But you need not close one document to open another; you can create a new document at any time while you are working with Word. When you are ready to create a new document, click the New button on the toolbar, shown here in the margin.

This button creates a new document, with the initial name of Document# (with the # representing the next unused document number). These document numbers help you identify the one you want to use, even before you have saved it with a unique name.

WARNING: If you do not save your new document before exiting Word, you will lose the entire document. Word does prompt you to save changes before you exit it.

The other way you can create a new document is to select the File | New command. This opens the New dialog box, which has options for document tools such as templates and summary information. Using a *template* provides some additional structure to the document, since a template is a pattern that affects formatting and may even provide some of the document text. You will learn all about Word templates in Chapter 4. When you select OK in the New dialog box with the Normal template selected, Word creates a new document just as if you used the New button on the toolbar.

Create and use templates when you want to give a set of documents a consistent appearance. Chapter 4 has more information about creating templates and using them. You can also use a Word wizard that will help you create several types of documents. There are wizards for legal pleadings and other types of documents that function as templates with a little extra assistance. Another option in a new document is to provide summary information. "Summary Info" in Chapter 4 tells you about creating and displaying document summaries; "Find File" tells you how you can search summary information to find the documents you want.

Switching Among Documents

When you have more than one document open, you need to be able to switch to the document you want. Two quick methods for doing this are the Window menu and CTRL+F6.

The bottom portion of the Window menu lists the documents currently open on your screen. Each of the documents has a number next to it; you can either type this number or click on the document name to switch to one of these open documents. In Word for Windows 6 there is a limit of nine document names that can display in the Window menu although the number open is only limited by available memory. If you have more than nine open you will see an option for More Windows to see additional documents.

Pressing CTRL+F6 switches from one document window to the next, following the same order in which documents are listed at the bottom of the Window menu.

When you want to be able to see several documents at once, look at "Windows" in Chapter 4. "Viewing Documents" in Chapter 4 explains other options that let you change how you display documents. When you display several document windows at once, you can switch to the document you want by clicking it.

Entering Text

After opening a new document, you will want to enter text or other elements in that document. Entering text in an electronic Word for Windows document is the same as typing a document on a typewriter or writing it with a pen on paper—with certain differences. You can correct anything on the screen without having to retype the entire document. Also, you must use a different technique for marking the end of lines and paragraphs.

Typing in the Document Window

Most of the techniques for typing with a computer are just like typing with a typewriter. For example, each time you press a key on the keyboard, the character on the key—a letter, number, or punctuation symbol—appears on the screen. If you press SHIFT, the capital letter (or the top character on the key) appears. Although Word doesn't impose many restrictions on what you enter in a document window, you will want to follow the usual rules for grammar and punctuation. Be sure to read the following box containing "Rules for Entering Numbers."

Some other things work differently when you're typing on a computer. For example, on a typewriter, you have to press the Return key at the end of each line to mark its end. Word, however, will automatically wrap the line of text when you run out of space at the right margin, and move down to the next line. You only press the ENTER key (the Return key's counterpart) when you want to signal the end of a paragraph. Because Word wraps text to fit the width of the lines, you can change margins after typing text, and the text will automatically size itself to the new margins. You also can let Word handle the page breaks; the program will automatically add a page break when the text fills a page.

When you lock the Shift key down on a typewriter, the letter keys you type produce all uppercase characters, and other keys produce their top characters. With the computer, when you press the CAPS LOCK key, the letter keys will produce capital letters; however, you still have to press SHIFT to access the upper characters for the other keys. Also, pressing SHIFT does not release the CAPS LOCK in the same way that it releases the Shift Lock on the typewriter.

Ending a Paragraph

To end a paragraph or short line in Word, press ENTER. When you press ENTER, you move to the next line, and an invisible symbol (¶) is entered in your document. Figure 2-1 contains several lines of text where ENTER was pressed to end the line.

CAUTION: Do not press ENTER to mark the end of a line within a paragraph. If you do so, you will have great difficulty formatting your document later, and you will lose one of the great advantages of using a word processor—automatic word wrap.

If you want to see the paragraph symbols (¶) that indicate where you have pressed ENTER to move to the next line, or view other "invisible" characters such as TAB, look at "Nonprinting Characters" in Chapter 4.

Rules for Entering Numbers

Numbers are sometimes written as digits and sometimes spelled out in words. The following guidelines provide examples of when each method of recording numbers is most popular:

- Express monetary amounts as digits.

- Enter both words and numbers in legal documents, as in "one hundred fifty (150)."

- Use digits to represent measurements, ages, percentages, and decimals.

- Use words for numbers that start a sentence.

- In formal documents, spell out numbers that require one or two words.

- Use hyphens to separate compound words, such as "fifty-four."

- Use words for indefinite numbers, as in "Millions of people are affected."

- Numbers requiring three or more words should be expressed as digits, as in "253" or "21 million."

- In less formal documents, numbers below ten are always written as words ("three, four, five") unless they are combined in a sentence with numbers above ten, in which case they are all expressed with digits ("1, 25, and 53").

- Add an *s* to make digits plural, and either *s* or *es* for plurals of words that represent numbers.

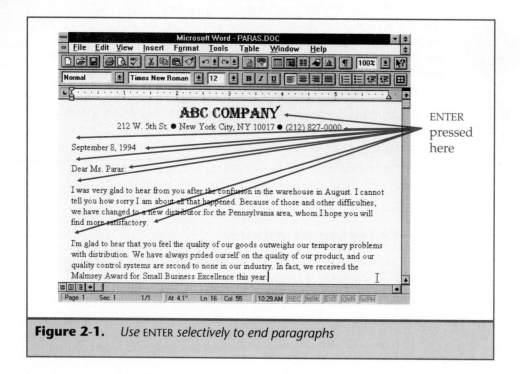

ENTER
pressed
here

Figure 2-1. *Use* ENTER *selectively to end paragraphs*

Using the Tab Key

Pressing the TAB key in Word moves you to the next tab stop, just as it does on a typewriter. Tab stops are positions on the page that you can easily move to by pressing TAB. In new documents, default tab stops are set every 1/2 inch. When you press TAB, the insertion point moves to the next tab stop, and aligns the characters you type next with that tab position.

On a typewriter, you use a tab to indent the beginning of paragraphs. You can still do this in Word, but it's easier to use paragraph formatting, which lets you start a paragraph without pressing TAB. You'll find out how to do this in Chapter 3.

When you want to align text in Word, use TAB, not the SPACEBAR. Since Word can use attractive proportional fonts (these control the width of the characters), each character does not occupy the same amount of space. So if you use the SPACEBAR to align text, you will have jagged alignment, since each character does not use the same amount of space as an empty space. When you use TAB, the space used is an absolute measurement, and so the text always aligns on the same location on the page.

Word's initial tab stops are set every 1/2 inch, but you can change them. "Tabs" in Chapter 4 tells how to do this, and explains right, center, and decimal tabs that change the alignment of the text that you enter at a tab stop. Rather than using TAB *to create a table within a document, check out "Tables" in Chapter 4, which describes an easier method.*

Editing a Document

No one creates a perfect document with the first draft. You will often need to edit your documents, either to refine your organization, correct mistakes, or reuse a document in a somewhat different context. Word gives you many efficient tools that make editing a simple task. Among other things, you can delete entire sections of text, copy them, or move them to different locations in your document.

Navigating Within a Document

The first step in learning how to edit your document is knowing how to move around in it, as well as quickly through it.

Moving with the Mouse

Moving within a document using the mouse is easy: You point and click at a location in the document, and the insertion point moves there.

If the text you want to see is not currently displayed, use the document window's scroll bars to get there. Click the scroll bar up- and down-arrow buttons to move one line up or down. Click to either side of the scroll box to move one window of text in that direction. Drag the scroll box to a new position in the scroll bar to move to that position in the document (this method involves some guesswork). Once you've displayed a new part of the document, click to move the insertion point to the exact desired location. Horizontal scrolling works the same way if the document is too wide to display on the screen all at once.

CAUTION: The scroll bar changes the part of the document that is displayed but does not move the insertion point. Before you enter any text after scrolling, remember to click to move the insertion point to the place where you want the text to appear.

Moving with the Keyboard

The keyboard offers a variety of methods for moving in a document. When you move with the keyboard, you move the insertion point itself, rather than just changing the display of the document. Here is a list of the movement keys:

Key	Moves You To
HOME	The beginning of the line
END	The end of the line
PGDN	One window down in the document
PGUP	One window up in the document
CTRL+HOME	The beginning of the document
CTRL+END	The end of the document
CTRL+LEFT ARROW	The beginning of the current or previous word
CTRL+RIGHT ARROW	The beginning of the next word
CTRL+UP ARROW	The beginning of the current paragraph or the previous one
CTRL+DOWN ARROW	The beginning of the following paragraph

These keystrokes may be very confusing at first, but rest assured they will quickly become familiar and easy to use. Most Windows applications use the same keystrokes for similar movements.

TIP: For a shortcut in moving through very long documents, see "Outlines" in Chapter 4.

Moving to a Specific Page

In a long document, you will need to be able to quickly move from one page to another. Word lets you move to a specific page in a document using the Go To command. You can also move to other types of markers using this command, as you'll learn in Chapter 4.

To use Go To, select Edit | Go To or press F5; this opens the Go To dialog box. The Page option will already be selected. In the Enter Page Number text box, type the number of the page you want to move to, and select Go To. The insertion point will move to the beginning of the text on that page.

You can even type the + or - key in the Enter Page Number box, followed by a number, to move a specific number of pages forward or backward in the document. For example, typing **+2** and selecting Go To moves you two pages forward from the current location.

TIP: You can move to any of the last three locations where you made editing changes in a document. Press SHIFT+F5 *to cycle through the last three editing locations.*

Making Corrections

As you type, you may find that you have misspelled words, used the wrong words, or simply mistyped something. Making corrections with Word is simple: You simply delete the characters on the screen and enter new ones.

Use the mouse or arrow keys to move the insertion point to the mistake that you want to correct. Position the insertion point just before or just after the characters to be deleted. Press DEL to delete the characters to the right of the insertion point, or press BACKSPACE to delete the characters to the left of the insertion point. If you want to delete one whole word, Word provides a shortcut. Press CTRL+BACKSPACE to delete the word before the insertion point, or CTRL+DEL to delete the word after the insertion point.

After deleting the incorrect characters, you'll want to enter the correct ones. Just type them, starting with the insertion point at the correct location. Word inserts the characters you type at the insertion point.

You can also replace characters using the *overtype* mode.(You can tell whether you are in overtype mode when you see OVR in the status bar, in either black or bright display. The OVR entry is dimmed, or grayed out, when you are not in overtype mode.) In overtype mode, Word does not make space for the new characters you type. Instead, new characters replace the old characters. If you are inserting the same number of characters that you are deleting, using overtype mode is faster than deleting the old text and inserting the new. To switch to overtype mode, press the INS key (or, in Word 6 only, double-click the dimmed OVR in the status bar). To switch back to the default insert mode, press INS or double-click the OVR indicator again.

NOTE: If you delete a word at the end of a sentence or immediately before a closing parenthesis, colon, semicolon, question mark, or exclamation mark, Word 6 also deletes the space before the word, so the punctuation mark moves to the end of the word before the one you just deleted.

Selecting Text

You have learned how to manipulate a single character of text, but you can also work with many characters at the same time—by *selecting* the text before taking an action. Selected text appears highlighted on your screen. Once text is selected, you can delete it, format it, copy it, or move it.

Selecting with the Mouse

Selecting text with the mouse lets you quickly choose the text you want to work with. First, move the mouse pointer to the beginning of the text you want to select and drag to the end of the text you want to select. The text between the point where you started to drag and where you release the mouse button becomes highlighted, marking it as the selected text. Another way to do this is to click the beginning of the text you want to select, to move the insertion point there. Then hold down the SHIFT key while you click the end of the text to select. All of the text in between the two clicks will be highlighted.

If you change your mind about what you are selecting, just click at another location in the document, or release the SHIFT key and press any arrow key.

Another way to use the mouse for selecting text is by using it with the *selection bar*. The selection bar—the blank area at the left of the text area—lets you select large areas of text quickly. When the mouse pointer is in the selection bar, it looks like an arrow pointing to the right, as shown here:

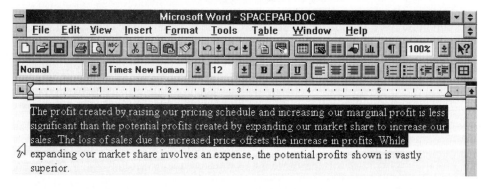

When you click the selection bar, the line of text immediately to the right of the pointer is selected. Click and drag the mouse up or down in the selection bar, and all of the lines to the right of where you drag in the selection bar will be selected. Another method is to click the selection bar multiple times: Clicking once selects the current line, twice selects the current paragraph, three times selects the entire document.

Here are some more options: To quickly select a word, just double-click it. Triple-click in the same spot, and you select the entire paragraph. To select an entire sentence, hold down CTRL when you click anywhere in the sentence.

Selecting with the Keyboard

To select text using the keyboard, you use the SHIFT key in combination with the movement keys. For example, pressing END moves the insertion point to the end of a line of text, but when you press SHIFT+END, you select all of the text from the insertion point's original location to the end of the line. You can use any of the movement keys or movement key-combinations with SHIFT to select text.

To select an entire document, press CTRL and the 5 key in the middle of the numeric keypad.

Another way to select text with the keyboard is using the Extend key (F8). Press F8, and the EXT indicator appears in the status bar. (To turn Extend off, press ESC.) Then you can press the arrow keys to indicate the area of text you want to select.

Press F8 repeatedly, and you select a progressively larger section of text—first the word your insertion point is on, then that sentence, then that paragraph, then the section, and then the entire document. To reverse directions, selecting progressively smaller sections of text, press SHIFT+F8 repeatedly.

You can also type a character after pressing F8, and Word will select all the text between the insertion point and the next occurrence of that character in the document. For example, if you press F8 and then type a period, you'll select from your current location to the end of that sentence.

If you change your mind about what you are selecting with the keyboard, you can use the arrow keys to leave out part of your original selection if you haven't as yet released the SHIFT key. If you have finalized your selection, make a new selection of the text you want to include.

TIP: When you already have text selected and you type more text, Word's default action is to replace the selected text with the text you are typing. However, Word has an editing option that you can change if you do not want text you type to replace any text you have selected.

Moving and Copying Text by Dragging and Dropping

Word provides a neat mouse shortcut for moving and copying text within a document. Once you have selected text you want to move to another location, drag the mouse from the selected text to where you want it moved. When you start dragging, the status bar will show the question, "Move to where?", and the mouse pointer will be accompanied by a dashed bar indicating where the selected text will be inserted, as well as a box just below that. Here's how the pointer looks in the following screen segment:

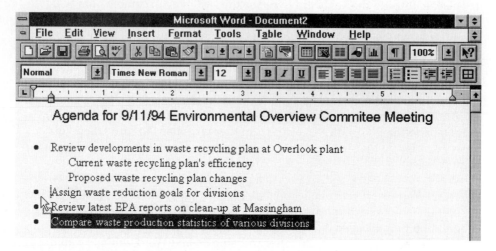

When you release the mouse, the selected text is moved to where the dashed bar is.

Copying selected text by dragging and dropping works the same way, except you hold down the CTRL key while you drag the selected text to a new location. The pointer will be accompanied by a + to the right, indicating that you are copying rather than moving. Also, the status bar says "Copy to where?". This drag-and-drop method of rearranging your document is quick and easy.

Deleting Selected Text

You can also select text that you do not want in its current location and delete it. You can delete text so that it is completely erased, or you can *cut* the text. When you cut text, it is removed from its current location in the document, but it can be *pasted*, or reinserted into a document.

If you no longer want the text and wish to erase it completely, select it and press either the DEL or BACKSPACE key.

If you want to paste the text you are cutting into another location, you have two options: the Windows Clipboard and Word's Spike feature.

Cutting Text to the Clipboard or the Spike

Word and most other Windows applications use the Clipboard—a temporary storage location for cut data. You can put data into the Clipboard and take data from it. The Clipboard stores data from one source at a time, so when you put something into the Clipboard, you are discarding whatever was there before. The Clipboard is emptied when you leave Windows.

Word's Spike is another special location in memory. The Spike, too, holds data temporarily, but it only works within Word. The Spike lets you move data from one location to another among Word documents only.

The Spike has a few other differences from the Clipboard. When you add something to the Spike, it is appended to the end of the current Spike contents, with paragraph breaks in between all the separate items added to the Spike. The Spike lets you pick up text from different parts of a Word document and then dump all of it into another location. The Spike is emptied when you leave Word or when you put the Spike's contents into a document, with CTRL+SHIFT+F3 as described shortly in "Inserting Text."

When you select and cut text, it is sent either to the Clipboard or to the Spike, as follows:

■ To cut to the Clipboard, select the Cut command, either by clicking on the Cut tool on the toolbar or by selecting Edit | Cut. The selected text is deleted from your Word document, and placed in the Windows Clipboard. From the Windows Clipboard you can paste it to another Windows application, or into a Word document.

> *WARNING: When you cut or copy text to the Clipboard, the previous contents of the Clipboard are erased. You cannot cut two different selections of text to the Clipboard, and then insert them both elsewhere.*

■ To cut to the Spike, press CTRL+F3. The selected text disappears from its current location in the document and is added to the Spike's current contents. From there it can be inserted into any open Word document.

Inserting Text

When you cut text, either to the Windows Clipboard or to Word's Spike, you can paste (insert) that text into a Word document. This is a helpful technique when you are reorganizing a document. When you paste text, it is placed at the insertion point's location—even in overtype mode. So, whether you are pasting from either the Clipboard or the Spike, you should always begin by moving the insertion point to where you want the text placed.

When the text you want to paste is in the Clipboard, you can either click the Paste button in the toolbar or select Edit | Paste. Word reads the contents of the Clipboard into your Word document at the insertion point's position. The text remains on the Clipboard, so if you want to paste it in another location in your document or into another document, simply reposition the insertion point and use the Paste command again. The text will stay in the Clipboard until you cut or copy in a different piece of text.

When the text you want to paste is in the Spike, position the insertion point where you want the text placed and press CTRL+SHIFT+F3. All the contents of the Spike will be inserted into your document. If you have cut several selections of text onto the Spike, all of those selections will appear, in the same order in which you added them to the Spike. When you paste text from the Spike in this way, the Spike is emptied.

When you want to paste the same text from the Spike to several locations, you need to use another method of pasting text from the Spike. Rather than CTRL+SHIFT+F3, type **spike** where you want the text pasted, press the SPACEBAR, and press F3. Word replaces the word "spike" with the contents of the Spike. To insert the Spike's contents in another location, type **spike** again and press F3, or press CTRL+SHIFT+F3.

Copying Text

You can copy text to the Clipboard without deleting it from its original location in your document. For example, if an address is used twice in a letter, you can copy the first occurrence of the address into another location, without having to type it again, and without its being deleted from the first location. You cannot copy text to the Spike.

The only difference between copying and cutting is how the text gets to the Clipboard. Whether the text was copied or cut to the Clipboard, you paste the text into your document in the same way.

To copy text to the Clipboard, select the text as you do for cutting. Then click the Copy button on the toolbar or select Edit | Copy. At this point you will not see a change in your document; the selected text remains where it is and stays selected. However, a copy of that text is now in the Clipboard. Move your insertion point to where you want the copy to be inserted, and use the Paste command as described above in "Inserting Text."

NOTE: You can even paste the data you copy into the Clipboard into a document in another application. The steps to insert the data into the other application depend on the other application. See Chapter 4, for details on copying to the Clipboard.

Undoing Edits

If you make an edit by mistake or change your mind, Word can undo the effect of the last several edits you have made. You can restore text you have deleted, remove text you have pasted, and reverse the effect of other commands. The Undo feature also helps you recover from a mistyped command, such as pressing Y instead of N when prompted to confirm a command.

To undo your last action, either click the Undo button on the toolbar or select Edit | Undo. Note that the Undo menu command will change to indicate the command you last executed. For instance, the Undo menu command might read "Undo Paste," "Undo Delete Word," or "Undo Typing." You can also press CTRL+Z or ALT+BACKSPACE to undo an action, although with this method you do not see a description of what you are undoing.

If you need to reverse the effect of more than one action, click the arrow next to the Undo button in the toolbar. You'll see a drop-down list box that lists many of the edits you have made, in the reverse order in which you made them. When you click one of these actions, all of the changes—from the last one made to the one you clicked—are undone.

The Undo command does have limitations:

■ Undo only remembers a limited number of changes, based on the amount of RAM (Random Access Memory) available.

■ You can undo changes you make to your document on the screen, but you cannot undo changes that go beyond Word itself. For example, if you save a document over one you already have on disk, Undo cannot restore the disk file you have just overwritten.

■ For Undo to remove the effect of a change you have made, you must use Undo immediately in Word for Windows 2, or before the change is forgotten by Word for Window 6. The oldest changes are forgotten when there is no more memory to add new changes.

Besides using Undo to reverse the effect of an action, you can also use Redo to reapply an action that you undid. See "Undoing and Redoing Actions" in Chapter 4 for more information about this feature. You may also want to look at "Repeating Actions" in Chapter 4 to see how you can have Word apply the same edits in several places.

Saving and Opening Your Documents

If you do not save your document to a disk file, the work you have put into it disappears when you close the document window or exit Word. Saving to a disk file lets you keep your document so that you can use it again later. The documents you no longer want to work with can be saved and closed to get them out of your way. Then, to work with them again you have to open them. The commands that save, close, and open documents have several shortcuts, summarized in Table 2-1.

CAUTION: Save often. A power surge or other incident can make your computer stop or crash, and you will lose any unsaved work. See "Save Options" in Chapter 4 to learn how to create timed back-ups of your documents as you are working.

Saving for the First Time

When you save a document for the first time, you need to give it a name. To save a document, select File | Save or Save As, or by using one of the shortcuts in Table 2-1. Word opens the Save dialog box, where you will provide a name for

Command	Toolbar Icon	Function Key Combination	Ctrl Key Combination
File	Save	💾	SHIFT+F12	CTRL+S
File	Save As		F12	
File	Close		CTRL+F4	CTRL+W
File	Open	📂	CTRL+F12	CTRL+O
File	New	🗋		CTRL+N

Table 2-1. *Shortcuts for Saving, Closing, and Opening Documents*

the document. This dialog box also lets you designate where the file is saved (directory and drive) and whether it is saved in another application's format.

Type the name for the document in the File Name text box. A filename must be no more than eight characters long; use only letters, numbers, and the underscore character. Choose a name that describes or suggests the contents of the document. For example, a letter to Jean Muraski might be named MURASKI. The list box below File Name lists all the files in the current directory. Filenames also have a three-character filename extension, separated from the main filename by a period. You do not have to provide an extension, because Word will add .DOC to the end of the filename you type. Filename extensions often indicate the format of how the data is saved. For example, .DOC represents a Word document.

TIP: You can use a different filename extension by typing it with the name, as in SALES.REP. As a rule, however, it's best to allow Word to add the default extension. Word automatically looks for documents with that extension.

Once you select OK in the Save dialog box, Word saves the document in a disk file, using the name you have provided. The document's filename also appears in the title bar, as well as in the Window menu.

If you want to save a file and store it in another directory or on another drive, look at "Saving Files" in Chapter 4 for how to change the location of where a file is saved. This section of Chapter 4 also has information about saving a file in different formats so you can use them with other applications.

Subsequent Saves

You do not have to provide the filename every time you save a document. For subsequent saves after the first one, Word uses the settings from the first time you saved the document. You do not see the Save dialog box, though you do see the message on the status bar telling you that Word is saving your file. You will see the message without the dialog box on subsequent saves whether you use the menu or the Save button on the toolbar.

If you want to save a file again with a different filename, location, or type, you cannot use the File | Save command to do this. Instead, use the File | Save As command or one of its shortcuts. Saving with the Save As command does not delete the original file from the disk; it simply creates another copy of the document using a different name. The Save As dialog box has the same options as the Save dialog box.

Closing the Document

When you have finished working with a document, you will want to put it away, or close it. This is just like removing a letter from your desk. If you do not put Word documents away, they may get in the way of the documents you do want to work with; moreover, when you leave long documents open, they slow down Word's performance.

To close a document window, move to that document (making it active) and select the File | Close command or use one of its shortcuts. If the active document has not changed since the last time you saved it, Word will immediately close the document window. If you have changed the document since the last time you saved it, Word will ask you if you want to save your changes. If you select Yes, Word saves the changes just as if you used the File | Save command. If you select No, your changes are discarded. If the document has never before been saved, selecting Yes causes Word to display the Save As dialog box. You can then make the settings necessary to save the file in that dialog box, or choose Cancel to return to the active document without saving or closing.

Opening an Existing Document

Once you save a file to a disk, you can open it and work with it again. When you open a file, you are reading it into your computer's RAM.

REMINDER: *Be sure to save the file again after opening it and editing it, or you will lose the changes that you made.*

To open a file, select the File | Open command or use one of its shortcuts. You will see the Open dialog box, in which you can select the file you want to open. This dialog box has many of the same options as those for saving a file. In the File Name text box, you can type the name of the file you want to open, or you can select it from the File Name list box. When you have designated the correct file, select OK to open the file in a new document window.

Checking the Spelling and Grammar of Your Document

Word's spell feature locates misspelled words in your document and suggests the correct spelling. The speller also locates words with unusual capitalization, and repeated words. Certainly you can search the document for these mistakes yourself, but using the speller ensures that you do not accidentally overlook any.

To check the spelling in your document, select the Tools I Spelling command, or press F7, or click the Spelling button on the toolbar, shown here in the margin.

When you start the spell-check by choosing Spelling from the Tools menu, Word looks at the words in your document and compares them against the contents of Word's dictionary. When Word encounters what it thinks is a misspelled word, it opens this Spelling dialog box:

At this point, the option you select tells Word what you want to do about the misspelled word.

■ For most misspellings, Word supplies suggestions for the possible correct spelling of the word. If you want to use one of the suggestions, highlight it in the Suggestions list box and select Change. You can also type a replacement in the Change To text box before you select Change.

■ By selecting Change All instead of Change, Word will replace every occurrence of the incorrect word with the suggested word you have selected or entered.

■ If you want to leave the word as is, select Ignore. If you want Word to ignore all future occurrences of the word while you are spell-checking, select Ignore All.

■ You may want to add the word to Word's dictionary by selecting the Add button; if you do this, every time the word subsequently appears during a spell-check, Word will know how to spell it. You may want to add proper names, acronyms, and technical terms.

When a document does not contain any misspelled words or when Word has finished the spell-check, you'll see a message, "The spelling check is complete." Select OK to close this message box. If you did not start the spell-check at the beginning of the document, when Word reaches the end of the document it will ask you if you want to check the document starting at the beginning.

THE AUTOCORRECT FEATURE   The Spelling dialog box in Word for Windows 6 has a wonderful feature called AutoCorrect. This feature automatically corrects your "favorite" spelling mistakes (that is, the ones you tend to make most frequently). When you check the spelling of a document and a word is consistently misspelled, select AutoCorrect. Now, every time you type the misspelled word, Word automatically alters it to the correct spelling. Word already has a few automatic spelling corrections set up for you. To see AutoCorrect in action, type **teh** and a space, and watch Word convert it to *the* followed by a space.

Word lets you customize how the speller works. For example, you can create custom dictionary files; you can also purchase dictionary files for other languages or that contain specialized terms for various professions. To learn more about these features, look up "Spelling" in Chapter 4. Also, "AutoCorrect" in Chapter 4 describes the options available for changing how AutoCorrect works.

Using the Grammar Checker

Word does not check for misused words; for example, if *their* is used instead of *they're*, Word won't identify it as incorrect as long as it's spelled correctly. The Tools | Grammar command can help you review your document for this type of error; however, even if you use Word's grammar-checker, you should always proof your document yourself to catch mistakes the computer cannot identify.

If you are responsible for putting together an important report, for instance, and you haven't had much writing practice lately, you may want to review a good source of grammar guidelines to give your writing a professional appearance. The box in this chapter, "Rules for Comma Placement," can help clarify at least one aspect of your writing.

Rules for Comma Placement

Commas separate elements of sentences to make the meaning clearer. They are also used to separate phrases that are nonessential and provide an aside from the main theme of the sentence. Correctly used, commas help add clarity to your sentences; when commas are missing or misused, they cause the reader to achieve less-than-perfect understanding of your material. Always use commas in these situations:

- To separate two parts of a compound sentence, as in "The weather was dismal, but we went despite it."

- After introductory phrases such as "Loved by all,...", "Founded in 1901,...", and "Gripped by fear,..."

- To separate the city name from the state or country, as in "Cleveland, Ohio" and "Frankfurt, Germany."

- To separate each of three or more entries, as in "Peter, Paul, and Mary" and "red, green, or yellow."

- To isolate the name when an individual is addressed directly, as in "No, Jane, I cannot give you a raise this year."

- Between consecutive modifiers: "a beautiful, gentle child."

- To separate an individual's name from an employer's name, as in "Jeff Pepper, of Osborne/McGraw-Hill."

- To separate nonessential clauses from the rest of a sentence. If the sentence makes sense without the clause, use commas. For example, "Scott Rogers, you must admit, is a dedicated, hard-working employee."

- To isolate *too* and other such words and expressions that help effect a transition: "He, too, was striken ill while abroad."

- When omitting the comma would cause confusion, as in "To a great cook like Betty, Crocker's new book would be useless."

Printing the Document

After you have created, edited and saved a document, you will probably at some point want to print it. Printing a document in Word is as simple as selecting a command. When you are ready to print, or press CTRL+P, or select File | Print. You will see the Print dialog box, where you can make the appropriate settings and select OK. (You'll learn more about these settings in Chapter 4, "Printing.") Word then prints your document. Click the print button, shown here in the margin, to print if you want to use the default settings.

The way Word for Windows prints documents is different from how DOS-based programs do it. Word works with Windows and its Print Manager to print your documents. When you select the Print command, Word and Windows act together to open the Windows Print Manager, which then handles sending information to the printer. Word and Windows tell the Print Manager the data you want to print and how it should be printed. Windows supplies the printer information your printer needs to print your data, and the Print Manager stores this information in a temporary file. Once this is done, you can continue working with Word. The Print Manager handles sending the document to your printer, so you do not have to wait until your document finishes printing before you continue to work on a document.

The Print dialog box has many options for changing how much of your document you print, how many copies, and so forth. "Printing" and "Print Options" in Chapter 4 contain more information about changing how Word prints the document. Many of the changes you make to a document are formatting changes, to make the printed version look better. Chapter 3 describes some basic formatting, and Chapter 4 covers specific information about all of the formatting available for your Word documents.

Changing the View

You can change how your document is displayed while you are editing it. The two most common editing views are *normal view* and *page layout view.* Normal view is what you have seen so far as you have worked through Chapter 1 and 2. Some Word screen elements, such as pictures, tables, and hidden characters, display differently in normal versus page layout view. Page layout view shows you how the document will look when you print it. Figure 2-2 shows the same document in both normal view and page layout view.

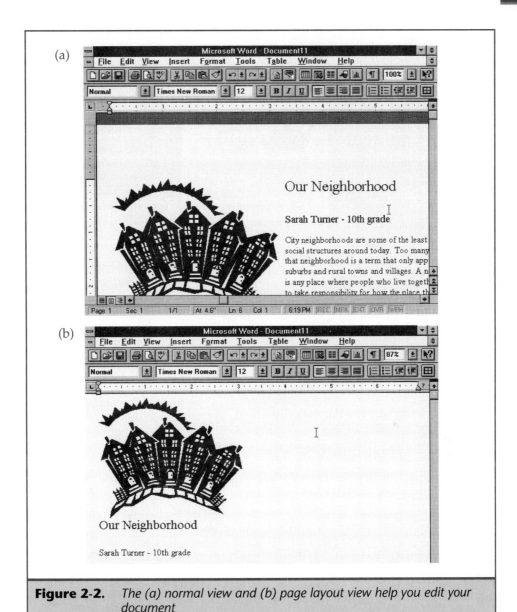

Figure 2-2. *The (a) normal view and (b) page layout view help you edit your document*

To switch to normal view, select View | Normal or click the Normal View button at the left end of the horizontal scroll bar. To switch to page layout view, select View | Page Layout or click the Page Layout View button which is the second button from the left end on the horizontal scroll bar.

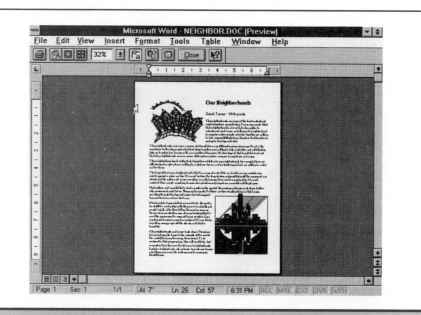

Figure 2-3.   *A previewed document*

You can also *preview* what the printed output from a document will look like by selecting the Print Preview button in the toolbar or by selecting the File | Print Preview command. Word displays a representation of the document as Word will print it, as shown in Figure 2-3. You can click the Print button on the toolbar to print the document as it currently appears. To exit the preview of the printed document, press ESC or click the Close button.

Word also has an outline view and a master document view. Outline view is described further in Chapter 4. Master document view is described under "Templates" in Chapter 4. You can also view a document at various magnification levels, when you want to see the document larger or smaller than it appears when printed. "Viewing Documents" in Chapter 4 has more information about changing the magnification level and other options for previewing a document.

CHAPTER 3

Formatting Documents

Word's *formatting options* allow you to control the appearance of your documents. Up to now you have learned about Word features that focus on entering text, and making sure it's error free, well-organized, spelled correctly, and grammatical. The only formatting actions discussed so far have been pressing ENTER to end a short line or a paragraph, and pressing TAB to indent the first line of a new paragraph. With just these fundamentals you can create a memo or a report, since Word has some default format options for essential elements such as margins and tab stops. These default formats provide an acceptable page layout for basic documents, and you have been using these defaults in your work so far. Now it's time to explore a few more elaborate formatting options that will let you add visual impact to your documents.

Word for Windows offers a full range of formatting features. *Character formatting* allows you to change the appearance of one or more characters. You can display characters in a particular style, size, or font. *Paragraph formatting* lets you define the type of margins, indents, tabs, borders, and alignment you want to implement for a single paragraph or a set of paragraphs. With the *page layout options*, you can change the appearance of an entire page or the whole document, including its margins, paper size, and orientation.

In this chapter you will learn the principles of all three types of formatting. In many instances there are several ways to apply the formatting, although only the simplest approach is presented in this chapter. Chapter 4 offers additional formatting options. You'll want to read all the Ready for More paragraphs in this chapter, which call your attention to some of the more advanced formatting options that you can explore after mastering the basics.

Rest assured, however, that with just the basics presented in this chapter, you can effect some dramatic changes in your documents, as shown in Figure 3-1's preview of one page, before and after formatting. Although the preview's small text size does not clearly show that the text on both pages is the same, it's easy to see how the formatting added to the page on the right has considerably improved the appearance of the page.

Character Formatting

When you format characters, you are changing the appearance of individual letters or symbols. You can change the formatting of one character, a group of characters, or every character in your document. Character formatting options let you change the size of characters, the font or typeface used for characters, or the style of characters, by adding enhancements such as boldface or underlining. Character formatting gives you the greatest ability to control the appearance of your document and its impact on readers. You will quickly find these character formatting features indispensable. Notice how the character formatting of the document in Figure 3-2 prevents the document from looking boring.

You apply all character formatting in the same ways. One way is to set the format of characters and then type them. Your formatting affects only the text your type next, even if the insertion point is in the middle of an existing paragraph. Or, to change the character formatting of existing text, you must select the text before setting the format.

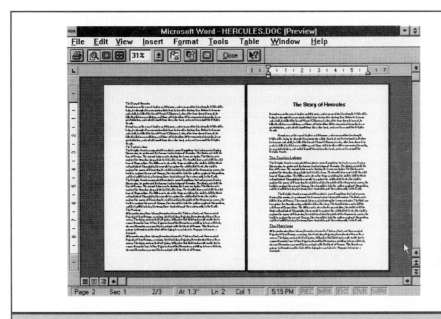

Figure 3-1. *Text with and without formatting*

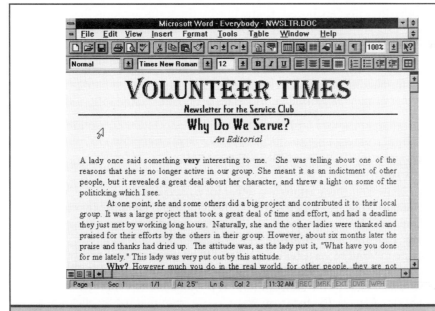

Figure 3-2. *Character formatting adds interest to your document*

Word for Windows offers you several ways to change formatting options, so you can choose the method that works best for you. As mentioned earlier, only the easiest methods are covered in this chapter: You will use the Formatting toolbar (called the *ribbon* in Word for Windows 2) for most settings, because the toolbar is the easiest way to accomplish most formatting tasks. You will use the Font dialog box (called the Character dialog box in Word for Windows 2) only for settings that cannot be changed using the Formatting toolbar. If you are interested in using other methods for invoking character formatting, refer to the "Fonts" section in Chapter 4.

Font Settings

The most noticeable feature of a character is its font. Fonts are sets of alphabetic, numeric, or symbolic characters in various typefaces. For example, if your handwriting were converted to fonts, cursive and printing would be two separate fonts. The fonts you select for your document go a long way toward setting its tone, whether it is traditional, modernistic, or simply fun.

Fonts are either serif, sans serif, or decorative. Serif fonts have little lines or curves, called serifs, at the top and bottom of letters.

- ■ Serif fonts are usually used for the major body of text in a document because they are "anchored" to the line by the serifs, making them easier to read. Also, since serif fonts are typically used in printed material, readers have more experience reading them.

- ■ Sans serif fonts have no anchoring lines. Conventionally, san serif fonts are used for headlines and short sections of text. They can be harder to read at length, but they have a clean line that stands out against serif text.

- ■ Decorative fonts are highly embellished or distorted and provide a graphical element in your document. Never use decorative fonts for more than a few words, because they are hard to read.

In Figure 3-2, the Volunteer Times is a decorative font. It is very pretty but you would not want to use this font for the entire document. The next two lines use the Kino MT font that is a sans serif font that does not have serifs. The rest of the text uses the Times New Roman font that is a serif font.

To change the font of your text, first move the insertion point to where you plan to enter new text, or select the existing text you want to format. Next, click the arrow button for the second-from-left drop-down list box on the Formatting toolbar (ribbon). Choose the font you want to use from that list by clicking it.

CAUTION: Avoid using more than three fonts in a document. Using too many fonts creates a document that is visually confusing your readers.

Size Settings

Another way to change the appearance of text is to change its size. Many fonts come in a variety of sizes. Some fonts only have a few standard sizes, but others are scalable, which means they can be scaled to a number of different sizes. A font's size is specified as the font's height, measured in points. (A point is 1/72 of an inch.) Height rather than width is used to measure, because some fonts have characters that vary in width.

The height specification is the height of the font's capital letters. A typical height for a text font you might use in a letter or report is 10 points. In *proportional fonts*, the letters have different widths even though the height of the capital letters is set the same. When you use a proportional font, an *I* takes up less space than a *W*. Some fonts have the same width for each letter and are called *monospaced fonts*. The width of the characters in a monospaced font is the same, always providing the same number of characters per inch. Look at a sample for a font to see if the characters are all the same size or proportionally sized.

TIP: Use proportional fonts in most text, since they are easier to read. Monospaced fonts are often used in tables, where you want figures or text to line up precisely. All of the TrueType fonts (marked with a TT in Word's Font list) are proportional. TrueType fonts are software fonts that come with Windows or are purchased separately. Printer fonts are built into your printer and can be proportional like TrueType fonts, or monospaced, such as Courier.

To change font size, begin by positioning the insertion point or selecting some text. Click the down-arrow button in the third-from-left drop-down list box in the Formatting toolbar (ribbon). The sizes available for the chosen font appear in this list. Click on a size in the list. If the font is scalable, you can type a font size in this box to have Word scale the font to that size instead of selecting a size.

Look up "Fonts" in Chapter 4 for more information on changing the font size and to get a better understanding of various font characteristics.

Character Style Settings

A third way to emphasize text is to apply character *styles*. There are many character styles, but in all cases a style is applied to the particular size and font that is already established for the text. Word offers the familiar boldfacing, italic, and underlining styles, as well as several other character styles. There are Bold, Italic, and Underline buttons available on the Formatting toolbar (ribbon). Other character styles can only be applied using the Font (Character) dialog box, available through the Format|Font (Character) command.

The less common character styles that Word for Windows provides include Strikethrough, Small Caps, All Caps, and a variety of Underlines in addition to a single underline. Strikethrough places a horizontal line through the text; Small Caps displays lowercase letters as uppercase letters of a smaller font size; and All Caps displays all the text as uppercase letters. The default type of Underline is a single underline beneath all characters and spaces. You can also choose to underline words only with a single line, or to use a double-underline, or (Word for Windows 6 only) to use a dotted underline.

NOTE: You will want to use character styles sparingly to emphasize important text. It is important to apply your style options in a consistent fashion. The box called "Guidelines for Using Character Styles" offers some principles for applying character styles that conform to commonly accepted conventions. If you use the style options as suggested here, their ability to increase the reader's attention to particular details is greatly enhanced.

To apply boldface, italic, or underlines to your text, begin by positioning the insertion point or selecting some text. Next, click the appropriate button in the Formatting toolbar (ribbon). The button for Bold has a boldfaced **B**, the Italic button has an italicized *I*, and the Underline button contains an underlined U. (These buttons are toggles. If bold, italic, or underline formatting has already been applied to selected text, clicking the appropriate button will turn the formatting off.)

To add other character styles to text, begin by positioning the insertion point or selecting some text. Then select Format|Font (Character). Select the check box for the style you want to use. If you are choosing an alternate underline style, you'll need to select it from the Underline drop-down list box. When you finish choosing the styles you want, select OK to apply them.

You can look up each of the style options in Chapter 4 to get more information. Try some of these topics: "Bold," "Italics," "Underline," "All Caps," "Small Cap italics," and "Text Color."

Guidelines for Using Character Styles

Changing a character style to boldface, underline, or italic can add visual interest and emphasis to document text. Avoiding overuse and inconsistent application of these features is an important element in the professional appearance of your document. Here are some ideas for applying these styles in your documents:

- *Italic*
    1. Words and expressions from other languages
    2. A word being defined in a sentence, as in "The word *bare* is sometimes misspelled *bear*"
    3. Letters used as words, as in "Dot your *i*'s and cross your *t*'s"
    4. A term discussed in a sentence, as in "The term *gothic* has different meanings to different people"
    5. Titles of books, magazines, journals, movies, and plays
- **Boldface**
    1. To add emphasis to report headings and letterheads
    2. To add emphasis to text in informal documents such as newsletters
    3. To distinguish user input when creating documentation for computer applications
- Underline
    1. To separate subtotals and totals in a column of numbers
    2. In place of italics if italics are not available

Position Settings

You can change the vertical positioning of text, moving it above or below the normal line of text. *Superscript* text is raised just above the normal line of text; *subscript* text appears just beneath the normal line of text. Super- and subscript text is usually also reduced in size. Word calculates the precise size and position change individually for each font. A typical use for super- or subscript text is in formulas and in chemical symbols, such as H_2O.

To change text to sub- or superscript, position the insertion point where you want to enter the text or select existing characters. Select Format | Font (Character) and mark the Subscript or Superscript check box; then select OK.

See "Super/Subscript" in Chapter 4 for information on specifying the size or position of sub- or superscript text.

Paragraph Formatting

When you format a paragraph, you are designating how the paragraph will appear on the page. You can set the alignment of the lines in the paragraph, the spacing between the lines in the paragraph, the spacing between paragraphs, the indentation for the entire paragraph, and the indentation of just the first line.

As with character formatting, there are several ways to change paragraph formatting settings. This chapter emphasizes techniques using the Formatting toolbar and the ruler to applying some paragraph formatting. Spacing between lines and between paragraphs, however, must be set using the Paragraph dialog box, displayed with the Format | Paragraph command. In Word for Windows 6, these changes are in the Indents and Spacing tab as shown here:

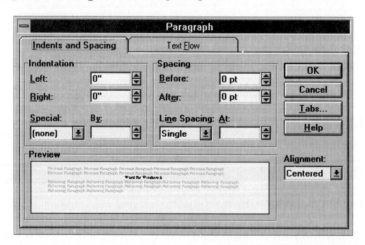

When you set a paragraph format, the format applies to the paragraph containing the insertion point, or for all paragraphs in which there is some selected text. If you create another paragraph after an existing paragraph by pressing ENTER, the new paragraph has the same format as the preceding one.

Other paragraph formatting features not covered in this chapter determine how page breaks affect the paragraph, the tab settings, and whether line numbers appear. Look in Chapter 4 under "Alignment," "Indents," "Pagination," and "Spacing" for further information on these and other paragraph formatting features.

Alignment Settings

The *alignment* of a paragraph determines how the ends of the paragraph's lines align with the margins of the page. You can left-align a paragraph to start the text at the left margin, leaving a "ragged edge" on the right side of the page. You can right-align the paragraph so that the left side is ragged. When you center-align the paragraph, you get an equal amount of space between each margin and the beginning and end of the lines. You can also justify the paragraph, so that the space between words is adjusted to fill the line completely, creating smooth left and right edges to the paragraph that are even with the left and right margin settings. Figure 3-3 shows paragraphs with each of these four alignments.

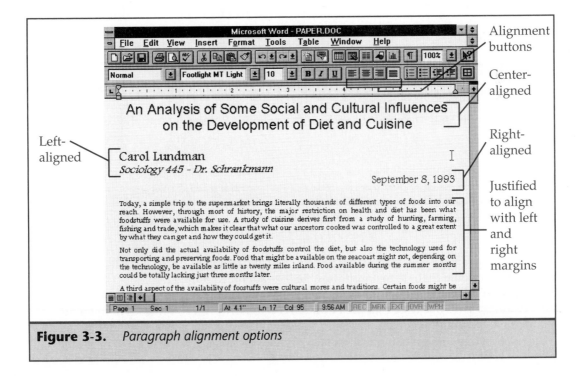

Figure 3-3. *Paragraph alignment options*

To change the alignment of a paragraph, click on one of the four alignment buttons on the Formatting toolbar (ribbon). (These are the buttons to the right of the Underline button.) The lines on the buttons indicate the alignment each represents.

Indentation Settings

Indentation allows you to temporarily alter the location of text in relation to the current margin settings. With Word for Windows you can set the indentation of a paragraph from either the left or right margin, and you can specify a separate indentation for the first line of a paragraph.

To set the indentation for an entire paragraph or set of paragraphs, first position the insertion point or select the paragraphs to be indented. If you are using Word for Windows 2, you may need to click on the symbol at the left end of the ruler until the indentation marks are displayed. Next, find the double triangle in the ruler that indicates the left and first line indent. In Word for Windows 2 you drag the bottom of the two triangles to the desired location on the ruler to set the left indent for all of the lines in the paragraph:

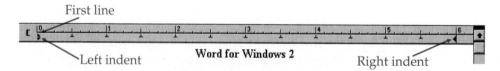

On the other hand, in Word for Windows 6 you drag the bar beneath the two triangles, shown in the following illustration. To set the right indent for the paragraph, drag the single triangle at the right edge of the ruler to the desired location.

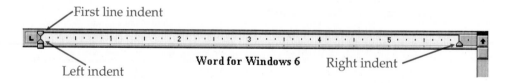

To change the left indent for just the first line of a paragraph, drag the top of the double triangle that indicates the left indent. To set the left indent for everything *but* the first line, drag the bottom triangle in Word for Windows 6, or press SHIFT while dragging the bottom triangle in Word for Windows 2. To move the top *and* bottom of the double triangle together, even if they are separated in the ruler, move the bottom triangle as if you were changing the left indent for the entire paragraph. If the top and bottom triangles are in different locations when you do this, the bottom arrow will move to where you drag it, and the top arrow will move to a new position that is the same distance from the bottom arrow as before.

Spacing Settings

Spacing indicates how close together lines are placed in the document. You can set two types of spacing for your document: the space between the lines within a paragraph, and the spacing between paragraphs. When you increase line spacing, you increase the amount of white space between the text lines within a paragraph. When you increase the space between paragraphs, you add extra white space between paragraphs.

Changing Spacing Within a Paragraph

When you want to change the line spacing within a paragraph, first position the insertion point or select the paragraph. Then select Format | Paragraph, which opens the Paragraph dialog box. Choose a setting in the Line Spacing drop-down list box.

There are two types of options for setting line spacing. You can either work with Word's calculations for the correct line spacing, or you can specify a line spacing to use. The Line Spacing default options are as follows:

- For Single, Word calculates the height of each line based on the height of the capital letters in the largest font used on the line.

- If you select 1.5 Lines or Double, Word simply multiplies the height it calculates for Single by 1.5 or 2.

- You can also select Multiple and enter a value in the At text box, to have Word multiply the calculated height for the line by the value you enter. This lets you do double, triple, or quadruple spacing.

You can also specify line height more precisely:

- Choose the At Least option, and enter a value in the At text box indicating the minimum line height you want Word to use. Word is able to increase the line spacing if needed to accommodate a large font.

- If you choose Exactly and enter a value in the At text box, Word must use that value as the line height, even if this means printing one line on top of another.

Changing Spacing Between Paragraphs

You can add extra space before or after your paragraph. This is commonly done in block-style business letters, in which there is no other way to indicate separate paragraphs. To set space before or after a paragraph, select the paragraphs to be affected or position the insertion point. Select Format | Paragraph and enter a measurement in either the Before or the After text box in the Spacing area of the dialog box. The Before value designates how close the paragraph will be to the preceding paragraph. The After value designates how close the next paragraph will be to the formatted paragraph.

Page Formatting

When you specify page layout options, you control how the text is arranged on the page. You can set the size of the margins, that is, the distance between the edge of the text and the edges of the paper. You can designate what size of paper the text is formatted for, and whether the long or short edge of the paper is at the top (orientation).

Page formatting is done through the Page Setup dialog box, displayed by the File | Page Setup command (Format | Page Setup in Word for Windows 2). Unless you want to change the page formatting options for your entire document, you will want to first position the insertion point on the first page for which you want to change the settings, or select some text from each page for which you want to change the settings.

Margin Settings

The margins of your document are the areas of space between the edge of the paper and the edge of the text. There are four margins on every page: top, bottom, left, and right. You can set each one individually.

If you are planning to print on both sides of the paper, you will want to use mirror margins, in which the margins of facing pages mirror each other. When you use mirror margins, you set inside and outside margins rather than left and right ones. You can also define a *gutter,* which is the amount of the page you expect to lose if the pages of your document will be bound.

To change the margins, begin as usual by positioning the insertion point, or selecting the pages to be affected. Then select File | Page Setup (Format | Page

Setup in Word for Windows 2). Select the Margins tab or option button. Choose
your settings as described just below, and select OK to apply the new margins.

Enter the desired margin measurements in the Top, Bottom, Left, and Right
text boxes. The effect of your settings is shown in an example page in the
Preview box (Sample box in Word for Windows 2). You can see these settings on
the Margins tab shown here:

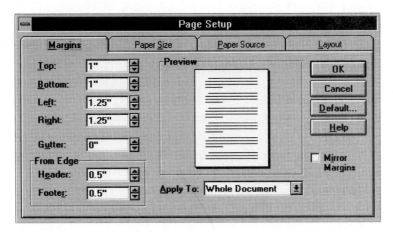

To create mirror margins, select the Mirror Margins check box (Facing Pages
in Word for Windows 2). Notice that the Left and Right text boxes change to
Inside and Outside, and that there are now two example pages in Preview. The
Inside margin measurement is used for the right margin of even-numbered
pages, and the left margin of odd-numbered pages. The Outside setting is used
for the left margin of even-numbered pages and the right margin of
even-numbered pages.

If you plan to bind your pages along the left side, you will need to allow
extra margin space there, since some of the page will be hidden by the binding.
To allow extra space for binding, enter a value in the Gutter text box. This value
is added to the inside or left margin. Defining the gutter and margin space
separately allows you greater flexibility in reformatting the document if you
change to a different binding technique, or change the format of the pages.

Page Size Settings

You can control both the size and orientation of the page that Word uses when
formatting the document. You probably work with standard letter-size pages, 8
1/2 by 11 inches, most of the time. All the predefined Word templates used for

creating new documents use this size. When you print an envelope, or on paper of a different size, it's important to specify that size because Word uses page size in conjunction with other settings (such as margins) to determine where to place text.

To change the paper size for a page in your document, first position the insertion point or select the pages that will use the new size. Then select File | Page Setup and click the Paper Size tab. (In Word for Windows 2, you select Format | Page Setup and then the Size and Orientation radio button.)

Choose a paper size from the Paper Size drop-down list box. Word offers several standard paper sizes. If you are using paper of a different, nonstandard size, enter the paper's measurements in the Width and Height text boxes. Remember that the width of the paper is the measurement of the top of the page, and the height measurement is the side of the page.

As usual, select OK to use the new settings.

Orientation Setting

The orientation of the page determines whether the short edge of the paper is at the top or on the side. *Portrait orientation* uses the width measurement for the top of the page, and the height measurement for the side. With 8 1/2-by-11-inch paper, the top of the page is 8 1/2 inches, and 11 inches is the length of the document. When you change to *landscape orientation*, these measurements are reversed. Working in landscape mode is like writing on a standard sheet of paper that is turned sideways. Portrait orientation is used for most documents; landscape mode is often used with large tables, where the 11-inch width of the page is required in order to show many columns and use a font size that is readable.

Changing the orientation of a page is easy; begin by positioning the insertion point or selecting some text on the pages to be affected. Select File | Page Setup and click the Paper Size tab. (In Word for Windows 2, select Format | Page Setup and the Size and Orientation radio button.) Choose Portrait or Landscape (notice that the values in the Width and Height text boxes exchange places). Then select OK.

THE
COMPLETE

REFERENCE

PART TWO

Commands

4

CHAPTER

Word Commands

This chapter is a comprehensive A through Z reference to all the features found in Word for Windows 2 and 6. Each entry in the chapter includes a description of the feature along with other information such as the procedure for using it, an explanation of the options available, helpful hints, as well as possible applications. Entries are classified alphabetically by the name of the Word feature, but cross-references are used generously throughout. This makes it easy for you to look up a feature if you know the Word command or even just a generic word-processing term that refers to it.

Abbreviations

You can speed up your typing by substituting abbreviations in place of certain frequently used long words, names, and titles. For example, you can use the abbreviation ANSI in place of American National Standards Institute. If the use of abbreviations is not appropriate in your document, you can type the abbreviation and have Word automatically substitute the full name represented by the abbreviation. In the case of the ANSI abbreviation just mentioned, for instance, after the document is typed you can use the Replace feature to replace all occurrences of ANSI with the full name, American National Standard Institute. In Word for Windows 6, the AutoCorrect or AutoText features make it even easier to type an abbreviation and replace it with the complete text.

Some abbreviations are widely used in technical documents, business memos, interoffice correspondence, and catalogs, and will not need to be replaced. The box in this chapter, "Common Abbreviations," lists some abbreviations that you can use with confidence that they will be recognized.

For more information on how to replace abbreviations with the names they represent, see "Find and Replace," "AutoText," and "AutoCorrect."

Common Abbreviations

In the lists of abbreviations that follow you will want to take special note of capitalization and whether or not a period is used. The forms shown for each abbreviation are the ones in common use today, but for some words, there are several acceptable variations. The use of periods, again, conforms to standard usage, but many references drop nearly all periods in abbreviations, while some use periods in all abbreviations. You may want to see if the organization or group you are working with uses a single style manual so you can match your abbreviations to that style.

Word	Abbreviation	Word	Abbreviation
abbreviation	abbr.	Association	Assn.
account	acct.	associate	assoc.
additional	addl.	assistant	asst.
also known as	a.k.a.	attachment	att.
amount	amt.	balance	bal.
anonymous	anon.	building	bldg.
Accounts Payable	AP	care of	c/o
Accounts Receivable	AR	collect on delivery	c.o.d.
		continued	cont.

Word	Abbreviation	Word	Abbreviation
central standard time	cst or CST	Not available/ Not applicable	NA
Chief Executive Officer	CEO	pacific standard time	pst or PST
Chief Financial Officer	CFO	package	pkg.
Company	Co.	pound or pounds	lb.
credit	cr.	purchase order	PO
debit	dr.	return on investment	ROI
department	dept.	ounce	oz.
discount	dis.	quart	qt.
eastern standard time	est or EST	quarterly	qtr.
		seconds	sec.
enclosure	enc.	self-addressed, stamped envelope	SASE
feet/foot	ft.		
for example	e.g.	standard	std.
free on board	f.o.b.	temperature or temporary	temp.
gallon	gal.		
inclusive	inc.	Universal Product Code	UPC
Incorporated	Inc.		
miles per gallon	mpg or MPG	volume	vol.
miles per hour	mph or MPH	with	w/
mountain standard time	mst or MST	without	w/o
		year	yr.

Accelerator Keys

Accelerator keys is a another term for shortcut keys. See "Shortcut Keys."

Accepting Revisions

See "Revision and Annotation Merging" and "Comparing Versions."

Active Document

The *active document* is the one that currently contains the insertion point. When you type text or select commands, you affect the active document. You activate a document by clicking it or by selecting the window containing it from the Window menu.

Add/Edit Routing Slip

See "Electronic Mail."

Adding Borders to Graphics or Text

See "Borders and Shading."

Adding Numbers

See "Math Calculations."

Addresses for Routing Documents

See "Electronic Mail."

Advance

In WordPerfect, you use the Advance feature to position text or graphics precisely on a page. In Word for Windows, you do this by inserting a frame around the text or graphic and then positioning the frame. For information on positioning frames, see "Frames."

   In Word for Windows 6, you can also use the ADVANCE field for the same effect. See "Fields" for more information on how to use the ADVANCE field.

ADVANCE Field

The ADVANCE field positions text precisely. For more information, see "Fields."

Aligning a Frame

When you align a frame, you set its position on a page. See "Frames" to learn how to align or position frames.

Aligning Text

See "Alignment," "Tabs," "Sections," and "Frames" for information on aligning text.

Aligning Pages

See "Margins," "Page Setup," "Page Size and Orientation," and "Paper Source."

Alignment

Word offers you four ways to align paragraphs between the left and right margins. You can left-align, right-align, center or justify paragraphs in Word. Alignment of text between the left and right margins is a Paragraph formatting option.

Procedures

Alignment is a Paragraph format option, applied using either the Formatting toolbar (ribbon), the Paragraph dialog box, or shortcut keys. When you change the alignment, the new alignment affects the paragraph where the insertion point is, or all paragraphs containing some selected text. If you press ENTER within a paragraph, creating a new paragraph, the new paragraph has the same alignment as the previous one.

Begin by selecting text or positioning the insertion point to indicate the paragraphs you want to realign. Then choose one of the following procedures.

TIP: *To revert to the default paragraph alignment, press* CTRL+Q. *This removes all direct paragraph formatting from the affected paragraphs, not just the alignment.*

With the Formatting Toolbar (Ribbon)

Click on one of the following alignment buttons in the Formatting toolbar (ribbon). The first button left-aligns, the second centers, the third right-aligns, and the fourth justifies.

With the Paragraph Dialog Box

1. Select Format | Paragraph, or, in Word for Windows 6 right-click the document area and select Paragraph from the shortcut menu.

2. In Word for Windows 6, select the Indents and Spacing tab, if necessary.

3. Choose a setting from the Alignment drop-down list box, and select OK.

With the Shortcut Keys

Press one of the four shortcut key-combinations shown in the following table:

Shortcut	Result
CTRL+L	Left-aligns paragraphs
CTRL+E	Centers paragraphs
CTRL+R	Right-aligns paragraphs
CTRL+J	Justifies paragraphs

Hints

Here are some hints about how alignment works and how it affects paragraphs which are indented.

What Alignments Look Like

When you change the alignment of a paragraph, you are changing how the words are arranged on the line between the left and right margins or indents. Figure 4-1 shows centered, right-aligned and justified paragraphs used to create a flyer; this screen is in Page Layout view.

■ In left-aligned paragraphs, each line starts at the left margin or indent, and looks ragged along the right side because each line has a slightly different length.

Figure 4-1.   *Examples of alignment*

■ Centered paragraphs have ragged edges on both the right and left sides. The center of each line is the midpoint between the left and right margins or indents.

■ In right-aligned paragraphs, each line ends at the right margin or indent, so the left edge appears ragged.

■ In justified paragraphs, Word adjusts the space between words to make each line start at the left margin or indent and end exactly at the right margin or indent. The last line of the paragraph is left-aligned.

Indented Paragraphs

When you apply an indent to a paragraph, you are effectively adding an additional margin to that paragraph. The alignment for the paragraph uses the additional margin for aligning the paragraph; therefore, the text is aligned using the indent rather than the margin set with the margin feature. For example, if you create a first-line indent of .5 inch and then justify the paragraph, the first line begins .5 inch to the right of the left margin, instead of at the left margin.

Applications

Left-alignment is the most common alignment for text documents because it is easiest to read.

Justified text works well in printed material such as books, brochures, and newspapers. Justification should be used sparingly in documents that contain technical or long words, unless you are also planning to use hyphenation. Otherwise, you will have the occasional line that contains only one or two long words, and a lot of white space.

Centering works best for titles, page numbers, and other headings. Remember that you can center paragraphs that contain only a single line. Do not center substantial sections of body text, because it is difficult to read for more than a few lines.

Right-alignment adds a modern flair to text, but should be used sparingly because it is more difficult to read than left-aligned or justified text. Frequently, right-alignment is used in sidebars, which are thin columns of text that appear to one side of a wider column of main body text, providing explanations, quotations, or further insights to the main discussion.

Related Topics

Indents
Margins
Page Setup
Sections
Styles

All Caps

All Caps is a Character formatting option that displays all characters as uppercase. All Caps can provide emphasis in titles and headings, and can be used in scripts and speeches to make them easier to read.

Procedures

All Caps can be applied to new or existing text. To apply it to new text, first add the format and then type the text. To apply it to existing text, select the text and then add the style. Next are the procedures for adding and removing All Caps.

With the Font Dialog Box

1. Select Format | Font (Character in Word for Windows 2), or, in Word for Windows 6, right-click the mouse and select Font, to open the Font dialog box.

2. In Word for Windows 6, select the Font tab if necessary.

3. Select the All Caps check box to turn the option on if you are applying this format, or to turn it off if you are removing this format. Select OK.

With the Keyboard

Press CTRL+SHIFT+A (CTRL+A in Word for Windows 2) to toggle the All Caps format on and off.

Hints

In Word for Windows 2, another way to open the Character dialog box is to double-click on a blank spot of the ribbon. In Word for Windows 2 you cannot open a shortcut menu by right-clicking the document area.

You can put all text in capital letters as you type by pressing the CAPS LOCK key before typing.

To cycle through three capitalization options, select text and then press SHIFT+F3. As you press this key-combination, the selected text changes from all lowercase letters, to initial capitals (the first letter of each word uppercase and the rest lowercase), and then to all uppercase. However, if you select a whole sentence or paragraph before using SHIFT+F3 to cycle through capitalization options, you do not get initial caps on all words in the sentence or paragraph. Word recognizes sentences and keeps only the first letter of the sentence capitalized.

Removing Formatting

Another way to remove All Caps is to select the text and press CTRL+SPACEBAR. This removes all character formatting from the selected text, not just All Caps.

Related Topics

Fonts

Alphabetizing

See "Sorting."

Alt Key

When you are using the keyboard, you use the ALT key in combination with other keys to select from menus and dialog boxes and to carry out commands and macros. Press ALT when the insertion point is in a document to activate the menu bar, and then press the key for one of the underlined letters in the menu titles to open that menu. To select a command or option in a dialog box, press ALT and the key for the underlined letter in that command or option.

For information on how to use the ALT key with function keys, see "Function Keys."

Related Topics

Function Keys
Shortcut Keys

Annotation

Annotations are initialed comments that can be added to a document and are typically used to let readers other than the author make comments to a document that has been locked. (In a locked document the text is protected from changes except by the document's original author.) Annotations are indicated in the text of the document by an *annotation mark*, which consists of the initials of the user who entered it and a sequential number. The text of the annotation does not appear in the document, but in a special annotation pane.

Procedures

The following procedures will tell you how to prepare your document for annotations, how to create them, and how to edit and work with them.

A

Locking and Unlocking a Document

You use annotations with locked documents. After you lock a document to prevent other people from changing it, annotations allow people reviewing the locked document to make comments and suggest changes. The method for locking documents depends on whether you are using Word for Windows 2 or Word for Windows 6.

In Word for Windows 6, when you lock a document, no one can make changes to the text. Anyone can turn off this protection, however, unless you also set a password when you lock the document. The password must be provided in order to unprotect the document. To protect a document in Word for Windows 6:

1. In the document to protect, select Tools | Protect Document to open the Protect Document dialog box.

2. Select Annotations. The other option buttons protect the document in different ways.

3. If you want to prevent another user from turning off your document protection, enter a password in the Password text box. The password can be up to 15 characters long. When you type the password, Word displays asterisks instead of the actual characters, so type the password carefully. When you're done, select OK.

TIP: Don't forget to record the password somewhere, so you won't forget it.

To unprotect a Word for Windows 6 document:

1. Select Tools | Unprotect Document.

2. If you assigned a password when you protected the document, you will have to provide the password before the document is unprotected.

Word for Windows 2 treats locking documents differently: Documents are locked as part of being saved. When a locked document is opened, Word compares the author name, as recorded in the Summary Info dialog box, to the user name for the application, as recorded in the User Options dialog box. This means you can actually alter any document by modifying your user name to match its author name. When the user and author names are the same, Word for Windows 2 lets you modify the text of the document. When the author and user names don't match, only annotations can be added to the document.

The steps for locking/unlocking a document in Word for Windows 2 are the following:

1. In the document you want to lock, select File | Save (File | Save As if the document has already been saved).

2. Select the File Sharing command button, to open the File Sharing dialog box.

3. Select the Lock File for Annotations check box to lock the document, or clear the check box it to unlock it. Then select OK.

4. You can also enter a password in the Protection Password text box. This means readers who can provide the password can open the document, but the document is still locked for annotations only. As a rule, you'll want to *either* assign a password *or* lock the document for annotations, but don't do both.

5. Select OK again to save the document.

Inserting Annotations

When you insert an annotation, Word adds an annotation mark to your document, formatted as hidden text. The annotation mark consists of the user's initials and a sequential number. The annotation text itself appears only in the annotations pane.

1. Move the insertion point to where you want to insert an annotation mark.

TIP: *In Word for Windows 6, if you select text before inserting an annotation, that text will be selected and highlighted when someone views or goes to that annotation. This can help the person reading your annotation recognize which text is referred to in the annotation.*

2. Select Insert | Annotation. Word inserts an annotation mark at the insertion point, and opens the annotations pane.

3. Type the annotation text, as shown in Figure 4-2.

4. Close the Annotations pane, by clicking Close or pressing ALT+SHIFT+C.

   If you want to return to the document window without closing the annotations pane, click on the document text or press F6. To switch back to the annotations pane, select Insert | Annotation again, click on the open annotations pane or press F6.

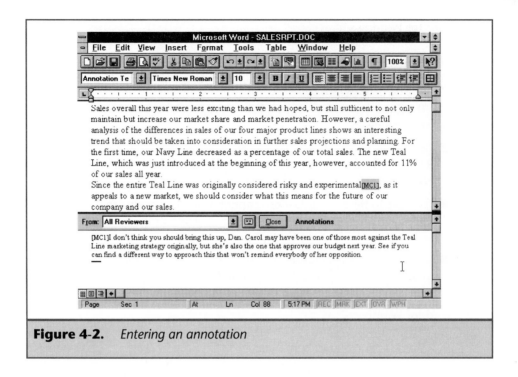

Figure 4-2.   *Entering an annotation*

Displaying Annotation Marks

Annotation marks are formatted as hidden text. To display them in the document, you have to display hidden text. You can do this temporarily by selecting the Show/Hide button on the Formatting toolbar (ribbon), or by changing the View settings using the Tools | Options command.

Viewing Annotations

To view annotations, open the annotations pane either by selecting View | Annotations, or double-clicking on an annotation mark in the document.

   In Word for Windows 6, you can choose to view all annotations, or only those of a single reviewer. To view selected annotations, choose that reviewer's name in the From drop-down list box in the Annotations pane's toolbar. You can open this list box by clicking it or by pressing ALT+SHIFT+R.

Going To an Annotation

Use the Edit | Go To command to move to a specific annotation quickly. Go To works differently in Word for Windows 2 and 6.

In Word for Windows 6:

1. Select Edit | Go To or press F5.

2. Select Annotations from the Go To What list box.

3. Use the Enter Reviewer's Name list box to specify the annotation you want, as follows:

   ■ To move to the next or last annotation, leave the default entry, Any Reviewer, in the Enter Reviewer's Name drop-down list box and select Next or Previous.

   ■ To move to the next or last next annotation of a specific reviewer, select the reviewer from the Enter Reviewer's Name drop-down list box before selecting Next or Previous.

   ■ To move to a particular numbered annotation, type that number in the Enter Reviewer's Name text box and select Go To.

In Word for Windows 2:

1. Select Edit | Go To or press F5 twice.

2. In the Go To text box, type **a** to move to the next annotation, or **a** and a number to move to that numbered annotation.

3. Select OK to go to the specified annotation.

Editing Annotations

To edit an existing annotation, click the annotations pane or press F6. (If the pane is not already open, you'll need to select View | Annotations first.) Then edit the annotation. You can either close the annotations pane or leave it open, as instructed earlier in "Inserting Annotations."

Deleting Annotations

1. Display the annotations marks, by selecting View | Annotations or by clicking the Show/Hide button in the Standard toolbar. Move to the mark for the annotation you want to delete.

2. Highlight the annotation mark in the document window, and press DEL or BACKSPACE. The annotation mark and the annotation are deleted.

A

Pasting Annotations into Text

You can paste the text of an annotation from the annotations pane into the document by cutting or copying the annotation in the pane to the Clipboard, moving to the document window, and pasting. (Remember that the document will have to be unprotected in order for you to paste in annotations.)

Printing Annotations

You can print annotations with the document or by themselves.

1. Select File | Print.

2. Select the Print What (Print in Word for Windows 2) drop-down list box.

   ■ *To print the document with its annotations* select Document from this drop-down list box to print the annotations and the text.

   ■ *To print only annotations* select Annotations and skip to step 4.

3. Select Options then the Annotations check box, to print annotations with the document text.

4. Select OK to print.

   When you print both the document and annotations, the annotations start on a new page after the text. The annotation text appears after the page number of the annotation mark, the user's initials, and an annotation number.

Creating or Reviewing Voice Annotations

In Word for Windows 6, you can create and review voice annotations, assuming you have the appropriate sound equipment installed in your computer. To record voice annotations, you need both a sound board and a microphone installed, but you only need the sound board to review voice annotations.

   Creating voice annotations is not much different from creating text annotations. If you want to create a combined text and voice annotation, start by entering a text annotation as usual, then put the insertion point next to the annotation mark in the document, and insert the voice annotation using the following steps:

1. Position the insertion point for inserting the voice annotation.

2. Select Insert | Annotation, and click the Insert Sound Object button in the Annotations pane's toolbar.

3. Record your voice annotation, using the instructions for recording that came with your sound board.

4. If, when you finish recording, Word displays a message asking if you want to update the sound object, select Yes.

5. Select Close or return to the document window.

Listening to sound annotations is also very similar to viewing your text annotations.

1. Select View | Annotations.

2. In the Annotations pane, double-click the sound symbol for the voice annotation you want to hear.

3. When you're finished, select Close or return to the document window.

Hints

Use annotations to get feedback from a number of people on a draft of a document. Word's annotations are easier to read and review than handwritten notes on printouts of the document.

You can also use annotations to get responses on proposals. Send the protected document file to everyone who may need to comment on the proposal, and request their comments. When the files come back to you, you can print the reviewer's comments and begin making any necessary adjustments to your proposal. Of course, you first need to check that your reviewers use Word for Windows, and know how to add annotations.

Related Topics

Electronic Mail
Footnotes and Endnotes
Viewing Documents

ANSI Codes

The ANSI codes are a set of 256 characters standardized by the American National Standards Institute. Most fonts use this set of characters, so when you change fonts in your document, the characters stay the same. For example, if you type a J in Times Roman font and then switch to Arial, the J does not become a Z because both fonts use the same code for J.

Some fonts, usually called *symbol fonts,* do not correspond to the ANSI set of characters. For example, if you type a *J* in the Times Roman font and then change to the Wingdings font, your *J* becomes a smiley face.

See "Special Characters" for instructions on inserting symbol font characters so that they do not change when you switch fonts.

Anchoring

You can lock the position of a frame by anchoring it to a paragraph, character, or page. See "Frames" for more information.

Antonyms

An antonym is word that is the opposite of another word. Use the Thesaurus to find antonyms for words in your documents. See "Thesaurus" to learn more about this feature.

Append

See "Spike" for information on how to cut or copy multiple items and paste (append) them as a unit.

Arranging Records

See "Sorting."

Arrow Keys

The arrow keys are used to navigate in documents (that is, to move the insertion point). For more information on using these keys, see "Moving the Insertion Point."

ASCII Text Files

ASCII text files contain characters only, with no formatting, and no end-of-line or other extraneous special characters. You can save or retrieve ASCII text files in

Word for Windows. Many programs can work with ASCII text files; so when you need to work with data in a program that cannot use the Windows Clipboard, such as a DOS-based program, save the file in an ASCII-format text file.

ASK Field

The ASK field prompts for information during a mail merge. See "Mail Merge" and "Fields."

Attaching Templates to Documents

See "Templates."

Attributes

If you are familiar with WordPerfect 5.1 or earlier, you may be accustomed to assigning colors to represent different types of characters, and calling these color assignments *attributes*. In all views of Word for Windows, character formatting such as boldfacing, italic, and font size are displayed just as they will print, so you do not need to assign attributes. Some people refer to character formatting as character attributes.

For more information on Word for Windows views, see "Views." For more information on characters styles, see "Character Formats" in this chapter, or review the "Character Formatting" section in Chapter 3.

Audio

You can record and use sound clips with Word for Windows 6, if your system has a sound board. See "Sound" for more information.

AUTHOR Field

The AUTHOR field is used to insert the name of the author into the documents. See "Fields" for more information.

Authorities

A *table of authorities* is used in a legal brief to list citations of court decisions and other legal documents, and their location within the brief. The citations are sorted by type of source, so that citations referring to different levels of the court system appear separately. For example, a table of authorities might include individual tables for citations from the Supreme Court, federal courts, and state courts; federal and state laws and regulations; and legal commentary.

Word for Windows 2 and 6 create tables of authorities differently. In Word for Windows 6, you use the Table of Authorities feature (explained in its own section of this chapter). There is no specific feature in Word for Windows 2 for creating tables of authorities. You can construct tables of authorities in Word for Windows 2 using bookmarks with Sequence and Reference fields. See "Bookmarks" and "Fields" later in this chapter for a complete explanation of these features.

> *TIP: Microsoft distributes a free package called "Legal Resource Kit," which includes a Word for Windows 2 macro that makes it easier to create tables of authorities in that version of the program.*

AutoCaption

See "Captions."

AutoCorrect

AutoCorrect is a new Word for Windows 6 feature that automatically corrects many standard typographical mistakes. For instance, AutoCorrect will automatically do the following, as you type:

- Replace straight quote marks (primes) with "curly quotes"
- Make sure names of days and first words in sentences are capitalized
- Correct words where you have capitalized the first two letters
- Replace abbreviations with the words they represent
- Correct standard typographical errors

See the box, "Rules for Creating Correctly Spelled Plurals," for guidance on some mistakes you might make, so that you can create AutoCorrect entries for them.

Procedures

Before you can use AutoCorrect, you need to turn it on. If you want AutoCorrect to fill out abbreviations and correct standard errors, you first need to tell AutoCorrect what you want substituted.

Turning AutoCorrect On and Off

1. Select Tools | AutoCorrect.

2. Select the check boxes to indicate which features of AutoCorrect you want to use. If you want to turn AutoCorrect off, clear all of these check boxes. Then select OK.

Creating an AutoCorrect Entry

1. If you want to replace errors or abbreviations with long sections of text, or with text that contains formatting, begin by creating the replacement text and selecting it.

2. Select Tools | AutoCorrect.

3. In the Replace text box, enter the typographical error or abbreviation to be replaced.

4. In the With text box, enter the correct or expanded version of text. If you selected text before opening the AutoCorrect dialog box, that text now appears in the With text box. Also, the Plain Text and Formatted Text option buttons are activated. Select the appropriate option button:

   ■ Plain Text saves the text without formatting, so that it takes on the formatting that surrounds it when it is entered.

   ■ Formatted Text saves the text with its current formatting, so that it is always inserted with that formatting.

5. Select Add and then OK.

A

Rules for Creating Correctly Spelled Plurals

Although plurals are normally formed by adding *s* or *es* to the singular form of the noun, there are a number of exceptions. Some of the more common exceptions are

- When a noun ends in a *y* preceded by a consonant, change the *y* to *i* and add *es*. For example, *trophy* becomes *trophies*. If a vowel precedes the *y*, you can simply add an *s*. For example, "She received more than 20 toys for Christmas."

- If the singular form of the noun ends in a silent *s*, the plural does not require the addition of a second *s*, although the *s* is typically pronounced in the plural form. For example, "General Smith's Special Forces Corps will receive their new orders on the same day as all the other corps on the base."

- Letters are made plural with either *s* or *'s* depending on whether they are uppercase or lowercase. For example, "Cross all your t's," and "The degrees will be conferred for the Ph.D's on Thursday."

- Some singular nouns that end with an *o* preceded by a consonant take *es* to form the plural, and others simply take an *s*. For example, "Why did you direct the movers to put the pianos in the same room with the crates of potatoes?"

- Words ending in *ch* or *sh* form their plural with *es*. For example, "There are four churches in our community," and "I broke two dishes last night."

- Nouns that end in *s*, *x*, or *z* typically form plurals with *es*. For example, "We sent twelve faxes to him last week."

- Abbreviations normally are made plural by adding an *s* to the singular form. For example, "Col. 1 contains the answer, but the answer can be found in cols. 1 and 2." or "The YWCAs in Akron chose to centralize child care at the West Exchange Street YWCA."

- Proper names or nouns use an *s* or an *es* to create the plural. Never change the original spelling of the name or nouns when you make the plural. For example, "There are two Marys and three Felixes living in Winnebagos."

- Hyphenated words change from singular to plural by making the most important word plural. For example, "All the mothers-in-law were presented corsages," and "Follow-ups are scheduled on Wednesdays." Compound words that are spelled open (with a space rather than a hyphen) follow the same rule.

- Words of foreign derivation frequently use the foreign form for their plural. For example, "I measured the radii of the circles."

Deleting or Editing an AutoCorrect Entry

1. If you want to replace the text supplied by an AutoCorrect entry with formatted text or a long text section, begin by creating and selecting the replacement text.

2. Select Tools | AutoCorrect.

3. In the list box under Replace Text as You Type, highlight the entry to be replaced.

4. To edit the entry, enter a new replacement text in the With text box, and then select Replace. To delete the entry, select Delete. Then select OK.

Options

The following options are available with AutoCorrect.

Change 'Straight Quotes' to "Smart Quotes"

Select this check box to have Word for Windows automatically replace straight quotation marks (primes or foot marks) with "smart quotes" (curly quotation marks).

Correct TWo INitial CApitals

Select this check box to have Word for Windows automatically correct words beginning with two capitals so only the initial letter is capitalized.

Capitalize First Letter of Sentences

Select this check box to have Word automatically capitalize the first word in a sentence. Word will capitalize any word following a period, question mark, or exclamation mark that is preceded by a character and followed by a space.

Capitalize Names of Days

Select this check box to have Word for Windows automatically capitalize the days of the week when they are spelled out. If the day of the week is abbreviated, as in *Mon*, the word will not be capitalized.

Replace Text as You Type

Select this check box to have Word for Windows automatically replace text with other text, using the AutoCorrect entries that you have provided. Even if this check box is turned off, Word still replaces quotation marks and corrects capitalization.

Hints

There may be situations where you have created an AutoCorrect entry to replace certain text, but sometimes you want to enter that text without having Word correct it. In this case, you need to turn AutoCorrect off, enter the text, and then turn AutoCorrect back on. For example, if you needed to enter *teh,* perhaps to demonstrate something or as a non-English word, you would turn AutoCorrect off, type **teh**, and then turn AutoCorrect back on, to prevent it from "correcting" *teh* to *the.*

Related Topics

AutoText
Find and Replace
Spelling

AutoFormat

AutoFormat is a Word for Windows 6 feature that analyzes your document, making changes and applying styles based on its interpretations. AutoFormat can quickly convert a plain document into an attractively formatted document with little effort on your part.

Procedures

You can AutoFormat your document automatically, with or without reviewing it.

Formatting Your Document Automatically

1. Create the document.

2. Select Format | AutoFormat and then OK.

3. To review the changes made to your document, select Review Changes. The revision marks, which indicate where the document was changed, appear in the document, and the Review AutoFormat Changes dialog box appears above the document. In this dialog box you can choose to move to the next or last revision, or to reject any one change. When you are done, select Cancel.

4. If you want to use another set of styles in the document, select Style Gallery to get the Style Gallery dialog box. Choose a template from the Template list box, and examine the Preview of box to see how your document will look formatted with this other template. Select OK when you are ready, and the currently highlighted template will be used for the document.

5. To accept the changes made, select Accept. You can also choose to reject all of the changes made, by selecting Reject All.

Formatting Your Document Automatically Without Reviewing

If you do not wish to review the changes made by Word when it AutoFormats your document, and then press CTRL+K or select the AutoFormat button:

Options

Before letting AutoFormat format your document, you can define how you want Word to do this. Select the Options button in the AutoFormat dialog box, which opens the Options dialog box. You can also reach this dialog box by selecting Tools | Options and selecting the AutoFormat tab. By default, all of the AutoFormat options are turned on.

Preserve

Select the Previously Applied Styles check box when you don't want AutoFormat to apply new styles to paragraphs that are already formatted with styles.

Apply Styles To

Choose Headings, Lists, or Other Paragraphs to designate which types of paragraphs you want AutoFormat to apply styles to. By default, all three of these check boxes are selected.

Adjust

When the Paragraph Marks, Tabs and Spaces, or Empty Paragraphs check boxes are selected, Word will adjust these aspects of your document to make formatting more efficient. With Paragraph Marks selected, excess paragraph marks are removed where word wrap is more appropriate. With Tabs and Spaces selected, spaces are replaced with tabs and excess tabs are removed. With Empty Paragraphs selected, blank paragraphs are deleted between paragraphs with certain types of formats.

Replace

When these check boxes are enabled, AutoFormat replaces text to make your document look better. The Straight Quotes with Smart Quotes option tells Word to supply curly quotes in place of straight quotes (primes or foot marks). With the Symbol Characters with Symbols option, Word replaces characters such as *R* with ® and *th* with ™. The Bullet Characters with Bullets option tells Word to replace symbols used for bullets, such as * or -, with actual bullet symbols, such as •.

Related Topics

Styles

AUTONUM Field

Use the AUTONUM field to insert paragraph numbers automatically. See "Fields" for more information.

AUTONUMLGL Field

Use the AUTONUMLGL field to insert legal format paragraph numbers automatically. See "Fields" for more information.

AUTONUMOUT Field

Use the AUTONUMOUT field to insert Outline format paragraph numbers automatically. see "Fields" for more information on this and other fields, and "Outlines" for information on how outlines work.

AutoText

AutoText is a Word for Windows 6 feature that lets you enter text into your document faster. You create an AutoText entry that defines what you will type in the document, and the text that you want to replace it. Unlike AutoCorrect, with AutoText you can choose when to have Word add the new text.

AutoText in Word for Windows 6 does same thing as the Glossary feature in Word for Windows 2. (To see how to use the Word for Windows 2 Glossary feasure, see "Glossary.")

Procedures

First create an AutoText entry. Then you can type text in the document and use AutoText to replace that text.

Creating an AutoText Entry

1. Enter the text you want to use as an AutoText entry in the document and select it. This is the actual text that you want inserted into the document.

2. Select Edit | AutoText or click on the AutoText button, shown in the margin.

3. Edit the text in the Name text box. This is what you will type into the document and that AutoText will replace. Make sure that this name is meaningful, so that you can easily remember it while you are typing your document.

4. By default, AutoText entries are available to all documents. If you want to restrict this AutoText entry so that it is only available to documents created with a certain template, choose that template from the Make AutoText Entry Available To drop-down list box.

5. You can choose to save the replacement text with the current formatting or without it, by selecting Formatted Text or Plain Text. If you select Plain text, when the text is inserted, it will adopt the formatting of the text it replaces.

6. Select Add.

Using AutoText

1. Type the name of the AutoText entry.

2. With the insertion point within or next to the AutoText name, press F3 and click on the AutoText button or select Edit I AutoText and Insert. Word replaces the AutoText name with the text you assigned to that name.

For example, in Figure 4-3 the company letterhead, which combines the company logo, slogan, and address, was inserted by typing an AutoText entry called **logo** and pressing F3. Now the user is ready to create the letter by simply typing it. Consider using AutoText to create your own letterhead when its text and graphic will also be used in flyers, memos, or other documents in different locations (see "Hints" in this section). Normally, a letterhead that will only be used for letters would be saved as a template.

Editing or Deleting AutoText Entries

1. If you want to replace the AutoText entry's replacement text, enter and format the new text.

Figure 4-3.   *Text and graphic entered using AutoText*

2. Select Edit | AutoText.

3. In the Name list box, highlight the name of the AutoText entry you are editing or deleting.

4. Select Add to edit the entry or Delete to delete it. If you select Add, Word displays a dialog box asking if you want to replace the current AutoText entry. Select Yes to do so.

5. Select OK.

Hints

AutoText can be used to insert either text and graphics. For example, you might save a company logo as an AutoText entry, and use "logo" as the name.

If you use AutoText to insert a field, make sure to update the field by pressing F9 immediately after inserting the field. The field will display whatever it contained when you created the AutoText entry, rather than the up-to-date setting.

Related Topics

AutoCorrect
Find and Replace
Glossary

AUTOTEXT Field

The AUTOTEXT field inserts an AutoText entry into the documents. See "AutoText" and "Fields" for an explanation of this and other fields.

Automatic Backup

See "Saving Files."

Automatic Font Substitution

There are two occasions when Word for Windows may automatically substitute one font for another. One is when you do not have both a screen and printer font for the font you choose. This other is when you retrieve a document that uses a font you do not have.

Fonts have various commands to tell your printer how to print them, and to tell your computer monitor how to display them. If your printer has sets of fonts installed, but has no equivalent *screen fonts* to tell your computer how to display them, Word will use the closest available screen font to display the font on your monitor. "Closest" does not mean exact, however, so the appearance may well differ. Also, if you have installed screen fonts on your computer, but do not have the equivalent *printer font* to tell your printer how to create them, your printer will use the closest available printer font. If your printed document does not match what is appearing on your screen, switch to a font for which you *do* have both the screen and printer versions.

If you retrieve a document that uses fonts not available on your system, Word will automatically substitute the font it thinks is closest, either in display or printing. You can either accept the substitutions, or change the font using the usual font formatting methods.

In Word for Windows 6, you have another choice for dealing with this situation: You can select Tools | Options, select the Compatibility tab, and then Font Substitution. Using the Font Substitution dialog box, change the font assigned to substitute for the font in the document. The advantage to doing this is that if you save the document with your changes, and retrieve it on another computer that does have the missing fonts installed, the document will not need reformatting. The file still uses the fonts that were missing on your system. See "Compatability Options" for more information on this font substitution feature.

Automatic Saving

See "Saving Files."

Backnotes

Backnotes is another name for endnotes. See "Footnotes and Endnotes."

Backspace Key

Use the BACKSPACE key to delete text: Position the insertion point after the text to delete and press BACKSPACE. Unlike the DEL key, which also deletes text, BACKSPACE removes text *behind* the insertion point.

Backup

See "Saving Files."

BARCODE Field

Use the BARCODE field to insert a bar code for a zip code into your document. See "Fields" in this chapter for information.

Bending Text

See "WordArt."

Block

See "Selecting Text."

Block Protecting

In WordPerfect, block protection is a feature that keeps lines or paragraphs together on a page. See "Keeping Paragraphs Together on the Page" or "Keeping Lines on the Same Page" under "Pagination" for the equivalent features in Word for Windows.

Bold

Bold, or boldface, is a character style that produces heavy, dark characters. Bold is often used to provide emphasis in titles, headings, and important text.

Procedures

Bold can be applied either as you are typing, or after you have typed the text. To apply Bold while typing, you add the format, type the text to be affected, and then remove the format. To apply Bold to existing text, select the text to formatted and then add the style.

Adding and Removing Bold with the Font Dialog Box

1. In Word for Windows 6, select Format | Font to open the Font dialog box. Or you can right-click the mouse at the insertion point to open the shortcut menu, and then select Font to open the Font dialog box.

   In Word for Windows 2, select Format | Character to open the Character dialog box. Or you can double-click on a blank spot of the Ribbon.

2. In Word for Windows 6, select Bold in the Font Style list box. In Word for Windows 2, select the Bold check box in the Style area. If you are removing Bold, choose another style in the list box, or select the check box again to clear it. Then select OK.

Adding and Removing Bold with the Toolbar

To either add or remove Bold, click on the Bold button (shown in the margin) in the Formatting toolbar.

Adding and Removing Bold with the Keyboard

To either add or remove Bold, press CTRL+B.

Hints

Another procedure for removing Bold from text is to select the text, and press CTRL+SPACEBAR. This removes all character formatting from the selected text.

Many dot-matrix printers print boldface text by overprinting it, or by printing the text a second time, offsetting it slightly to make the lines of the letter thicker. If the bold style is not printing to your satisfaction, consult your printer's manual for options to change the way bold is created.

Related Topics

Character Formats
Fonts

BOOKMARK Field

Use the BOOKMARK field to insert text marked with a bookmark in another section of the document. See "Fields" for more information about this field. See "Bookmarks," just below, for more about working with bookmarks.

Bookmarks

Use Word's bookmarks feature to mark a position or some text in a document. You can reference these bookmarks in field names, or use them to quickly find a specific location in a document.

Procedures

The following procedures will tell you how to insert, move, delete or go to bookmarks.

Inserting and Moving Bookmarks with the Dialog Box

1. Put the insertion point where you want to insert the bookmark. To mark text rather than a position in the document, select the text.

2. Select Edit | Bookmark (Word for Windows 6) or Insert | Bookmark (Word for Windows 2), to open the Bookmark dialog box.

3. Type the name of the bookmark in the Bookmark Name text box. If you are moving the bookmark from a previous reference, select the bookmark name from the Bookmark Name list box.

   Bookmark names can be up to 40 characters long in Word for Windows 6 or 20 characters in Word for Windows 2. You can only use letters, numbers, and underscore characters in the name.

4. Select Add or OK.

Inserting or Moving Bookmarks with Shortcut Keys

1. Put the insertion point where you want the bookmark. To mark text rather than a position in the document, select the text.

2. Press CTRL+SHIFT+F5. In Word for Windows 6, the Bookmark dialog box appears; in Word for Windows 2 a prompt appears in the status line.

3. Type the name of the bookmark in the dialog box (or after the prompt in Word for Windows 2), or select it from the Bookmark Name list box if you are moving the bookmark reference.

    The name can be up to 40 characters long in Word for Windows 6 and 20 characters long in Word for Windows 2; use only letters, numbers, and the underscore character.

4. Press ENTER or select Add.

Removing Bookmarks

1. Select Edit | Bookmark (Word for Windows 6) or Insert | Bookmark (Word for Windows 2), to open the Bookmark dialog box.

2. Highlight the name of the bookmark you want to delete in the Bookmark Name list box, and select Delete.

Going To Bookmarks with the Menus

1. Select Edit | Go To (or you can press F5 in Word for Windows 6), to open the Go To dialog box. In Word for Windows 6, select Bookmark from the Go To What list box.

2. Type the bookmark name in the Go To text box or select it from the Go To drop-down list box, and select OK.

NOTE: In Word for Windows 6, you can also simply highlight the bookmark in the Bookmark dialog box and select Go To.

Going to Bookmarks with Shortcut Keys

1. Press F5. In Word for Windows 6, the Go To dialog box appears; in Word for Windows 2 a prompt appears in the status bar.

2. In Word for Windows 6, follow the steps given just above for using the dialog box. In Word for Windows 2, type the bookmark name in the status bar.

3. Press ENTER.

Hints

Bookmarks may seem a minor feature by themselves. However, bookmarks can be used by other Word for Windows functions to greatly enhance your productivity and flexibility. You can use bookmarks with fields to create cross-references, for example, and to calculate values in your document. You can use them to copy text or graphics from one part of your document to another. You can also use bookmarks to move quickly to a specific part of the document using the Go To feature, or to mark text for copying into another document.

Related Topics

Cross-references
Fields
Mail Merge

Borders and Shading

You can add borders around paragraphs or graphics. Frames often have borders.

Procedures

The methods for adding a border using a dialog box are essentially the same in Word for Windows 2 and 6. However, Word for Windows 6 offers the shortcut of using the Borders toolbar.

Borders can be applied to a single paragraph, a set of paragraphs, cells in a table, a graphic, or to a frame. These options are described further in "Options," following this section.

Applying Borders with the Borders Toolbar

In Word for Windows 6, you can apply borders and shading using the Borders toolbar, shown here:

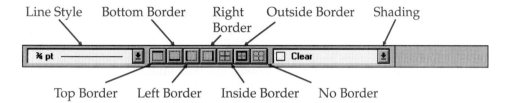

Line Style   Bottom Border   Right Border   Outside Border   Shading

Top Border   Left Border   Inside Border   No Border

1. Display the Borders toolbar by clicking the Borders button, the last button in the Formatting toolbar.

2. From the Line Style list box, choose a type of line for the border.

3. Choose one of the border buttons to designate the border part. The border part will use the last selected line style.

4. Choose a shading from the Shading list box.

5. Put away the Borders toolbar by selecting the Borders button again.

Applying Borders with the Menus

1. Select the item that you want to have the border.

2. Select Format I Borders and Shading (Format I Border in Word for Windows 2), to open the Paragraph Borders and Shading dialog box. The options in this dialog box depend on the type of item that you selected in step 1.

TIP: In Word for Windows 6, you can right-click a frame and select Borders and Shading to quickly open the dialog box.

3. Set the borders to apply with the border sample. The borders indicated with markers are what will appear in the document. You can select the border parts using the mouse or the keyboard:

   ■ With the mouse, click the border part that you want. To select multiple borders, press SHIFT while clicking.

■ With the keyboard, press ALT+R to move to the Border Sample. Then press the arrow keys to cycle through the possible selections.

TIP: One shortcut for defining where you want borders to appear is to select one of the preset border options. The options available depend on the item you selected before opening the dialog box.

4. After selecting a border part, choose a line type under Line in the dialog box. If you choose None, the line is removed.

5. Choose a color for the line from the Color drop-down list box. If color is not supported by your monitor or printer, the line may appear in a shading or pattern used to represent the color, or the color setting may be ignored.

6. If you started by selecting a paragraph or paragraphs, you can specify how close the text will be to the border by entering a value in the From Text text box.

7. Select OK.

Removing Borders

To remove a border, follow the steps given above for applying borders, and select "None" for the line type of each border that that you want to remove.

Applying and Removing Shading

You can apply shading to paragraphs and tables, but not to graphics. Shading changes the color or pattern of the background.

1. Select the paragraphs or cells you want to shade.

2. Select Format | Borders and Shading (Format | Border in Word for Windows 2), and select the Shading tab or button.

3. Select Custom to specify options for shading the selected object. Or select None to remove shading.

4. Choose an option from the Shading list box (Pattern drop-down list box in Word for Windows 2). Choices include a percentage shading, or a line pattern.

5. Select a color from the Foreground drop-down list box, which is the color that appears above the Background color.

6. Select a color from the Background drop-down list box, which is the color that appears behind the Foreground color.

7. Select OK (twice in Word for Windows 2) to return to the document.

If you selected colors, and you have a non-color printer, Word tries to simulate the colors using shading. If it cannot, or if your printer cannot print graphics, no shading is applied.

Options

Different border and shading options are provided, depending on what type of object you are applying them to.

Applying Borders to Paragraphs and Frames

When you add borders to paragraphs, the border settings become part of the paragraph formatting. In addition to the standard options for where borders can appear, you can specify how close the border comes to the paragraph text, and add lines between paragraphs.

Paragraph borders use the same indent settings as the paragraph to which they are applied. Paragraphs that have different indents have separate borders. To allow paragraphs with separate indents to be inside the same border, convert the paragraphs to a table, and apply the format to the table.

In Figure 4-4, all five paragraphs were selected at once, and the preset option Shadow was applied (The shadow effect is more apparent when the text is printed than when it is on screen). However, because of the different indents, you see three different shadow boxes on the page. Notice that the second paragraph in the third shadow box has a different left margin indent. Since the first-line indent is the same as the left margin indent of the surrounding paragraphs, this paragraph uses the same border.

You can also see in Figure 4-4 that a border can come very close to your text. You can increase the distance between the text and border by changing the value in the From Text text box in the Borders dialog box. This value measures the distance in points, which are 1/72 inch, so you can fine-tune the distance between the text and border.

You can also add lines between paragraphs, whether you selected one paragraph or many. To add lines between paragraphs, select the line between the paragraphs in the Border Samples. When you add a line between paragraphs to a single paragraph, the line will appear when you create a new paragraph.

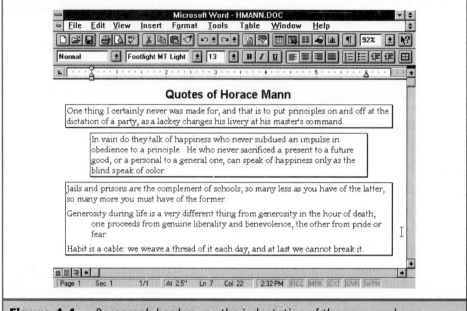

Figure 4-4.   *Paragraph borders use the indentation of the paragraph*

NOTE: You cannot create both a frame border and a paragraph border for text within a frame. Only one border is allowed.

Applying Borders to Pictures

You can apply borders to pictures or graphics that you add to your Word document. Notice that there are no options for creating lines between pictures, or for setting the distance between border and picture. You can, however, create white space between a graphic and its border, but not by changing the Border settings. Instead, you apply *negative cropping* to the graphic, as described under "Graphics."

You can also add a frame around a graphic, but that frame cannot have a border separate from the graphic border. The border applied to the graphic becomes the only border for both the graphic and frame. To create special effects, however, you can add graphics to tables. In the table, you can apply a graphic border and a table border.

Applying Borders to Tables

What you see in the Border Sample depends on whether you select a single cell, a single row, a single column, or cells from multiple columns and rows. If you select cells from multiple columns and rows, the Shadow preset option becomes Grid.

You can combine graphics and text with tables, and use borders to create interesting effects, as you can see in Figure 4-5. In this figure, the first row of the table has double-line borders at the top and bottom. The figures are inside single, thin-line boxes. The text paragraphs are bordered by a double-line on the left.

Related Topics

Frames
Graphics
Pictures

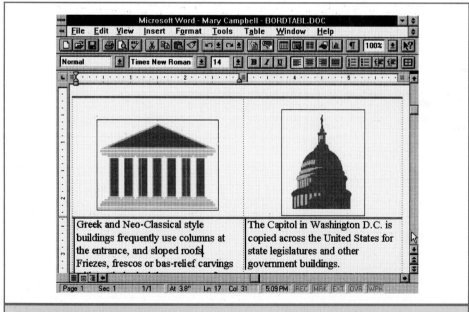

Figure 4-5. *Examples of table, paragraph, and graphic borders*

Boxes

See "Borders and Shading" and "Frames."

Breaks

You can insert page breaks (see "Pagination"), column breaks (see "Columns"), and section breaks (see "Sections") in your document.

Bulleted List

To quickly create bulleted lists, use Word's Format | Bullets and Numbering command, as described in "Lists" later in this chapter.

Bullets

Bullets are graphic symbols that are typically used to mark items in lists where numbering is not appropriate. You can insert bullets using the Insert | Symbol command, or you can convert a number of paragraphs into a bulleted list using Word for Windows's Format | Bullets and Numbering command. For instructions on converting paragraphs into bulleted lists, see "Lists."

Calculations

See "Math Calculations."

Callouts

A *callout* is text with a line that points to some element in a picture or chart. In Word for Windows 6, you can create callouts using the Drawing toolbar. For information on using the Drawing toolbar and creating callouts, see "Drawing on a Document."

Cancel

Almost all dialog boxes contain a Cancel button. Selecting this button closes the dialog box without applying any selections you have made in that dialog box. You can select Cancel by clicking the button or pressing ESC.

Capitalization

You can change the capitalization of text in your document in the following ways:

- Press SHIFT and a letter key to type the capital of that letter.
- Press CAPS LOCK; the CAPS indicator appears in the status bar. All letters you type will be capitals. To turn off CAPS LOCK, press the key again.
- Apply the All Caps character format to text (see "All Caps").
- Select the text to be affected and press SHIFT+F3 repeatedly. This cycles the selected text between all capitals, all lowercase, and initial capitals (in which only first letter of each word is capitalized or, if you selected more than one sentence, only the first letter in each sentence is capitalized).
- In Word for Windows 6, you can select the text, select Format I Change Case, choose a capitalization option, and select OK.

Captions

In Word for Windows 6, you can add *captions* that number similar objects and include a short description or title for figures, tables, or other objects in a Word document.

Procedures

You can create individual captions, or have Word automatically create captions for objects of a specific type.

Creating Individual Captions

1. Select the object you want a caption for—a picture, frame, table, or other object inserted into your document.

CAUTION: You can insert captions without selecting an object, in which case the caption is simply part of the normal text. However, the caption then serves no purpose.

2. Select Insert | Caption.

3. Choose a label from the Label drop-down list box. If none of the labels there are appropriate, you can select New Label, type a new label, such as "Chart" or "Photograph," and select OK.

4. From the Position drop-down list box, choose a location for the caption. You can put a caption above or below the object it labels.

5. If you do not want to use the default numbering system for objects, select Numbering.

   a. Select a new numbering system from the Format drop-down list box.

   b. To include chapter or section numbers in the caption—for instance, Table 2-4 would be the fourth table in the second chapter or section—select Include Chapter Numbers. Then choose the heading level to indicate chapter beginnings, and the separator to use between chapter and object numbers.

   c. Select OK when you are done. If you have not yet divided your document into chapters, Word reminds you to.

6. The Caption text box displays the current text of the caption, using the label and numbering format you selected. If you want to add a title or description to the caption, type it in the Caption text box.

7. Select OK to insert the caption for the currently selected object.

A caption for a graph in your document might look like the one above the pie chart in Figure 4-6.

Creating Captions with AutoCaption

1. Before inserting any of the objects you want to caption automatically, select Insert | Caption.

2. Select AutoCaption.

3. In the Add Captions While Inserting list box, select the check boxes for the items you want numbered together.

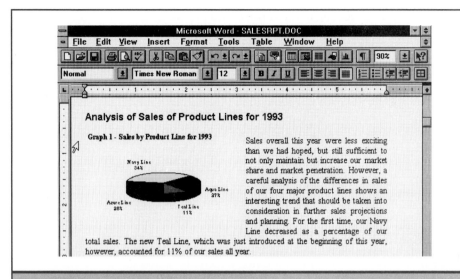

Figure 4-6.   *Use captions to label graphics*

For example, to add captions to all pictures added to your document, you could select Paintbrush Picture and Microsoft Word 6.0 Picture together, because all pictures would be numbered together. You would not include Quattro Pro Notebook, because you would want that labeled separately.

4. Under Options, you can choose where the caption is to appear, the text of the label, and a numbering format. You can also create a new label for the type of object you are working with. These options all work the same as described above for "Creating Individual Captions."

5. Select OK.

Hints

Word numbers each object with the same label sequentially; all the objects labeled with "Table" are in one list, all objects labeled with "Figure" are in another, and so forth.

To add text to a caption created with AutoCaption, just move to the caption in the document window and type the additional text you want to use.

If you delete an object that has a caption, you do not delete the caption. You will have to delete the caption separately. You delete a caption by highlighting the text and fields which make the caption and pressing DELETE or BACKSPACE. Word renumbers the captions after you delete one.

Captions are created using Sequence fields; see "Fields" in this chapter for details.

Related Topics

Fields
Graphics
Objects
Tables

Cartridges

Most printers have installed printer fonts, which are stored in the printer's memory rather than the computer's. You can expand the variety of printer fonts on most laser printers by installing printer cartridges containing the necessary information for the added fonts. These fonts must also be installed in your system, so that Word and other Windows applications can access them. For a complete explanation on installing font cartridges, consult the documentation that comes with your cartridge.

Center Page

You can center the text between the top and bottom margins by changing the vertical alignment of the page or section. See "Sections" for more information.

Center Text

See "Alignment" and "Tabs."

Centimeters

Word's default unit of measurement is inches. However, you can change the default setting to centimeters. You can also enter specific measurements in centimeters at any time by including the centimeter abbreviation, cm, after the measurement.

See "General Options" for details on changing the default measurement unit.

Changing Case

See "All Caps" and "Capitalization."

Changing the Directory

You can easily change the default directory for storing Word document files.

Procedures

In Word for Windows 6, you change this location using dialog box selections; in Word for Windows 2, you change the WIN.INI file.

Follow these steps in Word for Windows 6:

1. Select Tools | Options and select the File Locations tab.

2. In the File Types list box, highlight Documents.

3. Select Modify.

4. Choose a new directory, and select OK.

Follow these steps in Word for Windows 2:

1. Select Tools | Options.

2. Select the WIN.INI icon in the Category list box.

3. Select Microsoft Word in the Application drop-down list box.

4. From the Startup Options list box, select the line that starts DOC-PATH=. If there is no such line, enter **DOC-PATH** in the Option text box.

5. In the Settings text box, enter the drive and directory you want to use as the default.

6. Select Set and OK.

Hints

Use one directory for all of your currently-in-use Word for Windows documents, so that they are easy to retrieve and save. If all of them are in the same directory, you won't need to change directories to save or retrieve files. However, over time this directory may become quite crowded. To prevent this, set up a regular schedule for transferring files you are not using to another directory or to archival floppy disks.

Changing the Font

See "Fonts."

Chapter Numbers

You can include chapter numbers in the page numbers, captions, and indexes or tables of contents of your documents. Before doing so, you need to set up *chapters* in your document.

Procedures

Chapters in Word for Windows are sections of text that begin with a paragraph, usually a chapter title or number, that has a specific heading-level style applied to it. The heading level you use to indicate the beginning of chapters is irrelevant, as long as that heading level is not used for any text other then the text marking the beginning of chapters. To make outlining your document easier, use the Heading 1 or Heading 2 styles, so that any headings within a chapter are of a lower-level heading.

When you create page numbers, caption numbers, and indexes or tables of contents, you can choose to include the chapter numbers. The steps needed to include the chapter numbers are described within these specific features, since the exact steps are different for each feature. When you include chapter numbers choose the level of the heading indicating the beginning of each chapter as part of those features.

Related Topics

Captions
Index
Page Numbers

Character Formats

Character formats change the appearance of the characters in your document. You can change formats such as

- Font or font size (see "Fonts")
- Attributes such as boldface or underlining (see "Bold," "Italics," "Strikethrough," "Hidden Text," "Italics, Small Caps," "All Caps," and "Underline")
- Text color (see "Text Color")
- Placement of the text above or below the baseline (see "Super/Subscript")
- Spacing between the characters (see "Spacing Characters")

Characters per Inch

Characters per inch, or cpi, is a way of measuring the size of monospaced fonts, in which each character takes up the same space on a line. Word does not use cpi, but rather measures fonts by determining the height of the font in points, which are 1/72 inch. See "Fonts."

Charts

Graphs are occasionally referred to as charts. For instructions on creating and editing a graph, see "Graphs."

Check Spelling

See "Spelling."

Clearing Tabs

See "Tabs."

Click

See "Mouse Pointer."

Clip Art

Clip art refers to graphic images saved in a file and available for use in computer programs. Word for Windows comes with several pieces of clip art, as does Windows itself. You can also purchase sets of clip art with specific themes, such as business, transportation, and holidays, from various companies. See "Graphics" for information on importing and using clip art files in your Word for Windows documents.

Clipboard

The Windows Clipboard enables you to copy and move text, graphics, and other data within a Word for Windows document, between Word for Windows documents, or between Word for Windows and other applications, as shown in Figure 4-7.

Most Windows applications can access the Clipboard. You can use the Clipboard to copy data from other applications to Word documents, or from Word documents to most other applications. Because of this, you can easily import graphics, text, and other information into a Word document, or export that information into another application's document. The one restriction on this operation is the type of data the other application can support.

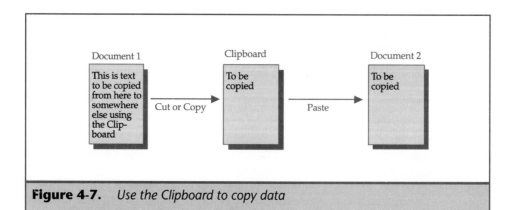

Figure 4-7.   *Use the Clipboard to copy data*

For example, you can export text from a Word document into a Paintbrush file using the Clipboard. However, you must first select the Text tool in Paintbrush and a location on the drawing, so that Paintbrush can accept text data. Because Paintbrush is a graphics application, it cannot accept text without this step.

How It Works

The Clipboard is a Windows feature that can be used in Word and in others Windows applications. You can also use the Clipboard to move text and other objects between Windows applications and some DOS applications which can run in a window.

When you cut or copy to the Clipboard, the items you selected are read to the Clipboard in the format they are currently in. When you paste them into your document, they are simply read back into a document, just as if they were being entered originally.

The Clipboard can paste items in any format the original application supports, as well as in their original format. You can also use the Clipboard to create OLE or DDE links between applications.

Procedures

The following steps explain how to copy and move text using the Clipbard, and how to insert material from the Clipboard using different formats.

Moving (Cutting) with the Clipboard

1. Select the text or graphics you want to move.

2. Select Edit | Cut, or press CTRL+X, or click the Cut button in the Standard toolbar.

3. Place the insertion point where you want the text or graphics to appear.

4. Select Edit | Paste, or press CTRL+V, or click the Paste button in the Standard toolbar.

Copying with the Clipboard

1. Select the text or graphics you want to copy.

2. Select Edit | Copy, or press CTRL+C, or click the Copy button in the Standard toolbar.

3. Place the insertion point where you want the text or graphics copied.

4. Select Edit | Paste, or press CTRL+V, or click the Paste button from the Standard toolbar.

Pasting Something in a Different Format

By default, Word pastes text or graphics into your document using the original format—that is, the format of the source of the pasted object. For some types of objects, you can choose a different format when you paste into a Word document, using the Edit | Paste Special command. This feature is most useful when you want to use a specific format for inserting a graphic or when you want to link and embed the object.

1. Cut or copy the objects (text, graphics, or other data) to the Clipboard, from Word or another Windows application.

2. Place the insertion point where you want the data to appear in the Word document.

3. Select Edit | Paste Special, to open the Paste Special dialog box shown here:

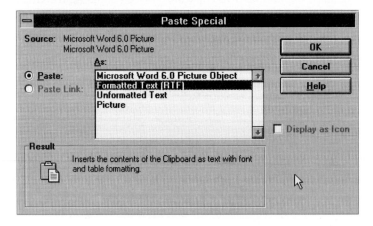

4. Choose a format from the As list box (Data Type in Word for Windows 2); this is the format that will be used when the object is pasted in.

5. Select the Paste radio button. (The Paste Link button is used to create a link to the original application, that is, the source of the pasted objects. Links are explained under "Object Linking and Embedding.")

Related Topics

Drag and Drop
Object Linking and Embedding
Spike

Closing Files

When you are finished using a document, you can close the document window containing it. This removes the file from your computer's memory. To edit the document again, you have to reopen it.

Procedures

1. To close a file, select File | Close.

TIP: You can also close a document window by double-clicking on the document window's control menu box in the upper-left corner.

2. If the document has never before been saved, or you have changed since it was last saved, Word displays a dialog box asking you if you want to save the file. Select Yes to save the document, or No to close the window without saving.

3. When you select Yes and the document has never before been saved, Word opens the Save As dialog box, where you specify a name and location for the file. If the document has been previously saved, Word saves the document with the same filename.

TIP: File names are eight characters long, and should be limited to letters, numbers, and the underscore character.

Hints

If you choose <u>N</u>o when Word prompts you to save your changes, all your edits are lost and cannot be recovered. Even if you have enabled the Automatic Save feature, those changes, too, are lost. The Automatic Save feature saves to a temporary file, which can only be recovered when you are restarting Word after an unexpected system crash or reboot procedure that clears everything in memory. The temporary backup copy is discarded once you request a save operation, even if you choose not to save the file.

Related Topics

Exiting Word
Opening Files
Saving Files

Collapsing Text

You can expand or collapse an outline to display various levels of outline entries or body text within the outline. For information on this, see "Outlines."

Color

See "Text Color."

Columns

In Word for Windows you can create two types of columns: table columns and newspaper-style columns. In tables, text is arranged in columns and rows. Newspaper-style columns "snake" from the bottom of one column to the top of the next, as in magazine and newspaper columns. See "Tables" in this chapter to learn about table columns. Newspaper-style columns are discussed here.

Figure 4-8 shows one example of how columns can be used in a newsletter. Notice that the columns are unequal in width, allowing the main story to run in the large column on the left, with a less-significant story in the narrower column

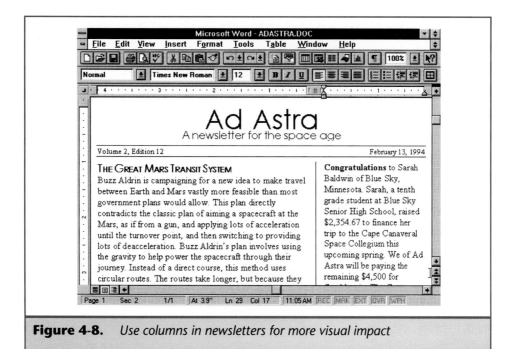

Figure 4-8. *Use columns in newsletters for more visual impact*

on the right. Columns are often used in newsletters both to increase visual interest, and because you can fit more text on a page with the careful use of columns.

TIP: If you have not used columns before, read the "Hints" section on columns before reading the procedures.

Procedures

There is one major difference between creating columns in Word for Windows 2 and 6: In Word for Windows 2, all columns in a section must be the same width. In Word for Windows 6, you can create columns of different widths.

WARNING: If you are not in Page Layout view, your columns will not appear as side-by-side columns. In Normal view, your columns appear using the correct width, but not all on one page. Instead, they appear after each other, separated by a column break line. Your text is actually formatted as columns, but doesn't appear that way on the screen in this mode.

Creating Columns with the Standard Toolbar

When you use the Standard toolbar, the columns created are spaced 1/2 inch apart and are applied to the document section containing the insertion point or the selected text.

TIP: See "Sections" for an explanation of what Word document sections are and how they effect formatting.

1. Put your insertion point in the section you want to format into columns, or select some text from each of the sections to format.

2. Click the Columns button in the toolbar; Word displays this columns grid:

3. In the columns grid, click and drag to the right to select the number of columns you want. Word allows you as many columns as it can fit on your selected page size, without letting the columns or the spaces between them become smaller than 1/2 inch.

Creating or Editing Columns with the Menus (Word for Windows 6)

1. Put your insertion point where you want columns to begin or in the column you want to edit.

2. Select Format | Columns.

3. Enter the number of columns you want, up to 45, in the Number of Columns text box.

    Initially, each column is the same width, and the space between columns is 1/2 inch. Word may actually create fewer columns, if there isn't enough room on your selected page size.

4. To change the columns widths or spacing between them, enter the measurements in the first Width or Spacing text boxes. When you are using varying widths for columns and spaces between them, start by clearing the Equal Column Width check box, then enter the measurements in the Width or Spacing text boxes for each column.

TIP: *The Spacing text box for each column refers to the space which appears after that column.*

5. To add a solid line in the space between columns, select the Line Between check box.

6. To have Word insert a column break at the insertion point, in order to start a new column, select Start New Column. The text after the insertion point appears at the top of the next column.

7. In the Apply To drop-down list box, select what part of the document you want the column settings applied to, and select OK.

Creating or Editing Columns with the Menus (Word for Windows 2)

1. Put the insertion point where you want columns to begin or in the column you want to edit.

2. Select Format | Columns.

3. Enter the number of columns you want in the Number of Columns text box. You can have up to 100 columns across a page.

4. In the Space Between text box, enter the distance between each column.

5. To include a solid line in the space between columns, select the Line Between check box (this was done in Figure 4.8).

6. If you want a new column started at the insertion point location when you close the dialog box, select Start New Column. Word will insert a column break to break the current column. The text following the insertion point appears at the top of the next column.

7. In the Apply To drop-down list box, select the portion of the document you want the column settings applied to, and select OK.

Adjusting Column Widths with the Ruler

Since you can have unequal columns in Word for Windows 6 but not in Word for Windows 2, there are some differences in the way the ruler works for adjusting column widths. The ruler for both versions of the program works the same way only if you have *not* turned off the Equal Column Width check box in the Columns dialog box in Word for Windows 6.

In Word for Windows 2, or in Word for Windows 6 if you have specified equal columns, when you adjust the width of one column, all other columns are also adjusted so that the columns still reach from the left to the right margin, the columns are all of equal width, and the space between columns is the same. To adjust column widths with the ruler, you must use the mouse.

1. In Word for Windows 2, you may need to click on the symbols at the end of the ruler until the ruler is showing the margin or column markers. (These markers look like heavy square brackets.)

2. Drag either column marker to the position you want it to hold. Word rearranges the column markers for the other columns so that the columns and the space between them are all equal, and the columns fill the page from margin to margin.

   In Word for Windows 2, you drag the column-marker brackets. In Word for Windows 6 you drag the entire gray area indicating the space between columns.

   If you turned off the Equal Column Width check box in Word for Windows 6, you can change a column width by dragging the dark gray area in the column marker shown below, and moving the entire column marker. Change the width of the space between columns by dragging the thin gray boxes at each side of the column marker as shown here:

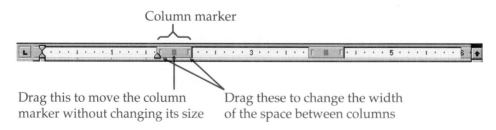

Column marker

Drag this to move the column marker without changing its size

Drag these to change the width of the space between columns

Balancing Columns

When you reach the end of a section or a document that is formatted with columns, you may find that the length of the columns is too uneven. You can make Word for Windows 6 balance the columns so that they are as close as possible to the same length, given the number of lines and line height. Figure 4-9 shows the visual effect of unbalanced and balanced columns.

1. Position your cursor at the end of the text in columns.

2. Select Insert | Break.

3. In the Break dialog box, select the Continuous option button, and then OK.

NOTE: If you want to start a new page after the columns, do not select Next Page in the Break dialog box. Instead, select Continuous as instructed in step 3 above, and add a hard page break after the continuous section break.

Hints

Word for Windows 2 keeps all newspaper-style columns within a section at the same width. The space between the columns is also the same all the way across. If you want uneven columns in Word for Windows 2, you must use tables (see "Tables").

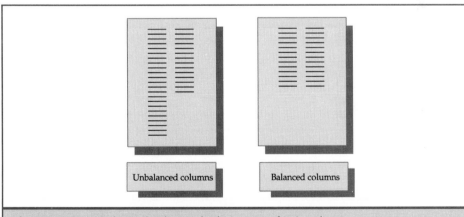

Figure 4-9.   *Balanced columns look more professional*

In Word for Windows 6, when you turn off the Equal Column Width option in the Columns dialog box, you can create columns of unequal width and with unequal space between.

Viewing Columns

Columns are displayed differently in Normal view and Page Layout view. In Normal view, columns are not displayed side-by-side as they are in Page Layout view. In Normal view, at the end of each column a column break appears, followed by the next column, in the same position on the page.

Column Breaks

You can insert a column break, causing the text after the break to move to the top of the next column. Insert column breaks by pressing CTRL+SHIFT+ENTER or by selecting Insert | Break, choosing the Column Break option, and OK.

Selecting Columns of Text

You can select columns of text using either the keyboard or the mouse.

- To select a column of text with the mouse, start at one corner of the column you want to select. Drag the mouse from there to the opposite corner.

- To select a column of text using the keyboard, position the insertion point in one corner of the column you want to select. Press CTRL+SHIFT+F8. Use the arrow keys to move to the opposite corner. You can also use HOME to move the beginning of a line in the column, and END to move to the end of a line. When you are in Normal view, you can use PGUP and PGDN to move your selection a screen up or down; this doesn't work in Page Layout view.

Related Topics

Margins
Tables

Comments

See "Annotation" and "Hidden Text."

COMMENTS Field

The COMMENTS field inserts the contents of the Comments text box from the Summary Info dialog box into the documents. See "Fields" and "Summary Info" for more information.

COMPARE Field

Use the COMPARE field to compare two values and determine if they are the same or different. See "Fields" for more information.

Comparing Versions

You can compare two versions of a document by adding *revision marks* to the document. Revision marks indicate where the two documents are different, by marking deleted, added, replaced, and moved text. You can have Word mark revisions as you are making them, or add the revision marks using a saved file as the original version of the document.

Figure 4-10 shows revision marks in a document, added while the document was edited. Notice the strikethrough text indicating deleted text, new text marked with underlining, and the revision bars on the outside edge to let you locate changes faster.

Procedures

The following procedures tell you how to add, customize and review revision marks in your document.

Adding Revision Marks while Editing

1. Open the document you are going to revise.

2. Select Tools | Revisions (Tools | Revision Marks in Word for Windows 2).

3. Select the Mark Revisions While Editing check box (Mark Revisions in Word for Windows 2). If you turn this option off, Word will stop marking revisions.

4. Select OK.

5. Edit your document, and you will see the revision marks appearing as you work.

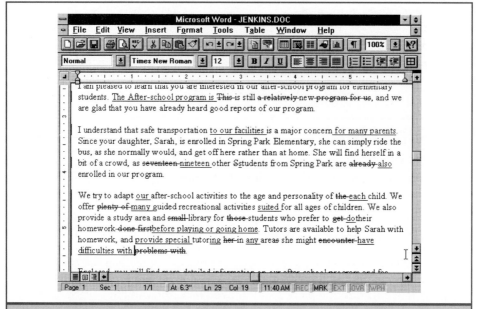

Figure 4-10.   *Reviewing the revisions in a document is easier when changes are marked*

Adding Revision Marks after Editing

1. Open the revised document.

2. Select Tools | Revisions and then Compare Versions (Tools | Compare Versions in Word for Windows 2), to open the Compare Versions dialog box. The options of this dialog box are the same as the Open dialog box.

3. Select the name of the file that is the original version of the document, and then OK. Word reads the two files and adds revision marks to the open document, marking how the open document is different from the original one.

Designating Revision Marks Settings

1. Select Tools | Revisions and then Options (Tools | Revision Marks in Word for Windows 2).

2. To tell Word how to mark new text, use the Mark drop-down list box under Inserted Text (in Word for Windows 2, work with the option buttons under Mark New Text With). You can choose bold, italic, underlined, or double-underlined, or no marks at all. In Word for Windows 6, you can also choose a color for the marks from the Color drop-down list box. The default is to let Word pick a different color for each author who works on the document.

3. In Word for Windows 6 you can tell Word how to mark deleted text. Use the Mark drop-down list box under Deleted Text. You can choose hidden or strikethrough formats. You can also choose a color from the Color drop-down list box. (In Word for Windows 2, you cannot choose how deleted text is marked; it is always marked with strikethrough.)

4. Specify where you want revision bars located (to indicate revised paragraphs), by choosing from the Mark drop-down list box. (In Word for Windows 2, you work with option buttons under Revision Bars.)

5. Select OK twice (just once in Word for Windows 2).

Reviewing and Accepting/Rejecting Revisions

You can accept or reject individual revisions or deletions, or all revisions in a document.

1. In a document with revision marks, select Tools | Revisions (Tools | Revision Marks in Word for Windows 2).

2. Select Review (Search in Word for Windows 2).

3. In Word for Windows 6, Word opens a dialog box that you can use to search for revision marks. Review the revisions by selecting Find or Find to move forward or backward through the document to the revision marks.

   In Word for Windows 2, you move to the next occurrence of revision marks; continue to step 4.

4. Accept or reject each revision.

   In Word for Windows 6, select Accept to keep or Reject to discard each revision. If you change your mind, you can select Undo Last to reverse the last acceptance or rejection you made.

   In Word for Windows 2, select Accept Revisions or Undo Revisions to accept or reject each revision. To move to the next revision mark, select

Search again. If you change your mind, select OK in the Revision Marks dialog and then select Edit | Undo.

5. When finished, select Cancel.

Accepting or Undoing All Revisions

1. In Word for Windows 2, select a section of text to accept/undo the revisions in that section. Otherwise, you must accept or reject all revisions in the document.

2. Select Tools | Revisions (Tools | Revision Marks in Word for Windows 2).

3. Select Accept All (Accept Revisions in Word for Windows 2) to keep all the revisions made to the document, or Reject All (Undo Revisions) to discard all the revisions made to the document.

TIP: You can use Edit | Undo if you find you've accidentally selected the wrong option.

4. Select OK.

Hints

Compare copies of legal documents, to ensure that you are aware of all changes to a document before you sign off on it. It would be very easy for a reviser to accidentally remove a vital phrase without quite realizing it.

Whether you compare versions of a document or have Word mark revisions while you edit, Word does not mark revisions to formatting, only revisions to the text.

Compatibility Options

Word for Windows lets you convert files created by other programs so you can use them in Word. However, since many features work somewhat differently in various programs, the compatibility among formats is not complete. Word for Windows 6 lets you change settings called Compatibility options that determine how Word for Windows handles certain features so that it can work more like the program used to create the file originally. You can also substitute a screen font if the original font that was used is not available on your system.

Procedures

The Compatibility options do not change the file in question. Instead, they change how Word works with that file. If you save the document in its original format from Word for Windows 6, and open it again in the original program used to create it, the Compatibility options will not have changed anything in the file.

1. Select Tools | Options and select the Compatibility tab.

2. If there are fonts used in the document that are not available for Windows on your system, select Font Substitution.

3. In the Missing Document Font list box, highlight the font you don't have.

4. In the Substituted Font drop-down list box, select the font you want to use in place of the missing font.

   NOTE: Select Default in the Substituted Font list box to tell Word to determine which font is closest to the missing one and use it. Remember, this does not change the font assigned to the text, but merely the font used to display the text because the original font is missing.

5. Select OK. If you want to change the font actually used to format the text in question, select Convert Permanently instead.

6. In Recommended Options For drop-down list box, choose the program used to create the file originally.

   Word displays a selection of check boxes for options that can be adapted in the Options list box. The program that you choose in Recommended Options For list box (step 6, above) determines which of these check boxes are selected or cleared. These are the recommended options for making Word work more like the selected program, but you are free to turn individual options on or off to suit yourself, your working style, or to simulate a program not included in the Recommended Options For list box.

7. When you are happy with the settings, select OK.

   NOTE: There are a limited number of settings you can change through Compatability Options. These settings are designed to let you match the way some other popular word processors create documents, but they won't turn Word into those programs.

Related Topics

Opening Files

Compose

Composing characters is a WordPerfect term referring to the process of entering characters that cannot be typed at the keyboard. See "Special Characters" for information on the equivalent process in Word for Windows.

Concordances

Concordances are files containing lists of words to be included as entries in indexes. See "Index" for more information.

Conditional End of Page

Conditional end-of-page is a WordPerfect feature for keeping paragraphs or lines together on a single page. See "Pagination" for information on the equivalent process in Word for Windows.

Continuation Notice

Footnotes and endnotes that appear on more than page use *continuation notices* to tell readers that there is more text. See "Footnotes and Endnotes" for more information.

Control Panel

The Control Panel is a Windows application used to control many settings and features for Windows and applications that run under Windows. You use the Control Panel to install fonts, install new printers, customize the colors used on the screen, and many other tasks. You will want to review your Windows documentation for instructions on using the Control Panel.

Controlling Pagination

See "Pagination."

Convert Text to a Table

See "Tables."

Converting Files

See "Opening Files."

Copy

See "Drag and Drop," "Clipboard," and "Spike."

Copying Formats

You can copy paragraph and character formatting from one section of text to another. Word for Windows offers the Format Painter button on the Standard toolbar, to make copying formatting even easier.

Procedures

You can copy character or paragraph formatting using the Format Painter or other options.

Copying Formatting with the Format Painter Tool

1. Select the text with the formatting you want to copy.

   ■ Select text only, and the formatting of the first character will be copied.

   ■ Select text and a paragraph mark, and the formatting of the first character as well as the paragraph formatting will be copied.

■ Select only a paragraph mark, and the paragraph formatting only will be copied.

2. Click the Format Painter button on the Standard toolbar. To copy the formatting to multiple locations, double-click the button.

3. Select the text you want to apply the copied formatting. To copy the formatting to another location, select another passage of text to format. If you double-clicked the Format Painter button, click the button again to stop applying the selected format.

Copying Paragraph Formats

Paragraph formats are saved with the paragraph character at the end of the paragraph. Copying this paragraph character also copies the paragraph formatting.

1. Select the paragraph mark at the end of the paragraph whose format you want to copy.

2. Select Edit | Copy, or press CTRL+C, or click the Copy button in the toolbar.

3. Put the insertion point at the end of the paragraph you want to have the copied format.

4. Select Edit | Paste, or press CTRL+V, or click the Paste button.

Copying Character Formats in Word for Windows 6

You can copy character formats using the Format Painter tool, as described above, or using these shortcut keys:

■ To copy the formatting, select the formatted text and press CTRL+SHIFT+C.

■ To paste the formatting, select the text to format and press CTRL+SHIFT+V.

Copying Character Formats in Word for Windows 2

In Word for Windows 2 you can only copy character formats with the mouse.

1. Select the text you want to have the copied format.

2. Press CTRL+SHIFT, and click on a character with the format you want to copy. Word formats the text you selected in step 1 with the same character formatting as the character you clicked in step 2.

Hints

Copying formats can be useful in limited circumstances; however, you will want to explore Word for Windows's styles to apply formats. When you apply styles, you can quickly change the formatting of all text formatted with that style, rather than copying formats each time you want to change the formatting in your document.

Related Topics

Styles

Count

Word counts the number of words in your document each time you save it, and records that value as part of the document's summary information. See "Summary Info" for instructions on finding out how many words there are in your document.

Create a New Directory

You can create a new directory for storing Word documents, using the Windows File Manager. In Word for Windows 6, there is also a way to create a new directory while changing the default directory for Word documents.

Procedures

You can create the new directory for organizing your files using Word for Windows 6, or using the Windows File Manager.

Creating a New Directory from Word for Windows 6

1. Select Tools | Options and click the File Locations tab.

2. In the File Types list box, highlight Documents.

3. Select Modify and then New.

4. Enter the path name for the new directory in the Name text box and select OK.

5. Select OK again to return to the document.

CAUTION: *Note that this new directory is now the default directory for saving and retrieving your Word for Windows 6 documents.*

Creating a New Directory with the Windows File Manager

1. Start the File Manager. (The File Manager program item is usually found in the Main program group in the Program Manager.)

2. Click the disk icon representing the drive on which you want to create a new directory.

3. In the directory tree, move to the directory in which you want to create the new subdirectory.

4. Select File | Create Directory, to open the Create Directory dialog box.

5. Enter the directory name in the Name text box. Directory names can be up to eight characters long. You should use only letters, numbers, and the underscore character in this name.

6. Select OK.

Hints

You may want to create a new subdirectory for your WINWORD directory to store all document files, or create several subdirectories to divide your document files by purpose or type. If you create a subdirectory to store your working Word files, you may want to change the default Word directory, so that accessing the files will be easier.

Related Topics

Changing the Directory
File Location Options
WIN.INI Options

CREATEDATE Field

Use the CREATEDATE field to insert into a document the date and time it was first saved. See "Fields" for more information.

Cropping a Graphic

Cropping a graphic means to cut it down, as you would trim a photograph. Cropping is usually done to isolate a specific part of the graphic, or to remove unwanted white space at the edges. See "Graphics" for more information.

Cross-references

Cross-references appear in one location of the document telling you where in the document you can find related information. In Word for Windows 2, cross-references are created by combining bookmarks and fields; in Word for Windows 6 you use dialog box options. Word for Windows 6 provides many more options for creating cross-references.

Procedures in Word for Windows 6

In Word for Windows 6, cross-references are created using dialog box options. You can reference footnotes or endnotes, text formatted with certain styles, bookmarks, equations, figures, and tables.

Inserting a Cross-reference

1. Place the insertion point in the document where you want to insert the cross-reference.

2. Type any lead-in or explanatory text you want to appear, such as "For further information see."

3. Select Insert | Cross-reference.

4. In the Reference Type list box, choose the type of object or text you are referring to.

5. In the Insert Reference To list box, choose the type of reference you want to enter in the text.

6. In the For Which list box, select the specific object or text you are referring to.

7. Select Insert.

Procedures for Word for Windows 2

In Word for Windows 2, cross-references are created using bookmarks to indicate the text you want to reference, and fields to insert the reference into your document.

Cross-referencing a Page

To create a cross-reference that refers to bookmarked text and shows the page number of the text:

1. Insert a bookmark in the document to mark the text or location to be referenced.

2. Move to the place where you want the cross-reference to appear.

3. Insert a PageRef field type, by pressing CTRL+F9 to insert the field characters and then typing **pageref** and the bookmark name.

4. Press F9 to update the field, if necessary. You may also need to select View | Field Codes to display the cross-reference rather than the field code.

For example, you may mark a paragraph with the bookmark name "Trends." On another page, following the text

See also:page

you would insert the field code {**pageref trends**}. The cross-reference would then read

See also: page 12

Cross-referencing Text

To create a cross-reference that uses the actual text being referenced:

1. Insert a bookmark in the document to mark the text or location to be referenced.

2. Move to the place where you want the cross-reference to appear.

3. Insert a Reference field type, by pressing CTRL+F9 to insert the field characters and then typing **ref** followed by the bookmark name.

4. Press F9 to update the field, if necessary. You may also need to select View | Field Codes to display the cross-reference rather than the field code.

For example, you may mark some text with the bookmark "rule12." In another location, following the text

Rule 12 reads

insert {**ref rule12**}. The cross-reference would then read

Rule 12 reads "No smoking of tobacco or other substances legal or illegal are permitted inside this facility."

Cross-referencing Styles

To cross-reference text with a particular style applied to it:

1. Apply the style that you want to refer to.

2. Move to the place where you want the cross-reference to appear.

3. Insert a StyleRef field type, by pressing CTRL+F9 to insert the field characters and then typing **styleref** followed by the style name in quote marks.

4. Press F9 to update the field if necessary. You may also need to select View | Field Codes to display the cross-reference rather than the field code.

For example, you may apply the Heading 1 style to a paragraph of text. In another location, following the text insert {**styleref "heading 1"**}. The cross-reference would then read

The Origin of the Profit Motive

if that were the text formatted with the Heading 1 style.

Cross-referencing Sequenced Items

You can cross-reference items in a sequenced list. To create such a list, insert a Sequence field code for each item you want to number, and include a list identifier for each type of item you mark with Sequence fields. For example, you can add Sequence fields at each table, graphic, or graph in your document. Each type of item would be numbered sequentially throughout the document.

1. Insert a Sequence field for the object, by pressing CTRL-F9 and entering **seq** followed by a list identifier, such as **graphs**.

2. Highlight the object and apply a bookmark to it, such as **sales**.

3. Move to the place where you want the cross-reference to appear.

4. Insert another Sequence field, by pressing CTRL-F9 and entering **seq** followed by the list identifier and the bookmark, as in **graphs sales**}. You may want to insert this field code with explanatory text, as in **"See Graph {seq graphs sales} for a graphic display of our sales increases."**

5. Press F9 to update the information. You may also need to select View | Field Codes to display the cross-reference rather than the field code.

The final display in the above example would read "See Graph 6 for a graphic display of our sales increases."

Hints

For Page Cross-references

Remember to use the Tools | Repaginate Now option in Word for Windows 2 before printing your document, so that the cross-references refer to the correct page numbers.

Related Topics

Bookmarks
Fields

Cursor Movement

The insertion point is sometimes called a *cursor.* You can use the keyboard to move the insertion point in your document, or you can use the mouse. For a full explanation of the keyboard options for moving the insertion point, see "Moving the Insertion Point."

Custom Dictionary

See "Spelling."

Customized Page Numbers

See "Page Numbers." You may also want to look at the explanation of the Page field type under "Fields."

Customizing Menus

See "Menu Options."

Customizing the Keyboard

See "Keyboard Options."

Customizing the Toolbar

See "Toolbar Options."

Customizing Word for Windows

You can customize Word for Windows in many ways. The related topics in the following list explain how to customize the various features.

NOTE: *In the following table, Winword means Word for Windows.*

See This:	About Customizing This:
AutoFormat	How AutoFormat works with your document (Winword 6 only)
Comparing Versions	How revisions are marked (Winword 6 only)
Compatibility Options	How Word converts files (Winword 6 only)
Edit Options	How you edit documents (Winword 6 only)
File Location Options	Where Word expects to find files (Winword 6 only)
General Options	General features
Grammar Options	How Word checks the grammar in your documents
Keyboard Options	The shortcut keys
Menu Options	Word's menus
Print Options	How Word prints documents
Save Options	How Word saves files
Spelling Options	How Word checks spelling in your document
Toolbar Options	The toolbars
User Info Options	The information Word maintains about you
View Options	The screen display for Word
WIN.INI Options	The startup options for Word for Windows 2

Cutting

See "Drag and Drop," "Clipboard," and "Spike."

Dashes

You add em and en dashes when you want a longer dash than the hyphen provides. Use the steps for entering these characters described under "Special Characters."

Database Field

The DATABASE field inserts the result of a database query into the document in Word for Windows 6. For more information on this, see "Databases."

D

Database Toolbar

The Database toolbar provides many of the tools you will want to use when working with a database in a document. Most of the time you use a database to supply the variable information that another document uses in a mail merge. Displaying the Database toolbar in Word for Windows 6 is done following the same steps as displaying any other toolbar. You can easily add the toolbar by selecting the View | Toolbars command, the Database check box, and OK. Once the Database toolbar appears, select from the following buttons to work with the data you have in the database. Word for Windows 2 does not have a Database toolbar but you can use the table features to add records and fields, delete records and fields, and sort the records in a database.

Button	Button Name	Function
	Data Form	Displays a data form to enter new records into a database
	Manage Fields	Lets you add, remove, and rename the fields in a database
	Add New Record	Adds a new row to the database for you to enter another record
	Delete Record	Removes the selected row from the database
	Sort Ascending	Sorts the records in ascending order by the field containing the insertion point
	Sort Descending	Sorts the records in descending order by the field containing the insertion point

Button	Button Name	Function
	Insert Database	Inserts an external database into the current document
	Update Fields	Updates fields in the table
	Find Record	Searches a field in the database for an entry you provide
	Mail Merge Main Document	Switches to the main document that uses the database as its source for data

Related Topics

Databases
Mail Merge
Toolbars

Databases

You use databases for Word's mail merge features. Word will accept the data for mail merge from Word documents, documents that Word can open with File I Open as well as Excel and 1-2-3 spreadsheets and Access databases. You can also open database files using DDE (Dynamic Data Exchange) and OLE (Object Linking and Embedding) features to display other databases in a Word for Windows document.

You can insert data from a database into your Word for Windows 6 document. When you use the database feature, the database can be any file that Word can read which contains information you want to insert into your document; anything from a Microsoft Access database to a WordPerfect document. The word "database" is used to describe how the file is being used, rather than the format the file is in.

Procedures

1. Position your insertion point where you want the information from the database to appear. This information will be formatted in a table.

2. Select Insert I Database.

3. Select Get Data.

4. Select the file you want to use as the database and OK, to open it. The options available are the same that you can use for opening any file.

   Depending on the type of file you are attempting to open, you may now be prompted to select a range of data from a spreadsheet, or the specific table or query from the database. If you are, select the appropriate unit of data to insert.

TIP: If you do not know about working with spreadsheets and databases, but need to use this feature, it will be worthwhile to find the documentation or a book on these applications and learn a little.

D

5. Select Query Options to set rules for which data you want to use. You can choose to filter records, sort records, or select fields, depending on the tab you select in the Query Options dialog box. After setting options in this dialog box, as described below, select OK.

   ■ Select Filter Records to create a series of comparative rules to control which records are used. For each rule, select the field to compare in the Field box, how the comparison is to be done in the Comparison box, and enter the text or data to compare the field to in the Compare To box. You can combine rules with And or Or. And requires that both rules be met while Or requires that either rule be met.

   ■ Select Sort Records to sort the records into an order before they are inserted into the current document. You can define three keys. For each key, select which field is being sorted, and whether the sort is ascending or descending. The lower keys are used when the higher level key results in a tie.

   ■ Select Select Fields to set which fields to insert. You can use Select, or Select All to transfer fields from the Fields in the Data Source list box to the Selected Fields list box. Use Remove or Remove All to remove fields from the Selected Fields list box.

6. Select Table AutoFormat to format the table that will appear in the current document. This feature works exactly like the Table AutoFormat feature described under "Tables."

7. Select Insert Data. Word displays a final dialog box with some last settings you can make for the data. Select OK when you are finished to actually insert the data.

■ Select All or From to set whether all or a limited number of records is inserted. If you select From, enter the first and last record number in the From and To text boxes.

■ Select the Insert Data as Field check box to insert all of the data and the table as a DATABASE field.

Hints

You will want to insert the data as a field if you need to be able to update the data. For example, you may insert the data from a spreadsheet into a report created in a Word document. If this report needs to be recreated regularly, such as a monthly sales report, you will find it easier if you use a field.

When you insert the data as a field, any formatting you apply to the table in the document is lost when you update that field. When you do want to insert data as a field, make sure that you use the Table AutoFormat feature to format the table, ensuring that you do not lose the formatting, or add * mergeformat to the DATABASE field.

Related Topics

Inserting Files
Mail Merge
Object Linking and Embedding
Opening Files
Saving Files
Tables

Data Field

The DATA field identifies the field containing the data for print merge in Word for Windows 2. For more information on this, see "Print Merge."

Date and Time

You can insert a date or time in your document. The date or time can be entered as text or as a field. When you add the date or time as a field, the field displays the current date or time, and is updated each time you print the document. Depending on the viewing options you have set for fields, the dates and times appear as the codes Word uses to represent these dates and times or as the dates and times that the fields represent.

Procedures

You can insert the Date or Time field using the menus, shortcut keys, or, in a header or footer, using a toolbar button.

Using the Menus

1. Select Insert | Date and Time, opening the Date and Time dialog box.

2. Select a format for displaying the date and/or time from the Available Formats list box. By selecting one of the listed formats, you are selecting whether you are adding the date, the time, or, in Word for Windows 6 only, both. The different purposes for different date and time formats are described in the box "Rules for Using the Correct Date Format."

    Word for Windows 6 also has an Insert as Field check box that you select to add a Date or Time field to the document in place of the text of the current date or time. In Word for Windows 2, Word adds the DATE or TIME field rather than the text of the current date or time. Select OK.

Using Shortcut Keys

■ Press ALT+SHIFT+D to insert a DATE field.

■ Press ALT+SHIFT+T to insert a TIME field.

In Word for Windows 2, these key combinations insert the DATE or TIME field. In Word for Windows 6, these key combinations insert either the text or the field for the date and time depending on whether the Insert as Field check box was selected the last time you used the Insert | Date and Time command.

The date or time you add has the same date or time format as the last date or time you added to a document. When you have not added a date or time, the date initially has the format of Month/Day/Year using two digits for each part and the time initially has the format of Hour:Minute AM or PM with two digits for the hours and minutes. You can change the default format that these key combinations present by changing the default time and date settings in Windows with the Control Panel.

Rules for Using the Correct Date Format

Word supports many different date formats. Each of them is useful in different situations. If you want your documents to look professional, it is important to know when to pick a specific format. The following rules will help you decide the correct format whether you are inserting a date with Word or typing a date in a sentence.

- Never use abbreviations when placing a date in the date line of a letter. For example, use March 23, 1994 not Mar 23, 1994.

- If you use only two of the three date components, no comma is needed. For example, May 1994 or May 5.

- Decade references are always plural and written in numbers as in 1970s or the '70s.

- Dates used in a sentence are typically written in a month, day, year sequence. For example, the open house is scheduled for October 5, 1994. An altered day, month, year style is used in military correspondence and in foreign countries. For example, General Smith has scheduled a meeting on 2 July 1994 for all base personnel. Note the absence of a comma in military style dates.

- Interoffice correspondence, business forms, and other informal notes are the only places where all numeric date entries are appropriate. For example, "Let's try to reschedule for 8/8/94."

- When the day precedes the month, the ordinal form is normally used. For example, "The movers are scheduled to come on the 12th of August." If you rewrite the sentence with the day following the month, the ordinal form is not appropriate. For example, "The movers are scheduled to come on August 12."

- In formal documents always write the day and year in words. "The *twenty-first* of April *nineteen hundred ninety-four* is a memorable date." The year number can also be expressed as one thousand nine hundred ninety-four.

In a Header or Footer

When you are entering a header or footer, Word shows an extra toolbar (only in Normal view in Word for Windows 2). You select the Date or the Time button from this toolbar to enter a Date or Time field in your header. This toolbar and the date and time added to a header are shown here:

Hints

Use a DATE and TIME field instead of text, in a header or footer, when printing drafts of documents. The date and time on the document ensure that you are reviewing the most up-to-date draft, instead of an older one which might still be sitting on your desk.

In Word for Windows 6, when you move the insertion point to any part of the DATE or TIME field, the entire date and time is highlighted. Any changes you make to the shaded area are replaced when you print the document. When you insert the text of the current date or time, you can edit the text just as if you typed the characters for the date and time yourself. You can also update a DATE or TIME field by moving to it and pressing F9.

Related Topics

Databases
Headers and Footers

Date and Time Formats

See "Date and Time."

DATE Field

The DATE field inserts the current date. For more information on this, see "Date and Time."

dBASE

dBASE is a popular data management program. Word can access files saved by dBASE II, III, and IV or files saved by other programs in these formats. dBASE files have a .DBF extension. Word converts the .DBF file to a Word table as it opens it. For more information on accessing databases; see "Databases." To work with this table, use Word's table features described under "Tables." You cannot save Word documents in a .DBF file.

The table's data appear as in Browse mode in dBASE. Each line in the table is a record and each column is a field. The column widths are the same as the field widths set in dBASE. Word shows the entire table, even if it is wider than the current page width. You need to modify the page size or edit the table if it is too wide to print on the current page.

Hints

You can use dBASE data in mail merge documents such as address labels and form letters.

DCA/RFT

DCA/RFT is the file format used by DisplayWrite and IBM 5520. Word can convert a file from this format when you open the file. See "Opening Files."

DDE

See "Object Linking and Embedding."

DDE Field

The DDE field inserts the contents of a DDE link to data from other Windows applications in Word documents created before Word for Windows 2. For more information on this, see "Object Linking and Embedding."

DDEAuto Field

The DDEAUTO field inserts the linked contents of a DDE link to data from other Windows applications in Word documents created before Word for Windows 2. For more information on this, see "Object Linking and Embedding."

Decimal Alignment

See "Tabs."

D

Default Directory

Word's default document directory is the directory Word displays when you first open or save a file during a work session. Word assumes that this is the directory containing your document files. When you first install Word, the default directory is the directory containing the Word program files. You change the default directory for Word for Windows 2 by adding a line to the WIN.INI file as described in "WIN.INI Options." To set the default directory for Word for Windows 6, look at "File Location Options."

Default Options

See "Options." Many of Word's customizations are described with the features they alter.

Default Settings

See "Options." Many of Word's customizations are described with the features they alter.

Default Toolbar

The default or Standard toolbar is the toolbar saved in the Normal template. This toolbar is available to all documents. You can modify the toolbar, and save the modified toolbar so that it is available for all files, or only a single template. For more information on modifying the default toolbar, see "Toolbar Options." The

Standard toolbar used initially by most Word for Windows documents is described further under "Standard Toolbar."

The default toolbar in Word for Windows 2 is shown here:

The 22 buttons on the default Toolbar carry out different commands. They are explained in Table 4-1. The buttons are listed from left to right on the Toolbar.

Delete Directory

You cannot delete a directory from within Word. You have to delete directories from DOS, Window's File Manager, or some other file management program.

Delete Files

See "File Management."

Delete Formatting

See "Removing Formatting."

Deleting Text

You can delete text from your document permanently or delete text from your document intending to place it at another location. To learn how to delete text, and then replace it in another location, another document, or another application, see "Clipboard" and "Spike."

Procedures

You can delete one character, one word, or selected text by following the instructions on page 152.

Button	Name	Action	See
	New	Creates a new document using the Normal template	New Document
	Open	Opens the file you select	Opening Files
	Save	Saves the current document	Saving Files
	Cut	Cuts the selected text to the Clipboard	Clipboard
	Copy	Copies the selected text to the Clipboard	Clipboard
	Paste	Pastes the Clipboard contents into the document	Clipboard
	Undo	Undoes the last action	Undoing and Redoing Actions
	Numbered List	Converts the selected text into a numbered list	Lists
	Bulleted List	Converts the selected text into a bulletted list	Lists
	Unindent	Moves the left indent to the previous tab stop	Indents
	Indent	Moves the left indent to the next tab stop	Indents
	Table	Inserts a table	Tables
	Column	Inserts newspaper columns	Columns
	Frame	Inserts an empty frame	Frames
	MSDraw	Starts the Microsoft Draw application	Drawing on a Document

Table 4-1. *Word for Windows 2 Default Toolbar*

D

Button	Name	Action	See
	MSGraph	Starts the Microsoft Graph application	Graphs
	Envelope	Creates an envelope to print with your document	Envelopes
	Spelling	Checks the spelling in your document	Spelling
	Print	Prints your document	Printing
	Zoom Whole Page	Displays the document in page layout view to show the whole page	Viewing Documents
	Zoom 100%	Displays the document at full size in normal view	Viewing Documents
	Zoom Page Width	Displays the document in the current view to show its whole width	Viewing Documents

Table 4-1.   *Word for Windows 2 Default Toolbar (continued)*

To Delete One Character

■ Position the insertion point after the character and press BACKSPACE.

■ Position the insertion point before the character and press DEL.

To Delete One Word

■ Position the insertion point after the word and press CTRL+BACKSPACE.

■ Position the insertion point before the word and press CTRL+DEL.

To Delete Selected Text

1. Select the text you want to delete.

2. Press DEL or BACKSPACE.

Hints

You can restore text you accidentally delete by selecting Edit | Undo. If you have carried out another command—anything other than moving the insertion point—between deleting the text and selecting Undo, the text cannot be restored in Word for Windows 2. In Word for Windows 6, Word tracks the changes you make so you can undo one or more of the changes you have made.

Related Topics

Clipboard
Drag and Drop
Spike
Undoing and Redoing Actions

Deleting Documents

See "File Management."

Dialog Boxes

Dialog boxes are special windows. You provide specifics for carrying out commands by selecting options in dialog boxes. Certain elements are common to all dialog boxes.

Options

You must select a dialog box element to make a change to its setting. You select, or move to, a dialog box element by clicking it with the mouse, or by pressing TAB and SHIFT+TAB so the dialog box element you want is highlighted or has an extra outline. Also, one letter in each part of a selectable element's label is underlined, just as one letter in all menu commands is underlined. You select or move to a dialog box element by pressing ALT and the underlined letter.

Text Boxes

You enter text in text boxes. For example, in the Open dialog box, enter a filename to open in the File Name text box, shown here:

When the entire entry in the text box is highlighted, your entry will entirely replace the existing entry. Some text boxes are connected to list boxes. When you select an item in the list box, it appears in the text box. Other text boxes are followed by double arrows. By clicking on these arrows, or by pressing the UP ARROW or DOWN ARROW in these text boxes, you change the number that appears in the dialog box.

List Boxes

There are two basic types of list boxes: list boxes and drop-down list boxes. List boxes are a set size and display several options, such as the Go to What list box, shown here:

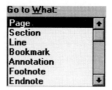

Drop-down list boxes initially look like text boxes followed by a down arrow button. Opening the drop-down list box displays the list box beneath the original box. After you a make a selection, the drop-down box closes again, and only the current setting is displayed.

Drop-down list boxes also come in two types. When the arrow is actually attached to the box, as in the Search drop-down list box shown below, you can only select an option from the list. Typing any character moves to the first item in the list that starts with the same character. If the arrow is slightly detached from the box as in the Find What drop-down list box shown below, you can either select an option from the drop-down list, or you can type an entry.

Check Boxes

Check boxes turn a feature on or off. When a check box is selected, the box has a large X in it, and the feature is active. When it is cleared, the box is empty, and the feature is inactive. For example, the dialog box shown above has the Match Case and Find Whole Words Only check boxes. They are selected or cleared independently of one another.

Option Buttons

Option buttons appear in sets. Option buttons are sometimes called radio buttons. Each option button in a set indicates a possible setting for the feature. For example, in the Tabs dialog box, there are two sets of option buttons, which are shown below. Selecting an option button in a set clears the other option buttons.

Command Buttons

You select command buttons to carry out an action. Most dialog boxes, have at least three buttons: OK, Cancel, and Help buttons. Selecting OK closes the dialog box and carries out the command using the settings you have made in the dialog box. Selecting Cancel closes the dialog box, but does not carry out any command. Selecting Help displays help information about the dialog box.

Command buttons always have some text on them that indicates what they do. If there are ellipses (three periods) after the text, selecting the button opens another dialog box in which you can make further settings.

Tabs

Word for Windows 6 has divided options in some dialog boxes into tabs that organize the dialog box options. You can switch between tabs to change which set of dialog box options you are working with. You switch between tabs by clicking them or pressing CTRL+TAB until the tab you want is in front. When a letter in the tab name is underlined, you can select the tab by pressing ALT and the underlined letter. With the Tools | Options command, you can also type the first letter of the tab. Tabs look like this:

D

Dictionaries

See "Spelling."

Directories

Directories are part of the structure on your disk. You use directories to organize the files on your disk in a logical fashion. Directories can contain other directories, which are called *subdirectories*. All disks have a *root directory*, which is the initial directory on the disk.

The series of directories and subdirectories between the drive letter and a specific file is called a *path*. Directories in a path statement are separated by backslashes (\). For example, C:\WINWORD6\DATA\FINANCE\STMT94.DOC, is found on the C drive's disk, in the WINWORD6 directory, then in the DATA directory, and in the FINANCE subdirectory. A root directory is indicated by only a backslash after the drive letter as in C:\ or in front of the filename as in \STMT94.DOC.

You should organize your Word documents and other document files in directories and subdirectories to make them easier to find. For example, you could put all of your Word files in one directory, and all of your Excel files in another directory. Alternatively, you can organize all of your files by purpose, putting all of your personal files, from whatever application, in one directory, all of your financial files in a second, and all of your sales information in a third.

For more information about directories, and how to create them or use them, see your DOS documentation. See "File Location Options" for setting the directories Word uses.

Display

To change the display of what you see on the screen, look at "View Options" as well as "Toolbars" for changing the appearance of the toolbars. To change how parts of your document appear, look under the document feature you want to customize. This includes character formats, paragraph formats, and page setup.

Display Print Queue

Word for Windows uses a print queue. Like other Windows applications, Word uses the Windows Print Manager to manage print jobs. You view the print queue using the Windows Print Manager.

When Word prints a document, it does not send the information directly to the printer. Instead, Word opens the Windows Print Manager, and prints the document to a temporary file. The Print Manager then sends the formatted document to the printer in the background while you continue to use Word or another Windows application. If you want to see the print queue or change the print order of various files, you do so in the Windows Print Manager.

For more instructions on using the Windows Print Manager, see your Windows' documentation.

DisplayWrite

DisplayWrite is one of the document formats Word accepts to bring documents into Word when you open the file. See "Opening Files."

Document Compare

See "Comparing Versions."

Document Margins

See "Margins."

Document Summary

See "Summary Info."

Document Templates

See "Templates."

Document Window

A document window is a window that appears within the Word windows and contains a document. Like other windows, it has a title bar, a control menu button, and sizing buttons. Word for Windows 2 only lets you have nine document windows open at once but in Word for Windows 6, you can have as many as you have memory for.

Procedures

You can move, size, arrange, and switch between your Word document windows.

Moving Between Open Windows

- Click on a portion of the open window when the windows are not maximized.
- Select Window, and then the window.
- Press CTRL+F6 or SHIFT+CTRL+F6 until the window you want is on top.

Opening a Second Window

You can open a second window for the same document file. This lets you use separate windows for looking at different sections of the same document.

1. Make the current window active by moving to it.
2. Select Window | New Window.

   You can also split one window into two parts called *panes.* The steps for this are described in "Viewing Documents."

Arranging Windows

To have Word size and arrange your open document windows so that you see all of each window, as shown in Figure 4-11, select Windows | Arrange All.

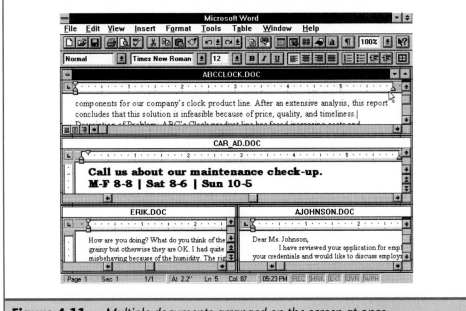

Figure 4-11.   *Multiple documents arranged on the screen at once*

Sizing the Active Document Window

Windows has a few quick sizing options you select using the sizing buttons in the document window's title bar. Clicking the Maximize button, double-clicking the document window's title bar, selecting Maximize in the document window's control menu, or pressing CTRL+F10 expands the window to fill the Word application window. You display the control menu by clicking the control menu box or pressing ALT+–. You can also reduce document windows to an icon in Word for Windows 6 by clicking the Minimize button or selecting Minimize in the document window's control menu.

To make a window any size you want, drag the window border to a new location. If you do not see a window border, click the Restore button first. You can also size a window by selecting Size from the document window's control menu or by pressing CTRL+F8. Then, press an arrow key to move to the window border in the arrow's direction. The subsequent arrow keys you press will move that border. When you press ENTER, the window is sized to the selected size.

You cannot size minimized or maximized windows. You may need to select Restore from the document window's control menu or press CTRL+F5 before you size it. You can also restore a window size by clicking its Restore button in the title bar or by double-clicking the window's icon. You also cannot make document windows larger than they appear when you maximize them.

Moving Document Windows

Drag the document window to where you want the window placed.

You can also move a window by selecting Move from the document window's control menu or by pressing CTRL+F7. Then, press the arrow keys until the window outline is where you want the window placed. When you press ENTER, the window is moved to the outlined position.

You cannot move maximized windows. You can move a window so part of it does not appear within the Word window but moving a window cannot move the window outside of the area used by the Word application window.

Hints

You want document windows to be large enough so you are comfortable working with the text. Often, unless you are working with multiple documents at once, you will want to leave the document windows maximized to see as much as possible of the current document. You may want to show two documents simultaneously when dragging and dropping text between documents in Word for Windows 6.

Appearance

When the document window is not maximized, the ruler, if displayed, appears in the document window rather than the application window. The document window does not include menu bars, ribbons, or toolbars. Each window has its own scroll bars. Only the active window in Word for Windows 6 shows the Normal View, Page Layout View, and Outline View buttons.

When a document window is maximized, the document title appears in the application window's title bar. The document window's control menu box appears at the left end of the menu bar. The document window's sizing buttons appear at the right end of the menu bar.

Related Topics

Windows

DOS Text

Most applications can save their files in a DOS text or ASCII format. DOS text or ASCII files contain no coding or formatting. Only ASCII characters are included in the file. Word can open DOS text files. Saving data as a DOS text file and opening it is often the least confusing method of transferring information from a non-Windows application into Word. Also, you can write programs for Basic or Pascal in Word and then save the file in the DOS text format for future use. To save a document in a text format, look at "Saving Files."

Dot Leaders

See "Tabs."

Double-Click

See "Mouse Techniques."

Double-Sided Printing

If your printer handles double-sided printing, you can print double-sided by selecting that Paper Size option. If double-sided pages are not an option on your printer, insert the pages in the printer twice. To print a double-sided document when your printer does not support double-sided printing in Word for Windows 6, print all the odd pages, flip the paper, then print the even pages. To do this, select File | Print and select Odd Pages from the Print drop-down list box in Word for Windows 6. Then select OK.

Once the odd pages are printed, put the pages back into the printer so printing occurs on the opposite side of the paper. For a dot-matrix printer, this means turning the paper around and rethreading it through the printer. In a laser printer, you will need to flip over the paper. Next, print the even pages. Select File | Print and select Even Pages from the Print drop-down list box. Then select OK. If you plan to bind the double-sided pages, see "Margins" about adding a binding offset.

A neat trick for printing on two sides of the page using a laser printer is after you print the odd pages, remove the pages without rearranging them, leaving page one at the bottom of the stack. If the last page is an odd-numbered page, remove this page from the stack as you put the pages back into the laser printer's feeding tray with the printing face down. Also remember to keep track of which way the top of the page should face. When you print the even pages on a laser printer when page one is at the bottom of the stack, select the Reverse Print Order check box for Print options. This little trick means you do not have to rearrange pages so page one is at the top, then page three, and so on.

Double Spacing

See "Spacing."

Double Underline

See "Underline."

Draft View

Word has a draft view that is faster than its other views; however, this view does not show all of the formatting the document uses. Look at "Viewing Documents" for the different types of ways to view your document including the draft view.

Drag

See "Mouse Techniques."

Drag and Drop

Word for Windows offers the ultimate in convenience for moving and copying text, a feature called Drag and Drop, which uses the mouse. In Word for Windows 6, you can drag and drop text between documents as long as both documents are simultaneously visible.

Procedures

Instructions on how to use the Drag and Drop feature are described below.

Copying Text with Drag and Drop

1. Select the text to copy by dragging the mouse across it.

2. Hold down the CTRL key.

3. Point the mouse at the selected text and press the mouse button.

4. Drag the text to a new location then release the mouse button.

Moving Text with Drag and Drop

1. Select the text to move by dragging the mouse across it.

2. Point the mouse at the selected text and press the mouse button.

3. Drag the text to a new location in your document, and then release the mouse button.

Related Topics

Clipboard
Mouse Techniques
Spike

Drawing Boxes and Lines in a Paragraph

See "Borders and Shading."

Drawing on a Document

Word lets you draw on a document. The drawing can be simple objects such as rectangles, lines, and circles, or can be very complex. You can also insert other file types as pictures into Word. Drawing in Word for Windows is very different depending on the version you are using.

Procedures

The Microsoft Draw features you will use to create your drawings are described below.

Drawing in a Word for Windows 2 Document

1. Select Insert | Object.

2. Select Microsoft Drawing from the list box and OK.

3. Draw the object in Microsoft Draw.

4. Select File | Update.

5. Select File | Exit and Return to Document Name.

    To change the drawing later, double-click the drawing or select Edit | Microsoft Drawing Object.

Drawing in a Word for Windows 6 Document

Click the Drawing button in the Standard toolbar.

You can also display this toolbar just like you display other toolbars—select the View | Toolbars command, the Drawing check box, and OK.

Word displays a Drawing toolbar like the one shown in Figure 4-12. Using this toolbar, you can draw on top of the document. The tools available on this toolbar are described under "Drawing Toolbar." For example, the text callouts to the two faces in Figure 4-12 were added using the Drawing toolbar. Most of the tools for drawing match features present in most drawing packages.

Drawn objects do not appear in normal view so when you display the Drawing toolbar, Word will switch you to the page layout view. If you have the Drawing toolbar displayed and then switch to normal view, when you select a button on the Drawing toolbar, Word will prompt you to select whether you want to switch to page layout view before continuing.

Hints

Holding down SHIFT while you draw a line only draws lines in 30- and 45-degree increments. Holding down SHIFT while you draw an ellipse or a rectangle makes the ellipse or rectangle a circle or square. If you press CTRL+SHIFT while you draw an ellipse, you will draw a circle around the point you select before you drag the circle away from the center.

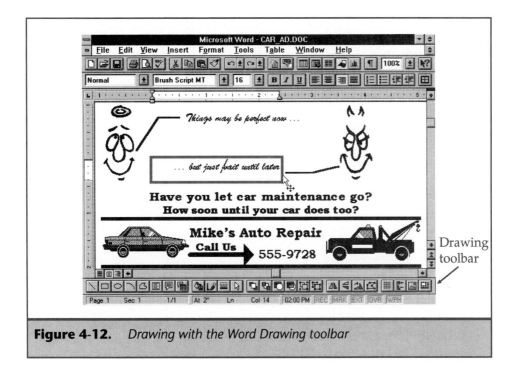

Figure 4-12. *Drawing with the Word Drawing toolbar*

Double-clicking a Drawing toolbar button in Word for Windows 6 makes the tool remain selected until you click another button or type text. Use this feature to draw multiple lines, rectangles, ellipses, arcs, or freeform shapes.

When the Select Drawing Objects button is selected, drag the mouse over a rectangle to select the drawn objects included in the rectangle. You can also select multiple objects using the Select Drawing Objects button by holding down SHIFT while you click each object you want to add or remove from the current selection.

Microsoft Draw

When you are drawing in Microsoft Draw in Word for Windows 2 documents, you will want to perform basic graphic editing. Microsoft Draw uses its own toolbar as well as commands to create your drawing. The basic graphics editing features and how they are used in Microsoft Draw are listed in Table 4-2.

Button or Menu Command	Graphics Feature
	Selects objects to be altered
	Draws a straight line
	Draws an ellipse or circle
	Draws a rectangle or square with rounded corners
	Draws a rectangle or square
	Draws an arc
	Draws a freeform shape over the area you drag the mouse
	Adds a box of text
Select Color after Fill	Sets the interior color of filled objects
Select Color after Line	Sets the border and line color
Draw I Line Style	Sets the style of the lines
Edit I Bring to Front	Puts selected drawn objects in front of all others
Edit I Send to Back	Puts selected drawn objects behind all others
Draw I Group	Puts selected drawn objects into a group so further customization, sizing, and placement affects all objects in the group equally
Draw I Ungroup	Ungroups a group of objects in a group so you can change the objects individually
Draw I Rotate/ Flip I Flip Horizontal	Flips the selected objects so what was on the left side is on the right and vice versa
Draw I Rotate/ Flip I Flip Vertical	Flips the selected objects so what was on the top is on the bottom and vice versa

Table 4-2. *Basic Drawing Functions in Microsoft Draw*

Button or Menu Command	Graphics Feature
Draw | Rotate/ Flip | Rotate Right	Rotates the selected objects 90 degrees right
Draw | Rotate/ Flip | Rotate Left	Rotates the selected objects 90 degrees left
Edit | Edit Freeform	Lets you adjust the points that define the selected objects
Draw | Snap to Grid	Causes subsequently placed drawn objects to start at the nearest grid point
File | Import Picture	Adds a picture from another file into drawing
Text | Font	Sets font of selected text
Text | Size	Sets size of selected text

Table 4-2. *Basic Drawing Functions in Microsoft Draw (continued)*

Related Topics

Drawing Toolbar
Layering Text and Graphics

Drawing Toolbar

The Drawing toolbar provides many of the tools you will want to use to draw in a Word for Windows 6 document. These tools provide the drawing capabilities. Display this toolbar by clicking the Drawing button in the Standard toolbar. Once the Drawing toolbar appears, you draw on a document by selecting the buttons and where you want to draw. Some of the buttons require that you select the drawn objects to change before you use the buttons on the Drawing toolbar. Word for Windows 2 does not have a Drawing toolbar since you create the drawn object separately in Microsoft Draw. The Drawing toolbar has the buttons with the associated functions shown in Table 4-3.

You can also change the appearance of a drawn object by right-clicking it and selecting Drawn Object Properties, by double-clicking it, or by selecting it and using the Format \| Drawing Object command.

Button	Name	Function
	Line	Draws a straight line using the starting and ending points you provide
	Rectangle	Draws a rectangle using the two corners you provide
	Ellipse	Draws an ellipse or circle using the two points you provide
	Arc	Draws an arc using the starting and ending points you provide
	Freeform	Draws a freeform shape over the area you drag the mouse
	Text Box	Adds a text box to contain text or other effects for text that you want separated from the main part of a document
	Callout	Inserts a box of text that points to an object in the document
	Format Callout	Sets the appearance of the callout including how many lines can connect the callout to what it points to, the gap between the line and the text box, the angle, the length, the drop, whether the callout has a border, whether Word handles attaching the line between what you are pointing to and the callout, and whether the callout has an accent bar
	Fill Color	Sets the color of filled object drawn with Rectangle, Ellipse, Arc, Freeform, Text Box, and Callout buttons
	Line Color	Sets the color of lines drawn with Line and the border for filled objects drawn with Rectangle, Ellipse, Arc, Freeform, Text Box, and Callout buttons
	Line Style	Sets the style of the lines drawn with Line and the border for filled objects drawn with Rectangle, Ellipse, Arc, Freeform, Text Box, and Callout buttons
	Select Drawing Objects	Selects objects you click to be altered by the other buttons

Table 4-3.   *Word for Windows 6 Drawing Toolbar*

Button	Name	Function
	Bring to Front	Puts selected drawn objects in front of all others
	Send to Back	Puts selected drawn objects behind all others
	Bring in Front of Text	Puts selected drawn objects in front of document text
	Send Behind Text	Puts selected drawn objects behind document text
	Group	Puts selected drawn objects into a group so further customization, sizing, and placement affects all objects in the group equally
	Ungroup	Ungroups a group of objects in a group so you can change the objects individually
	Flip Horizontal	Flips the selected objects so what was on the left side is on the right and vice versa
	Flip Vertical	Flips the selected objects so what was on the top is on the bottom and vice versa
	Rotate Right	Rotates the selected objects ninety degrees to the right
	Reshape	Lets you adjust the points that define the selected freeform objects
	Snap to Grid	Causes subsequently placed drawn objects to start at the nearest grid point
	Align Drawing Objects	Aligns selected drawn objects relative to one another or the page
	Create Picture	Inserts a picture just like selecting Insert	Picture or puts selected drawn objects into a picture
	Insert Frame	Adds a frame around the selected drawn objects or adds an empty frame

Table 4-3.   *Word for Windows 6 Drawing Toolbar (continued)*

D

Related Topics

Drawing on a Document
Frames
Toolbars

Dropped Capitals

Word for Windows 6 can create dropped capitals like the ones that you see at the beginning of books, magazines, and newspapers. To create the same effect in Word for Windows 2, you insert the initial capital letter in a frame as described under "Frames."

Procedures

1. Move to the paragraph where you want the dropped capital.

2. Select Format | Drop Cap.

3. Select Dropped as the style when you want the initial capital to occupy the beginning of the next several lines or In Margin when you want the initial capital to cause the paragraph to be indented by the space the capital requires.

4. Select the font for the initial capital from the Font drop-down list box when you want it to be a different font than the rest of the text.

5. Select the number of lines of document text the initial capital occupies in the Lines to Drop text box. This sets the size of the initial capital but you can change it later by selecting the initial capital and changing its font size.

6. Select how much distance you want between the document text and the initial capital after Distance from Text.

7. Select OK.

If you select more than one character before you select Format | Drop Cap, all the selected characters will be accented as shown in Figure 4-13. *Once* was created by selecting *Once* and then using Format | Drop Cap to make it drop in the margin (where the graphic image is added). The *F* later in the text is added by making it a dropped capital that uses three lines.

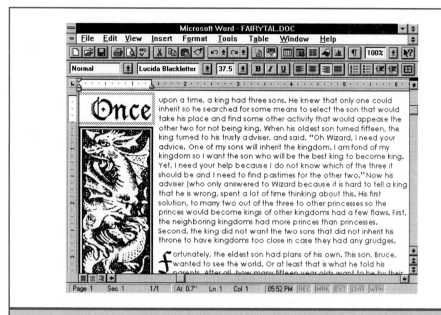

Figure 4-13. *Creating dropped capitals and dropped words*

Hints

If you need to alter the placement of the dropped capital on the page, do it by changing the paragraph formatting. You can also drag the margins on the rulers to shift a dropped capital's position. You can also change the alignment of a dropped capital without affecting the alignment of the paragraph that the dropped capital introduces. You change the font and size of the dropped capital using Font and Font Size in the Formatting toolbar.

If you no longer want a dropped capital used, select the dropped capital and select the None option under Position.

Drop-Down Lists

Drop-down lists in a form make form completion easier by providing a list of predefined choices. Look at "Forms" for how to include drop-down lists in the forms you create.

Edit Options

Word has several customization settings that change how you edit documents. These options are on one of the tabs in the Tools | Options command.

Procedure

1. Select Tools | Options.

2. Click the Edit tab.

3. Change the options described below. Select OK.

Options

The Edit options let you set how Word works when you are editing your documents.

Typing Replaces Selection

If this check box is selected, and you type while text is selected, your typed entry replaces the selected text. When this check box is cleared, the selected text becomes unselected so anything you type does not replace that text. Set this according to your preference for whether you want any selected text replaced when you start typing. By trying it both ways, you will find a preference.

Drag-and-Drop Text Editing

When this check box is selected, copy and move text by dragging it and dropping it with the mouse. When this check box is cleared, you cannot use this method of rearranging your text.

Automatic Word Selection

When this check box is selected, Word selects the entire word, when you select part of a word. When this check box is cleared, only the selected part of the word is included. For example, if the insertion point is before the *m* in automation and you select *m* through the beginning of the next word with this check box selected, Word selects "automation." If this check box is cleared, Word selects "mation."

Use the INS Key for Paste

When this check box is selected and you press INS, Word pastes the Clipboard's contents at the insertion point. When this check box is cleared and you press INS, you switch between insert and overtype mode.

Overtype Mode

When this check box is selected, overtype mode is in effect so the characters you type replace the characters at the insertion point's location. When this check box is cleared, you are in insert mode. You can switch to overtype mode by pressing INS (assuming the Use the INS Key for Paste check box is cleared). You can continue switching between insert and overtype mode in Word for Windows 6 by double-clicking the OVR indicator on the status bar.

Use Smart Cut and Paste

When this check box is selected, it lets Word intelligently remove spaces before punctuation marks when you delete words before punctuation marks. When this check box is cleared, Word only deletes the text you select.

Allow Accented Uppercase

When this check box is selected, Word assumes that accented characters at the beginning of words are acceptable. When this check box is cleared, features such as changing case and spelling assume that the first character in a word should have any accent mark removed.

Picture Editor

Selects the editor used to edit pictures. The options you have depend on the Word components and other applications you have installed on your computer.

Edit | AutoText

See "AutoText."

Edit | Bookmark

See "Bookmarks."

Edit | Clear

See "Clipboard" and "Spike."

Edit | Copy

See "Clipboard" and "Spike" as well as "Object Linking and Embedding" for when to use this command to share data between applications.

Edit | Cut

See "Clipboard" and "Spike" as well as "Object Linking and Embedding" for when to use this command to share data between applications.

Edit | Find

See "Find and Replace."

Edit | Glossary

See "Glossary."

Edit | Go To

See "Moving the Insertion Point."

Edit | Links

See "Object Linking and Embedding."

Edit | Object

See "Object Linking and Embedding."

Edit | Paste

See "Clipboard" and "Spike" as well as "Object Linking and Embedding" for when to use this command to share data between applications.

Edit | Paste Special

See "Clipboard" and "Spike" as well as "Object Linking and Embedding" for when to use this command to share data between applications.

Edit | Redo

See "Undoing and Redoing Actions."

Edit | Repeat

See "Repeating Actions."

Edit | Replace

See "Find and Replace."

Edit | Select All

See "Selecting Text."

Edit | Undo

See "Undoing and Redoing Actions."

Editing Documents

Editing is the process of creating and formatting a document. If you are unfamiliar with the steps involved in the process, see Chapters 1, 2, and 3 for a quick explanation of the basic features of editing. When you have read those chapters, you will be ready to return to this chapter, and research specific areas of interest.

Related Topics

Shortcut Keys

EditTime Field

The EDITTIME field inserts the amount of time a document is edited. For more information on this, see "Fields."

Electronic Mail

Word can work with Microsoft Mail and other mailing systems to route Word documents to other users. Word and Microsoft Mail can work together so you can send a document to one or many other Word users. Each of the document recipients can make revision marks on the document and send them back to you or to the next person in a chain of recipients. Since Word and Microsoft Mail do much of the work, all you have to do is tell Word the document to send, to whom you want it sent, and whether you want each recipient to be sent the document at once or whether you want one recipient to look at it and pass it on to the next one.

If you want to send a Word file without using Microsoft Mail, you can probably mail the file electronically anyway. Most electronic mail systems let you attach a file to a message. You attach your Word document to a message and have the message and the attached file sent to the desired recipient. However, this is done through the electronic mail system and is not as convenient as the steps described above.

Procedure

The following procedures describe how to route a document to multiple users and how to use Word to send electronic mail.

Routing a Document

1. Open the file to send.

2. Select File | Add Routing Slip.

3. Select the Address button.

4. Select the names of the people you want to receive the Word document and the Add button for each name.

5. Select OK.

6. Type any entries in the Subject and Message text boxes that you want included in the document.

7. Select One After Another when you want the same document sent serially from one named addressee to the next or select All At Once when you want to send the Word document to all addressees simultaneously.

8. Select other options that include the following:

   ■ *Remove*   Removes the highlighted name from the list of addressees.

   ■ *Move*   Moves the highlighted name in the list of addresses up or down in the list.

   ■ *Return When Done*   Tells Word that after a recipient reviews the document that their copy of Word for Windows will send the copy of the document back to you.

   ■ *Track Status*   Tells Word to send a message back to you when the document is sent to the next person in the list.

   ■ *Protect For*   Protects users from making changes to the document that are not marked as changes. When Annotations is selected, document recipients can only make annotations to the document. When Revisions is selected, document recipients can make changes but they all use revision marks that cannot be turned off. When Forms is selected, document recipients can only make changes in the form fields.

   ■ *Reset/Clear*   Removes the settings made in other parts of the dialog box.

9. Select Route to send the document to the selected recipients or select Add Slip if you want to continue editing the document before you select File | Send to send the document to the selected recipients.

   Before the document is sent to the selected recipients, you can edit the routing slip by selecting File | Edit Routing Slip.

Sending Electronic Mail

1. Select File | Send.

   If the Mail as Attachment check box for General Options of the Tools | Options command is selected, the current document is picked up as an attachment to the note and you can see the Word icon for the document you are adding. If the Mail as Attachment check box is cleared, the contents of the document are added as the note's contents.

2. Type the addressees to send the note to, in the To and Cc text boxes.

   You can also add names for the To and Cc text boxes by selecting Address. For each addressee to add, highlight the name then select To to add it to the To text box or Cc to add it to the Cc text box. Then select OK to return to the Send Note dialog box. You can compare the addressees in the To and Cc text boxes to the names you have in your address book for your mail system by selecting the Check Names button. The names in the To and Cc text boxes that Word finds are underlined. You will see a message if one or more of the addressees are not in your address book.

3. Type the subject for the note in the Subject text box.

4. Change the message shown at the bottom. You can also select Attach and select a file to include as an attachment. Use this option when you want to attach a file other than the current one.

   You can also insert the contents of a file by moving to the message area and using the Edit | Insert from File command.

5. Select Send.

Related Topics

Annotation

EMBED Field

The EMBED field represents an embedded object in a Word for Windows 2 document. For more information on this, see "Object Linking and Embedding."

Encapsulated Postscript Files

Encapsulated Postscript Files, or EPS, is one of the file formats Word accepts for graphic images. You add these files as pictures to your Word documents. Look under "Graphics" for more information about bringing image files, such as those in an EPS format, into a Word document.

The way EPS files display in your Word documents depends on whether the file also includes a TIFF or WMF format picture of the EPS contents. If the EPS file does not contain a TIFF or WMF format image as part of its file, then the EPS file appears in your Word document as a boundary box indicating that the file is an EPS file. When you print a document with an EPS file, if you have a PostScript printer, the PostScript image is printed. If you do not have a PostScript printer, Word prints the TIFF or WMF format image if the EPS file has one. If you do not have a PostScript printer and the EPS file does not include a TIFF or WMF format image, the printed document has an empty box indicating where the image is placed in the document.

Embedded Objects

Embedded objects are objects such as text, graphs, or pictures that are created by another application and embedded in Word. The object, and all its relevant information, are saved in your Word document. You start the application used to create the object from within Word, edit the object, and then close the other application to continue working with Word. For more information, see "Object Linking and Embedding."

Embedding

Embedding allows you to add objects such as text, graphs, or pictures created by another application in your Word document. Embedded objects are saved in your Word document although you use the other application to modify the embedded objects. For more information, see "Object Linking and Embedding." Word includes several supplementary applications that can be used to create embedded objects. These applications are WordArt, the Equation Editor, Microsoft Graph, and, in Word for Windows 2, Microsoft Draw.

Related Topics

Drawing on a Document
Equations
Graphics
Object Linking and Embedding
WordArt

Enclosures

When you are creating mail merge documents such as form letters to which you want to add enclosures, use the INCLUDETEXT field to include the selected documents in the final version of the form letters. See "Fields" for how to use the INCLUDETEXT field.

Endnotes

Endnotes let you attribute the source of your information in a document. Unlike footnotes, endnotes are placed at the end of your document. Word handles arranging and placing the endnotes for you. The features for endnotes are the same as footnotes and are described under "Footnotes and Endnotes."

Entering Special Characters

You can enter special characters besides the ones on your keyboard. The steps for doing this are described under "Special Characters."

Envelopes

Word makes it easy for you to create envelopes that can be printed just like your other print documents. Word can pick up addresses from your document to make entering the data easier. The envelope can either be printed at once or added to your document.

Procedures

This section provides information on the various ways you can create and print an addressed envelope.

Creating An Addressed Envelope

1. Select the address in your document. If you do not select the address before the next step, Word searches the document for text that looks like an address. Word uses any set of several short lines as the address for the envelope. If you are uncertain that Word will pick up the appropriate address, select the text containing the address.

2. Select Tools | Envelopes and Labels. In Word for Windows 2, select Tools | Create Envelope or click the Envelope button from the toolbar. Word opens the Envelopes and Labels or the Create Envelope dialog box. In the Envelopes and Labels dialog box, you may need to select the Envelopes tab to see the options you want for addressing envelopes.

3. Check the address in the Delivery Address (or Addressed To in Word for Windows 2) text box. The text box currently contains the address you selected or the address Word picked up from the document. You can enter new text, edit it, or delete it.

4. Enter your return address in the Return Address text box if necessary. Word saves the return address as the default return address and automatically uses it the next time.

5. Change the options described in the next section. In Word for Windows 6, many of these options do not appear until you select the Options button.

6. Select Print or Add to Document. When you select Print Envelope, Word immediately prints the envelope you have defined. When you select Add to document, Word adds the envelope as a separate section at the beginning of your current document. This section has the page number 0 (zero), so it does not disturb the page numbering for the remainder of your document.

   If you have changed the return address, when you complete the dialog box Word prompts for whether you want to save that return address as the default mailing address. Select Yes to save the address with the user information. Select No and the address is not used as the return address the next time. The default return address is one of Word's User Info options.

E

You can see how Word converts the information in the dialog box into an envelope by looking at Figure 4-14. Word has handled placing the contents of the addressee and return address in their correct locations.

Options

The following options are either part of the Envelopes and Labels or the Create Envelope dialog box, or are available when you select Options. Word for Windows 6 divides the options in the Envelope Options dialog box between the Envelope Options and Printing Options tabs.

Envelope Size

This drop-down list box selects the size of the envelope. The list includes a variety of sizes of envelopes including United States and European standard sizes.

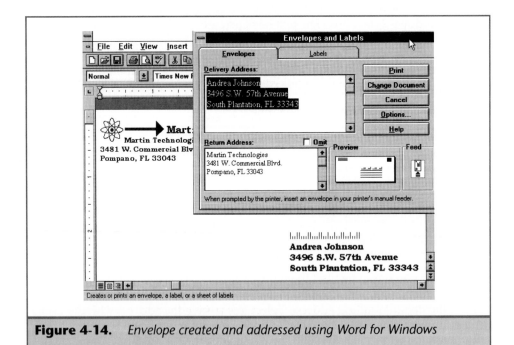

Figure 4-14.   *Envelope created and addressed using Word for Windows*

Omit or Omit Return Address

When this check box is selected, Word omits printing a return address on the envelope such as when the envelopes already have a preprinted return address. When this check box is cleared, Word prints the return address on all envelopes.

Delivery Point Bar Code

When this check box is selected, Word for Windows 6 adds the POSTNET bar code for the addressee's ZIP code. The POSTNET bar code helps the post office promptly deliver the letter and can save you money with mass mailing. Daisy-wheel printers cannot print a POSTNET bar code.

FIM-A Courtesy Reply Mail

When this check box is selected, Word for Windows 6 adds the Facing Identification Mark that identifies the front of the envelope to make presorting quicker for the post office when you are including a delivery point bar code. Daisy-wheel printers cannot print a POSTNET bar code.

Delivery Address

These options set the style and position of the address entered in the Delivery Address text box. Selecting Font and the font style and size sets the delivery address's font and style. You can also select the Default button from the dialog box Font displays to make all envelopes created with the same template as the current document use the same font style and size. From Left and From Top set the distance from the upper-left corner of the envelope where Word starts the delivery address. The default of Auto lets Word place it according to the envelope's size.

Return Address

These options set the style and position of the address entered in the Return Address text box. You have the same options as Delivery Address.

Feed Method

These options tell Word how envelopes are inserted into the printer. The six boxes select the alignment in the printer's feeder. The Face Up and Face Down radio buttons select whether you are putting envelopes face up or face down in the printer. Clockwise Rotation selects whether you are putting the envelopes in a reverse direction. Initially the options selected match what Word assumes works best for your printer so you only need to change the options if you want to feed the envelopes into the printer differently.

Feed From

This drop-down list box lets you select how the envelopes are inserted into the printer. You have any of the options listed to choose from, although the options Word lists depend on the printer you are using.

Hints

Even if you use envelopes with the return address preprinted, you can use the return address field to include your initials or name. This lets the recipient of your letter or mailed document know exactly who at your company mailed the letter.

Make sure to use the correct two letter abbreviation for the state. As a reminder, these are listed in the box "State Code Abbreviations."

If you want to add further formatting to an envelope, add the envelope to the document. Once the letter is in the document, you can use other Word features such as adding graphics to the document.

In Word for Windows 6, you can also change the appearance and position of addresses on an envelope by changing styles. For example, documents using the Normal template use styles named Envelope Return and Envelope Address for positioning and appearance of envelopes. Changing the definition of the styles changes the appearance of envelopes. If you modify these styles in a template file, you will change the appearance of all envelopes created for documents using that template.

Related Topics

Mail Merge
Printing
Styles

State Code Abbreviations

State abbreviations are commonly used on most correspondence. You can use this handy list to look up the code for any state, the District of Columbia, or United States territories:

State	Abbreviation	State	Abbreviation
Alabama	AL	Montana	MT
Alaska	AK	Nebraska	NE
Arizona	AZ	Nevada	NV
Arkansas	AR	New Hampshire	NH
California	CA	New Jersey	NJ
Colorado	CO	New Mexico	NM
Connecticut	CT	New York	NY
Delaware	DE	North Carolina	NC
District of	DC	North Dakota	ND
Columbia		Ohio	OH
Florida	FL	Oklahoma	OK
Georgia	GA	Oregon	OR
Guam	GU	Pennsylvania	PA
Hawaii	HI	Puerto Rico	PR
Idaho	ID	Rhode Island	RI
Illinois	IL	South Carolina	SC
Indiana	IN	South Dakota	SD
Iowa	IA	Tennessee	TN
Kansas	KS	Texas	TX
Kentucky	KY	Utah	UT
Louisiana	LA	Vermont	VT
Maine	ME	Virginia	VA
Maryland	MD	Virgin Islands	VI
Massachusetts	MA	Washington	WA
Michigan	MI	West Virginia	WV
Minnesota	MN	Wisconsin	WI
Mississippi	MS	Wyoming	WY
Missouri	MO		

E

Environment Defaults

If you have used WordPerfect, you are accustomed to changing how WordPerfect behaves by changing the environment defaults. In Word, you change these settings somewhat differently. In the table below, the first column lists the WordPerfect environment defaults and the second column lists the topics in this chapter you should refer to for the comparable information in Word.

WordPerfect Environment Default	Word Topic
Allow Undo	Undoing and Redoing Actions (Undo is always available)
Back-Up Options	Save Options
Beep Options	Control Panel
Cursor Speed	Control Panel
Document Management/Summary	Save Options and Summary Info
Fast Save	Save Options
Format Document for Default Printer on Open	No parallel since Word does this automatically
Hyphenation	Hyphenation
Language	Foreign Language Support
Units of Measure	Control Panel
WordPerfect 5.1 Keyboard	Control Panel
Auto Code Placement	No parallel since Word handles where formatting starts and stops
WordPerfect 5.1 Cursor Movements	General Options
Delimited Text Options	Mail Merge

EPS

EPS (Encapsulated Postscript) is one of the many file formats Word accepts for graphic images. You add EPS files as pictures to your Word documents. Look under "Graphics" for more information about bringing graphics files, such as those in EPS format, into a Word document. See "Encapsulated PostScript Files" for information on how these files display in your Word documents.

EQ Field

The EQ field creates an equation similar to ones created with the Equation Editor. For more information on this, see "Fields."

Equation Editor

See "Equations."

Equations

Use Word's supplementary application, the Equation Editor, when you need to enter an equation or formula into a document. The Equation Editor creates equations using mathematical and typesetting conventions. Since the equation is treated as a separate unit, any editing you do in your document has no effect on it. The Equation Editor is designed to make entering and placing mathematical characters easy.

Procedures

The following instructions describe how to use the Equation Editor to create an equation.

E

Starting the Equation Editor

1. Select Insert | Object.

2. Select Microsoft Equation 2.0 or Equation from the list and OK.

3. Enter the equation. Figure 4-15 shows the Equation Editor with an equation completed.

4. Select File | Exit and Return to Document Name.

5. Select Yes to update the equation in the Word document.

Editing the Equation

Double-click the equation or select Edit | Equation Object in Word for Windows 2.

In Word for Windows 6, you can either edit the equation by opening the Equation Editor as a separate application or by editing the equation within Word and letting the Equation Editor replace Word's menu and toolbars. You edit the equation in its own application window by selecting the equation, right-clicking the equation and selecting Open Equation or by selecting the Edit | Equation Object | Open command. The Equation Editor includes a View menu that you do not have when you edit the equation as described below. To leave the Equation Editor, you can use the File | Exit command.

To edit an equation within Word for Windows 6, right-click the equation and select Edit Equation or select the Edit | Equation Object | Open command. The Word for Windows 6 menu is replaced by the Equation Editor menu and the Word toolbars disappear as the Equation Editor toolbar appears. You continue to work with the Equation Editor until you click outside of the area the equation uses.

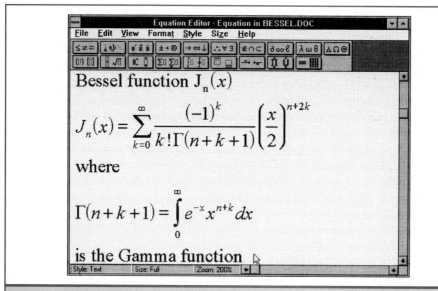

Figure 4-15. *Equations created with the Equation Editor*

Entering an Equation

When you enter an equation in the Equation Editor, you are filling in slots. *Slots* are areas in the Equation Editor that you fill with characters and symbols. You can add more slots by adding templates as described below. Equation Editor templates such as fractions and matrices are combinations of symbols and empty slots. The insertion point covers the slot you are currently working with. Press TAB or ENTER to move to the next slot or SHIFT+TAB to go back to the previous slot. HOME and END move the insertion point to the beginning and end of a slot. Empty slots have an outlined box. An equation with empty slots looks like this:

$$\sum_{\square}^{\square} \square$$

The procedure for entering an equation depends on what you want to enter. You can enter letters, numbers, and symbols. You can also insert templates. Click or use the arrow keys to move to the part of the equation you want to edit. Symbols, templates, and embellishments are added using the *palettes*, which are the 19 buttons shown in the toolbar (see Figure 4-15). The palettes and the different items they add to an equation are shown in Table 4-4. To enter characters or symbols, or to set a position, follow one of these steps:

■ To enter numbers and letters, type the numbers and letters. To include spaces in the text, select Style | Text and then type the text.

■ To enter a symbol, click a palette containing the symbol you want. Drag the mouse to the symbol. Clicking another palette or part of the window unselects the chosen palette. When a palette is selected it looks like this:

■ To enter some symbols, select a style in the Style menu and type the character that creates the character you want. For example, select Style | Greek and let the Equation Editor convert the letters you type into their Greek characters. You can do this with symbols which are also inserted with the palettes.

■ To select a template, click the palette containing the template. Then click the button on the palette for the template. Clicking another palette or part of the window unselects the chosen palette. When you add templates, you see outlined boxes for the slots to fill with other characters.

■ To select an embellishment such as primes, click the palette containing the embellishment. Then click the button on the palette for the embellishment. Clicking another palette or part of the window unselects the chosen palette. The embellishment applies to the last character or symbol entered.

For example, to add the $J_n(x)$ at the top of Figure 4-15, start by typing **J**. For the subscripted n, click the third palette in the second row which has templates for subscript and superscript positions. Click the second button in this palette and the Equation Editor adds an outline that is below the J. Type **n** and press RIGHT ARROW to move out of the slot. Next, click the first button in the first palette in the second row to add the parentheses. The size of parentheses inserted with a template is adjusted better than if you type them. Next, type **x** as the contents of the parentheses and press RIGHT ARROW. The rest of the formula is added the same way; using palettes to add templates for positioning options and symbols.

Formatting with the Equation Editor

The Equation Editor has several commands for changing the appearance of equations. By default, the Equation Editor uses settings that match the most commonly used typesetting and mathematical conventions. You can change several of these settings to get desired results. You can change font typefaces, font size, spacing, and alignment.

Palette	Adds
![relational symbols palette]	Relational symbols such "not equals" or "approximately"
![spaces and ellipses palette]	Spaces and ellipses
![embellishments palette]	Embellishments such as primes and arrows
![operators palette]	Draws mathematical operators such as $\times$ and division signs
![arrows palette]	Arrows
![logical symbols palette]	Logical symbols
![set theory palette]	Set theory symbols
![miscellaneous palette]	Miscellaneous symbols such as infinity and the degree symbol
![lowercase greek palette]	A lowercase Greek letter
![uppercase greek palette]	An uppercase Greek letter
![brackets palette]	Template to put entries inside parentheses, braces, and brackets
![fractions palette]	Template for fractions and radicals
![superscript palette]	Template to include superscript and/or subscript slots
![summation palette]	Template for summation with possible superscript and subscript slots
![integrals palette]	Template for integrals with possible superscript and subscript slots
![underbar palette]	Template for underbar and overbar slots

Table 4-4. *Equation Editor Palettes*

Palette	Adds
→ ←	Template for underarrow and overarrow slots
∏ ∪	Template for products and set theory expressions
☐☐☐ ▦	Template for matrices

Table 4-4.   *Equation Editor Palettes (continued)*

The style of the characters is defined several ways. Some of the symbols require specific fonts because only those fonts provide the desired characters. You can change the font of other text items. The easiest way to change the font is to select Style | Define. Choose a typeface for each style, and choose whether it uses boldface or italics. Then select the style from the Style pull-down menu and type the entries that use that style. If the style you want does not appear, select Style | Other, then select a typeface and whether characters using that typeface are also boldfaced or italicized.

The easiest way to set the font's size is to select Size and a font size description. Select Size | Define to set the exact size the assigned to each font size descriptions. You can override the font size by selecting Size | Other and then typing the point size you want and OK.

You can either set the typeface and size before you enter the affected characters or you can select the characters and then the commands. You select characters in the Equation Editor just like you select text in Word—drag the mouse across the characters you want to select or use SHIFT and the arrow keys.

Change the spacing to stretch or squeeze an equation to fit a particular space. Set the spacing by selecting Format | Spacing. From the Spacing dialog box, you can set the distance between lines of equations, the horizontal and vertical distance between elements in a matrix, how high superscript characters are raised, how low subscript characters are dropped, the distance between a limit and the symbol using the limit, and whether the settings you enter become the new defaults. The spacing defaults are relative so they match the size of the characters. You can see a sample of the spacing you are setting with the diagram on the right side of the dialog box.

When several equations are in one Equation Editor object, you need to set an alignment between them. The most used alignment options are set with the Format menu. Using the options at the top of the Format pull-down menu, you can left-align, center, right-align, or align according to the equals sign or decimal point. The alignment you select applies to all of the equations in the Equation Editor object.

Shortcut Keys for the Equation Editor

The Equation Editor has many shortcut keys you can use to make selections. Table 4-5 shows the shortcut keys for menu commands. Table 4-6 shows the shortcut keys for entering popular symbols. Table 4-7 shows the shortcut keys for popular templates. Table 4-8 shows the shortcut keys for popular embellishments.

Besides the key combinations listed in the tables, the Equation Editor has a few other key combinations. If you want to insert a tab character in a slot, press CTRL+TAB. You can also press CTRL+G when you want only the next character to use the Symbol style, and press CTRL+B when you want only the next character to use the matrix-vector style.

TIP: The Equation Editor also has shortcut keys to enter any symbol or template when you know its palette number and the number of the button within the palette. To insert a symbol, press CTRL+SHIFT+S, type a number between 1 and 9 for the palette number, followed by a number between 1 and 32 for the button number within the palette, and press ENTER. To insert a template, press CTRL+SHIFT+T, type a number between 1 and 9 for the palette number, followed by a number between 1 and 32 for the button number within the palette, and press ENTER.

Menu Command	Keyboard Shortcut
File I Update	F3
File I Exit and Return to Document	ALT+F4
Edit I Copy	CTRL+C
Edit I Clear	DEL
Edit I Cut	CTRL+X
Edit I Paste	CTRL+V
Edit I Select All	CTRL+A
Edit I Undo	CTRL+Z
View I 100%	CTRL+1
View I 200%	CTRL+2
View I 400%	CTRL+4
View I Redraw	CTRL+D
View I Show All	CTRL+Y
Format I Left	CTRL+SHIFT+L
Format I Center	CTRL+SHIFT+C
Format I Right	CTRL+SHIFT+R
Style I Math	CTRL+SHIFT+=
Style I Text	CTRL+SHIFT+E
Style I Function	CTRL+SHIFT+F
Style I Variable	CTRL+SHIFT+I
Style I Greek	CTRL+SHIFT+G
Style I Matrix-Vector	CTRL+SHIFT+B

Table 4-5.   *Shortcut Keys for Equation Editor Commands*

Symbol	Keyboard Shortcut
∞	CTRL+S I
→	CTRL+S A
∂	CTRL+S D
≤	CTRL+S <
≥	CTRL+S >
×	CTRL+S T
∈	CTRL+S E
∉	CTRL+S SHIFT+E
⊂	CTRL+S C
⊄	CTRL+S SHIFT+C

Table 4-6. *Shortcut Keys for Symbols in the Equation Editor*

Symbol	Template	Shortcut Keys
(⠿)	Parentheses	CTRL+9 or CTRL+0 or CTRL+T (or)
[⠿]	Brackets	CTRL+[or CTRL+] or CTRL+T [or]
{⠿}	Braces	CTRL+{ or CTRL+} or CTRL+T { or }
	Fraction	CTRL+F or CTRL+T F
⠿/⠿	Slash fraction	CTRL+/ or CTRL+T /
	Superscript (high)	CTRL+H or CTRL+T H
	Subscript (low)	CTRL+L or CTRL+T L
	Joint sub/ superscript	CTRL+J or CTR+T J

Table 4-7. *Shortcut Keys for Templates in the Equation Editor*

E

Symbol	Template	Shortcut Keys
	Integral	CTRL+I or CTRL+T I
	Absolute value	CTRL+T |
	Root	CTRL+R or CTRL+T R
	nth root	CTRL+T N
	Summation	CTRL+T S
	Product	CTRL+T P
	Matrix template (3 × 3)	CTRL+T M
	Underscript (limit)	CTRL+T U

Table 4-7. *Shortcut Keys for Templates in the Equation Editor* (continued)

Hints

Sketch out the equation you want to enter before you start the Equation Editor. The sketch helps you figure out which the symbols and position options you want in the Equation Editor and it gives you an idea of how the final result should look.

Embellishments	Keyboard Shortcut
Overbar	CTRL+SHIFT+-
Tilde	CTRL+~ (CTRL+" on some keyboards)
Arrow (vector)	CTRL+ALT+-
Single prime	CTRL+ALT+'
Double prime	CTRL+" (CTRL+~ on some keyboards)
Single dot	CTRL+ALT+.

Table 4-8. *Shortcut Keys for Embellishments in the Equation Editor*

You do not need SPACEBAR to add spaces between parts of an equation. Most of the time the Equation Editor adds spaces appropriately. When you do want to add spaces with SPACEBAR, select Style | Text first. While you can type symbols such as brackets and parentheses, use the palettes instead. The Equation Editor sizes and spaces characters added with the palettes to match typographical and mathematical conventions, preventing later spacing problems. You can nudge some things by pressing CTRL and an arrow key, as when you grab part of an equation, but use this only when the equation is completed and you are fine-tuning its appearance.

Working with an equation may be easier if you zoom it. You can enlarge an equation by selecting View | 200% or View | 400%. Select View | 100% to see the equation at its actual size. If the equation has clutter remaining as you edit the equation, select View | Redraw. To make the overall equation(s) larger or smaller, drag one of the four corners of the Equation Editor object while you are in Word.

You can enter more than one equation in an Equation Editor object. Press ENTER at the end of the equation to start the next line. Use multiple equations to group the equations together.

When you have more complex equations than you can create with the Equation Editor, consider getting MathType. MathType is an enhanced version of the Equation Editor. It provides features such as macros, customizable palettes, formatting that changes by pressing TAB, a TEX interface, and saving equations in EPS and WMF files. MathType is provided by Design Science. You can contact the company at (800)827-0685.

To print your Equation Editor equations correctly, your printer must be able to print scalable fonts. The Equation Editor includes several TrueType fonts. All TrueType fonts are scalable. Use only the Equation Editor fonts, or other scalable fonts. The scalable fonts must be sent to your printer, which makes printing take longer. However, these fonts give you the same appearance on paper that you see on your computer's monitor. If you change printers after you install the Equation Editor, you may need to reinstall the Equation Editor so these TrueType fonts are available. Reinstalling Equation Editor is often the best solution if you have problems with equations printing or displaying incorrectly.

If you want to enter equations in other Windows' applications, use the Clipboard in the Equation Editor to copy the equation from the Clipboard. Then switch to the other application and paste the equation into that application's document. Applications that let you insert objects into their documents may include the Equation Editor in the list of acceptable objects to add. You can add the equations through these applications. However, you cannot run the Equation Editor independently.

E

Related Topics

Object Linking and Embedding

Erasing

You erase text as described under "Deleting Text." You can also erase files as described under "File Management" in this chapter.

Errors

If you run into a problem while working with Word, Word will display a message. These messages let you select OK to leave the message and continue working with Word. You can also select Help to display the Help window with information about the message that Word has just displayed. You can also look at Word's Message Index (Error Messages in Word for Windows 2). The Message Index includes most of Word's messages, which, when selected, will display more about what caused the message.

Excel

Excel is a spreadsheet application designed for the Windows environment. Word can open Excel files, converting them into Word format as they are opened. For more information on opening these files, see "Opening Files" and "Inserting Spreadsheets." You can also embed Excel spreadsheets into Word documents and link Excel spreadsheets into Word documents. Word lets you start Excel from within Word by clicking the Microsoft Excel button in the Microsoft toolbar. You can also create a Microsoft Excel object that you want as part of your Word document by clicking the Insert Microsoft Excel Worksheet button in the Standard toolbar. Once you start Microsoft Excel, you are using Excel, not Word. You leave Excel and return to your Word document by selecting File | Exit and Return to *Document Name*. A Word document with an Excel embedded document might look like Figure 4-16.

TIP: *You need to have Microsoft Excel for Windows installed on your computer to take advantage of sharing data between Word and Excel.*

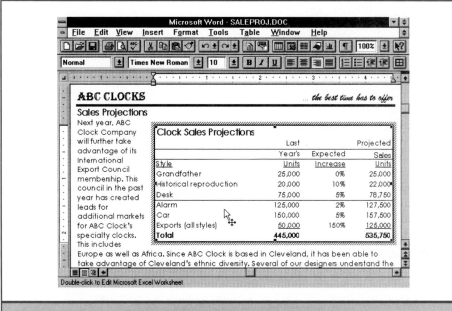

Figure 4-16.　*Excel worksheet embedded in a Word document*

E

Exchanging Data

See "Object Linking and Embedding."

Exclude Dictionary

See "Spelling."

Executing Macros

See "Macros."

Exiting Word

You must exit Word whenever you want to quit using Word completely. This removes Word from active memory and releases the memory for other applications.

Procedures

Exiting Word and closing Word's application window mean the same thing. If you close the application window, Word is exited. Exit Word following any of these procedures:

- ■ Select File | Exit.
- ■ Double-click the application window's control menu box.
- ■ Press ALT+F4.

After doing any of these, the Word application window closes. To use Word again, you need to restart the application. When you exit Word, open documents that have not changed since they were saved close automatically. Word prompts you about saving documents that have changed since they were last saved or which were never saved. Select Yes for each document that you want to save and No for the documents you do not want to save. If the document has never been saved before, Word opens the Save As dialog box for you to specify a filename.

Expanding and Collapsing Outlines

See "Outlines" for details on creating and using outlines.

Exporting Word Documents

Exporting Word documents puts a Word document into another format that other applications can use. Word can save documents in other formats by selecting a different file type in the Save File as Type drop-down list box. This drop-down list box and the other options for saving a file are described under "Saving Files."

EXPRESSION= Field

The EXPRESSION= field returns the result of an expression or formula. For more information on this, see "Fields."

Fast Save

See "Saving Files."

Faxes

You can use Word to make faxing documents easier in several ways. Word has templates that guide you through creating fax cover letters. In Word for Windows 6, select the Faxcovr1 or Faxcovr2 templates when you create a new document. These templates have ready-made fax forms into which you can insert the data applicable to the fax you are sending. There is also a Fax Wizard you can use to guide you through creating a fax cover letter. In Word for Windows 2, select the FAX template. With either the FAX template or Fax Wizard, you just enter the information that Word prompts for, and Word will handle placing it in the document.

You can use Word with a fax board to fax Word documents directly from your computer to another fax. To do this, you select Printer in the Print dialog box and choose the fax board option from the list. To make this option available, you must install your fax board into your computer and in Windows. The directions that come with the fax board will guide you through these steps.

You can set Word to do a mail merge to only records with fax numbers, as described in the following section.

Procedures for Mail Merges to Records with Fax Numbers

The procedure for setting up a mail merge to use only records with fax numbers has the same steps as for selecting the records you include in a mail merge using other criteria. The procedures for Word for Windows 2 and 6 are different.

In Word for Windows 6

1. After setting up the main and data documents, select Tools | Mail Merge.

2. Select Query Options.

3. In the Field column, select the field with the fax number, and choose Is Not Blank in the Comparison column. Select OK.

4. Select Close or Merge.

In Word for Windows 2

1. After setting up the main and data documents, select File | Print Merge.

2. Select Merge and then Record Selection.

3. In the Field Name list box, choose the field with the fax number, and in the Is list box choose Not Blank.

4. Select Add Rule and OK.

5. Select Close or OK.

Related Topics

Mail Merge
Print Merge
Printing

Fields

Fields are special codes. When Word prints a document, it substitutes something for each code in your document. For example, you can enter a date code in your document, and whenever you print the document, Word will substitute the current date in the code's location.

A field code consists of the following:

The opening field character, which is a { (curly brace)
The field code
Instructions, if required
General switches, if desired
The closing field character, which is a } (curly brace)

All Word fields are listed under "Options" in this section, after the "Procedures" section. Each field's description includes the field code, a description of what it inserts into your document, and explanation of the possible instructions for that field. General switches, which most fields can use, are explained under "Other Options," after the "Options" section.

For information on specific fields used in mail or print merges, see "Mail Merge" and "Print Merge" later in this chapter. If you want more information about a particular field than what is described here, press F1 for help and select Search to find the help information on the field.

Procedures

This section gives the procedures for the various ways of entering fields in a document; displaying the results of field codes; updating, editing, and formatting the results of field codes; moving among field codes; printing field codes; locking a a field; and unlinking a field from the updating process.

Entering a Field with the Menus

In addition to entering a field with the Insert I Field command described here, some fields can be inserted in other ways. For example, the Date and Time fields can be inserted using shortcut keys, or using the Date and Time command from the Insert menu. The fields that are not normally added with the Insert I Field command described below are instead added by using other Word features, such as using the Tools I Mail Merge command, Insert I File, or Edit I Paste Special commands.

1. Move the insertion point to the location in the document where you want the field added.

2. Select Insert I Field, to open the Field dialog box shown here:

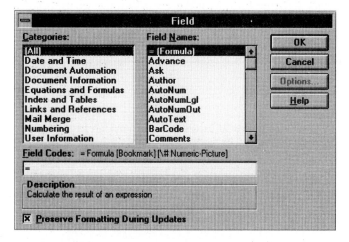

The Field Names list box displays the fields belonging to the category selected in the Categories list.

3. In Word for Windows 6, you can change which fields are listed in the Field Names list box by selecting a different category under Categories. Then select a field from the Field Names list box (Insert Field Type list box in Word for Windows 2).

Notice that the field code for the selected field appears in the Field Codes text box. Above this text box, Word displays other instructions the field code can use. Below the Field Codes box is a description of the code's purpose.

4. If needed, specify the options or instructions to add to the field code. The method for doing this will depend on the version of Word for Windows you are using.

   ■ In Word for Windows 6, select the Options button and then choose from the options that are displayed for the field. Select OK to return to the Field dialog box. The Options button is dimmed when the selected field does not use additional options or instructions.

   ■ In Word for Windows 2, choose instructions from the Instructions list box and then select Add. (The Instructions list box will be dimmed when the selected field does not offer additional instructions.)

NOTE: Besides using either method described above, you can also type the options, switches, and instructions in the text box after the field name.

5. Specify whether you want Word for Windows 6 to replace the field's formatting when it updates the field. If you want Word to keep the field's formatting when it is updated, select the Preserve Formatting During Updates check box; turn off the check box when you want the formatting to be replaced.

6. Select OK.

Word now inserts the field into the document. Depending on your settings, Word displays either the field code or the field's result. See the upcoming procedure for "Switching Between Codes and Results" to learn how to change what Word displays. If you see the field codes, you can see how Word added the { and } for you.

Entering a Field with Shortcut Keys

You can type the field name and any codes for a field you want to add into the document rather than using the Insert | Field command. Use this method of adding the field when you know the field code you want to add as well as any switches you want to add.

1. Move the insertion point to the location in the document where you want the field added.

2. Press CTRL+F9 to insert the opening and closing field code symbols, { and }. (You cannot type these characters on the keyboard, because Word will not recognize them as field codes.)

3. Type the field name and any options, switches, and instructions between the field code symbols.

4. Press F9 to update the field.

When you press F9, Word interprets the entry from the { to the } added by pressing CTRL+F9 and updates the field you have entered. Depending on your settings, Word displays either the field code or the field's result. If Word does not understand what you typed in step 3 and Word is displaying field results, you may see a message such as "Error!" or "Error: Bookmark not defined."

TIP: You can change text you already have in a document into a field code. You can add a field by typing the field name and its options or instructions, selecting the field name and options or instructions, and pressing CTRL+F9.

Nesting Fields

You can use a field as part of the instructions for another field; this is called *nesting* fields. You can nest up to 20 fields in this fashion.

To insert a field within another field, position the insertion point directly after the field code of the existing field. Then insert the nested field using one of the methods described above.

Switching Between Codes and Results

You can switch between displaying the field codes and displaying the results of those field codes, using either the menus or shortcut keys.

- ■ You can press SHIFT+F9 to toggle between field codes and results. The toggle changes all fields in a document.

- ■ To use the menus in Word for Windows 6, first select Tools | Options, then the View tab, the Field Codes check box, and OK. In Word for Windows 2, select View | Field Codes to toggle between field codes and results.

- ■ In Word for Windows 6, you can also right-click the field and select Toggle Field Codes from the shortcut menu. This only affects the current field.

NOTE: In Word for Windows 6, if you display the field's results, when you move the insertion point to any part of the field's result, the entire field is grayed out.

Updating Fields

Updating a field makes the field's value the most current value. To update the results of a field code, you can either

- Press F9 with the insertion point inside the field.
- Right-click the field and select Update Field from the shortcut menu (Word for Windows 6 only).

Word will also update the field's contents when you print the field. This assumes that Word is set to update fields when printing. To turn on this setting, select File | Print and then Options, select the Update Fields check box, and OK.

Editing Fields

You can edit field codes just as you would edit other text in the document. You cannot edit the field results, however, because Word updates them and replaces them with the new field results.

1. Toggle your display so you see the field codes (see "Switching Between Field Codes and Results," just above).

2. Move the insertion point inside the field code, and modify the field code or instructions as needed.

3. When you're done, update the field, and then toggle back to displaying field results to check that the results are what you want.

Formatting Field Results

You can apply formatting directly to field results by selecting all or part of the field results and applying the format as you would to normal text. However, when you update the field, you may lose the formatting. Word for Windows 6 lets you designate whether a field will keep its formatting; you do this when you add the field with Insert | Field. Turn on the Preserve Formatting During Updates check box, and the field results will retain the formatting as the field results change. If this check box is cleared, the field contents may have new formatting after the field is updated.

You can also use the * mergeformat switch to tell Word to use the same formatting for a particular field after it is updated. Add the *mergeformat switch at the end of the field instructions, as in

{TIME *mergeformat}

This switch is the only way you keep the formatting. In Word for Windows 6, this switch is automatically added for you when the Preserve Formatting During Updates check box is selected. In Word for Windows 2, you must add this switch yourself. For more information about general switches, see "Switches" under "Options," below.

Moving Among Fields Only

You can quickly move from field to field in your document, without having to search through the text to find the codes. When using this feature, you will not be able to move to fields that Word automatically formats as hidden text (the Index Entry, TOC Entry, Referenced Document field types).

■ Press F11 to move to the next field.

■ Press SHIFT+F11 to move the previous field.

REMINDER: *If your keyboard does not have an F11 key, press* ALT+F1 *instead.*

Printing Field Codes

In some situations you may want to print your document showing the field codes rather than the field results. For instance, you might do this as documentation for a mail merge document, or to print a quick draft version of the document. Here are the steps:

1. Select File | Print, to open the Print dialog box.

2. Select Options, to open the Options dialog box displaying the print options.

3. Select the Field Codes check box.

4. Select OK twice to close the Options dialog box and then print the document.

REMINDER: *Don't forget to turn off the Field Codes check box after you've finished printing field codes, so that Word will return to printing your document with the field results.*

Locking or Unlocking a Field

You can lock a field to temporarily prevent Word from updating it. This allows you to preserve the previous result of the field. If you manually try to update the field, Word will beep at you. For example, if you have a {USERNAME} field in a document that you want to continue to show your name even when someone else is working on the document, you would lock the {USERNAME} field.

1. Move the insertion point to inside the field.

2. Press CTRL+F11 to lock the field so that its results cannot be updated. Press SHIFT+CTRL+F11 to unlock a field so that its results can be updated again.

Unlinking a Field

To permanently prevent Word from updating a field's results, you can *unlink* the field. Most fields are linked to information; for example, the Time field is linked to your system's internal clock. Unlinking the field means that it can no longer access that source of information and thus cannot be updated at all. The field code of an unlinked field still appears when you show field codes instead of field results.

CAUTION: *You cannot relink a field after unlinking it.*

To unlink a field, move the insertion point inside the field and press CTRL+SHIFT+F9.

Options

This section contains a list of the available fields. For each field there is an example of the field code, an explanation of its purpose and its instructions, and any specific switches used with the field. For an explanation of the general switches that all fields can use, see "Other Options" at the end of this section. Fields relating to mail merge are also mentioned here, but are more thoroughly explained in "Mail Merge."

■ The field code itself appears in all capitals, with options or instructions in lowercase.

■ If instructions or arguments are optional rather than required, they appear inside square brackets: [ ].

■ Any value that will be replaced by variable information appears in italic. For example, "*NewValue*" would be replaced by something else when you actually enter the field. If "NewValue" is optional, the instruction would read ["*NewValue*"].

■ Spaces shown in field codes are not optional. You must include spaces between the field code and the options and between different options.

TIP: Many of the fields use commas and backslashes for specific purposes. When you need to include a comma or backslash for a different purpose, include an extra backslash. For example, a filename used within a field code might look like C:\\WINWORD6\\TEXT.DOC.

The = Field

You can use the {=} field to evaluate an expression. After the =, you enter the formula you want calculated. You can use operators, functions, and bookmark names for the data you want the field to evaluate. An example might be

{=.07*Subtotal}

where Subtotal is the bookmark that contains a number you want multiplied by 7 percent.

You can use the following operators and functions in your = fields.

NOTE: In the following table, "on left" means before the operator or function; "on right" means after the operator or function.

Operator	Effect
+	Adds value on left to value on right
–	Subtracts value on right from value on left
*	Multiplies value on left times value on right
/	Divides value on right by value on left
^	Raises value on left to the power of the value on right
%	Treats value on left as a percentage
=	Equals TRUE when value on left equals value on right
<=	Equals TRUE when value on left is less than or equals value on right

Operator	Effect
<	Equals TRUE when value on left is less than value on right
>=	Equals TRUE when value on left is greater than or equals value on right
>	Equals TRUE when value on left is greater than value on right
<>	Equals TRUE when value on left does not equal value on right

Function	Purpose
ABS(x)	Returns the absolute value of x
AND(x,y)	Equals TRUE when both x and y are true; equals FALSE in other cases
AVERAGE()	Returns the average of the values in parentheses
COUNT()	Counts the number of values in parentheses
DEFINED()	Equals TRUE when bookmark in parentheses is a defined bookmark
FALSE	Equals a FALSE value to use as comparison with TRUE
IF(x,y,z)	Equals y when x is true, and z when x is false
INT(x)	Returns the integer of the sum of x
MAX()	Returns the largest value among values in parentheses
MIN()	Returns the lowest value among values in parentheses
MOD(x,y)	Returns the remainder when value of x is divided by value of y
NOT(x)	Equals TRUE when x equals FALSE; equals FALSE when x equals TRUE
OR(x,y)	Equals TRUE when either x or y are true; equals FALSE when both are false
PRODUCT()	Multiplies the blocks of values in parentheses and totals the products
ROUND(x,y)	Rounds the value of x to the number of digits set by y
SIGN(x)	Returns 1 if value of x is positive, or –1 if x is negative, or 0 if x equals 0
SUM()	Totals the values in parentheses
TRUE	Equals a TRUE value to use as comparison with FALSE

ADVANCE

The {ADVANCE} field in Word for Windows 6 shifts the text on the remainder of the line a number of points in any direction you select. After ADVANCE you enter the direction you want the text shifted: \l for left, \r for right, \u for up, \d for down, \x for left from the left margin of the column or frame, and \y for down from the top margin of the column or frame. After this switch is the number of points you want the entry shifted in that direction. For example, the field code

    T{ADVANCE \D2 }E{ADVANCE \u2 }X

produces T$_E$X. Notice that the second ADVANCE field code is after the *E* so the *X* is on the same level as the *T*.

ASK

The {ASK} field prompts the user to enter information during a mail merge. That text is then assigned a bookmark. You can use this field to take the text typed by the user and insert it into the merged document. See "Mail Merge" later in this chapter for more information.

AUTHOR

See "INFO."

AUTONUM

The {AUTONUM} field automatically numbers the paragraph on a particular level of an outline. This field is normally at the beginning of each paragraph you want numbered. This field cannot be nested inside an IF field, or locked or unlinked. The field's result is the paragraph's number. When Word counts the paragraphs to calculate the result, Word counts all paragraphs that are at the same outline level, starting fresh each time a paragraph with a higher outline level is encountered. For example, an {AUTONUM} field in the eleventh paragraph would result in 11.

AUTONUMLGL

The {AUTONUMLGL} field automatically numbers paragraphs in the legal format, which displays all outline levels for the paragraph. This field cannot be nested inside an IF field, or locked or unlinked. The field's result is the paragraph's number, including all outline levels. For example, an {AUTONUMLGL} field might show a result of 2.3.1; the paragraph referred to here is in the first third-level paragraph under the third second-level paragraph, under the second first-level paragraph. Legal documents use this numbering system to number paragraphs and outlines.

AUTONUMOUT

The {AUTONUMOUT} field automatically numbers paragraphs in the outline format. This field cannot be nested inside an IF field, or locked or unlinked. The field's result is the number or letter for the heading's position within an outline. When you use this field on a paragraph that does not have an outline level, it has the same result as the {AUTONUM} field. For instance, *II.* is the second first level paragraph in a document, and *B.* is the second second-level paragraph under a first-level heading. You can also easily add outline numbering using bullets and numbering as described under "Lists."

AUTOTEXT

The {AUTOTEXT} field in Word for Windows 6 returns the contents of an AutoText entry. Using this field instead of replacing the AutoText entry will update the document if the AutoText entry changes. After AUTOTEXT you enter the name of the AutoText entry to insert, as in {AUTOTEXT Call_Me}. The document will contain the expanded version of the AutoText entry, Call_Me.

BARCODE

The {BARCODE} field in Word for Windows 6 returns the POSTNET delivery-point bar code, using the information entered after BARCODE or the contents of the given bookmark. For example, {BARCODE 44406} displays its result as the POSTNET delivery-point bar code for ZIP code 44406. POSTNET delivery-point bar codes help the Post Office deliver mail promptly. When you are doing mass mailings, using the POSTNET delivery-point bar code may provide a discount for postage.

This field can use the following switches:

Switch	Result
\b	Tells Word that the information after BARCODE is a bookmark name.
\f	Tells Word to add a facing identification code. Follow \f with **"a"** when you want a courtesy reply mark. Follow \f with **"c"** when you want a business reply mark.
\u	Tells Word that the address is for the United States.

Bookmarks

The Bookmark field, {*bookmark*}, returns the contents of the named bookmark. For example, if you have a bookmark named Sales that contains $569,349, inserting {Sales} as a field code will produce $569,349 as the field's results. You cannot use Insert | Field to add this field, so use CTRL+F9 instead and type the bookmark name before you press F9 to update the field.

If the bookmark includes a paragraph mark, then the paragraph that uses this field takes the same paragraph formatting. If the bookmark name matches the name of another Word field, put REF and a space before the bookmark name so Word knows to use the bookmark's contents rather than the other field.

Word for Windows 6 has three switches you can use with this field:

- Use \f when you want the bookmark to include footnotes and endnotes from the text in the bookmark and you want Word to increment their number when they appear as part of the field.

- Use \n when you want paragraph numbering from the text in bookmark to also appear where the text appears again as the {*bookmark*} field's results.

- Use \! when you want to limit the updating of fields within the text selected by the {*bookmark*} field. This switch is described under {INCLUDETEXT}.

COMMENTS

See "INFO."

COMPARE

The {COMPARE} field in Word for Windows 6 returns a 1 when the comparison of the two expressions using the operator you provide is true, or a 0 when it isn't. The {COMPARE} field uses this format:

{COMPARE *expression1 operator expression2*}

Both expressions can be bookmarks, text in quotes, numbers, or results from other fields. The operator can be =, <=, <, >=, >, or <> as described for the = field. You can use the ? to represent any single character in either expression, and the * to represent zero or more characters in either expression.

For example, {COMPARE State="Ohio"} returns 1 when the bookmark State contains the text Ohio.

F

CREATEDATE

See "INFO."

DATA

The {DATA} field specifies the file that contains the data to put in the main document in a mail or print merge. See "Mail Merge" later in this chapter for a full explanation of creating merged documents.

DATABASE

The {DATABASE} field inserts a database query's results in a Word for Windows 6 document. You can use this field to insert an SQL database query into a Word document. You may also add this field when you use the Insert | Database command.
 This field uses several switches:

■ Use the \c switch followed by the directions to the other application for the query you want included in Word.

■ You can tell Word the location of the database using the \d switch; include two backslashes in the path information where you would otherwise use one, so Word will recognize the pathname.

■ To include the SQL instructions that select the database records to insert as the field's result, include \s and the SQL instruction as part of the field information. *SQL instructions* are the Standard Query Language that databases can use to select data.

■ To apply a Table AutoFormat format to the field's results, use the \l switch followed by the name of the table.

■ The \b switch selects the part of the last table format to be used by the results of the query. After \b is a number: 0 to use no table formatting; 1 to include the borders; 2 to include the shading; 4 to include the font; 8 to include the color; 16 to include the best fit settings; 32 to include the heading row; 64 to include the last row; 128 to include the first column; and 256 to include the last column.

■ To specify the range of records from the database included in the query, use \f followed by the first record, and \t followed by the last record.

DATE

The {DATE} field displays the date when the field was last updated. Use this field to insert the current date in a document. The resulting date is usually displayed in the default date format for Windows, but you can use the Date-Time Picture switch (described in "Other Options") to format the date in another fashion. You can also include the \l switch when you want the {DATE} field to use the same date and time format as the last {DATE} field.

The {DATE} field can be added in more than one way, as described in "Date and Time" earlier in this chapter.

DDE

The {DDE} field is for DDE links from earlier versions of Word for Windows. Word now uses the {LINK} field. See "Object Linking and Embedding" later in the chapter.

DDEAUTO

The {DDEAUTO} field is for automatically updated DDE links from earlier versions of Word for Windows. Word now uses the {LINK} field. See "Object Linking and Embedding" later in the chapter.

EDITTIME

See "INFO."

EMBED

The {EMBED} field embeds an object in your Word document file. Word adds this field for you when you embed an object. See "Object Linking and Embedding" later in the chapter for more information.

EQ

The {EQ} field creates an equation in Word for Windows 6, similar to ones you can create with the Equation Editor. The {EQ} is useful if you did not install the Equation Editor or you want to add a formula in-line with other text. When a formula is fairly complex, however, the Equation Editor is easier to use. You can double-click the {EQ} field to start the Equation Editor with the equation that this field creates.

This field uses many switches to tell Word the equation you want to create.

THE \A SWITCH   This switch draws a two-dimensional array using the entries in the parentheses that follow. The numbers for the array are separated by commas and fill up the array's size one row at a time. You can also use \al after \a when you want the array elements left-aligned; \ar when you want the array elements right-aligned; or \ac when you want the array elements centered. When you want to set the vertical or horizontal spacing between the array element, use \a and then the \vs or \hs switches and a number of points. If the array has more than one column, include \co between \a and the opening parentheses for the number of columns in the array. For example, the field code {EQ \a \co3 (5, 6, 7, 1, 2, 3)} creates the following:

5 6 7
1 2 3

THE \B SWITCH   This switch draws parentheses or other characters around the element in parentheses. Without any switches modifying \b, \b draws parentheses. You can set the left side of the matching characters with \lc\ and a character, and the right side with \rc\ and a character. Another option is to set the character with \bc\ and a character. If the character after \c\ is an opening (, {, [, or <, Word draws the matching closing symbol around the element. If it is another character, Word uses the same character for both sides. For example, {EQ \b \bc\[(\a \co2 (1, 2, 3, 4))} returns

$$\begin{bmatrix} 1\,2 \\ 3\,4 \end{bmatrix}$$

THE \D SWITCH   This switch adjusts the position of the next entry (often it is something else created by the {EQ} field. At the end of the \d switch is an empty set of paretheses. You can include the following switches between the \d and the opening parentheses: \fo and a number of points to move forward the next element; \ba and a number of points to move backward the next element; and \li() to draw a line from the affected element to the next character.

THE \F SWITCH   Use \i f followed by two entries separated by commas to place the first entry as a fraction's numerator and the second entry as the fraction's denominator. For example, {EQ \f (7,8)} creates the fraction ⅞.

THE \I SWITCH   Use \i to create an integral sign ∫. After the \i are parentheses containing the lower limit, the upper limit, and the expression after the integral symbol, separated by commas. Before the opening parentheses, you can include \su to change the integral sign to a summation sign; \pr to change the integral sign to a pi character; \in to place the upper and lower limits to the right of the sign so the expression is more in line with the text; \fc \ and a character to place the character as a fixed-size character in place of the integral sign; or \vc \ and a character to place the character as a variable-size character in place of the integral sign.

THE \l SWITCH   The \l switch treats the series of elements entered in parentheses after the \l as a single element. Use this switch to create a series of entries that other switches will treat as a single unit.

THE \o SWITCH   With the \o switch you can combine characters by putting one on top of another (overstriking). Following \o are the characters that will be put on top of one another, in parentheses and separated by commas. Between the \o and the opening parentheses you can include \al to left-align the boxes that hold each overstruck character; \ac to center the boxes that hold each overstruck character; or \ar to right-align the boxes that hold each overstruck character.

THE \r SWITCH   The \r switch followed by one element in the parentheses puts the element in parentheses under a radical sign. You can also have two elements in parentheses, separated by commas, to tell the \r switch to put the first element above the radical sign and the second element under the radical sign.

THE \s SWITCH   The \s switch positions a single element as a superscript or subscript character. If you put multiple elements in the parentheses following the switch, the first element is superscript, and the next elements are placed in order below the first one and left-aligned. If you only use one element for this switch, you can also include the following switches to modify how the \s switch operates: \ai and a number of points to add above the line within the paragraph; \di and a number of points to add below the line within the paragraph; \up and a number of points to move the element up; and \do and a number of points to move the element down. Word for Windows 2 cannot use \ai or \di. For example, Sales{EQ \s \do3 (last year)} displays as Sales$_{\text{last year}}$.

THE \x SWITCH   You can add a box around an element by putting it in parentheses preceded by \x. If you want to specify the sides of the box you are drawing, insert one of the following between the \x and the element in parentheses: \to to draw the line that is the top of the box; \bo to draw the line that is the bottom of the box; \le to draw the line that is the left side of the box; or \ri to draw the line that is the right side of the box.

You can include a series of the switches detailed above, and nest them to create the equation you want. For example, the field

{EQ \r(3,\f(81,16))

returns this equation:

$$\sqrt[3]{\dfrac{81}{16}}$$

FILENAME

See "INFO."

FILESIZE

See "INFO."

FILLIN

The {FILLIN} field prompts the user to enter text that is inserted as the field's result. See "Mail Merge" later in the chapter for more information.

FTNREF

In Word for Windows 2, the {FTNREF} field returns the footnote number of a footnote in the document. See "Footnotes and Endnotes" later in the chapter for a full explanation.

GLOSSARY

The {GLOSSARY} field in Word for Windows 2 inserts the contents of a previously created glossary entry. This field code takes the format

{GLOSSARY *name*}

where name is the name of the glossary entry. Word for Windows 6 uses the {AUTOTEXT} field. See "Glossary" in this chapter for more information.

GOTOBUTTON

The {GOTOBUTTON} field displays text that, when double-clicked, moves to another location. Macros and interactive documents use this field to quickly move to another location. You can also select a {GOTOBUTTON} field by moving the insertion point to the text to be moved and pressing ALT+SHIFT+F9. This field takes the format

{GOTOBUTTON *destination DisplayText*}

where *destination* is the location where you want to go to when you select the field. This destination can be anything you would specify after selecting Edit | Go To or pressing F5, such as a bookmark or page number. *DisplayText* is either the text or graphic to appear as the field. DisplayText can use another field such as {*bookmark*} or {INCLUDEPICTURE} when you want to put the contents of the bookmark or picture on the button.

The results of this field might look like this:

Clicking any of the phrases, such as Production Report, quickly moves you to the described location in the document.

IF

The {IF} field compares two values. The result of the comparison determines which of the two values is displayed in the document. See "Mail Merge" in this chapter for more information.

IMPORT

In Word for Windows 2, the {IMPORT} field displays the contents of a graphics file. Word for Windows 6 uses the {INCLUDEPICTURE} field. On screen, the file displays a low-resolution bitmap image of the graphics file. When you print the document, the image is printed at full resolution. This field takes the format {IMPORT *filename*}, where *filename* should include both the path and name of the file. For example,

{IMPORT c:\\winword\\clipart\\2darrow2.wmf}

would display the image in the 2DARROW2.WMF file.

If your {IMPORT} field results are not what you expect, check that you provided the correct path to the graphics file, that you installed the correct graphics converters, and that Word knows where to find those graphics converters. The information about the graphics converters is stored in WIN.INI.

INCLUDE

In Word for Windows 2, the {INCLUDE} field inserts text from another document into the document containing the field. Word for Windows 6 uses the

{INCLUDETEXT} field. You can insert either the entire document or just the contents of a bookmark. This field takes the format

{INCLUDE *filename* [*bookmark*]}

where *filename* is the name of the file that you want to insert, and *bookmark* is the section of the document you want to insert. If you do not use a bookmark name, Word inserts the entire document as the field's results.

You can include a \c switch and the converter you want Word to use to import the inserted document into the current document. Use \! when you want to limit the updating of the fields within the text selected by the {*bookmark*} field (this switch is described under {INCLUDETEXT}).

TIP: You can take changes that you have made in the field results of an {INCLUDE} or {INCLUDETEXT} field and apply them to the source document. Either press CTRL+SHIFT+F7, *or select Tools | Macro and select Commands or Word Commands from Macros Available in, UpdateSource in Macro Name, and OK.*

INCLUDEPICTURE

The {INCLUDEPICTURE} field inserts a graphic image from another file into the Word for Windows 6 document. Usually you do not insert this field yourself but instead let Word insert it for you when you use the Insert | Picture command and select the Link to File check box. You will only see this field code if you select the picture and press SHIFT+F9. This field takes the format

{INCLUDEPICTURE *filename*}

where *filename* is the name of the graphics file that you want to insert.

After the filename, you can include a \c and the graphics converter you want Word to use. You can also include \d when you do not want the image stored within the document. If field results display as Error! instead of the picture, check that you have used the correct filename and that the graphics converter Word uses for the file is correct and installed.

INCLUDETEXT

In Word for Windows 6, the {INCLUDETEXT} field inserts text from another document into the document containing the field. The difference between the {INCLUDE} field and the {INCLUDETEXT} field is that the {INCLUDETEXT} field will also include graphics from the source document file. You can insert either the entire document, or just the contents of a bookmark.

This field uses the format

{INCLUDETEXT *filename* [*bookmark*] *switches*}

where *filename* is the name of the file to insert, and *bookmark* is the section of the document you want to insert. If you do not use a bookmark name, Word inserts the entire document as the field's results.

Use the \c switch with the converter you want Word to use to bring the inserted document into the current document.

Use the \! switch to limit the updating of fields within the text that this field brings from another location. When you use this switch, the fields that are within the text inserted by the {INCLUDETEXT}, {bookmark}, and {REF} fields are not updated until the document containing the original text updates them. Without the \! switch, fields that are part of the text inserted by the {INCLUDETEXT}, {bookmark}, or {REF} fields are updated when you print that part of the document.

INDEX

The {INDEX} field represents where Word will put an index created from index entry fields ({XE}) in the document. For further description of creating an index, see "Index" later in this chapter.

INFO

The {INFO} field inserts data from the Summary Info dialog box into your document. You can also use this field to change the data in the Summary Info dialog box, and to insert the data in your document. This field takes the format

{[INFO] *InfoType* ["*NewValue*"]}

INFO is optional, because the *InfoType* value is what Word actually needs in order to know the information you want the field replaced with.

InfoType is the kind of summary information that you want inserted, such as author, comments, createdate, edittime, filename, filesize (Word for Windows 6 only), keywords, lastsavedby, numchars, numpages, numwords, printdate, revnum, savedate, subject, template, and title. Note that these are also separate fields as well. Some of these are shown in the Summary Info dialog box, and can be set by you. The others are values which Word calculates for your document and appear when you select Statistics from the Summary Info dialog box.

NewValue, which should be enclosed in quotes if it is text, is the information you want copied back into the Summary Info dialog box. When you include NewValue as part of the INFO or one of the information type fields, the field both replaces the entry and displays the new entry. You can use *NewValue* for the author, comments, keywords, subject, and title fields of Summary Info; other information type fields will ignore any entry for *NewValue*.

KEYWORD

See "INFO."

LASTSAVEDBY

See "INFO."

LINK

The {LINK} field creates a link with a document file created by another application. See "Object Linking and Embedding" in this chapter for more information.

MACROBUTTON

The {MACROBUTTON} field displays text that, when selected, starts a macro. For a full explanation of how this field works, see "Macros" later in the chapter.

MERGEFIELD

The {MERGEFIELD} field inserts a field from a data file into the main document in a merge. See "Mail Merge."

MERGEREC

The {MERGEREC} field inserts the number of the current merge record. See "Mail Merge."

MERGESEQ

The {MERGESEQ} field inserts the number of the current merge record according to its order within the records merged. See "Mail Merge."

NEXT

The {NEXT} field moves the mail-merge process to the next record. See "Mail Merge."

NEXTIF

The {NEXTIF} field moves the mail-merge process to the next record, depending on a condition. See "Mail Merge."

NOTEREF

In Word for Windows 6, the {NOTEREF} field returns the footnote or endnote number of a footnote or endnote in the document. See the section on "Footnotes and Endnotes."

NUMCHAR

See "INFO."

NUMPAGES

See "INFO."

NUMWORDS

See "INFO."

PAGE

The {PAGE} field inserts the page number for the page containing the field. You can use the Numeric Picture switch (*) to control how the page number appears, as described in "Other Options" later in this section. In addition to inserting this field yourself, you can insert it using the Insert | Page Numbers command. See "Page Numbers" later in this chapter for an explanation of adding the current page number to a document.

PAGEREF

The {PAGEREF} field inserts the page number where a bookmark is located. You can use this field to create cross-references. The field code takes the format

{PAGEREF *bookmark*}

where *bookmark* is the name of the bookmark being referenced. You can use the Numeric Picture switch (*) to control how the page number appears, as described in "Other Options" later in this section.

PRINT

The {PRINT} field sends printer instructions to your printer. This field takes the format

{PRINT "*code*"}

where *code* is the printer instructions. These instructions vary by printer, so you must use your printer's manuals to learn the code you want to use. This field works well with PostScript printers and Hewlett-Packard LaserJet Series II or III. Other printers may not be able to use this field.

PRINTDATE

See {INFO}.

PRIVATE

Word for Windows 6 creates this field for you when you add a document in another format into Word for Windows. This field contains the information Word needs to convert it back to its previous format. Do not change this field.

QUOTE

The {QUOTE} field inserts text. This field interprets the text as a possible code, rather than as what appears when you type. For example, entries not in quotes are assumed to be code numbers for the ANSI character set, or to be part of a hexadecimal value when preceded by 0x. The format for this field is {QUOTE *LiteralText*}. For example, the field code

{QUOTE Word for Windows 153}

produces the result

Word for Windows(™)

Word interprets the 153 as an ANSI code for ™

RD

The {RD} field indicates a document to be inserted as part of the current document for the purpose of generating index entries, tables of contents, and tables of authorities. After RD is the name of the document to include. This field does not display any result, but rather causes the indexes, tables of contents, or tables of authorities to include entries from the named document. You use this field to combine several documents into one for index entries, tables of contents, and tables of authorities; see also "Master Document" later in the chapter.

REF

See "Bookmarks" in this section.

REF INTERN_LINK*n*

Word for Windows 2 adds the {REF INTERN_LINK*n*} field to your documents when you use the Edit | Paste Special command to copy and link text from one location to another within the same document. The n in INTERN_LINK is the sequential number Word assigns to the internal link. In Word for Windows 6, Word will add the {LINK} field instead.

REVNUM

See "INFO."

SAVEDATE

See "INFO."

SECTION

The {SECTION} field inserts the section number where the field is located.

SECTIONPAGES

The {SECTIONPAGES} field inserts the total number of pages in the section where the field is located.

SEQ

Use the {SEQ} field to number items or sections of text in your document. You can create sets of items, such as graphics, photographs, and tables, and track the correct number for each item in each set. You can also use this field to automatically number sections or chapters in your document, as well as create cross-references to items or objects numbered using this field.

This field takes the format

{SEQ *identifier* [*bookmark*]}

where *identifier* is the name you provide for the set of items you are sequencing. For example, in a document using the {SEQ} field to number chapters, graphics, and tables, you might use chapter, figs, and table for the identifiers. In this example, the first time you enter {SEQ figs}, the field result would be 1, representing the first figure. The second {SEQ figs} code would show a field result of 2, and so on throughout the document. If you inserted {SEQ chapter} between these two {SEQ figs} field codes, its field result would be 1, since it would be the first SEQ field code for the chapter sequence.

When you include a bookmark in a SEQ field, the field's result is the sequence number of the item marked by the bookmark. For example, in a table with the bookmark name of Sales_Table, the field {SEQ table Sales_Table} returns the number of the table at Sales_Table, rather than the next number in the table sequence.

Word offers several switches that you can use to further customize the text inserted using the {SEQ} field:

- When you use the \c switch, Word does not use the next number in the sequence for this field's result. Instead, the field result is the current sequence number, which is the last one that appeared in your document.

- When you use the \h switch, Word hides the field result of the {SEQ} field. Use this switch to advance the sequence list without displaying the incremented sequence number. You can refer to that item in the list in a cross-reference.

- When you use the \n switch, Word proceeds to the next number in the sequence. This is the default setting when you do not use any switches.

- When you use the \r switch, you are telling Word to restart the numbering in that specific sequence list, starting with the number after the \r. For example, if you enter {SEQ figs \r 14}, the field result is 14. The {SEQ} fields after this one that use the same identifier would increment normally, starting at this number.

SET

The {SET} field assigns a bookmark to defined text. Any field that references that bookmark will insert or use that text. The format is

{SET *bookmark* "*text*"}

where bookmark is the name of the bookmark assigned to the text, and text is the text marked by the bookmark.

For example, in a rental contract, when you need an address repeated several times, enter the field

{SET address "2006 Waterbury Rd. #3"}

Each time a field references the address bookmark, Word will insert 2006 Waterbury Rd. #3. This field is useful in forms and in mail merges.

SKIPIF

The {SKIPIF} field makes Word skip an item if a particular condition is true. This field is often used in mail merges. See "Mail Merge."

STYLEREF

The {STYLEREF} field inserts text from the previous paragraph that uses a defined style. This field does not work with character format styles. This field takes the format

{STYLEREF "*StyleIdentifier*" *switches*}

where *StyleIdentifier* is the name of the style you are looking for, already assigned to text within the document.

You can use the \l switch to find the last paragraph on the current page using the specified style, even if it comes after the field. You can also use the \n switch in Word for Windows 2 when you want the copy of the paragraph that this field returns to include the paragraph numbering from the original paragraph.

SUBJECT

See "INFO."

SYMBOL

The {SYMBOL} field inserts a symbol or a string of characters. The format of this field is

{SYMBOL *CharNum*}

where *CharNum* is the decimal or hexadecimal code for the symbol you want to insert. You can define the symbol by specifying the ANSI code using decimal or hexadecimal numbers, or you can type a character. After Char/Num, you can use these switches:

- The \f switch sets the font the symbol uses which can change the characters available.

- The \s switch sets the size of the symbol that the field inserts. After \s is the number of points for the height of the character.

- In Word for Windows 6 you can use the \h switch to set the line height; after the \h is the number of points to set the height.

For example,

{SYMBOL 255 \f "Wingdings" \s24}

creates a small Windows logo that is 1/3 inch high. You can also change the font, size, and line height attributes for this symbol by selecting only the field code or its result and applying formatting with the Word menu commands, shortcuts, or toolbars. This field offers an alternative to using the Insert | Symbol command to add unusual symbols to a document. See "Special Characters" for more information.

TA

The {TA} field represents an entry to appear in a table of authorities. See "Table of Authorities" for instructions.

TC

The {TC} field represents an entry to appear in the table of contents. See "Tables of Contents and Figures" for instructions.

TEMPLATE

See "INFO."

TIME

The {TIME} field inserts the current time (or the time when the field was last updated). You can use the Date-Time Picture switch described under "Other Options" in this section to control the time's format. As a default, Word uses the default Windows time format. You can insert this information in a variety of ways other than by using this field; see the section on "Date and Time" for more information.

TITLE

See "INFO."

TOA

The {TOA} field is replaced by a table of authorities using entries defined in other locations in the document. See "Table of Authorities" for instructions.

TOC

The {TOC} field is replaced by a table of contents that references the headings and other table of contents entries in the document. See "Tables of Contents and Figures" for instructions.

USERADDRESS

The {USERADDRESS} field inserts the user address that appears under Mailing Address in the User Info options for the Tools | Options command. In Word for Windows 6, you can include text after USERADDRESS when you want something different to appear as the user address without changing the setting for the user address set with the Tools | Options command.

USERINITIALS

The {USERINITIALS} field inserts the user initials that appear under Initials in the User Info options for the Tools | Options command. In Word for Windows 6, you can include text after USERINITIALS when you want something different to appear as the user initials without changing the setting for the user initials set with the Tools | Options command.

USERNAME

The {USERNAME} field inserts the user name that appears under Name in the User Info options for the Tools | Options command. In Word for Windows 6, you can include text after USERNAME when you want something different to appear as the user name without changing the setting for the user name set with the Tools | Options command.

XE

The {XE} field marks entries to appear in an index. See "Index" for more information about creating index entries.

Other Options

Word has three general switches that can be used with most fields, described in the sections that follow.

Format Switch: *

You can use the * switch to set the format of a field result. You can designate character case, numeric format, and character formatting.

To set the case of the field's result when it is text, enter one of the following after the switch: *upper* to cause the entire field result to appear in uppercase, or *lower* for lowercase letters; *firstcap* to capitalize the first letter in the first word and leave the rest of the field in lowercase; or *caps* to capitalize the first letter in each word and leave the other letters in lowercase. Here are examples:

Field Entry	Result
{subject *upper}	SHOWS THE DIFFERENT FORMATTING FOR FIELD RESULTS
{subject *lower}	shows the different formatting for field results
{subject *firstcap}	Shows the different formatting for field results
{subject *caps}	Shows The Different Formatting For Field Results

You can also control how a number is presented. Using the * format switch, you can designate arabic numbers, cardinal or ordinal numbers, roman numbers, alphabetic numbers, hexadecimal numbers, or as text. Examples of these settings are shown here:

Field Code Entry	Result
{ NUMPAGES * Arabic * MERGEFORMAT }	1
{ NUMPAGES * Ordinal * MERGEFORMAT }	1st
{ NUMPAGES * Roman * MERGEFORMAT }	I
{ NUMPAGES * Alphabetic * MERGEFORMAT }	A
{ NUMPAGES * Cardtext * MERGEFORMAT }	one
{ NUMPAGES * Ordtext * MERGEFORMAT }	first
{ NUMPAGES * Hex * MERGEFORMAT }	1
{ NUMPAGES * Dollartext * MERGEFORMAT }	one and 00/100

You can set character formatting using the * switch. The field switch *charformat causes the entire field result to use the character formatting applied to the first character after the {. For example, if you enter {Filename * charformat} in the document named REPORT, the field result is *REPORT.DOC*.

The field switch *mergeformat tells Word to combine new and old formats when you change or update the field. Any formatting applied to the prior field result will apply to an updated field result. If there is no previous result to the field, Word uses the format of the first character after the { to format the result.

For example, suppose you enter a {SUMMARY} field to display the document summary. If you enter {SUMMARY * charformat} and you make the first sentence boldface and then update the result, the entire summary will be in boldface. If you enter {SUMMARY * mergeformat}, only the first sentence is in bold and the rest is not. If you do not use either * charformat or * mergeformat, the formatting you apply to the field or field's result disappears the next time the field is updated.

Date-Time Picture Switch: \@

The \@ switch controls how fields that show a date or a time display their result. You use this switch to create a picture that you want the field result to match. This picture is composed of the elements shown in Table 4-9. Most fields that add dates and times display options to select one of several popular date and time formats. As an example, you can have the field code {SAVEDATE \@ "dddd', 'MMMM' 'dd', 'yyyy"} and the document is last saved on 05/05/94, this field displays the result Thursday, May 5, 1994. The text in the single quotes tells Word to include the spaces and commas so Word knows it is not a code in the date and time format.

Character	Effect
m	Minutes without leading zeros
mm	Minutes with leading zeros
h	Hour of 12-hour clock without leading zeros
hh	Hour of 12-hour clock with leading zeros
H	Hour of 24-hour clock without leading zeros
HH	Hour of 24-hour clock with leading zeros
d	Day number
dd	Day number with leading zero for single-digit days
ddd	Three-letter abbreviation for day name
dddd	Day name
M	Month number
MM	Month number with leading zero for single-digit months
MMM	Three-letter abbreviation of month name
MMMM	Month name
yy	Last two digits of year
yyyy	Year number
AM/PM	Uppercase AM and PM indicate morning and afternoon hours
am/pm	Lowercase am and pm indicate morning and afternoon hours
A/P	Uppercase A and P indicate morning and afternoon hours
a/p	Lowercase a and p indicate morning and afternoon hours

Table 4-9. *Date-Time Picture Elements*

Do not include spaces in your date-time picture. If you want spaces between the date-time picture elements, you must enclose the entire date-time picture inside quotation marks. Then you can include spaces or other characters in your date-time picture, and they will appear in the field results.

You can include a sequence value (such as the results of the {SEQ} field) in your date-time picture. To do this, enclose the identifier name in accents grave (`).

TIP: You can assign formats to the individual parts of a date, time, or number by formatting the characters in the date-time picture or number picture switch. Since the characters in the pictures have a one-to-one correspondence with the characters in the field result, Word matches the field result formatting with the formatting assigned to individual characters in the pictures.

Number Picture Switch: \#

Use the \# switch to create a number picture that sets the appearance of the field's result when it is a number. Following the \# are a series of characters that represent the character positions in the field's result. This picture is composed of the elements shown in Table 4-10.

For example, using the switch \# "#,##0.00" for a field that returns 1642.6 will cause the field result to be displayed as 1,642.60.

Character	Effect
0	Displays the number in that place using 0 if a digit is not present.
#	Leaves the number in that place blank if not needed.
x	Truncates or rounds the digits on each side of the decimal point. When x is to left of decimal point, digits to left of x are truncated. When x is to right of decimal point, digits to right of x decide whether digit in x's position is rounded up or down, and the extra digits do not appear.
.	Represents the decimal point.
,	Represents the thousands separator.
+	Displays + in front of positive numbers and – in front of negative ones.
-	Displays = in front of negative numbers and nothing in front of positive ones.

Table 4-10.   *Numeric Picture Elements*

Table 4-10 indates that for the decimal point and thousands separator, the period and the comma are used. The characters for these two purposes are set by the Windows Control Panel. After the decimal point, you will want to use the # or 0 character to indicate how many digits you want after the decimal point.

You can also have more than one format after \# to tell Word to format positive numbers and negative numbers differently. Two formats separated with a semicolon tell Word that the first format applies to positive numbers and the second one applies to negative numbers. Three formats separated with a semicolon tell Word that the first format applies to positive numbers, the second one applies to negative numbers, and the third one applies to zero. For example,

    \# "#,###;(#,###);zero"

displays positive numbers with a comma separating the thousands and no digits after the decimal point, negative numbers the same way except they are enclosed in parentheses, and zeros as the text "zero".

You can include additional text in your number picture, such as the zero shown in the above example. The dollar sign, or other appropriate characters, can be included in a number picture and will be used in the field results. If you want to include spaces or other characters and you don't know if Word will understand that they are part of the number format, put the format in quotes. When you want to specify that text appears in the field result exactly as it appears in the number format, enclose it in accents grave (`). You will also use accents grave to enclose an identifier name used with a {SEQ} field used to produce the value of one of the identified sequences you are using in your document.

Figures

See "Graphics".

File Formats

Most applications use their own formats for storing their data. Since applications are designed to accomplish different tasks, they need to store your data in specific formats. Also, application developers have designed individual formats to handle the data their applications use.

Word can share data with many popular applications because it can read the various formats. When Word sees that a file you open is not in Word's own format, it will convert the file to Word format. When you save a document in

Word, the Save File as Type drop-down list box offers you a choice of file types; your selection determines the format for saving your file. Word can also use graphics file formats, so you can put pictures in your documents. When you add the picture, Word converts it from one of many popular graphics image formats into Word's own format for graphics.

Related Topics

Opening Files
Saving Files

File Location Options

Word uses several types of files as you work with your documents. In addition to the program's own files, Word uses document files for your data, clip art files for graphics you can add to the documents, and template files to provide models for the appearance of your documents. To use these files, Word needs to know where to find them. These file locations in Word for Windows 6 are designated by File Location options available through the Tools | Options command. The settings for the file locations are saved in the WINWORD6.INI file in your Windows directory.

In Word for Windows 2, Word assumes that document files, automatically saved back-ups, clip art, and templates are in the same directory as WINWORD.EXE. When you start Word you can tell it to start with another directory, by including that directory as the Working Directory for the program item; or you can start Word by opening a Word for Windows file that is in another directory.

Word for Windows 2 dictionary files are either in the directory containing WINWORD.EXE, in the MSAPPS\PROOF directory, or in the directory set by TOOLS-PATH in the WIN.INI file.

The tutorial files are in the WINWORD.CBT subdirectory in the directory where WINWORD.EXE is located. These are the defaults for when no directory is otherwise specified. You can set a directory for Word for Windows 2 to use when you do not want Word for Windows 2 to use the default location. Word for Windows 2 saves its file location settings in the WIN.INI file in your Windows directory.

Procedures

In Word for Windows 6, you set the file location settings following the steps described below. In Word for Windows 2, you set the file location settings by changing the settings in the WIN.INI file. Doc-path sets the location for documents, DOT-path is for templates, AUTOSAVE-path is for backups of documents, Spelling is for spelling, Hyphenate is for hyphenation, Thesaurus is for the thesaurus, Grammar is for grammar, and Programdir is for the Word for Windows 2 program files. See "WIN.INI Options" for changing the file location options as well as other customization options.

1. Select Tools | Options and then the File Locations tab.

2. Select the type of files and the directory you want to change in the File Types list box. The types of files and their purpose include the following:

Documents	Where you keep most of your documents
Clipart Pictures	Where you want Word to look for graphics images when you use commands such as Insert	Picture
User Templates	Templates that are your own (versus shared with other users)
Workgroup Templates	Templates that you share with other users
User Options	Where Word records your customizing options, in the file WINWORD.OPT
AutoSave Files	Where Word puts the automatically saved files that are emergency back-ups in case your system fails
Dictionaries	Dictionary files used for checking the spelling of documents
Tutorial	Word's tutorial files (if they are installed)
Startup	Templates and add-in programs that Word automatically loads

3. Select Modify. Then either type the directory where you want to store the selected type of files, or use the Directories list box and Drives drop-down list box to select a new location. You can also create the directory you want by selecting New and typing a name for the directory.

4. Select OK.

5. Repeat steps 2 through 4 for each directory location you want to change.

TIP: The file locations you specify can be altered. For example, when you select a particular drive and/or directory when you save or open a file, you change the directory of that file. Word will continue using the new directory and drive you select during the Word session.

File Management

With Word's file management tools, you can find files using any information, and open, delete, print, or copy multiple files.

Procedures

The following procedures tell you how to locate and work with files in Word for Windows 2 and Word for Windows 6.

Finding Files in Word for Windows 2

1. Select File | Find File, to open the Find File dialog box (Figure 4-17).

The left half of the Find File dialog box lists the files selected by the current search. At the top of the dialog box, Paths Searched tells you the directory of the files listed, and Sorted By displays how the files are ordered. The right half of the dialog box shows a preview of the document highlighted on the left. This dialog box can also display the document contents, statistics, summary information, or title as described under "View" below.

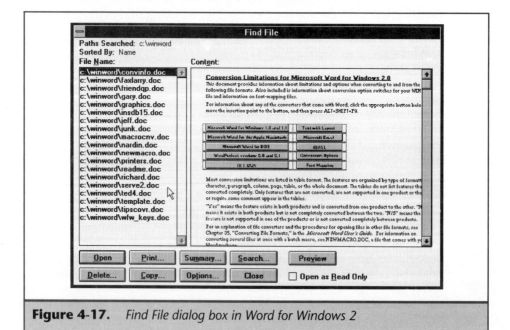

Figure 4-17.   *Find File dialog box in Word for Windows 2*

2. If the files you want are not showing in the File Name list box, select Search. In the Search dialog box, you can change the search criteria. The options in this dialog box are described later, under "Options" in this section.

3. Carry out the desired action with the selected file(s). You can print, open, copy, or delete the file(s), as described later, under "Options" in this section.

4. When you are finished working with the files, select Close.

Finding Files in Word for Windows 6

1. Select File | Find File, to open the Search dialog box (illustrated later, under "Options").

2. Select OK from the Search dialog box to display the Find File dialog box (Figure 4-18). You may need to select a location, such as \WINWORD6, for the directory to search before you can select OK.

NOTE: The next time you select File | Find File, Word will display the files selected with the last search you performed, and will show you the Find File dialog box (Figure 4-18) instead of the Search dialog box.

The Listed Files list box on the left of the Find File dialog box shows a diagram of the files that Word is looking at. The icons may be disk drives, folders for directories, or papers for documents and other types of files. On the right is a display of information about the file highlighted on the left. In Figure 4-18, the right side is a preview of the document. Word can also display summary information or file information similar to a disk management program such as the File Manager, as explained later in the "Options" section. The other command buttons, used to perform actions or change the display of files, are also explained in that section.

3. If the files you want are not showing in the List Files list box, select Search. In the Search dialog box, you can change the search criteria. The options in this dialog box are described under "Options" below.

4. Carry out the desired action with the selected file(s). You can print, open, copy, or delete the file(s). For more information on these operations, see "Options" below.

5. When you are finished working with the files, select Close.

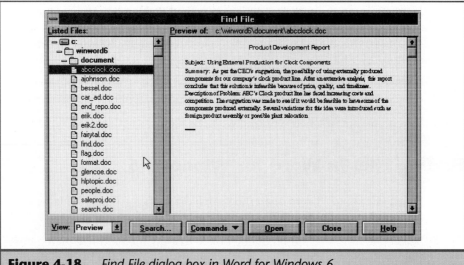

Figure 4-18. *Find File dialog box in Word for Windows 6*

Options

The following sections describe the command options available in the Find File and Search dialog boxes.

Open

Select Open to open the files selected in the Listed Files or File Name list box. In Word for Windows 6, you can also select Commands and Open Read Only to open the files without the ability to save the files using the same name. In Word for Windows 2, Word opens the files as read-only when you select the Open as Read Only check box.

Delete

In Word for Windows 6 you can delete selected files by selecting Commands and then Delete or by pressing DEL. In Word for Windows 2 you can delete selected files by selecting Delete. Word prompts you to confirm that you want to delete the files; select Yes to delete the files, or No to abort the deletion.

Print

Select Commands and then Print (or just Print in Word for Windows 2) to print the files selected in the Listed Files or File Name list box. Word displays the Print dialog box, which is identical to the dialog box for the File | Print command. Choose the settings in this dialog box and then select OK. The print options you choose will apply to all documents that you print from this dialog box. Word opens these files and prints their contents.

Copy

Select Commands and then Copy (or just Copy in Word for Windows 2) to copy the files selected in the Listed Files or File Name list box. This opens the Copy dialog box, where you can either type the directory where you want to copy the selected type of files or use the Directories list box and Drives drop-down list box to select a new location. You can also use the New button to create a new subdirectory.

The copied files have the same name as the original files unless you include a new filename in the Path text box. If you select multiple files to copy, instead of including a filename, you can modify part of the filename using wildcard characters in the Path text box, indicating portions of the old file name that will not change when the copied file is created. You cannot copy several files to a single filename. For example, you could select files EFR1.DOC, EFR2.DOC and EFR3.DOC, and enter MVC?.* in the Path text box after selecting the appropriate drive and directory. When you copy the files, the copies are called MVC1.DOC, MVC2.DOC and MVC3.DOC.

Summary

Select Commands and then Summary (or just Summary in Word for Windows 2) to change the summary information of the selected file in the Listed Files or File Name list box. Word opens the Summary Information dialog box just as if you had opened the file and selected File | Summary Info. In this dialog box you can change the summary information used to identify the file. See "Summary Info" in this chapter for a complete explanation of the Summary Info fields. If multiple files are selected, you will only change the summary information of the first file.

Sorting

Select Commands and then Sorting in Word for Windows 6 (or just Options in Word for Windows 2) to change the sort order of files in the Listed Files or File Name list box. From the Options dialog box, under Sort Files By, you can select Author, Creation Date, Last Saved By, Last Saved Date, Name, or Size option buttons to determine how the files are sorted in the Find File dialog boxes. Select OK, and Word reorders the listed files. When multiple directories of files are listed, each directory is sorted separately. Word sorts all of the files listed, even when you have selected only a few before sorting.

View

Select the View drop-down list box in Word for Windows 6, or Options in Word for Windows 2, to change how the files are displayed on the right side of the Find File dialog box.

In Word for Windows 6, selecting Preview displays the contents of the highlighted file. Selecting Summary displays the summary information and document statistics for the highlighted file. You can select File Info to display the title and file information for all of the files listed in the window.

In Word for Windows 2, the options on the right half of the Options dialog box change the displayed information. Selecting Content displays the contents of the highlighted file. You can select Summary Info to display the document summary information or Statistics to display the document statistics on the highlighted file. Selecting Titles displays only the file name and the title from the summary information for all of the files listed. The display does not change until you select OK.

Search

Select Search to open the Search dialog box, shown just below. Here you define the files you want displayed in the Find File dialog box. Word has many options for designating what files you want to find and where you want to search.

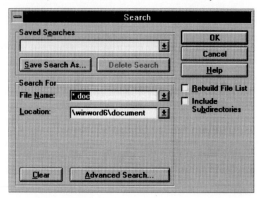

This is the same dialog box you see in Word for Windows 6 the first time you use the File | Find File command. This dialog box defines the display of files for the Find File dialog box. Several of the search options do not appear until you select the Advanced Search button. In Word for Windows 2, all of the search options appear in the Search dialog box. After you have specified the search you want Word to perform, select Start Search in Word for Windows 2 or OK in Word for Windows 6.

The following sections describe the search options you can use to select which files are shown in the Find File dialog box.

FILE NAME AND TYPE   To search for a specific filename or extension, type the filename in the File Name text box. In Word for Windows 6, you can open the drop-down list box and select a file type to alter the extension, to find a particular type of files. In Word for Windows 2, select the file type from the Type drop-down list box, to update the filename in the File Name text box.

For example, entering EFR?.* in the File Name list box will find files such as EFR3.DOC, EFR4.WK3 and EFRT.XLS. However, Word would not find the file EFR010.DOC. For this case you would enter EFR* and select Word Document (*.doc) from the Type drop-down list box. Word will then find EFR3.DOC and EFR010.DOC, but not EFR4.WK3.

Word for Windows 6 lets you enter more than one file name to find, separated with commas. For example, you can enter ***.doc,*.dot** to find both Word documents and template files.

LOCATION   You can customize your search so that Word looks for files in one or more drives or directories. In Word for Windows 6, you set the search location using the Search dialog box and the Location tab from the Advanced Search dialog box. In Word for Windows 2, all of the search options appear in the Search dialog box.

In Word for Windows 6, in the Search dialog box select a drive in the Location drop-down list box. You can select one of the drives in the list box or type in the drive and directory location. Another option is to select Advanced Search and the Location tab. From this dialog box, you can easily select the drives and directories to search. Use Directories and Drives to choose the drive and directory to search, and select Add. You can also select a directory in the Search In list box; use Remove to remove a directory from the path list or Remove All to clear all of the drives and directories listed. Selecting OK returns you to the Search dialog box and enters the chosen locations, separated with semicolons, in the Location drop-down list box. When you want Word to also search the subdirectories within the directories you select, turn on the Include Subdirectories check box. For example, if you are searching your WINWORD6 directory for document files, including the subdirectories in the search will also find document files in every subdirectory under the WINWORD6 directory.

In Word for Windows 2, in the Search dialog box select the drives you want searched in the Drives drop-down list box. Initially, Drives is set to Path Only, so Word searches for files only in the drives listed in the Path text box. In the Path text box, edit each of the paths to be searched, separated by semicolons. As a shortcut, select Edit Path and use that dialog box to select a list of paths in the Path text box, before selecting Add to add the selected drive/directory to the list. You can also choose a directory in the Search Path list box; use Delete to remove a directory or Delete All to clear all of the drives and directories listed in Path. Besides selecting Path Only in the Drives drop-down list box, you have a few other options: You can choose to search any particular drive; All Local Drives searches all the hard drives in your computer; All Drives searches all fixed or hard drives your computer has access to, including network drives. Word does not search your floppy drives when All Drives is selected. The only way to include a floppy drive in the search is to include that drive letter in the Path text box.

SUMMARY INFO AND TEXT   Word will search for files that contain specific text, or specific Summary Info entries. You can search for files created by a specific person, or containing certain keywords. To search Summary Info in Word for Windows 6, select the Advanced Search button and then the Summary tab. In Word for Windows 2, make your entries in the bottom half of the Search dialog box.

When you have entries in the Title, Author, Keywords, or Subject text boxes, Word searches for files with that text in the summary information. For example, if you enter Mary Smith in the Author text box, Word finds the files with Mary Smith recorded as the author in the Summary Info. You can also select the Match Case check box to find only Summary Info entries with the same case as your search criteria.

Enter text in the Containing Text text box (Any Text in Word for Windows 2) to have Word find files containing that text, either as Summary Info or as part of the file's contents. For instance, if you enter Mary Smith in the Any Text text box, Word find letters written to Mary Smith and reports with Mary Smith recorded as the author.

With the Summary Info fields, you can use special characters to help you find the entries you want. Just as you can use ? and * to represent one or zero or more characters in a file name for selecting the files to search in the File Name text box, you can also use these characters in the text boxes for the Summary Info you are searching for. Here are the characters you can use:

Character	Result
?	Matches any character in that position
*	Matches zero or more characters in that position
"*text*"	Finds *text* as a phrase rather than looking for individual words
\	Matches the next character (usually one of the other special characters) as it appears, so * matches *
,	Joins words or phrases, so Word finds files matching either word or phrase
& or space	Joins words or phrases, so Word finds files matching both words or phrases
~	Matches words or phrases that do not match the entry after the ~

In Word for Windows 2, you can use these special characters to find documents that contain particular text. In Word for Windows 6, you can use pattern matching in the Containing Text text box. Pattern matching for text in the document is just like pattern matching when you are searching a document with Edit | Find. The special characters can be typed in, or you can choose them by selecting the Use Pattern Matching check box and then Special. See "Find and Replace" in this chapter for more information.

DATES   You can search for files based on when they were originally created or saved, as well as who saved them. You can search for files created before or after specific dates, or between two dates. In Word for Windows 6, these options are available when you select Advanced Search from the Search dialog box and then click the Timestamp tab. In Word for Windows 2, all of these options are in the Search dialog box.

The date text boxes are divided into two sections in the dialog box. You can search for files created on or after a date, or saved on or after a date:

- ■ *Created*   Under Created (Date Created in Word for Windows 2), in the From text box (After in Word for Windows 2) enter the cutoff date on or after which the files were initially created. In the To text box (Before in Word for Windows 2) enter the cutoff date on or after which the files were initially created. Word will find only files created on or between the From date and the To date. You can also supply just the From date to find files created on or after a specific date, or just the To date to find files created on or before a specific date.

- ■ *Saved*   To find files based on when the document was most recently saved, you enter the dates as described above for creation dates, except you use the From and To boxes under Last Saved rather than Created (Before and After under Date Saved in Word for Windows 2). For example, if you entered 2/11/94 in the From text box and 2/14/94 in the To box, Word will search for files that were last saved on or after February 11 and on or before Valentine's Day.

You can also find files according to who worked with them. This is *in addition to* using the Author summary information as described above in "Summary Info and Text." In Word for Windows 2, you do this by typing an entry in the Saved By text box. In Word for Windows 6, you type the name in the By text box below Last Saved or Created on the Timestamp tab. When you save a document, Word records the user name, and remembers the user name when the document was created and when it was last saved. These user names are part of the User Info options set with Tools | Options. For example, if you enter Mary Smith in the

Saved By text box, Word will search for documents last saved with Mary Smith recorded as the user, whether or not she is listed as the author.

OPTIONS   When you use Search to specify search criteria, you can have Word either replace the list of found files displayed, or add to it. In Word for Windows 6, first select Advanced Options and then the Summary tab. To specify what you want Word to do with the found files list, select from the Options drop-down list box.

■ Choose Create New List, and the most recently found files will replace the ones currently displayed.

■ Choose Add Matches to List, and the most recently found files will be added to the files already displayed.

■ Choose Search Only in List, and Word limits its search to the files already displayed. The files currently displayed in the Find File dialog box are pruned to only include the ones that match the additional criteria.

In Word for Windows 6, from the Search dialog box you can also turn on the Rebuild File List check box when you want the newly selected files to replace the currently listed files; turn this option off when you want the newly selected files to be added to the ones currently displayed.

SAVING A SEARCH   Once you have set up a search that you plan to use repeatedly, you can save the search criteria. Saved searches are easily repeated. For instance, say you keep all your Word documents in three directories, and frequently use a search that only gets *.doc files from those three directories.

To save a search in Word for Windows 6, select the Search button, then Save Search As, and type a description for the files selected by the current search criteria; then select OK. Later, when you want to use the same search, choose the name of the search from the Saved Searches drop-down list box. Word will make the search criteria in this dialog box and the Advanced Search dialog box match the saved search criteria. To discard the saved search, select it from the Saved Searches drop-down list box and choose Delete Search.

Hints

The foregoing discussion of search options has focused on one search feature at a time, but you will get the best use out of Word's Search features when you combine them. For example, you might use a combination of search criteria to find all files created before 01/01/93, by Mary Campbell, in the \WINWORD and \WINWORD\DOCUMENT directories.

With file operations such as copying, deleting and printing, you can work with multiple files. To select multiple files, move to the first one and hold down the SHIFT key while either moving to or clicking the last file you want to select. Or hold down CTRL to select a noncontiguous group of files. All of the files you select will be included in the next file operation. If you select Open in Word for Windows 2, Word will open as many of the selected documents as possible, up to its limit of nine.

If you want to list all of your Word documents, specify the root drive of the disk as the location to search, *.DOC for the filename, and then search all directories. Once you have the Word documents listed, you can back them up by copying them to floppy disks.

Use the Preview or Contents view of a document to make sure you are opening, deleting, or printing the right document.

 TIP: If you accidentally delete the wrong file, you may be able to recover it using another utility, and if you discover your error before another file uses the disk space previously occupied by the unintentionally deleted document.

Related Topics

Summary Info

File Naming

See "Saving Files."

File Sharing

Word lets you share documents and data in several ways. When you are working with other users, you can password-protect your documents so they cannot be unintentionally revised, as described in "Saving Files." If you want to share your documents with others to receive their comments, look at the suggestions under "Faxes" and "Annotation". To share data in one document with other documents, follow instructions in "Object Linking and Embedding." "Opening Files" has various information about opening shared files, such as those on a network.

File|Close

See "Closing Files."

File|Exit

See "Exiting Word."

File|Find File

See "File Management."

File|List of Last Four Open Files

See "Opening Files."

File|New

See "New Document."

File|Open

See "Opening Files."

File|Page Setup

This Word for Windows 6 command displays a dialog box with four page tabs that change settings for how the document is laid out on a page. These options are further described under, "Margins," "Page Size and Orientation," "Sections," and "Paper Source."

File|Print

See "Printing."

File|Print Merge

See "Mail Merge."

File|Print Preview

See "Viewing Documents."

File|Print Setup

See "Printing."

File|Save

See "Saving Files."

File|Save All

See "Saving Files."

File|Save As

See "Saving Files."

File|Summary Info

See "Summary Info."

File|Template

See "Templates."

F

Filenames

See "Saving Files."

Filling in Text and Graphics

See "Borders and Shading."

Fill-in Fields

See "Fields."

Filtering

See "Mail Merge" for information on filter records that are included in the mail merge process; see "Sorting" to filter the data that Word sorts.

Find and Replace

Use the Find feature to locate specific instances of text or formatting in your document. Use the Replace feature to locate specific text or formatting and replace it with other text or formatting.

Procedures

Using Word's Find or Replace features, you can search for text, including special characters; search for text with certain formatting applied; and search for certain formatting without specifying text. When you search for text with formatting, you define both the text and the formatting that you want to find, and Word finds only instances of that text with that formatting.

With the Replace feature, you can also specify text or formatting to replace the text or formatting that you find. You specify text, formatting, or both, to replace the text, formatting, or both that you find. If you find text and replace it with formatting, the text is not deleted; the formats you specify are applied to it.

Finding Text or Formatting

1. Select Edit | Find, or press CTRL+F in Word for Windows 6, to open the Find dialog box (Figure 4-19).

> *NOTE: If you have used Find during the current session, the dialog box displays your old settings. You have to delete them before entering new ones.*

2. Specify the text or formatting you want to find, using the options described under "Options" in this section.

3. Select the direction in which you want Word to search through the document. In Word for Windows 6, choose All, Up, or Down from the Search drop-down list box; in Word for Windows 2, select the Up or Down option buttons. Up or Down starts from the insertion point's position. The All option searches the entire document, starting from the insertion point and returning to the top of the document if necessary.

4. Set any other criteria you want, as described in "Options."

5. Select Find Next to locate the first occurrence of the specified text or formatting. Word highlights the first occurrence, but the Find dialog box does not close.

6. You can continue searching in two ways. Select Find Next again; or select Close, closing the Find dialog box, and then press SHIFT+F4. This key-combination repeats the last Find command, and Word finds the next occurrence of the search text or formatting.

Replacing Text or Formatting

1. Select Edit | Replace, or press CTRL+H in Word for Windows 6, to open the Replace dialog box. (If you are starting from the Find dialog box, you can switch to the Replace dialog box in Word for Windows 6 by selecting the Replace button; you cannot then switch back to the Find dialog box.) The Replace dialog box looks just like the Find dialog box in Figure 4-19, except that you can now make an entry for the replacement.

> *NOTE: If you have used the Replace feature during the current Word session, your old settings still appear in the dialog box. You have to delete these settings before entering new ones.*

Figure 4-19.   *Find dialog box in Word for Windows 6*

2. Specify the text or formatting you want to replace, using the options described under "Options" in this section.

3. Specify the replacement text or formatting. Enter the text after Replace With, and use the buttons along the bottom of the dialog box to select the formatting.

4. Select Find Next to locate the first occurrence of the text or formatting. Word highlights the first occurrence, and the Replace dialog box remains open. Select Replace to replace that occurrence with the substitute text or formatting you specified. To replace all occurrences of the search text or formatting, select Replace All. Word moves through the document and does all the replacements at once, and leaves the Replace dialog box open.

5. Select Close to close the Replace dialog box.

Options

Word has many options in the Find/Replace dialog box. These options help you to only find the text and/or formatting you want without having to look at more of the document than intended.

Find What/Replace With

In Find What, enter the text you want to locate, and in Replace With enter any text you want to use as a replacement. (If you want to find or replace formatting instead of or as well as text, look at the "Format" section just below.) You can enter up to 255 characters in both Find What and Replace With. Below these boxes will be descriptions of any formatting you have designated for the text you have entered there. You can use the shortcut keys to set character and paragraph formatting for the text you enter in these boxes. This formatting appears below the text boxes as if you used other options in the dialog box to set the formatting you want to find or replace. In Word for Windows 6, if you want to use one of the entries you searched for in a previous session, open the drop-down list box and select the one you want from the list.

When you search for formatting only, without entering any text for Find What, Word finds any text with the specified combination of formats. If you do enter text for Find What and then specify formats to find, Word only finds instances of the formatting when it is applied to the specified text; Word will not find the formatting when it is applied to other text. If you do not specify a format for Word to find, but you do enter text in Find What, Word finds the specified text regardless of its format.

SEARCHING WITH WILDCARDS   You can use wildcard characters when you searching for text. The * character takes the place of any number of characters; so if you enter cereb*, Word locates words such as *cerebellum, cerebral,* and *cerebrospinal.* The ? character takes the place of any one character; so if you enter ?ally, Word locates words such as *tally, rally,* and *dally.*

SEARCHING FOR AND REPLACING SPECIAL CHARACTERS   Besides entering the exact characters you want to find, you can enter other types of characters in the Find What and Replace With boxes.

In Word for Windows 2, the easiest special characters to use are ? and *, and they work as described just above in "Searching with Wildcards."

You can also search for and replace special characters such as paragraph markers, tabs, and hard page returns. In your entry for Find What or Replace With, enter your choice of the character codes shown in Table 4-11. Most of the codes require that the characters be entered using the upper or lowercase characters you see in Table 4-11. Also, notice how some special characters can only be used in the text to search for or in its replacement.

Word for Windows 6 does not use the ? and * characters in the Find What or Replace With boxes. You can see in Table 4-11 that Word for Windows 6 can use more special characters. You select the Special button and then the special character you want to add, without having to remember what to type. Use the other Find and Replace features just as you do when searching for normal text.

Characters to Enter	Matches
^?	(? question mark in Word for Windows 2) Any character in Word for Windows 6 (Find What only)
?	Any character in Word for Windows 2 or a question mark in Word for Windows 6
^#	Any digit (0-9) in Word for Windows 6 (Find What only)
^$	Any letter (A-Z, a-z) in Word for Windows 6 (Find What only)
^&	Contents of the Find What text box in Word for Windows 6 (Replace With only)
^a	Annotation mark in Word for Windows 6 (Find What only)
^b	Section break in Word for Windows 6 (Find What only)
^c	Clipboard contents (Replace With only)
^d	Field in Word for Windows 6 (Find What only)
^d	Hard page breaks and section breaks in Word for Windows 2
^e	Endnote mark in Word for Windows 6 (Find What only)
^f	Footnote mark in Word for Windows 6 (Find What only)
^g	Graphic in Word for Windows 6 (Find What only)
^l	End-of-line character created by SHIFT+ENTER in Word for Windows 6
^m	Manual page break created by CTRL+ENTER in Word for Windows 6, or contents of Find What (Replace With only) in Word for Windows 2
^n	End-of-line character in Word for Windows 2 or column break in Word for Windows 6
^p	Paragraph mark
^s	Nonbreaking space
^t	Tab character
^w	White spaces (nonbreaking spaces; paragraph, section, and hard page breaks; tab, end-of-line, and end-of-cell characters)
^-	Optional hyphens
^~	Nonbreaking hyphens
^	Caret
^+	Em dash in Word for Windows 6
^=	En dash in Word for Windows 6
^0nnn	ANSI character, where nnn is ANSI character code
^nnn	ASCII character, where nnn is ASCII character code
^1	Graphic in Word for Windows 2

Table 4-11.   *Entries to Find Special Characters*

Characters to Enter	Matches
^2	Footnote in Word for Windows 2
^3	Footnote separator in Word for Windows 2
^5	Annotation mark in Word for Windows 2
^9	Tab in Word for Windows 2
^10	Line feed in Word for Windows 2
^11	New line in Word for Windows 2
^12	Page or section break in Word for Windows 2
^13	Paragraph mark in Word for Windows 2
^14	Column break in Word for Windows 2
^19	Field in Word for Windows 2

Table 4-11. *Entries to Find Special Characters (continued)*

F

Find Whole Words Only

Select the Find Whole Words Only check box (Match Whole Word Only in Word for Windows 2) when you want to find only occurrences of the complete word—nothing more and nothing less—that you entered in the Find What. With this option enabled, Word does not find instances of the Find What text that are part of another word. For example, if you type the word real after Find What and then turn on Find Whole Words Only, Word finds every instance of the word real in your document, but skips words like *really, arboreal,* and *real-estate.*

Match Case

Select the Match Case check box when you want to find only text whose case exactly matches what you have entered in Find What. With this option enabled, Word only finds instances of the word with the same pattern of capitalization as the one you entered. For example, if you enter Pre-Raphaelite for the Find What and then turn on Match Case, Word will find *Pre-Raphaelite* but not *pre-raphaelite, Pre-raphaelite,* or *pre-Raphaelite.*

Sounds Like

Select the Sounds Like check box if you want Word to find text that sounds like your entry in the Find What box. For example, if you turn on Sounds Like and enter ther in Find What, Word will find *their, there,* and *they're.* Use this technique when you want to find a word and you're not sure how it is spelled.

Use Pattern Matching

Word for Windows 6 can use *pattern matching*. In pattern matching, Word looks for text that has the same pattern as the pattern you enter in the Find What box. To use pattern matching, select its check box.

Pattern matching has even more choices for selecting the types of characters you are looking for. These additional choices are listed in Table 4-12. They also appear when you select the Special button to add them to the Find What or Replace With boxes.

Characters to Enter	Effect
?	Matches any character in that position
*	Matches zero or more characters in that position
[x-y]	Matches any character in that position in the range x to y, where x and y are characters
[...]	Matches any character in the brackets, so [abc] matches the character a, b, or c
[!...]	Matches any character that does not appear in the brackets, so [!abc] matches any character except a, b, or c
[!x-y]	Matches any character that is not in the range from x to y, so [!a-c] matches any character except a, b, or c
{n}	Matches n occurrences of the previous character, so Michel{2}e matches *Michelle* but not *Michele*
{n,}	Matches n or more occurrences of the previous character so Michel{1,}e matches *Michelle* and *Michele*
{n,m}	Matches between n and m occurrences of the previous character, so 50{1,3} matches 50, 500, and 5000 but not 50000
@	Matches one or more occurrences of the previous character, so 50@ matches 50, 50000 and 5000000
<(characters)	Matches words that start with *characters*, as in <cab to match *cab*, *cable*, and *cabinet*
>(characters)	Matches words that end with *characters*, as in >tion to match *action* and *elocution*
\	Matches the next character as it appears, so \@ matches @

Table 4-12.   *Special Entries for Pattern Matching*

No Formatting/Clear

To clear any of the formatting settings you have made for Find What or Replace
With entries, select No Formatting in Word for Windows 6, or Clear in Word for
Windows 2. In the Replace dialog box, when you select this button, you only
clear either the formatting for the text to find or its replacement—depending on
the last text box or drop-down box you used. You can see which formatting these
buttons will clear by looking at the text that appears above them.

Format

The Format option selects the formatting you want to find or replace. (In Word
for Windows 2, you must select the formatting to find or replace using separate
buttons for Character, Paragraph, and Styles.) Then, in either version of Word,
the formatting you selected to be found or replaced appears beneath Find What
or Replace With, depending on which was active when you selected Format. You
can see where the formatting applies by looking at the text that appears above
the buttons.

In Word for Windows 6, once you select Format, you can choose from font,
Paragraph, Language, or Style, to display a Find Font, Find Paragraph, Find
Language, or Find Style dialog box. The first three dialog boxes look and behave
just like the dialog boxes you use when you are setting the font, paragraph
formatting, and language of text. The only difference you will notice is that check
boxes are grayed out, and list boxes do not show their selections. Only the
formatting selections you make are remembered as formatting you want to find.
For example, you can select Format, Font, and 10 for Size to find any text 10
points high, regardless of the font. The Find Style dialog box only has a list box
containing the available styles and a description of the highlighted style to
select the style to find. To finish choosing the format or style to find or replace,
select OK.

In Word for Windows 2, you select from Character, Paragraph, or Styles to get
a Find Character, Find Paragraph, or Find Style dialog box. The Find Character
and Find Paragraph dialog boxes look and behave just like the Character and
Paragraph dialog boxes you use to set character or paragraph formatting. The
only difference you will notice is that check boxes are grayed out, and that list
boxes do not show their selections. Only your formatting selections are
remembered as formatting you want to find. For example, you can select
Paragraph, then Line Spacing, and Double to find any text that is double-spaced,
regardless of any other paragraph formatting. The Find Style dialog box only has
a list box containing the available styles and a description of the highlighted style
to select the style to find. To finish choosing the format or style to find or replace,
select OK.

F

TIP: In Word for Windows 6, use the toolbars and keyboard shortcuts described in "Shortcut Keys" to apply formatting to entries in the Find What and Replace With boxes. For example, while the Find and Replace dialog boxes are displayed, choosing a font from the Formatting toolbar adds that font to the format you are finding or replacing, as if you had selected Format and Font. You can use the Formatting toolbar buttons for style, font, font size, bold, underline, italic, and paragraph alignment, and their keyboard shortcuts, as well as keyboard shortcuts for all caps, subscript, superscript, underline, double-underline, hidden, small caps, and for removing character formatting. Word also accepts keyboard shortcuts for single-, double-, and 1 1/2 spacing, and for removing paragraph formatting.

Hints

Use Word to find and replace all sorts of formatting and text. This feature can eaily fix your most commonly made mistakes. You can also have Word replace text with graphics to quickly add frequently used graphics to a document.

Use Find and Replace to Fix Common Mistakes

If you frequently make the same mistakes, you can use Word's find and replace tools to fix them. For example, if you use the wrong homonym, you can use Word to find the ones you frequently misuse and select the ones you want Word to replace. The box "Problem Homonyms to Watch For" lists the most commonly misused homonyms.

Word can also find extraneous phrases. As you look over documents you have written, you may find that you have unnecessarily used certain phrases, or overused others. The box "Correcting Wordiness and Redundancy" lists some common phrases that can be shortened to clarify your writing.

Undoing Replacements

Before using the Replace feature, save your document. If you replace text or formatting incorrectly, you can always close the window without saving, open the unchanged copy of your document, and try again.

TIP: *This can be a lifesaver if you accidentally select Replace before specifying the replacement text or formatting. When you use Replace without specifying replacement formatting or text, the selected text is deleted (that is, replaced with nothing). Saving first is especially useful because the Undo command is somewhat limited when used with Replace. After you use Replace, the Undo command only undoes the last replacement. If you used Replace All, the Undo command replaces all of the changes made.*

Correcting Wordiness and Redundancy

When you are working against a tight deadline, you might find it difficult to take sufficient time rewriting your initial draft. When you are short on time, sometimes you miss opportunities to remove unnecessary words and redundant phrases. Each of us has our own set of problem phrases that can appear in our writing; following are some typical examples. Once you identify the phrases that cause you problems, you can use Word's search and replace features to eliminate them from your writing.

Problem	Correction
He plans to call at 3:00 P.M. *in the afternoon.*	He plans to call at 3:00 P.M.
Always call 911 *in the event of an emergency*	Always call 911 if there is an emergency.
We would like *to call your attention to* our special 50%-off sale.	We would like to notify you of our special 50%-off sale.
A salad *can be used for* a quick meal.	A salad is a quick meal.
She *is a woman who* is always on time.	She is always on time *or* She is always punctual.
We need to discuss wages, benefits, retention rates, *and so forth.*	We need to discuss wages, benefits, and retention rates.
Silicon *can be used for* repairing the window track.	Silicon can repair the window track.
Pollution *is a topic that* interests me.	Pollution interests me.
She proceeded down the aisle *in a quiet manner.*	She proceeded quietly down the aisle.
John *is able to* go to school.	John can go to school.

F

Problem Homonyms to Watch For

Homonyms are words that sound the same but have a different spelling and meaning. Even when you know the correct use for each word in a homonym group, your brain can play tricks as you are hurrying to complete an important document. Word's spelling checker will not find these errors in usage as long as each one is correctly spelled. Word's grammar checker will find some but not all of them. Even when grammar checker does find one of these errors, Word may think it is a grammatical error for a reason other than an incorrect homonym. In addition to using Word's tools, you will need to proof your documents carefully to find homonym errors; consider using the Search function, too, if you have a recurring problem with one or two.

Here are ten homonym groups that frequently cause problems.

by, buy	I walk *by* his house each day.
	I need to stop at the store to *buy* milk.
chord, cord	If you play the first *chord* of the song, I will try to guess the tune.
	Do you have a piece of *cord* with which to tie the package?
cue, queue	Without the *cue* card, she couldn't remember her lines.
	Fans began to *queue* up hours before the ticket booths opened.
feat, feet	It was a *feat* of daring to jump from the cliff.
	How many *feet* are in one yard?
flair, flare	She has a *flair* for decorating.
	The police helped light a *flare* to mark the accident.
in, inn	John is *in* the dining room.
	We would like to stay at a cozy *inn* this weekend.
its, it's	The group wants to renew *its* vendor's licence.
	It's too late to go to the movies.
led, lead	He *led* the horse to water.
	Lead poisoning can come from exposure to some paint.
their, there, they're	*Their* luggage was lost.
	There are five houses on the street.
	They're not here yet.
to, too, two	He went *to* the meeting.
	She asked for a raise, *too*.
	The *two* boys went to the office picnic.
whole, hole	I can't believe he ate the *whole* pie.
	You have a *hole* in your glove.

Replacing Text with Graphics

You may have a small piece of clip art, such as an icon, that you plan to use frequently in your document. Rather than inserting the art repeatedly as you create your document, enter some special text instead as a placeholder, such as Art1. After you are finished editing, you can replace the placeholder with the art automatically. First, copy the art to the Clipboard. Then open the Replace dialog box, and enter the placeholder text in the Find What box, and type ^c for Replace With. Then select Replace or Replace All. Word replaces placeholder text with the graphic from the Clipboard.

Another option is to insert the graphic in the document once, and name the graphic with a bookmark. When you want the same graphic to appear in other locations, use the {bookmark} field code. (See "Fields" for more information.) Using a field instead of using Edit | Replace to put insert multiple copies of the graphic makes the document size smaller; also, any edits, such as changes made with Format | Picture, apply to each appearance of the icon.

Searching from the Middle of a Document

When Word reaches the end or beginning of the document while searching, it does not stop searching. Instead, it displays a message box asking you if you want to continue searching at the beginning (if you're searching down) or end (if you're searching up) of the document. Select Yes, and Word continues until it has searched the entire document. Select No, and Word stops the find or replace operation.

Searching for Multiple Formats

When you specify a combination of formats to find, Word only locates text that has *all* those formats. For example, if you are searching for bold text in a double- spaced paragraph, Word will not find bold text in a paragraph with single spacing. Be careful that you do not define formatting that may not be appropriate.

Deleting Text

Here's a technique for deleting all instances of some particular text. Put the text you want to delete in the Find What box, and leave Replace With empty. Select Replace (or Replace All), and the next occurrence of the text (or all occurrences) will be deleted. Word for Windows 6 has smart deletion, so if the text appears at the end of the sentence or has some punctuation mark, Word removes the extra space after deleting the text.

F

Related Topics

ASCII Text Files
ANSI Codes
Character Formats
Grammer Checking
Paragraph Formats
Spell Checking

Find File

See "File Management."

Finding and Replacing Text, Formatting, and Special Characters

See "Find and Replace."

First Pages

In some documents, you may want to treat the first page differently. This includes giving the first page an odd page number; in many books, each chapter starts on an odd page so the first page is on the right side. Word has several features that you may want to employ for creating the first page of a document.

When you want a page to start on the right side, use the Insert | Break command described under "Pagination." The "Page Numbers" section describes how you can designate the page number appearance, the starting page number, and whether you want the page number to appear on the first page. "Headers and Footers" tells you how to specify a different header and footer for the first page.

Floating Toolbars

See "Toolbars."

Flush Left and Flush Right

See "Alignment" and "Tabs."

Fonts

Fonts are a set of characters in a particular style. Figure 4-20 shows several fonts in use. You can set both the font and the size of that font. Windows offers you a variety of fonts that can be scaled to any size, and your printer probably offers additional fonts. You can also install fonts that you buy from software stores, to expand the available font selections on your system.

Before you can use a font in Word for Windows, you must have the font installed in Windows. Word for Windows 6 includes several fonts that the installation program will install for you. Fonts can be enhanced with various features such as bold, underline, and italic, as described for these features in the sections of this chapter.

Figure 4-20.   *Too many fonts can be distracting and unattractive*

Procedures

A font can be selected to take effect as you are typing, or after the text is typed. To choose the font while typing, select the font and then type the text; when you are ready, select a different font or revert to the default font. To choose a font for typed text, select the text to format and then select the font.

Selecting a Font/Font Size with the Formatting Toolbar

1. Open the Font drop-down list in the Formatting toolbar by clicking its down-arrow button, or press CTRL+SHIFT+F.

2. Select a font by clicking it, or by highlighting it and pressing ENTER.

3. Open the Font Size drop-down list in the Formatting toolbar by clicking its down-arrow button, or press CTRL+SHIFT+P.

4. Choose a font size by clicking it, by highlighting it and pressing ENTER, or by typing the size and pressing ENTER.

Selecting a Font/Font Size with the Ribbon (Word for Windows 2)

1. Open the ribbon's Font drop-down list by clicking the down-arrow button or pressing CTRL+F.

2. Select a font by double-clicking it or by highlighting it and pressing ENTER.

3. Open the ribbon's Points drop-down list by clicking its down-arrow button or pressing CTRL+P.

4. Choose a font size by highlighting it and pressing ENTER, or by double-clicking it. If the font is scalable, such as the TrueType fonts that come with Windows, you can type a size into the Points text box.

Selecting a Font/Font Size with the Menus

1. Select Format | Font (Format | Character in Word for Windows 2), to open the Font dialog box.

2. Select a font in the Font list box.

3. Select a font style in the F<u>o</u>nt Style list box (Word for Windows 6 only).

4. Select a size for the font in the <u>S</u>ize list box (<u>P</u>oints drop-down list box in Word for Windows 2), or type a size in this text box.

5. Select OK.

Hints

A document's normal font is set by the Normal style. To change the font for an entire document at once, modify this style. See "Styles" for more information.

Make the font's appearance fit the document. For example, Matura MT Script is inappropriate for most business correspondence, but it may be just what you need for printing invitations to a party.

Don't use too many fonts in the same document. Switching fonts frequently makes the document harder to read and distracts the reader from the content.

To help make font selection easier, the Font drop-down list in the Word for Windows 6 Formatting toolbar shows you the fonts already in use in the document at the top of the list, as well as placing them alphabetically in their normal position in the list, as you can see here:

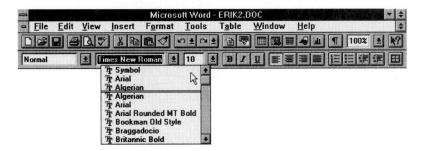

Font sizes measure the height of the font, and are listed in points (1/72 inch). Some fonts are scalable to any size, from 1 to 1,638 points in .5-inch increments; others only have a limited number of sizes. The Points drop-down list box on the Formatting toolbar or in the Font dialog box shows the available point sizes. If the font is scalable, you can also enter a value in this text box. You can even enter a size that is not listed, such as 11.5.

If you designate a size that does not appear in the Points drop-down list box, and the font is not scalable, the font is displayed and printed in the closest available size of the font.

You can expand your font selection by installing soft fonts and add-on printer fonts. *Soft fonts* are installable programs that create fonts. *Printer fonts* can be cartridges or disks of fonts that you install directly to your printer. When you seek to expand your font selection, look for scalable fonts that can be enlarged or reduced to many sizes, because they add versatility. If your needs are simple, however, a few useful nonscalable fonts may suffice.

TrueType fonts have an advantage: On your screen they look just as they do when printed. The disadvantage is that printing with TrueType fonts may take longer than with other fonts, such as the fonts your printer provides. Word tells you which type font you are selecting: TrueType fonts have double-T symbols next to them in the Font list, and printer fonts have a small printer next to them. Fonts available from other sources may have other icons. Fonts with no icons include plotter fonts, designed for working on plotters, and screen fonts, designed for displaying data on the screen.

The following key-combinations are also available to change the size of text you will type or that you have selected:

Shortcut Key	Function
CTRL+SHIFT+>	Selects the next larger font size in the font size list
CTRL+SHIFT+<	Selects the next smaller font size in the font size list
CTRL+[	Decreases font size by one point
CTRL+]	Increases font size by one point

Related Topics

Character Formats
Styles

Footers

Footers are text that appears at the bottom of every page. See "Headers and Footers."

Footnotes and Endnotes

Footnotes and endnotes are references that you can place at the bottom of a page or another location in your document. They provide commentary or documentation about your text.

Procedures

In Word for Windows 6, you can create both endnotes and footnotes in the same document. In Word for Windows 2, you create one set of notes and then format them as endnotes or footnotes.

Creating a Note

To create a note, you must first insert a note reference mark in the text that identifies text with a related note. The second step is to enter the text of the note.

1. Position the insertion point where you want the note reference mark.

2. Select Insert | Footnote. In Word for Windows 6, select Footnote or Endnote to determine the type of note you are creating.

TIP: In Word for Windows 6, you can quickly add a note by pressing ALT+CTRL+F *or an endnote with* ALT+CTRL+E.

3. If you want automatically numbered notes, select AutoNumber (Auto-Numbered Note in Word for Windows 2). Select Custom Mark (Custom Footnote Mark in Word for Windows 2), and then enter your note reference mark in the text box, using up to ten characters (numbers, letters, or symbols). In Word for Windows 6, select Symbol to enter a nonkeyboard symbol. Select OK.

NOTE: When renumbering notes that are numbered automatically, Word skips notes with custom marks.

4. If you are in Normal view, Word opens the note pane, and you enter the note text in this pane. If you are in Page Layout view, Word moves the insertion point to where the note will print, and you enter the text there.

5. When you finish entering the note text, leave the Note pane and return to the document:

   ■ In Normal view, click the Close button, or press ALT+SHIFT+C, or double-click the split bar, or select View | Footnotes. To return without closing the pane, click on the document or press F6.

■ In Page Layout view, either click the document or use the arrow keys to move into the document text.

Editing a Note

In Page Layout view, move to the note text in the note pane, and edit it. In Normal view, open the note pane by selecting View | Footnotes, and then edit the note.

Deleting a Note

To delete a note, delete its note reference mark in the document, by selecting it and pressing DEL or BACKSPACE.

Moving a Note

To move a note, move its note reference mark using the Clipboard. Both the note reference mark and the note text are moved at the same time. (For instructions on changing where notes are printed, see "Location" under "Options" in this section.)

1. Select the note reference mark for the note you want to move.

2. Cut the note reference mark to the Clipboard.

REMINDER: *You can cut to the Clipboard by selecting Edit | Cut, by clicking the Cut button on the toolbar, or by pressing* CTRL+X.

3. Move the insertion point to the new location for the note.

4. Paste the note reference mark back into the document.

REMINDER: *You can paste from the Clipboard by selecting Edit | Paste, by clicking the Paste button on the toolbar, or by pressing* CTRL+V.

Copying a Note

To copy a note, copy the note reference mark to the Clipboard and then paste it back into your document. Both the note reference mark and the note text are copied.

1. Select the note reference mark for the note you want to copy.

2. Copy the note reference mark to the Clipboard.

REMINDER: You can copy to the Clipboard by selecting Edit | Copy, by clicking the Cut button on the toolbar, or by pressing CTRL+X.

3. Move the insertion point to where you want the note.

4. Paste the note reference mark back into the document.

REMINDER: You can paste from the Clipboard by selecting Edit | Paste, by clicking the Paste button on the toolbar, or by pressing CTRL+V.

Specifying Note Locations and Numbering

1. Select Insert | Footnote.

2. Select Options. In Word for Windows 6, select the All Footnotes or All Endnotes tab, depending on the settings you want to change.

3. From the Place At drop-down list box, choose where you want the notes to appear.

4. In Word for Windows 6, select a numbering method from the Number Format drop-down list box.

5. Enter the number of the first note in the Start At text box.

6. By default, Word numbers notes continuously throughout the document. To start numbering notes again after each section break in your document, select Restart Each Section. In Word for Windows 6, on the All Footnotes tab you can select Restart Each Page to start numbering footnotes again on each page.

7. Select OK.

Designating Note Separators

Word uses three types of note separators: The *separator* appears above the notes, separating them from the body text. The *continuation notice* appears after the notes, indicating they are continued on the next page. The *continuation separator* appears above the continued notes on that page. Notes are continued onto the next page when one page has too many notes to fit comfortably, and they can be fit onto the next page.

The default separator is a 2-inch line starting at the left margin. The default continuation separator is a line extending from the left to right margins. Word does not use a default continuation notice, but you can add one.

In Word for Windows 6, select Footnote Separator, Footnote Continuation Separator or Footnote Continuation Notice to open a note pane that displays the current separator or notice. In Word for Windows 2, select Separator, Cont. Separator or Cont. Notice to open a note pane that displays the current separator or notice. To delete the separator, highlight it and press DEL. Replace it with any characters or graphic elements. If you want to reset the note separator to its default, click the Reset button or press CTRL+SHIFT+R.

Designating Note Separators in Word for Windows 6

In Word for Windows 6, you cannot designate note separators until you have added that type of note into your document.

1. Add a footnote or endnote to the document.

2. Open the note pane by selecting View | Footnotes.

3. Select a type of note from the Notes drop-down list box in the pane's button bar. The options in the list box depend on what notes you have added to your document. If you have inserted both footnotes and endnotes, you can choose All Footnotes or All Endnotes to display the appropriate set in the note pane. The Separator, Continuation Separator, and Continuation Notice options are for the set of notes currently displayed in the pane.

4. Select the continuation separator or notice you want to edit.

5. Edit or create the continuation separator or notice using any of the usual text editing tools.

TIP: You can create lines as footnote or endnote separators by creating paragraph borders.

6. Close the note pane by selecting Close or pressing ALT+SHIFT+C.

DESIGNATING NOTE SEPARATORS IN WORD FOR WINDOWS 2

1. Select Insert | Footnote.

2. Select Options.

3. Select Separator, Cont. Separator, or Cont. Notice. Word opens the appropriate pane.

4. Create the continuation notice or separator you want to use.

TIP: You can create lines as footnote or endnote separators by creating paragraph borders.

5. Select Close from the note pane button bar.

Hints

Some of Word's features that make working with endnotes and footnotes more useful include dragging and dropping the notes to move and copy them, putting notes in columns, formatting the notes, hiding them, referencing note numbers in another location and indexing them.

Drag and Drop Notes

You can move notes using drag and drop. Drag the note reference mark from its current location to where you want it, and release the mouse button. The note itself will move to the appropriate place, even though you have not actually moved the note's text. If you are using automatically numbered note reference marks, Word will renumbers the repositioned note.

Notes in Columns

When you add notes to text in columns, Word places the notes for that column's text at the bottom of the column. For the purpose of notes, Word essentially treats each column as a separate page.

Note Formatting

Notes and note reference marks are formatted using the Footnote Reference, Endnote Reference, Endnote Text, and Footnote Text styles. By default, the two note text styles use the Normal style's font in 10 point. The two note reference styles use the Normal style's font in 8 point and superscript. To change the formatting for all notes and reference marks, simply change these styles. The box "Footnote Forms" describes the format most commonly used for various source material.

You can also apply the usual formatting features and techniques for formatting text in your notes. For example, to apply italic to text in your note, you can use the Italic button on the toolbar or ribbon, or press CTRL+I.

Viewing Notes

How you view notes depends on the Word view you are using. In Page Layout view, the notes are displayed on the page where Word will print then. To edit them, you move the insertion point to their location and edit them as you do text. If you double-click a note reference mark, Word moves your insertion point to the note text. You can return to the note reference mark's location by pressing the Go Back key, SHIFT+F5.

In Normal view, you have to open the Note pane to view notes. You can do this in several ways: Select View | Footnotes, or double-click a note reference

---

Footnote Forms

Many professional societies have their own specialized style conventions for footnotes and endnotes. You will need to follow the style of the organization or group for whom you are writing. If you are writing an academic paper, you will probably be asked to follow the conventions of Turabian style, the Modern Language Association, or the Chicago Manual of Style. If you need a reference for your general business writing you can use these general rules for the two most common types of references:

For books:

[1] Author name, <u>book title</u> (place of publication: publisher name, publication year), page numbers if applicable.

[1] John Smith, <u>Lazy Days of Summer</u> (New York: Wonder Press, 1993), 301-325.

For magazine articles:

[1] Author name, "article title," <u>magazine name</u> (publication date): page numbers.

[1] Emily Richards, "Watching Stars by Day," <u>Star Watcher Gazette</u> (July 1993): 57-59.

mark, or press SHIFT while dragging the split pane icon down. In Normal view, pressing F6 switches the insertion point between the note pane and the document without closing the note pane. As you switch between notes in the note pane, the view of the document in the top of the window changes to show the part containing the note reference containing the insertion point.

Suppressing Notes

You can choose to have notes (endnotes only in Word for Windows 6) print at the end of each section of your document or print all notes from every section at the end of the document. When you suppress notes for a section, they appear at the end of the next section, as if they were part of that second section. For example, the first section of a document has three columns and the next section of the document has no column division, suppressing the endnotes in the three-column section puts the endnotes for the three-column section with the endnotes for the section that does not have the column division. Supressing notes is done on a section by section basis rather than applying it to the entire document.

To suppress notes in a section, move the insertion point to that section, or select text in all the sections where you want to suppress notes. In Word for Windows 6, select File | Page Setup and the Layout tab, select the Suppress Endnotes check box, and OK. This check box is only available if you have already formatted endnotes to appear at the end of sections instead of the end of the document. In Word for Windows 2, select Format | Section Layout and then the Suppress Footnotes check box. Select OK to return to your document.

Referencing Notes

You can create a cross-reference to another note using the NOTEREF field type. To use this field type, you must first insert a bookmark in the note you want to reference. Then enter a {NOTEREF} field in the note containing the reference. The NOTEREF field type takes the format

{NOTEREF "*bookmark*"} in Word for Windows 6
or
{FTNREF "*bookmark*"} in Word for Windows 2

where *bookmark* is the bookmark name in the note that you are referencing. The field's result is the number of the note containing the bookmark.

For more information on inserting fields and bookmarks, see "Bookmarks" and "Fields."

Indexing Footnotes

In Word for Windows 6, you can index text that appears in footnotes or endnotes the same way that you index document text. You cannot index text in footnotes in Word for Windows 2. See "Index" for more information.

Related Topics

Bookmarks
Fields
Index
Sections

Forcing Text to a Page

See "Sections."

Foreign Language Support

When you work with text in a language other than English, you tell Word's proofing tools to use a different dictionary for that text. You can also tell Word that you want to use a different language for documents created with a template.

Procedures

1. Select the text in the other language.

2. Select Tools | Language, to open the Language dialog box (Format | Language in Word for Windows 2).

3. Choose a language from the Mark Selected Text As list box, and select OK.

NOTE: If you want Word to skip over the selected text during grammar and spell checking, choose the no proofing option, the first item in the list box. Use this option for tables of abbreviations, sections of programming code, or other types of text that you want Word's proofing tools to skip over.

If you want the language you are selecting to be the default language for documents created with a particular template, select Default (Use as Default in Word for Windows 2) from the Language dialog box. Word prompts you to confirm that you want that language to be the default for all new documents created using the same template as the one used in the document you are working on. If you select Yes, every document subsequently created using that template will be formatted for that language. If you select No, the default language is not changed.

Hints

When you are using a proofing tool, such as the Spelling Checker, Grammar Checking, or Thesaurus, Word automatically switches to the dictionary of the language the text is formatted as. If you do not have a dictionary for that language, Word displays a dialog box telling you that it cannot locate the dictionary. After you select OK from this dialog box, Word skips the formatted text, and proceeds to the next text in the document.

To purchase alternate language dictionaries for use with Word, contact Microsoft through the phone numbers in your program documentation.

Related Topics

Grammar Checking
Spelling
Templates
Thesaurus

Form Letters

See "Mail Merge" and "Print Merge."

Format

See "Character Formats," "Paragraph Formats," "Sections," "Columns," "Borders and Shading," "Frames," or the name of a particular format you want to apply.

Format|AutoFormat

See "AutoFormat."

Format|Borders and Shading (Border in Word for Windows 2)

See "Borders and Shading."

Format|Bullets and Numbering

See "Lists."

Format|Change Case

See "Capitalization."

Format|Character

See "Character Formats," "Italics," "Bold," "Underline," "Strikethrough," "All Caps," "Small Capitals," "Super/Subscript," "Spacing Characters," "Text Color," and "Fonts."

Format|Columns

See "Columns."

Format|Drawing Object

See "Drawing on a Document."

Format | Drop Cap

See "Dropped Capitals."

Format | Font

See "Fonts."

Format | Frame

See "Frames."

Format | Heading Numbering

See "Outlines."

Format | Language

See "Foreign Language Support."

Format | Page Setup

See "Margins," "Paper Size and Orientation," and "Paper Source."

Format | Paragraph

See "Paragraph Formats," "Spacing," "Pagination," Indents," and "Alignment."

Format | Picture

See "Graphics."

Forma**t**|**S**ection Layout

See "Sections."

F**o**rmat|**S**tyle

See "Styles."

F**o**rmat|Style **G**allery

See "Styles."

F**o**rmat|**T**abs

See "Tabs."

Formatting an Index

See "Index."

Formatting Toolbar (Ribbon)

The Formatting toolbar (the ribbon in Word for Windows 2) lets you quickly apply many of the most popular formatting changes to text in a document. Adding the Formatting toolbar to your display is done following the same steps as for any other toolbar. Select View | Toolbars, then the Formatting check box, and then OK. Like other toolbars, you can customize the Formatting toolbar, as described in "Toolbar Options." Once the Formatting toolbar appears, you can click its buttons (see the table below) to apply formatting to selected text, or the text you are about to enter.

Toolbar Button	Name	Function	Described In
Normal ⬇	Style	Selects a style to apply	"Styles"
Times New Roman ⬇	Font	Selects a font to apply	"Fonts"
10 ⬇	Font Size	Selects a point size to apply	"Fonts"
B	Bold	Applies boldface	"Bold"
I	Italic	Applies italic	"Italic"
U	Underline	Applies underlines	"Underline"
▤	Align Left	Left-aligns paragraph	"Alignment"
▤	Center	Centers paragraph	"Alignment"
▤	Align Right	Right-aligns paragraph	"Alignment"
▤	Justify	Aligns paragraph on left and right sides	"Alignment"
▤	Numbering	Adds sequential numbers to paragraph	"Lists"
▤	Bullets	Adds bullet characters to paragraph	"Lists"
▤	Decrease Indent	Indents paragraph to previous tab stop	"Indents"
▤	Increase Indent	Indents paragraph to next tab stop	"Indents"
▦	Borders	Displays the Borders toolbar	"Borders and Shading"

Procedures

The Formatting toolbar is intended for the mouse. However, some of the buttons in the Formatting toolbar can be can be used by the keyboard. Other features available through the Formatting toolbar have keyboard shortcuts to use when using the mouse is not convenient.

Using the Formatting Toolbar (Ribbon) with the Mouse

1. Select the text to format, or move the insertion pointer to where you want to enter the formatted text.

2. Click the button for the formatting you want.

3. Make any selections that the button shows such as selecting the font, size, or style to apply to the text.

Using the Formatting Toolbar (Ribbon) with the Keyboard

Most of the Formatting toolbar buttons have keyboard shortcuts. These shortcuts either activate the button in the toolbar or apply the formatting that the button provides. The buttons and their key-combinations are listed in the following table:

NOTE: The buttons that do not have a keyboard shortcut are Numbering, Bullets, and Borders. You can apply the formatting that these buttons provide by using the Format | Bullets and Numbering command and the Format | Borders and Shading command.

Toolbar Button	Key-Combination
Style	CTRL+SHIFT+S
Font	CTRL+SHIFT+F
Font Size	CTRL+SHIFT+P
Bold	CTRL+B
Italic	CTRL+I
Underline	CTRL+U
Align Left	CTRL+L
Center	CTRL+E
Align Right	CTRL+R
Justify	CTRL+J
Decrease Indent	CTRL+SHIFT+M
Increase Indent	CTRL+M

Related Topics

Ruler
Toolbars
Toolbar Options

Forms

Use Word to created *printed forms* (forms to be printed and then filled out by hand or typewriter), or *on-line forms* (forms to be completed on a computer and then printed.

Printed forms are created using text editing commands, tables, borders, and symbols. Printed forms are not covered here in depth; see "Applications" in this section for an example form and the features used to create it.

On-line forms use fields and macros to prompt the user through the process of completing the form, and to adapt the form to the information entered. On-line forms in Word for Windows 2 are created using fields and macros, rather than any features especially designed for forms. Word for Windows 6 includes specific on-line form features, such as the Forms toolbar and new form fields. This section focuses on on-line forms using Word for Windows 6's new form features, although an example Word for Windows 2 form is also shown under "Applications," along with instructions for creating it.

Procedures

In Word for Windows 6, forms are created using standard formatting features, special form fields, and macros. The form fields let you add text, check box fields, and drop-down list box fields to your form. Word for Windows 6 provides a Forms toolbar with buttons for some of the more common tasks in creating a form.

Displaying the Forms Toolbar

To display the Forms toolbar, right-click on a blank space in another toolbar, and select Forms from the shortcut menu. You can also select Insert | Form Field, and Show Toolbar. The Forms toolbar is shown below; for full descriptions of the buttons, see "Forms Toolbar."

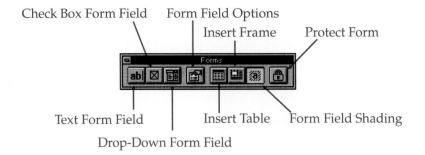

Check Box Form Field Form Field Options
Insert Frame Protect Form

Text Form Field Insert Table Form Field Shading

Drop-Down Form Field

Adding Form Fields with the Menus

1. Lay out your form.

   Create the document to include the information other than the form fields you will be adding. You can add form fields as you create the form in a document since you can always move form fields if you rearrange your form.

2. Position the insertion point where you want a field to appear, and select Insert | Form Field.

3. Select Text, Check Box, or Drop-Down, depending on the type of field you want to insert. The types of form fields are discussed later in "Options."

4. Select Options, and specify the options for this field, as described later in "Options."

5. When you're done, select OK twice.

TIP: Another way to add form fields while the Forms toolbar is displayed is to click the Text, Check Box, or Drop-Down Form Field button from the toolbar.

Specifying Options for Form Fields

1. Move the insertion point to the field.

2. Open the Form Field Options dialog box by either double-clicking the field, right-clicking and selecting Form Field Options from the shortcut menu, or clicking the Form Field Options button in the Forms toolbar.

3. Make your settings, as described in the "Options" section.

4. Select OK.

Locking the Document

The form fields that you add to your document do not act as form fields until you have locked your document as a form. To do this, click the Protect Form button on the Forms toolbar. You can also select Tools | Protect Document, then Forms, and OK. When you protect a form with the Tools | Protect Document command, you can prevent anyone from unlocking the document by adding a password when you lock the document. This password will have to be provided before the document can be unlocked. To unlock a form, select Tools | Unprotect Document or click the Protect Form button on the Forms toolbar. If a password is used to protect the form, you must supply the password before the form is unlocked. While a form is locked, you can only move from field to field in the form so you skip over everything else in the form.

TIP: If you lock a template, all documents created with that template are locked.

To prevent a section of the document from being locked, select Tools | Protect Document, then Forms, and then Sections. Clear the check boxes for the sections you don't want to lock. When you're done, select OK twice.

Options

A form can use many different types of fields. These fields are often identical to the items you use in a dialog box to make a selection. These different fields have their own settings that let you select how an entry is made, its initial value, and any limits on the entries you make.

Types of Form Fields

In Word for Windows 6 you can insert three types of form fields: text, check box, and drop-down list fields. In addition, there are six types of text fields, which you select by changing the options for that text field.

REGULAR TEXT FORM FIELD   Use a Regular text form field where any type of text might be inserted—letters, numbers, or symbols. You can set a default entry.

NUMBER TEXT FORM FIELD   Use a Number text form field when the entry is always going to be a number. Only numbers can be entered, and you can set a specific format for those numbers.

DATE TEXT FORM FIELD   Use a Date text form field when the entry is always going to be a date. Only valid dates can be entered, and you can set their display format. You can also set a default date.

CURRENT DATE OR TIME TEXT FORM FIELD   Use a Current Date or Current Time text form field to have Word supply the date or time the form is created or printed. You can set the format for the date or time, and choose whether these fields will be updated when the form is printed.

CALCULATION TEXT FORM FIELD   Use a Calculation text form field to total numbers or perform other calculations. You can enter a specific calculation in this field, and choose whether the total will be updated when the form is printed.

CHECK BOX FORM FIELD   Use a check box form field to get yes or no answers.

DROP-DOWN FORM FIELD   Use a drop-down form field to limit users' selection to a list of acceptable options for the field.

Options for Text Fields

The options for text fields include the type of text field, its initial value, the maximimum length of the entry, any format, when a macro is run, the bookmark name for the field, and help text.

TYPE   Select one of the six types of text form fields, described under "Types of Form Fields" above, from this drop-down list box.

DEFAULT/EXPRESSIONS   The title of this text box changes depending on the type of text form field selected for Type. In this box, enter the default entry for the field, whether it is a name, a date, or a value.

MAXIMUM LENGTH   Enter the field's maximum length in this spin box, or select Unlimited (the default).

FORMAT   The name of this drop-down list box, and the available formats, change depending on the type of text field selected for Type. Depending on the field, this list box offers date and time formats, capitalization formats, or number formats.

RUN MACRO ON   Word can run a macro when the insertion point enters or leaves the field. After Entry, select the macro to run when the insertion point enters this field; after Exit, enter the macro to run when leaving the field. These drop-down list boxes contain the macros you have in your document or template.

FIELD SETTINGS   In the Bookmark text box, enter a bookmark name that macros will use to reference the field. The default name is simply the field type and a sequential number. To prevent users from filling in this field, turn off the Fill-in Enabled option.

ADD HELP TEXT   Select Add Help Text to open the Form Field Help Text dialog box. Select Status Bar to designate help that will appear in the status bar when the insertion point is in the field, or Help Key to designate help that will appear when the user presses F1 from this field. Whichever tab you select, you can choose None to provide no help; AutoText Entry and an entry name to display the text of that entry; or Type Your Own, and type the help text into the text box. You can enter up to 255 characters' worth of advice to the user.

Options for Check Box Fields

The options for check box fields include the size of the check box, its initial value, when a macro is run, the bookmark name for the field, and help text.

CHECK BOX SIZE   Select Auto to make the text box the same size as the surrounding text, or Exactly to specify a check box size in points.

DEFAULT VALUE   Select Not Checked or Checked to specify the default setting for the check box form field.

RUN MACRO ON   Select the macro to run when the insertion point enters this field after Entry, and the macro to run when leaving after Exit. These drop-down list boxes contain the macros you have in your document or template.

FIELD SETTINGS   In the Bookmark text box enter a valid bookmark name to use in macros. Turn off the Fill-in Enabled option to prevent users from selecting or clearing this field.

ADD HELP TEXT   Select Add Help Text to open the Form Field Help Text dialog box. Then select the Status Bar or Help Key tab. On the tabs, choose None to provide no help; AutoText Entry and an entry name to display the text of that AutoText entry; or Type Your Own and up to 255 characters of help text in the text box.

Options for Drop-Down Fields

The options for drop-down fields include the items available in a drop-down list box, when a macro is run, the bookmark name for the field, and help text.

EDIT THE DROP-DOWN LIST   You can add items to the drop-down list, remove them, order the list, and edit items on it. Begin by entering items for the list in the Drop-Down Item text box, and select Add. The items then appear in the Items in Drop-Down List that lists all of the available choices for the drop-down list box in the form. Each item is added to the end of the list.

Sort the list by highlighting the item to move and selecting the Up or Down Move buttons beside the list. To remove an item from the list, highlight it and select Remove. To edit an item, highlight it, edit it in the Drop-Down Item text box, and select Add again.

RUN MACRO ON   After Entry, select the name of the macro to run when the insertion point enters this field; after Exit, select the macro to run when leaving the field. These drop-down list boxes contain the macros you have in your document or template.

FIELD SETTINGS   In the Bookmark text box enter a valid bookmark name to use in macros. Turn off the Fill-in Enabled option to prevent users from selecting this field.

ADD HELP TEXT   Select Add Help Text to open the Form Field Help Text dialog box. Then select the Status Bar or Help Key tabs. On the tabs, choose None to provide no help; AutoText Entry and an entry name to display the text of that AutoText entry; or Type Your Own and up to 255 characters of help text in the text box.

Applications

You can use forms for several purposes. You can create printed forms using Word's formatting. Word for Windows 2 can combine forms and macros to have a macro guide you through providing the information you need in a document. Word for Windows 6 takes advantage of the form capabilities so you can use the document as an interactive form.

Creating a Printed Form

Printed forms are meant to be filled out after they are printed. For example, the form shown in Figure 4-21 is printed, handed out to customers, and then returned after completion.

This form was very easy to create. The letterhead and the headings for each section are simply paragraphs. The sections that customers will complete are tables. A border was applied to the bottom of the cells in the second column of each table. In the first table, the second cell in the last two rows were split, making four cells in those two rows.

TIP: To create attractive check boxes in a printed form, try inserting symbols such as circles, boxes, and diamonds. Using unfamiliar shapes can add a unique flair to your form.

Creating an On-line Form with Word for Windows 2

In Word for Windows 2, you can create on-line forms using fields and macros that begin executing as soon as you open the document. Though you do not have all the special options that Word for Windows 6 has for creating on-line forms, they are still relatively easy to create.

For example, Figure 4-22 shows an on-line form created in Word for Windows 2 for recording telephone orders from Jame's Party Supplies catalog. When a document is opened using the order form template, a macro immediately begins, which moves from field to field. The macro continues adding lines to the lower part of the form to accommodate all of the ordered items, until the operator enters a zero, telling the macro to go to the last information in the form.

Creating an On-Line Form with Word for Windows 6

In Word for Windows 6, you can easily create a form to be completed on screen. For example, see Figure 4-23, which is a legal document. Each of the gray areas that you see is a form field. Those containing text are drop-down form fields, and are currently displaying the default settings for those fields. The drop-down list of the first field is displayed.

This document is locked, so pressing TAB or SPACEBAR moves you to the next field. Only form fields and sections of the document that were unprotected can be altered.

F

Gabrielle's
Wedding Invitations
212 Severn Way ♥ Akron, OH 44302
Tel: 216/722-3939 ♥ Fax: 216/722-4040

WEDDING INVITATION FORM

PERSON ORDERING

Name _____

Street Address _____

City, State, Zip _____

Phone (Day) _____ Phone (Evening) _____

Pick Up Date _____ Deposit _____

INVITATION

Paper Seleted _____

Design Selected _____

Inviters (Parents) _____

_____

Name of Bride _____

Name of Groom _____

Date and Time _____

Location (address) _____

RSVP AND RECEPTION INVITATION

RSVP Form _____

RSVP Address _____

City, State, Zip _____

Reception Address _____

State, City, Zip _____

Location _____

Time _____

FAX OR DROP OFF THIS FORM. CALL OUR MAIN OFFICE WITH ANY QUESTIONS.

Figure 4-21. *A printed form*

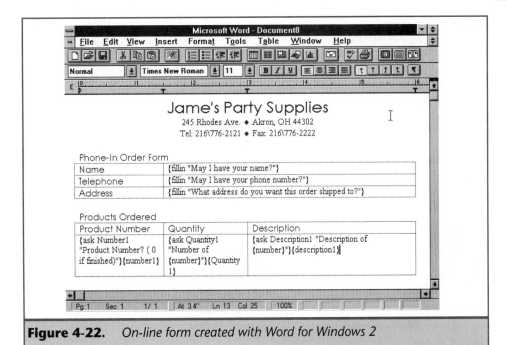

Figure 4-22. *On-line form created with Word for Windows 2*

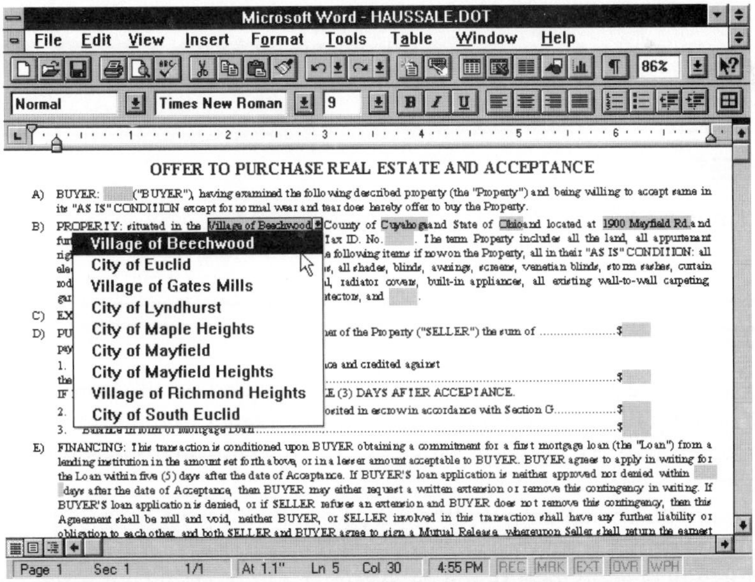

Figure 4-23. *On-line form created with Word for Windows 6*

Forms Toolbar

The Forms toolbar offers shortcuts for features useful in creating on-line forms. The purpose of each button is explained in the table below.

Toolbar Button	Name	Function
ab|	Text Form Field	Inserts a text form field with default options
⊠	Check Box Form Field	Inserts a check box form field with default options
	Drop-Down Form Field	Inserts a drop-down form field with default options
	Form Field Options	Opens the Form Field Options dialog box for the current form field
	Insert Table	Inserts a table
	Insert Frame	Inserts a frame
	Form Field Shading	Toggles between shading and not shading form fields
🔒	Protect Form	Toggles between locking and unlocking documents for forms

Formulas

See "Equation Editor" and the "EQ" field under "Fields."

FoxPro

FoxPro is a database management application designed for the Windows environment. Word can insert a FoxPro database, converting it into a Word table as it is opened. To work with this table, use Word's table features, described in the section on "Tables" in this chapter. Each line in the table is a record, and each column is a field. The column widths are determined by the field widths in FoxPro. Word shows the entire table, even if it is wider than the current page width. You will need to modify the page size or edit the table if it is too wide to print on the current page.

You can also embed FoxPro databases into Word documents and link FoxPro databases into Word documents. Word lets you start FoxPro from within Word by clicking the Microsoft FoxPro button in the Microsoft toolbar. Once you start FoxPro, you are using FoxPro, not Word, and you must follow FoxPro's menu and features.

Related Topics

Databases

Fractions

You can create fractions by inserting a symbol, using the Equation Editor, or using the {EQ} field.

The Insert I Symbol command can add symbols for ¼, ½, and ¾. These fractions appear the same size as the surrounding text.

You can also create fractions using the Equation Editor (see "Equation Editor").

The third option, using the {EQ} field, does not have as many complex options as the Equation Editor, but the fraction appears in line with other text. With the insertion point where you want the fraction, press CTRL+F9, and then type **EQ \f(x,y)** where x is the numerator of the fraction and y is the denominator of the fraction. Press F9. This last option lets you create simple fractions such as ⅞.

Frame-Positioned Object

See "Frames."

Frames

A *frame* is a box containing an object that appears in your document, such as a selection of text. You can move this frame to any position you want on the page. Use frames to position both text and graphics on your page. Putting text or graphics in a frame lets you wrap text around the contents of the frame.

Once a frame is added to a document, it can be moved and sized. Some items in Word are automatically in frames. For example, creating a dropped capital with the Word for Windows 6 command Format I Drop Cap puts the dropped capital in a frame.

Procedures

To use a frame, you need to add it to a document, either to surround existing text or graphics or add it and then add the contents you want inside the frame. Once you have the frame, you can move and size it to change how the framed contents appear in the document. You can also change the format of the frame so document text wraps around the frame's contents.

Inserting Frames

1. To frame objects that are already in your document, select them. You can select text, graphics, and tables. If you want to insert an empty frame, do not select anything; just move the insertion point where you want the frame placed.

2. Select Insert | Frame. Word for Windows 2 has a Frame button on the toolbar; the button has the white box and black lines around it.

3. If you are in Normal view, Word prompts you to change to the Page Layout view so you can see where the frame appears on the page. Select Yes to do so, or No to remain in Normal view.

If you selected something before inserting the frame, Word now adds the frame around the selected objects, large enough to surround the objects. If you are inserting an empty frame, you have to indicate the size of the frame for Word.

When you insert an empty frame, Word changes the pointer to a plus sign, which you use to indicate the correct size and position of the frame.

■ With the mouse, point to where you want one corner of the frame, drag the mouse to the diagonally opposite corner, and release the mouse button.

■ With the keyboard, use the arrow keys to move the pointer to one corner of the frame, press ENTER, move to the diagonally opposite corner, and press ENTER again. You can move the pointer with the arrow keys, or by pressing SHIFT and the arrow keys to move larger distances.

TIP: When working with frames, use the Page Layout view. This view shows the frame and surrounding text in the same location where the text and frame contents will appear when you print the document. Normal view displays the frame and its contents separately from the text beside which it will appear. Some features, such as wrapping text around a frame, do not appear unless you are in Page Layout view.

Moving a Frame

Follow these steps to move a frame with the mouse:

1. Switch to Page Layout view.

2. Position the mouse pointer inside the frame. The pointer turns into a four-headed arrow plus the pointer.

3. Drag the frame to its new position. The dotted line around the frame moves with the mouse pointer, but the text won't move to the new location until you release the mouse button.

Follow these steps to move a frame with the keyboard:

1. Switch to Page Layout view.

2. Position the insertion point inside the frame using the arrow keys.

3. Select Format | Frame, to open this Frame dialog box:

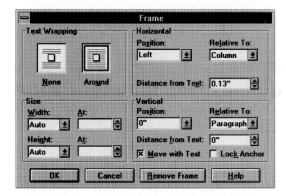

4. Under Horizontal and under Vertical, enter your choices determining the horizontal and vertical positions of the frame, as explained under "Options" in this section. Then select OK.

Sizing a Frame

Follow these steps to size a frame with the mouse:

1. Click on the frame to select it. Eight sizing handles appear on the frame, at each corner and in the middle of each side, as shown in Figure 4-24.

2. Move the insertion point to one of the sizing handles. When the mouse pointer is correctly positioned, the mouse pointer turns into a double-headed arrow.

3. Drag the sizing handle so that the frame is the size you want it.

Follow these steps to size a frame with the keyboard:

1. Using the arrow keys, position the insertion point inside the frame.

2. Select Format | Frame, to open the Frame dialog box shown earlier.

3. Under Size, make selections and enter choices to set the size of the frame, as explained under "Options." Then select OK.

Wrapping Text Around a Frame

Move the insertion point to the frame. Then select Format | Frame, or select Format Frame from the shortcut menu when you right-click the frame, to open the Frame dialog box. Under Text Wrapping, make the selections to determine

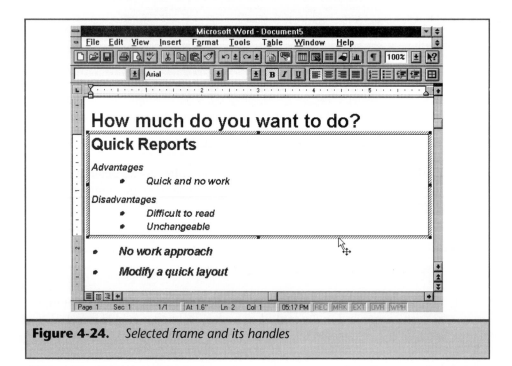

Figure 4-24.   *Selected frame and its handles*

how the text wraps. These choices are explained under "Options" below. When you're done, select OK.

Options

There are variety of options in the Frame dialog box for formatting a frame. You can choose how text wraps around the frame, the size of the frame, and its position.

Text Wrapping

Choose None or Around. With None, the text will not appear beside the frame (as in Normal view). Choose Around, and if there is at least 1 inch of space between the edges of the frame and the margins of the document, Word will place text beside the graphic. Using the Vertical and Horizontal options, you can control how close to the graphic the text is positioned. Figure 4-25 shows a frame with text wrapped around it.

Figure 4-25.   *Frames with text wrapped around*

Size

Set the size of the frame by defining its width and height:

■ Select Auto in the Width or Height drop-down list boxes to let Word determine the best size for the frame based on its contents.

■ Choose Exactly for either Width and Height and then enter a measurement in the At text box. When you choose Exactly, the frame's size does not change as the frame's contents shrink and expand.

■ Choose At Least in the Height drop-down list box and enter a value in the At text box. Word will not reduce the frame to less than this height, but it will increase the frame's height if needed.

Horizontal

The options under Horizontal set the horizontal position of the frame. You define the exact position of the upper-left corner of the frame in terms of distance from the margin or the edge of the paper. You can also specify how close the text can come to the edges of the frame when it is wrapped around the frame.

First, select Page, Margin, or Column from the Relative To drop-down list box; this tells Word where to start measuring. Word measures from the left edge of the paper when you select Page, from the left margin when you select Margin, or from the left margin of the column when you select Column.

Next, select one of the distance choices in the Position drop-down list box or type in the measurement. The left side of the frame is placed at this distance from the object you select in the Relative To list box. For example, if you choose Paper from the Relative To list box and enter 3" in the Position text box, the left side of your frame is positioned at 3 inches from the left side of the paper. You will typically want to use Margin for Relative To, and an option such as Left or Right to put the frame against the left or right margin.

When you select Around, you can also control how close the text can come to the sides of the frame, by entering a measurement in the Distance from Text text box. The text will come no closer than that distance to the sides of the frame, giving you a margin around the frame.

Vertical

Using the Vertical options, you can set the vertical position of the frame, either by defining the vertical position of the upper edge of the frame, or by keeping it with the text that surrounds it. You can also designate how close the text comes to the top and bottom of the frame.

Choose Paragraph, Margin, or Page from the Relative To drop-down list box to set the frame's relative placement to the top of the paragraph, the top margin, or the top of the page. Then select one of the position options from the Position drop-down list box, or type a measurement.

To control how close the text comes to the top and bottom edges of the frame, enter a measurement in the Distance from Text text box. You can use this text box to create a margin around the frame to make a graphic or other framed item stand away from the surrounding text.

Turn on the Move with Text check box to make the frame move up or down as you add text above or below the frame's position. Turn on Lock Anchor, and the frame remains with the current paragraph.

> *TIP:* *Dragging a frame in the Page Layout view of a document changes the horizontal and vertical positions to Page so the frame is placed on the page relative to the page's dimensions rather than the margin or column edge. Word also changes the distances in the Position drop-down list boxes to the actual distance from the top or left side of the page to the top or left side of the frame.*

Removing the Frame

Select Remove Frame to remove the frame from the document. The frame's contents will appear just before the first paragraph the frame was in.

Hints

Use frames to precisely control the position of text and graphics on your page. When printing on forms, you need to determine exactly where your text is going to appear, so that it prints in the correct location on the page. Frames help you to ensure that your printed form looks professional.

You can also use frames to insert graphics and tables into newsletters, brochures, and other documents in an interesting way. You can wrap text around a frame, allowing you to include graphics, as shown in Figure 4-25, that stretch across columns.

Create drop-capitals with frames in Word for Windows 2. To create drop-capitals, put the first letter in a frame and then modify its font or size. The frame should have text wrap-around, a left horizontal position, a vertical position relative to the paragraph, and should move with the text.

Remember that frames are not the same as borders. If you want a visual frame around the contents of a framed object, select the frame and add a border with the Format | Borders and Shading command or the Borders toolbar. The Borders command has options that also set the distance between the border and the text. The distance between the frame's border and the surrounding text is set with the Format | Frame command.

A frame's size and position do not determine the size and position of the frame's contents. To change the portion of a graphic that appears within a frame, or enlarge it or reduce it, do not try to do it by moving or sizing. Instead, change its scaling, using the Format | Picture command. This command also can crop the graphic from the sides, top, or bottom, when you want to change the section of the graphic that appears in the frame.

Text contents inside a frame can have formats different from those of the surrounding text. Text inside a frame can use most of the formatting you apply to a document. The frame gives the effect of having a miniature document inside another.

If you plan to spend time formatting the contents of a frame, you may want to create the frame's contents in another document, frame it, copy it to the Clipboard, and then paste both the frame and its contents into the other document. This way, you can apply the formatting you want to the frame's contents without worrying that you are including other document contents you do not want.

Related Topics

Borders and Shading
Captions
Graphics
Margins

Function Keys

The function keys are the keys labeled F1 through F10 or F12. These keys provide shortcuts for carrying out Word commands. They can be combined with the ALT, CTRL, and SHIFT keys to expand the range of choices. The keys and the commands they execute are shown in the following table.

NOTE: Some keyboards do not have the F11 *and* F12 *keys. On these keyboards, press* ALT+F1 *for* F11 *and* ALT+F2 *for* F12. *For key-combinations such as* SHIFT+F12, *press* ALT+SHIFT+F2.

Function Key	Action
F1	Open a Help topic regarding the Word operation you are currently doing
SHIFT+F1	Change the mouse pointer so you can click the part of the screen about which you want more information
F2	Move the selected text and graphics to the location you select before pressing ENTER
CTRL+F2	Preview the current document in Word for Windows 6, or set the font to the next larger size in Word for Windows 2
SHIFT+F2	Copy the selected text and graphics to the location you select before pressing ENTER
CTRL+SHIFT+F2	Set the font to the next smaller size in Word for Windows 2
F3	Insert a Word for Windows 2 glossary entry
CTRL+F3	Cut text or graphics to Word's Spike
SHIFT+F3	Cycle the selected text through lowercase, uppercase, and proper case (initial-cap)
CTRL+SHIFT+F3	Insert the Spike's contents and clear the Spike
F4	Repeat previous action
ALT+F4	Close application window, exiting Word
CTRL+F4	Close the current document window
SHIFT+F4	Repeat the last Find or Go To command
F5	Go to an annotation, bookmark, field, line, page, or section
ALT+F5	Restore application window to its previous size
CTRL+F5	Restore document window to its previous size
SHIFT+F5	Go to a prior insertion point position
CTRL+SHIFT+F5	Open the Bookmark dialog box to insert a bookmark
F6	Go to the next pane
ALT+F6	Go to the next document window
CTRL+F6	Go to the next document window
SHIFT+F6	Go to the previous pane
ALT+SHIFT+F6	Go to the previous document window
CTRL+SHIFT+F6	Go to the previous document window
F7	Check the selected text's spelling

F

Function Key	Action
CTRL+F7	Move a document window if it is not maximized
SHIFT+F7	Open the Thesaurus dialog box
CTRL+SHIFT+F7	Update all links
F8	Extend a selection in extend mode
CTRL+F8	Size a document window
SHIFT+F8	Shrink a selection in extend mode
CTRL+SHIFT+F8	Select a column of text
F9	Update the selected fields
ALT+F9	Minimize the application window
CTRL+F9	Insert an empty field
SHIFT+F9	Toggle between showing field codes or field results
ALT+SHIFT+F9	Select a field as if you double-clicked it
CTRL+SHIFT+F9	Replace a field with its last result
F10	Activate the menu bar
ALT+F10	Maximize application window
CTRL+F10	Maximize current document window
SHIFT+F10	Display shortcut menu for the selected object in Word for Windows 6, or activate a Word for Windows 2 Annotation, Outline, Header/Footer, or Macro toolbar
CTRL+SHIFT+F10	Activate the Word for Windows 2 ruler
F11	Go to the next field
CTRL+F11	Lock a field
SHIFT+F11	Go to the previous field
CTRL+SHIFT+F11	Unlock a field
F12	Open the Save As dialog box
CTRL+F12	Open the Open dialog box
SHIFT+F12	Save the current document
CTRL+SHIFT+F12	Open the Print dialog box

General Options

You can set some general default options for Word.

Procedures

1. Select Tools | Options.

2. Select the General tab (icon in the Category box in Word for Windows 2).

3. Select or clear the check boxes or select a new unit in the Measurement Units drop-down list box to make the default settings. The options are explained under "Options" below.

4. Select OK.

Options

Word for Windows 2 and 6 offer different options. Many of the General options in Word for Windows 2 are offered on the Edit tab of the Options dialog box in Word for Windows 6, and are therefore covered under "Edit Options." When the same option has a different name in Word for Windows 2 and 6, the Word for Windows 6 option is listed with the Word for Windows 2 option included in parentheses.

Background Repagination

Clearing this check box means that Word does not repaginate when you pause. Background repagination is always on in Page Layout view and Print Preview, no matter what this setting is. Select this check box to have Word recalculate page breaks whenever you pause typing or editing. Pages are always repaginated when you switch to Page Layout view or Print Preview.

Typing Replaces Selection (Word for Windows 2 Only)

Select this check box to have selected text deleted when you start typing the replacement text. When this option is off, Word moves the selected text to the left when you enter replacement text, retaining both the old and new text. See "Edit Options" for the equivalent command in Word for Windows 6.

Drag-and-Drop Text Editing (Word for Windows 2 Only)

Select this check box to move text by dragging selected text with the mouse. When it is cleared, you must use either the Spike or the Clipboard to move text. See "Edit Options" for the equivalent command in Word for Windows 6.

Confirm File Conversions (Word for Windows 2 Only)

Select this check box when you want to confirm the file format when opening files saved in a non-Word for Windows 2 format. When it is cleared, Word converts the file based on its extension without prompting for confirmation. When the file name extension and the actual format do not match, the file either does not convert at all, or converts incorrectly. See "Opening Files" for the equivalent command in Word for Windows 6.

Use INS Key to Paste (Word for Windows 2 Only)

Select this check box to paste the contents of the Clipboard into the document by pressing INS. With this setting activated, you cannot switch between insert and overtype modes. When this check box is cleared, INS only switches between insert and overtype modes. See "Edit Options" for the equivalent command in Word for Windows 6.

Overtype Mode (Word for Windows 2)

When this check box is selected, characters that you type replace the characters in front of the insertion point. When this check box is cleared, characters in front of the insertion point are moved to the right to make room for characters being entered. See "Edit Options" for the equivalent command in Word for Windows 6.

Help for WordPerfect Users (WordPerfect Help)

With this check box selected, each time you press a function key, Word interprets it as a WordPerfect 5.1 command, and offers help on how to carry out the same procedure with Word.

Navigation Keys for WordPerfect Users (WordPerfect Document Navigation Keys)

When this check box is selected, Word reacts the same way WordPerfect does to the keys used for moving the insertion point. When this is cleared, these keys react as explained in this book.

Blue Background, White Text (Word for Windows 6 Only)

Select this check box to have Word display your document as blue on white. This does not affect any other color assignments in Windows, as changing the colors in the Windows Control Panel would do.

Beep on Error Actions (Word for Windows 6 Only)

Clear this check box to stop Word from beeping whenever an error occurs. Select the check box to have it beep again.

3D Dialog and Display Effects (Word for Windows 6 Only)

Clear this check box to have Word stop using a 3D effect in dialog boxes and other display elements. Select it to return to the 3D display.

For example, Figure 4-26 shows the Break dialog box with and without the 3D effects.

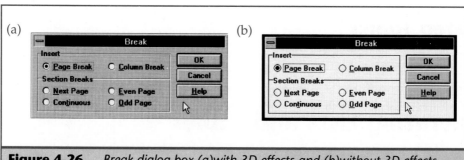

Figure 4-26.   *Break dialog box (a)with 3D effects and (b)without 3D effects*

Update Automatic Links at Open (Word for Windows 6 Only)

Clear this box to prevent Word from automatically updating any links to other files in a document when it is opened. When selected, Word will update those links in the process of opening the file. See "Object Linking and Embedding" for an explanation of how linked documents work.

Mail as Attachment (Word for Windows 6 Only)

Clear the check box to have Word use your documents as the text of messages sent using an electronic mail system from Word rather than attaching your document as a separate file.

Recently Used File List (Word for Windows 6 Only)

Clear this check box to stop displaying recently used files at the bottom of File menu. The value in the Entries text box indicates how many files are displayed. Nine is the maximum.

Measurement Units

The unit chosen in the Measurement Units drop-down list box is the one Word assumes is used in dialog boxes and uses to display the ruler. You can enter measurements in other units when you add the unit's code after the measurement.

Related Topics

Edit Options

Generating Lists and Tables

See "Tables of Contents and Figures," "Index," or "Table of Authorities."

Global Search

See "Find and Replace."

Global Templates

See "Templates."

Glossary

A glossary entry is a frequently used set of text or graphics which you have stored, along with the name. You can enter the text or graphic by typing the name and activating the glossary feature, to replace the name with the entry. The Glossary feature is called the AutoText feature in Word for Windows 6, and is explained under that heading.

Procedures

The first step in using the glossary is to define the glossary entry. Then you can insert the glossary entry wherever is convenient. You can edit the glossary entry's contents or name, or delete the glossary entry when it is no longer useful.

Defining a Glossary Entry

1. Select the text, graphic, or combination you want to repeatedly insert into a document. Remember to select the paragraph character to apply paragraph formatting.

2. Select Edit | Glossary, to open the Glossary dialog box. The text you selected appears after Selection. If you selected a picture or graphic, the field for that picture or graphic is displayed instead of the picture itself.

3. Type a name, up to 31 characters long, in the Glossary Name text box. To avoid complications, don't add spaces to the name.

4. Select Define.

If the current document uses the Normal template, Word automatically stores the glossary entry with the Normal template, making it available for all documents.

If the current document uses another template, Word may prompt you to specify where the glossary entry is to be stored. When you select Define, Word opens another Glossary dialog box.

Select the "as Global" option button, and Word saves the glossary entry with the Normal template, making it available in all documents. When you quit Word, Word displays a dialog box prompting you to confirm that you want to save the changes to the global glossary settings. Select Yes to save all the glossary changes you have made for future use. Select No, and you will lose the glossary entries.

If you select the "in Template" option button, the glossary entry is stored with the template used by the current document. The glossary entry is available only for documents created with this template. When you close the current document, or the last open document that uses this template, Word prompts you to confirm that you want to save the template. Select Yes to store the new glossary entries with the template for future use, or select No and lose the new glossary entries.

Inserting a Glossary Entry with Menus

1. Put the insertion point where you want the glossary entry's contents.

2. Select Edit | Glossary.

3. Highlight the glossary entry name in the Glossary Name list box.

4. To insert the glossary entry's contents with formatting select Insert. Select Insert as Plain Text to insert the glossary entry's contents without any formatting, causing it to pick up the formats applied to the surrounding text.

Inserting a Glossary Entry with Shortcut Keys

1. Type the glossary entry name in your document, making sure it is preceded by a paragraph character or a space.

2. Put the insertion point at the end of the name, and press F3.

Editing a Glossary Entry's Contents

1. Insert the contents of the glossary entry, and edit it.

2. Select the edited glossary entry.

3. Select Edit | Glossary.

4. Highlight the glossary entry's name in the Glossary Name list box.

5. Select Define. Word prompts you to confirm that you want to redefine the glossary entry. Select Yes to use the new contents or No to keep the old contents.

Changing a Glossary Entry's Name

1. Insert the glossary entry's contents and select them.

2. Select Edit | Glossary.

3. Highlight the glossary name from the Glossary Name list box, and select Delete.

4. Type the new name in the Glossary Name text box and select Define.

Deleting a Glossary Entry

You may find that after a while, certain glossary entries become obsolete, and need to be deleted from your templates to keep your templates uncluttered.

1. Select Edit | Glossary.

2. Highlight the glossary entry to delete in the Glossary Name list box.

3. Select Delete

4. Select Close.

Printing Glossary Entries

1. Open a new document using the template containing the glossary entries you want to print. To print the global glossary entries, any template will do.

2. Select File | Print.

3. Select Glossary in the Print drop-down list box.

4. Select OK.

Hints

You can use Word's Spike to gather selected text and graphics from your document and copy or move them to a new location. If you only need a few copies of text or graphics, consider using the Spike or the Windows Clipboard instead of a glossary entry.

Use glossary entries for items to insert repeatedly and at different times. For example, use an art file containing a scanned signature instead of signing all letters. Saving this signature as a glossary entry for a Letter template and inserting it will be faster than signing form letters.

You can also use glossary entries for frequently repeated text to ensure that the text is consistently entered. For example, an equation, a section of a contract, or a frequently used paragraph in letters could be entered and edited once, and then made into a glossary entry, for frequent, error-free use.

Remember that glossary entries can include formatting, as well as text and graphic elements. You use glossary entries for frequently repeated text and graphics with complicated formatting that you do not want to create each time.

Related Topics

AutoText
Clipboard
Fields
Spike

Glossary Entries

See "Glossary."

Go To

See "Moving the Insertion Point."

GOTOBUTTON Field

See "Fields."

Grammar Checking

You can use Word's grammar feature to check your document for grammatical errors, spelling mistakes, and poor grammatical style. You can control which grammar rules are checked by changing the options for this command.

Procedures

1. Put the insertion point at the beginning of the document. To check only a section of the text, select it instead.

2. Select Tools | Grammar. Word immediately begins checking your document, one sentence at a time.

3. When Word finds a sentence that violates the rules of grammar and style it is checking for, it displays the Grammar dialog box. The sentence containing the possible error appears in the Sentence text box. The words of the error are bold. The possible corrections appear in the Suggestions list box.

4. If you do not understand the error that Word is pointing out, select Explain. Word provides an explanation of the rule of grammar the sentence may violate.

5. Select a change from the Suggestions list box or highlight it and select Change to change the sentence.

    Select Ignore to have Word skip the current problem and continue checking the grammar. Select Ignore Rule to have Word ignore the grammar rule it is using for the remainder of the grammar check. Select Next Sentence to have Word skip the current sentence and move to the next one Word finds a problem with.

6. When Word finishes the grammar check it displays a set of *readability statistics* about the document. Select OK to close this dialog box.

Unless you select text beforehand, Word checks the grammar of your document from the insertion point to the end of the document. If the insertion point was not at the beginning of the document, when Word reaches the end of the document, it asks you if you want to start checking from the beginning of the document. When you select No, the Readability Statistics dialog box appears. When you select Yes, Word continues checking the document from the beginning, and finishes when it returns to where it originally started.

Options

You have several options for what action you can take when Word flags text as grammatically incorrect.

G

Ignore

Select this button to have Word skip the problem it found in the sentence. Only this specific error is ignored. Any other errors in the sentence are flagged, and any other violations of the same rule of grammar are flagged.

Change

First highlight a suggested change in the Suggestions list box. Next, select Change to have Word change the text of your document as described in the Suggestions list box, removing the error. You can also select Change after selecting Sentence in Word for Windows 6 changing the sentence with the grammar error.

Remember that Word does not actually understand English, and will mark some correct text as wrong. If you do not understand why Word has flagged some text, select Explain to find out how Word thinks your document is incorrect. You may find that Word did not accurately interpret the construction of your sentence. For example, users of English seem to use adverbs and adjectives interchangeably at times, because of where the word appears in the sentence. Word may misinterpret what word the adjective or adverb modifies, and therefore tell you to change to a different modifier. See the box, "Rules for Adjectives and Adverbs" to find rules that will help you determine whether Word's advice is right or wrong.

Rules for Adjectives and Adverbs

Adjectives always modify nouns, and adverbs always modify verbs. Although these rules can never be broken there are many instances in English when it is easy to confuse the modifier needed. The following rules will help you make the right choices:

■ When the form of the verb "to be" is followed by a word describing the sentence subject, an adjective is used. For example, "He is tired." When you substitute another descriptive verb such as looks or feels, an adjective is still used. For example, "He looks tired."

■ Adjectives and adverbs have more than one form depending on whether they are used to refer to one item or action, to compare two, or to differentiate when more than two are referred to in the comparison. The three forms are called positive, comparative, and superlative. Many adjectives form their comparative form with *er* and their superlative with *est*. Comparative is used to compare one thing or person against another and superlative is used to compare one

Rules for Adjectives and Adverbs (*continued*)

person against a group or another person. These forms should never be interchanged.

■ Never use adverbs that do not add additional meaning to the verb. For example, "We will unite together to fight this problem" should be written as "We will unite to fight this problem."

■ Good and well are frequently used incorrectly. *Well* is the adverb, and *good* is the adjective. For example, compare "Sharon stayed home from school since she was not feeling *well*" and "The new secretary received a *good* grade in the computer class."

■ Some adjectives and adverbs have irregular forms. Be especially careful when using the comparative and superlative forms. For example: *good, better, best.*

■ Latter and last are frequently confused. Latter is used when discussing two objects and last when there are a group of more than two. Of the two desserts you mentioned, I will have the *latter*. The *last* dessert on our menu is the most popular.

■ Adverbs can normally be formed by adding *ly* to an adjective although there are some adjectives that end in *ly*. For example, he was a lowly servant in the household.

■ Adjectives and adverbs with many syllables normally form their comparative and superlative forms with *more, most, less,* and *least*. For example, "He was the *most* troublesome lad at the school."

■ Do not use two negative adverbs together. For example, "We never hardly planted in the garden before" is wrong. It should be "We hardly planted in the garden before" or "We never planted in the garden before."

■ Keep adjectives and adverbs as close as possible to the word they modify.

G

Next Sentence

You may have a sentence that you know Word will find several errors in, but do not want to change. Select Next Sentence when the first error in the sentence is flagged. Word then skips to the next sentence, ignoring any further errors.

Use this command when checking elements in a table, since the table entries probably are not complete sentences. Also, this command is useful when you use quotations that do not conform to Word's grammar rules, or when intentionally creating an ungrammatical sentence for emphasis.

Ignore Rule

Word checks your document using many grammatical rules. At times, you may not want to apply all the rules to your document. For example, a personal letter does not need to be as grammatically accurate as a business proposal.

When Word uses a grammar rule you do not want to apply to your document, select Ignore Rule. Word no longer applies that rule of grammar to your document.

Explain

When you select Explain, Word displays a dialog box containing an explanation of the error currently flagged. Word does not explain how your sentence is incorrect. Instead, Word explains the rule of grammar your sentence supposedly violates including examples. Press ESC or double-click the control menu button to return to the Grammar dialog box.

Options

Selecting Options opens the Grammar Options dialog box, from which you can select the set of grammar rules you want applied to your document, and whether you want readability statistics to appear when you are done. These features are described fully under "Grammar Options."

Hints

Remember that Word is only a computer program, not an English professor. A sentence or phrase flagged as incorrect isn't necessarily incorrect. Word has difficulty understanding unusual phrasing or odd sentence construction. Sometimes, its corrections will seem nonsensical to you. Remember to use the grammar checker as a guide to potential errors, but not as the final arbiter of what is correct.

For example, Word might run into difficulty with pronouns. See the box, "Rules for Using Pronouns Correctly" to see some rules that govern how pronouns should be used. Word may not catch all of your violations of these rules, or it may flag as incorrect a usage that fits these rules. Remember to consider Word's suggestions carefully, but in light of your own grammatical understanding.

Rules for Using Pronouns Correctly

Pronouns are tricky because they come in several forms. You first need to decide whether to use first, second, or third person (I, you, he/she). You also need to decide whether you want the singular or plural form of that person (I/we, you/you, he/she/it/they). The last decision is which case to use depending on the pronouns within the sentence. The subject of a sentence uses nominative case, objects of the sentence or of a preposition use objective case, and possessive case is used to denote ownership. There are also many different types of pronouns: personal pronouns, relative pronouns, and possessive pronouns. All of the rules are too numerous to list here but these are some of the important ones:

- A plural pronoun should be used when it refers to more than one word. For example, *"Dave* and *I* propose we begin to write the book immediately" or "*Dave* and *Carol* think *they* will be able to join us on Thanksgiving."

- If the pronoun is intended to reference only one of the words, the singular form will be used: "*John, Dave,* or *Mark* will give up *his* day off to insure that we have adequate staffing on Saturday."

- Pronouns used in comparisons are tricky and are best determined by pretending to finish the sentence with extra words. For example, "Dave writes better than I." When you change the sentence to "...than I write," it is clear that the pronoun cannot be *me.*

- The form of the pronoun is the object form when the pronoun is the object of a sentence or the object of a preposition. For example, "John invited *Karen* and *me* to the opera on Saturday" and "Let's keep the secret between *you* and *me.*"

- Possessive pronouns and similar contractions are sometimes confused but are very different words. For example, "The cat is washing its paws." You cannot substitute *it's* which means *it is.*

- Use *which* and *that* to refer to things. Use *that* when the clause it introduces is required for a meaningful sentence and *which* when the sentence is meaningful without the clause. For example, "The house that sold last week was on the market for three weeks." Compare that to "Karen's new listing, which I saw last Thursday, may be just the right house for you."

- Use *who* and *that* when referring to people. These words parallel the use of *which* and *that* for required and nonrequired clauses in rule 6.

Rules for Using Pronouns Correctly (*continued*)

- The relative pronoun *whose* and the contraction *who's* meaning *who is* are often confused. For example, "Whose coat is this?" versus "Who's the better writer?"

- The indefinite pronouns, *everyone* and *anyone*, are always singular and require a singular verb. For example, "Everyone at the office tries to please the new director."

- For clarity, pronouns such as *it* or *they* may have to be replaced by a noun. For example, "Money, security, and pleasant working conditions are important to most employees; they are important to a productive workplace." It is unclear whether the employees or the rewards are important. You could rewrite the part of the sentence to read, "these *conditions* are important to a productive workplace."

Related Topics

Grammar Options
Spelling
Thesaurus

Grammar Options

You can set options for Words grammar checking using the Grammar Options dialog box.

Procedures

You can open this box in two ways.

Setting Options While Grammar Checking

1. Start checking grammar, to open the Grammar dialog box.

2. Select Options.

3. Change the settings described under "Options" below as you prefer.

4. Select OK.

Setting Options with the Menus

1. Select Tools | Options.

2. Select the Grammar tab (icon from the Category box in Word for Windows 2).

3. Change the settings described under "Options" below as you prefer.

4. Select OK.

Options

While the same basic options appear in both Word for Windows 2 and 6, they are set up differently.

Use Grammar and Style Rules

In Word for Windows 6, select the set of grammar rules you want to enforce from this drop-down list box. The preset options include Strictly (All Rules), For Business Writing and For Casual Writing. There are three potential custom settings, which are initially set to enforce all rules.

In Word for Windows 2, select one of the three options buttons under this heading to select which group of grammatical rules you want to enforce. You can choose Strictly (All Rules), For Business Writing, or For Casual Writing, all of which have a preset selection of rules. While there are no custom sets, you can customize these sets of rules.

Check Spelling

In Word for Windows 6, you can clear this check box to prevent Word from checking spelling as it checks the grammar in your document. In Word for Windows 2, "Spelling Errors" is a check box in the Grammar list box that can be selected or cleared.

Show Readability Statistics

Clear this check box to prevent Word from displaying the Readability Statistics dialog box when it finishes checking the grammar in your document.

G

Customize Settings

You can customize the sets of grammar rules to fit your own needs, as described above. To begin customizing, you select Customize Settings, to open a new dialog box.

Start by selecting the set of rules you want to customize from the Use Grammar and Style Rules drop-down list box. The other dialog box elements then display the current settings for that set of rules.

Word divides the rules up into two sets, Grammar and Style. In Word for Windows 6, you must select the Grammar or Style option button to display those rules in the list box. In Word for Windows 2, there are two list boxes. The list boxes contain check boxes for each of the rules that can be applied. Select the check boxes for the rules you want to enforce and clear the check boxes for those you do not want to use.

When you find a grammar or style rule that you do not understand, select Explain. Word displays a dialog box that explains the currently highlighted rule. Press ESC to close this dialog box, or double-click the control menu box.

Select the number of words that can come between "to" and an infinitive verb in the Split Infinitives drop-down list box. If more words than you specify come between "to" and an infinitive verb, Word flags the text as an error. You can choose to allow up to three words.

Select the number of nouns that can follow each other in the Consecutive Nouns drop-down list box. You can allow up to four in a row before Word will flag the nouns as an error. Select the number of prepositional phrases that can follow each other in the Prepositional Phrases drop-down list box. You can allow up to four in a row.

In Word for Windows 6 only, you can have Word flag as an error any sentence that has more than a set number of words by entering the maximum number in the Sentences Containing More Words Than text box.

If you decide that you don't like the set of rules you have created, or if you change settings accidentally, select Reset All, restoring the default settings for all the sets of rules.

Hints

The following is an explanation of the different grammar options and readability statistics that may help you decide how to use these features.

Grammar Options

You want to flag split infinitives because they can make sentences difficult to understand. They can, however, be used in casual writing to make a point. You will want to flag consecutive nouns because when several nouns appear in a row

Graph   *313*

G

the first ones are usually being used to modify the last one. Your reader may not understand how the modifying nouns interrelate. Use adjectives to modify nouns instead of other nouns.

Avoid using many prepositional phrases in a row because they are also confusing. Unless the sentence is very well constructed, your readers will quickly lose track of which noun is being modified by each of the propositional phrases.

Readability Statistics

The Readability Statistics dialog box displays three types of statistics: counts, averages, and indexes. The Counts area shows the number of words, characters, paragraphs, and sentences in the document. The Averages area shows the average number of sentences per paragraph, words per sentence, or characters per word.

The Readability area shows a set of standard statistical indexes used to determine the readability of your document: the percentage of sentences with passive verbs, and several indexes. Word for Windows 6 uses the Flesch Reading Ease, Flesch-Kincaid Grade Level, Coleman-Liau Grade Level, and Bormuth Grade Level, where Word for Windows 2 offers the Flesch Reading Ease, Flesch Grade Level, Flesch-Kincaid, and Gunning Fog indexes.

The Flesch Grade Level and the Flesch-Kincaid indexes use the word length in syllables and sentence length to calculate the reading skill necessary to read the document, expressed in grades. The Coleman-Liau and Bormuth Grade Levels use word length in characters and sentence length to calculate a grade level. The Flesch Reading Ease index provides a percentage score indicating how easy the text is to read. The Gunning Fog index tells you how difficult the text is.

Related Topics

> Grammar Checking
> Spelling
> Thesaurus

Graph

When you want to create graphs to include in Word for Windows, you can create them using the Word's supplementary application, Graph. These graphs are included in your Word document as embedded OLE or DDE objects.

There are two document windows in Graph, the Datasheet and the Chart. The Datasheet displays your data, while the Chart displays the chart created from that data.

Procedures

You can use Graph to create a graph using data in a Word table, data you enter into Graph, or data saved with another program that you can import into Graph. After creating the first graph, you can change the type of graph, and add or remove elements such as arrows and text, legends, data labels, and labels along the axes.

Creating a Graph from a Table

1. Select the table containing the information you want to graph in Word for Windows.

2. Click the Insert Chart button on the Standard toolbar. You can also select Insert | Object, highlight Microsoft Graph in the Object Type list box, and select OK. In Word for Windows 6, you may need to select the Create New tab in the Object dialog box.

   Word now opens Graph, and creates a graph using the data in the table you selected.

3. Edit or format your graph so that it looks the way you want it.

4. Select File | Exit and Return.

5. When prompted about updating the graph in your documents, select Yes.

The graph appears in your document as an embedded object. You can add a frame, delete, or relocate the graph just as you would any other embedded object. For more information on embedded objects, what they are, and how they work, see "Object Linking and Embedding."

Editing a Graph

Editing a graph is just like editing any other embedded object. You can open Graph from within Word, edit it, and then close Graph, updating the graph in the document.

■ Double-click on the graph in your Word document.

Graph | **315**

■ Highlight the graph, and select Edit | Object | Edit in Word for Windows 6 or Edit | Microsoft Graph Object.

Options

The steps above explain how to create a simple graph, but Graph offers some other options which can customize your graph, or create it differently.

Creating a Graph Without a Table

You can enter your data directly into Graph, or you can retrieve a file of data saved with Excel, Works, Multiplan, 1-2-3, or Symphony, or one that has been saved in a format compatible with one of those programs.

1. Open Graph without selecting a table of data.

2. You can type data into the datasheet window, which will be used to create the chart. Entering data into the datasheet is done the same way you enter data into a Word table.

3. You can import data by selecting File | Import Data or File | Open Microsoft Excel Chart if you are opening data saved with Excel.

   You can open any ASCII file that uses either comma or tab characters to separate fields, or any file with the .WKS, .WK1, .WR1, .XLS, or .SLK extensions.

TIP: When you import data, you can import up to 256 columns and 4,000 rows of data. Some spreadsheets may contain more data than that, so make sure that the information you want is actually within the first 256 columns and 4,000 rows, or you won't be able to import it.

4. Format and insert your graph as usual.

Changing Graph Types

You can change the type of graph that displays your data. Graph offers a variety of different two and three-dimensional graph styles. To change a graph type, select a general type of graph from the Gallery menu, to open a dialog box which displays specific graph types. For example, selecting 3-D Column displays the following dialog box.

G

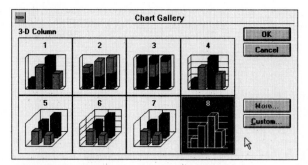

Select the specific type of graph you want to use and select OK to change the chart.

Rearranging Data Series

You can manipulate how your numbers are displayed and used in your graph by making selections from the DataSeries menu. From this menu you can choose data to use as labels for the x-axis in an x-y graph, include or exclude specific rows or columns of data from the chart, have the graph treat rows or columns as the shape of series of related data, and, in combination graphs, assign specific series of data to the main chart or the overlay.

TIP: It is often difficult to visualize what is meant by a data series in a graph. Remember that the contents of the legend are each a label of one data series. So if North appears in the legend, and all the information for North appears in a single row, then your data series are arranged in rows.

Some of these options will not be available, depending on the graph type you are using and what is selected when you open the menu. You must select a column or row before you include or exclude it or plot it on the x-axis, and you must select a data series before you add it to a main or overlay chart.

Adding Graph Elements

You can add elements to your graph, such as arrows, data labels, titles, grid lines, and axis labels. These elements are added by selecting them from the Chart menu and responding to the dialog boxes. The chart in Figure 4-27 uses these table elements, and labels them.

Unattached text is entered differently than chart or axis titles. Instead of selecting a menu command, just make sure that Chart is the active window, and that no text is selected, and start typing. You can move this text to a new location when you are finished.

Graph   *317*

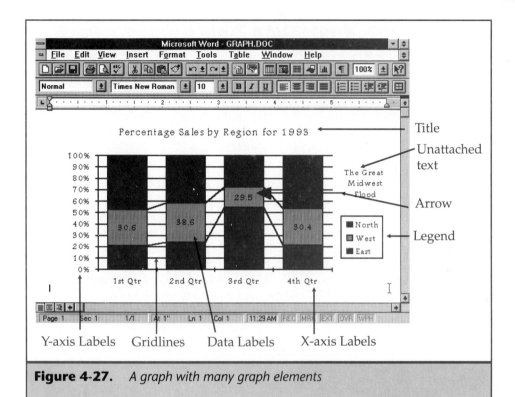

Figure 4-27.   *A graph with many graph elements*

Formatting Graph Elements

Each element of the graph has many different features that you can format. To
format these elements, first select them, and then select an available option from
the Format menu. The options available depend on the element currently
selected, since some options are simply not appropriate to certain elements. For
example, you can change the scale for your axes, but it would be useless to try
changing the scale for your legend.

*TIP: You can tell an element is selected when the selection boxes appear
around it.*

Working with Single Data Points

You can work with a single data point in your chart by pressing CTRL and clicking it. After it is selected, you can format it, just as you can format other graph elements. If you are in a 2D line, column, or bar chart, a black square appears along with the white handles. Drag this black handle to change the value of the data point, changing the entry in the datasheet as well.

Hints

Charts can make it easier to spot trends in sets of numeric data. They also allow you to create a great impact with very few words, because the relationship between the factors being graphed is intuitively clear. However, in most business or professional settings, the actual numbers used to create the graph are also very important and should be included in an easy-to-read table along with the chart.

Use arrows and unattached text together to create callouts to refer to anomalous situations in your graph. For example, your readers may not instantly remember when major flooding occurred in the Midwest, which means they probably won't understand sudden sales drops in that period, unless you provide an explanation. Adding this explanation to the graph makes the impact immediate.

Related Topics

Tables

Graphics

Graphics are pictures or other images that you bring into Word. You can add graphics to provide visual interest to a wide variety of documents.

Procedures

You can insert graphic images into your Word documents. Once they are inserted you can adjust their sizes, or crop them, to focus on a single element of the image.

Inserting Graphics

Use the following steps to insert a graphic using the Insert | Picture command. You can also insert graphics using the Clipboard, as described under "Clipboard."

1. Put the insertion point where you want the graphic to appear.

2. Select Insert | Picture, to open the Picture dialog box.

3. Use the File Name, Directories, and Drives boxes to find the file for the graphic you want to insert. If you cannot find the file using these boxes, then use Find File. This opens the Find File dialog box described under "File Management."

4. If the picture does not appear in the Preview box, select Preview Picture. In Word for Windows 2, you must select Preview for each file you want to preview.

5. If you want to import the graphic as a DDE or OLE object, select the Link to File check box.

   In Word for Windows 6, when you decide to import the graphic, you choose whether or not to save the picture with the file by selecting the Save Picture with Document. If this is not selected, the link must be renewed each time you open the file.

6. Select OK to insert the graphic.

Selecting Graphics

Before you can work with a graphic in Word, you need to select it. Click on the graphic, put the insertion point before the graphic and press SHIFT+RIGHT ARROW. You can tell when the graphic is selected because it is marked with eight handles.

Sizing Graphics with the Mouse

Select the graphic, and drag a handle until the box is the right size and release it.
    When you size a graphic, it maintains the same relative distance from the margin. If you resize a graphic using one of the corner handles, the height-to-width proportion of the graphic stays the same. If you resize it using one of the handles in the middle of a side, you change the height-to-width proportion.

TIP: Watch the status bar to see the percentage of change in the size of the picture as you resize it.

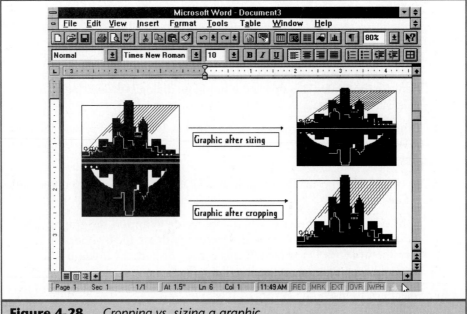

Figure 4-28. *Cropping vs. sizing a graphic*

Cropping Graphics with the Mouse

Select the graphic, press SHIFT, and drag a handle. The mouse will change shape when you are cropping instead of sizing.

If you crop outwards, you add white space around the image in the picture. If you are creating the graphic yourself, with Microsoft Word or another program, try to do any cropping there. Cropping and sizing graphics in your document makes your document much larger.

See Figure 4-28 as a way of understanding the difference between sizing and cropping a figure.

Sizing and Cropping Graphics with the Menus

1. Select the picture.

2. Select Format | Picture. Word tells you the original height and width of the graphic under Original Size. Use this as a comparison as you make changes.

3. Crop a graphic by entering measurements in the text boxes under Crop From. You can crop from the Top, Bottom, Left, or Right.

4. Size a graphic either by percentages of the original size or by specific measurements. Change the percentages in the Width and Height text boxes or specify measurements in the Width and Height text boxes.

5. Select Reset to return the graphic to its original settings.

6. Select OK to apply your changes.

Hints

The following hints on editing, positioning, framing, and converting imported graphics may help make your work with graphics images somewhat easier.

Editing Imported Graphics

Your ability to edit imported graphics depends on whether your graphic is in a raster (bitmapped) or a vector format. *Raster* images are recorded as many dots of color. Each dot is recorded individually. *Vector* images are recorded as lines, using mathematical formulas to represent each line that is in the image.

Raster images are commonly available. However, raster image files are larger than vector images files, and the images more difficult to edit. Vector image files are smaller, and the images are much easier to edit. You can use the drawing feature in Word for Windows 6 to edit many vector images.

If you have raster images and want to be able to edit them, you will need to convert them to a vector format. To do this, you need a graphics program with a trace feature, which can trace your raster image and create a vector image from it. This will be especially useful if you have a scanner, which creates art by scanning it in, because scanned images are always raster images.

Supported Graphics Formats

Word can import any graphic for which it has the correct graphic import filter installed. The graphic import filter is the file that tells Word how to read the format.

Currently, Word has graphic import filters for the following graphics file formats. However, Microsoft frequently adds new graphic import filters, so you should check the README.DOC file in your WINWORD directory. This file will tell you if your release of Word has further graphic import filters.

Filename Extension	Format
.WMF	Windows Metafile
.EPS	Encapsulated Postscript
.TIF	TIFF (Tagged Image File Format)
.CGM	Computer Graphics MetaFile
.HGL	HP Graphics Language
.WPG	DrawPerfect
.DRW	Micrografx Designer 3.0/Draw Plus
.PCX	PC Paintbrush
.BMP	Windows Bitmaps
.DXF	AutoCAD 2-D Format
.PLT	AutoCAD Plotter Format
.PIC	Lotus 1-2-3 Graphics

If you cannot import a file in one of these formats, you may not have installed the graphic import filter when you installed Word. To check this in Word for Windows 6, select Help | About Microsoft Word, and System Info. Select Graphic Filters in the Choose a Category drop-down list box and review the installed graphics filters. To check this in Word for Windows 2, select Tools | Options. Select the WIN.INI icon from the Category box. In the Application drop-down list box, select MS Graphics Import Filters. The Startup Options list box shows all the installed graphics import filters. If the import filter is not installed, you need to run Setup to install it, as described in Appendix A.

Applying Borders to Graphics

You apply borders to graphics, to surround them with a box or to add a line to one side of the graphic. See "Borders and Shading" for a full explanation of how to apply borders.

Positioning Graphics

When you first insert a graphic, it appears on the line of text just like another character. This means that you can position the graphic just like text. If you want to have more control of the graphic's exact position, insert a frame around it, and then position the frame using the methods described under "Frames."

Related Topics

Drawing on a Document
Frames
Object Linking and Embedding

Gridlines

Table gridlines let you see which cell you are working in. For more information on showing or hiding table gridlines, see "Tables."

Hand Feeding Pages

See "Printing."

Hanging Indents

See "Indents."

Hard Hyphen

A hard hyphen is a hyphen that causes a word not to break at the end of the line.

Procedures

1. Put the insertion point where you want a hard hyphen.

2. Press CTRL+SHIFT+HYPHEN. You will see a regular hyphen or a long hyphen depending on if you are displaying nonprinting characters.

Hints

You can control how hard hyphens are displayed by setting Word's Options for displaying nonprinting characters. If you choose to show optional hyphens, hard hyphens are displayed as longer than normal hyphens, marking them as hard hyphens. If you choose not to display optional hyphens, hard hyphens are shown as regular hyphens, so that, visually, there is no way to distinguish between hard and normal hyphens in your document.

To change the default determining whether or not optional hyphens are displayed, select Tools | Options, and then select View. Select or clear the Optional Hyphens check box. To change this setting temporarily, select the Show/Hide button to display all special characters.

Related Topics

Hyphenation

Hard Page Break

A hard page break forces Word to start the following text at the top of a new page. You can insert a hard page break by pressing CTRL+ENTER. See "Pagination" for more information.

Hard Space

Insert a hard space between two words you do not want separated when Word wraps the line. The hard space keeps the words from being separated.

Procedures

1. Put the insertion point where you want the hard space.

2. Press CTRL+SHIFT+SPACEBAR.

Hints

Use hard spaces when you have two words that should not be separated, such as elements of a name, or a title and a name. For example, you would want to keep Ms. Brown together on one line, rather than splitting the words between two lines.

Displaying Hard Spaces

You can set how hard spaces are displayed by setting Word's options for displaying nonprinting characters. If you choose to show spaces, hard spaces are displayed as degree signs. Regular spaces are shown with a small dot. If you choose not to display spaces, there is no way visually to distinguish between hard and normal spaces in your document.

To change the default determining whether or not spaces are displayed, select Tools | Options, and View. Select or clear the Spaces check box. To change this setting temporarily, select the Show/Hide button to display all special characters.

Headers and Footers

Headers and footers are text and/or graphics that appear at the top or bottom of every page. Headers and footers are good ways to include page numbers or identify information for pages in your document.

Since the procedures for working with headers and footers are different in Word for Windows 2 and 6, the two sets of procedures are covered separately here.

Procedures for Word for Windows 6

The following procedures explain how to work with headers and footers in Word for Windows 6.

Creating or Editing Headers and Footers

1. Select View | Header and Footer. Word switches to Page Layout view, if necessary, to display a header in a nonprinting box of dotted lines, and displays the floating Header and Footer toolbar, shown below

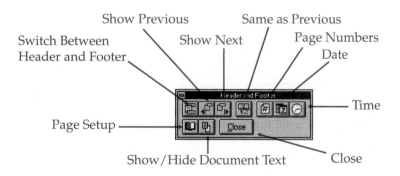

TIP: *If you are in Page Layout view, and you want to edit an existing header or footer, you can double-click on the header or footer area to activate it and open the Header and Footer toolbar.*

2. When you want to create or edit a footer on the current page, select the Switch Between Header and Footer button.

3. When you want to edit a header or footer that starts on a previous or later page, select the Show Next or Show Previous buttons in the toolbar.

4. Create the header or footer using the same techniques for creating and formatting text or graphics that you would use in the main document.

   You can also insert a field for the page number, the time, or the date using the Page Numbers, Time, or Date buttons in the toolbar.

5. To have the current header or footer appear only on specific pages, select the Page Setup button, and then the Layout tab. Select Different Odd and Even and OK.

   The current header or footer will appear on only odd or even pages, depending on the type of page it is on now. Use the Show Next or Show Previous buttons to move to the next kind of page, and create the header or footer for that.

6. Select Different First Page on the Layout tab if you want no header or a unique header or footer for the first page of the document or section. If the current header or footer is not on the first page of the section or document, use the Show Next or Show Previous buttons to move to the header or footer area on that page, and create it there.

7. Select Close or double-click in the document.

If your document is divided into sections, the header and footer carry over into each section by default, so that you only need to create one header and footer for the entire document.

Deleting Headers and Footers

1. Select View | Header and Footer or, in Page Layout view, double-click on the header or footer area.

2. Select the contents of the header or footer.

3. Press DEL or BACKSPACE.

4. Select Close or double-click on the document area.

If the header or footer in the next section is linked to the one deleted, the later one is also deleted. You can break the link by selecting the Same as Previous button.

Vertically Positioning Headers or Footers

Headers and footers appear respectively in the top and bottom margins of your document. If your header or footer is very long, Word readjusts the top or bottom margin to allow enough room for it.

1. Select View | Header and Footer, or double-click in the header or footer area in Page Layout view.

2. Move to the header or footer you want to reposition using the Show Previous or Show Next buttons, if necessary.

3. Drag the margin markers in the vertical ruler to adjust the size of the header or footer box. If you move the header down, or the footer up, into the area used by the document text, Word readjusts the document's margins so that it does not print on top of the document text.

4. Select Close.

TIP: You can also increase or reduce the space between headers or footers and body text by changing the margins of the body text. If you make the top margin smaller, for example, the body text comes much closer to the header text.

Horizontally Positioning Headers or Footers

Headers and footers use all the space from the left and right margin, just like body text. Headers and footers have two preset tab stops, a center tab in the center of the page and a right aligned tab at the right margin, which you can use for aligning text. You can also align the paragraphs in the header or footer by creating new tab stops or by using indentation.

Linking and Unlinking Headers and Footers

If your document is divided into sections, you do not need to create new headers and footers for each section. Instead, Word creates links so that you only need to create one header or footer for the entire document. Even if you use different headers or footers for odd and even pages, you only need to define one odd header for the entire document, no matter how many sections there are.

You can unlink headers and footers by moving to a header or footer in a section, and selecting the Same as Previous button so it does not appear depressed. The nonprinting text "Same as Previous," which appeared at the top of the header or footer, disappears but the text of the header or footer remains. You can then edit the header or footer to customize it for that section of the document and any later sections.

To reestablish the link between a header and footer and that of the previous section, select the Same as Previous button again, while editing the header or footer. You will be prompted about losing the current text, and using that of the previous section. Select Yes.

Procedures for Word for Windows 2

The following procedures explain how to create and work with headers and footers in Word for Windows 2.

Creating or Editing Headers and Footers

Headers and footers are a part of a section's formatting. They are carried over from one section to the next automatically. If you make changes in the first section's header or footer, the changes apply to all the sections. However, if you create a header or footer in a later section, earlier sections do not use that header or footer. Follow these steps to create or edit headers and footers:

1. In Normal view, select View | Header/Footer.

2. Select the Different First Page check box to use a unique header or footer on the first page of a document or section. The entries "First Header" and "First Footer" appear in the Header/Footer list box.

3. Select the Different Odd and Even Pages check box to use different headers or footers for odd and even numbered pages. The entries "Odd Header," "Odd Footer," "Even Header," and "Even Footer" appear in the Header/Footer list box.

4. Select an entry in the Header/Footer list box and OK to create or edit it.

TIP: If you are in Page Layout view, selecting OK displays a frame in your document in which you enter the header or footer, not the header or footer pane. You don't have many of the options that are available in the header or footer pane.

If you are in Normal view, Word opens the header or footer pane that includes the Header/Footer bar shown below, which contains several options useful in creating a header or footer.

5. Enter your header or footer. Your header or footer can include text and/or graphics. You can use the usual character and paragraph formatting options in the header or footer. You can quickly insert fields for page number, date, and time by selecting the buttons in the Header/Footer bar, with the default formats.

TIP: To select the Header/Footer bar options with the keyboard, press SHIFT+F10 *and the mnemonic.*

6 Close the header or footer pane by selecting Close. To switch to the document without closing the pane, click on the document or press F6.

Deleting Headers and Footers

1. Select View | Header/Footer.

2. Select the header or footer you want to delete from the Header/Footer list box and press OK.

3. Select the entire contents of the header or footer.

4. Press DEL.

5. Select Close or click on the document.

Vertically Position Headers or Footers with the Dialog Box

1. Select View | Header/Footer.

2. Enter a measurement for the distance between the header or footer and the top or bottom of the page in the Header or Footer text box. Select OK.

Vertically Position Headers or Footers with the Mouse

1. Select File | Print Preview.
2. Select Margins.
3. Point the mouse at the header or footer and drag it to its new location.
4. Select Cancel.

Horizontally Position Headers or Footers

Headers and footers use the same margins as the main text of the document. You can change the alignment of the text or graphics in the header by changing the paragraph format of the text, indenting it, or using tab stops. Headers and footers are automatically formatted with a center tab centered between the margins and a right-aligned tab at the right margin.

Linking to Previous Headers and Footers

By default, headers and footers are linked, so that you only need to enter one header or footer to format the entire document, even if it is divided into many sections. If you use different odd and even page headers or footers, they are still linked to the odd or even headers or footers of previous sections. However, when you change a header or footer in a section, the link to the previous section's headers or footers is broken, since the text is no longer identical. Follow these steps to link to previous headers and footers.

1. Open the header or footer pane for the header or footer you want to link to that of the previous section.
2. Select Link to Previous from the header/footer bar. If the current header or footer is already linked, the button is not available for selection.
3. When Word prompts you to confirm that you want to delete the current header or footer and replace it with the header or footer of the previous section, select Yes.
4. Select Close.

Formatting Page Numbers in Headers and Footers

You can quickly change the format of the page numbers that you insert in headers or footers.

1. Select View | Header/Footer.

2. Select Page Numbers.

3. Select a numbering option from the Number Format drop-down list box. You can select from Arabic numbers, upper- and lowercase letters, and upper- and lowercase Roman numbers.

4. Select Continue from Previous Section to keep the page numbering consistent through sections. To restart page numbering in the current section with a specific number, select Start At and enter the number in the text box.

5. Select OK.

6. Select OK again to return to the document, or continue creating your header or footer as usual.

Options

The Header and Footer toolbar in Word for Windows 6 offers shortcuts to several useful features.

Button	Action
Switch Between Header and Footer	Switches the insertion point between the header and footer of the current page
Show Previous	Shows the header or footer of the previous section
Show Next	Shows the header or footer of the next section
Same as Previous	Deletes the current header or footer and links to the one in previous section
Page Numbers	Adds a field inserting the page number at the insertion point
Date	Adds a field inserting the current date at the insertion point
Time	Adds a field inserting the current time at the insertion point
Page Setup	Opens the Page Setup dialog box for the current section
Show/Hide Document Text	Switches between showing and hiding the text of the document while you edit the header or footer
Close	Closes the header and footer pane

H

Applications

Creative use of headers and footers can help you create unique documents. You can use headers or footers that appear on the side instead of the top or bottom of the page, or create watermarks which appear in the background of the main text.

Headers at the Side

Headers and footers contain text or graphics that appear at the top or bottom of each page. However, you can change a header or footer so that the text or graphic appears at the side of the page, rather than at the top or bottom. You can use this feature to create special effects in your document.

For example, see Figure 4-29, which shows the Print Preview of a letterhead. The large *Gabrielle Fox* down the left side of the letterhead is actually part of the header. Using this feature you can create exciting letterheads, and other documents.

Create this letterhead by adding a WordArt object at the beginning of the footer, and then the address. Then close the header/footer pane and switch to Page Layout view. Select the WordArt object, and insert a frame to contain it. Size and move the object along the left side of the page, since it is no longer confined to the footer area. Change the margins of the document so that the WordArt

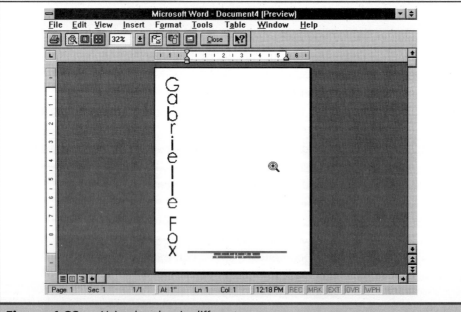

Figure 4-29. *Using headers in different ways*

objects fits entirely inside the margin. In this letter, the address remains at the bottom of the page.

Watermarks

Watermarks, which are graphics or text appearing in the background of a document, usually in a light color or gray, can be created as headers and footers. To create a watermark, you can insert a frame around a graphic or text in a header or footer and use the Send Behind Text button in the Drawing toolbar to move the graphic or text behind the main body of the document. You can position the frame containing the text or image to use as a watermark at any point on the page, instead of just within the header or footer boundaries. The advantage of creating a watermark as part of a header or footer is that it then appears on every page.

Related Topics

Drawing on the Document
Frames
Page Numbers
Sections Watermarks

Headings

See "Outlines."

Help

You can use Help to get information on all aspects of Word. You will find that the on-screen help is complete and extremely useful.

Procedures

There are many ways for you to access Help.

Opening the Help Index

You can open Help for Word showing the index, the first screen. From this screen you select or search for other topics.

- Press F1 within your document without selecting anything.
- Select Help | Help Index.

Getting Help on the Current Task

You can open Help while you are carrying out a task to get help on that task and its options by pressing F1 with a dialog box open or after highlighting a menu command.

Getting Help on a Key or Screen Region

You can also open Help to explain a command, key, or screen region.

- Press SHIFT+F1 and choose a menu command with the mouse or keyboard, press a key or key combination, or click on a region or object on the screen.
- In Word for Windows 6, click on the Help button in the Standard toolbar and then select a menu command or button with the mouse or press a key or key combination.

Options

Help is a separate application with its own menus, commands and toolbar. When you open it, one topic of information is displayed. You can move from that one topic to other topics to find the topic that fully answers your questions.

Switching Topics with Hotspots

Hotspots are the green, underlined text in a Help topic. Use hotspots to move to other topics or to display definitions of terms. When the hotspot's underline is solid, selecting it displays the topic referred to. When the hotspot's underline is dotted, selecting it displays a definition of the term, as you can see here:

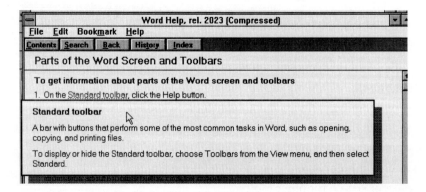

You select a hotspot by clicking it, or pressing TAB until it is highlighted then ENTER.

TIP: *The mouse pointer becomes a hand when it is pointing to a hotspot.*

Searching for Topics

You search for topics by providing Help a keyword. Help displays a range of possibly related topics that you can explore to find the answer to your questions.

1. In Help, select Search, to open the Search dialog box.

2. Type a word in the word text box or highlight an option from the word list box. If you cannot find the word you are looking for, try again with a related word.

3. Select Show Topics. The topic list box now displays a series of topics.

4. Highlight the topic you want to see, and select Go To. The new topic appears in Help.

Viewing Topics While Using Word

Help often provides step-by-step instructions that you may want to view while working with Word.

In Word for Windows 6, these step-by-step instructions are shown in a special How To window. To view it while working in Word, select On Top. The How-To window now appears on top of any other window you are working with, even though it is not the current application window.

In Word for Windows 2, you can display the Help application window with the Word for Windows window by changing the sizes of the Help window and the Word window so that you can see both of them at the same time.

To change the size of a Help window, you first need to ensure that it is not maximized. You can click on the Restore button or select Restore from the application window's control menu to do this. Then, you can drag the border of the window with the mouse to size it. Alternatively, you can select Size from the application window's control menu, use the arrow keys to reposition the window's border, and then press ENTER.

For further information on sizing windows, see "Sizing Windows" in Chapter 1.

H

Printing Topics

Another way to view the step-by-step instructions while working with Word is to print the topic. That way you have a hard copy of the instructions to look at while doing the process.

To print a topic, follow these steps:

1. Display the topic.

2. Select Print (File | Print in Word for Windows 2) in the Help or How To window.

Moving Back to Topics

While in Help, you can move back to the last topic you looked at, or you can move back to any of the Help topics you looked at since you started Help. You can move to the Help Index at any time, whether or not you have viewed it in the current Help session.

■ Select Back to move to the last topic you looked at.

■ Select History to open the History window, which displays all the topics viewed since you opened Help. Select one to move to it.

■ Select Index to display the index of topics.

■ Select Contents to return to the display of Help contents.

Getting Help on Help

Window's Help provides Help about itself. Press F1 in the Help window to display help on Help. To return to Help about Word for Windows, select History and a topic about Word.

Related Topics

Help | About Microsoft Word
Help | Getting Started (Word for Windows 2)

Help|About Microsoft Word

In Word for Windows 6

Selecting this command displays the About Microsoft Word dialog box, which tells you which release of Word and its supplementary programs you are using. You can also select System Info, which starts a program that lets you see many details about Word.

To use System Info, highlight the category of information you want to see in the Choose a Category drop-down list box. The list box below shows the current setting for that category. You can choose Run to open a program that will allow you to make changes to this information, Print to print the settings, or Save to save the information in an ASCII file. Select Close to close this window when you are finished.

In Word for Windows 2

Select Help | About to view the About dialog box, which displays some information about Word and your computer system. Make sure to display this dialog box when you call Microsoft's support line for help with Word since they will request some of this information.

Related Topics

Help

Help|Contents (Word for Windows 6)

See "Help."

Help|Examples and Demos (Word for Windows 6)

Select this command to see a series of topics for which Word can display an example or a demonstration. Select a topic to see the example or demonstration. Select Close to return to Word.

H

Help|Getting Started (Word for Windows 2)

When you select Help | Getting Started, Word starts a application that introduces you to the Word screen, basic Word skills, and can give you a brief lesson on Word productivity. This application is designed to help someone who is new to Windows, word-processing, and/or Word.

Help|Index

See "Help."

Help|Learning Word

When you select Help | Learning Word, Word starts an application that introduces you to some of Word's features. This application is designed to help someone who is new to Word for Windows learn more about what features are available for use. Learning Word introduces you to formatting, editing, proofing, tables, frames and pictures, and viewing and printing. These features are not covered in depth, but you will have a chance to carefully walk through the steps with Word prompting you through each step of the process.

Help|Quick Preview (Word for Windows 6)

Select this command to see a brief preview of Word for Windows 6's new features, tips for WordPerfect users, or an introduction to the Word screen.

Help|Search for Help On (Word for Windows 6)

Select this command to display Help when the Search dialog box is already open. See "Help" for instructions on using the Search dialog box to find information.

Help|Technical Support (Word for Windows 6)

Select this topic to find information on how to contact Microsoft Corporation for information on using Word.

Help|Tip of the Day (Word for Windows 6)

Select this command to see a series of tips that can be displayed when you start Word.

Help|WordPerfect Help

This command provides help to people who have already mastered WordPerfect.

Hidden Text

Hidden is a character format that produces text that (by default) will not appear when your document is printed or in the Page Layout view. You may use hidden text to include notes about your document that are meant for you, or for a co-author, or to hide text that you are considering deleting.

Procedures

The Hidden character style can be applied as the text is being typed or after it is typed. To apply it while typing, select the feature, type the text to be affected, and then remove the feature. To apply the format to typed text, select the text, and then add the style.

1. Select Format | Font (Character in Word for Windows 2).

TIP: In Word for Windows 6, you can also right-click the document and select Font. In Word for Windows 2, you can double-click on a blank spot of the ribbon.

2. Select the Hidden check box. Clear it to remove the hidden format. Select OK.

Hints

Hidden Paragraph Characters

If the paragraph character at the end of a paragraph of hidden text is not also formatted with the Hidden text style, the extra line appears in your document even through the hidden text does not. Remember to format both the paragraph you want to hide and its paragraph character.

Removing Formatting

Another procedure for removing the Hidden style from text is to select the text and press CTRL+SPACEBAR. This removes all character formatting from the selected text.

Applications

The hidden text format may not appear useful at first glance, but as you work with Word more, you will find many uses for the feature.

For Updating Your Document

Some documents you create may need to be re-created periodically. Monthly or quarterly reports, project completion reports, or sales memos may use mostly the same text with only a few changes each time. Use hidden text to include notes in your document telling you, or another person, where to get the information.

For Collaborating on Documents

You may find yourself working with another person in creating a document. Many large reports are not created by one person, but by a group of people, all of whom need to work together on a document. Use the hidden text format to include text you want added to the document.

Related Topics

Character Formats

Hide Text

See "Hidden Text."

Highlighting Text

See "Selecting Text."

Horizontal Lines

See "Borders and Shading."

Horizontal Ruler

See "Ruler."

Horizontal Scroll Bar

See "Scroll Bars."

Hyphenation

You can use hyphens between words to combine them, as in *forget-me-not*. You can also put hyphens in words so they can be broken in two by the end of a line. You can add hyphens in your document or let Word add hyphens to words for you, after appropriate settings have been selected.

See the box "Rules for Hyphenation" for instructions on how words should be hyphenated in English. Word will be using these rules for hyphenating, but you will want to know them when you choose to use manual hyphenation.

Procedures

You can let Word hyphenate documents automatically, or you can have Word prompt you for where to hyphenate words.

Rules for Hyphenation

When you turn on hyphenation in Word you can have Word add hyphens automatically where they are appropriate. You can also elect to approve their location and insert them manually. Although this latter approach provides an additional measure of control, you will want to follow some basic rules if you choose the manual approach. Let these simple rules guide you in deciding where hyphens should go:

- Always use the syllable marks provided by Word in choosing a location. Words should never be split anywhere other than a syllable break.

- Divide words after prefixes or before suffixes rather than within them.

- Limit the number of lines that end in hyphens to no more than 20-25 percent of the lines on the page.

- Three consecutive lines should never end in hyphens.

- Hyphens should not be used in the last line of a paragraph or a page.

- Syllables should always have at least two and preferably three letters divided from the rest of the word.

- Contractions should not be hyphenated.

- Abbreviations such as AICPA, ASCII, and *indef.* should never be hyphenated.

- Long numbers can be split after a comma if you need to break them.

- Choose divisions that do not make real words that might be confusing. For example, *be-atific* (*be* is a word) would be better hyphenated as *bea-tific*.

Hyphenating Automatically

1. Put the insertion point at the beginning of the document or select the text to hyphenate.

2. Select Tools | Hyphenation.

3. Select the Automatically Hyphenate Document check box in Word for Window 6 or clear the Confirm check box in Word for Windows 2.

4. Clear the Hyphenate Words in CAPS (Hyphenate CAPS in Word for Windows 2) check box to prevent Word from hyphenating words that are all capitals.

5. Enter a measurement in the Hyphenation Zone (Hot Zone in Word for Windows 2) text box setting how much white space is allowed at the end of each line.

6. In Word for Windows 6, enter a value in Limit Consecutive Hyphens To, to limit the number of consecutive lines that can be hyphenated. Select OK.

Word now proceeds to hyphenate the text in the document automatically. When Word for Windows 2 finishes hyphenating text, a message box saying "Hyphenation Complete" is displayed. Select OK to return to the document. Word for Windows 6 does not display a message.

Hyphenating Manually

1. Move to the beginning of your document or select the text to hyphenate.

2. Select Tools | Hyphenation.

3. Make the setting selections you want regarding hyphenating words in capitals, the size of the hyphenation zone, and the number of consecutive hyphenated lines.

4. Select Manual (in Word for Windows 2, make sure that Confirm is selected) and select OK.

5. Word displays a word in the Hyphenate At text box, with hyphens at each place the word can be hyphenated using the rules of the current language. The highlighted hyphen is the one Word wants to insert. Move the highlighted hyphen to change where the word is hyphenated.

6. Select Yes when the hyphen is placed correctly. Word inserts the hyphen and continues checking the document. Select No to leave the word unhyphenated and continue checking the document.

7. When Word for Windows 2 finishes hyphenating text, a message box saying "Hyphenation Complete" is displayed. Select OK to return to the document. Word for Windows 6 doesn't display any message.

H

Hints

The following are some hints that explain how hyphenation works in Word, which may help you work with hyphenation more effectively.

Hyphenation or Hot Zone

The *hyphenation zone* is a percentage of the length of the line running along the right end of the line. Word attempts to have some text in the hyphenation zone of every line. If the hyphenation zone of one line is empty, Word hyphenates the first word of the following line so there is text in the hyphenation zone. For example, in Figure 4-30, Word will hyphenate the word "Hyphenation" since the hyphenation zone on the prior line is empty.

The narrower your hot zone is, the more hyphenated words you have. When you increase the width of the hot zone, you have fewer hyphenated words, but the right margin of your page is more ragged.

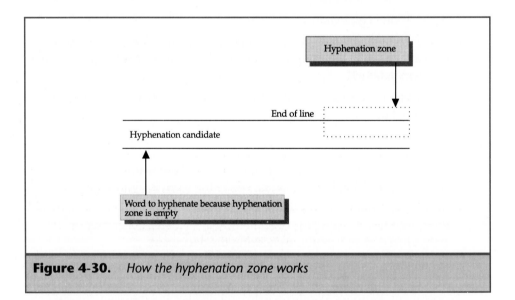

Figure 4-30. *How the hyphenation zone works*

Types of Hyphens

Word uses three types of hyphens: regular hyphens, hard or nonbreaking hyphens, and optional hyphens. Regular hyphens are inserted using the - key on your keyboard. These hyphens always appear and always print. If one appears in a word near the end of a line, Word automatically breaks the word after the hyphen and wraps the second word down to the next line.

Hard, or nonbreaking, hyphens, are inserted by pressing CTRL+SHIFT+—. When you have inserted a hyphen in a word, or between two words, they are not broken apart by word wrapping, unless Word breaks them at some other location in the word. Nonbreaking hyphens print as normal hyphens, but when you display optional hyphens or special codes, they appear as longer than normal hyphens.

Optional hyphens are inserted to tell Word where a word can be broken if it needs to be. You can insert these optional hyphens by pressing CTRL+—. Optional hyphens do not print unless the word is broken at the optional hyphen at the end of the line, when printed as normal hyphens. If you display special codes or optional hyphens, you will see these hyphens as longer than usual hyphens.

When to Hyphenate

Do not hyphenate immediately after entering text. As a rule, it is better to write and edit all of your text, and then layout your page before hyphenating. This is because if you change column width, or add or remove words from a paragraph, you have to re-hyphenate the document to have the hyphenation complete. Hyphenation should be one of the very last things that you do in creating a document.

I-J

IF Field

See "Mail Merge."

IMPORT Field

See "Fields."

Importing Graphics

See "Graphics."

INCLUDE Field

The Include field type is used to include text from another document at its position. For a full explanation of this field type, see "Fields."

INCLUDEPICTURE Field

See "Fields."

INCLUDETEXT Field

See "Fields."

Indents

When you change the indent for paragraphs, you are effectively adding extra margin settings for that paragraph. You can set indentation for the entire paragraph and a separate indent for the first line only.

Procedures

Indents are paragraph formats. When an indent is changed, it affects the paragraph containing the insertion point, or all selected paragraphs. If you press ENTER in a paragraph, creating a new paragraph, the new paragraph has the same indentation as the original.

Changing Indents with the Dialog Box

1. Mark the paragraphs you want to format by selecting text in each or by putting the insertion point in one.

2. Select Format | Paragraph or right-click in the document and select Paragraph.

3. Select the Indents and Spacing tab if necessary.

4. Enter a measurement in the Left text box to set the left indent. Enter a positive number to move the paragraph in from the margin. Enter a negative number to move the paragraph out into the margin area.

5. Enter a measurement in the Right text box to set the right indent.

6. Set any special indents.

   ▪ In Word for Windows 6, select First Line or Hanging from the Special drop-down list box and enter the indent in the By text box.

   ▪ In Word for Windows 2, enter a measurement in the First Line text box.

7. Select OK.

Changing Indents with the Ruler

1. Mark the paragraph you want to format by selecting text in each or by putting the insertion point in one.

2. In Word for Windows 2, click the symbol at the left end of the ruler until the ruler displays the paragraph scale, as shown below.

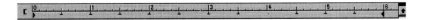

TIP: In Word for Windows 6, the ruler always displays the indentation arrows.

3. Drag the indent markers to where you want the paragraph indented.

I-J

   In Word for Windows 6, the left indent marker is a double arrow. You can move both arrows by dragging the bar underneath. Drag the lower arrow to set the paragraph's left indent. Drag the upper arrow to set the indent for the first-line of the paragraph.

   In Word for Windows 2, the left indent marker is a double arrow. Dragging the double arrow sets the left indent for all lines. To set the first line indent separately, press SHIFT and drag. Only the upper arrow, marking the first line indent, will move.

Changing Indents with Shortcut Keys

1. Mark the paragraph(s) you want to format by selecting text in each one or by placing the insertion point in a single paragraph.

2. Press the shortcut keys shown below to format the selected paragraphs.

Word for Windows 2

Shortcut	Result
CTRL+N	Changes left and first line indent to the next tab stop to the right
CTRL+M	Changes left and first line indent to the next tab stop to the left
CTRL+T	Changes the left indent only one tab stop to the right (hanging indent)
CTRL+G	Changes the left indent only one tab stop to the left

Word for Windows 6

Shortcut	Result
CTRL+M	Changes left and first line indent to the next tab stop to the right
CTRL+SHIFT+M	Changes left and first line indent to the next tab stop to the left
CTRL+T	Changes the left indent only one tab stop to the right (hanging indent)
CTRL+SHIFT+T	Changes the left indent only one tab stop to the left

Changing Indents with the Formatting Toolbar

In Word for Windows 6, you can also use the two buttons shown here from the Formatting toolbar to change the indent of a paragraph.

Select the one on the left to move your indent one tab stop to the left and the one on the right to move your indent one tab stop to the right.

Hints

The following hints on using negative indents and the ruler in Word for Windows 2 may help you work with indents better.

Negative Indents

You can move the indent of a paragraph into the margins of your document. If you are using the menus, you would do this by entering a negative number in the indent text boxes instead of a positive number. With the ruler, simply move the indent markers outside the margins. You might do this to provide emphasis for headings or introductory paragraphs.

Using the Ruler with the Keyboard (Word for Windows 2)

Shortcut	Result
CTRL+SHIFT+F10	Make the ruler active
LEFT ARROW	Move the ruler cursor a small amount to the left
RIGHT ARROW	Move the ruler cursor a small amount to the right
CTRL+LEFT ARROW	Move the ruler cursor a greater amount to the left
CTRL+RIGHT ARROW	Move the ruler cursor a greater amount to the right
SHIFT+LEFT ARROW	Move the ruler cursor left of zero on the ruler
HOME	Move the ruler cursor to zero on the ruler
END	Move the ruler cursor to the right end of the column
L	Set the left indent at the position of the ruler cursor
R	Set the right indent at the position of the ruler cursor
F	Set the first-line indent at the position of the ruler cursor
ENTER	Apply the ruler settings and return to the document
ESC	Cancel the ruler settings and return to the document

Applications

Hanging indents are commonly used in bibliographies, to emphasize the authors of the works cited and separate each entry. In a hanging indent the first line of a paragraph starts at the left margin, but the rest of the paragraph is indented one tab stop (usually .5 inches) to the right.

In Word for Windows 6, you can create hanging indents by selecting Hanging Indent from the Special drop-down list box and entering the amount you want the text indented from the first line in the By text box.

In Word for Windows 2, use a positive indent for the body of the paragraph, but a negative indent for the first line. The indent for the first line must be the same measurement as the indent for the rest of the paragraph, but the number must be negative. This returns the first line to the left margin.

If you are using the ruler, creating a hanging indent is even easier. Press SHIFT and drag the left indent marker to the correct location. You can also create a hanging indent using the shortcut keys shown above in the procedure using shortcut keys.

Related Topics

Margins
Paragraph Formats

Index

An index is a list of items marked in the text and the page number on which they appear. An index is created using a combination of Index and Index Entry fields, in which Index Entry fields mark text or objects to include and the Index field marks where the collected index entries are to appear.

Procedures

In addition to the procedures described here, you can insert the Index and Index Entry field codes directly into your document. When you do that, you have further customization options. See "Options" about entering fields.

Marking an Index Entry

1. Select the text to include as the entry in the index or put your insertion point where you want an entry.

2. Press ALT+SHIFT+X or select Insert | Index and Tables | Index | Mark Entry in Word for Windows 6, or select Insert | Index Entry in Word for Windows 2.

3. If necessary, enter the text to appear in the index in the Main Entry text box (Index Entry in Word for Windows 2).

   To create a subentry, enter the parent entry in the Main Entry text box, and the subentry in the Subentry text box, in Word for Windows 6. In Word for Windows 2, type the parent entry in the Index Entry text box and then a colon and the subentry.

4. Select the page reference to appear in the index. You have several options:

   ■ To have the index reference the current page, select the Current Page option button in Word for Windows 6. Since this is the default in Word for Windows 2 nothing needs to be selected.

- You can have the index refer to a range of pages. In Word for Windows 6, select the Page Range Bookmark option button, then the bookmark for those pages in the drop-down list box. In Word for Windows 2 select the name of the bookmark marking those pages in the Range drop-down list box.

- In Word for Windows 6 only, you can also choose to create an index entry to serve only a cross-reference by selecting the Cross-reference option button and entering the other index entry this should reference in the text box.

5. Select the Bold check box to boldface the entry's page number in the index.

6. Select the Italics check box to italicize the entry's page number in the index.

7. Select Mark (OK in Word for Windows 2).

Automatically Marking Index Entries (Word for Windows 6 only)

In Word for Windows 6, you can have Word automatically insert index entries by creating and using a concordance file. A concordance file contains words or phrases you want referred to in the index and the text to appear in the index for those references. You can then have Word automatically go through your document and mark the text for entry in the index.

1. Select Insert | Index and Tables, and, if necessary, the Index tab.

2. Select AutoMark.

3. Select the concordance file. Select OK.

Word will now mark index entries in your document, using the concordance file entries.

Creating a Concordance File (Word for Windows 6 only)

A concordance file can be used in Word for Windows 6 to automatically mark text for indexes as described above.

1. Open a new file.

2. Create a two-column table by selecting Table | Insert Table, and selecting OK.

3. In the first column, type text you want referenced in the index, using the capitalization used in the document. Since Word can only find exact matches, you may have multiple entries to match when the word or phrase appears in the middle of the sentence (*whale*), at the beginning of a sentence (*Whale*), or as a plural (*whales, Whales*).

4. Press TAB to move to the second column.

5. Type the entry to appear in the index. You may have multiple words you want referenced under the same index entry. For example, *orca, dolphin, cetacean,* and *whale* might all appear under *whale* in your index.

6. Repeat steps 3 through 5 until you have included all the text and index entries.

7. Save the document.

Inserting an Index in Word for Windows 6

1. Put your insertion point where you want the index.

TIP: Insert the index at the end of your document so that it does not affect pagination and on a new page so it stands out clearly. Often indexes are often formatted as two columns, even when the main document is not, to fit more of the short entries in less space.

2. Select Insert | Index and Tables, and then the Index tab, if necessary.

3. To have subentries below the parent entry and indented, select Indented. To have subentries on the same line as the parent entry, select Run-in. The effect of any of your formatting selections for the index is shown using the sample index in the Preview list box.

4. Select a format from the Formats drop-down list box to choose a set of styles to use with the index.

5. To move the page numbers for index entries to the right margin, select Right Align Page Numbers. After selecting this check box, you can select

a style of line to run from the index entry to the page number from the Tab Leader drop-down list box.

6. To format your index with multiple columns, enter the number in the Columns text box, and select OK.

Inserting an Index in Word for Windows 2

1. Put your insertion point where you want the index, and select Insert | Index.

2. To have subentries below the parent entry and indented, select Normal Index. To have subentries on the same line as the parent entry, select Run-in Index.

3. In Word for Windows 2, select None to not mark each letter group, Blank Line to add a blank line at the start of each new letter or Letter to display the appropriate letter for each letter group. Select OK.

Options

Indexes are created with Index and Index Entry fields, which are entered with all of the coding when you mark index entries and insert your index. When you enter the field codes directly, without using the menus, you have some further options for customizing your index. To learn about entering fields directly, see "Fields."

Index

The Index field type collects the text and page numbers from Index Entry field types in the document and creates an index using those entries. Word offers a number of switches you can use to maintain control over the index's format.

The Index field type takes the format

{INDEX [*switches*]}

where *switches* are the switches you can use to control the format of the index, and are described below. In the default index, in which you do not use switches, subentries are indented beneath entries, page numbers are separated from text by a space and from each other by commas.

\B   The \b switch collects index entries only from pages marked with a bookmark. For example, {INDEX \b chap1} will create an index for the pages marked with the bookmark, chap1.

\C   The \c switch formats the index in columns. For example, {INDEX \c 3} would create a three-column index.

\E   The \e switch lets you set up to three characters to separate index entries from page numbers. For example, enter {INDEX \e "..."} to separate index entries and page numbers with ellipses.

\F   The \f switch creates an index using the specified entries only. For example, enter {INDEX \f "a"} to index only entries that include \f "a" in the entry field. The "a" is an identifier included in the entry field and the index field specifically so you can create an index from a subset of all index entries.

\G   The \g switch lets you set the character to separate pages in a range. For example, {INDEX \g -} separates the first and last pages in a range with a hyphen.

\H   The \h switch lets you set characters that are inserted as headings for the letter groups in the index, such as an A that appears before the list of index entries that start with A. You can use any alphabet character, any other character, or a space. These must be enclosed in quotation marks.

TIP: If you include a letter of the alphabet as part of heading, Word advances to the next letter in the alphabet automatically when it reaches a new letter group in the index.

\L   The \l switch lets you set the character that separates page numbers in the index. You must enter the character separator and any spaces in quote marks. For example, enter {INDEX \l "; "} to separate page numbers by a semicolon and a space.

\P   The \p switch creates a partial index covering only part of the alphabet. Use this switch with a very large document or index so you do not run out of memory while creating the index. For example, {INDEX \p a-b} creates an index for the *a* and *b* letter groups of entries.

\R   The \r switch creates an index in which subentries are on the same line as their parent entries. A colon follows parent entries, while subentries are separated by semicolons. The line wraps around if necessary.

\S   The \s switch lets you use sequence numbers in your index. Sequence numbers, defined using the Sequence field type described under "Fields," separate your document into parts that are used with indexes, tables of contents, and other referencing fields. With the \s switch, your index entries display a sequence number, a separator, and a page number.

For example, enter {INDEX \s section} to use sequence numbers using the sequence named *section.*

\D   The \d switch, always used with the \s switch, sets the characters that separate sequence numbers from page numbers. You can use up to three characters. Remember to enclose the separator character in quote marks.

Index Entry

The Index Entry field marks entries to include in an index. You must specify the text to appear in the index. The total Index Entry field code can be no more than 64 characters long.

The Index Entry field uses the field code format {XE "*text*"[*switches*]}. *Text* is the text that actually appears in the index. *Switches* are the switches that let you control the index entry, and are described below.

Indexes can have up to seven levels of subentries. You indicate a subentry in text by separating each level of entry with a colon, for example, Whales:carnivorous:orca.

TIP: To use a colon in an index entry, put a \ (backslash) before it.

\B   The \b switch bolds a page number of this index entry only. You could boldface page numbers referring to graphics or tables to distinguish them. If your index page numbers are already formatted bold, this switch removes the bold.

\F   The \f switch defines the index entry as being of a specific type. An example is {XE \f "a"}. You can create an index of only one type of index entries.

\I   The \i switch italicizes the page number of this index entry only. Again, use this to distinguish between references to different types of entries in your document. If your index's page numbers are already formatted as italics, this switch removes that format from the page numbers of the entry.

\R   Use the \r switch to mark ranges of pages, by following it with a bookmark name that refers to those pages, for example, {XE Copying Disks \r diskcopy}.

\T   Use the \t switch to give Word text to use in place of page numbers for this entry. For example, enter {XE DISKCOPY \t See Copying Disks} to create a cross-reference in the index.

Hints

Indexes normally start on a new page at the end of the document, so that they are set apart from the body of the text and do not affect the text's formatting. Since the entries in an index are usually quite short, it is common to use multiple columns, letting you fit more index on fewer pages with much less wasted space.

In Word for Windows 6, you can index text found in the body of your document or in footnotes or endnotes. In Word for Windows 2, you can only index text found in the body of your document.

Related Topics

Bookmarks
Table of Authorities
Table of Contents and Figures

INFO Field

See "Fields."

Initial Caps

See "Capitalization" or "Dropped Capitals."

Insert Mode

See "INS Key."

INS Key

The INS key switches Word between the insert and overtype modes, which affects what happens when you type with the insertion point before characters. In the insert mode, Word moves text after the insertion point right, making space for the new text. In the overtype mode, what you type replaces the existing text. When you are in the overtype mode, the status bar displays "OVR". In Word for Windows 6, you can also switch between the insert and the overtype mode by double-clicking on the OVR indicator in the status bar.

In the overtype mode, hidden characters and graphics are treated just like other characters. For example, if the insertion point is just before a graphic in the overtype mode, and you type a character, the graphic is replaced by the character.

Insert|Annotation

See "Annotation."

Insert|Bookmark

See "Bookmarks."

Insert|Break

See "Pagination," "Columns," or "Sections."

I-J

Insert|Caption

See "Captions."

Insert|Cross-reference

See "Cross-reference."

Insert|Database

See "Databases" in this chapter.

Insert|Date and Time

See "Date and Time."

Insert|Field

See "Fields."

Insert|File

See "Inserting Files."

Insert|Footnote

See "Footnotes and Endnotes."

Insert|Form Field

See "Forms."

Insert|Frame

See "Frames."

Insert|Index and Tables

See "Index."

Insert|Index Entry

See "Index."

Insert | Object

See "Object Linking and Embedding."

Insert | Page Numbers

See "Page Numbers."

Insert | Picture

See "Graphics."

Insert | Symbol

See "Special Characters."

Insert | Table of Contents

See "Table of Contents and Figures."

I-J

Inserting a Date

See "Date and Time."

Inserting Files

Use the Insert | File command to import all or part of another file into the current file.

Procedures

1. Move to the location in the document where you want the other file to appear.

2. Select Insert | File, to open the File dialog box.

3. Using the File Name, Directories, and Drives boxes, select the file you want to insert in your document. You can select any type of file that Word can open.

4. Select Confirm Conversions if the file is not saved in Word for Windows 6 format, and you want to confirm Word's interpretation of what format the style is saved in.

5. If you want to insert only a part of the file, enter it in the Range text box. You can enter a bookmark, a range name, a range, or other identifier in this text box.

   TIP: *The bookmark, range, or identifier is created in the program the file was originally created in and depend on what that program is.*

6. To create a link to the file, select the Link to File check box. For a full explanation of what a link is, see "Object Linking and Embedding."

7. Select OK.

Hints

You can use the Insert | File command to insert the contents of a spreadsheet, as described here. However, you may also want to see "Databases" for other methods of inserting information from a spreadsheet.

Inserting Spreadsheets

Inserting a spreadsheet is just like inserting any other file into a Word document. However, since the organization of a spreadsheet is somewhat different than that of another word processing file, there are some variations.

In step 5, you can select to insert the entire file, or a part of the file. To select a part of a spreadsheet, you must know which range of cells in the spreadsheet you want to use. The easiest method is to name a range of cells in the spreadsheet. You can enter the range, specified the same way you specify the range in the spreadsheet program, in the Range text box, or enter the range name, making sure to match the spelling and punctuation of the name you assigned that range in the spreadsheet.

If you do not specify a range in step 5, a dialog box appears after you select OK that lets you select a named range from the spreadsheet or specify a range. The advantage of waiting to this point to select the range is that you can choose the named range, making sure that the name is correct.

The process of naming a range of cells in your spreadsheet depends on which program you are using to create the spreadsheet, so you will want to consult that spreadsheet's documentation.

Related Topics

Object Linking and Embedding
Opening Files

Inserting Spreadsheets

You can insert or open spreadsheets for which you have a valid converter file. Word for Windows ships with converter files for Lotus 1-2-3 and Microsoft Excel files, but you can get others. See "Opening Files," "Inserting Files," or "Object Linking and Embedding" for a further explanation of how to insert spreadsheets into your Word document.

Insertion Point

The insertion point is the blinking upright line that appears in your document. This line indicates where you are in the document at the moment. When you type text, it appears at the insertion point's location. The insertion point may also be called the cursor. If you are unfamiliar with the insertion point, or how to move it, see Chapter 1.

Install

Installing Word, or any of its ancillary files, is done using the Word Setup program. A full explanation of how to install Word, and how to use the Setup program to install further components, is given in Appendix A .

Italics

Italics is a character format that produces slanted text. You may use italicized text to provided emphasis for new terms or for explanatory text.

Procedures

The Italics style is applied either as text is typed, or after it is typed. To apply it while typing, add the format, type the text, and then remove the format. To apply it to typed text, select the text and add the style.

Adding and Removing Italics with the Menu

1. Select Format | Font (Character in the Word for Windows 2), or in Word for Windows 6, right-click the document area and select Font.

2. Select the Italic check box. Clear it to remove the format. Select OK.

Adding and Removing Italic with the Mouse

Select the Italic button from the Formatting toolbar, to toggle the Italic format on or off.

Adding and Removing Italic with the Keyboard

Press CTRL+I to add or remove the Italic format.

Hints

Another way to open the Character dialog box in Word for Windows 2 is to double-click on a blank spot of the ribbon.

Removing Formatting

Another procedure for removing italics from text is to select the text and press CTRL+SPACEBAR. This removes all character formatting from the selected text.

Related Topics

Character Formats
Fonts

Justification

See "Alignment."

Kerning

See "Spacing Characters."

Keyboard Options

You can change the assignment of macros or commands to various key combinations.

Procedures for Windows 6

1. Select Tools | Customize.

2. Select the Keyboard tab if necessary.

3. Select a category of things you want to assign shortcut keys to from the Categories list box. You can choose to assign shortcut keys to commands, macros, fonts, AutoText entries, styles, or common symbols.

4. Select the specific item you want to assign a shortcut key to from the Commands (Macros, Fonts, AutoText, Styles, or Common Symbols) list box. The Current Keys list box displays the keys currently assigned to this item.

5. In the Press New Shortcut Key text box, press the key combination you want to use for the currently highlighted item. The keys' current assignment displays beneath this text box when you press keys.

6. Select or enter a template in the Save Changes In drop-down list box to indicate which template these keyboard assignments are saved with.

   If they are saved with the Normal template, they will be available for all documents. Otherwise, they are only available for documents created with the template they are saved in.

7. Select Assign, to assign the shortcut key displayed in the Press New Shortcut Key text box to the selected item.

8. Select Remove to unassign the shortcut key highlighted in the Current Key list box.

9. Select Reset All to return to the default key assignments.

10. Select Close to return to the document and save your key assignments.

K

Procedures for Windows 2

1. Select Tools | Options in Word for Windows 2.

2. Select the Keyboard icon from the Category box.

3. Select Commands or Macros depending on what you want to assign key combinations to.

4. Select Global to make key assignments available to all documents, or Template to make them available only with the current template.

5. Select the key to assign to an item using the options under Shortcut Keys, using the Ctrl and Shift check boxes and the Key drop-down list box.

6. Select the macro or command to assign to the key combination, using the Commands or Macros list box. The Current Keys For list box shows the keys the selected command or macro is currently assigned to.

7. Select Add to assign the command or macro to the keystroke combination. To delete the key assignment, select Delete. To return to the default key assignments, select Reset All. Select OK.

Select Delete to delete the key assignment you selected in the Current Keys For list box.

Select Reset All when you want to restore most of the original Word key assignments in the NORMAL.DOT template. When you select this command while another template is active, that template's key assignments are set to the same as the NORMAL.DOT key assignments.

Related Topics

Shortcut Keys

Keywords

See "Summary Info."

KEYWORDS Field

See "Fields."

Labels

You can create mailing labels using the Mail Merge and Print Merge features. See "Mail Merge" for more information.

Landscape Printing

Landscape printing prints the page with the widest side of the paper at the top. See "Page Size and Orientation and Printing."

Language

See "Foreign Language Support."

LASTSAVEDBY field

Displays the date the current document was saved. See "Fields."

Layering Text and Graphics

When you look at a document in Word for Windows 6, you can visualize one sheet of paper on which your text and graphics are placed. Although everything appears to be integrated on one sheet, Word actually has three "layers," with one layer above the text and one layer below it. Think of these layers as sheets of mylar that allow the entries on all three layers to be visible.

Procedure

When you draw on a document with the Draw feature, the object you create is automatically placed on the layer above your text. These steps explain how to move a drawing object you have drawn using the Drawing toolbar to the layer above or below your document text.

1. Select the object.

2. Click the Drawing button in the Standard toolbar.

L

3. Select the Send Behind Text button from the Drawing toolbar to move the object behind your text. You can also select the Bring in Front of Text button when you want the selected drawn objects moved from behind text to in front of it. These buttons are shown in the margin.

Figure 4-31 shows a document with a drawing of a cat and a feeding dish behind the text. The feeding dish was drawn using the Line, Arc, and Ellipse buttons on the Drawing toolbar. The cat came from the CAT.WMF file in the CLIPART directory. The cat is added as the contents of a text box that was drawn using the Text Box button on the Drawing toolbar. Once the feeding dish was drawn and the cat added, these objects were selected; then the Send Behind Text button was selected to put them behind the document text. Notice that you do not need to put the document text in a text box. When you move a drawn object behind text, you are putting it behind the main text of the document.

NOTE: *You may also need to use the Send Behind Text and Bring in Front of Text buttons to make drawn objects appear on top of embedded objects.*

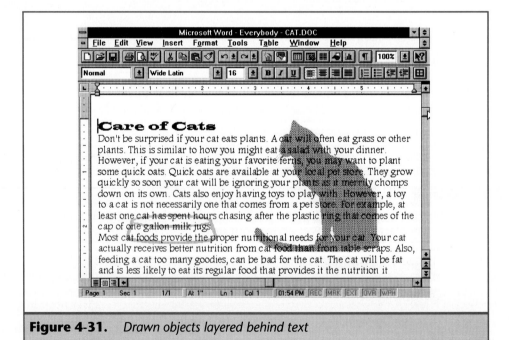

Figure 4-31.   *Drawn objects layered behind text*

Hints

Imported graphics are always placed on the layer with the text and cannot be moved behind or in front of text. If you want to create a watermark logo with an imported graphic, or you want to put an imported graphic behind text, you will need to put it in a text box using the Text Box button in the Drawing toolbar, rather than putting the imported graphic in a frame.

Related Topics

Drawing on a Document
Drawing Toolbar
Watermarks

Layout

See "Margins," "Page Size and Orientation," "Paper Source," and "Sections."

Leading

See "Spacing."

Left-Alignment

See "Alignment."

Left Justification

See "Alignment."

Legal Documents

Word provides a wizard for creating legal pleadings. To use it, all you need to do is select File | New and choose the Pleading Wizard. Use the dialog boxes for your entries.

Word also will help you create a table of authorities for your legal documents, as described under "Table of Authorities."

Letter Spacing

See "Spacing Characters."

Line Draw

With WordPerfect, you use Line Draw to draw lines and other shapes on your page. With Word, you can use Draw features or borders and frames for the same effects. See "Drawing on a Document" and "Borders and Shading."

Line Numbers

Word can print line numbers in the left margin of your documents. This feature is often used in legal documents and is also useful, for example, in a document that will be discussed in a meeting. Word assigns a number to each line of text, but not to any extra spacing between lines that is achieved with a spacing value greater than 1. Header and footer lines are not numbered, nor are the blank lines before and after paragraphs. Word also does not number lines in headers, footers, footnotes, and endnotes.

In Word for Windows 6 you use File Page Setup to add line numbers; in Word for Windows 2 you use the Format | Section Layout command. The page numbers appear in Page Layout view and Print Preview. Since the line numbers are in the left margin, in Page Layout you may need to shift the document display to the left in order to see the numbers.

Procedures

The procedure for adding line numbers is different in Word for Windows 6 and 2, but the same options are available in both versions of the program. Line numbering is a format that you assign to sections of your document; when you select the parts of your document to assign line numbers, follow these guidelines:

■ When your document is not divided into sections, line numbers will be added to the whole document.

■ When your document is divided into sections, move the insertion point to the section, or select text in each of several sections, that you want to have line numbers.

■ To number just a few lines of your document, select those lines only. Word will add section breaks before and after them when you apply this format.

Adding Line Numbers in Word for Windows 6

1. Select the section of the document to be numbered.

2. Select File | Page Setup, the Layout tab, and the Line Numbers button.

3. Select the Add Line Numbering check box.

4. Designate any options you want to use for line numbers, as described below in "Options."

5. Select OK twice. Figure 4-32 shows a document with line numbers.

Adding Line Numbers in Word for Windows 2

1. Select the section of the document to be numbered.

2. Select Format | Section Layout, and the Line Numbers button.

3. Select the Add Line Numbering check box.

4. Designate any options you want to use for line numbers, as described below in "Options."

5. Select OK twice.

Options

Following are the options Word offers for customizing a document's line numbers.

STARTING WITH A NUMBER OTHER THAN 1   You can enter a number in the Start At text box to assign it as the number of the first line. This number starts the line numbering for the entire section. Whether or not this number displays depends on the increment that you choose. For example, if you enter 2, then set the increment as 3, the numbering works like this:

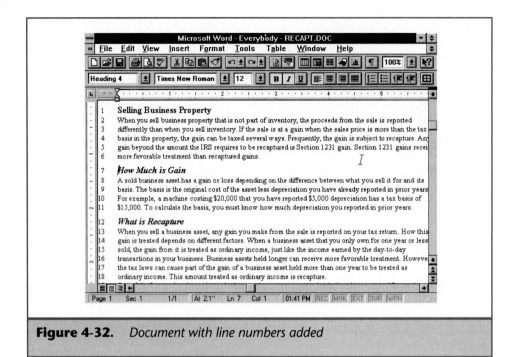

Figure 4-32. *Document with line numbers added*

Actual Line Number	Line Number Displayed
1	
2	3
3	
4	
5	6
6	
7	
8	9
9	
10	

USING AN INCREMENT OTHER THAN 1   You can choose to number every other line, every third line, and so on. Set the numbering increment in the Count By text box. For example, if you enter 3 in this text box, Word numbers lines with 3, 6, 9, 12, and so on.

THE DISTANCE BETWEEN NUMBERS AND THE TEXT You can designate the amount of space between the right side of the line numbers and the left side of the text, by entering a distance measurement in the From Text text box. The default of Auto is .25 inch, unless you are using newspaper style columns, where the default is .13 inch. This setting does not change the margins for the text; rather, the line numbers appear within the margin. If you set this distance at more than the margin width, the line numbers will not appear.

THE LOCATION TO START NUMBERING Word can start line numbering on each new page, at each new section, or from the beginning to the end of the document. Designate this by selecting the Restart Each Page, Restart Each Section, or Continuous (Continue in Word for Windows 2).

Hints

You can quickly number paragraphs rather than individual lines, using the Numbering button in the Formatting toolbar that adds paragraph numbers. See "Lists" for more information about numbering paragraphs.

You can suppress line numbering for specific paragraphs. When you suppress line numbering in a paragraph, Word skips the paragraph when numbering lines, as if the paragraph were not there. To do this, move the insertion point to the paragraph (or select text in several paragraphs) that you don't want to be numbered, and select Format | Paragraph. In Word for Windows 6, also select the Text Flow tab. Then select the Suppress Line Numbers option.

Related Topics

Page Numbers

Line Spacing

See "Spacing."

LINK Field

The LINK field displays the contents of data in another file. See "Fields or "Object Linking and Embedding."

Linking

See "Object Linking and Embedding."

Lists

You can easily create numbered or bulleted lists with Word. These lists are useful for listing steps in a procedure or highlighting important points or agenda topics.

Procedures

The procedures for creating lists are different, based on whether you are creating a bulleted or numbered list, and whether you are using Word for Windows 2 or 6.

Creating a Bulleted or Numbered List in Word for Windows 6

1. Select the paragraphs to which you want to add bullets or numbers.

2. Select Format | Bullets and Numbering. You can also right-click the selected paragraphs and select Bullets and Numbering from the shortcut menu.

3. Select the Bulleted, Numbered, or Multilevel tab, depending on what you want to put in front of the list items.

    When you select the Multilevel tab, the level added to the paragraphs will depend on the indentation of the paragraph or the tabs at the beginning of the paragraph. The paragraphs with the least indentation or fewest tabs will have the highest level numbering.

4. Select the type of bullet, number, or multilevel labeling that you want in your list, and then select OK.

NOTE: If you do not see a list option that you want, you can create one as described below under "Options." You can choose the character used for the bullets or numbers, as well as their size and placement. If you want to set levels using styles, use the Outline features described under "Outlines."

Figure 4-33 shows a document with bullets added to several paragraphs, to create lists.

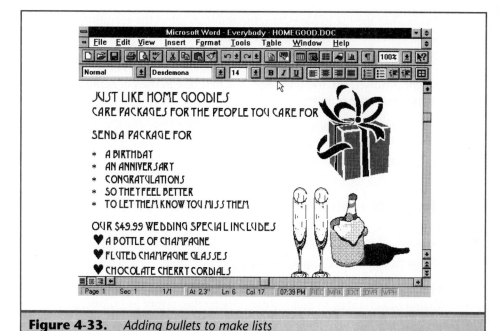

Figure 4-33.   *Adding bullets to make lists*

Creating a Bulleted List in Word for Windows 2

1. Select the paragraphs you want to format as a bulleted list.

2. Select Tools | Bullets and Numbering.

3. Select the Bullets option button; the Bullets and Numbering dialog box changes to display the options that apply to bullets.

4. Under Bullet Character, choose a bullet style. If you don't like the bullets presented there, you can select New Bullet, opening the Symbol dialog box, from which you can select another bullet.

5. Designate a size for the bullets by entering a font size in the Point Size text box.

6. If you want to replace the bullets in a bulleted list with other bullets, or the numbers in a numbered list with bullets, select the Replace Only Bullets check box. Leave this option off when you do not want to add bullets to paragraphs that do not already start with numbers or bullets.

L

7. If you want the list to have hanging indents, select the Hanging Indent check box. (In this style, the bullet appears at the page margin, the text of the first line begins some distance away, and the other lines in the paragraph align with the start of text in the first line. When Hanging Indent is turned off, the lines after the first line in the paragraph are aligned with the bullet.)

   To designate the alignment of the lines after the hanging indent, enter a value in the By text box.

8. Select OK.

Creating a Numbered List in Word for Windows 2

1. Select the paragraphs you want to turn into a numbered list.

2. Select Tools | Bullets and Numbering.

3. Select the Numbered List option button; the Bullets and Numbering dialog box changes to display the options that apply to numbered lists.

4. Choose a format for the numbers from the Format drop-down list box.

5. In the Separator drop-down list box, select a character to appear between the paragraph numbers and the paragraph text, or enter one in the text box.

6. In the Start At text box, enter the number for the first item in the list.

7. If you want to replace the numbers in a numbered list with other numbers, or the bullets in a bulleted list with numbers, select the Replace Only Numbers check box. Leave this option off when you do not want to add numbers or bullets to paragraphs that do not already start with numbers.

8. If you want the list to have hanging indents, select the Hanging Indent check box. (In this style, the number appears at the page margin, the text of the first line begins some distance away, and the other lines in the paragraph align with the start of text in the first line. When Hanging Indent is turned off, the lines after the first line in the paragraph are aligned with the number.)

   To designate the alignment of the lines after the hanging indent, enter a value in the By text box.

9. Select OK.

Creating Numbered or Bulleted Lists with the Toolbar

Select the paragraphs you want to format as a bulleted or numbered list. Then click the Bullets or Numbering button on the toolbar.

When you select these buttons, Word automatically creates a list with a hanging indent of .25 inches. If the paragraphs you selected were already formatted as a numbered or bulleted list, Word prompts you to confirm that you want to replace the current numbers or bullets. Select Yes to replace them.

Removing Bullets and Numbers

If you want to convert paragraphs from a list back to regular text, select the paragraphs, then select Format | Bullets and Numbering (Tools | Bullets and Numbering in Word for Windows 2), and then the Remove command button.

Options

In Word for Windows 6, when you select Modify from the Bullets and Numbering dialog box, you can change the characters used for the bullets or numbers, their size, and their position. The dialog box changes to offer appropriate options for bullets or numbers.

SPECIFYING THE APPEARANCE OF BULLETS OR MULTILEVEL BULLETS
The top of Bullet Character area selects the actual character of the bullet. Select from the characters shown or select Bullet and choose a symbol from the Symbol dialog box. Point Size sets the size of the bullet or number. The default is Auto, rather than an actual point size, which lets Word determine the bullet or number size depending on the size of the adjacent text. Use the Color drop-down list box to choose the color of the bullet or number.

SETTING THE APPEARANCE OF NUMBERS   Under Number Format, enter any text you want to appear before and after the number in the Text Before and Text After text boxes. Remember to include any blank spaces you want in this text. Set the style of the number to one of the choices listed in the Number drop-down box. To change the font of the number and text, select Font and choose a font. You can also set the starting number of the series with the Start At text box.

CHOOSING THE POSITION OF THE NUMBER OR BULLET   In the Bullet Position or Number Position section of the dialog box, you select the position of the bullet/number Word will add. Choose the alignment from the Alignment of

L

List Text drop-down list box; designate the amount of space between the left margin and the bullet/number with Distance from Indent to Text, and the amount of space between the bullet/number and the text with Distance from Number to Text; and specify the indentation of the rest of the paragraph by turning Hanging Indent check box on or off.

When you select the Multilevel tab before you select Modify, the options presented are slightly different. Since you can choose the identification of each individual level, you must first select the level you want to change from the Level list box. The other settings match the current settings for the selected level. You can also have a level adapt the number and position options from the prior level, by selecting either Nothing, Numbers, or Numbers and Position from the Include from Previous Level drop-down list box.

Hints

Arrange your list with the most important entries first.

TIP: You can quickly add bullets or numbers to selected paragraphs using the Bullets or Numbering buttons in the toolbar. In Word for Windows 6, you can also make a paragraph start with a bullet by pressing SHIFT+CTRL+L.

Related Topics

Outlines

Locate

See "Find and Replace."

Lock Documents or Files

You can lock a document using a password when you save the file, or lock a document so that only its original author can edit it. See "Locking and Protecting Documents," "Saving Files" and "Annotation" for explanations of these features.

Locking and Protecting Documents

There will be times that you do not want your documents edited. To prevent editing, you can lock your document, protecting it against changes. There are several different ways to lock your document, and each method has a slightly different effect on how your document can be edited.

Word for Windows 6 offers you the ability to use a password with a file to prevent unauthorized users from accessing it, and to lock a master or subdocument to prevent changes. Word for Windows 6 also offers you the ability to protect a document for annotations, revisions or forms. Protect a document for annotations, and only annotations can be added to the document. No other changes can be made. Protect a document for revisions, and all changes made to the text are marked. Protect a document as a form, and you can only move between form fields in the document, not changing any other text. When you protect a document, you can use a password so that it cannot be unprotected by a user.

Word for Windows 2 offers you the ability to use a password to prevent unauthorized users from opening the file. You can also lock a document for annotations, not permitting any changes except annotations in the file. In Word for Windows 2, while you can choose to mark revisions, you cannot use a password to make sure that the mark revisions feature is not turned off.

Procedures

Word for Windows 2 and 6 offer a variety of ways to lock your documents against other users or to protect it against undocumented changes. In Word for Windows 2, all protecting is done in the process of saving the document, and these protection are options are described as follows in "Saving a Document with Passwords." In Word for Windows 6, there are further protection features, for annotations, merge revisions, forms and master documents, which are set separately.

Saving a Document with Passwords

1. Select File | Save or Save As.

2. Select the directory you want to save the file in using the Directory and Drive boxes.

3. Enter the name for the file in the File Name text box.

4. Select Options or File Sharing, make your protection settings as described below, and select OK.

L

In Word for Windows 2, you can now set a password or lock the document for annotations:

Protection Password Type a password of up to 15 characters in the text box, and the document cannot be opened by anyone unless they provide this password. When you select OK from the File Sharing dialog box, you must enter the password again and select OK to confirm.

Lock for Annotations Select this check box, and when any other user opens your document, they will only be able to insert annotations.

In Word for Windows 6, you can now set how the document file is locked:

Protection Password Enter a password in this text box, and the file cannot be opened unless the password is supplied by the person attempting to open it. When you select OK from the Options dialog box, you must enter the password again and select OK to confirm.

Write Reservation Password Type a password in this text box, and the person opening the document can either provide the password and open the document normally, or open the document without the password as read-only. Read-only documents cannot be saved using the same file name. When you select OK from the Options dialog box, you must reenter the password and select OK.

Read-Only Recommended Select this check box to have Word display a message when the user attempts to open this document recommending that they open it read-only. However, the user can still choose, without using a password, to open the document normally.

5. Select OK to save the document with the file protection settings you have defined.

Protecting for Annotations, Revisions or Forms (Word for Windows 6 Only)

1. Select Tools | Protect Document.

2. Select what you want to protect the document for:

Revisions Select this option button, and Word lets you edit the document, but marks all changes made. You can change how revisions are marked using the Tools | Revisions command.

Annotations Select this option button, and you cannot edit your document. However, you can insert annotations.

Forms   Select this option button, and you cannot edit or move to text in your document. You can move between and make selections or entries to form fields. When this option button is selected and the document has more than one section, the Sections button is selectable. (This button is used as described in step 4.)

TIP: You cannot protect your document in more than one way at one time.

3. To ensure that your document stays protected, enter a password in the Password text box. Before the document can be unprotected, this password has to be supplied.

4. Select Sections, when the Forms option button is selected, if you want to let users edits certain sections of your document. Clear the check boxes for the sections you want unprotected from the Protect list box. Then select OK.

REMINDER: Sections are divided using section breaks.

5. Select OK to protect the document.

Removing Document Protection (Word for Windows 6 Only)

You can remove document protection by selecting Tools | Unprotect Document. If you supplied a password when protecting the document, Word now prompts you for the password. If you do not supply the correct password, the document is not unprotected.

Locking and Unlocking Master and Subdocuments

Master documents are documents that contain field references to other Word documents, called subdocuments. Subdocuments appear in the master documents, as if they were portions of the master document. When you open a master document that you created, it and all the subdocuments that you created are unlocked, while any subdocuments in it that you did not create are locked.

You can also choose to lock the master document or the subdocuments, even if you did create them. Locked documents cannot be edited until they are unlocked.
   To lock or unlock a master or subdocument:

1. Put the insertion point in the master document outside any subdocuments, or in the subdocument you want to lock or unlock.

2. Click the Lock Document button on the Master Document toolbar.

Hints

As you can tell by reviewing the steps given above, protecting a document is of little use for maintaining security unless you include a password. These non-password protection features are not used to protect against unauthorized changes so much as against accidental changes. These protection features are a tool to let you work with documents, without having to worry that you will accidentally delete or change text beyond revision. This is particularly important when you are reviewing technical or legal documents, or when you are reviewing a document shared among several different people.

Passwords are case-sensitive. For example, SAFE, Safe, and safe are treated as three different passwords.

When security is an issue, and you are attempting to prevent documents against unauthorized access or changes, you need to use the passwords. The downside to using passwords is that if you forget your passwords those documents are no longer available to you. If you use passwords, be sure to record them in a secure location. Another alternative is to keep copies of the file, saved without a password, on a disk kept in a secure location as backups.

The terms *read-only* and *read-write* refer to how you can open documents. Documents opened with read-write, which is the usual way of opening documents, can be edited and saved. Files opened read-only can be edited, but if you want to save the document, you must use a different filename.

Related Topics

Annotation
Comparing Versions
Forms
Master Documents
Opening Files
Saving Files

Logical Operators

See "Equations."

Lotus

The Lotus Development Corporation publishes the popular 1-2-3 spreadsheet program. Word can open spreadsheets files created in 1-2-3, as described in "Opening Files." You can open files with the .WK1 and .WK3 formats. You can also embed 1-2-3 for Windows objects in Word files; see "Object Linking and Embedding."

Lowercase

See "Capitalization."

Macro Toolbar

The Word for Windows 6 Macro toolbar has buttons for running and recording macros, but most of its buttons are to help you edit your macros. Following are descriptions of the Macro toolbar buttons:

Toolbar Button	Name	Task Performed
Logo	Active Macro	Selects the macro to be active and affected by the buttons on the Macro toolbar
	Record	Records your commands and actions and adds them to the macro
	Record Next Command	Records the next command you select and adds it to the macro
	Start	Runs the macro
	Trace	Runs the macro and highlights each statement as it is performed
	Continue	Continues macro execution after a pause
	Stop	Halts macro execution
	Step	Steps through the macro one statement at a time

M

Toolbar Button	Name	Task Performed
	Step Subs	Steps through the macro one subroutine at a time
	Show Variables	Shows the variables in a macro when you are running it, so you can see their current value
	Add/ Remove REM	Adds and removes REM from the selected lines; converting them between statement and remarks
	Macro	Displays the Tools	Macro command's dialog box
	Dialog Editor	Starts the Dialog Editor application to create a dialog box for the macro to use

Word for Windows 6 also has a Macro Record toolbar that has only a Stop and Pause button. The buttons in the Word for Windows 2 Macro toolbar include Start, Continue, Step, Step SUBs, Trace, and Vars. They perform the same feature as the buttons in the Word for Windows 6 Macro toolbar. They have underlined letters so you can select the button by pressing ALT+SHIFT and the underlined letter.

NOTE: For more details on working with macros, and the functions of these toolbar buttons, see Chapter 7.

Related Topics

Macros

MACROBUTTON Field

The MACROBUTTON field displays text that, when selected, starts a macro. For a full explanation of how this field works, see "Macros" in this chapter.

Macros

A *macro* is a set of instructions that tell Word how to perform a task. You can tell Word to record the selections you make from Word menus and store them as a macro, then replay this macro when you want to quickly perform the task.

When you record a macro, Word converts your menu selections to WordBasic commands. With some additional technical guidance and practice, you can also write your own WordBasic instructions that extend macro capabilities even further. If you take this approach, you can add *logic* to your commands to test for specific conditions, or create your own dialog boxes and process user input.

The macros you create are stored with the NORMAL template accessible by all documents, or with another template attached to your current document. After you finish recording a macro, you will need to choose File | Save All to save the template along with any macros that you have stored in it.

This section focuses on the macro recorder feature of Word. Chapter 7 provides some additional macro examples as well as a discussion of some more advanced techniques for creating and testing macros.

Procedures

The basic steps in creating and using a macro are recording it, editing it, and running it. You can also stop and restart the macro recording, rename the macro, and assign it to a toolbar, menu, shortcut key, or button in the document.

Recording a Macro

1. Set up a document so it has the conditions you plan to have in effect when you use the macro.

2. When you are ready to start recording, activate the macro recorder by double-clicking the status bar button REC in Word for Windows 6, or choosing Tools | Macro and selecting the Record button. (In Word for Windows 2, select Tools | Record Macro.)

3. Type a name for the macro in the Record Macro Name box, or accept the name Word suggests. Do not include spaces, periods, or commas in your macro name. When your macro name is acceptable, the OK button will become available.

4. In Word for Windows 2, if you want to use a key-combination to run this macro, type the letter in the Shortcut Key drop-down list box or select it from the list. In Word for Windows 6, there are more options for specifying, while you are recording it, how a macro will run, so follow the instructions under "Assigning a Macro to a Toolbar, Menu, or Shortcut Key" in this section.

5. If you want to, type up to 255 characters in the Description box as an optional description of the macro.

M

6. Choose OK to close the dialog box.

7. Perform the actions you want recorded. In Word for Windows 6, notice that the mouse pointer now has a cassette tape next to it, and your workspace now contains a Macro Record toolbar with buttons for Stop (the one with the square) and Pause (the one with the two lines and a circle).

WARNING: When performing these actions, you will want to work carefully, avoiding mistakes and mistyping. Though you can correct any errors by editing the macro, the process of creating it is easier when there are not mistakes to correct.

In Word for Windows 6, when you want to pause while recording a macro—for instance, to add data to your document so your macro will have the entries it needs to work on, or if you just want to check out a few button options without recording them—you can use the Pause command and then resume recording when you are ready. Just click Pause in the Macro Record toolbar, perform the actions that you do not want recorded, and click Pause again to restart the recording process.

8. When you have performed all the steps of your task, click the Stop button in the Macro Record toolbar or double-click REC on the status bar. The Macro Record toolbar disappears. (In Word for Windows 2, select Tools | Stop Recorder.)

WARNING: Word does not record mouse clicks, except for clicks to select menu commands and dialog box options. Most of the time, Word will beep when you try doing something with a mouse that Word cannot record in a macro.

Running a Macro

Macros are often attached to a key, toolbar button, or menu; however, if this is not the case, you will need to run the macro from the Macro dialog box.

NOTE: Word offers buttons in the Macro toolbar that you can use when running a macro to control how quickly it runs. These are used when you are testing a macro to make sure there are no mistakes. You will find more information about the Step, Step Subs, Trace and Show Variables buttons in Chapter 7 "Macros."

1. Select Tools | Macro.

2. In Word for Windows 6, if you don't see the macro you want, select a different macro source from the Macros Available In box.

3. Select the macro to run in the Macro Name box, and then select OK.

Assigning a Macro to a Toolbar, Menu, or Shortcut Key

The quickest way to access a macro is by assigning it to a toolbar, menu, or shortcut key. In Word for Windows 2, you must create the macro and then assign it, in two separate operations if you want to assign it to a toolbar or menu. In Word for Windows 6, you can assign the macro when you create it.

NOTE: *In both Word for Windows 2 and 6, to assign macros you have already created to a toolbar, menu, or shortcut key, follow instructions in "Toolbar Options," "Menu Options," and "Keyboard Options" in this chapter.*

In Word for Windows 6, when you assign a macro you are creating to a toolbar, menu, and shortcut key, the procedure is the same as creating a macro as described above in "Recording a Macro," except you have a few more steps to perform. Start by following the steps given above for recording a macro. When you select OK in the Macro dialog box, as mentioned in step 6 above, the Record Macro dialog box appears. In this dialog box:

1. Select Toolbars, Menus, or Keyboard, depending on where you want the macro assigned. Then specify how you want the macro assigned.

   If you selected Toolbars in step 1, drag the macro from the list box containing the macro name to the desired position on any of the available toolbars. Then, from the Custom Button dialog box, choose one of the buttons. (You can also select Edit to create a new custom button.) If you select Text Button, enter the text you want to appear on the button in the Text Button Name text box. Select Assign.

   If you selected Menus in step 1, select where the macro appears as a menu command. From the Change What Menu drop-down list box, select the menu where the macro will appear as a command. From the Position on Menu drop-down list box, select the position for the macro in the menu; the default is Auto, to let Word decide where it is placed. You can also use this drop-down list box to see the underlined letters of the menu commands already in the menu; the underlined letters have an ampersand (&) in front of them. In the Name on Menu text box, you can

M

alter the macro name to what you want to appear on the menu; this includes putting an & in front of the character you want underlined. You can also select Menu Bar and add another menu to the menu system, and add the macro to that menu. Select Add to add the macro to the menu.

If you selected Keyboard in step 1, press the key-combination you want to use for the macro while in the Press New Shortcut Key text box. Examine the text under Currently Assigned To to see if some other macro or Word function is assigned to the key-combination you chose. If another function uses the key-combination, press BACKSPACE to remove the key-combination and enter a different one. Select Assign to assign the key combination.

2. When you are satisfied with your choices, select Close.

3. Perform the actions you want recorded to execute the task.

4. After you have performed the last step of the task, click the Stop button in the Macro Record toolbar, or double-click REC on the status bar.

Assigning a Macro to a Button in the Document

Another option for executing a macro is to assign it to a "button" in your document.

1. Move to the position in your document where you want the macro button, and select Insert | Field.

2. Select the MACROBUTTON field from the Field Names list box (Insert Field Type list box in Word for Windows 2). It now appears in the Field Codes text box.

3. In Word for Windows 6, select Options.

4. In the Macro Name list box (Instructions list box in Word for Windows 2), select the macro to run when the button is clicked. This list box contains macro instructions for most Word commands, as well as the macro names you see in the Macro dialog box (displayed with the Tools | Macro command). The macro name appears in the Field Codes text box as part of the MACROBUTTON field.

5. In the Field Codes text box, type the text you want to see as the macro button. For example, the final entry in the Field Codes text box might be something like this:

   MACROBUTTON TotalAllNumbers [Double-click here to calculate the totals].

6. Select OK twice (once in Word for Windows 2).

At this point, you can run the macro by double-clicking the button, or by moving to the button and pressing ALT+SHIFT+F9. For example, the result of assigning the TotalAllNumbers macro to a button, as described in step 5 above, will look like this in the finished document:

Summary Report [Double-click here to calculate the totals]

NOTE: *If you see the field code instead of the assigned macro text, press* SHIFT+F9 *to switch from displaying field codes to field results.*

Moving or Copying Macros to Another Template in Word for Windows 6

Word automatically stores new macros in the NORMAL.DOT template, making the macros available in all documents. Macros that you only need for specialized applications can be copied or moved to other templates.

1. Select Tools | Macro.

2. Choose the Organizer button.

3. In the Macros Available In box on the *left* side of the dialog box, select the template where the macro is now stored.

NOTE: *You may need to use the Close File button under Macros Available In box if another template is open. Then select the Open File button and open the desired template.*

4. In the Macros Available In on the *right* side of the dialog box, select the template to which you want move or copy the macro.

NOTE: *You may need to use the Close File button if you have another template open. Then use the Open File button to open the desired template.*

M

5. In the In or To list box of macro names, select the macro you want to move or copy. (When you select a macro from either list box, that list box becomes the In list box and the other list box becomes the To list box. This lets you copy from either source of macros to the other.)

6. Select the Copy button.

7. If you are removing the original macro, select the Delete button; if you are copying the macro, you can skip this step.

8. Select the Close button.

Renaming a Macro

1. Select Tools | Macro.

2. Choose the Organizer button. (Word for Windows 2 users, skip to step 4.)

3. In the Macros Available In box on the *left* side of the dialog box, select the template where the macro is stored.

NOTE: You may need to use the Close File button under Macros Available In box if another template is open. Then select the Open File button and open the desired template.

4. Select the macro name you want to change.

5. Choose the Rename button, type the new name, and select OK.

6. Select the Close button.

Editing a Macro

1. Select Tools | Macro.

2. In Word for Windows 6, if the macro you want is not displayed, select the source of macros you want to edit from the Macros Available In box.

3. Select the macro to edit in the Macro Name box, and then select Edit.

4. Make your changes to the macro.

Figure 4-34 shows a macro opened for editing. Most of the macro instructions in this case are for menu commands, so the macro statement for Format | Draw Object command includes all of the possible settings that can be made for the text box the command is formatting. When you edit a macro, Word gives you the Macro toolbar, which provides many of the features you will need when you are editing a macro.

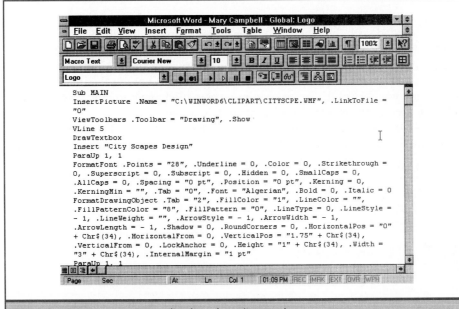

Figure 4-34. *A macro, edited to show instructions*

5. Close the macro window just as you would close a document window.

6. When prompted, select Yes to save the edited macro.

Using Macros Supplied With Word for Windows 6 as Models

Word for Windows 6 provides a number of existing macros. These macros are stored in the CONVERT.DOT, LAYOUT.DOT, MACRO60.DOT, and TABLES.DOT templates. If you load one of these templates as a global template, you can use its macros in your document. You can also use the Organizer to copy any of these macros from its template to the NORMAL.DOT template, or to a template of your own.

M

NOTE: *If you did not do a complete Word for Windows installation, you may need to run the setup program again to copy these templates containing macros to your disk.*

Hints

Macros recorded with the macro recorder require conditions while they are recorded to be the same as the conditions under which they will work. This is because the task is actually performed as the macro is recorded. For instance, if you are creating a macro to copy the two paragraphs following the insertion point, when you record the macro you must actually have two paragraphs following the insertion point in your current document.

If you hear a beep when you are recording a macro, it may be that Word does not record actions performed with a mouse (except for clicking to select menu commands and dialog box options). You may want to move the mouse out of reach while recording the macro, in case you forget and reach for it out of habit.

To make a macro from another template available in the document you are using, add the macro's template as a global template. See "Templates" for complete instructions.

Related Topics

Fields
Keyboard Options
Macro Toolbar
Menu Options
Organizer
Templates
Toolbar Options

Mail Merge

Word's Mail Merge feature lets you combine text in a main document with variable data stored in a data source. Mail Merge can dramatically accelerate and simplify the process of creating many similar copies of a document. Your data source can have hundreds or thousands of entries — typically names and addresses — that are combined with unchanging text in the main document to create customized letters, mailing labels, or advertisements. Figure 4-35 illustrates the process of merging records in a data source with a form letter to create many customized letters.

In Word for Windows 6, merge features are referred to as Mail Merge. In Word for Windows 2, the merge features are called Print Merge, and are described in "Print Merge" later in this chapter.

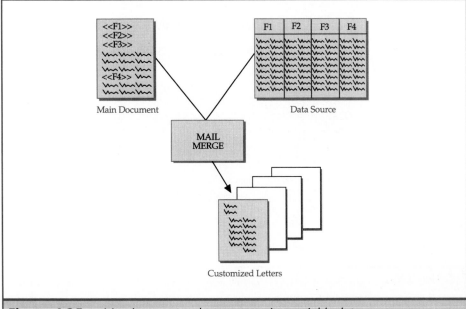

Figure 4-35.   *Merging creates documents using variable data*

Procedures

The Mail Merge Helper dialog box, a wizardlike helper that guides you through the required steps, is shown in Figure 4-36. This helper provides options for each step in the merge. You cannot select the final merge step until you have defined a main document and a data source with entries.

Creating the Main Document

The main document for a merge can be an existing document or a document you create from the Mail Merge Helper. To use an existing document, be sure to open it *before* activating the Mail Merge Helper.

M

1. Choose Mail Merge from the Tools menu, opening the Mail Merge Helper dialog box.

2. Select Create.

3. Select the type of main document you want Word to set up from the Create drop-down list. You can create a main document formatted for Form Letters; Mailing Labels; Envelopes; or Catalog for catalogs or other lists.

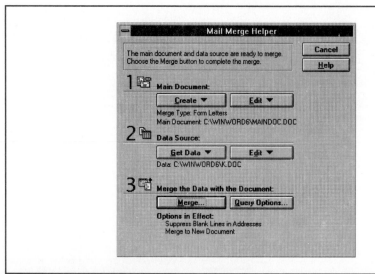

Figure 4-36.   *The Mail Merge Helper dialog box walks you through the merge operation*

Alternatively, select Restore to Normal Word Document to have Word break the connection between this document, assuming it is an existing main document, and the data source, making it a normal document again.

4. Choose the Active Window button to create the main document in the active window, or the New Main Document button to open a new window for creating the main document.

   The Active Window button is the Change Document Type button if the current document is already a main document.

5. Select Edit under Main Document in the Mail Merge Helper dialog box, then select the name of the document, and create your main document.

   The Mail Merge toolbar appears while you are creating or editing a mail merge main document or data source.

6. Select the Mail Merge Helper button from the Mail Merge toolbar to return to the Mail Merge Helper dialog box.

Mail Merge Helper

Creating and Maintaining the Data Source

The data source is a file containing the variable information to be inserted into a main document during a mail merge operation. Normally, the data source is organized into a table, with each type of variable information in a column and is known as a *data field*. Every row in the table contains one entry for each field in the table and is called a *data record*. You can enter values directly into the table or use a form for your entries.

Figure 4-37 displays a Data Form dialog box, used to enter data for a form letter. This dialog box makes it easy to enter complete data source entries. You can use the scroll bar at the side of the form to look at all of the data fields. You can also use the Record arrow buttons and text field at the bottom of the box to look at a different record. Data records are included in the data source in the order you enter them, though you can also sort and otherwise rearrange them when you work with the data source.

1. Select Get Data from the Data Source section of the Mail Merge Helper dialog box.

2. Choose your data source from the drop-down list box: Create Data Source to create a new data source; Open Data Source to open an existing data source and use it; or Header Options to set options regarding a separate header file. (Headers are described under "Header Files" later in this section.)

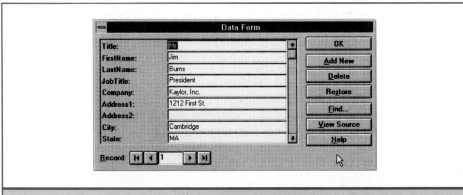

Figure 4-37. *Enter your data records in the Data Form dialog box*

M

NOTE: The remaining steps of this procedure assume that you selected Create Data Source in step 2.

3. Word displays field names in the Field Names in Header Row box in the Create Data Source dialog box shown below. These field names identify the fields that occur in each record of the data source.

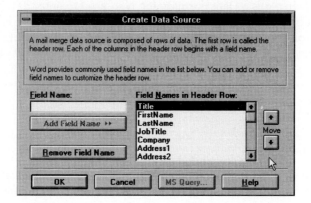

■ To add a field, type the field name in the Field Name text box and select Add Field Name. A field name can be up to 40 characters long; you may use only letters, numbers, or the underscore character. The first character must be a letter, and spaces are not allowed.

■ To remove a field, highlight the field name in the list box and select Remove Field Name.

■ To move a field in the list, highlight the field and reposition it using the up- and down-arrow buttons beside the list.

4. When the Field Names in Header Row list box shows the field names you want in the correct order, select OK. The Save Data Source dialog box appears. Type a new filename for the document in the File Name box, and select OK.

5. Word now allows you to edit the data source or enter a new document. Select Edit Data Source to enter the variable information for the merge. You enter this data in a Data Form dialog box, like the one shown in Figure 4-37.

6. Enter the variable information for this record into the text boxes labeled with the field names. Use TAB or SHIFT+TAB to move between the fields. Select Add New to enter the record and move to the next one.

As you are entering records, if you want to move to an earlier or later record, use the arrow buttons next to Record at the bottom of the Data Form, or enter the number of a particular record in the text box. Select Delete to remove the current record, and select Restore to restore an edited record to its most recent state. Find lets you search the records in the data source file for specific information, and View Source lets you view the entire document containing this source data.

7. Select OK when you are finished entering variable data. You can always return to the data source to enter further variable data later.

Using Fields in the Merge

You can add fields to your main document to control how your merge will occur. *Merge fields* indicate where contents of the data source are inserted into your final documents. *Word fields* can prompt you to enter data to include in your merge document, or can process information from your data source in a particular way, for instance, skipping records or displaying certain text.

Inserting Merge Fields

Merge fields allow you to place the variable data wherever you want it in the main document. When the merge is performed, the merge fields are converted to the values in the record being processed.

1. In the Mail Merge Helper dialog box, choose Edit under Main Document and select the main document you want to edit.

2. Position the insertion point where, in the main document, you want the variable information to be placed in the merged document.

3. Click the Insert Merge Field button in the Mail Merge toolbar.

 REMEMBER: *The Mail Merge toolbar appears when you are creating or editing a Mail Merge main document.*

M

4. Select a merge field from the list presented. Word inserts the field into your document surrounded by chevrons << >>. In Figure 4-38, fields have been added in the address block and salutation line. Merge fields are the fields that you created in your data source.

5. Repeat steps 2 through 4 until you have added all the fields you need.

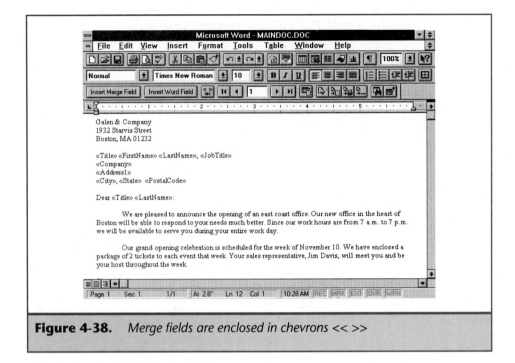

Figure 4-38. *Merge fields are enclosed in chevrons << >>*

6. Select File | Save to save the file.

7. Click the Mail Merge Helper button in the Mail Merge toolbar.

INSERTING WORD FIELDS   You can select the following Word fields from the Mail Merge toolbar:

When you select a field from this list, Word displays a dialog box in which you provide the information needed to create the field. For example, the dialog box for the Fill-in field is shown here:

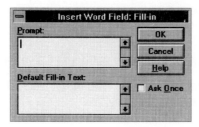

When you enter a Word field in the main document, you see the field's results rather than the field code. Or you can select Tools | Options and the View tab, and then the Field Codes check box under Show. When you change this setting, the field codes are displayed, as you can see in Figure 4-39. This main document uses only MERGEFIELD fields, which are inserted using the Insert Merge Field button in the Mail Merge toolbar.

To insert Word fields, follow these general steps:

1. In the Mail Merge Helper, select Edit under Main Document.

2. Position the insertion point where you want to insert the field.

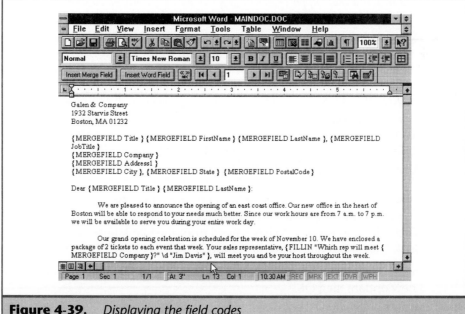

Figure 4-39. *Displaying the field codes*

3. Click the Insert Word Field button in the Mail Merge toolbar.

4. Choose the field you want to use.

5. Complete the dialog box for the field and select OK.

6. Click the Mail Merge Helper button in the Mail Merge toolbar to return to the Mail Merge Helper dialog box.

Executing the Merge

When you have entered all the records in the data source and created the final version of your main document, you are ready to complete the merge operation.

1. In the Mail Merge Helper dialog box, select Merge under Merge the Data with the Document, opening the Merge dialog box.

2. Select the location for the merge output in the Merge To drop-down list box. You can choose New Document or Printer.

NOTE: If you have an e-mail system installed that supports the messaging application programming interface (MAPI) or the vendor-independent messaging (VIM) standard, an Electronic Mail option will also appear. If you have a fax card installed that supports MAPI or VIM, an Electronic Fax option will appear.

3. To specify which records are to be merged, you can select the All option button under Records to be Merged, or you can select From and enter the first and last record to merge in the From and To text boxes.

WARNING: If you choose to specify records to be merged, make sure you know which records you are selecting, by opening the data source file and reviewing it. You may have sorted or reorganized your records, and left the sorted data source document open or saved it with changes. Word will use that list in the merge, so be sure that's what you want before you execute the merge.

4. If you don't want Word to print lines that are empty because a field is empty, select Don't print blank lines when data fields are empty, under When Merging Record. To have Word print the blank lines, select Print blank lines when data fields are empty.

5. To specify how Word handles merge error, select Check Errors and choose a new option, then OK.

6. Choose <u>Q</u>uery Options to select which records are merged by designating criteria for the records to match. See "Specifying Query Options to Choose Records" later in this section for more information.

7. Select <u>M</u>erge to execute the merge.

If you chose to merge to a new document (step 2), the merge documents will appear in the Word window behind the Mail Merge Helper. Close the Helper and review the merged records before printing the documents. Figure 4-40 shows one of the mail merge letters.

Options

Word provides many ways to customize your mail merges.

Word Fields

When creating the main document, select Word fields from the Insert Word Field button's drop-down list box. The fields you insert with this button let you alter

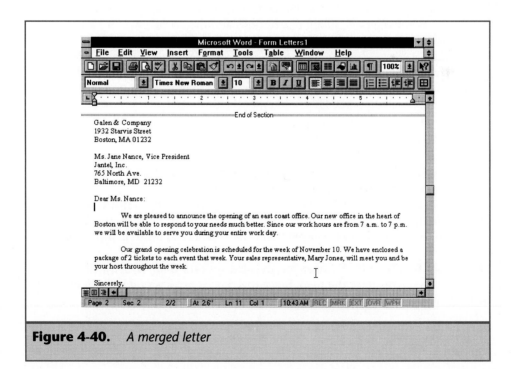

Figure 4-40. *A merged letter*

the merge in various ways. The names of the Word fields for mail merges that appear in this list are not the names you would look up in your documentation, or that appear in your document when the field codes are displayed. The following table explains the Word fields and their results:

Word Field	Field Code Inserted
Ask...	ASK field
Fill-in...	FILLIN field
If...Then...Else	IF field with the TextIfFalse argument
Merge Record #	MERGEREC field
Merge Sequence #	MERGESEQ field
Next Record	NEXT field
Next Record If...	NEXTIF field
Set Bookmark...	SET field
Skip Record If...	SKIPIF field

The following paragraphs describe the Word fields and switches as if you were actually typing the fields, rather than the dialog box elements you can use when inserting them from the Word fields list box in the Mail Merge toolbar. The relationships between the dialog box options and the actual switches are self-explanatory.

ASK FIELD   The ASK field is used to prompt the user for input while Word is merging documents. The input is used to control the merge program, or is inserted into the document. This field takes the format

{ASK *bookmark* "*prompt*"}

where *bookmark* is the bookmark assigned to the text, and *prompt* is the text that appears on the screen asking the user for the input.

You can use this field with the \o switch, to have Word prompt you only once when the merge begins, rather than for each record in the merge. Use the \d switch to specify the default text that is used when no input is provided.

FILLIN FIELD   The FILLIN field prompts the user for data, which will be displayed as the result of the field. Since this data is not assigned a bookmark, it is not available for use by other fields. This field uses the format

{FILLIN "*prompt*"}

where *prompt* is the text that prompts the user to the text that will be displayed.

Use the \d switch to specify the default data that is used when no input is provided. You can also use the \o switch to have Word prompt you only once in the merge, rather than for each iteration of the main document.

IF FIELD Use the IF field to compare two expressions and then insert text depending on the results of that comparison. The format is

{IF *expression operator expression* "*TrueText*" "*FalseText*"}

where *expression* is what is being compared. This can be text, numbers, or a bookmark. The *operator* is the type of comparison being made (see the table of operators just below). "*TrueText*" is the field's result if the comparison is true. "*FalseText*" is the field's result if the comparison is false.

Operator	Purpose
=	Equals
>	Greater than
<	Lesser than
>=	Equal to or greater than
<=	Equal to or lesser than
<>	Not equal to

The following shows the dialog box for the IF field:

MERGEREC AND MERGESEQ FIELDS The MERGEREC field result is the number of the current data file record. You can use this field to number the documents you create with the merge, or use it for further merge programming. This field uses no switches.

The result of the MERGESEQ field, which is very similar to MERGEREC, is the number of the current data record among the records actually being used. If you have chosen to skip some fields, or limited the number of fields being used, this number will be different from the one inserted with the MERGEREC field.

NEXT FIELD   The NEXT field advances the merge to the next record in the data source, but displays no result of its own. It uses no switches.

NEXTIF FIELD   The NEXTIF field advances the merge to the next record if a comparison is true. It combines the features of the NEXT and IF fields. It uses the format

{NEXTIF *expression operator expression*}

where *expression* is the text, number, or bookmark to be compared. The operators used are described in the preceding IF field.

SET FIELD   The SET field is used to assign a bookmark to data, which can then be inserted at any point in the document. This field uses the format

{SET *bookmark "data"*}

where *bookmark* is the name of the bookmark to which the data is going to be assigned, and which will be used to insert that text throughout the document. The *data* argument is the data to be assigned to the bookmark.

SKIPIF FIELD   The SKIPIF field is used to skip records while merging, thus creating no merged document for the skipped records. This field takes the format

{SKIPIF *expression operator expression*}

where *expression* is the text, numbers, or bookmarks to be compared, and *operator* specifies the comparison to be made. All the operators listed for the IF field can be used. When the comparison is true, Word cancels the merged document created for the current record. It starts the merge again at the beginning of the main document, using the next record. Therefore, no document is created for the data record that was skipped, and a complete document is created for the next data record.

Specifying Query Options to Choose Records

Word let you select the data source records to be used in the merge, using *query options*. The Query Options dialog box allows you to base your specifications on values in multiple fields.

1. In the Mail Merge Helper, select Query Options under Merge the Data with the Document.

2. Select the Filter Records tab if it is not on top. It looks like this:

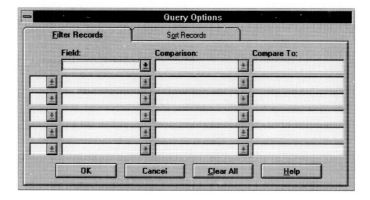

3. Open the drop-down list for Field, and select a field name from the data source.

4. Open the drop-down list for Comparison, and select from the comparison operators presented.

5. In the Compare To box, type an entry to be used with the Comparison operator.

6. To look at another entry, choose And or Or, using the drop-down arrow at the left of the next line of text boxes. This sets the relationship between the current rule and the next.

7. Repeat steps 3 through 6 for the next field you want to query.

8. When you have finished your specifications for the record selection, choose OK.

M

Organizing the Data Source

You can choose to sort the data source file from the values in one to three fields. These fields are called *sort keys*. The first one is specified as Sort By. The second as Then By and the third as Then By. Word only looks at the second sort key when there are duplicate entries for the first Sort By field and the third key when there are duplicate entries in the second. Specifying extra sort keys allows you to have tie-breakers.

1. From the Mail Merge Helper, select Query Options under Merge the Data with the Document.

2. Select the Sort Records tab.

3. Open the drop-down list in the Sort By box to display the list of fields in the data source, and choose the field you want to use for the primary sort key.

4. Choose Ascending to sort from A to Z and 1 to 9, or choose Descending to sort from Z to A and 9 to 1.

5. If you want to sort by a second field, repeat steps 3 and 4, using the Then By field. Repeat step 3 again, with the Then By field, if you need to specify a third key.

Header Files

You can store the information on field names in a file separate from the data source file. The advantage of using a header file is that you can ensure that field names are the same for many different data sources. The disadvantage is that you have to ensure that the fields are in the correct order for all of those different data source files, or the header file will cause confusion.

To create a header file, select Header Options from the Get Data list box in the Mail Merge Helper. You can choose to open a header file to use with the main document and data sources, or you can choose to create a header file the same way you create a list of field names for a data source. You select the source of the data to use with a header file.

Hints

There are some hints to make working with the Mail Merge feature easier and more productive.

Using Data from Another Source

You may already have data in a file that is acceptable to Word as a data source for a merge. Word supports Microsoft Access and Microsoft Excel files as data sources. Also, you can use files in a database package for which you have an ODBC (Open Database Connectivity) driver in your Windows directory. Word supplies these drivers for Paradox, FoxPro, and Access. You can use other files for which you have a converter. Word for Windows supplies converters for previous versions of Word for Windows, Word for the Mac, and Word for DOS, as well as for Lotus 1-2-3 and WordPerfect 5.x.

To open a data source from another application:

1. In the Mail Merge Helper, select Get Data under Data Source.

2. Select Open Data Source.

3. Select the filename in the Open Data Source dialog box.

4. If you want to choose the conversion method rather than allowing Word to choose it, select the Confirm Conversions check box and pick the conversion method you want to use.

5. Select OK.

Using E-Mail to Distribute Merged Documents

If you plan to distribute merged documents via fax or e-mail, you will want to use the Query Options dialog box to choose only those records that have an entry in the fax number or e-mail address fields. See "Specifying Query Options to Choose Records" earlier in this section and "Electronic Mail."

Organizing Data in a Different Way

Data source tables are limited to 31 data fields. When you need to create records with more fields, you can create a document that includes the header row entries and the records beneath them as paragraphs. *Delimiters* are used to mark the end of each field in these records. Your delimiter can be either a tab character or a comma.

It is important to use the same delimiter in all records in your data source. Make sure that the fields appear in the same order for each record. You need the same number of fields in each record, although a field can be left empty as long as the delimiters are correctly positioned. If your field contains a punctuation mark such as a comma or period, make sure that you enclose the fields in quotation marks.

M

Ensuring That Non-Variable Text is Correct

An important part of creating your main document is making sure that it reads correctly when merged. An important part of creating a data source is making sure that it contains *all* of the data that needs to be varied. While names and addresses are obvious forms of data that can vary, there are some other issues that are not so obvious.

For example, many people new to merges forget to include a title to use in salutations in the data source files and main documents. Consider the response to your letter, however, if you send out seven letters in which the salutation reads "Mr. *Name*," but three of the letters should be sent to "Ms. *Name*." Three of your recipients will develop a bad opinion of you or your company.

Do not limit yourself to Mr. and Ms. in your titles. Many officials and special professions have specific forms of address which are correct. Addressing people appropriately makes them more likely to give your message a fair hearing. See the Rules Box "Forms of Address" for some forms of address you will want to remember to use, when appropriate.

Nobody actually enjoys being the recipient of a "form letter". By using the merge process creatively, you make your documents look more personal, without actually taking more time to create the documents. The trick is taking the time originally, when creating the data source, or the main document, to record all possible bits of information, and then to use them effectivly in the merge document. For example, a travel company might want to record clients' last vacation spot, and use that text in writing letters about scheduling their next year's vacation.

One thing you should be extremely careful about is making sure that the data source is correct. Nothing causes a worse impression that mispelling a person's name, or incorrectly identifying their company in a merge document. This adds to the reader's feeling of being treated impersonally. This is most important with merge documents because the printed copy is normally not proofread again. You should regularly proofread data sources that you use often, to check for incorrect or multiple entries. Make sure that people's names and titles are spelled correctly. If you are using abbreviations for degree and professional associations in your mail merge, make sure that these are correct, so that you do not present a sloppy image. The rules box "Rules for Abbreviating Degrees and Professional Assocations" will help you keep these correct.

Forms of Address

If you are writing to Mr. Smith, it is easy to tell how to address your letter. If you are writing to an important official, a clergyman, or a dignitary you might not be as certain how you should address your letter. The entry that you use in the address block sometimes matches the salutation but at other times it is different. The list that follows provides an acceptable alternative for many of these special situations. The address form is used in the address block at the top of the letter. The salutation form is preceded by the word "Dear."

Individual	Address Form	Salutation Form
Ambassador to the U.S.	His Excellency ... Ambassador of ...	Ambassador ...
U.S. Ambassador	The Honorable ...	Ambassador ...
Rear Admiral	Rear Admiral ...	Admiral ...
Lieutenant General	Lieutenant General ...	General ...
U.S. President	The President	Mr. President
Former U.S. President	The Honorable ..	Mr. ...
U.S. Senator	The Honorable ...	Senator ...
Court Judge	The Honorable ...	Judge ...
Mayor	The Honorable ...	Mayor ...
Catholic Bishop	The Most Reverand ... Bishop of ...	Bishop
Catholic Priest	The Reverand ...	Father ...
Episcopal Bishop	The Right Reverand ... Bishop of ...	Bishop
Minister without PhD	The Reverand ..	Mr. ...
Rabbi	Rabbi ...	Rabbi ...

Related Topics

Fields
Mail Merge Toolbar
Print Merge

M

Rules for Abbreviating Degrees and Professional Associations

When you are creating a mailing list you will want to be certain that you use the correct abbreviations for academic degrees and professional associations that you reference. These rules can guide you to the correct entries:

- Academic degrees use periods but no spaces in the abbreviations. For example B.A. Ph.D., J.D., L.L.M., M.D., and M.B.A.

- M.B.A. is written without periods when it is used generally to refer to a specific type of training, as in the job market for MBA's is much better this year.

- Abbreviations for religious orders such as the Jesuits use the same form as academic degrees as in S.J.

- Professional credentials are normally recorded in all capitals without periods as in CPA representing Certified Public Accountant and CFP representing Certified Financial Planner.

- When degree abbreviations follow a name you do not use titles such as Mr. Ms. or Mrs. For example, you can use George P. Jones, Ph.D. or Mr. George P. Jones but would not use Mr. George P. Jones, Ph.D. Other more specific titles such as President, Chancellor, or Provost can be used along with the degree abbreviation.

Mail Merge Toolbar

The Mail Merge toolbar provides access to many of the special Mail Merge options while you are working with a Mail Merge main document or data source. You can use its buttons for inserting fields in a main document, for moving among fields when working with a data source file, and so forth. Here is a list of the Mail Merge toolbar buttons:

Button	Button Name	Purpose
Insert Merge Field	Insert Merge Field	Lets you select a merge field to insert
Insert Word Field	Insert Word Field	Lets you select a Word field to insert
« » ABC	View Merged Data	Toggles between showing codes and data from the data source
⏮	First Record	Displays the first record
◀	Previous Record	Displays the previous record
	Go to Record	Lets you enter the record to display
▶	Next Record	Displays the next record
⏭	Last Record	Displays the last record
📋	Mail Merge Helper	Opens the Mail Merge Helper dialog box
📋	Check for Errors	Runs the merge, checking for errors and creating no output
📋	Merge to New Document	Runs the merge, storing the merged document to a new document window
📋	Merge to Printer	Runs the merge, sending the merged document to the printer
📋	Mail Merge	Opens the Merge dialog box letting you set merge options
🔍	Find Records	Finds a record in the data source that contains the specified data
📝	Edit Data Source	Displays the Data Form dialog box for editing the data source

Managing Files

See "File Management."

Margins

With Word, you can set the top, bottom, left, and right margins of a page all at the same time. You can create mirror margins for double-sided documents and add a gutter when you plan to bind the document.

Procedures

Margins are an element of page formatting; you can change them using the menus or in Print Preview. You can set the left and right margins using the ruler.

Changing Margins with the Menus

You can set the margins for a whole document, from a specific page to the end of the document, or for a section. If you select text before changing margins, you can specify the margin settings for that selected text only; Word will make the selected text a section and set the margins for that section.

1. Select File | Page Setup (Format | Page Setup in Word for Windows 2).

2. Select the Margins tab or option button, if necessary.

3. Enter your margin settings in the Top, Bottom, Left, and Right text boxes.

   ■ To create mirror margins, select the Mirror Margins check box (Facing Pages in Word for Windows 2). The Left and Right text boxes change, becoming the Inside and Outside text boxes. The inside margin is the right margin for even-numbered pages, and the left margin for odd-numbered pages; the outside margin represents the other side margins.

   ■ To reserve part of the page for binding your document, enter the width of the binding area in the Gutter text box. This value will be added to the inside or left margin value.

4. Select the part of the document to which you want to apply these margins, from the Apply To drop-down list box.

5. In Word for Windows 6, enter the minimum distance between headers or footers and the page edge, in the Header and Footer text boxes. (Headers and footers appear between the document margin and the page edge. This setting effectively sets a margin for the headers and footers.)

6. Select OK.

Changing Margins with the Ruler

Margins changed with the ruler affect the selected section of the document, or the entire document if no section breaks have been inserted.

In Word for Windows 6, switch to Page Layout view by selecting View | Page Layout or clicking the Page Layout View button. Then drag the margin to its new location on either the vertical or horizontal ruler. The margin is the division between the gray and white areas on the ruler. When the mouse is positioned over it, it becomes a two-headed arrow. To position the mouse, assuming you have not created indents, point at the spot between the left and first line indent markers. There is no separate visual indicator, such as the arrows marking indents, of the margin location.

In Word for Windows 2, click on the bracket symbol at the left end of the ruler, if necessary, until the ruler shows the margin markers, which look like square brackets. Then drag the left or right margin marker to its new position. Since there is no vertical ruler, you cannot set the top and bottom margin with the ruler.

Changing Margins in Print Preview in Word for Windows 2

You can alter all four margins in Print Preview. As when you use the ruler, the new settings affect the current section, or the entire document if no section breaks have been inserted.

1. Select File | Print Preview.

2. Select Margins in the Print Preview toolbar. The margins are indicated by gray lines appearing on the page. Each line has a black handle at the left or bottom end.

3. Select the line for the margin you want to move, by clicking on the margin handle or pressing TAB until it is highlighted.

4. Move the margin line to its new location by dragging its handle or using the arrow keys and pressing ENTER.

5. Press ENTER or click outside the page to update the display of your document.

M

Hints

When you want to change the margins for a single paragraph, use the Indent paragraph format. This lets you establish what are effectively temporary margins for the paragraph.

Related Topics

Indents
Page Size and Orientation
Ruler
Sections
Viewing Documents

Master Document Toolbar

When you select the Master Document view, Word displays the Outline and
Master Document toolbars. The outlining buttons let you change the outline you
are creating for the master document, altering the levels of entries in the outline
or expanding and collapsing the outline branches, setting which text you actually
see. The right side of the toolbar is the Master Document toolbar and contains
the buttons for working with subdocuments. You can use these buttons to merge
a subdocument or to split or join subdocuments. See "Master Documents" for
more information.

The following table explains the function of each button:

Button	Button Name	Purpose
←	Promote	Makes the selected heading one level higher
→	Demote	Makes the selected heading one level lower
⇒	Demote to Body Text	Makes the selected heading body text
↑	Move Up	Moves the selected heading up in the outline
↓	Move Down	Moves the selected heading down in the outline
+	Expand	Shows lower level headings and body text under the current heading
−	Collapse	Hides lower level headings and body text under the current heading
1	Show Heading 1	Shows only level one headings in the document
2	Show Heading 2	Shows through second level headings in the document

Button	Button Name	Purpose
3	Show Heading 3	Shows through third level headings in the document
4	Show Heading 4	Shows through fourth level headings in the document
5	Show Heading 5	Shows through fifth level headings in the document
6	Show Heading 6	Shows through sixth level headings in the document
7	Show Heading 7	Shows through seventh level headings in the document
8	Show Heading 8	Shows through eighth level headings in the document
All	All	Shows all headings in the outline
	Show First Line Only	Toggles between showing all body text and only the first line
	Show Formatting	Toggles between showing formatting or using a draft font
	Master Document View	Opens the Master Document toolbar
	Create Subdocument	Makes the selected headings into a subdocument
	Remove Subdocument	Makes the selected subdocument part of the main document
	Insert Subdocument	Opens a file and inserts it as a subdocument
	Merge Subdocument	Combines the selected subdocuments into a single subdocument
	Split Subdocument	Splits the current subdocument into two documents at the insertion point location
	Lock Document	Locks or unlocks the document for editing

Master Documents

Word for Windows 6's Master Document feature is the ideal solution for working with large documents. Master documents help you take projects that might be unwieldy because of their length and organize them into smaller pieces, called *subdocuments*. You can control the formatting for the entire project by setting format options in the master document, but you can also work on the individual subdocuments. For example, you can use a master documents to split a writing project into subdocuments among several individuals, yet ensure the consistent overall appearance of the combined project.

Since master documents work with outline features, it is easy to organize the final document after all the subdocuments have been written.

Procedures

There are several procedures for working with master documents that are unique to master documents, and some, though similar to those used in working with normal documents need to be modified when working with master documents.

Creating a Master Document

1. Select File | New.

2. Select View | Master Document.

3. Create an outline, using the heading styles 1 though 9.

NOTE: See "Outlines" for the procedures used to create outlines.

4. Select the outline headings and text to be used in creating the subdocuments. The first heading level selected should be the heading level that marks the beginning of subdocuments. When you create subdocuments, as described in the following steps, each occurrence of this heading level is the beginning of a new subdocument, and headings and text that are part of a branch begun by a heading of this level are part of the subdocument.

5. Click the Create Subdocument icon on the Master Document toolbar. Figure 4-41 shows a master document after subdocuments have been created for the outline.

6. Select File | Save As, specify a filename for the master document, and click OK to save the master document and all of its subdocuments.

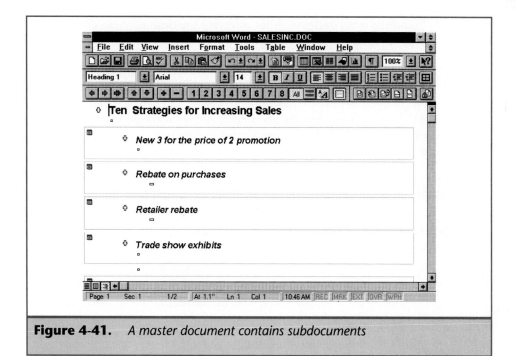

Figure 4-41. *A master document contains subdocuments*

Word creates a unique name for each subdocument, using the first eight characters of the outline heading if it is unique. If it is not unique, Word adds numbers or characters to make it unique. For example, if the headings were Article 11, Article 12, and Article 13, Word might use the first four characters followed by a unique four-digit number, as in ARTI8765, ARTI9504, and so forth.

Formatting a Master Document

You can apply formatting to either the master document or its subdocuments, and your choice will affect what gets formatted. To set the format for the entire document, choose the format settings in the master document. If you want the formatting to affect only one subdocument, choose your format settings from the subdocument.

M

Printing a Master Document

If you want to see all the detail of your master document, print the document in Normal view. If you want to see just an outline of the document, print from the Master Document view, first using the Expand and Collapse buttons on the toolbar to control the level of detail. After selecting the desired view, choose File | Print, select the desired options, and then OK.

Opening a Subdocument

You can open subdocuments by choosing File | Open. You can also open subdocuments from within a master document, and you should use this approach whenever you plan to rename a subdocument; otherwise, the link to the master document will be broken.

Renaming a Subdocument

1. Open the subdocument by double-clicking its icon in the master document.

CAUTION: It is important that you open the subdocument from within the master document, or the link between the master document and subdocument will be destroyed.

2. Choose File | Save As, type the new subdocument name, and click OK.

3. Close the subdocument.

Reorganizing Master Documents

You must have the master document open to reorganize it. You will probably find it easiest to work in Master Document view. You can move, combine, and join subdocuments, incorporate other Word documents, change a subdocument into a master document, and delete subdocuments.

MOVING A SUBDOCUMENT   Click the subdocument icon in the master document, and drag it to the new location to reorganize the master document.

ADDING AN EXISTING WORD DOCUMENT AS A SUBDOCUMENT
1. Move the insertion point to the place in the master document where you want to insert the new subdocument.

2. Click the Insert Subdocument button, opening the Insert Subdocument dialog box. This dialog box presents elements you are familiar with from the Open dialog box.

3. Select the name of the document you want to insert, and then OK.

4. If needed, change the outline level of the new subdocument entry.

SPLITTING A SUBDOCUMENT   It's easy to divide a subdocument into two documents, to enable different people to work on the two sections. Just move the insertion point to the location where you want to make the split, and click the Split Subdocuments button. Choose File I Save As to save the new subdocuments and the changed master docments.

MERGING SUBDOCUMENTS   To combine subdocuments, they must be adjacent. Reposition them, if necessary, and then follow these steps:

1. Click the subdocument icon of the first subdocument to be merged.

2. Press SHIFT, and click the subdocument icons of any other adjacent subdocuments to be merged.

3. Click the Merge Subdocument button on the Master Document toolbar.

DELETING A SUBDOCUMENT   Select the subdocument icon, and press DEL or BACKSPACE. Since the subdocument is deleted, the subdocument icon no longer appears.

Hints

Here are some hints to help you work with master documents and subdocuments.

Page Numbering

If you want to sequentially number all the pages in a master document, Word will handle the task for you automatically. If you want some sections to have numbers that do not follow the sequence of the rest of the master document, you can change the numbering within the subdocument.

Access to Subdocuments

When you open a master document, Word only opens the subdocuments for which you are the author with read/write access. Subdocuments authored by someone else are opened as read-only. To make changes to a subdocument that you did not author, you will need to use the Unlock button on the Master Document toolbar before you can make a change.

M

NOTE: If you want to lock your subdocuments more effectively, you will need to use different methods. See "Locking and Protecting Documents" in this chapter for procedures for locking your document in different ways.

Applications

Master documents are typically used for long reports or books; the subdocuments contain large sections of the report or chapters of the book. Master document features make it easy to ensure a consistent look to the completed document—even when your work on it is not all done at the same time, or when the sections are written by several individuals.

Math Calculations

Word for Windows will perform math calculations in your documents. You can perform the calculation with numbers entered in tables, by inserting formulas in other cells of the table, as explained in "Tables" in this chapter. Or you can use field and insert the results of an expression into the document, as described under "Fields."

Word for Windows 2 offers a third alternative, not available in Word for Window 6: You can calculate equations entered in your document. This third method is described in the following section.

Procedure

1. Enter the formula in your Word for Windows 2 document. Use the operators shown below along with the numbers to be calculated. The numbers and operators can be arranged horizontally or vertically, or can occur among other text.

Operator	Function
+ or a space	Addition
- or ()	Subtraction
*	Multiplication
/	Division
%	Percentage
^	Calculates a power or root. 2^3 would be 2^3.

2. Select the formula to calculate.

TIP: *If the formula is arranged vertically, select it by dragging across it with the right mouse button.*

3. Select Tools | Calculate.

The calculation's result appears in the status bar for a few seconds. Then Word copies the result to the Clipboard. Paste that result into your document or any other document.

Applications

This feature is useful when you need a one-time calculation that you do not intend to repeat. You can use this feature much like you would use the Windows Calculator, without the inconvenience of leaving your document to enter the formula.

Related Topics

Fields
Tables

Maximize

Maximize a window to make it as large as possible in your screen. A maximized window takes the entire screen for an application window, or the entire application window for a document window.

Procedures

There are three ways to maximize:

■ Click on the Maximize button, shown here in the margin.

■ Open the Control menu by clicking on the button at the left end of the title bar (or press ALT+SPACEBAR for the application window or ALT+ – (minus) for the document window), and select Maximize.

M

■ Press ALT+F10 for an application window or CTRL+F10 for a document window.

Related Topics

Minimize
Windows

Menu Options

You can customize Word's menus to suit your own needs, or to accommodate a particular template, by assigning macros and commands to the menus; in Word for Windows 6, you can also assign AutoText, styles, and fonts. For example, you might add a custom menu to a template, providing the specific commands useful in that document, like the Shortcuts menu shown in Figure 4-42.

Procedure in Word for Windows 6

1. Select Tools | Customize, and the Menus tab if necessary.

2. In the Categories list box, choose the category of elements you want to assign to menus: commands, macros, fonts, AutoText entries, styles, or common symbols.

3. From the Commands (Macros, Fonts, AutoText, Styles or Common Symbols) list box, choose the specific item you want to assign to a menu.

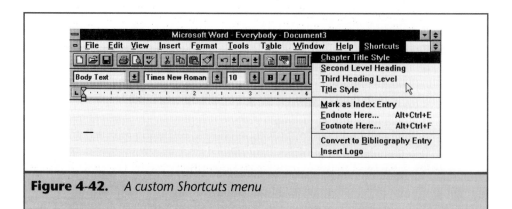

Figure 4-42.   *A custom Shortcuts menu*

4. From the Change What Menu drop-down list box, choose the menu to which you want to assign this item.

5. In the Position on Menu drop-down list box, specify where you want the item to appear.

6. In Name on Menu, enter the text to appear on the menu for this item.

> *TIP: Enter an & before a letter in the menu option to underline it .*

7. To change the menus available, select Menu Bar:

   ■ To add a new menu, enter its name in the Name on Menu Bar text box, choose a position in the Position on Menu Bar list box, and select Add.

   ■ To change the name of a menu, enter its new name in the Name on Menu Bar text box, select the menu in the Position on Menu Bar list box, and select Rename.

   ■ To remove a menu, highlight it and select Remove.

   ■ Select Cancel when you are done.

8. In the Save Changes In drop-down list box, select the template this menu is to be saved in. If it is saved with the Normal template, the menu is available for all documents. Otherwise, the menu is only available for documents created with the template the menu is saved in. Only the Normal template and other templates attached to the current document are shown in this list box.

9. Select Add to add the item to the menu. (Or select Remove to remove the selected item, or Reset All to return to the default menu.)

10. Select Close to return to the document and save your menu assignments.

Procedures for Word for Windows 2

M

1. Select Tools | Options.

2. Select Menus from the Category box.

3. Select either Commands or Macros, depending on which you want to assign.

4. Under Context, select Global to make the menu assignment globally available, or Template to make it available only with the current template.

5. From the Menu list box, choose the menu to which you want to assign the macro or command.

6. In the Menu Text text box, type the text for the menu item, entering an & before the character to be underlined.

7. From the Commands or Macros list box, choose the command or macro to assign.

8. Select Add to assign the command or macro to the menu. (Or, to delete the menu assignment, select Delete. To restore the default menus, select Reset All.)

9. Select OK.

Related Topics

Keyboard Options
Toolbar Options

Merge

See "Mail Merge" or "Print Merge."

MERGE Field

See "Mail Merge" or "Print Merge."

MERGEFIELD Field

See "Mail Merge" or "Print Merge."

MERGEREC Field

See "Mail Merge" or "Print Merge."

MERGESEQ Field

See "Mail Merge" or "Print Merge."

Microsoft Draw to Import Graphics

See "Drawing on a Document" and "Graphics."

Minimize

When you minimize a window, you reduce it to an icon. This clears space on the desktop and saves some memory.

NOTE: You can minimize document windows in Word for Windows 6 only.

Procedures

There are two ways to minimize:

■ Click the Minimize button, shown here in the margin.

■ Open the control menu by clicking the button at the left end of the title bar, or press ALT+SPACEBAR for an application window or ALT+ – for a document window, and select Minimize.

Related Topics

Maximize
Windows

M

Modifying WIN.INI

See "WIN.INI Options."

Mouse Installation and Customization

You need to install your mouse before you can use it. In Windows, you can also customize some mouse setup features to make it work better for you.

Procedures

You install and customize your mouse in Windows.

Installing the Mouse

1. Attach the mouse to your system, as described in the documentation that comes with your mouse and computer.

2. Start Windows.

3. Select the Main program group from the Window menu.

4. Using the arrow keys, highlight the Windows Setup program item icon and press ENTER.

5. Select Options | Change System Settings.

6. Select a mouse type from the Mouse drop-down list box. If you select any option except Other Mouse, you do not need to install the mouse driver that came with your mouse, because Windows has those mouse drivers built in. Before selecting Other Mouse, make sure you have the disk with the appropriate mouse driver. Windows will prompt you to supply the drive containing that disk. Enter it and select OK, and Windows copies the driver to your hard drive.

TIP: Mouse drivers are files that tell your computer how to communicate with the mouse.

7. Select OK, and then Options | Exit.

   The mouse is now ready to use, and will use the default options. You can also customize the mouse to change those default settings.

Customizing the Mouse

1. From the Main program group, select the Control Panel program item.

2. Select Settings | Mouse, or click the Mouse icon.

3. Move the scroll box in the Mouse Tracking Speed scroll bar, to set the speed for the movement of the mouse pointer on the screen as you move the mouse across your desktop.

   A slower tracking speeds means you can place the mouse more precisely, because the pointer moves a little while the mouse moves a lot. A faster tracking speed makes the mouse pointer move faster, requiring less desk space for rolling the mouse.

4. Move the scroll box in the Double Click Speed scroll bar, to determine how quickly you have to click the mouse in order for the computer to interpret it as a double-click.

   A slower double-click speed can help a person with arthritis or other mobility problems, because the two clicks that make a double-click can be further apart. Otherwise, setting a faster double-click helps prevent two single clicks from being mistakenly recognized as a double-click.

 TIP: Test the double-click speed you've selected by trying to double-click in the TEST box. The box will be highlighted when Windows recognizes the two clicks as a double-click.

5. To reverse the roles of the left and right mouse buttons, select the Swap Left/Right Buttons check box. This is to accommodate those using the mouse in their left hand.

6. Select the Mouse Trails check box to have Windows display mouse pointers trailing behind the main mouse pointer when you move the mouse. This feature does not affect the mouse's operation, but can be fun.

7. Select OK, and then Settings | Exit.

Related Topics

Mouse Pointer
Mouse Techniques

M

Mouse Pointer

The *mouse pointer* indicates the location of the next mouse action on the screen. The mouse pointer may change its shape, to tell you what the program is expecting you to do next. Table 4-15 explains the various appearances of the mouse pointer, and tells you what you can do with the mouse when it has that shape.

Related Topics

Mouse Installation and Customization
Mouse Techniques

Mouse Pointer	Function
	Selects objects
	Gets help on the next command or object selected
	Tells you to wait while the computer finishes a command
	Sizes a window
	Sizes a frame or object
	Creates a frame
	Drags and drops text
	Moves a table's gridlines
	Creates a pane

Table 4-15. *Mouse Pointer Shapes and Their Actions*

Mouse Techniques

The mouse is a device used for pointing at elements on the screen and selecting them. A mouse is the most common type of pointing device, but you can also use a trackball, stylus, or other device for the same purposes. A mouse makes using Windows and Word for Windows easier, because you can make selections without typing. Your selections can be based on what is on the screen, rather than what you know about the program.

Procedures

When you move the mouse device, the mouse pointer, which is the small icon on the screen, moves around the Word window. When an instruction in this book says to move the mouse to or point to a certain location, it means use the hand-held mouse to move the mouse pointer to that location on the screen.

Dragging

Use dragging to move an object around on the screen, or to select text.

1. Point the mouse at an object you want to move (drag). When you are selecting text, you point the mouse at the beginning of the text you want to select.

2. Press the left mouse button and hold it down.

3. Without releasing the left mouse button, move the mouse pointer to where you want the object dragged.

4. Release the mouse button.

TIP: When you drag across text, you are dragging from the beginning to end of the text to select it, rather than moving an object to another location. You can also drag text that is already selected, to move or copy it as described under "Drag and Drop" in this chapter.

M

Clicking

Clicking is most often used to highlight or select an object. Simply point the mouse pointer at the button or other object you want to select, and press and quickly release the left mouse button once.

In Word for Windows 6, you can also use right-clicking. Right-clicking is the same procedure as clicking, except that you use the right mouse button instead of the left one. In Word for Windows 6, right-clicking a toolbar or the document area opens a shortcut menu.

Double-Clicking

Double-clicking is most often used to execute a menu command or select an option in a menu or dialog box. Point the mouse pointer at the item you want to select or execute, and click and release the left mouse button twice, quickly.

To designate how quickly you must click the mouse button twice for it to register as a double-click, use the Windows Control Panel as described under "Mouse Installation and Customization."

Related Topics

Mouse Installation and Customization
Mouse Pointer

Move

See "Clipboard," "Drag and Drop," and "Spike."

Moving the Insertion Point

The insertion point marks your location in your document. Whatever actions you take in Word occur at the insertion point's location. When you type text, it appears at the insertion point. When you change a format setting, it effects the text at the insertion point. Therefore, it is important that you be able to easily move the insertion point where you need to go in your document.

Procedures

You can move the insertion point in several different ways: with the keyboard, the mouse, and the Go To command.

Moving with the Keyboard

The available keys and key-combinations for moving the insertion point are listed in Table 4-16.

Moving with the Mouse

If necessary, use the scroll bars to display the position in the document where you want to move the insertion point to. Using the scroll bar changes what part of the document is displayed, but does not actually move the insertion point itself. Use the scroll bar by clicking the scroll bar on either side of the scroll box, or dragging the scroll box along the scroll bar. Then click on the location you want the insertion point to appear.

Moving with the Go To Command

1. Select Edit | Go To or press F5 (twice in Word for Windows 2).

2. Indicate where you want to go:

Keys	Moves Insertion Point To
UP ARROW	The line above
DOWN ARROW	The line below
RIGHT ARROW	The character to the right
LEFT ARROW	The character to the left
CTRL+RIGHT ARROW	The word to the right
CTRL+LEFT ARROW	The word to the left
HOME	The beginning of a line
END	The end of a line
CTRL+UP ARROW	The paragraph above
CTRL+DOWN ARROW	The paragraph below
PAGE UP	Text one window above
PAGE DOWN	Text one window below
CTRL+PAGE UP	The text at the top of the window
CTRL+PAGE DOWN	The text at the bottom of the window
CTRL+HOME	The beginning of the document
CTRL+END	The end of the document

Table 4-16.   *Keyboard Methods for Moving the Insertion Point*

M

■ In Word for Windows 6, select the type of item you want to move to in the Go To What list box (such as page, annotation, or footnote). Then select the specific item in the Enter drop-down list box. The name of this box changes depending on the item type you chose.

■ In Word for Windows 2, enter where you want to go to in the Go To text box, or select a bookmark to move to from the Go To list box. Table 4-17 lists codes you can enter representing locations to which you want to move.

3. Select Go To (or OK in Word for Windows 2).

TIP: In Word for Windows 6, if the item selected in the Enter drop-down list box is "Any Object," "Any Footnote," or another "Any" entry, you can select Next or Previous.

Moving with the Go To Shortcut Key (F5) in Word for Windows 2

1. Press F5. A prompt appears in the status bar, but the Go To dialog box does not appear.

2. Specify where you want to move the insertion point, using the codes given above in Table 4-17. You cannot select a bookmark name.

3. Press ENTER.

Hints

These are some hints for using the Go To command in Word for Windows 2.

Moving Relatively in Word for Windows 2

Usually, the destinations you specify with the Go To command are counted from the beginning of the document. You can use + (plus sign) and - (minus sign) to specify destinations relative to your current position. For example, to move to the 21st line after the insertion point's current location, enter **1+21**. To move to the 21st line of the document, no matter where you start from, enter **121**.

Go To Code	Goes To
a	The next annotation
a and an annotation number	That annotation
Page number alone	That number
f	The next footnote
Bookmark name	The bookmark
f and a footnote number	That footnote
l and a line number	That number
p	The next page
p and a page number	That number
s	The next section
s and a section number	That section
% and a number	That percentage of the way through the document

Table 4-17. *Go To Codes for Word for Windows 2*

Combining Destination Codes in Word for Windows 2

You can combine Go To destination codes to indicate more specifically where you want to go. For example, enter **S2P7** to go to the seventh page of the second section. You can even combine codes, using the + sign in the largest item in the code. For example, you can enter **P+3L2** to move second line on the third page after your current location.

Related Topics

Scroll Bars

M

Multiple Copies

You can print multiple copies of your document at once. See "Printing."

Negative Indents

Negative indents move text closer to the edge of the paper and are used to create hanging indents, or to move entire paragraphs into the margin. See "Indents."

New Document

When you open a new document in Word, you choose a template to define the document's default settings and formats.

Procedures

1. Select File | New.

2. To open a new Word document, leave Document selected. To open a new template, select Template.

3. Select a template from the Template list box (Use Template in Word for Windows 2). Templates contain styles, AutoText entries, toolbars, and macros that help you create a certain type of document.

TIP: In Word for Windows 6, names in this list followed by the word "Wizard" will help you create your new document with a set of specific features.

4. Select OK.

Hints

 You can open a document using the Normal template by clicking on the New button on the Standard toolbar, shown here in the margin.

Some templates have macros that begin when the new document is created, such as the Wizards in Word for Windows 6, or the FAX templates in Word for Windows 2. When you select a new document using these templates, you are prompted by dialog boxes to enter certain information about your document, such as an author name, a fax number, or a date, before you are able to edit the new document directly.

Related Topics

Templates
Wizards

New Page

See "Pagination."

New Page Number

At any point in your document, you can restart the page numbering at any number you choose. See "Page Numbers."

Newspaper-Style Columns

The NEXT field merges data in a mail merge without starting a new document. See "Mail Merge."

NEXT Field

See "Fields."

NEXTIF Field

The NEXTIF field decides whether to create a mail merge document for a data record based on a condition. See "Mail Merge."

Nonbreaking Hyphen

See "Hard Hyphen."

N

Nonbreaking Spaces

See "Hard Space."

Nonprinting Characters

Nonprinting characters are characters that you can see on your screen, but which do not appear in your document when it is printed. You can choose to display or hide these nonprinting characters. Figure 4-43 shows many nonprinting characters that are normally hidden.

Procedures

You can choose whether or not to display nonprinting characters. You can also change the default display to include or exclude these characters.

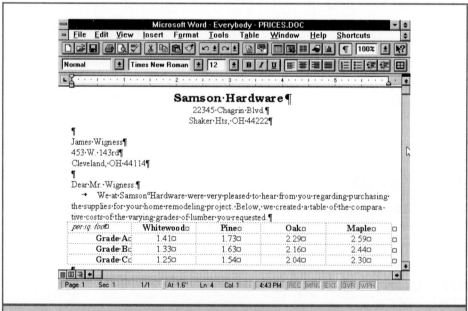

Figure 4-43. *Displaying nonprinting characters*

Displaying Nonprinting Characters

 You can toggle between showing and hiding nonprinting characters. Click the Show/Hide button on the Standard toolbar, shown here in the margin.

Changing the Default Display

You can specify which nonprinting characters are displayed by default. Then, when you toggle the display as described above, you switch between displaying all nonprinting characters, and displaying only the nonprinting characters you have chosen to display by default.

1. Select Tools | Options, and the View tab or icon.

2. Select or clear the appropriate check boxes under Nonprinting Characters to set up your default display.

3. Select OK.

Hints

Nonprinting characters are displayed with the symbols shown in Table 4-18.

Item	Displays As
Spaces	Small dots
Hard Spaces	Degree symbols
Tabs	Right-arrows
Paragraphs	Paragraph symbols
Optional hyphens	Long hyphen (em dash)
Nonbreaking hyphens	Double hyphen
Hidden text	Dotted line underneath
New line	An arrow pointing left

Table 4-18. *Nonprinting Character Display Codes*

N

It's a good idea to display nonprinting characters when editing a document. These characters help you see where you have used spaces, tabs, and other features to create your document. However, when you are laying out your document, aligning text and positioning frames, it's best to hide all nonprinting characters so that you can be sure that the document will print as you see it on the screen.

Related Topics

View Options

Normal View

See "Viewing Documents."

NOTEREF Fields

The NOTEREF field returns a footnote or endnote reference mark or bookmark. See "Footnotes and Endnotes."

Numbered Lists

See "Lists."

Numbering

See "Page Numbers."

Numbering Across Documents

See "Master Documents."

Object Linking and Embedding

Object Linking and Embedding (OLE) and Dynamic Data Exchange (DDE) are the technologies used by Windows and Windows applications to share data, through either linking or embedding. OLE and DDE let you add pictures, charts, and other data objects created in another application to your Word document, as well as put Word documents into files in other applications. With OLE and DDE you can effectively add the functionality of other software to the program you are using.

TIP: OLE and DDE work the same way, but OLE is the term used in Windows 3.1. Since OLE and DDE work behind the scenes, you won't need to understand the actual differences between them to use them both. If you are really interested in them, see your Windows documentation.

Linking vs. Embedding

Using OLE and DDE, you embed or link data objects into your Word document, and embed or link Word data objects into the data of other applications. You decide whether to link or embed the object; the difference is solely based on the original location of the data that you are sharing.

When you *link* an object, the *data object* you are sharing is stored in its own file using the format of the application that created it. That application, the *source application*, is used to edit the data. Word and other applications can include the data in their own documents by linking to that file. When you see a data object in a Word document, you are seeing a picture of data stored in another file that uses a different format. When you edit the data object from the Word document it is linked into, you open the source application (which opens the file), then make your changes, and save the edited data into the same file. Then the data object in the Word document is updated to reflect the new contents of the linked file. You can still use the source application to work with the data file separately from Word. For example, you can link a Paintbrush file containing a company logo into a Word document. This Paintbrush file can be edited in the Paintbrush application or by starting the Paintbrush application from Word. The same file, containing a copy of the logo, can be linked into many different Word documents, or into Excel worksheets and Access database reports.

When you *embed* a data object into a Word document, the data object is actually stored in the Word document. You still use the source application to edit the data; however, the data is provided to the source application from the Word document, rather than the source application opening a separate file that contains the data. You cannot use other applications to edit the data, nor can you include the data in other documents unless you link or embed the Word

0

document containing the embedded data object. The object in the Word document is the original copy of the data. For example, when you embed an Excel worksheet into a Word document, the worksheet is edited using Excel, but the data is stored as part of (embedded in) a Word document. Other applications cannot edit the Excel spreadsheet.

If you plan to use a data object only in a single Word document, embed it in that document. An embedded data object is stored in the document that uses it, even though the data is saved in the format of another application. When you plan to use the data in many different applications, you want to link (instead of embed) the object. Linking is also the best method if you plan to use the data in several locations within a single document. When the linked object is edited and saved in its original file, all documents or applications that have a link to that file use the updated version in their data links.

Before you can share data between applications, the applications must have embedding or linking capability. Some applications can only provide data, some applications can only accept data, some can do both, and some can do neither. Applications that can accept data to embed or link are called *client applications.* Applications that can provide data to embed or link are called *server applications.* Word for Windows can be both client and server. Word for Windows 2 and 6 also provide four applications that can supply objects you embed into Word documents: Microsoft Graph creates graphs, WordArt creates enhanced text, and Equation Editor creates equations. In Word for Windows 2, the Draw application creates drawings; in Word for Windows 6, Word's drawing capabilities are integrated in the word processor.

Special Fields Used to Share Documents

When you embed or link data objects in Word, you may see the LINK, EMBED, and INCLUDE fields in your documents. Most fields insert something into the Word document that contains them, and these fields are no exception. These fields insert the data object displayed in the field's location. You do not have to be concerned with the switches in these fields. The Word commands that modify embedded or linked objects make the necessary changes to these fields.

TIP: As mentioned in the "Fields" section earlier in this chapter, you can switch between displaying field codes and field contents in your documents. Press SHIFT+F9, *or select* Tools | Options, *and then turn on or off the Field Codes check box option in the View tab.*

Procedures

The following procedures will tell you how to link or embed an existing file or part of an existing file into your Word document, as well as how to create and insert an embedded object without leaving Word. You will also learn how to set the format of an object when it is linked or embedded into your Word document, and, if you are using Word for Windows 6, how to change the format in which an embedded object is stored.

Creating an Embedded Object

You can create and insert an embedded object without ever leaving Word.

1. Move the insertion point to where you want the object to start.

2. Select Insert | Object.

3. From the Object Type list box, choose the application for the type of data you want to add, and select OK. The application opens. The applications available in this list box are all the server applications Word has found.

4. At this point, you can proceed to create the data you want to appear in the embedded object, using the application you selected in step 3.

5. Choose Exit from the File menu to close the application you are using to create the embedded object. In some applications, this command may appear as Exit and Update.

Depending on how the application appears when you open it, there may not be a File menu to select Exit from. For example, some applications (such as WordArt with Word for Windows 2) operate using a dialog box. In this case, select the OK button. Some applications (such as WordArt in Word for Windows 6) change Word's toolbars and menus. In these cases, you can leave the source application by clicking a part of the document that is not part of the embedded object. In either case, when prompted about updating or saving the changes, select Yes. You return to your document, and the embedded object appears in the document.

Inserting an Embedded or Linked Object in Word for Windows 6

You can insert a file as an embedded or linked object, without opening the application used to create the file in Word for Windows 6. In Word for Windows 2,

0

you can only create embedded and linked objects from a file using the Clipboard, as described next.

1. Move the insertion point to where you want the object to start.

2. Select Insert | Object and the Create from File tab.

3. Select the file you want, using the File Name text box, the Directories list box, and the Drives drop-down list box—just as if you are opening a file.

4. If you want the inserted object to be linked to the Word file, select the Link to File check box; if you want the object embedded into the current document, clear the check box.

5. Select OK to add the object to the document. The object is linked if the Link to File option is on, or embedded if the option is off.

If you decide you want to be more selective about the part of the linked file that appears in the Word document, use the Edit | Links command and change the contents of the Item text box (see "Changing Settings for Linked Objects" later in this section).

Embedding or Linking Data using the Clipboard

In both Word for Windows 2 and 6, you can embed or link data objects by starting the application used with the data and copying the data to the Clipboard.

1. In the source application, display and select the data that you want to share.

2. Choose Copy from the source application's Edit menu to copy the selection to the Clipboard.

3. Switch to Word, and move the insertion point to where you want to insert the data from the Clipboard.

4. Choose Edit | Paste Special to display the Paste Special dialog box like the one shown here:

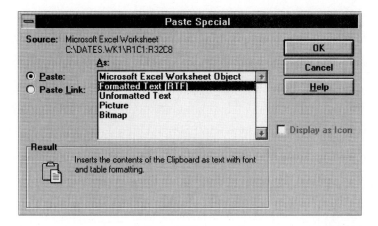

In Word for Windows 6, select the format to use when pasting the Clipboard data into Word from the As list box. The formats listed depend on the source of the data since they are the formats the source application can support. Select either the Paste or the Paste Link button. Choose Paste, and Word either embeds or copies the object into your document. Paste Link links the data using the selected format. Paste Link is only available if you can link to the source file.

In Word for Windows 2, select the format to use when pasting the Clipboard data into Word from the Data Type list box. The formats listed depend on the source of the data. You can also select either the Paste button to embed the object, or Paste Link button to create a link. Paste is only available when the selected type of data can be copied or embedded, and Paste Link is only available when the selected type can be linked.

5. Select the format you want the data object to use.

6. Select OK to add the object.

Figure 4-44 shows several objects added to a Word document. They look different because we have selected different formats for pasting them.

If you choose a format that contains the word *Object* and select the Paste option button, you will embed the object. If you select the Paste Link option, you will create a link from the Word document to the source file.

O

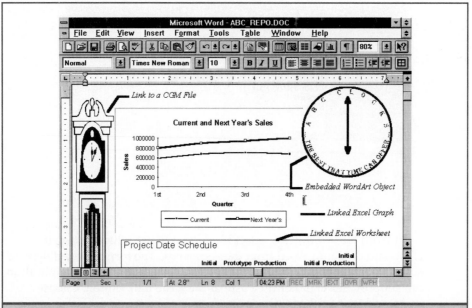

Figure 4-44.   *Linked and embedded objects in a Word document*

TIP: When you are creating the data to link, save the file before creating the link. Word needs to know the name of the linked file so that it can update the data object using the file.

Embedding Part of an Existing File

1. Display and select the portion of data that you want to embed in the source application.

2. Choose Copy from the source application's Edit menu to copy the selection to the Clipboard.

3. Switch to Word, and move the insertion point to where you want to embed the data.

4. Choose Edit | Paste Special and then OK. The data from the source application is embedded, assuming the application is a server and Word can accept the format.

Editing an Embedded or Linked Object from Word

The following are several ways to edit OLE or DDE objects from within Word.

- Double-click the object. (Note: Sound and video-clip objects cannot be edited this way, because double-clicking them will play them. Nor can linked text be edited by double-clicking.)

- Select the object, and then select Edit | *ObjectName* Object, where *ObjectName* is the name of the object's source, such as Microsoft Graph. If the object is a linked object, the command will be Edit | Linked *ObjectName* Object. Some objects do not include their name in the command. In Word for Windows 2, you will open the other application with the data that you see in the Word document. In Word for Windows 6, you must also select Edit to edit the object while remaining in Word, or Open to open the other application and work with the object there; Edit is only available for some types of objects.

- Open the source file containing the linked object, using the creating application. For example, to edit an Excel worksheet object that appears in a Word document, open Excel and the worksheet. When you return to the document in Word, the document with the link to the worksheet will display the modified version of the worksheet.

- In Word for Windows 6, select the object, and then Edit or Open from the object's shortcut menu. Select Edit to edit the object in Word, or Open to open the other application and work with the object there. Edit is only available for some types of objects.

Figure 4-45 shows an embedded object being edited from Word. The shaded area in the Word document is where the object will appear in the document. In this embedded object, since it uses an entire file, using more of the Excel worksheet makes the embedded object larger within the Word document.

Changing the Format of an Embedded Object in Word for Windows 6

In Word for Windows 6, you can change the format of an embedded object. You cannot do this in Word for Windows 2.

1. Select the object whose format you want to convert, or any object using the format you want to change.

O

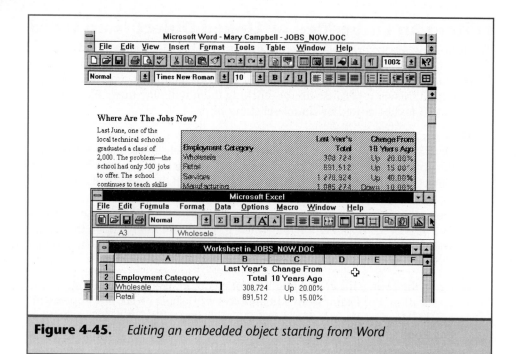

Figure 4-45.   *Editing an embedded object starting from Word*

2. Select Edit | *ObjectName* Object | Convert, where *ObjectName* is the name of the object's source.

3. You can choose to convert the current object to another format, or you can choose a new application to use for editing or opening all objects in the document that use the format of the selected object.

   While the Convert To option button is selected, choose the type of object you want the selected object converted to from the Object Type list box. Change the application used to edit all objects with the same format as the currently selected object by selecting the Activate As option button and choosing the object type from the Object Type list box that normally uses the application you want to use.

   For example, if you want an embedded Excel worksheet to appear in a Word document and you don't plan to make any changes to it, you can select Microsoft Word 6.0 Picture as the Object Type for the embedded object. Word converts the embedded Excel worksheet object into a picture of the data. After making this type of conversion, you cannot revert to the previous object type.

4. Select OK to make the change.

TIP: In Word for Windows 2 and 6 you can convert an embedded object into a picture by selecting the object and pressing CTRL+SHIFT+F9.

Changing Settings for Linked Objects

When you change the settings for linked objects, you can change the nature of the link itself. You can choose when to update the link, break the link, or change what the link is to.

1. Select Edit I Links to open this Links dialog box:

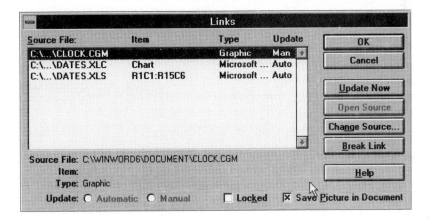

2. From the Source File list box (Links in Word for Windows 2), select the linked object to change.

3. Select the link options that you want to change, as described just below. Then select OK to return to the document (if necessary).

Here are the link settings you can specify:

■ The Automatic or Manual option buttons let you control when Word checks the linked data to include any changes. With Automatic, Word updates every time the data in the linked file changes. Manual updates the linked data only when you use the Edit I Links command and select Update Now, or when you move to the field and press F9 or select Update

Link from the field's shortcut menu. To prevent subsequent updates to the linked data, select the Locked check box. The linked data will not change until you use Edit I Links again and clear this check box.

■ To convert the contents of the link into the text or picture as it appears in Word, select Break Link (Cancel Link in Word for Windows 2). This breaks the link between the data in Word and the source data file. Select Yes to confirm that you indeed want to break this link, and the Word document will then contain either the text or a picture of the data in the source file. Another way to do this is to move to the field code for the linked data and press CTRL+SHIFT+F9.

■ To work with the data in the linked file, select Open Source. This is the same as double-clicking the object, selecting Edit I Linked *ObjectName* Object I Open, or selecting Open from the field's shortcut menu.

■ If you want to change the file or the part of the file from which the linked object comes, select Change Source (Change Link in Word for Windows 2). In the dialog box, use the File Name text box, Directories list box, and Drives drop-down list box to specify the filename, if necessary. In the Item text box you can enter or modify the location of the file the object is linked to.

■ In a Word for Windows 6 document, you can designate that the saved file will be smaller. To do this, turn off the Save Picture in Document option. When this check box option is enabled, the document retains a picture of the data. When it is turned off, Word only stores the link information in the document, not the data that the link represents.

Options

In Word for Windows 6, you can display the embedded or linked object as an icon, rather than display the actual data. To do this, select the Display as Icon check box in the Paste Special dialog box. The icon for the inserted object is usually the icon of the application that created it. Just double-click the icon to edit the data that the icon represents. This icon makes the data always available without having it displayed on the screen.

You can also change the icon that Word uses for the embedded or linked object. When you use the Edit I Paste Special or the Insert I Object command and select the Display as Icon check box, Word shows you the Change Icon button. Select this button, and you see another dialog box where you can select the icon to represent the embedded or linked object. Choose one of the displayed icons in the Icon list box, or select Browse to see another file containing icons, or enter your own special caption to appear below the icon by entering new text after Caption.

If you change your mind about whether or not to display an object as an icon, use the Edit | *ObjectName* Object | Convert command again and change the setting of the Display as Icon check box.

Hints

If you want to have some position options for the embedded or linked object, add a frame around it. Frames and their options are described under "Frames."

To make the embedded or linked object smaller or larger, the usual method is to select Format | Picture and change the percentage of scaling. "Graphics" in this chapter explains several features for Word pictures that you can use on the pictures of embedded and linked objects that appear in your Word documents.

Embedding and linking does not increase the number of applications installed on your computer. Word can only work with embedded and linked objects created with applications you have installed.

You can format the results of linked or embedded text if the object type allows it. If you are allowed to select individual characters, words, and paragraphs, you can use Word's formatting features to enhance the appearance of the text. For example, in a linked worksheet, you might want to format the table's headings. The "* mergeformat" that you may see as part of the field code for the linked or embedded data tells Word to keep the formatting applied to embedded data or update linked data.

To make Word data available in another application, you need to copy it to the Clipboard, as described under "Clipboard" in this chapter. Several Microsoft applications can work with Word data. Word for Windows 6 has a Microsoft toolbar that you can use to quickly switch to other Microsoft applications. By selecting buttons in this toolbar, you can start Microsoft Excel, PowerPoint, Mail, Access, FoxPro, Project, Schedule+, and Publisher, assuming these applications are installed.

TIP: Word provides several applications that create embedded objects. The Equation Editor, Graph, and WordArt, and Draw in Word for Windows 2, all create embedded objects.

Related Topics

Clipboard
Drawing on a Document
Equations
Frames

0

Graph
Graphics
Inserting Files
WordArt

OLE

See "Object Linking and Embedding."

On-line Forms

On-line forms are forms meant to be filled out on the screen and then printed. The ways in which Word for Windows 2 and 6 handle form creation are quite different. See "Forms" for more information.

Opening Files

You can open disk files in a Word document window without closing files that are already open. You may open up to nine files at one time in Word for Windows 2, and as many files as your computer's memory can accommodate in Word for Windows 6.

Procedures

The following procedures explain how to open a Word for Windows file or a file created in another application.

Opening a Word for Windows File

1. To open the Open dialog box, select File | Open, or press CTRL+F12, or select the Open toolbar button, or press CTRL+O in Word for Windows 6.

2. Choose the drive and directory for the location of the file you want to open.

The File Name list box shows the files available in the specified directory, with the filename extension selected in the List Files of Type drop-down list box. Change the Directories list box and the Drives drop-down list box to list files in a different location. When you change the drive and directory from this dialog box, Word uses the selected drive and directory for the remainder of your Word session.

In the Directories list box, the file folder icon for the current directory is open, and the current subdirectories appear below it. To open a subdirectory, double-click it, or press the arrow keys until it is highlighted and press ENTER. To move to an undisplayed directory, select a directory above the open directory. The open directory is then closed, and the directory you chose is opened, with the subdirectories of the newly opened directory displayed below it. Continue moving through directories until you reach the document you want to open.

3. Select the file you want to open from the File Name list box, or type its name in the File Name text box.

The File Name list box shows the files available in the specified directory, with the filename extension selected in the List Files of Type drop-down list box. To look for files with extensions not listed, in File Name enter *. followed by the extension, and select OK. The File Name list box then displays the files in the current directory with that extension.

Another way to open a file from another drive or directory is to enter the full path and filename of the file you want to open in the File Name text box. This way you can open a file in another drive or directory without changing the directory of files that Word will display next time you open the Open dialog box.

4. In the List Files of Type drop-down list box, select the type of files you want to see. Your selection here determines what files will be listed in the File Name list box. The default is to list files in the Word for Windows format (.DOC files). To list documents with a different extension, choose that extension from this drop-down list box.

5. Select any options you want for opening the file.
   Two options are the Read Only check box and the Find File button. When you open a file in read-only status, you cannot save the changed version to the same filename. If you want to save a changed version of this file, you must give it a new name. Find File helps when you are unsure of the name of the file you want to open. This button displays the Find File dialog box described under "File Management." Use Find File to look at the contents of a file before you open it, as well as to search for text that is contained in the document. An option found only in Word for Windows 6 is Confirm Conversion, which is explained under "Opening a Non-Word for Windows File."

6. Select OK to open the file. You also select OK when you double-click a file in the File Name list box.

O

Opening a Non-Word for Windows File

You can also open a file that is not in Word for Windows format. To do so, follow steps 1 through 5 above. Once you select OK, Word will look at the file and realize that the file is not in a Word for Windows format. In Word for Windows 2, Word then opens the Convert File dialog box. In Word for Windows 6 you only see the Convert File dialog box when you select the Confirm Conversion check box in the Open File dialog box.

The Convert File dialog box lists the possible formats that Word will accept, and Word's guess for the appropriate format will be highlighted. Select OK if the selection is correct, or make another selection before you select OK. In Word for Windows 6, when the Confirm Conversion option is turned off, Word automatically selects the format of the file without your input. You will not see the prompt for a format type unless Word is not sure of the format of the file you are opening.

After the format of the document is selected by you or Word, Word converts the file from its original format to Word for Windows's format. If Word requires any further information to assist in the conversion, it prompts for that information. A message appears on the status line telling you the percentage of the ongoing conversion process Word has completed.

To open a Word for DOS 5.5 document in Word for Windows 6, select the Confirm Conversion check box and select Word for MS-DOS 6.0 as the format to convert the document from.

Hints

The following are some tips that may make opening files faster or more accurate.

Shortcuts to Opening Files

At the bottom of the File menu, Word displays the names of the last four files you opened, as shown here:

```
1 ERIK2.DOC
2 OUTLINE.DOC
3 A:\GREENER.DOC
4 PEOPLE.DOC

Exit
```

To reopen one of those four files, select it from the menu. You can select one of these menu options either by double-clicking it, or highlighting it and pressing ENTER, or by typing the number that precedes the filename.

You can designate how many files—up to nine—Word for Windows 6 will remember for displaying at the bottom of the File menu. Select Tools | Options, then the General tab, and enter a new number after Recently Used File List.

You can also open one or more files at a time, by specifying the files to open from the Find File dialog box and selecting Open. See "File Management" in this chapter for more information.

Default Document Location

Word assumes that the next file you want to open is in the same directory as the last directory you specified for a file-selection command. When you first start Word, it uses its initial directory.

■ Word for Windows 6 assumes your documents are in the directory set with Tools I Options, the File Locations tab, File Types, and Documents. These file options are described in "File Location Options" in this chapter.

■ Word for Windows 2 assumes that documents are in the directory set by INI path in the WIN.INI file, unless you tell Word to start with another directory by including that directory as the Working Directory for the program item when you start Word, or if you start Word by opening a Word for Windows file that is in another directory. The options you can set with WIN.INI are described in "WIN.INI Options."

Designating How Word Converts Documents

If you want to change the settings for how Word for Windows 6 converts files that are in another format, these options are described under "Compatibility Options." Word for Windows 2 does not have these settings.

Using Documents on a Network

When you are working on a network and want to open a document, you select it just like any other document. This probably will include selecting the drive with the network in the Drives drop-down list box. You can only save the document to a network drive if you have the network's permission—as set by the network administrator, rather than in Word. To protect your documents from other users' changes, assign a password or use Word's annotation features. See "Saving Files" and "Annotation."

Related Topics

Annotation
Closing Files
Compatibility Options

0

File Location Options
File Management
Saving Files

Optional Hyphens

See "Hyphenation."

Options

Word has many settings that you can change to make Word operate the way you want it to. Most of these options are set with the Tools | Options command. Since there are so many options, and because Word for Windows 2 and 6 have their own names for options, they are categorized and described individually in this chapter as shown in the table below.

See This:	About Customizing This:
AutoFormat	How AutoFormat works with your document (Winword 6 only)
Comparing Versions	How revisions are marked (Winword 6 only)
Compatibility Options	How Word converts files (Winword 6 only)
Edit Options	How you edit documents (Winword 6 only)
File Location Options	Where Word expects to find files (Winword 6 only)
General Options	General features
Grammar Options	How Word checks the grammar in your documents
Keyboard Options	The shortcut keys
Menu Options	Word's menus
Print Options	How Word prints documents
Save Options	How Word saves files
Spelling Options	How Word checks spelling in your document
Toolbar Options	The toolbars
User Info Options	The information Word maintains about you
View Options	The screen display for Word
WIN.INI Options	The startup options for Word

Organizer

Word for Windows 6 has an Organizer that lets you transfer styles, AutoText, toolbars, and macros among templates and documents. You can also delete these items and rename them with the Organizer. The Organizer does not create these items but rather lets you share them among your Word documents and templates. Use the Organizer to copy these items among the templates you use, so that documents based on the templates will have these items available. You can also copy these items from the current document to its template, for the use of other documents using the same template.

Procedures

1. Select Format | Style and then Organizer, or select Tools | Macro and then Organizer. Word displays a dialog box that looks like this:

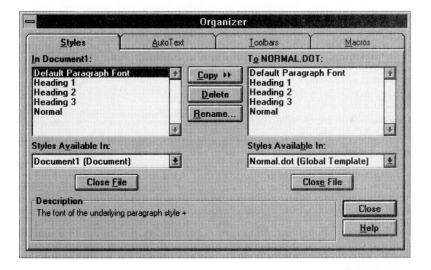

2. Use the Organizer to work with the styles, AutoText entries, toolbars, and macros.

3. Select Close to leave the Organizer.

Your activities in step 2 above will depend on what you want to do. The tabs all have the same elements, since they are only changing the Word feature you are working with. Select the styles, AutoText entries, toolbars, or macros you want to work with from either the In list box or To list box. You can change the template that appears in either list by using the Close File button below the list box. Once you select Close File, it changes to Open File.

When you select Open File, you can choose a template or document file whose items you want to work with. For example, the In list box can show the contents of a template or a document when you want to copy one particular document's styles for use in other documents created with a template. When NORMAL.DOT is not the selected file, you can also choose from the Available In drop-down list box and switch between NORMAL.DOT and the template or document that is currently open.

- To delete a style, AutoText entry, toolbar, or macro, choose it in the list and then select Delete. You will be asked to confirm that you want to delete the selected item. Select Yes to delete it, Yes to All to delete all selected items without further confirmation, No to skip over deleting the listed item as well as Cancel and Help.

- To rename a style, AutoText entry, toolbar, or macro, select it in the list and then select Rename. Type a new name and select OK.

- To copy a style, AutoText entry, toolbar, or macro, select it in the In list box and then select Copy. The selected item is copied into the template in the To list box.

Organizing Data and Documents

Word has several organization features you can use for your documents. "File Management" describes how you can use the File | Find File command to locate and work with specific documents. "Sorting" covers sorting data within a document, including how to organize the data you will use for Mail Merge.

Orientation

See "Page Size and Orientation."

Orphans

See "Pagination."

Outlines

Word's Outline feature provides a hierarchical format to a document, letting you work with the headings in the outline to organize and rearrange the document. By displaying only the headings, you can quickly move to a specific part of the document. You can also use outline headings to rearrange the document's text, and to quickly execute formatting tasks. Word's Outline view shows the different levels of headings and the text that belongs to each one. By applying outline headings to your document and using the Outline view, you have a new way of working with your document.

Procedures

When you create an outline, all paragraphs are marked as either headings or as body text. Word offers you nine levels of headings styles. Any paragraph that is not a heading is body text. The following procedures tell you how to create, edit, or print an outline.

Switching to Outline View

Select View | Outline, or click the Outline View button at the left of the Word for Windows 6 horizontal scroll bar. To switch back to Normal view, select View | Normal or click the Normal View button at the left of the Word for Windows 6 horizontal scroll bar.

Creating a New Outline

1. Open a new file.

2. Switch to Outline view by selecting View | Outline. The Outline toolbar replaces the ruler, as shown here:

3. Type a heading. Word assigns the Heading 1 format automatically.

4. Press ENTER to end the first paragraph, and type another heading or a few lines of text. Note that paragraphs are automatically formatted at the same level as the paragraph that precedes them.

O

5. Change the level of the heading you just typed, or convert the paragraph text to body text, using either the mouse or the keyboard. The buttons and key combinations you can use to do this are shown in Table 4-18.

6. Repeat steps 4 through 6 until you have created your entire outline document. You can have up to nine levels of headings in your document. Figure 4-46 illustrates an outline, without body text.

Toolbar Icon	Key Combination	Result
←	ALT+SHIFT+LEFT ARROW	Switches to next higher level
→	ALT+SHIFT+RIGHT ARROW	Switches to next lower level
⇒	ALT+SHIFT+5 (the 5 on numeric keypad)	Converts to body text
↑	ALT+SHIFT+UP ARROW	Moves up one position in the outline
↓	ALT+SHIFT+DOWN ARROW	Moves down one position in the outline
+	ALT+SHIFT++ or + on numeric keypad	Expands to next higher level
−	ALT+SHIFT+− or – on numeric keypad	Collapses to next lower level
1 to 8	ALT+SHIFT+*level number*	Displays outline only through level number specified
All	ALT+SHIFT+A or ALT+SHIFT+*	Expands or collapses the entire outline
≡	ALT+SHIFT+L	Shows either all text or just the first line
ᴬ/A	/ (on numeric keypad)	Shows or hides character formatting

Table 4-18.   *The Outline Toolbar*

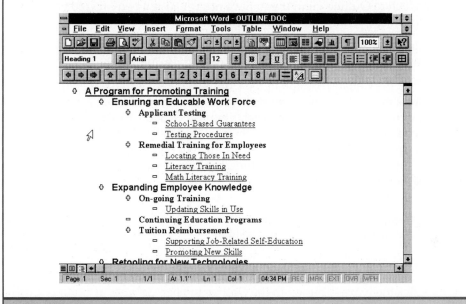

Figure 4-46.   *Outlined document, showing several levels used at once*

Outlining an Existing Document

1. Open the document you want to outline.

2. Switch to Outline view by selecting View | Outline.

3. Move to the paragraphs you want to use as headings, and change them to the appropriate heading level. You can do this by selecting icons on the toolbar or by pressing the keys shown in Table 4-18. Another way to do this is to drag the square bullet in front of a paragraph to the appropriate indentation for the level you want to use.

Collapsing and Expanding Heading Levels

To *collapse* or *expand* the branches of the outline means to hide or show the body text and headings under the current heading. Branch is a term used in outlines which refers to the body text and headings under a specific heading. Collapsing and expanding do not affect the headings and text elsewhere in the outline that are not subordinate to the heading you collapse or expand.

O

1. Switch to Outline view. If you have not yet added body text to your document, it may look something like Figure 4-46.

2. Move to the last heading in a branch. For example, in Figure 4-46 you could move to the first third-level heading, "Applicant Testing."

3. Click the Collapse button in the Outline toolbar, or press ALT+SHIFT+–, or press the – key on the numeric keypad. The body text that is lower than the current one disappears. Each time you click the Collapse button (or press either key-combination), the next higher level of heading disappears. You cannot collapse the current paragraph. When you collapse the entire branch, nothing appears on the level under the current paragraph, as shown here:

> ✧ **Ensuring an Educable Work Force**
> ✧ **Expanding Employee Knowledge**

4. Move to one of the collapsed headings.

5. Click the Expand button in the Outline toolbar, or press ALT+SHIFT++, or press the + key on the numeric keypad. The highest level of headings under the current paragraph reappears. Keep clicking the Expand button (or pressing either key-combination) until you see all the levels you want.

Collapsing or Expanding Heading Levels

To expand all collapsed headings and body text under a heading, double-click the + in front of the heading. If all headings and text under that heading are already expanded, your double-click will collapse them all.

Displaying Selected Heading Levels

Instead of individually collapsing or expanding branches, you may want to display only through a particular level heading in your document. You can do this with either the mouse or the keyboard:

■ Click on the numbered button in the Outline toolbar to display only headings through that level.

■ Press ALT+SHIFT followed by the level number, to display only headings through that level; for example, ALT+SHIFT+3 shows only the first three levels.

Selecting Outline Branches

When you want to select text in Outline view, you can use most of the usual selection methods. Also, keep the following guidelines in mind:

■ You cannot select part of two paragraphs. When your selection extends from one paragraph to another, all of both paragraphs are selected. For example, if you drag to select the last sentence in one paragraph and the first sentence in the next paragraph, when you release the mouse button the entire contents of both paragraphs will be selected.

■ When you click in the selection bar, you select the paragraph beside the mouse pointer, as usual. When you double-click in the selection bar in Outline view, however, the heading and all its subordinate headings and body text are selected.

■ When you click on the + in front of a paragraph, you select that paragraph as well as all the headings and body text paragraphs under it.

Moving Outline Branches

In Outline view, you can easily move a heading, and all of its subheadings and body text, within the document. You can change the level of the headings in the branch up or down just as easily.

Begin by moving to the highest-level heading in the branch you want to move, and then select it. If the heading's subheadings and body text are displayed, and you want to move them as well, double-click the + before the heading to select them all. Only the part of the outline that is selected is moved. If subheadings are collapsed, selecting the heading automatically selects the subheadings.

■ To move the branch up in the outline, click on the Move Up button in the Outline toolbar or press ALT+SHIFT+UP ARROW.

■ To move the branch down in the outline, click on the Move Down button in the Outline toolbar, or press ALT+SHIFT+DOWN ARROW.

■ You can also move a heading, along with its subheadings and text, up or down by dragging the + or – in the selection bar for the heading. Word displays a line marking where the branch will move when you release the mouse, as shown in the following:

```
    ✦  Windows
              ▫  Windows is not actually an operating system by itself since it enhances the ...
    ✧  OS/2
              ▫  OS/2 is an operating system designed to overcome many of the limitations in ...
    ✧  Applications
```

Promoting or Demoting Branches to Other Levels

Move to the highest-level heading in the branch you want to promote or demote. If the heading's subheadings are displayed and you want them promoted as well, double-click the + before the heading to select them, too.

- ■ To increase the heading and its subheadings by one level, click the Promote button in the toolbar or press ALT+SHIFT+LEFT ARROW.

- ■ To decrease the heading and its subheadings by one level, click the Demote button in the toolbar or press ALT+SHIFT+RIGHT ARROW.

Subheadings that are not selected are not changed. When you have hidden subheadings, selecting the heading automatically selects the subheadings.

TIP: You can also promote and demote branches by dragging the symbol in front of a heading to the left or right. When you drag body text to the left, you change it into a heading. When you drag the symbol for a heading level all the way to the right, it changes the heading to body text.

Deleting Branches

Move to the highest-level heading in the branch that you want to delete, and select the part of the outline to delete. If the heading's subheadings and body text are displayed and you want them deleted as well, double-click the + before the heading to select them, too. Only the part of the outline that is selected will be deleted. When you collapse subheadings, selecting the heading automatically selects the subheadings.

When you're ready, delete the entire heading, including its paragraph character and selected subheadings and body text, by pressing DEL or BACKSPACE.

Reducing the Body Text Display

This is a useful feature that makes reorganizing a document easier and lets you quickly find the text you want. Switch to Outline view. Then press ALT+SHIFT+L in Word for Windows 6 or ALT+SHIFT+F in Word for Windows 2. Your document will look like Figure 4-47. The ellipses at the end of the lines of body text indicate that the document has more text for each paragraph.

Adding Outline Numbers in Word for Windows 6

1. Select the part of the outline you want numbered. (To select the entire outline, you can press CTRL+5 using the 5 key on the numeric keypad.) Only the headings that you can see are numbered, so you can also determine which headings are numbered by expanding and collapsing parts of the outline.

2. Select Format | Heading Numbering to open the Heading Numbering dialog box.

3. Choose the style of outline numbering you want from one of the boxes, and select OK.

Figure 4-48 shows an outline that has numbers added.

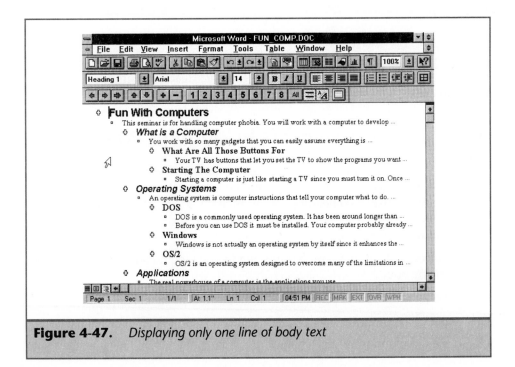

Figure 4-47. *Displaying only one line of body text*

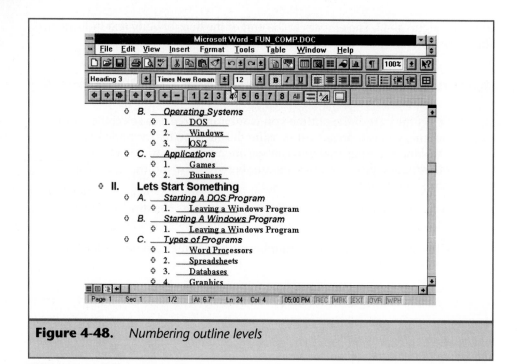

Figure 4-48.   *Numbering outline levels*

To remove outline numbers, select the part of the outline from which you want the outline numbers removed, select Format | Heading Numbering, and select Remove.

Adding Outline Numbers in Word for Windows 2

1. Select the part of the outline you want numbered. (To select the entire outline, you can press CTRL+5 using the 5 key on the numeric keypad.) Only the displayed headings are numbered, so you can also designate which headings are numbered by expanding and collapsing parts of the outline.

2. Select Tools | Bullets and Numbering to open the Bullets and Numbering dialog box.

3. Select the Outline option button at the top of the dialog box.

4. Select a type of outline numbering from the Format drop-down list box. As you highlight each option, Sample shows you how it looks.

When you select Learn by Example, Word applies the labeling system used for the first instance of each heading to the remainder of the headings. For example, if your first level-one heading has a "1." before it, Word would use arabic numbers to mark all level one heads.

5. Select the options you want for the outline numbering, as described just below, and select OK.

■ Auto Update increments the numbers as you promote and demote levels, as well as when you add and remove headings. Word does this using field codes such as {AUTONUMOUT}.

■ Replace Only Numbers adds outline numbers only to headings that currently have a number.

■ Hanging Indent By adds the outline numbers as hanging indents, by changing the paragraph's indentation.

Figure 4-48 shows an outline that has numbers added.

To remove outline numbers you have added, select the part of the outline from which you want the outline numbers removed, select Tools I Bullets and Numbering, the Outline option button, and then Remove.

Printing an Outline

When you print a document from Outline view, only the displayed elements of the outline are printed.

NOTE: *Print Preview, of course, still shows the entire outline.*

1. Switch to Outline view.

2. Collapse or expand branches to display only the paragraphs you want to print.

3. Select File I Print, and select the print options you want to use.

4. Select OK to print the outline.

Hints

When you need to have an outline as well as a document (for instance, when you are submitting an academic paper or an outline of a speech for a conference), switch to Outline view after finishing the document, and collapse branches so that only the headings show. Then print the outline. This is much easier than creating an outline as a separate document.

Using Outlines to Create Documents

Create an outline of your document first, and then fill in the document with the body text. By creating the outline first, you can be sure that you have covered all of the major topics you want to deal with, and you will avoid spending time writing text that you have to eventually remove as irrelevant.

Moving Around in Long Documents

Use the Outline view to move quickly through large documents. Switch to Outline view, display only high-level headings, move to the heading closest to the text you want to work with, and then either expand that text or switch back to Normal view.

Using Styles and Headings

When you set the heading levels for an outline, you are assigning styles to the paragraphs containing the headings. The heading styles are Heading 1 to Heading 9, to match the heading level. You can quickly format all headings of a specific level by changing the formatting applied with that style. This lets you maintain consistent formatting for headings throughout the entire document.

Use outlining to add headings to a document even when you do not necessarily need the other Outline view features. The same Heading 1 through Heading 9 styles that Word uses for outline headings can be helpful in headings for documents. If you later want to change the headings' appearance just change the styles.

TIP: Using text marked with heading styles, you can use your outline to create the document's table of contents. See "Table of Authorities" for more information.

Changing Outline Styles

In Word for Windows 6, you can modify the outline's styles so that they supply exactly the features you want. To create an outline style, select Modify from the Heading Numbering dialog box (opened by selecting Tools | Heading Numbering). From the Level list box, select each outline level that you will use for the outline style you are creating, or click each outline level in the Preview box. Then, for the selected outline level, change the other options in the dialog box to change how the outline will appear.

Under Number Format, enter any text to appear before the number in the Text Before and Text After text boxes. Remember to include any blank spaces you want in the entry. You can also choose a style of numbering from the choices listed in the Bullet or Number drop-down box. To change the font of these entries, select Font and choose a font. You can also set the starting number of the series, with the Start At text box. If this level of outline headings includes the number or number and position of the previous heading, select an option from the Include From Previous Level list box.

In the Number Position section of the dialog box, select the position of the number Word will add. Choose from these options: use the Alignment of List Text drop-down list box to control the alignment; designate the amount of space from the left margin to the number with the Distance from Indent to Text option; designate the amount of space between the heading number and the text in the Distance from Number to Text option; and use the Hanging Indent check box to set whether the rest of the paragraph at the heading level is indented. You can also select the Restart Numbering at Each New Section option when you want Word to restart counting after each higher-level heading.

Once you have finished changing the outline style, select OK, and Word uses the new style you have created. You can modify the style by selecting Format | Heading Numbering and Modify again without selecting one of the boxes displaying outline styles. If you select one of the outline style boxes, that style replaces the style you have created.

Related Topics

Lists
Printing
Styles

Outline View

When you switch to Outline view, the ruler is removed and the Outline toolbar appears in its place. The text in your document is arranged in an outline. Some paragraphs are headings, which means that one of the nine headings styles has been applied. Other paragraphs are body text. In Outline view, you can control what levels of text are displayed, reposition entire sections or branches of the outline, and promote or demote them as you reorganize your document. For a full explanation of the Outline view features, see "Outlines."

O

Outline Numbering

See "Outlines."

Outline Toolbar

The Outline toolbar lets you quickly set the outline levels in a document in Outline view, and determine the parts of the outlined document that you see. This toolbar appears when you switch to Outline view (by selecting View | Outline or clicking the Outline View button to the left of the document's horizontal scroll bar). Like other toolbars, you can customize the toolbar to change the buttons available on it, as described in "Toolbar Options." The buttons of the Outline toolbar are listed in Table 4-18.

The Master Document View button switches to Master Document view and uses the unused portion of the Outline toolbar for the Master Document toolbar.

Overtype Mode

See "INS Key."

Padlock

See "Master Documents."

Page Break

See "Pagination."

PAGE Field

The PAGE field inserts the page number for the page containing the field. For more information, see "Fields."

Page Formats

See "Margins," "Page Size and Orientation," and "Paper Source."

Page Layout

See "Margins," "Page Size and Orientation," and "Paper Source."

Page Layout View

See "Viewing Documents."

Page Numbers

You can add page numbers to your document, specify the first page number, and designate the format of page numbers.

Procedures

You can add page numbers by themselves, or you can add them to headers and footers, which is done differently in Word for Windows 2 and 6.

Inserting Page Numbers Alone

1. Move the insertion point to where you want the page number added, and select Insert | Page Numbers, opening the Page Numbers dialog box.

2. Select an option under Position to set the position of the page number. With Top of Page (Header), the header contains the page number; with Bottom of Page (Footer), the footer contains the page number.

   In Word for Windows 6, using the Insert | Page Numbers command adds the page number to an existing header or footer. In Word for Windows 2, using this command will replace any previous header or footer after Word gets your confirmation.

3. Select an Alignment option to set how the page number is aligned in the header or footer. The choices include Right, Center, and Left, as well as Inside and Outside in Word for Windows 6, to put the page number on different sides of the page for odd and even pages. The page number is aligned using tab characters.

4. In Word for Windows 6, you can enable the Show Number on First Page check box if you want the page number to appear on the first page.

5. Select Format to open the Page Number Format dialog box and specify the format of the page number.

   a. Select a format from the Number Format drop-down list box. You can use arabic numbers, upper- or lowercase letters, or upper- or lowercase roman numbers.

   b. Select the initial page number for the current section under Page Numbering. Choose the Continue from Previous Section option to have the first page in the current section use the page number following the last page of the previous section. To use a specific page number, select the Start At option button and enter the first page number for the section in the Start At text box.

6. In Word for Windows 6, you can include chapter numbers with the page number. To include the chapter number:

   a. Select the Include Chapter Number check box and choose the style from the Chapter Starts with Style drop-down list box that is used to mark when a new chapter begins.

   b. Select the character that separates the chapter number from the page number in the Use Separator drop-down list box.

7. Select OK twice to return to the document.

When you return to the document, Word creates a header or footer containing a page number field alone, formatted as you defined. The header or footer contains only the PAGE field.

TIP: You can also add a page number by pressing ALT+SHIFT+P. This key combination adds the PAGE field to the document, and Word substitutes the field with the current page number. You can also use the Insert | Field command when you want to set the format of the page number.

Adding Page Numbers to Headers or Footers in Word for Windows 2

You can add page numbers to headers or footers that contain other entries.

1. Select View | Header/Footer while in Normal view, to open the Header/Footer dialog box.

2. To set the format of the page numbers or the first page number in the current section, select the Page Numbers command button to open the Page Number Format dialog box. This is the same dialog box described in the foregoing section for the Insert | Page Number command. Select OK when you are finished, to return to the Header/Footer dialog box.

3. In the Header/Footer list box, select the header or footer you want to edit or create, and select OK to open the header or footer pane.

4. Enter the text or graphics you want to appear in the header or footer if necessary.

5. Move the insertion point to where you want the page number, and click the Page Number button on the Header/Footer toolbar or press SHIFT+ALT+P. Word inserts a PAGE field code into the header or footer. (Unless you have turned on the field code display with View | Field Codes, however, you will see "1.")

6. Select Close to close the header or footer pane, or press SHIFT+F10+C. You can also return to the document without closing the pane by pressing F6.

NOTE: *If you want to add the page number from the Page Layout view, you can double-click any existing header or footer to edit it, but you will have to add the page number using the default format by pressing SHIFT+ALT+P.*

Adding Page Numbers to Headers or Footers in Word for Windows 6

Here are the steps to add page numbers to headers and footers in Word for Windows 6:

1. Select View | Header and Footer from Normal view. Or, in Page Layout view, you can double-click any existing header or footer.

2. Enter the text or graphics you want to appear in the header or footer.

3. Move the insertion point to where you want the page number, and click the Page Numbers button on the Header and Footer toolbar or press SHIFT+ALT+P. Word inserts a PAGE field code. (Unless you have turned on the display of field codes, however, you see "1.")

4. If you want the page number to have a different format, select Insert | Page Numbers and Format. Once you select the page number's format, select OK and Close.

5. Select Close to finish editing the header or footer, or select one of the views from the View menu.

TIP: You can also insert and format a page number in Word for Windows 6 headers and footers using Insert | Page Numbers. Besides using this command to set the format of the number, you can put the page number in a frame, which may give you more options for positioning and appearance.

Hints

You can also insert page numbers in a document by inserting the PAGE field code yourself. For a full explanation of this field type, see "Fields."

Related Topics

Fields
Headers and Footers

Page Orientation

See "Page Size and Orientation."

Page Setup

See "Margins," "Page Size and Orientation," and "Paper Source."

Page Size and Orientation

When setting the size and orientation of your page, you can choose from certain standard paper sizes or specify a custom size. You can set the page size and orientation for a whole document, from a particular page forward to the end of the document, or for a section.

Procedure

1. Select File | Page Setup and the Paper Size tab (or Format | Page Setup and the Size and Orientation option button in Word for Windows 2) to open the Page Setup dialog box.

2. If the paper you are going to use is a standard size, select it from the Paper Size drop-down list box. The height and width of that paper size will appear in the Height and Width text boxes. If your paper is a not a standard size, enter its width and height in the Width and Height text boxes.

3. Select either the Portrait or Landscape option button, depending on how you want to feed your paper into your printer. Portrait mode uses the narrow side of the paper as the top; Landscape mode uses the long side of the paper as the top. Figure 4-49 shows an example of both portrait and landscape orientations.

4. Select the part of the document in which you want to use the new page size or orientation, from the Apply To drop-down list box. Then select OK.

   ■ With Whole Document, the entire document uses the designated page size and orientation.

   ■ With This Section or Selected Sections, the section containing the insertion point or the selected text uses the designated settings.

   ■ With This Point Forward or Selected Text, Word inserts a section break just before the insertion point or before and after the selected text, and the new section uses the new settings.

Hints

Word uses the defined paper size to format your document and repaginate it. You can mix page sizes and orientations: For example, you can write a letter and

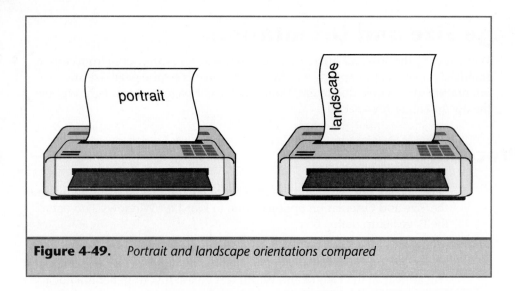

Figure 4-49.   *Portrait and landscape orientations compared*

include an envelope for it in the same document, by changing the page size and orientation of the last page and entering the information for the envelope in this last page. Also, if you are creating a report that includes wide tables or graphics, you can switch to landscape for a single page to accommodate the wide table, and then return to portrait for the remainder of the document.

Related Topics

Envelopes
Margins
Pagination
Paper Source
Printing

PAGEREF

The PAGEREF field inserts the page number a bookmark is on. For more information, see "Fields."

Pagination

Word automatically breaks your document into pages, based on the page size and margin settings. You can also add manual page breaks, keep lines or paragraphs together on a page, start a page with a specific paragraph, and allow or disallow widow and orphan lines. Page breaks are *soft page breaks* when Word adds them for you, or *hard page breaks* when you add them yourself. These page breaks look different in Normal view, as you can see from this document:

Soft page break is above the text and a hard page break is below the text
Page Break

Procedures

The following procedures will explain how to turn automatic pagination on and off, how to paginate your document manually, and how to insert and remove hard page breaks. These procedures also explain how to keep text together on one page and prevent awkward or unattractive page breaks.

Turning Off Automatic Pagination

By default, Word automatically breaks your document into pages by inserting soft page breaks as you are typing. You can turn this on and off for all views except Print Preview and Page Layout, which always have automatic pagination. Turning it off can accelerate Word's performance, depending on the size of the document and the editing changes you are making.

To turn off automatic pagination, select Tools | Options, and select the General tab or the General icon in the Category list box. Then turn off the Background Repagination check box option, and select OK. If you want to restart automatic pagination, just check this box again.

Repaginating Manually in Word for Windows 2

To repaginate your document manually, select Tools | Repaginate Now, or switch to Print Preview or Page Layout view.

NOTE: *There is no equivalent command in Word for Windows 6, because Word for Windows 6 is always repaginating your document.*

Inserting and Removing Hard Page Breaks

■ Press CTRL+ENTER, or select Insert | Break and select OK.

Hard page breaks do not move if a page has more or less white space. In Normal view, these page breaks look different from the soft page breaks that Word displays to show where text is split between pages.

■ Move to the page break character in Normal view, and press DEL or BACKSPACE.

If the page break exists because the paragraph has a page break before it as part of its formatting, the only way to remove the page break is by using the Format | Paragraph command and clearing the Page Break Before check box (on the Text Flow tab in Word for Windows 6).

Keeping a Paragraph at the Top of a Page

You can apply a paragraph format that keeps a hard page break just before that paragraph, so that it always starts a new page. When this format is enabled, it affects the paragraph the insertion point is in, or all selected paragraphs. If you press ENTER in a paragraph, creating a new paragraph, the new one has the same setting as the previous one.

■ Select Format | Paragraph, and the Text Flow tab in Word for Windows 6. Select the Page Break Before check box, or clear this box to remove the format. Then select OK.

Keeping Paragraphs Together on the Page

You can apply a paragraph format that keeps the formatted paragraph on the same page as the next paragraph. Word moves any soft page break that exists between these two paragraphs to a position before both of them, to prevent them from being separated. When this format is enabled, it affects the paragraph the insertion point is in, or all selected paragraphs.

You might use this feature for a title for a paragraph, so that the page does not break between the title and the subsequent text. If you press ENTER in a paragraph, creating a new paragraph, the new paragraph has the same setting as the previous one.

■ Select Format | Paragraph, and the Text Flow tab in Word for Windows 6. Select the Keep with Next check box, or clear this box to remove the format. Then select OK.

Keeping Lines on the Same Page

You can apply a paragraph format which prevents a paragraph from being broken in two by a page break. Word moves the soft page break to before the formatted paragraph to prevent it from being split. When this format is set, it affects the paragraph the insertion point is in, or all selected paragraphs. If you press ENTER in a paragraph, creating a new paragraph, the new paragraph has the same setting as the old.

■ Select Format | Paragraph, and the Text Flow tab in Word for Windows 6. Select the Keep Lines Together check box, or clear this box to remove the format. Then select OK.

Allowing Widows and Orphans

As a default, Word places page breaks to avoid leaving the first line of a paragraph alone at the bottom of a page (orphan) or the last line of paragraph alone at the top of a page (widow). You may need to change this if you need to print a specific number of lines on a page or reduce the number of pages you need to use.

In Word for Windows 2, follow these steps:

1. Select Tools | Options.

2. Select the Print icon in the Category box.

3. Clear the Widow/Orphan Control check box. If you do not want to allow widow and orphan lines, select this check box. Then select OK.

In Word for Windows 6, follow these steps:

1. Select Format | Paragraph, and make sure the Text Flow tab is selected.

2. Clear the Widow/Orphan Control check box. If you do not want to allow widow and orphan lines, select this check box. Then select OK.

Hints

Automatic pagination makes it easier for you to see how your document is laid out. On the other hand, you can work with long documents more quickly when this feature is turned off. When editing and entering long documents, turn it off and then restart it when you are ready to edit the pages. You will also find that Word performs faster when you edit and enter lengthy documents using Normal view versus Page Layout or Print Preview.

When a paragraph is the start of a new section of your document, keep the paragraph at the top of a page. Keep the paragraphs of a table together, to prevent the table from being split across pages.

Keeping the lines of a paragraph together whenever possible will prevent your readers from losing the train of thought because the page has to be turned.

Avoid widow and orphan lines whenever possible; they make your document look less professional, and much less readable if the page has to be turned at an odd point in the discussion.

Page Break Displays

In Normal view, soft page breaks, which Word inserts, appear as a light dotted line. Hard page breaks, which you insert, appear as a heavy dotted line. In Word for Windows 6, the words "Page Break" also appear in the middle of a hard page break line.

In Page Layout view and Print Preview, Word does not distinguish between soft and hard page breaks. These views represent each page of the document as it will appear when printed.

Related Topics

Margins
Page Size and Orientation

Panes

See "Viewing Documents."

Paper Source

You can designate the source of the paper used to print the first page of a section or the other pages in the same section. This option is effective only if your printer has multiple bins or trays, or both a single tray and a manual feeder for paper. For example, in a document that contains both an envelope and a letter, you can have Word print the envelope using paper from a manual feeder and then use the regular sheet feeder for the letter.

You can set the paper source for a whole document, or for a particular section. If you select text before changing the paper source, you can choose to change the paper source for the selected text only, in which case the selected text is turned into a specific section.

Procedure

1. Select File | Page Setup (Format | Page Setup in Word for Windows 2).

2. Select the Paper Source tab or option button if necessary. The Page Setup dialog box changes to present the Paper Source elements.

3. In the First Page list box, select the source of paper for the first page of the section. The available options depend on the printer selected. Most printers that Windows supports have at least a single tray and can also be fed manually. Other printers may have multiple trays or may not have a manual feeder. Some printers have an envelope feeder.

4. In the Other Pages list box, select the source of paper for the remainder of the pages in the section.

5. Select the part of the document you want the paper source settings to affect by choosing an option from the Apply To drop-down list box, and then select OK.

   ■ With Whole Document, the first page of the document uses the paper source chosen in the First Page list box, and the remainder of the document uses the setting of the Other Pages list box.

   ■ With Selected Text or This Point Forward, Word inserts a section break before the insertion point, or before and after the selected text, creating a new section. The first page of the new section uses the paper source specified in the First Page list box, and the rest use the setting in the Other Pages list box.

■ With This Section or Selected Sections, the current or selected sections use these settings.

Hints

Most letters today use letterhead for the first page only, and then blank sheets after that. You can use two separate trays of paper, one loaded with letterhead and the other with blank sheets, or you can manually feed the letterhead and then use the default tray for the blank paper.

Related Topics

Printing

Paragraph Formats

With Word, you can specify many formats that affect a paragraph of text, including its indentation, how page breaks affect it, and the spacing before, within, or after the paragraph.

See "Alignment," "Indents," "Pagination," and "Spacing" for detailed information on these paragraph formats.

Paragraph Marks

See "Nonprinting Characters."

Parallel Columns

See "Columns."

Passwords

See "Locking and Protecting Documents" and "Saving Files."

Pasting

See "Clipboard" and "Object Linking and Embedding."

PICT Files

PICT files, a Macintosh graphics format, are one of the file formats Word accepts for graphic images. You can add these files as pictures to your Word documents. Look under "Graphics" for more information about bringing image files such as these into a Word document.

Picture Command to Import Graphics

See "Graphics."

Pictures

See "Graphics."

Pie Charts

The pie chart is one of the graph types available in Microsoft Graph. See "Graph" for more information.

Pitch

Word for Windows measures font size using points rather than pitch. *Pitch* is used to describe font size by how many characters fit across a one-inch space. *Points* represent the height of the characters, with one point equaling 1/72 inch.

Placing Text Around a Framed Object

See "Frames."

Playing Macros

Macros perform a series of steps for you, such as typing or selecting Word features to apply to a document. See Chapter 8 for complete information on macros. "Macros" in this chapter describes how you run a macro in Word.

Point Size

See "Fonts."

Positioning

See "Equations" and "Frames."

Positioning Equations

See "Frames."

Positioning Graphics and Charts

See "Frames."

Positioning Objects

See "Frames."

Positioning Tables and Spreadsheets

See "Frames."

Positioning Text

See "Frames."

PostScript

Word accepts graphic image files in Encapsulated PostScript format (.EPS files). You can add these files as pictures to your Word documents. However, you cannot print these files unless you are using a PostScript printer. Depending on the file, you may not be able to display it, either. If the file is saved with an embedded TIFF file, that file is used to display the EPS graphic. If there is no attached graphic, you cannot even display the .EPS file without a PostScript printer. Look under "Graphics" for more information about bringing image files such as these into a Word document.

PowerPoint

Microsoft PowerPoint is a Windows application that can share data with Word. You can embed and link PowerPoint data in Word documents, as described in "Object Linking and Embedding." Word for Windows 6 also lets you start PowerPoint from within Word, by clicking the Microsoft PowerPoint button in the Microsoft toolbar. Once you start Microsoft PowerPoint, you are using PowerPoint, not Word, and you must follow PowerPoint's menu and features.

Preferences

Word has many settings that you can change to make Word operate the way you want it to. Most of these options are set with the Tools | Options command. Since there are so many options, and because Word for Windows 2 and 6 have their own names for options, they are categorized and described individually in this chapter as shown in the table below.

See This:	About Customizing This:
AutoFormat	How AutoFormat works with your document (Winword 6 only)
Comparing Versions	How revisions are marked (Winword 6 only)
Compatibility Options	How Word converts files (Winword 6 only)

See This:	About Customizing This:
Edit Options	How you edit documents (Winword 6 only)
File Location Options	Where Word expects to find files (Winword 6 only)
General Options	General features
Grammar Options	How Word checks the grammar in your documents
Keyboard Options	The shortcut keys
Menu Options	Word's menus
Print Options	How Word prints documents
Save Options	How Word saves files
Spelling Options	How Word checks spelling in your document
Toolbar Options	The toolbars
User Options	The information Word maintains about you
View Options	The screen display for Word
WIN.INI Options	The startup options for Word

Preview Print

See "Viewing Documents."

Primary Documents

See "Master Documents."

PRINT Field

The PRINT field sends instructions to your printer. For more information, see "Fields."

Print Merge

The Print Merge feature lets you combine text in a main document with variable data stored in a data file. The data file can have many records containing information which can be combined with the data in the main document to create customized documents such as letters, labels, or contracts.

The merging feature is called Mail Merge in Word for Windows 6, and is covered under that heading. This "Print Merge" section only covers the merge feature in Word for Windows 2.

Procedures

The basic steps of carrying out a print merge are quite simple. The first step is to create a data file. Then you create the main document, including the fields which mark where data will merge into the document. Then you tell Word to actually carry out the merge process.

Creating a Data File

You can create data files in Word or use data files created in other programs such as 1-2-3, dBASE, or WordPerfect. Data files include the specific data that will merge with the generic main document to create customized documents.

Data can be arranged in a Word table, or in other ways, as described under "Data Files Arranged as Paragraphs." Tables are the easiest way to create a data file in Word.

1. Select File | Print Merge.

2. Select Attach Data File.

3. Select Create Data File to start creating a data file using the Word table feature.

4. Create the list of fields to appear in your data file.

   ■ Add a field name to your list by typing the name in the Field Name text box and selecting Add.

   ■ Remove a field name from the list, by highlighting it in the Fields in Header Record list box and selecting Delete.

   Field names can use up to 31 characters, including letters, numbers, and the underscore character. Field names cannot include spaces.

5. Select OK.

6. Enter a name and location for the data file using the dialog box elements in the Save As dialog box. This is no different than saving a file by selecting File | Save As.

7. Select OK. Word displays the data file in the application window. The data file contains a table, the first row of which contains the field names you created in step 4.

8. Enter the data for the data file. Each row is a record which contains information that is used in one copy of a document. For example, the name, address, and phone number of a specific client such as ABC Co. would create one record. Each cell in a row contains a field, which is a single bit of information, such as the zip code for ABC Co. Make sure that the same type of information is entered in the same column in every row.

9. Select File | Save when you are finished creating the data file.

Creating a Main Document

The main document contains the information that does not change in each copy created by merging. It also includes the merge codes that tell Word where information from the data file is to be inserted.

1. Select File | New and OK to create a new file.

2. Select File | Print Merge.

3. Select Attach Data File. You want to attach your data file, even though you have not yet created the main document, because this will make inserting the merge codes easier.

4. Select the data file to attach using the File Name box, and the Directories and Drive Name boxes, then select OK.

    After Word attaches the file, it returns to the document. The Print Merge bar appears, just above the ruler. The buttons on this bar can make inserting merge codes and merging the document easier.

5. Enter the text and formatting of the main document as if you were creating a normal document.

    Any place you want to enter varying data, such as names or addresses, you need to include a merge field.

6. To insert your merge fields:

   ■ Select the Insert Merge Field button.

   ■ Select the field whose contents you want to insert in the Print Merge Fields list box.

   ■ Select OK.

7. Select File | Save to save your main document.

Merging Files

When you actually merge a document, you are telling Word to copy the information in the data file and add it to the main document at the merge fields. One copy of the main document is created for each record that needs to be merged.

The following steps assume that you have created both the data file and the main document, and that the main document is the current document when you start the steps.

1. Select File | Print Merge while in the main document.

2. Select Merge.

3. Select what you want to do with the merge results under Merge Results.

   ■ Select Merge to Printer to have Word send the merge results to the printer, without saving them in a new document.

   ■ Select Merge to New Document to have Word send the merge results to a new document, separating each copy of the merged document with a section break.

   ■ Select Only Check for Errors when you have programmed a complicated merge, and want to make sure that your merge contains no errors. No merge results are created.

4. You can select which records you want merged by selecting All or From under Print. If you select From, enter the number of the first record in the From text box and the number of the last in the To text box.

5. Select how you want empty fields treated under Treatment of Blank Lines Caused by Empty Fields.

   ■ Select Skip Completely to have Word ignore paragraph marks when the paragraph's contents are only an empty merge field and some punctuation or spaces.

   An empty merge field occurs when that particular record has no contents in that field. For example, some addresses take two lines for the street address while some take one. If you created a separate field for each line, and had an address which only used one line, selecting this option would have Word simply ignore the line in the main document which contained only the merge field that had no entry.

- Select Print Blank Lines to have Word go ahead and print blank lines created by empty merge fields.

6. If you want to select which records to merge by comparing the contents of a field to some specific setting, select Record Selection.

- Select the field to use to select records from the Field Name list box. For example, if you were creating form letters to send to customers in a single city, you would select City.

- Select how the field is to be evaluated from the Is list box. For example, you would select Equal To, if you want to send letters only to addresses which included a specific city.

- If the field needs to be compared to something, enter that into the Compared To text box. For this example, you could enter **Akron** to send letters only to clients in Akron.

- Select Add Rule to add this rule to the list of rules used for this merge.

- Select the And or Or option button if you plan to add more rules. These determine how the current rule, displayed after Merge Records When, interacts with other rules.
  Select And to have Word use only records that fit both rules, or Or to have Word use records that fit either of the rules.

- Select Clear Last Rule to remove the last added rule from the list, or Clear All Rules to remove all rules and have Word merge all of the records.

- Select OK when you are finished setting up rules.

7. Select OK to begin the merge.

Options

The procedures above explain the basic steps of doing a print merge. However, there are many advanced and alternate features which can customize how you do a merge.

Using Different Data Files

You are not restricted to using data files created using the procedure described above for your merges. You can also use data files created by other programs, or data files which are organized without a table. However, using the basic table-organized data file is the easiest method.

DATA FILES ARRANGED AS PARAGRAPHS   One alternative to organizing your data file as a table is to arrange it using paragraphs. For example, if you have more than 31 fields in your records, you cannot use a table, since Word tables cannot have more than 31 columns. Instead, you could arrange your records by separating fields with tab marks and records with paragraph marks. When you organize your file in this fashion, there are several rules you have to remember.

- The file must have a header record, which works like a header row.

- All records must have the same number of fields as the header record, though fields can be left empty.

- Use either tabs or commas to separate fields, but not both in the same file.

- Enclose the entire field in quotation marks if the field's contents include tabs, commas, line breaks, paragraph marks, or quotation marks.

- End each record with a paragraph mark, and make sure that there are no extra paragraph marks to confuse the merge.

DATA FILES CREATED BY OTHER PROGRAMS   You can use an Excel or 1-2-3 spreadsheet, dBASE database, or a WordPerfect 4 or 5 document as the data file for a merge simply by attaching it to your main document. (This assumes that the conversion filters which let Word translate these files into Word documents are installed, which they are by default.) The advantage of using these files is that you do not have to worry about reentering data which you already have in another format.

After you attach and convert these files, you need to make sure that these records are arranged properly. An Excel worksheet or dBASE file is formatted as a table, unless there are more than 31 fields. The data in other files is arranged in paragraphs, as described above.

If the original file does not have header information assigning a name to each field, you will need to add a header record as the first record or create and attach a header file. Header files are explained below.

Using Header Files

You do not always need to include the header information in a header row or record. You can also use a header file. A *header file* contains the information which normally appears in a header row or record. With a header file, you can use any one header row or record with any number of data documents. The advantage of using a header file is that you know that the spelling of the field names will be consistent, so that you can switch data files without having to worry about typographical errors in different files. You can also use header files to provide headers for documents, such as dBASE databases, which might not have headers.

P-Q

One problem with header files is that the information in each data file you use with the header file must be arranged in the same order. For example, you might have a data file in which the first three fields are Title, FirstName, and LastName, and a second file in which they are CompanyName, StreetAddress, and City. If you used the same header file for both files, your letters would be addressed to *Dear ABC Company Akron* instead of *Dear Mr. Landers*.

Programming a Word Merge with Fields

While you can create very flexible merges with the directions given so far, you can build even more flexibility into your merges using the Word fields in addition to the Print Merge fields.

Some of the commands you select using the dialog boxes insert fields, such as when you set Record Selections options in the main document to set which fields are used. You can also insert these fields directly, just as you can insert Print Merge fields. To insert them, select the Insert Merge Field button on the Print Merge bar while working in the main document, then select an option from the Word Fields list box and select OK.

The options you select in the Word Fields list box are not the same as the field types you would look up in your documentation, or those which appear as the field codes when the field is displayed. See the table below to find out what fields are inserted with the different selections.

Select	To Insert
Ask...	ASK fields
Fillin...	FILLIN fields
If...Then	IF fields
If...Then...Else	IF fields with the "TextIfFalse" argument
Merge Record #	MERGEREC fields
Next Record	NEXT fields
Next Record If...	NEXTIF fields
Quote...	QUOTE fields
Set Bookmark...	SET fields
Skip Record If...	SKIPIF fields

ASK FIELD   The ASK field takes the format of {ASK *bookmark* "*prompt*"}, and is used to prompt the user for input while Word is merging documents. The input is used to control the merge program, or it is inserted into the document. *Bookmark* is the bookmark the text is assigned, while *prompt* is the text which appears on the screen prompting the user to input text.

You can use this field with the \o switch, to have the field prompt the user once, when the merge begins only, instead of prompting for each record. Use the \d switch to set the default text, which is used when the user does not enter any input.

FILLIN FIELD   The FILLIN field prompts the user for text which is displayed as the result of the field. Since it is not assigned a bookmark, it is not available for use by other fields. This field uses the format {FILLIN *"prompt"*} in which *prompt* is the text that prompts the user to enter the text to be displayed.

You can use the \d switch to set default text to be displayed if the user does not enter anything. You can also use the \o switch to have Word prompt you only once in the merge, rather than for each iteration of the main document.

IF FIELD   Use the IF field to compare two expressions and then use different text depending on the results of that comparison. The format is {IF *expression operator expression "TrueText" "FalseText"*}. *Expression* is what is being compared. This can be text, numbers, or a bookmark. The operator is how the two expressions are being compared. You can use any of the operators shown in the following table:

Operator	Purpose
=	Equal
>	Greater than
<	Less than
>=	Equal to or greater than
<=	Equal to or less than
<>	Not equal to

"TrueText" is the field's result if the comparison is true. *"FalseText"* is the field's result if the comparison is false.

MERGEREC FIELD   The MERGEREC field result is the number of the current data file record. You can use this field to number the documents you create with the merge, or use it for further merge programming. This field uses no switches.

NEXT FIELD   The NEXT field advances the merge to the next record in the data field, but displays no result of its own. It uses no switches.

NEXTIF FIELD   The NEXTIF field advances the merge to the next record if a comparison is true. It combines the features of the NEXT and IF fields. It uses the format {NEXTIF *expression operator expression*}. *Expression* is the text, number, or bookmark to be compared. The operators used are described under the IF Field above.

QUOTE FIELD   The QUOTE field inserts literal text into the document and uses the format {QUOTE *"literaltext"*}. Literal text is meant to be inserted exactly as typed. Text in quote marks is inserted exactly as it appears, but decimal or hexadecimal numbers outside of quote marks are interpreted as the related ANSI code. For example, if the field was {QUOTE 14}, 14 would be interpreted as an ANSI code. ANSI code 14 is a column break, so the field would insert the column break into your document.

SET FIELD   The SET field is used to assign a bookmark to text, which can then be inserted at any point in the document. This field uses the format {SET *bookmark "data"*}. *Bookmark* is the bookmark the text is going to be assigned to, and which is used to insert that text throughout the document. *Data* is the text which is to be assigned to the bookmark.

SKIPIF FIELD   The SKIPIF field is used to skip records while merging, creating no merged document for the skipped records. This field uses the format {SKIPIF *expression operator expression*}. *Expression* is the text, number, or bookmarks to be compared, while *operator* sets how the expressions are compared. All the operators listed under the IF field above can be used. When the comparison is true, Word does not cancel the merged document created for the current record. It starts the merge again at the beginning of the main document, using the next record.

Related Topics

Fields
Mail Merge
Tables

Print Options

Word lets you define certain default settings for print operations.

Procedure

1. Select Tools I Options or the Options button from the Print dialog box.

2. Select the Print tab or the Print icon in the Category list box, displaying the dialog box shown here:

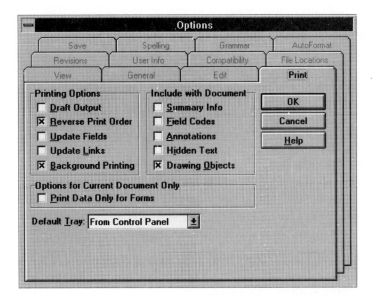

3. Select the options you want to change, as described in the following section, and select OK.

Options

The options that you can set for printing include settings for how Windows and Word interact to print your document, what Word includes in the document, and the location of the paper for the printing. Word for Windows 2 also lets you select whether a document has widows and orphans.

Printing Options

The check boxes under Printing Options control general features which affect the printing process.

DRAFT OUTPUT   When you enable the Draft Output option, Word prints the document's text without any formatting, and prints pictures or other graphics as blank frames. Depending on your printer, formatted text may print with underlining. Turn on this option when you simply want to proof your document faster and without formatting. Turn this option off again when you are ready to print the document with all of the selected formatting.

REVERSE PRINT ORDER   When you turn on Reverse Print Order, Word prints the document starting with the last page. (By default, Word prints from first to last.)

UPDATE FIELDS   Select the Update Fields check box when you want Word to update all fields in your document before it begins printing. This avoids printing a document with outdated information if you forgot to update all of your fields.

UPDATE LINKS   Select the Update Links check box when you want Word to update all links in your document before it begins printing. This ensures that the linked data in a document uses the latest version available.

BACKGROUND PRINTING   When you select Background Printing in Word for Windows 6, Word prints the document in the background so you can continue to work with Word while Windows prints the document. Turning off this option frees up memory and may accelerate the printing of your document.

Include with Document

The options under Include with Document let you control the types of ancillary information print with the document.

SUMMARY INFO   Turn on the Summary Info check box to have Word print the summary information about your documents on a separate page after the document.

FIELD CODES   When you select the Field Codes check box, Word prints the field codes rather than the results of the fields. If a document is not printing correctly, printing the document's field codes can help you figure out why.

ANNOTATIONS   Select the Annotations check box to have Word print all annotations, and the document pages they reference, on a separate page. You can use this list of annotations while reviewing a document, to help you correct or clarify it.

HIDDEN TEXT   When you select the Hidden Text check box, Word prints any text that is formatted as hidden. Usually, hidden text is not intended to print; it provides commentary or documentation within a document.

DRAWING OBJECTS   In Word for Windows 6, you can turn on the Drawing Objects option to print drawn objects, including objects added to your document such as clip art, graphics, and charts. Turn the option off to omit these objects from the printed document.

Envelope Options (Word for Windows 2 Only)

When you have installed a feeder specifically to feed envelopes into your printer, select the Printer's Envelope Feeder has been Installed check box. Word will then use the envelope feeder, rather than trying to feed the envelopes from another source.

Options for Current Document Only

The three options described next are only in effect for the document in which you select them. To use these settings for another document, you have to reselect them for that document.

PRINT DATA ONLY FOR FORMS (WORD FOR WINDOWS 6 ONLY)   When this check box is selected, Word prints only the data from the form. Turn on this option when you are printing data on preprinted forms such as invoices or insurance forms. For other types of documents, leave this option off.

WIDOW/ORPHAN CONTROL (WORD FOR WINDOWS 2 ONLY)   When this option is turned on, Word does not allow a single line of paragraph to occur alone at the top or bottom of page. Instead, Word forces the single line to join the other lines of the paragraph.

USE TRUETYPE FONTS AS DEFAULTS (WORD FOR WINDOWS 2 ONLY)
With Window 3.1 or higher, selecting Use TrueType Fonts as Defaults causes Word to use TrueType fonts when possible.

Default Tray

In Word for Windows 6, you can select the source of paper for the document sections that are not set separately with the File | Page Setup command. The available options depend on the printer selected.

TIP: If you see the option "From Control Panel" in this list box, it means Word is going to use the default setting in the Windows Control Panel.

Related Topics

Printing

Print Preview

See "Viewing Documents."

PRINTDATE Field

The PRINTDATE field returns the date a document was last printed. For more information, see "Fields."

Printer Fonts

Printer fonts are fonts that are installed in your printer's memory. See "Fonts."

Printing

The last step in creating a document with a word processor is usually to print it out onto paper for use. Printing, in Windows, involves sending the file (with the different codes used to tell the printer how to place and format text) to a temporary file. Window's Print Manager will then handle the process of sending the file to the printer while you continue working in Word or another application. The formatting and placement features you can use with a specific printer is controlled by the capabilities of that printer.

Procedures

The following procedures explain how to print your document, and how to change the default settings for the printer.

Printing Documents

1. From the file you want to print, select File | Print, to open the Print dialog box. You can also press CTRL+P or CTRL+SHIFT+F12.

2. In the Print What drop-down list box (Print in Word for Windows 2), select what you want to print. You can print the document, the document's summary information, the document's annotations, descriptions of the styles the document uses, the AutoText entries used by the document's template, or the key assignments and macros used by the document's template.

3. In the Copies text box, enter the number of copies you want to print.

4. Select one of the Range option buttons to specify the portion of the document you want to print:

   ■ All prints the complete document.

   ■ Current Page prints the page the insertion point is on. If you selected text before starting to print, this option button is called Selection, and it prints the selected text as if it were the complete document.

   ■ Select Pages to print a range of pages from the document. In Word for Windows 6, type the range to print in the adjoining text box, using a hyphen between the first and last pages in the range and commas between individual pages. For example, type **1,5-7,10** to print pages one, five, six, seven, and ten. In Word for Windows 2, enter the first page number in the From text box, and the last page number in the To text box.

5. In Word for Windows 6, select the part of the range to print from the Print drop-down list box. You can print all the pages in the selected range, just the odd pages, or just the even pages.

6. If you want to send the output to a permanent file, select the Print to File check box. Word will prompt you for the filename and location after you select OK.

NOTE: Selecting Print to File prints the document to a permanant file containing all of the printing codes. You can then copy this file to a printer, using DOS, and print it. You might do this to create a document on one system and then print it on another system that has a better printer but not the Word software.

7. When you are printing more than one copy and you want Word to automatically collate your copies, select the Collate Copies check box.

   For example, if you print a three-page document and request two copies, by default Word will print all the copies of the first page, then all the copies of the second page, and so forth, so that the printed pages are stacked 1, 1, 2, 2, and 3, 3. With Collate Copies selected, Word prints pages 1, 2, 3, and then another copy of pages 1, 2, 3.

8. If you need to change the setup of the printer you are using, select the Printer button (the Setup button in Word for Windows 2). Then follow the procedure explained below, under "Changing the Printer Setup."

9. You can select the Options button to change some of the default printing options in Word. See "Print Options."

10. Select OK to begin printing the document.

Figure 4-50 shows the beginning of a document printed several times, with different Print What settings. The header for each page describes the Print What setting for the page.

TIP: To print a document using the default settings, you can click the Print button in the Standard toolbar. Word immediately prints the document without displaying the Print dialog box.

Changing the Printer Setup

1. Select File | Print, and then the Printer button, to open the Print Setup dialog box. In Word for Windows 2, select File | Print Setup, or select the Setup button from the Print dialog box.

2. In the Printers list box, select the printer whose settings you want to change, and select Options (Setup in Word for Windows 2), to open the Setup dialog box. The elements of this dialog box are different for each printer, reflecting the printer's features. For example, the Setup dialog box for a Hewlett-Packard LaserJet III is shown in Figure 4-51. The changes you make here are the same as making them in the Windows Control Panel.

3. After making your changes to the printer setup, select OK to return to the Print Setup dialog box.

4. Select the printer you want to use from the Printers list box. In Word for Windows 6, select the Set as Default Printer.

5. Select Close (OK in Word for Windows 2) to close the Print Setup dialog box.

Hints

The following hints will help you to print more effectively and create better documents, and tell you what to do when common printer errors occur.

Document

Fun With Computers

This seminar is for handling computer phobia. You will work with a computer to develop basic computer skills. You will start a computer, start a few applications, and develop an awareness for the features a computer can provide. This course is not for learning a specific package. The computers you will use in this course have many different packages that may not necessarily match what you have at home. The skills you will develop in this course will help you feel comfortable using the computer.

What is a Computer

You work with so many gadgets that you can easily assume everything is computerized—especially if it isn't working

Summary Info

Filename:	FUNCOMP2.DOC
Directory:	C:\WINWORD6\DOCUMENT
Template:	C:\WINWORD6\TEMPLATE\NORMAL.DOT
Title:	Fun With Computers
Subject:	Class Seminar
Author:	Mary Campbell
Keywords:	Computers, seminar
Comments:	Handout for Fun With Computers to be taught at the Adult Education class
Creation Date:	9/29/93 05:10 PM
Revision Number:	2
Last Saved On:	9/29/93 05:10 PM

Figure 4-50. *Printed document, summary, styles, and annotations*

Annotations

Page: 1
[MC1]Sue, let's try stressing what the course is good for, rather than what it won't do for them.
Page: 1
[MC2]Missing period here.
Page: 1
[MC3]Sue, what's this sentence about?

Styles

Default Paragraph Font
    The font of the underlying paragraph style +

Head Topics
    Font: Bookman Old Style, 18 pt, English (US), Kern at 16 pt, Flush left, Line Spacing Single, Space Before 6 pt, Widow/Orphan Control

Heading 1
    Style for Next Paragraph: Normal

    Normal + Font: Arial, 14 pt, Bold, Kern at 14 pt, Space Before 12 pt After 3 pt, Keep With Next

Heading 2
    Style for Next Paragraph: Normal

    Normal + Font: Arial, 12 pt, Bold, Italic, Space Before 12 pt After 3 pt, Keep With Next

Figure 4-50.   *Printed document, summary, styles, and annotations* (continued)

Handling Printer Problems

When you select OK to start your print job, and your document does not print, check the following possible problems:

- Is the printer turned on? (This may sound stupid, but it's one of the two most common printer problems.)

- Does the printer have paper? (This is the other most common problem.)

- Is the printer ready to accept information? Most printers have a button that turns them on line. Usually, pressing this button when the printer

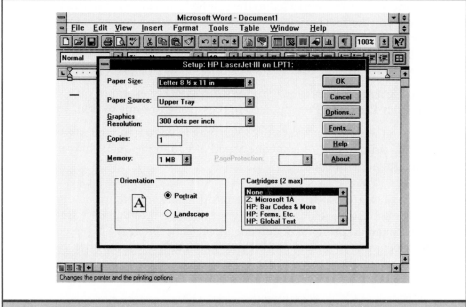

Figure 4-51. *Dialog box for setting the options for a printer*

is off line will begin the flow of information from the computer to your printer.

■ When you select File | Print, are the correct printer and the correct printer port selected?

> If the wrong printer is selected, simply reselect the correct printer as described under "Changing the Printer Setup" above.

> If the printer connection is wrong, use the Windows Control Panel to change it. If the printer you are using is not listed there, it is not installed, and you must install it before you can print to it.

> Switch to the Windows Print Manager application. If "Stalled" appears after the printer name, highlight the printer in the list (rather than the print *job*) and select Resume. You may need to do this, for example, after you have had to turn on the printer or put in more paper.

■ Are you using a printer switch box? If so, check that the printer switch box is turned to the setting for your computer.

■ Is your computer connected to the printer? This problem normally occurs when you are first setting up your printer or when you have moved furniture. A partially connected printer cable cannot send the information to the printer. You can reattach the cable using the screws or clips on the cable to secure it to your printer or computer.

■ Is there a message on your printer's display? For example, on a Hewlett-Packard IIP+, you need to press Alt-Continue to print legal paper.

■ Are you working on a network? You may have routed your output to the wrong print queue, or someone ahead of you in the queue may be printing a lengthy document.

As you can see, most printing problems are easily solved. In some situations, you may see a message telling you that your document cannot be printed. Select Retry to try again to print the document; select Cancel to leave the message and allow the document to remain in the Print Manager's queue, so after you have fixed the problem, the document can be printed.

Preview Before Printing

You can avoid having to reprint a document if it doesn't turn out the way you want, by previewing the document or using the Page Layout view of the document. These options show the document as it will appear when printed. See "Viewing Documents" for more information.

Confirming the Selected Printer

Look at the printer name that appears in the top of the Print dialog box. This is the printer Word will use when printing your document. The printer selection will determine how the printed document appears, because printers have their own individual features.

If you want to change the printer you are using in Word for Windows 6, select the Printer button, highlight the printer in the Printers list box, and select Set as Default Printer and Close. To change the printer you are using in Word for Windows 2, select the Setup button in the Print dialog box, highlight the printer in the Printer list box, and select OK.

Printing Drafts

You can print a draft version of your document by selecting the Draft Output check box in the Printer Options dialog box. Draft output prints faster because codes, which take longer to print, are not sent to the printer. What is not printed in draft mode will vary based on the type of printer you have.

For example, when you print draft output with a PostScript printer, both graphics and formatted text do print, because there is no gain in time by not doing so. On a laser printer, such as a Hewlett-Packard LaserJet III, formatted text will print, but not graphics. On a dot-matrix printer, graphics will print, and text is printed without formatting.

Printing Multiple Documents

You can print several documents at one time, without opening and printing each one separately, using the File | Find File command. Begin by selecting File | Find File, to open the Find File dialog box. In Word for Windows 6, select the files to print in the Listed Files list box, then select Print from the Commands drop-down list. In Word for Windows 2, select the files to print in the File Name list box, and then select the Print button. Choose the printing options and settings you want to use, and then select OK. Word prints each document consecutively.

For more information on using the File | Find File command, see "File Management."

Printing Merged Documents

In Word, you can create form letters that, when printed, can be combined with data files containing information that changes in each version of the letter. See "Mail Merge" for details.

Printing Envelopes

Printing an envelope is like printing any other document. You define, within a document, a page size that conforms to the envelope's measurements, and print the document normally. Word can create an envelope for printing quickly, using addresses you provide or that are found in your document. See "Envelopes" to learn how to create envelopes and "Paper Source" for how to make sure that the envelope page of your document is actually printed on an envelope.

Printing Mailing Labels

You can print one or many mailing labels using Word's mail merge feature. See "Mail Merge" for details.

Related Topics

File Management
Mail Merge
Print Options
Viewing Documents

Printing the Current Page

See "Printing."

Printing Multiple Copies

See "Printing."

PRIVATE Field

Word for Windows 6 creates this field for you when you add a document in another format into Word for Windows. This field contains the information Word needs to convert the file back to its previous format. Do not change this field.

Programs

You can add the functionality of other programs to Word for Windows 6. These add-in programs provide commands that can extend the features available to you. You can use add-in programs created by software publishers, and you can also write your own.

Procedures

To add-in a program, select File | Templates, then Add and the filename, and then the OK button.

When you're finished using an add-in, you can unload it using the File | Templates command, clearing the check box next to the add-in program name. Select Remove after selecting the add-in program will remove it from the list.

Project

Microsoft Project is a Windows application that can share data with Word. You can embed and link Project data in Word documents, as described in "Object Linking and Embedding." Word for Windows 6 also lets you start Project from within Word by clicking the Microsoft Project button in the Microsoft toolbar. Once you start Microsoft Project, you are using Project, not Word, and you must follow Project's menu and features.

Proofing

Word has several proofing tools, described in this chapter, to help improve your documents. Word can check the spelling in a document, as described under "Spelling." You can review your document for incorrect grammar, as described under "Grammar Checking." Word will look for synonyms, antonyms, and so forth, for the words in your document, as described under "Thesaurus." You can also display various statistics about your document, including the number of words, paragraphs, and pages, as described under "Summary Info."

Protecting Documents

See "Annotation," "Locking and Protecting Documents," and "Saving Files."

Publisher

Microsoft Publisher is a Windows desktop publishing application that can share data with Word. You can embed and link Publisher data in Word documents, as described in "Object Linking and Embedding." Word for Windows 6 also lets you start Publisher from within Word by clicking the Microsoft Publisher button in the Microsoft toolbar. Once you start Microsoft Publisher, you are using Publisher, not Word, and you must follow Publisher's menu and features.

Quick Keys

See "Shortcut Keys."

Quitting Word

See "Exiting Word."

Quotation Marks

Word can work with various types of quotation marks. When you check a document's grammar, Word verifies that you have both beginning and ending quotation marks. See "Grammar Checking" for instructions on turning this feature on and off. You can use the Insert | Symbol command to add specific quotation marks; for instance, you might need to use " " instead of " ". In "Special Characters" you can read about using this command. Word for Windows 6 can make smart quote replacements, so "text" becomes 'text.' To accomplish this you turn on the 'Straight Quotes' with 'Smart Quotes' check box in the AutoFormat options. More information about AutoFormat features are described in "AutoFormat."

QUOTE Field

The QUOTE field inserts literal text in a merged document. See "Mail Merge" and "Print Merge."

RD Field

The RD field indicates a document that is included as part of the current document for generating index entries, tables of contents, and tables of authorities. See "Fields" for more information.

Readability

See "Grammar Checking."

Read-Only

See "Opening Files" or "Locking and Protecting Documents" for information about opening documents in read-only status, so they cannot be changed and saved using the same filename. See "Master Documents" for information about locking and unlocking master documents and subdocuments so they are read-only.

Recompiling

You can *recompile* indexes, tables of authorities, tables of contents, and tables of figures. Recompiling updates these documents to include any new entries. To find out more about recompiling them, look at "Index," "Table of Authorities," and "Table of Contents and Figures."

Redlining

See "Comparing Versions."

Redoing an Action

Word can redo actions you have executed, just as it can undo them. See "Undoing and Redoing Actions" for more information.

REF Field

The REF field inserts the contents of a bookmark that has the same name as a particular field type, or creates a cross-reference. See "Fields."

REF INTERN_LINK Field

The REF INTERN_LINK field in Word for Windows 2 represents linked data added to your documents with the Edit | Paste Special command. See "Fields" for more information about fields, and "Object Linking and Embedding" for more information about using the Edit | Paste Special to link other data into your Word documents.

References

See "Cross references" and "Footnotes and Endnotes."

Removing Features

Just as you can add an option, element, attribute or other feature to a Word document, you can also remove them. The steps for removing a feature depend on the feature, and are explained with the particular feature's description in this chapter. For example, to find out how to remove a footnote, consult "Footnotes and Endnotes."

Removing Formatting

The formatting you add to text can be removed. Word has several shortcuts to make removing formatting easier.

Procedures

The following sections explain the shortcuts for removing character formatting and paragraph formatting.

Removing Character Formatting

Word offers four easy ways to remove character formatting from your text. You can remove specific features, or you can remove all of the formatting at once. Before removing character formatting, select the characters from which you want to remove highlighting. Then choose one of these techniques:

- Press the key-combination for the formatting you want to remove, such as CTRL+B to remove boldfacing. (Remember, most key combinations switch between applying and removing the format.)

- Open the Font or Character dialog box, and clear the settings you want to remove.

- Press CTRL+SPACEBAR to revert to the default character formatting of the style currently in effect for the text.

- Assign the Normal style to the text, using the Style button in the Formatting toolbar or by pressing CTRL+SHIFT+S (CTRL+S in Word for Windows 2) and selecting Normal from the list. This removes all prior formatting and applies the Normal style's formatting.

Removing Paragraph Formatting

First select the paragraph or paragraphs from which you want to remove formatting. Then do one of the following:

- Press CTRL+Q to remove the manual paragraph formatting and revert to the default paragraph formatting of the style currently in effect for the paragraphs.

- Assign the Normal style to the text, using the Style button in the Formatting toolbar or by pressing CTRL+SHIFT+S (CTRL+S in Word for Windows 2) and selecting Normal from the list. This removes prior formatting and assigns the Normal style's formatting.

Related Topics

Character Formats
Paragraph Formats

Renaming Documents

You can rename documents from the Find File dialog box, described under "File Management." You can also save a document with a new name using the File | Save As command, as described under "Saving Files."

Renumbering

See "Lists."

Reorganizing an Outline

See "Outlines."

Repagination

See "Pagination."

Repeating Actions

You can easily repeat the last action you did in your document, such as reapplying formatting to several passages of text, or inserting some text in several locations.

Procedures

You can repeat a command, or repeat the typing of some text.

Repeating Commands

Choose one of these techniques:

- ■ Press F4.
- ■ Press CTRL+Y.
- ■ Select Edit | Repeat. The Repeat command changes to match the action you can repeat—for instance, Repeat Formatting or Repeat Insertion. It

changes to Can't Repeat when the last action you performed is one that cannot be repeated.

REPEATING GO TO OR FIND   The Go To and Find commands are repeated differently than other commands: Press SHIFT+F4.

Repeating Text

Move your insertion point to where you want to insert another occurrence of the text you just typed, and press F4 or select Edit | Repeat.

Hints

When Word repeats text, it inserts the text you entered before you moved the insertion point. The text you have entered—not the action of moving the insertion point—is the action Word will repeat.

When you are repeating formatting, you must first select the text to which you want to apply the identical formatting.

Often, you will have to move the insertion point, or select text, paragraphs, or sections, before you repeat the last action. For example, if you want to repeat the action of entering an address, you need to move to where you want the second address before you choose to repeat the action.

Related Topics

Undoing and Redoing Actions

Repeating Formats

See "Copying Formats."

Replacing Text and Formats

See "Find and Replace."

Replacement Typing

See "INS Key."

Replacing Text in a Document

See "Find and Replace."

Resizing

Several features of Word documents can have their size adjusted, including toolbars displayed in boxes, columns, frames, graphics, tables, and windows. The steps for resizing depend on the feature, and are explained with the particular feature. For example, to find out how to change the size of a frame, look at "Frames" in this chapter.

Restoring

Word can restore the original version of something you have changed. See "Undoing and Redoing Actions" for more information. If you need to restore the original formatting to edited text or paragraphs, see "Removing Formatting."

Retrieve

See "Opening Files" or "Inserting Files."

Return to a Prior Editing Location

You can return to one of the three previous locations where you did some editing. Press SHIFT+F5, and Word cycles through the three prior editing locations and the current one. An "editing location" is where the insertion point was located when you made a change.

Return Characters

See "Nonprinting Characters" to see how you can display the special characters that end paragraphs in Word.

Reusing Entries

See "AutoText" if you have Word for Windows 6, or "Glossary" if you have Word for Windows 2.

Reversing Print Order

See "Printing."

Revision and Annotation Merging

When you share the same document with several people and they make their comments separately, you need some way to combine the different annotation and revision marks. Word lets you take one version of a file that contains annotation and revision marks and merge it with the current document. This feature lets you combine the revision marks from several documents into one that you can use to analyze and decide what revisions you want to keep. To use this feature, the changes in the other documents must be marked using Word's revision marks. You can make sure that other people add their changes using revision marks by protecting the document you give them.

Procedures

The procedures for merging revision marks are different for Word for Windows 2 and 6.

Merging Current Revision Marks in Word for Windows 6

1. Open the version of the document containing the revision codes you want to merge with another document.

2. Select Tools | Revisions and then the Merge Revisions button from Revisions dialog box. You can also select Tools | Revisions by double-clicking the MRK indicator in the status line.

3. Select the file that you want to receive the revision marks, and then OK. Selecting a file in this dialog box works just like selecting a file to open.

Word opens the document you selected in step 3 and merges into it the revision marks from the document you opened in step 1. Figure 4-51 shows a document with revision marks incorporated from several other documents.

NOTE: *When you are merging revision marks from subdocuments into the master document, you open the subdocuments in step 1 and select the master document in step 3.*

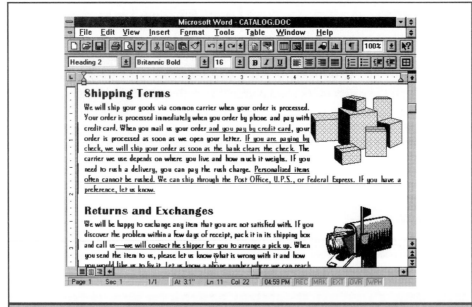

Figure 4-51.   *Document containing revision marks merged from several documents*

Once the revisions marks are combined into one document, you can apply the revisions using the Tools | Revisions command, as described in "Comparing Versions."

MERGING REVISIONS TO MAILED DOCUMENTS   If you have routed the document using Microsoft Mail to other Word users, when you receive the edited documents there will be a document icon in the returned mail message. When you double-click this icon, Word will ask if you want to merge the revision marks. When you select Yes, you can select OK again since the original document name is already selected. If you want to merge the revision marks with a different document, specify the document before selecting OK. You can double-click the document icons repeatedly to merge the other routed documents.

Merging Current Revision Marks in Word for Windows 2

1. Open the version of the document containing the revision codes you want to merge with another document.

2. Select Tools | Compare Versions.

3. Select the file into which you want the revision marks incorporated, and select OK. Do this just as you would select a file to open.

The document selected in step 3 is opened, and the revision marks from the document opened in step 1 are transferred to the newly opened document. At this point, you can apply and review the revisions using the Tools | Revision Marks command (see "Comparing Versions" in this chapter).

Compiling All the Revisions

Repeat the merge process for each document whose revision marks you want to merge. For example, suppose you have several copies of the document PROPOSE stored in different locations. Open one copy of PROPOSE, and follow the steps above for selecting another version of the PROPOSE document. Once the newly opened "control" document contains the revision marks, repeat the steps for another version of the revised PROPOSE document. Once you have repeated these steps to merge each version of the PROPOSE document, the current version will contain the revision marks from all of the versions of the document. At this point, you can close the revision versions.

Related Topics

Annotation
Comparing Versions

Revision Marks

See "Comparing Versions" and "Revision and Annotation Merging."

REVNUM Field

This field returns the revision number of a document. Each time you save a document, the revision number increases by one. This is the same revision number you see when you select File | Summary Info and choose Statistics. See "Fields."

RFTDCA

RFTDCA is a format used by IBM 5520 and DisplayWrite. See "Opening Files" and "Saving Files" for information on opening files saved in this format, or saving files in this format.

Ribbon (Word for Windows 2)

The ribbon lets you quickly apply many of the most popular formatting features to text in a Word for Windows 2 document. (Word for Windows 6 uses the Formatting toolbar instead of the ribbon.) The ribbon cannot be customized as you can a toolbar.

To display the ribbon, select the View | Ribbon command. From the ribbon, you can select from the following boxes and buttons to apply formatting to selected text or to text you are about to enter. The table also tells you the keystroke combinations that you can use in place of some of the boxes or buttons, and provides a cross-reference to the section of this chapter that describes the formatting feature.

Box or Button	Key-Combination	Function	Described In
Normal ▼	CTRL+S	Selects a style to apply	Styles
Times New Roman ▼	CTRL+F	Selects a font to apply	Fonts
10 ▼	CTRL+P	Selects a point size to apply	Fonts
B	CTRL+B	Boldfaces text	Bold
I	CTRL+I	Italicizes text	Italics
U	CTRL+U	Underlines text	Underline
☰	CTRL+L	Left-aligns a paragraph	Alignment
☰	CTRL+E	Centers a paragraph	Alignment
☰	CTRL+R	Right-aligns a paragraph	Alignment
☰	CTRL+J	Justifies a paragraph	Alignment
↑		Sets left-aligned tab	Tabs
↑		Sets center-aligned tab	Tabs
↑		Sets right-aligned tab	Tabs
↑.		Sets decimal-aligned tab	Tabs
¶		Shows or hides display characters	Nonprinting Characters

Procedures

You can choose to display or hide the ribbon. You can select buttons on the ribbon using the mouse or the keyboard, unlike Word for Windows 6's toolbars.

Displaying or Hiding the Ribbon

Use the View | Ribbon command to toggle between displaying and hiding the ribbon.

Using the Ribbon with the Mouse

First select the text to format, or move the insertion point to where you want the formatting to begin. Click the button for the formatting you want. When you open a list box, select the setting you want.

Keyboard Equivalents for the Ribbon

Most of the buttons in the ribbon have keyboard shortcuts, as shown in the earlier table. Pressing these key-combinations either selects the button in the ribbon or applies the formatting that the button provides. When you use the key-combinations for the style, font, and font size boxes, you must then select the style, font, or font size you want.

TIP: You can open the Character dialog box to apply font, font size, and style changes, by double-clicking part of the ribbon that does not contain a box or button.

Related Topics

Character Format
Formatting Toolbar (Ribbon)
Paragraph Formats
Ruler
Toolbars

Rich Text Format (RTF)

RTF, or Rich Text Format, is a format that most Microsoft applications can use for sharing data. Word can open and save files in an RTF format, as described under "Opening Files" and "Saving Files." You can also embed and link data that's in RTF format, to keep the formatting of the data as it is in its original location. RTF is one of the possible formats displayed with the Edit | Paste Special command; see "Object Linking and Embedding."

Right-Align Text

See "Alignment" and "Tabs."

Rotating

You can rotate text using WordArt, as described under "WordArt," and drawn objects as described under "Drawing on a Document." If you want to rotate graphics that are not drawn in Word, you must use a graphics package that can work with the picture to rotate it. Then you save the rotated version in a graphics file and insert it as a picture, or copy it via the Clipboard into the Word document.

Routing

See "Electronic Mail" for instructions on routing a document from one Word user to another, to let other Word users make comments to the same document.

Rows

See "Tables."

RTF

See "Rich Text Format (RTF)."

Ruler

Word's ruler is a bar on the screen that shows the position of margins, indents, tabs, and table boundaries. In the horizontal ruler you can change left and right margins, tabs, indents, and column boundaries. Word for Windows 6 also has a vertical ruler that appears in Page Layout view and Print Preview and lets you set top and bottom margins, header and footer position, and row heights in tables. The rulers appear at the top and left side of the document. When the document window is not maximized, the rulers are inside the document's window, rather than appearing below the menu bar, toolbars, and ribbon. The horizontal ruler does not appear in Master Document view or in Outline view.

Procedures

You can choose to show or hide the ruler, depending on what you are doing. The ruler works somewhat differently in Word for Windows 2 and 6. You can use the keyboard with the Word 2 ruler. Word 6 also supplies a vertical ruler in Page Layout view, if you choose to display it.

Hiding and Displaying the Ruler

Use the View | Ruler command to toggle between showing and hiding the ruler.

In Word for Windows 6, in most views, you hide and display *both* the vertical and horizontal rulers; you cannot have one without the other. In Normal view, selecting View | Ruler to display the ruler will show the horizontal ruler but not the vertical one.

The ruler uses the measuring system set by Word's general options. The section of the ruler that appears above a document matches the part of the document that is displayed. When you zoom to make the document look larger or smaller, the ruler proportionally increases or decreases, so an inch on the ruler is as wide as an inch on the document when it is printed, even if on the display it looks smaller or larger than an inch.

Using the Ruler with the Mouse in Word for Windows 6

The symbols for the ruler in Word for Windows 6 and the information they provide are labeled below:

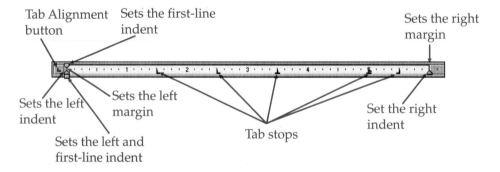

The ruler dynamically changes to match the paragraph, column, or table column containing the insertion point. A vertical ruler contains only the margin indicators that apply to the document, the table row, or to the header or footer. When you change margins, they apply to the entire section containing the insertion point; when you change indents and tabs, they only apply to the paragraph with the insertion point. If you want to set indents and tabs for multiple paragraphs, select the paragraphs before changing the indents and tabs with the ruler.

You can make the following changes using the mouse with the ruler:

- *To change the margins* for the selected page, column, or table column, drag the appropriate margin symbols to a new location on the ruler. Remember that for columns and table columns, you can set the margins for both the columns and for the spaces between the columns.

- *To change the indents* for the selected paragraphs or current paragraph, drag the indent triangles to new locations on the ruler. You can change the first-line indent independently of the left indent by dragging the first-line indent triangle. To change both the first-line and left indents by the same amounts, drag the little box below the left indent triangle. The indents are relative to the margin, so when you change the margins, the indents will change as well.

- *To set a tab,* click the Tab Alignment button for the type of tab you want to add. Each time you click the Tab Alignment button, the symbol on the button cycles among left-aligned, centered, right-aligned, and decimal tabs. When you insert a tab symbol, all default tabs before that tab symbol are deleted.

Using the Ruler with the Mouse in Word for Windows 2

The symbols that appear on the Word for Windows 2 ruler represent information that changes to match the paragraph, column, or table column containing the insertion point. When you change margins, they apply to the entire section containing the insertion point. When you change indents and tabs, they only apply to the paragraph with the insertion point. If you want to set indents and tabs for multiple paragraphs, select the paragraphs before changing the indents and tabs with the ruler.

You can make the following changes using the mouse with the ruler:

- *To change the information shown on the ruler,* click the symbols at the left end, beyond the zero. The ruler has three scales, as shown on the next page.

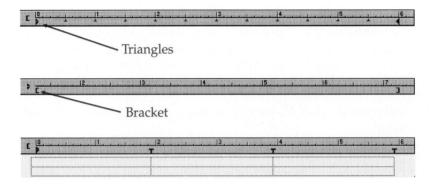

In the top ruler, which shows the *paragraph scale,* the triangles indicate the indents for the selected paragraphs. In the second ruler, which shows the *margin scale,* the [and] indicate the margins of the page or column. In the third paragraph, showing the *table scale,* the T indicates the divisions between the columns in a table.

- ■ *To change the margins* for the selected page or the page containing the insertion point, use the margin scale and drag the margin symbols to a new location on the ruler.

- ■ *To change the table boundaries* for the current cell, use the table scale and drag the table symbols to a new location.

- ■ *To change the indents* for the selected paragraphs or current paragraph, use the paragraph scale and drag the indent symbols to their new locations. You can change the first-line indent independently of the left indent by pointing only at the first-line indent triangle. To change both the first-line and left indents together, point at the left indent triangle and drag it. To change the left indent independently of the first-line indent, press SHIFT and then drag the left indent triangle.

- ■ *To set a tab,* activate the paragraph scale. Click the ribbon button for the type of tab you want to add, and then click the ruler where you want the tab to appear. When you insert a tab symbol, all default tabs before that tab symbol are deleted.

TIP: You can clear a tab stop in either version of Word by dragging the tab stop symbol down off the ruler. You can move a tab stop by dragging the tab stop symbol to a new location.

Using the Ruler with the Keyboard in Word for Windows 2

You can also use the keyboard with the ruler to set indents and tabs. The key-combinations to do this are shown in Table 4-20. You must activate the ruler before you can set tabs and indents with it. The changes you make to tabs and indents with the ruler affect all selected paragraphs, or the paragraph the insertion point is in.

Keystroke	Result
CTRL+SHIFT+F10	Activates the ruler and displays the ruler cursor
RIGHT ARROW	Moves the ruler cursor a small distance to the right
LEFT ARROW	Moves the ruler cursor a small distance to the left
CTRL+RIGHT ARROW	Moves the ruler cursor a greater distance to the right
CTRL+LEFT ARROW	Moves the ruler cursor a greater distance to the left
SHIFT+LEFT ARROW	Moves the ruler cursor to the left of the zero
HOME	Moves the ruler cursor to zero
END	Moves the ruler cursor to the right end of ruler
L	Sets a left indent at the ruler cursor's position
R	Sets a right indent at the ruler cursor's position
F	Sets a first-line indent at the ruler cursor's position
1	Makes the next tab stop left-aligned
2	Makes the next tab stop center-aligned
3	Makes the next tab stop right-aligned
4	Makes the next tab stop decimal-aligned
INS	Sets a tab stop at the ruler cursor's position
DEL	Deletes the tab stop at the ruler cursor's position
ENTER	Returns to the document and applies new settings
ESC	Returns to the document without applying new settings

Table 4-20. *Key-Combinations for Using the Ruler*

Opening Dialog Boxes with the Ruler

- Double-clicking a tab stop in the ruler displays the Tabs dialog box, as if you selected the Format | Tabs command. If there is no tab stop at the location where you double-click, Word adds one and then opens the Tabs dialog box.

- In Word for Windows 2, double-clicking a part of the ruler that cannot be interpreted as a tab stop or inside a section displays the Paragraph dialog box, as if you selected the Format | Paragraph command.

- In Word for Windows 6, double-clicking an indent marker in the ruler displays the Paragraph dialog box, as if you selected the Format | Paragraph command.

- In Word for Windows 6, double-clicking a part of the ruler that is not used for margins, indents, or tabs displays the Page Setup dialog box, as if you selected the File | Page Setup command.

Rules

See "Grammar Options" for instructions on changing the grammar rules Word uses when it proofs your documents. See "Columns," "Footnotes and Endnotes," and "Tables" when you want to set the lines and borders Word uses in columns, footnotes and endnotes, and tables. See "Mail Merge" for information about the changes you can make to selection rules when you are creating a mail merge document.

Running Macros

Macros can execute a series of steps for you, such as typing or selecting Word features to apply to a document. Chapter 7 explains how to create macros. "Macros" in this chapter tells how to run a macro in Word.

Save Options

You can set the Save options, the default options that affect the file saving process.

Procedure

You can open the Options dialog box for the default save options from the Tools menu or from the Save or Save As dialog boxes.

From the Tools Menu

1. Select Tools | Options.

2. Select the Save tab or icon.

3. Set the options as you want them. For information on these options, see "Options" below.

4. Select OK.

From the Dialog Boxes

Select Options from the Save or Save As dialog box as you save a file. Word opens the Options dialog box with the Save default options displayed. Select your options, described under "Options" below, and then select OK.

Options

The Save options change how Word saves your documents.

ALWAYS CREATE BACKUP COPY   Select Always Create Backup Copy to have Word create a copy of your document with the file extension .BAK each time you save it. The backup copy is the previous version of your document before you most recently saved it.

ALLOW FAST SAVES   Select Allow Fast Saves to have Word save only your changes to a document, rather than reformatting and saving the entire document each time. Fast saves save only the document changes you have made, so it is faster than a normal save. Fast save is the default setting.

Use a normal save before carrying out certain tasks. When you use a normal save, Word saves more complete information about your document. Use a normal save before compiling an index, converting your document to a new format, or transferring it to another application. You can use a normal save by clearing the Allow Fast Saves text box and then saving the document again.

PROMPT FOR SUMMARY INFO   Summary info is information about your document that you can use to help organize your files and for other purposes. Select Prompt for Summary Info to have Word prompt you for summary info when you first save each document.

See "Summary Info" for a description of this option.

PROMPT TO SAVE NORMAL.DOT (WORD FOR WINDOWS 6 ONLY)
Select Prompt to Save Normal.dot to have Word prompt you about saving changes to default settings for macros, AutoText entries, menus, shortcut keys, and toolbars in the NORMAL.DOT template each time you exit Word.

SAVE NATIVE PICTURE FORMATS ONLY (WORD FOR WINDOWS 6 ONLY)
Select Save Native Picture Formats Only to have Word save all graphics in your document in a Windows format only (assuming they have come from a different platform such as the Macintosh). Doing this saves space.

EMBED TRUETYPE FONTS (WORD FOR WINDOWS 6 ONLY)   Select Embed TrueType Fonts to have Word save TrueType fonts with the document they are used in, so that readers of the document can see it as you designed it, even if their system does not have those fonts installed.

SAVE DATA ONLY FOR FORMS (WORD FOR WINDOWS 6 ONLY)   Select Save Data Only for Forms to have Word save only the data from form documents so that you can use the information as a database. By default, the data and the form features are saved together.

AUTOMATIC SAVE EVERY   Most computer users know they should save often to prevent losing information when there is a power surge or program error. Very few users, however, actually do so, because it is easy to forget to save documents while working. Select Automatic Save Every to have Word save your document for you regularly. The interval between saves is the number of minutes you enter in the Minutes text box.

This feature does not replace saving the document as you normally would. The automatic save option saves documents as temporary files that can be opened only if Word was unloaded without exiting (such as when the power is interrupted or a bug causes your system to crash) and you have to reboot. When you exit Word properly, these temporary files are deleted. If Word was unloaded without exiting, the next time you open Word it will tell you that some recoverable files are available. Select OK to have Word resave those files as permanent Word files. You can then open them for use.

FILE SHARING OPTIONS FOR CURRENT DOCUMENT (WORD FOR WINDOWS 6 ONLY)   If your document is going to be shared with other users, you may want to control their access to it. Enter a password in the Protection Password text box to prevent the current document from being opened by someone who does not know the password. Enter a password in the Write Reservation Password text box to prevent other users from being able to save an edited version of your document, though they will be able to open the document. Select Read-Only Recommended to have Word suggest to users that they open your document as a read-only document, unless they have actual changes to make.

Related Topics

Saving Files
Forms

SAVEDATE Field

The SAVEDATE field returns the date a document was saved last. See "Fields."

Saving Files

One of the most important features of a word-processor is that a document you create and save as a file can be opened again and edited later. This fundamental advantage of a word-processor over a typewriter or other method of recording text is so basic that its importance is often unappreciated.

Procedures

Saving a document has different steps when you are saving it the first time, saving it subsequent times, saving it using new settings, and saving all open documents at once.

Saving a Document for the First Time

1. Select File | Save, click the Save button on the toolbar, or press SHIFT+F12 or CTRL+S, opening the Save or Save As dialog box.

2. Type the file's name in the File Name text box. The list box below displays the files in the selected directory.

   The filename must conform to the DOS filenaming conventions. A name may be no more than eight characters long, and may consist only of letters, numbers, and the underscore symbol. Do not include spaces.

   You don't need to include a filename extension. Word will add one for you. You only have to add an extension if you want one that is different from the default. The default file extension depends on the file format you select in the Save File as Type drop-down list box.

3. Use the Directories and Drives boxes to select another directory, if desired.

   The Directories box shows the root directory and a directory tree to the current directory. The file folder icon for the current directory is open, and the subdirectories of the current directory appear beneath it. Open a subdirectory by double-clicking it or by pressing TAB to highlight it and then pressing ENTER.

   Move to an undisplayed directory by selecting a directory above the open directory, closing the open directory and opening the one above it. The newly opened directory's subdirectories are displayed.

   When you have opened the directory you want to save the document in, check the File Name list box to ensure that the filename given for the current document is not already used in the directory.

4. Select a file format from the Save File as Type drop-down list box to set the format the file is saved in and the filename extension it uses. The default is the Word for Windows format, with a .DOC filename extension.

5. In Word for Windows 2, you can lock your document or supply a password by selecting File Sharing. These settings are explained under the following "Options."

6. Select Options to open the Options dialog box for the Save category. In this dialog box, you can change Word's default options relating to saving. In Word for Windows 6, you can also define passwords for the current document with this option. These settings are explained under "Save Options." Password protection and other file sharing options in Word for Windows 2 are described under the following "Options."

7. Select OK to save the file.

Resaving a Document with the Same Name and Format

Resaving a document with the same name and format is done using the same commands you used to save it originally.

- Click the Save button on the toolbar
- Press SHIFT+F12
- Press CTRL+S
- Select File | Save

Word saves the document to the same filename, without requiring any further information from you.

Resaving a Document with a New Name or Format

You can save a document with a new name or format by selecting File | Save As or pressing F12. The Save As dialog box is the same as the Save dialog box explained above. Make the appropriate selections from the dialog box options and select OK.

WARNING: If you save your file to the same name in the same directory, but with a different format, the original file is deleted and replaced by the one in the new format.

Saving Multiple Documents at Once

When you have multiple documents open at one time, you may find it difficult to remember which of these opened documents you have saved. To save them all at one time, select File | Save All. Word saves each file to its previously set filename and format. If a document was not previously saved, Word opens the Save As dialog box letting you assign a name and format.

Options

Word for Windows 2 has file sharing options that are set separately than other save options in Word.

File Sharing Options (Word for Windows 2 Only)

Set these options by selecting File Sharing in the Save or the Save As dialog box. They help you maintain your file's security.

LOCK FOR ANNOTATIONS   Select Lock for Annotations to lock your document so that other users can open but not edit it. Other users can, however, enter annotations. (To learn how to enter and use annotations, see "Annotation.") Although other users are unable to unlock your document, you can unlock it when you want to edit it. To unlock your document, open the File Sharing dialog box again, and clear the Lock for Annotations check box.

PROTECTION PASSWORD   Enter up to 15 characters in the Protection Password text box to use as a password for your document. No one can view or open your document without providing the password.

As you enter the password, only asterisks appear in the text box, preventing anyone watching you from seeing the password onscreen. After you select OK in the File Sharing dialog box, Word prompts you to confirm the password. Type the password again and select OK.

When you or someone else tries to open the file, Word prompts for the password. If the correct password is not provided, the file cannot be opened. When the File | Find File command is used to look for files, Word prompts for the password before letting a user view the file's contents.

FILE SHARING SETTINGS   To set the File Sharing settings, you must be the document's author. Word compares the name of author in the document's summary info with the name of the user in the User Info Options panel. If they don't match, the File Sharing settings can't be changed.

To change the program's user, select Tools | Options, then User Info from the Category box. Enter a new name in the Name text box. The original name is the one provided when Word was installed. Check the name of the document's author by selecting File | Summary Info. You can change this name to make the file accessible.

If the user and author names are the same, the document can be edited even if it is locked for annotations. To keep someone using your computer from changing your document, change the name of the document's author so that it doesn't match your user name.

Save Options

You can set several default options about saving a document using the Options dialog box, which can be opened by selecting Options in the Save or Save As dialog box. These options are explained under "Save Options" above. In Word for

Windows 2, the file sharing options set for a single document are set using the Save Options dialog box.

Related Topics

Closing Files
Compatibility Options
Exiting Word
Opening Files
Save Options

Scalable Fonts

See "Fonts."

Scaling Graphics

See "Graphics."

Screen Fonts

Screen fonts are fonts for displaying text onscreen. See "Fonts."

Scroll Bars

Scroll bars are used to move through a document. You can choose to display or to hide them.

Procedures

Horizontal and vertical scroll bars work in the same way, except that horizontal scroll bars move you left to right in the document, while vertical scroll bars move from top to bottom.

- Click the arrow at either end of the scroll bar to move in small increments in that direction. The vertical scroll bar moves you one line at a time, and the horizontal scroll bar moves you a small distance to the left or right.

- Click the scroll bar between the arrow and the scroll bar box to move one window in that direction.

- Drag the scroll bar box to a place on the scroll bar to move to approximately the same location in the document. The page number in the status bar will show the page that will be displayed when you release the mouse.

Options

Scroll bars consist of the scroll bar itself, the scroll arrows, and a scroll bar box, as shown here:

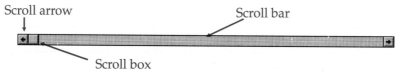

You can choose to hide or display the scroll bars by selecting Tools | Options and selecting the View icon or tab. Clear or select the Horizontal Scroll Bar or Vertical Scroll Bar check boxes to set whether these features appear.

Related Topics

View Options

Scrolling

Scrolling is the process of moving through a document to view the document and move the insertion point. You can do this using movement keys or the scroll bars. See "Scroll Bars" or "Moving the Insertion Point" to learn how to move in your document.

Searching a Document

See "Find and Replace."

Searching for a File

See "File Management."

Secondary Files

Secondary files, called datasources, are used during merges to provide text to be merged into a primary file. See "Mail Merge."

Section Breaks

See "Sections."

SECTION Field

The SECTION field returns the section number of the current section. See "Fields."

Section Formats

See "Sections."

SECTIONPAGES Field

The SECTIONPAGES field returns the total number of pages of the current section. See "Fields."

Sections

Sections break your Word document into smaller segments, which usually contain various formats. Some formats must be the same throughout a single section, so you must break the document into sections used just for these formats. Each section can have different margins, columns, page size and orientation, line numbering, page numbering, headers and footers, and endnote settings. For example, the newsletter shown in Figure 4-53 uses several different sections in order to have different columns and line numbers.

Procedures

In Word, you add section breaks where you want them. Changes to such features as margins, page size, page orientation, and number of columns are made using the File | Page Setup command (Format | Page Setup in Word for Windows 2). When you make these changes using this command, you have the choice of applying the change to the entire document, to the current section, or to the rest of the sections in the document. In Word for Windows 2, changes to vertical alignment, placing footnotes as endnotes, and line numbers are made using the Format | Section Layout command.

Inserting Section Breaks

1. Put your insertion point where the new section will begin.

2. Select Insert | Break.

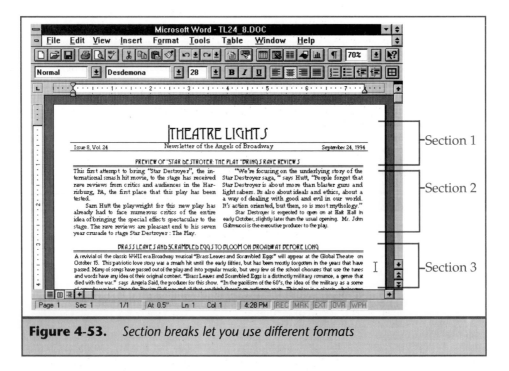

Figure 4-53. *Section breaks let you use different formats*

3. Select an option button in the Section Breaks area of the dialog box. These selections set where the first page of the section is:

   ■ Select Next Page to start a new page as the beginning of the next section.

   ■ Select Even Page to start with the next even-numbered page or Odd Page to start with the next odd-numbered page (you may end up with an extra blank page).

   ■ Select Continuous to start the new section on the current page.

4. Select OK.

Apply Section Formats

1. Put your insertion point in the section to format or select the text to format.

2. Select File I Page Setup and the Layout tab in Word for Windows 6 (select Format I Section Layout, opening the Section Layout dialog box in Word for Windows 2). The Apply to Section area of the dialog box indicates which sections are selected and will be affected by the changes you make.

3. Change where you want the section to start from the Section Start drop-down list box. It will have the current starting point for the section. Selecting a different option changes the section's starting location just as if you had selected the new option when you inserted the section break. You have the same starting location choices that you have when you insert a section break.

4. Select the vertical alignment of text in the section. Select Top to start the text at the top margin, Center to center it between the top and bottom margins, or Justified to have Word add space between paragraphs to make the text start at the top margin and end at the bottom.

5. When a document has endnotes that are placed at the end of each section, the Suppress Endnotes check box (Suppress Footnotes in Word for Windows 2) is available. Select this check box and the endnotes appear after the next section instead.

6. Select Line Numbers to add line numbers to the section and to set how they appear. Information on all the line numbering features is provided under "Line Numbers."

7. Select OK.

Hints

All section formats control how the pages of the section appear when printed. The effect of some of these formats, such as vertical alignment, is not apparent unless you use Print Preview to view them.

Vertical Alignment

Do not use different vertical alignments for sections that occur on the same page. When you choose to start sections continuously, multiple sections occur on a single page. If the sections have different vertical alignments, your text prints oddly, with each section laid out separately on the page and often overlapping other sections. Word for Windows 6 sets the vertical alignment as an option available with the File | Page Setup command.

Forcing Odd Pages

When you start a section on the next odd page, this forces Word to put that first page of text on an odd page. Chapters and sections of a report usually start on an odd page as a visual organizational signal. You force page breaks with the Insert | Break command in the same way as for dividing the document into sections.

Changing Page Breaks Between Sections in Word for Windows 6

To change where a Word for Windows 6 section starts, move to the beginning of the section, just after the section break, and insert a new section break using the section break page division you want. Then move to the old section break above the new one and delete it.

Copying Section Breaks

Section breaks can be copied to other locations in the document to apply the formatting specific to the section to another section in the document. Copy it to the Clipboard as described under "Clipboard."

Related Topics

Columns
Footnotes
Line Numbers

Margins
Page Numbers
Page Setup

Selecting Text

Selecting text is the process of telling Word that you want to do something with that text.

Procedures

Selecting Text with the Mouse

You can select text quickly with the mouse. Table 4-21 shows how you can use the mouse to select different amounts of text.

Selecting Text with the Extend Key

You can use the Extend key to select text.

1. Press F8, the Extend key. *EXT* appears in the status bar.

Do This	To Select
Drag mouse across text	The text you drag across
Press the SHIFT key and click text	The text from the insertion point to where you click
Double-click a word	The word you click
Press CTRL and click	The sentence you click
Drag in the selection bar	The lines beside where you dragged
Click in the selection bar	The line beside where you clicked
Double-click the selection bar	The paragraph beside where you clicked
Press CTRL and click in the selection bar	The entire paragraph
Drag with the right mouse button	A column of text

Table 4-21.   *Using the mouse to select text*

2. Select text by using the movement keys or by pressing F8 repeatedly to expand the selection. You can also extend the selection to a specific character by pressing it.

- Press the arrows and other movement keys to extend and contract the selection.

- Press F8 (the Extend key) repeatedly to extend the selection, as shown in Table 4-22.

- Press a character key to extend the selection to that character. Pressing the key again extends the selection to the next occurrence of that character.

3. Press ESC to end the extend mode.

Selecting Text with the Keyboard

Table 4-23 shows the key presses used to select text and the text that they select. You can combine these key presses. For example, you can press CTRL+SHIFT+END to select to the end of the current paragraph and then SHIFT+LEFT ARROW to keep from selecting the paragraph mark at the end.

Selecting Columns of Text

You can select columns or rectangles of text. This can be useful for selecting numbers arranged in a tabular column, as shown in Figure 4-54.

Press F8	To Select
Once	The current word
Twice	The current sentence
Three times	The current paragraph
Four times	The current section
Five times	The entire document

Table 4-22. *Using Extend to select text*

1. Press CTRL+SHIFT+F8. The status bar shows COL to indicate that you are in Column mode.

2. Use the movement keys to extend your column selection.

3. Press ESC when you wish to leave extend mode.

Hints

In extend mode you can use the Edit/Go To and Find commands to extend the selection. The selection extends from the insertion point's location to the text that you go to or find.

Other ways to select all of the text in the document are to select Edit | Select All or press CTRL+A.

Key Press	Selects
SHIFT+RIGHT ARROW	One character to the right
SHIFT+LEFT ARROW	One character to the left
SHIFT+UP ARROW	To the same position in the previous line
SHIFT+DOWN ARROW	To the same position in the next line
CTRL+SHIFT+RIGHT ARROW	To the end of the current word
CTRL+SHIFT+LEFT ARROW	To the beginning of the current word
SHIFT+END	To the end of the current line
SHIFT+HOME	To the beginning of the current line
CTRL+SHIFT+UP ARROW	To the beginning of the current or next paragraph
CTRL+SHIFT+DOWN ARROW	To the end of the current or next paragraph
SHIFT+PAGE UP	One screen up from the current position
SHIFT+PAGE DOWN	One screen down from the current position
CTRL+SHIFT+HOME	To the beginning of the document
CTRL+SHIFT+END	To the end of the document
CTRL+5 (num. keypad)	The entire document

Table 4-23.   *Selecting with keys*

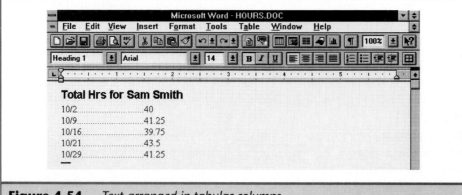

Figure 4-54.   *Text arranged in tabular columns*

SEQ Field

The SEQ field numbers items or sections of text in your document. See "Fields."

SET Field

The SET field assigns a bookmark to defined text. See "Fields."

Shading

See "Borders and Shading."

Shadowed Text

See "WordArt."

Sharing Data

See "Clipboard" or "Spike" for information on sharing data with other documents or applications. See "Saving Files" for information on security for document files shared with other Word users. See "Object Linking and Embedding" for information on sharing data with other applications.

Shortcut Keys

Shortcut keys are used to activate commands with the keyboard without having to use the menus. Word has many shortcut keys for different features. The features and the shortcut keys these features use are shown below.

Shortcut Keys for	See
Adding and updating fields	Fields
Adding special characters	Special Characters
Apply and remove font styles	All Caps, Bold, Italics, Small Capitals, Spacing Characters, Strikethrough, Super/Subscript, Text Color, Underline
Assigning styles	Styles
Changing the size and font	Fonts
Function keys	Function Keys
Moving in a document	Moving the Insertion Point
Moving in a table	Tables
Outlines	Outlines
Paragraph formatting	Alignment, Indents, Pagination, Spacing
Selecting text	Selecting Text

Besides the shortcut keys for the features described above, Word also has shortcut keys for many of its commands. The following table shows the shortcut keys you can use to select various menu commands in Word for Windows 6. The shortcut keys with an asterisk work in Word for Windows 2 as well as in Word for Windows 6. The ones without an asterisk only work in Word for Windows 6.

Command	Press
File I New	CTRL+N
File I Open	CTRL+O or CTRL+F12*
File I Close	CTRL+W
File I Save	CTRL+S or CTRL+F12*
File I Save As	F12*
File I Print Preview	CTRL+F2
File I Print	CTRL+P or CTRL+SHIFT+F12*
File I Exit	ALT+F4*
Edit I Undo	CTRL+Z or CTRL+2*
Edit I Repeat	CTRL+Y or F4*

Command	Press
Edit	Clear	DEL
Edit	Cut	CTRL+X* or SHIFT+DEL
Edit	Copy	CTRL+C* or CTRL+INS
Edit	Paste	CTRL+V* or SHIFT+INS
Edit	Select All	CTRL+A or CTRL+5*
Edit	Find	CTRL+F
Edit	Replace	CTRL+H
Edit	Go To	CTRL+G or F5*
Edit	Bookmark	CTRL+SHIFT+F5*
Edit	Links	Update Now	CTRL+SHIFT+F7
View	Normal	ALT+CTRL+N
View	Outline	ALT+CTRL+O
View	Page Layout	ALT+CTRL+P
Insert	Page Numbers	ALT+SHIFT+P
Insert	Annotation	ALT+CTRL+A
Insert	Date And Time	ALT+SHIFT+D
Insert	Footnote	Footnote	ALT+CTRL+F
Insert	Footnote	Endnote	ALT+CTRL+E
Insert	Index and Tables	Index	Mark Entry	ALT+SHIFT+X
Insert	Index and Tables	Tables of Authorities	Mark Citation	ALT+SHIFT+I
Insert	Field	TC Field	ALT+SHIFT+O
Format	Font	CTRL+D
Format	Change Case	SHIFT+F3
Format	AutoFormat	CTRL+K
Format	Style	CTRL+SHIFT+S (CTRL+S in Word for Windows 2)
Tools	Spelling	F7
Tools	Thesaurus	SHIFT+F7*
Table	Select Table	ALT+5*
Table	Table AutoFormat	ALT+CTRL+U
Window	Split	ALT+CTRL+S

Command	Press
Help	Contents	F1
Context-sensitive Help	SHIFT+F1

See "Keyboard Options" for information on changing existing shortcut keys or adding new ones.

SKIPIF Field

The SKIPIF field makes Word skip an item if a particular condition is true. See "Mail Merge."

Small Capitals

Small Caps is a character format that produces text in which letters typed as lowercase appear as capitals in the next smaller font size. Small caps are often used in titles and headings and in scripts and speeches.

Procedures

The Small Caps style can be applied as the text is being typed or after it is typed. To apply the style while typing, first add the format, then type the text, and then remove the format. To apply it to typed text, select the text to be formatted and then add the style.

Adding and Removing Small Caps with the Menu

1. Select Format | Font (Character in Word for Windows 2) or, in Word for Windows 6, right-click the selected text or insertion point location and select Font from the shortcut menu.

   TIP: *In Word for Windows 2, another way to open the Character dialog box is to double-click a blank spot of the ribbon.*

2. Select the Small Caps check box. Clear this box to remove the Small Caps format.

3. Select OK.

Adding and Removing Small Caps with the Keyboard

Press CTRL+SHIFT+K to add or remove the Small Caps format (CTRL+K in Word for Windows 2).

Removing Formatting

Another method for removing Small Caps from text is to select the text and press CTRL+SPACEBAR, removing all character formatting from the selected text.

Related Topics

Character Formats
Fonts

Snaking Columns

See "Columns."

Sorting

You can quickly sort tables or paragraphs in alphabetic order. In Word for Windows 2, you can only sort using a single field, while in Word for Windows 6 you have two additional fields, or sorting keys, that can be used to break ties. For example, if you have two people named Campbell in your list, you can use a second key to sort the Campbells by their first name.

Procedures

1. Select the text you want to sort. The text to select for different sorting tasks is shown in Table 4-24.

To Sort	Select
Whole document	Nothing
Selected paragraphs	The paragraphs to sort only
Whole table	Entire table
Whole tabular table	Entire table
One table column	That column only
One tabular column	That column only

Table 4-24.   *Text to select for sorting*

2. Select Table | Sort Text (Tools | Sorting in Word for Windows 2). When the insertion point is in a table, this command is Table | Sort Table.

3. Specify the sort field in the Sort By drop-down list box. This list box will list the available fields you can use to sort with such as Column 1 and Column 2. In Word for Windows 2, select the field from the Field Number spin box.

4. Select the type of sorting to do from the Type drop-down list box:

   ■ Select Date to have Word sort using text in a standard date format, ignoring any other text.

   ■ Select Number (Numeric in Word for Windows 2) to have Word sort using numbers, ignoring dates and other text.

   ■ Select Text (Alphanumeric in Word for Windows 2) and Word sorts both alphabetically and numerically, putting numbers and special characters before letters.

5. Select Ascending or Descending to choose how Word sorts your text, as shown here:

   Ascending sort
   A . . . Z 1 2 3

   Descending sort
   Z . . . A 3 2 1

6. In Word for Windows 6, if you selected enough text so that there is some to serve as a second or third key, the Then By and Then By drop-down list

boxes are available for specifying a second and third sorting key. Repeat steps 3 through 5 to set up these sort keys.

7. Word may assume that your table or list has a header row that should not be sorted. If you want the top row sorted along with the rest of the rows, select the No Header Row option button rather than the Header Row option button.

8. In Word for Windows 6, you must select Options to set the further sort options. In Word for Windows 2, the following options appear in the dialog box you are already working in.

9. Select Commas to have Word treat commas as marking the ends of fields. Select Tabs to have Word treat tabs as marking the ends of fields. In Word for Windows 6, select Other and enter another character used to mark the ends of fields in the text to sort.

10. Select Sort Column Only when you select a tabular or table column, and want to sort that column without affecting any other columns.

11. Select Case Sensitive to have Word separate lower- and upper-case when sorting text. Upper-case letters will come before lower-case letters.

12. Select OK (twice in Word for Windows 6) to sort the text.

Hints

Word has several features that make sorting easier. These features include using different fields for sorting, undoing a sort if the data is not sorted the way you want, and using acceptable date and time formats when you sort by date.

Fields

In ordinary sorting, only the first word in a paragraph or line may be used to determine the sort order. When you want to sort using a word other than the first word, the words in a line or paragraph must be separated into fields by a comma or tab or, in Word for Windows 6, by a character specified after selecting the Other option button in the Sort Options dialog box. Fields may also be created by using Word's Table feature. Then you can select which column in the table you want to use for sorting.

Undoing Sorts

You can undo a sort by selecting Edit | Undo Sort immediately after sorting. In Word for Windows 2, if you do anything else before selecting Undo, however, you cannot undo the sort. In Word for Windows 6, use the Undo button in the Standard toolbar to undo the sort and everything done since the sort.

If you save your document before sorting it, you can be assured of being able to restore your document if the sort does not work the way that you thought it would, even if you do some editing before realizing that the sort is incorrect. Simply close the current sorted document without saving it, and then open the original unsorted document again.

Date and Time Formats

When you choose to sort according to Date, Word sorts only those paragraphs or cells containing dates in certain recognizable formats like the ones shown below. If Word cannot find a date, that paragraph, row, or cell is sorted as if it contains nothing.

> 11/6/93
> 11-6-93
> 11 6 93
> November 6, 1993
> Nov. 6, 1993
> Nov 6
> 06-Nov-93
> November-93
> 11/06/93 3:30 PM

Related Topics

> Tables

Sorting Tables

See "Sorting."

Sorting Text

See "Sorting."

Sorting the File List

See "File Management."

Sound

You can add sound to your Word documents. To add the sound, your computer needs sound capabilities available with a sound card. Sounds can either be part of a document or part of the annotations in a document.

Procedures

Sounds can be added to a document as an embedded object or as voice annotations in Word for Windows 6. Voice annotations are an alternative to using written annotations. Voice annotations are usually created by one user and heard by another.

Adding an Embedded Sound Object

1. Move the insertion point to where you want the icon for the sound placed.

2. Select Insert | Object.

   You can add a sound object two ways.

   ■ Choose Sound from the Object Type list box with the Create New tab selected and OK. Word and Windows opens the Sound Recorder application. You can use the Edit | Insert from File command to insert a sound file as well as using other Sound Recorder application features to add the sound you want. When you have the sound you want, select File | Exit and Yes when prompted about updating the object.

   ■ Choose Sound from the Object Type list box with the Create from File tab and select the sound file to add as an object and OK.

   Word and Windows adds an icon for the sound object you have embedded into your document. To hear the sound, double-click the icon or select the icon and press ALT+SHIFT+F9.

Creating Voice Annotations

In Word for Windows 6, creating a voice annotation lets a user make comments about a documentation. To create voice annotations, you must have a microphone installed as well as a sound board.

1. Position the insertion point on the text the voice annotation will belong to.

2. Select Insert | Annotation, and click the Insert Sound Object button in the annotations pane's toolbar.

3. Record your voice annotation, using the instructions for recording that came with your sound board.

4. If, when you finish recording, Word displays a message asking if you want to update the sound object, select Yes. The document will have a icon for the sound object you just recorded.

5. Select Close or return to the document window.

When you want to listen to the voice annotations, look at the document's annotations. Double-clicking the sound icons will replay the recorded voice annotations.

Spacing Characters

With Word, you can control the spacing between the characters in your document by adding extra space to the right of a character. For example, see Figure 4-55 to see how you might use expanded spacing to make an attractive flyer.

Procedures

The spacing between characters can be applied either as the text is being typed or after it is typed. You can add the format, type the text to affect, then remove the format, or you can select the text to format and then add the format.

1. Select Format | Font (Character in Word for Windows 2) or, in Word for Windows 6, right-click the selected text or insertion point location and select Font.

2. In Word for Windows 6, select the Character Spacing tab.

3. Select Expanded or Condensed from the Spacing drop-down list box to add or remove space between characters. Select Normal to return to the default spacing.

Figure 4-55.   *Expanded character spaces make interesting effects*

4. Specify the distance to add or remove between characters in the By text box. You can enter between 0 and 1584 points (between .25 and 14 points in Word for Windows 2).

5. In Word for Windows 6, select the Kerning for Fonts check box to have Word automatically kern text, adding and removing space between individual pairs of letters to make them fit together better. Enter the smallest font size you want kerned in the Points and Above box.

6. Select OK.

Hints

You can change the spacing between characters for a special effect in a brochure or newsletter. This feature may work well if you are planning to superimpose the text on a graphic.

You can change the spacing between specific letter pairs throughout your document by using the Edit I Replace command, and replacing those character pairs with the same characters, but with different character spacing. You may need to change the character spacing of character pairs in camera-ready copy to make the text read more smoothly by taking out oddly placed gaps.

Related Topics

Character Formats
Find and Replace
Super/Subscript

Spacing

You can set two kinds of spacing for your paragraph with Word, line and paragraph spacing. Line spacing controls the space between the lines within the paragraph. Paragraph spacing controls the spacing between paragraphs. You can see these spacings marked in Figure 4-56.

Procedures

Both line spacing and paragraph spacing are paragraph formats. When these are set, the setting affects the paragraph the insertion point is in or all selected paragraphs. If you press ENTER in a paragraph, creating a new paragraph, the new paragraph uses the same spacing formats as the previous paragraph.

Setting Line Spacing

1. Select Format | Paragraph or, in Word for Windows 6, right-click the document area and select Paragraph.

2. In Word for Windows 6, select the Indents and Spacing tab.

3. In the Line Spacing drop-down list box, select Single, 1.5 Lines, Double, At Least, Exactly, or Multiple to set the line spacing. Word for Windows 2 also has an Auto option. For more information on these choices, see "Options" below.

4. If you selected either At Least or Exactly in the Line Spacing box, enter the number of points in the At spin box for these settings to use. If you selected Multiple in the Line Spacing box, enter the percentage of the single line size you want the paragraphs to use.

5. Select OK.

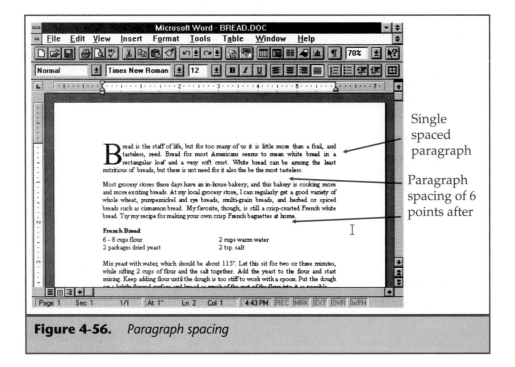

Figure 4-56.   *Paragraph spacing*

Setting Paragraph Spacing

1. Select Format | Paragraph, or, in Word for Windows 6, right-click the document area and select Paragraph.

2. Select the Indents and Spacing tab in Word for Windows 6.

3. To leave space before the paragraph, enter a measurement in the Before text box. Enter a measurement in the After text box to leave space after the paragraph.

   In Word for Windows 6, define the space before or after paragraphs in terms of points, which are 1/72 inch. Each click of the arrows that are part of this text box changes the value by 6 points. In Word for Windows 2, the space before and after paragraphs is measured in lines. You can enter fractions of lines to have smaller spaces before or after.

4. Select OK.

Options

There are different options for spacing lines within a paragraph:

- *Single, 1.5 Lines, Double* Sets one of these standard line spacings for the formatted paragraph.

- *At Least* Sets a minimum line spacing for Word to use. Word can expand the lines if necessary, but cannot decrease the line spacing below this measurement. You need to specify the line spacing in the At text box when you select this option.

- *Exactly* Sets an exact line spacing for Word to use. Word cannot expand or shrink the line spacing you specify in the At text box.

- *Multiple* (Word for Windows 6 only) Sets the spacing for the lines in the formatted paragraph based on a multiple of the font and font size. For example, 1 is the same as Single, but you can also use decimals such as 1.2 to have line height 120 percent larger than Single.

- *Auto* (Word for Windows 2 only) Sets the spacing for the lines in the formatted paragraph on the basis of the font and font size.

Hints

Double-spacing is often required for academic papers. It is also useful for drafts that you or a proofreader are reviewing, because changes can be marked in the space between the lines.

Related Topics

Paragraph Formats

Special Characters

Word can insert special characters or symbols. Special characters are those that print, and are part of normal fonts, but that do not have their own key on the keyboard, such as an é and a copyright mark. Symbols are usually selected from special decorative fonts, such as Wingdings or Zapf Dingbats. When you insert a symbol, you cannot change the font that it is in. Word for Windows 2 doesn't distinguish between special characters and symbols.

Procedures

You can insert special characters and symbols using a menu command. With frequently used special characters and symbols, you may want to assign a shortcut key so you can press the shortcut key to add the special character or symbol.

Inserting Symbols

1. Select Insert | Symbol.

2. In Word for Windows 6, select the Symbols tab.

3. Select the font you want to use in the Font drop-down list box. If you want to insert a standard character that cannot be typed at the keyboard, without defining a particular font, select Normal Text. Look for fonts with names like Symbol, Wingdings, or DingBats to find a set of different characters, such as those in Figure 4-57.

4. Highlight the character you want to use. As you highlight characters, a box displays them in a larger size. In Word for Windows 2, this box appears only when you point at the symbol and press the mouse button. Note that in Word for Windows 6 any shortcut keys for this character are displayed in the upper right corner of the dialog box.

5. Select Insert (OK in Word for Windows 2). In Word for Windows 6, continue inserting more characters or select Close.

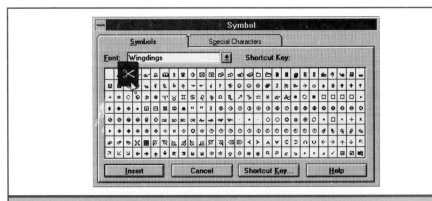

Figure 4-57.   *Different symbols in symbol fonts*

Inserting Special Characters

1. Select Insert | Symbol.

2. In Word for Windows 6, select the Special Characters tab.

3. Highlight the character you want to insert in the Character list box.

NOTE: In Word for Windows 6, the shortcut key for the character appears in this list box as well.

4. Select Insert (OK in Word for Windows 2). In Word for Windows 6 continue inserting more characters or select Close.

Changing Shortcut Keys in Word for Windows 6

1. Select Insert | Symbol.

2. Highlight the symbol or character associated with the shortcut key you want to assign or edit.

3. Select Shortcut Key.

4. Press the keys to use as shortcut keys with the insertion point in the Press New Shortcut Key text box.

5. Select OK.

6. Select Insert or Close.

Once the shortcut key is assigned, you can add it to any location in the document by pressing the key combination you pressed in step 4 above.

Hints

When you use special characters in Word, the special character appearance depends on the font. Symbols do not change when you change the font. Word for Windows 2 treats symbols differently as described below.

Symbols vs. Special Characters in Word for Windows 6

When you insert symbols in Word for Windows 6, these symbols are protected from changes in font. That is, although you can apply a new font size, position, or even (depending on the symbol or font) a format such as italics or underlining, you cannot change the font. The characters you insert as symbols are usually part of special fonts that do not include the usual letters and symbols that are part of standard font sets. If you were to change the font, you might change your "smiley face" (Wingdings) into a *J* (normal text).

Special characters, on the other hand, are characters that appear in most normal font sets, but that cannot be typed from the keyboard, such as em or en dashes or smart (curly) quotes. You can insert these characters from the Special Characters tab or from the Symbols tab, if you have selected normal text as the font. These characters can change fonts, since most font sets have the same characters. Your "smiley face" will not turn into a *J* when you switch to the next font.

Symbols in Word for Windows 2

When you insert symbols in Word for Windows 2, they are included in your document as a field code. This prevents you from accidentally changing the font for these characters and having your "smiley face" turn into a *K* because the font you changed to does not include these special symbols.

Related Topics

Fields
Keyboard Options

Spelling

Word's Spelling feature enables you to locate misspelled words in your document, and to replace them with correct ones. The Spelling feature also flags incorrectly capitalized words and repeated words.

Procedures

When you check the spelling in your document, you can check selected text or your entire document. The steps are the same. If you want to check a word, a sentence, a paragraph, or a page, select the text before activating the Spelling feature.

1. To activate the Spelling feature, select Tools | Spelling, select the Spelling button from the Standard toolbar, or press F7.

   The first word in the document or selected text that Word cannot locate in its dictionaries is highlighted, and the Spelling dialog box appears.

   The highlighted word also appears in the Not in Dictionary text box. The suggested replacement words appear in the Suggestions list box. Your next action will depend on whether or not you agree with Word's suggestions.

2. You can either correct the word that is flagged as misspelled or ignore it. You can also choose to add the word to a custom dictionary, correct all instances of the word, or ignore all instances of the word, depending on the option you select.

   ■ When the flagged word is wrong and the correct word is suggested, highlight the correct word in the Suggestions list box and select Change.

   ■ When the flagged word is wrong, and the correct word is not suggested, type the correct word in the Change To text box and select Change. You can click on the word in the Not in Dictionary text box to change the Change To text box to contain the flagged entry, if it makes entering the correct replacement easier. Select Change All if the word is consistently misspelled to have Word correct it each time it is encountered.

   ■ When the flagged word is correct, select Ignore. Select Ignore All to avoid flagging the word when it occurs again. Select Add to add the word to a custom dictionary so it is not flagged in other documents. You can change which dictionary the word is added to by selecting a dictionary from the Add Words To drop-down list box.

   ■ When the flagged word is one that is repeated, such as "the the," select Change, and Word will delete the second instance of the word.

   For a fuller explanation of each of these choices, see "Options" in this section.

3. After you select one of the options above, Word continues checking the document, highlighting the next word that cannot be found in the dictionary. Make a selection regarding the newly flagged word as described in step 2.

4. When Word finishes, it displays a message box saying "The spelling check is complete." Select OK to return to your document.

Options

When Word encounters a word that does not appear in its dictionaries, it highlights the word in your document and shows it in the Not in Dictionary text box in the Spelling dialog box. Word's suggested spelling appears in the Change To text box, and some alternate spellings appear in the Suggestions list box. You have a number of choices about what to do with the word in question.

CHANGE   To insert the correct word in place of the flagged word, make sure that the correctly spelled word appears in the Change To text box. You can select the correct spelling from the Suggestions list box or type it into the Change To text box yourself. Then select the Change button.

When Word flags an improperly capitalized word, selecting Change corrects the capitalization but does not change the spelling. When Word flags a repeated word, one of the words can be deleted.

CHANGE ALL   When you know that a flagged misspelling appears frequently in your document, select Change All instead of Change. Word will correct that word each time it finds it. However, Word does not correct the subsequent instances of the word until it reaches them. If you cancel the Spelling feature before reaching the end of your document, the later appearances of the misspelled word are not changed to the correct spelling.

IGNORE   When Word flags a word that is spelled correctly, select Ignore and Word skips the word in question. If the word appears again in your document, Word flags it again.

IGNORE ALL   When Word flags a correctly spelled word that reappears in your document, select Ignore All instead of Ignore. Word then ignores every appearance of the word, treating the word as though it occurred in the Word dictionaries. However, the next time you use the Spelling feature the word is flagged as usual.

ADD   Select Add to add the flagged word in the Not In Dictionary text box to the custom dictionary, letting you create a personalized dictionary for use in Word. For more information on custom dictionaries, see "Custom Dictionaries" in the Hints section.

UNDO LAST   Select Undo Last to undo your last correction. This feature works for the last five corrections, but it cannot go back and correct a word for which you chose Ignore or Ignore All.

SUGGEST Select Suggest to have suggestions provided for a word in the Change To text box. You can type the word in the Change To text and request suggestions as well as request suggestions for a flagged word.

ADD WORDS TO When you select Add, Word adds the word to the custom dictionary you selected in the Add Words To drop-down box.

OPTIONS Select Options to open the Options dialog box, in which you can set the defaults that the Spelling feature uses. These options are fully described under "Spelling Options."

AUTOCORRECT (WORD FOR WINDOWS 6 ONLY) Select AutoCorrect to replace the flagged word with the word appearing in the Change To text box, and to record the correction as an AutoCorrect entry. AutoCorrect can replace the word automatically when you type the word incorrectly spelled. This feature is described under "AutoCorrect."

Hints

Spelling in Word checks your document against dictionary files to find misspelled words. With documents that include such things as invoices and ones containing acronyms (words formed from the initial letters of a name), you can add these words to your dictionaries. You can create your own custom dictionaries as well as using ones from other sources such as dictionaries containing medical or legal terms. Word can suggest words when you use wildcard characters in the Change To text box. If a document contains foreign text, you can mark the language the section uses so Word can switch the language Word uses to check the text spelling.

How Spell Works

When you use the Spelling feature, Word compares words in your document with the words in its dictionary files. If a word is not found in a dictionary file, Word flags it as potentially incorrect. Word also flags words when the capitalization appears improper or if the same word occurs twice in sequence.

Word makes suggestions for flagged words by searching for words in its dictionaries that are similar in spelling or sound to the flagged word. You can select a suggested word to replace the incorrect one or type the correct word in the Change To text box.

Invoices and Acronyms

Word normally checks all words in your document that are not entirely composed of numbers. This means that Word checks words with some numbers, such as invoice numbers or IRS tax form titles. Word also flags acronyms, such as NAFTA or CINC-PAC, since they are usually not in the dictionary. You can set Word to ignore words containing numbers or words all in capitals (which includes most acronyms) by changing the Spelling options.

You can add acronyms you use regularly to your custom dictionary. If a word with numbers is one that you have to use frequently, such as an ID number or street address, such as 25th St., add it to the custom dictionary too.

Custom Dictionaries

Word automatically uses the standard dictionary when checking your text's spelling. As a default, Word also uses a custom dictionary file called CUSTOM.DIC, which is created when you first install Word. The CUSTOM.DIC file is initially empty. You will add words to this CUSTOM.DIC when you select the Add button while Add Words To is set to CUSTOM.DIC. You can create or purchase any number of other dictionary files to use as well as the CUSTOM.DIC custom dictionary. You can use only ten (four in Word for Windows 2) custom dictionaries at one time for checking the text of your document.

OPENING AND CLOSING CUSTOM DICTIONARIES   Word uses the open custom dictionaries when proofing your document's spelling. You can have up to ten custom dictionaries open at a time (four in Word for Windows 2).

The Custom Dictionaries list box in the dialog box Word displays when you select Options, displays the dictionary files in the default directory and any you have added to the list box. The original default directory, if Word was installed normally, is a directory containing the WINWORD.EXE file. The default directory can be the directory containing the WINWORD.EXE file, the directory specified by the TOOLS-PATH statement in the WINWORD.INI file for Word for Windows 2, or the MSAPPS\PROOF directory.

You can use a dictionary that is not listed in the Custom Dictionaries list box by selecting the Add button, specifying the full path and filename of the directory in the File Name text box, and selecting OK. The dictionary is added to the Custom Dictionaries list box.

Open dictionaries are highlighted in the Custom Dictionaries list box. You open a dictionary in the Custom Dictionaries list by clicking it, or by highlighting it and pressing ENTER.

You close a dictionary by selecting it again. Speed up the Spelling feature by closing dictionaries you do not need for the document you are checking.

If you open a new custom dictionary after starting the Spelling feature, the new dictionary is not used. You have to restart the Spelling feature to use the newly opened dictionary.

S

CREATING BLANK CUSTOM DICTIONARIES   Creating a new custom dictionary is as easy as opening one. Go to the Spelling tab in the Options dialog box, and select the New button (Add in Word for Windows 2). Enter the name you want for the dictionary file and select OK. The dictionary file is created in the default directory, unless you specify the full pathname for it.

CREATING CUSTOM DICTIONARIES   You can create custom dictionaries instead of simply using the Spelling dialog box to add words to an existing one. You may want to start out with all the acronyms or specialized terms that you use frequently. To do this, create a file that lists the words you want in your dictionary, with one word on each line and no extra spaces. Save the file with the filename extension .DIC, after selecting Text Only in the Save File as Type drop-down list box. Open this file as you would open other custom dictionaries.

When creating a custom dictionary, be aware of capitalization. When your entry is all lowercase, Word will recognize and avoid flagging it regardless of capitalization. If you enter a word in the dictionary with an initial capital, Word recognizes the word only if you enter it in your document with an initial capital or all capitals; the word will be flagged if you enter it all lowercase. If your dictionary entry is all capitals, Word recognizes the word only if it is all capitals. If you make your dictionary entry using an irregular capitalization, such as PostScript, Word recognizes the word only with exactly the same irregular capitalization. See Table 4-25 for examples of these rules.

EXCLUDE DICTIONARIES   An exclude dictionary is a special custom dictionary that lets you flag words you don't want in your documents. An exclude dictionary works the reverse of a normal dictionary. When Word finds a word in a regular dictionary, the word is not flagged. However, when Word finds a word in an exclude dictionary, Word flags the word.

Dictionary	Word Flags	Word Ignores
tree	trEe	tree, Tree, TREE
Spanish	spanish	Spanish, SPANISH
AWOL	awol, Awol	AWOL
d'Arcy	d'arcy, D'Arcy, D'ARCY	d'Arcy

Table 4-25.   *Custom Dictionary Entries Affect Flags*

An exclude dictionary consists of words you don't want in your documents even if they are correctly spelled. For example, Word recognizes and therefore does not flag most normal contractions. To ensure that you don't use those contractions, create an exclude dictionary containing them; the contractions will then be flagged. Another use is flagging mistyped words that are a correct spelling of another word. For example, in a book about databases, *field* is a commonly used word that might be regularly mistyped as *filed*. Add *filed* to an exclude dictionary to have all occurrences flagged so they are checked.

Create an exclude dictionary using the steps given above for creating a custom dictionary. However, save the file with the name MSSP2_EN.EXC and a file type of Text Only. The MSSP2_EN is the same name as the main dictionary file (MSSP2_EN.LEX).

Professional or Technical Dictionaries

You may want to purchase professional dictionaries. These dictionaries can be used with Word and contain medical, legal, or other technical terms for a specific field. The advantage is that you do not need to add words to a dictionary. These dictionaries have already been double-checked for correctness. Such dictionaries are created by Microsoft as well as by third-party software vendors.

Using Wildcard Characters

You can use wildcard characters when entering a word in the Change To text box to see Word's suggested spellings. Wildcard characters take the place of letters in the word you type, letting you look for related words. The ? character takes the place of any one letter. The * character takes the place of any number of characters.

For example, if you know the word starts with *pred*, but aren't sure how the rest of the word is written, type **pred*** and select Suggest. Word suggests a series of words starting with *pred*.

Spell Checking Foreign Text

You can use Word's spelling feature for a foreign language, as long as you have the dictionary for the language. First, you need to mark the text as being in a specific language with Tools | Language (Format | Language in Word for Windows 2). When the Spelling feature reaches text marked for another language, Word switches to the dictionary for that language. If you do not have the dictionary for a language, you cannot check the spelling of that language. You can call Microsoft to check on the availability of foreign language dictionaries.

To format a section of text as a different language, select the text first. Then use the Tools | Language (Format | Language in Word for Windows 2) and select the new language from the Mark Selected Text As list box.

Related Topics

Find and Replace
Foreign Language Support
Grammar Checking

Spelling Options

You can set the Spelling options, the default options which control how Word checks the spelling in your document.

Procedures

1. Select Tools | Options.

2. Select the Spelling tab or icon.

3. Make your settings as described under "Options" below.

4. Select OK.

TIP: Another way to set the Spelling options is to select Options from the Spelling dialog box.

Options

The following options are available in the Spelling tab in the Options dialog box.

Always Suggest

Clear the Always Suggest check box to prevent Word from suggesting correct spellings for flagged words. You can still request suggestions by selecting Suggest in the Spelling dialog box.

From Main Dictionary Only (Word for Windows 6 Only)

Clear the From Main Dictionary Only check box when you want Word to check your custom dictionaries to see if a word might be correctly spelled.

Words in UPPERCASE

Select the Words in UPPERCASE check box to have Word ignore words all in capitals when checking spelling in your documents.

Words with Numbers

Select the Words with Numbers check box to have Word ignore words with numbers in them while checking spelling in your document.

Reset Ignore All (Word for Windows 6 Only)

Select Reset Ignore All and Yes to remove all entries from the Ignore All list that Word creates when you select Ignore All from the Spelling dialog box in response to a flagged word. After selecting this, all the words Word had been ignoring in the current session are now flagged again.

Custom Dictionaries

This list box displays the names of custom dictionary files located in your proofing tools directory. Dictionaries with selected check boxes are open. In Word for Windows 2, open dictionaries are highlighted. Up to ten custom dictionary files can be open at a time (four in Word for Windows 2).

TIP: You can open a custom dictionary by clicking it or by highlighting it and pressing ENTER.

New\Add\Remove

Select Add to add a dictionary to the Custom Dictionaries list box or, in Word for Windows 2, to create a new custom dictionary file. Select New in Word for Windows 6 to create a new custom dictionary. Select Remove in Word for Windows 6 to remove the highlighted custom dictionary from the list.

In Word for Windows 6, after selecting Add, you can locate the dictionary file using dialog box options like those for opening a file normally. Select OK to add the dictionary file to the Custom Dictionaries list box. You can create a new dictionary file in Word for Windows 6 by selecting New and specifying the filename and directory before selecting OK. This file is automatically added to the list box.

In Word for Windows 6, you can remove a dictionary from the list without deleting or moving it by highlighting it in the list box and selecting Remove.

In Word for Windows 2, after selecting Add, type the name of a dictionary file in the Create text box and select OK. If this file does not already exist, it is created and added to the Custom Dictionaries list. If it does exist, it is added only to the Custom Dictionaries list. Include a file not in a default directory by including its complete pathname.

To remove a dictionary from the list in Word for Windows 2, you have to move or delete the dictionary file, so that Word cannot find the file when it starts checking spelling next.

Edit (Word for Windows 6 Only)

Select Edit to have Word open the highlighted dictionary as a Word document that you can edit. Word prompts you to confirm that you want to open the dictionary as a Word document. The dictionary is displayed as a single column list of words. When you are finished editing the file, simply select File | Close and the select Yes when asked if you wish to save the changed file.

Related Topics

Spelling

Spike

Word's Spike feature is somewhat like the Windows Clipboard, but offers some added advantages. You can cut text from your document and place it on the Spike, then insert it back into the document, just like the Clipboard. However, unlike the Clipboard, you can cut many selections to the Spike, without deleting the Spike's previous contents.

 WARNING: You cannot copy text to the Spike, only cut it.

Procedures

1. Select the text or graphic to be cut.

2. Press CTRL+F3 and Word cuts the selection to the Spike.

3. To paste the Spike's contents into the document and remove them from the Spike, put the insertion point where you want the Spike's contents and press CTRL+SHIFT+F3.

4. To paste the Spike's contents into the document without removing them from the Spike, put the insertion point where you want the contents. Make sure there is a space, tab character, or paragraph mark before the insertion point. Type **spike** and click the AutoText button, press F3 or ALT+CTRL+V.

Hints

The Spike is actually a special type of temporary AutoText or Glossary entry and, like these features, uses the F3 key to carry out its operations. In Word for Windows 6, you can also see part or all of the Spike's contents by selecting Edit | AutoText and highlighting Spike in the Name list box. All or some of the contents appear in the Preview box.

When you cut several selections of text to the Spike, the selections are stored in the order you cut them. That is, the first text you cut to the Spike is the first entry within the Spike, and so on so the last text in the Spike is the last selection of text you cut to the Spike. Each selection of text added to the Spike is separated with a paragraph mark.

Related Topics

AutoText
Clipboard
Glossary

Split Table

See "Tables."

Splitting a Document Window

See "Viewing Documents."

Spreadsheets

Spreadsheet applications create documents, called worksheets, that are arranged like Word's tables. Worksheets can carry out calculations using cell entries. Word can open Lotus 1-2-3 and Excel worksheet files. You can use fields to create spreadsheet-like tables that perform limited math calculations.

See "Opening Files" and "Tables" for more information on opening worksheet files, and performing math calculations in a table.

Standard Word Styles

Word has standard styles that are applied automatically, such as header and footer styles, footnote text and footnote reference styles, and index styles. You can change or remove these styles. See "Styles" for further information on what styles are and how they work.

Start a New Page

See "Hard Page Break" and "Pagination."

Statistics

See "Grammar Checking" or "Summary Info."

Strikethrough

Strikethrough is a character format that produces text with a horizontal line through its middle. You may use text with the Strikethrough style to indicate deleted or proposed text.

Procedures

The Strikethrough style can be applied while text is being typed or after it is typed. To apply while typing, add the format, type the text, then remove the format. To apply to typed text, select the text and then add the style.

1. Select Format I Font (Character in Word for Windows 2) or, in Word for Windows 6, right-click the document area and select Font.

2. Select the Strikethrough check box to apply the format or clear it to remove the format.

3. Select OK.

Hints

In Word for Windows 2, another way to open the Character dialog box is to double-click a blank spot of the ribbon.

Removing Formatting

Another procedure for removing Strikethrough from text is to select the text and press CTRL+SPACEBAR. This keystroke removes all character formatting from the selected text.

Related Topics

Character Formats
Comparing Versions
Fonts

Style Area

See "Styles."

Style Gallery

See "Styles."

Style Sheets

In Word for DOS all styles available for a document are stored in a separate document called a *style sheet*. In Word For Windows, styles can be stored in a template or in the document itself. See "Styles."

STYLEREF Field

The STYLEREF field inserts text from the previous paragraph that uses a defined style. See "Fields."

Styles

Styles are sets of formats that you can apply to text. The advantage to using styles instead of applying the formats directly is that you can easily change your entire document's formatting by changing the formatting assigned to a particular style. You can think of styles as the numbers in a paint by numbers set, as shown in Figure 4-58.

Word for Windows 6 updates the Style feature by adding character styles. *Paragraph styles*, which are the only styles you can create with Word for Windows 2, affect all of the text in a paragraph and can apply both paragraph and character formats. *Character styles* can be applied to only the text you select, even if it is only a single word, and apply only character formats.

Word for Windows 6 also has a new feature, AutoFormat, that will automatically apply styles to your document. You can use this feature as a shortcut for formatting your document. For more details of AutoFormat, see "AutoFormat."

Use styles any time you want to have a consistent look to text. For example, in a document that uses several long quotations, you would want these quotations to have the same paragraph formatting. Styles cannot solve all formatting issues. With quotes, you must enter them since a style does not include these characters. See the box "Rules for Quotes" about when you need to add quotes to a document.

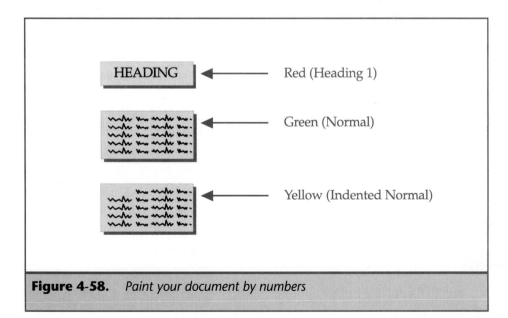

Figure 4-58.   *Paint your document by numbers*

Rules for Quotes

Quotation marks are always used around direct quotes but are never used for indirect quotes or paraphrased remarks. Here are some additional rules that commonly apply to the use of quotes.

- Enclose unfamiliar jargon in quotes, as in: Our networked guru even managed to "crash" the system.

- Misspelled words and slang, as in: Tommy's first grade teacher has been correcting his use of "ain't."

- Words that indicated stamping or marking, as in: the package was marked "Undeliverable."

- The definition of a word in italics, as in: *Multimedia* is "the creative combination of text, graphics, audio, and animation."

- Enclose chapter titles and magazine articles in quotes.

- Use single quotes within a quotation to mark text normally in quotation marks, as in: Sally said, "I just finished reading 'Sailing on the Great Lakes' in the *Forever Sailing* magazine and wondered if you would like to borrow it."

- Alternate between single and double quotes when quotes are nested, as in: Tonya said, "I was offended when Jim said, 'You have been wasting too much time repackaging parcels marked "Undeliverable"' and decided not to work late any more this week."

Procedures

Applying Styles with the Formatting Toolbar

1. Select the text to apply the style to.
2. Click on the Style drop-down list box on the Formatting toolbar.

TIP: In Word for Windows 6, press CTRL+SHIFT+S *to activate the Style drop-down list box. In Word for Windows 2, press* CTRL+S.

3. Select a style by double-clicking it or by highlighting it and pressing ENTER.

TIP: *In Word for Windows 6, paragraph style names in the Style list box are bold, while character style names are not.*

Applying Styles with the Menu

1. Select the text you want to format with the style.

2. Select Format | Style.

TIP: *Press* CTRL+S *twice in Word for Windows 2.*

3. Select a style name from the Styles list box (Style Name in Word for Windows 2).

4. Select Apply.

Creating Paragraph Styles with the Formatting Toolbar

1. Select text with formatting you want to save as a style.

2. Click on the Style box in the Formatting toolbar.

TIP: *Press* CTRL+SHIFT+S *in Word for Windows 6, or* CTRL+S *in Word for Windows 2, to activate the Style list box.*

3. Type a name for the style.

4. Click outside the Style list box, or press ENTER.

Creating Styles with the Menu

1. To create a paragraph style using formatting already applied to a paragraph, select that paragraph. When creating a character style in Word for Windows 6, do not select any text.

2. Select Format | Style.

TIP: Press CTRL+S *twice in Word for Windows 2.*

3. In Word for Windows 2, type a name for the style in the Style Name text box.

TIP: In Word for Windows 6, you can now create the style using the selected paragraph by typing the name in the Styles text box and selecting Apply.

4. Select New (Define in Word for Windows 2).

5. In Word for Windows 6, type a name for the new style in the Name text box.

6. In Word for Windows 6, select Character or Paragraph from the Style Type list box to set the type of style. If you selected text before starting to create the style, you can create only a paragraph style.

7. To use another style as the basis for this one, select the base style in the Based On drop-down list box.

    For example, to create a style named "Bibliography" that is the same as the Normal style, except that it has a shadow-box border and uses a larger font size, select Normal in the Based On drop-down list box and change those two formatting settings.

8. To apply a different style to paragraphs following paragraphs formatted with the style you are creating, select a style from the Style for Following Paragraph (Next Style in Word for Windows 2) list box.

    For example, if you create a style called "Section Head," you know that the paragraph after each section head is to be formatted with the style First Text. Select First Text in the Style for Following Paragraph list box (Next Style in Word for Windows 2). When you press ENTER ending a paragraph formatted with Section Head, the new paragraph is automatically formatted with First Text.

9. Select an option from the Format menu or, in Word for Windows 2, a button under Change Formatting to set the formats for the style. You can select Font (Character in Word for Windows 2), Paragraph, Tabs, Border, Language, Frame, and, in Word for Windows 6, Numbering. Character styles in Word for Windows 6 have only Font and Language. The dialog boxes that are opened are the same ones you use when formatting text directly.

10. For styles you use frequently, assign a shortcut key combination you can use to apply that style.

    In Word for Windows 6, select Shortcut Key, then highlight the style under Commands. With the insertion point in the Press New Shortcut Key text box, press the keys you want to use to apply the style. Select Close to return to the New Style dialog box.

    In Word for Windows 2, select or clear the Ctrl and Shift check boxes and then select a key from Key drop-down list box to construct a shortcut key.

11. Select the Add to Template check box to add the style you are creating to the document's template. Adding the style to the template makes it available to all documents created using that template. Adding a style to the Normal template makes it available to all documents.

12. Select OK (Add in Word for Windows 2) to add the style you just created to the document.

13. You can now create more styles by following steps 4 through 12.

14. Select Apply to close the dialog box and apply the highlighted style to the current paragraph. Select Cancel to close the dialog box and return to the document without applying a style to the text, and without losing the new style.

Editing Styles

1. Select Format | Style.

2. Highlight style in the Styles (Style Name in Word for Windows 2) list box.

3. Select Modify (Define in Word for Windows 2).

4. Change the formatting for the style as if you were creating the style. (The steps for changing formatting assigned to a style are described above under "Creating Styles with the Menu.")

5. Select OK (Change in Word for Windows 2).

6. Create or edit additional styles, or select Apply to apply the current style to the selected text, or select Cancel to simply close the dialog box.

Removing Styles

You can delete a style from a document.

1. Select Format | Style.

2. Highlight the style's name in the Styles (Style Name in Word for Windows 2) list box.

3. In Word for Windows 2, select Define.

4. Select Delete.

5. When Word prompts you asking whether you actually want to delete the style, select Yes.

6. Close the dialog box to return to the document, or continue creating or modifying other styles.

Renaming Styles

1. Select Format | Style, opening the Style dialog box.

2. Select the style's name in the Styles (Style Name in Word for Windows 2) list box.

3. Select Modify (Define in Word for Windows 2).

4. In Word for Windows 2, select Rename.

5. Type the style's new name in the Name (New Style Name in Word for Windows 2) text box.

6. Select OK.

7. Close the Style dialog box to return to the document, or continue creating and modifying other styles.

Copying Styles Between Documents in Word for Windows 6

To copy styles between documents in Word for Windows 6, use the Organizer feature. You can copy documents between any two documents or templates, regardless of which file is open when you open the Organizer.

1. Select Format | Style.

2. Select Organizer.

3. By default the In and To list boxes show the styles available in the current document and its template.

    When you want to copy styles between some other documents, select the Close File button under that list box, then select the Open File button and select the file to use.

4. Highlight the styles to copy.

5. Select Copy.

6. Select OK.

TIP: There are other uses for the Organizer. See "Organizer" for a full explanation of this feature.

Copying Styles from a Template in Word for Windows 6

Word for Windows 6 offers a new feature that lets you preview what your current document would look like with styles from various templates and then copies styles from a specific template into the current document.

1. Format your document with styles. Use the styles included with your template.

2. Select Format | Style Gallery.

3. Highlight a template in the Template list box. The Preview box shows how your document would look, formatted with that template's styles.

If you want to see an example document or a listing of the styles displaying their format, select Example or Style Samples instead of Document under Preview.

4. Select Browse to specify another directory containing templates that you might want to use.

5. Select OK to copy the highlighted template's styles into the current document, or Cancel to close the dialog box without copying the styles.

Copying Styles Between Documents in Word for Windows 2

You can copy styles between other documents or templates and the current document.

1. Open the documents or templates between other documents and the current document you want to copy styles.

2. Select Format | Style, opening the Style dialog box.

3. Select Define to display the formatting dialog box elements.

4. Select Merge, opening the Merge Styles dialog box.

5. Select a document or template file that you want to copy styles from or to using the File Name, Directories, Drives and Type boxes.

TIP: *If you are copying styles from the current document to its template, you do not need to select a filename.*

6. Select From Template to copy from the selected file to the current document. Select To Template to copy from the current document to the selected file.

7. Word warns you that styles in the target document or template are about to be replaced by the styles in the template or document you are copying from. Select Yes to continue copying styles, or No to stop the process.

8. Word returns you to the Style dialog box. You can continue to create and modify styles or close the dialog box.

Hints

To make working with styles easier, you can use style aliases or style families. Word automatically comes with several styles that Word applies to certain texts, such as footnotes, for you. You can display the paragraph style names in the margin.

Style Names

In Word for Windows 6, your full style name can be up to 253 characters long but cannot include a backslash(\), braces([]), or semicolon(;). Word does not distinguish between uppercase and lowercase letters in style names.

In Word for Windows 2, style names can be up to 20 characters long. You can use any character in a filename except for a backslash (\).

ADDING ALIASES TO STYLE NAMES (WORD FOR WINDOWS 6 ONLY)   In Word for Windows 6, you can provide short names, or *aliases*, for styles by typing a comma and the short name following the full name in the Name text box. This short name will appear in the Style list box or in the Style bar at the side of your document. You can then type the alias in the Style drop-down box to invoke that style.

Style Families

You can create families of styles that are based on the same style. Creating families of styles makes it easy to keep your document looking organized.

For example, you could create a style for the body text of your document that uses the font Arial at 10 points. You can then create styles for figure captions, tables, sidebars, headings, table of contents, and indexes that are based on this body text style which use the same font. If you change the font of the body text style to Times Roman, then all of these other styles change to Times Roman. Doing this maintains a uniform appearance throughout your document.

Standard Styles

Word has some standard styles that it automatically applies to certain types of text, such as tables of contents and footnotes. When you look at the Style box on the Formatting toolbar or the Styles (Style Name in Word for Windows 2) list box in the Style dialog box, you do not normally see these styles. However, you can modify these styles just as you can styles that you create.

To display these additional styles in Word for Windows 6, press SHIFT before clicking the arrow for the Style button in the Formatting toolbar, or select All Styles in the List drop-down list box in the Style dialog box.

To display these styles in Word for Windows 2, press CTRL+Y with the insertion point in the Style Name drop-down list box in the Style dialog box. After you press CTRL+Y, these further style names are displayed in this dialog box. Until you apply the style to text in the document, the style does not appear in the Style box on the ribbon.

Many of these styles are applied automatically, such as the styles for annotation text, captions, and index entries. Others, such as the Headings styles, you can apply.

Seeing Style Names in Your Document

When you use styles often, you may want an easier way to see which paragraph uses which styles. To do this, display the style names in a style area on the left side of your document in the normal view. To do this, select Tools | Options, select the View tab or icon, and enter a measurement in the Style Area Width text box. To remove the style area, reduce this measurement to zero. A style area is shown in Figure 4-59. Reducing the Style Area Width to 0 removes the style names.

Figure 4-59. *A style area displays style names*

Related Topics

AutoFormat
Organizer
Outlines

SUBJECT Field

The SUBJECT field returns the contents of the Subject document summary information. See "Fields."

Subscript

See "Super/Subscript."

Summary Info

Word stores summary information about each document you create. This includes information about when the file was created and last saved as well as statistics about the file's contents.

Procedures

1. Select File | Summary Info.

2. To add or edit summary information, make changes in the Title, Subject, Author, Keywords, and Comments text boxes, described under "Options" below. The information included in these text boxes should reflect characteristics of the document, making it easier to find if you should forget its filename.

3. To view the statistics about the document, select the Statistics button.

4. In Word for Windows 2, select Update to update the Statistics dialog box, which by default is updated each time you save or close the document. In Word for Windows 6, this dialog box is automatically updated when you open it.

5. Select OK to return to the Summary Info dialog box.

6. Select OK again to return to the document.

Options

The options for document summary information sets the document information Word retains with the document. The only setting you cannot change is the document statistics that Word calculates for you.

Title

Enter the title of your document in the Title text box.

Subject

Enter the subject of your document in the Subject text box.

Author

Word automatically includes the user name as the author name of your document. If you use the File Sharing features in Word for Windows 2 when you save the document, do not change this entry or you will be unable to edit the document later. If this is not a concern, you can edit the name of the author in the Author text box.

Keywords

Enter some of the document's keywords in the Keywords text box. Keywords are those that will help you identify the document quickly, such as the name of the addressee of a letter, or a product name or invoice number. Word will search documents for words entered as keywords to find a file you want.

Comments

Enter comments about the document in the Comments text box. Use this text box to provide clarifying information distinctly describing the document. A very specific description in this text box will make it easier to locate the precise file you want when you use the File | Find File command.

Statistics

Selecting the Statistics command button opens the Document Statistics dialog box, which shows you information about your document, including the amount of time spent editing it, how many times it has been saved, when it was last printed, and the number of characters, words, and pages it contains.

Hints

When your documents include summary information, you can use this information in different ways. You can print it separately from a document; you can insert it into a document through fields; and you can search for specific information to select the files you want to work with. To make sure a document includes summary information, you can tell Word when you save a document to prompt you for this information.

Printing Summary Info

You can print a document's summary info with the document or alone. To print a document's summary information, select Summary Info from the Print What list box in the Print dialog box. To print the Summary Info along with the document it describes, select the Summary Info check box in the Print tab of the Options dialog box.

Inserting Summary Info into the Document

You can insert items of Summary Info into your document using fields. These field codes insert the correct information from the Summary Info dialog box into your document. For further information on this feature see "Fields."

Prompting for Summary Info

By default, you have to select File | Summary Info to open the Summary Info dialog box. You can also set Word to prompt you to add summary information the first time you save a document.

To do this, open the Options dialog box by selecting Tools | Options, then selecting the Save tab or icon, and then selecting the Prompt for Summary Info check box. The first time you save each document, Word opens the Summary Info dialog box so that you can fill it in. If you do not want to supply summary information for a particular document, you can press ESC to close the dialog box and save the document.

Finding Documents

You can use summary information with the File | Find File command to find a document whose filename you have forgotten. See "File Management" for a full explanation of how to use this command.

Related Topics

Fields
File Management

Super/Subscript

Superscripted text appears above the line of the text and is used for marking footnotes and for exponents and other mathematical symbols. Subscript appears below the line of the text and is used in mathematical and scientific formulas as shown here:

$$a^2 \times b^2 = c^2 \text{ or } H_2O$$

Procedures

The Superscript or Subscript formats can be applied as the text is being typed or after it is typed. To apply these formats while typing, add the format, type the text, then remove the format. To apply it to typed text, select the text and add the format.

Adding and Removing Superscript or Subscript with the Menus in Word for Windows 6

1. Select Format | Font.

2. Select the Superscript or Subscript check box.

   By default, superscript or subscript text moves the baseline of the formatted text up or down three points.

3. Select the Character Spacing tab if you want to change how much of the text is superscript or subscript.

4. Select Raised (superscript) or Lowered (subscript) from the Position drop-down list box.

   Select Normal to return to the normal amount of superscripting or subscripting.

5. Enter the measurement in points in the By spin box. This measurement is how far the baseline of the formatted text is raised or lowered from the normal baseline.

6. Select OK.

Adding and Removing Superscript or Subscript with the Menus in Word for Windows 2

1. Select Format | Character.

2. In the Super/Subscript drop-down list box, select either Superscript or Subscript.

3. In the By text box, enter the number of points away from the baseline of text you want the formatted text moved.

4. Select OK.

Adding and Removing with Shortcut Keys

- Press CTRL+SHIFT++ to make text superscript.

- Press CTRL+= to make text subscript.

Related Topics

Equations
Spacing

Superscript

See "Super/Subscript."

Switches

See "Fields."

SYMBOL Field

The SYMBOL field inserts a symbol or a string of characters. See "Fields" and "Special Characters."

TA Field

See "Table of Authorities."

Table Columns

See "Tables."

Table Commands

The Table commands all relate to working with tables, with the exception of the Table | Sort command in Word for Windows 6. All of the table commands are described under "Tables", while the Word for Windows 6 Table | Sort command, which can be used to sort tables or text outside of a table, is described under "Sorting".

Table of Authorities

A table of authorities is used in legal briefs to list all citations of court decisions. The citations are normally sorted by different sources of legal authority, such as the Supreme Court, federal courts, state courts, federal laws and regulations, state laws and regulations, and legal commentary. Figure 4-61 shows an example of a very brief table of authorities. Word for Windows 6 offers a new feature that makes creating tables of authorities simple. Simply mark the citations in the text, assign them to a particular category, and then tell Word where to create the table.

The table of authorities feature does not appear in Word for Windows 2, although Microsoft offers a Legal Resource Kit free of charge that will install table of authorities macros. You can also create a table of authorities in Word for Windows 2 by using the SEQ and Reference fields (see "Fields" for more information on these).

Procedures

The following procedures indicate how to create and update tables of authorities in your document. When creating a table of authorities, you must first mark all the citations you want to include in the table, assigning each citation to the appropriate category. Then you insert the table and update it. You can modify the available categories to customize this feature to your needs.

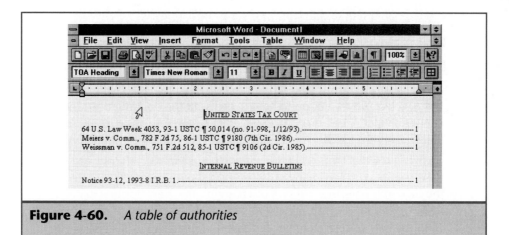

Figure 4-60. *A table of authorities*

Marking Citations

1. Select the first citation in the document.

   The first time a particular case or authority is cited in the text of a brief, it should be cited in the long form, which includes all necessary information for a reader to locate the source. When the same case or authority is cited later in your brief, it should be in the short form, such as *Kramer v. Kramer*, which lets the reader know to which previously cited case or authority the reference is being made.

2. Press ALT+SHIFT+I, or select Insert | Index and Tables, the Table of Authorities tab, and Mark Citation. The selected text appears in the Selected Text box and the Short Citation text box.

3. Edit the text in the Selected Text box to match how you want the long citation to appear in your table of authorities.

   TIP: You can include formatting features such as bold and underlining by using the shortcut keys.

4. Select Category and then the category you want to assign this citation to in the Category list box.

5. Edit the text in the Short Citation text box to match the short citations you have entered in the document.

6. Choose what you want Word to do with this citation.

- Select <u>M</u>ark to mark this particular occurrence of the citation.

- Select Mark <u>A</u>ll to have Word search for all appearances of the text in the <u>S</u>hort Citation text box, and mark all of them as citations.

7. Either select <u>N</u>ext Citation to have Word scan the document for the next citation, which Word recognizes because it contains "in re" or other terms usually found in citations, or select Cancel to quit marking citations.

If you see the TA field, Word is displaying the field codes rather than their results. You can change the codes to show the results by selecting the field and pressing SHIFT+F9 or changing the view options to not display field codes.

Modifying Categories

Word lets you use up to 16 categories of citation in a table of authorities. The first seven are already assigned names: Cases, Statutes, Other Authorities, Rules, Treatises, Regulations, and Constitutional Provisions, while the remaining ones are simply assigned numbers. You can change the names of any of the 16 categories to reflect the types of citations you need to include in your table of authorities.

1. In the Mark Citations dialog box, select Cate<u>g</u>ory.

2. Highlight the category in the <u>C</u>ategory list box.

3. Type a new name in the Replace <u>W</u>ith text box.

4. Select <u>R</u>eplace.

5. Continue until you have renamed all of the categories you need to, then select OK.

Inserting the Table of Authorities

1. Put the insertion point where you want to insert your table of authorities. If you are putting the table of authorities on the first page of a document, you may want a section break after the table of authorities so you can change the beginning number of the subsequent page to 1.

2. Select <u>I</u>nsert | Inde<u>x</u> and Tables.

3. Select the Table of <u>A</u>uthorities tab.

4. Select a format in the Formats list box. The effect of this format on a sample table is shown in the Preview box.

5. Clear the Use Passim check box if you do not want Word substituting "passim" for any page references with more than five references.

6. Clear the Keep Original Formatting check box to allow Word to override the formatting in the citation with the formatting applied with this feature.

7. Select the category to show tables for in the Category drop-down list box. You can insert tables for all categories or for any one category.

8. Select a tab leader from the Tab Leader drop-down list box to set the type of line between the citation and the page references.

9. Select Modify with Custom Style highlighted in the Formats list box to create a new format.

   Word formats your table of authorities by applying one style (TOA Headings) to the headings for each table, and a second style (Table of Authorities) to the citation and page references. After selecting Modify, you can modify these styles just as you would any other style. See "Styles" for instructions on modifying styles.

10. Select OK to insert your tables.

Updating a Table of Authorities

1. Select Insert | Index and Tables.

2. Select the Table of Authorities tab.

3. Select OK.

4. When Word asks if you really want to replace the current table, select Yes.

TIP: *A shortcut for updating your table is to put your insertion point in the table and press F9.*

Hints

Always mark citations for your tables of authorities after finishing the editing on your document, so that you are sure you've included all citations. Also, this gives you one last check that the first citation is in fact the long citation.

When you mark citations, Word inserts a TA type field. If you delete the citation, make sure that you also delete this field. To change how a citation's long or short form will appear, edit the TA field in the document, as described under "Fields." When you insert a table of authorities in your document, Word inserts a TOA type field. You can edit your table directly, but you will have to reenter all of your corrections after updating the table.

TA Fields

Word for Windows 6 marks text for tables of authorities with the {TA [*switches*]} field, which marks the text and sets the form of the table entry.

\B   The \b switch makes the page number in the table entry bold.

\C   The \c switch sets the category the entry belongs to.

\I   The \i switch makes the page number of the table entry italicized.

\L   The \l switch sets the text of the long form of the citation.

\R   The \r switch includes the range of pages marked with the given bookmark in the table entry.

\S   The \s switch sets the short citation form.

TOA Fields

TOA fields, which use the format {TOA [*switches*]}, insert a table of authorities in your document compiled from TA fields in your document.

\B   The \b switch compiles the table from the part of the document marked with the given bookmark.

\C   The \c switch sets the categories of entries for which tables are inserted.

\D   The \d switch defines the characters separating a sequence number and a page number and is used with the \s switch.

\E   The \e switch sets the characters that separate a table entry and its page number.

\F   Use the \f switch to remove the formatting applied to table entries in the document, so that table entries use the formatting of the table styles only.

\G   The \g switch sets the characters with separate page numbers in a page range.

\H   Use the \h switch to include the category as a heading for the table.

\L   Use the \l switch to set the characters separating page numbers when the entry has several page references.

\P   The \p switch uses "passim" as the page reference when there are five or more page references for a single entry.

\S   Use the \s switch to include a sequence number with the page number.

Related Topics

Fields
Styles

Table of Contents and Figures

You can create tables of contents using text marked with styles or fields. In Word for Windows 6, you can create tables of figures or other objects in your document for which you inserted captions.

Procedures

The following procedures explain how to create a table of contents, or, in Word for Windows 6 only, how to create a table of figures using text marked with styles. The final procedure also explains how you can mark table of contents or table of figures entries with fields.

Creating a Table of Contents

1. Put your insertion point where you want the table of contents.
2. Select Insert | Index and Tables (Table of Contents in Word for Windows 2).
3. Select the Table of Contents tab in Word for Windows 6.

T

4. Select the options in Word for Windows 6 that determine how the table looks:

   - Select a format for the table of contents from the Formats list box. A sample table of contents using these styles appears in the Preview box. If you highlight Custom Styles in this list box, you can select Modify and create new styles for each level in the table of contents.

   - Clear the Show Page Numbers check box if you don't want to include page numbers in your table of contents.

   - Clear the Right Align Page Numbers check box to have page numbers appear after the heading separated by a space.

   - Select the number of levels to appear in the table of contents in the Show Levels spin box.

   - Choose a tab leader from the Tab Leader drop-down list box to stretch from the entry to the page number.

5. Select the source of the table of contents entries. To use text marked with TC type fields as entries in your table of contents, select Options and Table Entry Fields. To use paragraphs formatted with specific styles as entries in your table of contents, select Options and Styles (Use Heading Paragraphs in Word for Windows 2).

   In Word for Windows 6, select a style to include by entering the level it uses in the table of contents in the TOC Level box after the style's name. All heading styles and all styles used in the document appear in this list.

   In Word for Windows 2, select All to use all heading styles in the table of contents, or enter the highest and lowest level styles to use in the From and To spin boxes. You can use only Word's nine built-in heading styles for table of content entries in Word for Windows 2.

6. Select OK twice (once for Word for Windows 2).

Creating a Table of Figures in Word for Windows 6

1. Put your insertion point where you want the table.

2. Select Insert | Index and Tables.

3. Select the Table of Figures tab.

4. Select the caption label you are creating a table for from the Caption Label list box.

5. Select a set of styles to use from the Formats list box. A sample table shows the effect of these styles in the Preview box. Highlight Custom Style and select Modify to create a new set of styles.

6. Clear the Show Page Numbers check box if you don't want to include page numbers in your table.

7. Clear the Right Align Page Numbers check box to have page numbers appear after the entry separated by a space.

8. Clear the Include Label and Number check box to keep Word from including the caption label and number in the table entry.

9. Choose a tab leader from the Tab Leader drop-down list box to stretch from the entry to the page number.

10. Select Options to set which entries the table is compiled from.

   ■ Select Style and then choose a style from the list box. The table is compiled using text marked with this style.

   ■ Select Table Entry Fields to compile the table from TC fields that use a specific identifier after the \f switch. Select a code that identifies the fields you want to use in this table from the Table Identifier list box. For example, if you leave the default of F, Word compiles the table of figures using TC fields that have the switch of \f F.

11. Select OK twice.

Adding Table of Contents Entries Using Fields

1. Move to the text you want for the table of contents entry or select the text if you do not want to use the entire paragraph.

2. Press ALT+SHIFT+O. The dialog box shows the paragraph's text or selected text as the table of contents entry.

3. Change the text to match the table of contents entry if you want something different than the current contents of the Entry text box.

4. Set the table identifier by selecting a letter from the Table Identifier drop-down list box. You can use different table identifiers to create separate tables of contents for different identifiers.

5. Set the table of contents level for the entry you are creating by selecting a number in the Level text box.

6. Select Mark to create the table of contents entry.

Hints

You can mark text with a TC field to include it in a table of contents, or create your table of contents with certain text styles. When you insert a caption, you insert a SEQ field, and you can use this field to create tables of figures.

TC

The TC field marks text for compiling into a table of contents or figures. It uses the format {TC "*text*" [*switches*]}. *Text* is the text to appear in the table. Nest an REF field to actually include document text.

\F   The \f switch marks the entry with a table identifier, which can be used to include the entry in only one table.

\L   The \l switch assigns a level to the table entry.

\N   The \n switch prevents the page number for this entry from appearing (Word for Windows 6 only).

TOC

The TOC field type collects TC entries or text marked with a particular style for a table of contents or other list. The field uses the format {TOC "*switches*"}.

TIP: Before updating a TOC field, hide your field codes so that the pagination is correct.

\A   The \a switch compiles the table without using caption labels or numbers.

\B   The \b switch compiles a table from entries in the part of your document marked with the bookmark.

\C   The \c switch compiles the table using SEQ fields with a specific table identifier. SEQ fields are inserted when you create a caption.

\D   The \d switch sets the characters used to separate sequence numbers and page numbers. Sequence numbers are added with the \s switch.

\F   The \f switch compiles a table using only TC entries with the given table identifier.

\L   The \l switch compiles a table using only TC entries with the levels given.

\O   The \o switch compiles a table using text formatted with the built-in heading styles given.

\P   The \p switch sets the character separating a table entry and its page number.

\S   The \s switch compiles a table using the sequence given, or a table that includes the sequence number.

\T   The \t switch creates a table using the styles given.

Related Topics

Fields
Outlines
Table of Authorities

Table of Contents with Fields

See "Table of Contents and Figures."

Table of Contents with Headings

See "Table of Contents and Figures."

Table of Figures

See "Table of Contents and Figures."

Tables

Tables are ways to arrange text. They consist of cells arranged in rows and columns, as can be seen in Figure 4-60. Text, numbers, or graphics can be entered into the cells. You can carry out mathematical calculations with numbers entered into cells, very much as you do with spreadsheet programs. Word for Windows 6 offers a new feature for formatting tables quickly, the Table AutoFormat feature.

In Figure 4-60 you can see how a table can arrange text in a readable fashion. You can also use tables when creating on-line or printed forms.

There is a long list of procedures for different operations you can do with tables. This long list does not mean that tables are difficult to understand or use, just that there is a great deal of flexibility in what you use tables to do, and how you carry out operations with the table.

Procedures

The following procedures will explain how to work with a table. They include steps for inserting tables and converting between text and a table, as well as

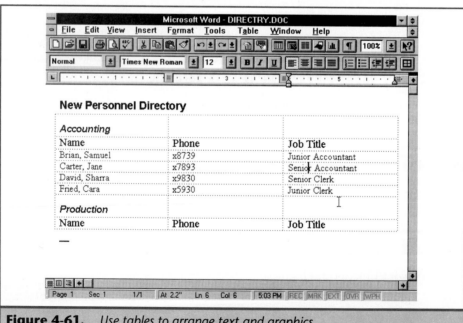

Figure 4-61.   *Use tables to arrange text and graphics*

steps for moving and selecting in a table. There are also procedures for inserting formulas for doing math in a table. Steps for adding or removing cells from a table are explained, along with how to split and merge cells and tables. You will learn how to format the rows and columns of a table, to display or hide gridlines, and to apply a set table format.

Inserting a Table with the Menu

1. Put the insertion point where you want a table.

2. Select Table | Insert Table.

   You can skip the following steps in Word for Windows 6 by using Wizard. The Table Wizard helps you create a formatted table by prompting you for information about how you want the table laid out. You can select Back or Next to move between the dialog boxes in the Wizard, and select Finish when you want it to insert the table.

3. Enter the number of columns you want for the table in the Number of Columns text box.

4. Enter the number of rows you want for the table in the Number of Rows text box. The default is 2 (1 in Word for Windows 2). You can easily add more rows, so this number does not need to be final.

5. Enter the columns' width in the Column Width text box. With Auto, the default, Word spaces the columns across the page.

   In Word for Windows 6, you can use the AutoFormat feature to format the table. This feature is discussed below.

6. Select OK.

Inserting a Table with the Toolbar

1. Put the insertion point where you want a table.

2. Click the Insert Table button on the Standard toolbar, and Word displays a grid pattern, as shown on the next page.

3. Drag across the grid so that the number of rows and columns you want in your table are highlighted, then release the mouse button.

Moving in a Table

Moving in a table is a little different than moving in normal text. You can move through a table quickly using the key presses shown in Table 4-26 or by clicking in the cell you want to move to with the mouse.

Converting Text to a Table

1. Select the text to convert into a table, making sure there are no hard page breaks selected, as well as having tabs or commas separating the data you want in separate columns.

2. Select Table | Convert Text to Table or click the Table button in the Standard toolbar.

Press	To Move to
TAB	The next cell
SHIFT+TAB	The previous cell
ALT+HOME	The first cell of the current row
ALT+END	The last cell in the current row
UP ARROW	The previous row
DOWN ARROW	The following row
ALT+PAGE UP	The first cell in the current column
ALT+PAGE DOWN	The last cell in the current column

Table 4-26.   *Keystrokes for Moving in a Table*

In Word for Windows 2, if Word clearly understands the division between sections of data, it automatically creates the table and splits the information into cells. The dialog box described in step 3 appears only if Word is not sure how to divide cells.

3. Tell Word how the text breaks into separate cells. Select Paragraphs, Tabs, or Commas to indicate where you want the information divided. In Word for Windows 6 you can also select Other, and provide a character used to divide the text, such as a slash or quotes.

 In Word for Windows 6, you can also set the total number of columns in your table and the column width and use the AutoFormat feature to format the table, as described under "Inserting a Table with the Menu" above.

4. Select OK. The entry in each cell in the new table ends at the character selected in the dialog box.

Converting a Table to Text

1. Select the rows of the table you want to make into text. The Table | Select Table command described below quickly selects all of the table.

2. Select Table | Convert Table to Text.

3. Tell Word how you want to divide the separate cells. Select Paragraphs, Tabs, or Commas to divide cells with paragraph breaks, tabs, or commas. In Word for Windows 6 you can also select Other, and provide a character used to divide the text, such as a slash or quotes.

4. Select OK. The entry in each cell now is separated by the character you selected in step 3.

Selecting in a Table

When you select a cell, row, column, or table, the entire table element is highlighted, not just the text or graphics within the cell.

SELECTING A CELL

■ Drag across the entire cell, including the end of cell character.

■ Click in the cell's selection bar at the left edge of the cell.

■ Move to the cell by pressing TAB, selecting all the text in the cell. Press SHIFT+RIGHT ARROW to include the end of cell character. When you display nonprinting characters, at the end of every cell is an end of cell character.

SELECTING A ROW

■ Click in the selection bar to the left of the row.

■ Double-click the selection bar of a cell in the row.

■ Select Table | Select Row with the insertion point in a cell of the row to select.

■ Drag the mouse across the entire row to include the end of row character to the right of the table's edge. When you display nonprinting characters, each cell has an end of cell character, and the same character appears at the end of the row as an end of row character.

SELECTING A COLUMN

■ Put the mouse above the column and click when the mouse pointer looks like a down-pointing arrow.

■ Drag the mouse across the entire column.

■ Select Table | Select Column with the insertion point in a cell in the column to select.

■ In Word for Windows 2, right click a cell in the column you want to select.

SELECTING A TABLE

■ Drag across all the columns or rows in the table, including the end of row characters.

■ Select Table | Select Table with the insertion point in the table.

■ Press ALT+5 (on the numeric keypad with Num Lock off) with the insertion point inside the table you want to select.

Inserting Formulas in a Table (Word for Windows 6)

1. Move to the cell you want the formula in.

2. Select Table | Formula. Word analyzes your table and may present a formula. If not, the Formula text box displays only an equal sign (=). The = is for the = field that you can use to create evaluated expressions (described under "Fields").

TIP: Word automatically provides a SUM formula if Word decides you are in a cell which, given the table layout, would logically sum values above or on the side. This SUM formula is sometimes called AutoSum, since it automatically appears.

3. Enter a formula using the four standard operators or by selecting a function in the Paste Function drop-down list box and inserting that function in the Formula text box. (The *standard operators* are + for addition, – for subtraction, * for multiplication and / for division.) Functions added with Paste Function drop-down list box are added to the Formula text box rather than replacing any existing function or operator. Cells can be referenced by cell names or bookmarks.

   Cell names are a combination of the number and letter assigned to each cell. Columns are labeled left to right starting with letter A. Rows are numbered from the top starting with 1. For example, in a table with five rows and three columns, the bottom right cell has the cell name C5. When you have multiple cells that you want in a formula, separate the cell names with commas, as in B2,B3. When you want a range or block of cells in the table in a formula, enter the cell name of the cell in the first row and column, then a colon, and then the cell name of the cell in the last row and column. For example B3:D4 includes cells B3, C3, D3, B4, C4, and D4.

4. Select a format for the formula result in the Number Format drop-down list box.

5. Select OK to insert the formula. Unless you have Word set to display field codes, the result of your formula will appear in the cell.

TIP: In Word for Windows 2, use the (Expression) field type to perform limited mathematical calculations in tables. See "Fields" to learn about the (Expression) field type.

Adding Cells to a Table

1. Mark where and how many cells you want to insert. Select a row or column below or to the right of where you want to insert another row or column. If you select multiple rows or columns, that is the number that will be inserted. To insert cells, select the number of cells to insert.

TIP: If you select nothing, you can insert any number of rows in Word for Windows 6, or any number of cells in Word for Windows 2.

2. Select Table | Insert Cells/Rows/Columns, or click the Table button in the Standard toolbar.

   If you selected rows or columns, they are simply inserted. If you selected a cell or cells, you must now select how those cells are inserted.

3. Select Insert Entire Row or Insert Entire Column to insert complete rows or columns. Select Shift Cells Right to insert the cells to the left of the selected cells while leaving the cells in the other rows in place. Select Shift Cells Down to insert the cells above the selected cells while leaving the other cells in the other columns in place. You will insert as many rows or columns as you selected cells in.

4. Select OK.

   TIP: *Press TAB in the last cell of a table to add a new last row.*

Deleting Cells from a Table

1. Select the cell, row, or column you want to delete. To delete the entire table, select the entire table.

2. Select Delete Cells/Row/Columns.

   If you selected rows, columns, or the entire table, they are now deleted. If you selected one or more cells, you must now tell Word how to delete them.

3. Select Shift Cells Left to delete only the selected cells and move those to the right into their place. Select Shift Cells Up to delete the selected cells and move the ones below up into their place. Select Delete Entire Row or Delete Entire Column to delete complete rows or columns. You will delete as many rows or columns as you selected cells in.

4. Select OK.

Setting Row Options

1. Select the row or rows to format.

2. Select Table | Cell Height and Width (Row Height in Word For Windows 2). In Word for Windows 6, the Row tab should be selected.

3. Select an option in the Height drop-down list box to set how the row height is determined.

   With Auto, the default, Word varies the row height to match the row's contents. Select At Least to enter a minimum height for the cell in the At text box. Select Exactly to enter the exact row height in the At text box. If the contents cannot fit in this height cell, you will not see that part that doesn't fit.

4. Enter how far the row should be indented from the left margin in the Indent From Left test box. This sets the cell's position rather than the indentation of the text within the cell.

5. Select an alignment, Left, Center, or Right to align the row with the page's margins.

6. To change settings for other rows, select Previous Row or Next Row. Select OK when you are finished changing settings.

Setting Column Width Options

1. Select the column or columns whose width you want to set.

   In Word for Windows 2, if you want to change the space between columns, you should select the rows for which you want to the change the space between columns.

2. Select Table I Cell Height and Width (Column Width in Word for Windows 2). In Word for Windows 6, the Column tab should be selected.

3. Enter the column's width in the Width for Column # text box. Select AutoFit to let Word select the column width.

4. Enter a measurement in the Space Between Columns text box.

5. Select Previous Column or Next Column to change these settings for other columns, or select OK when you are finished.

Setting Column Width with the Mouse

You can change the width of table columns using the mouse and the gridlines or the ruler.

- Drag the column gridline using the mouse.
- Drag the column marker on the ruler to a new location.

- Press SHIFT and drag the column gridline to the right of the selected cell or group of cells to resize those columns without resizing the entire table.

- Press CTRL and drag the column gridlines to the right of the selected cell or group of cells to resize the selected columns and the columns to the right.

Merging Cells

1. Select two or more cells on the same row to merge together.

2. Select Table | Merge Cells. Word merges the cells, as shown below. If the cells have contents, each cell's contents are separated with a paragraph mark. The merged cell is considered part of the column that the first selected cell is in.

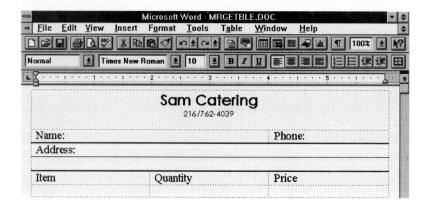

Splitting Cells

1. Select the cells you want to split. In Word for Windows 2, only cells that were merged can be split.

2. Select Table | Split Cell.

   In Word for Windows 2, Word splits the merged cell into the original cells, separating its contents at the paragraph marks.

3. In Word for Windows 6, enter how many columns you want the cell broken into and select OK.

Word for Windows 6 also breaks the text between the new cells at the paragraph mark. If there is only one, all the text appears in the first cell.

Merging Tables

Merge two tables by deleting any text or paragraph marks between the two tables.

Splitting a Table

1. Put the insertion point in the first cell of the planned second table.

2. Select Table | Split Table or press CTRL+SHIFT+ENTER. Word inserts a paragraph mark between the two tables.

Using Table AutoFormat in Word for Windows 6

1. Select Table | Table AutoFormat with the insertion point within the table you want to format.

   You can also start the Table AutoFormat feature by selecting AutoFormat in the Insert Table dialog box while inserting the table.

2. Select a set of formats from the Formats list box. These formats will be displayed in the Preview box with sample data.

3. Select the formatting features you want to use under Formats to Apply.

   You can choose to remove the Border, Shading, Font, Color or AutoFit formats. AutoFit sizes the columns to match the widest text they contain. For example, if you clear Font, your table is not specially formatted with the font saved with that format.

4. Select where you want special formatting applied under Apply Special Formats To.

   Special formats are applied to Heading Rows, the First Column, the Last Column, or the Last Row. When you clear one of these check boxes, that row or column uses the same formatting as the other rows or columns in the table.

5. Select OK.

Displaying Gridlines

Select Table | Gridlines to display nonprinting gridlines around the table that indicate the current column width and row height settings.

Hints

The following hints can help you work with tables effectively. They give you further guidance on how to format tables, how tables are constructed in Word, and how to make multi-page tables easier to read.

Formatting Table Contents

The table contents can be formatted using the same Word features you use for formatting other types of text. This includes using the Format | Font (Character in Word for Windows 2) and the Format | Paragraph command to change features such as character appearance and alignment. The box "Aligning Entries in Tables" describes several of the alignment conventions you will use on your tables.

End of Cell or Row Marks

End of cell or row marks indicate where the cell or row ends. You can choose to display or not display these marks. They are important because features may work differently depending on whether or not these marks are selected.

- Select the Show/Hide button in the Standard toolbar to toggle between showing and hiding these marks.

- If you choose to show paragraph marks by selecting Tools | Options and the View tab or icon, and then selecting Paragraph Marks, the end of cell and end of row marks will also be displayed.

Sorting in Tables

You can sort tables just as you can sort text. When you sort tables, each row is a record and each column is usually considered a field. You can sort a single column, without affecting other text, by selecting only that column and selecting the Sort Column Only check box. See "Sorting" for a complete explanation of the Sorting feature.

Numbering Cells in Tables

In Word for Windows 6, you can number the cells in your table using the numbered or bulleted list feature. To do this, select the cells you plan to number,

Aligning Entries in Tables

Table entries are difficult to read if they are not properly aligned. The following are some general conventions for aligning different types of entries.

Text	Left
Number without decimals	Right
Number with decimals	Decimal
Time with minutes	Colon
Beginning and ending time	Left
Percentages with decimals	Decimal
Percentages without decimals	Right
Money	Decimal
Text and numbers	Left

and click the Numbering button in the Formatting toolbar. In the Table Numbering dialog box, select whether you want to Number Across Rows or Number Down Columns.

If there are multiple paragraphs of text in a cell, Word will, by default, number each paragraph. If you want only one number in each cell, select the Number Each Cell Only Once check box. Select OK to number your table.

Applying Borders and Shading

You can apply borders and shading to cells, rows, columns, or tables separately from the borders and shading you apply to the contents of those cells. See "Borders and Shading" for instructions on how to apply borders and shading. You can also use the Table AutoFormat feature in Word for Windows 6 to apply many different formats to your table, including borders and shading.

Repeating Headings on Each Page

In Word for Windows 6, you can designate some rows, including the first row of the table, as heading rows. When a table breaks across pages, any heading rows are repeated at the top of each page. The advantage of using heading rows instead of copying that information over again is that when you change formatting features, such as margins, row height, or font sizes, you may change which row appears at the top of the next page. Using heading rows, you can be sure that the identifying information appears at the top of each page for ease of reading.

To designate rows as heading rows, select the rows, which must include the first row of the table, then select Table | Headings. If you ever want to remove this designation, select this command again. This feature does not work when you force a hard page break, such as by pressing CTRL+ENTER.

Entering Text and Formatting Inside Cells

You enter text and graphics inside cells normally. You can use any normal formatting features within a cell, such as paragraph and character formatting. For example, indentations in a cell measure distance from the edge of the cell.

TIP: *You cannot press TAB to enter a tab character in a cell. To enter a tab character, press CTRL+TAB.*

Cell References

Before entering formulas, you need to know how to reference other cells. When you use numbers in other cells, you must refer to those cells according to their names. Since all cells are intersections of a column and row, cell names consist of the letter of the column and the number of the row. For example, a cell in the third row of the fourth column is called "D3."

When you want to reference a range, or set, of cells, you have two choices. You can assign a bookmark to that range of cells and insert the bookmark in the formula, as described under "Inserting Formulas in a Table" above. Alternatively, you can reference the range of cells by the name of the first and last cells in the range.

There are two ways to reference a range of cells using cell names, depending on whether or not you want the formula to take into account added columns or rows. The easiest way is to reference the first and last cell in the range that you want to refer to, separating the cell names with a colon, as in A1:B3. Alternatively, you can repeat the row or column letter twice, separated by a colon, indicating you want to select the entire row or column. For example, use 1:1,2:2,3:3 instead of A1:B3 when you want to make sure that all of the cells in rows 1, 2, and 3 are included, rather than just A1 through B3.

All cell references must appear within parentheses, as in =sum(A1:A4).

Related Topics

Borders and Shading
Columns
Fields
View Options

Tabs

New documents in Word open with default tab stops. You can change the default tab stop interval, or create new tab stops in your document, using one of four alignments.

Procedures

Set tabs using the Tabs dialog box or the ruler. Tabs are a paragraph format, so position the insertion point in the paragraph you want to format, or select text in all paragraphs you want to format. When you create a new paragraph by pressing ENTER, the new paragraph uses the same tab stops as the original.

Changing the Default Tab Interval

1. Select Format | Tabs. You can also double-click a tab marker in the ruler.

2. Set the interval between default tab stops in the Default Tab Stops text box. This number is between 0 and 22.

3. Select OK.

Settings Tabs with the Ruler

1. Select the alignment for the tab. The tab alignment options are left, centered, right, and decimal.

   ■ In Word for Windows 6, click the Tab Alignment button until it displays the alignment you want to use.

   ■ In Word for Windows 2, click the tab alignment button for the alignment you want.

2. Click the tab stop's position on the ruler and a tab indicator of the chosen alignment appears at that position.

3. In Word for Windows 2, click the text to return to the document.

Setting Tabs with the Dialog Box

1. Select Format | Tabs. You can also double-click a tab marker in the ruler.

2. Enter the tab stop's distance from the left margin in the Tab Stop Position text box.

3. Select the Left, Right, Center, or Decimal option button. Word for Windows 6 also includes Bar. The effect of these tab alignments is explained in Table 4-27.

   When you enter more text than can fit to the right of the right and center tabs, the remaining text uses the paragraph alignment.

4. Select the type of line from the Leader area to appear between the tab and the character that precedes it.

5. Select Set to add the tab stop to the Tab Stop Position list box.

6. Remove a tab stop by highlighting it in the Tab Stop Position list box and selecting Clear. Remove all tab stops by selecting Clear All.

   The tab stops that you clear appear in the Tab Stops to be Cleared area. When you select OK to exit the dialog box, the tab stops are cleared.

7. Select OK.

Hints

All paragraphs are initially formatted with the default tab stops, all of which are left-aligned. When you create a tab stop, all default tabs between the left margin and that tab stop are cleared, so that the tab stop you create is the first one. To continue using the default tab stops between the left margin and the new tab stop, you need to set them yourself.

Alignment	Effect
Left	Left edge of text after tab aligned with tab stop.
Right	Right edge of text after tab aligned with tab stop.
Center	Center of text after tab aligned with tab stop.
Decimal	Decimal point with adjacent numbers aligned with tab stop. Other text right-aligned.
Bar	Inserts a vertical bar at the tab stop.

Table 4-27. *Effect of tab alignments*

In Word for Windows 2, the decimal-aligned tab cannot align words with a period in them, such as section numbers or invoice numbers. The character just before or after the decimal point must be a space or number. Otherwise, the decimal point in the text does not line up with a decimal tab. The same thing happens if no decimal point appears, or if the only adjoining characters are not numbers. In these cases, the decimal tab acts like a right-aligned tab.

Using the Ruler with the Keyboard in Word for Windows 2

You can set tabs using the ruler and the ribbon with the keyboard rather than the mouse. First, position the insertion point or select text appropriately.

1. Press CTRL+SHIFT+F10 to activate the ruler.

2. Position the ruler cursor at the tab's position by pressing LEFT ARROW or RIGHT ARROW.

3. Select the tab's alignment by pressing 1 for left-aligned, 2 for centered, 3 for right-aligned, or 4 for decimal tabs.

4. Press INS to set the tab stop.

5. When you finish creating all of your tab stops, press ENTER.

Related Topics

Indents

TC Fields

See "Table of Contents and Figures."

Templates

Templates are files that store text and graphics, AutoText (glossary) entries, macros, styles, toolbars, keyboard assignments, menus, and page layout settings. These settings or features are the defaults for all documents created using that template. Templates are models for documents, as shown in Figure 4-62.

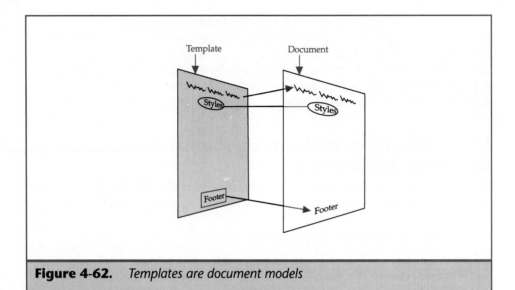

Figure 4-62.   *Templates are document models*

Procedures

The following procedures explain how to create a template, and how to attach a new template to a document.

Creating a Template

1. Select File | New to open a new document.

2. In the New dialog box, select the Template option button and select OK.

3. Add text or graphics or settings that every document created with this template is to use.

4. Select File | Summary Info and enter a brief description of the template's purpose in the Title text box. This description will appear in the New dialog box under Description when you highlight the template's filename on opening a new file.

5. Select File | Save. Enter the filename in the File Name text box and select OK to save the file. Word recognizes the .DOT filename extension as indicating Word template files.

Attaching a New Template in Word for Windows 6

In Word for Windows 6, you can switch the document template of the current document and add more than one global template. Then, you can share template features such as styles and macros between documents.

1. Select File | Templates. The document's current template appears in the Document Template text box, and all open global templates appear in the Global Templates and Add-Ins list box.

2. Select Attach to select a new template file. Select a template file and OK.

3. Select the Automatically Update Document Styles check box to have the new template's styles override those currently applied to the document.

4. Select the check boxes of any templates in the Global Templates and Add-Ins list box that you want available. Clear the check boxes of those you do not want available.

   ■ Select Add to select any other template files to add to the list box.

   ■ Select Remove to remove the highlighted template from the list box.

5. Select Organizer, discussed under "Organizer," to copy or remove styles, toolbars, AutoText entries, or macros from the template.

6. Select OK.

Attaching a New Template in Word for Windows 2

You can switch the document template of the current document to use the styles and macros of a different template.

1. Select File | Template.

2. Select a new template file from the Attach Document To drop-down list box.

3. Select OK.

Hints

The following hints explain how to use templates, where they are stored, how conflicts involving multiple templates for a single document are resolved, and how you modify a template from one of the documents created using it.

T

Using Templates

You can create macros that, once saved with a template, will start as soon as you open a new document using that template. For example, Word for Windows 2 comes with a template called FAX. As soon as you create a new document using this template, Word starts a macro that creates the document and has you enter the necessary information in a dialog box.

Templates can help you create documents faster because in the macro you have all of the correct formatting and any text or graphics that always appear in these documents.

Another advantage of using templates is that you can ensure that your documents will have a standard appearance. By using the same template for all reports, for example, you can make sure that all of your reports have similar information arranged in a similar fashion, with little effort.

Conflicts

When you have multiple templates available, you may have conflicting settings when there are multiple AutoText (glossary) entries with the same name. The document templates settings override those of any global template, while the Normal template, which is always available but does not appear in the Global Templates and Add-ins list box, overrides any other global templates. These other global templates override each other in alphabetical order, so that "ANNSTEMP" overrides settings in "YANSTEMP."

Template Locations

Word assumes that your templates are stored in the TEMPLATE subdirectory of the application directory in Word for Windows 6, or the application directory in Word for Windows 2. If you use a different location in Word for Windows 6, change the File Locations options with the Tools | Options command to tell Word where to find these files. If you use a different location in Word for Windows 2, add the DOT-path setting to the WIN.INI file using the Tools | Options command with the directory of the template files as the setting for this option.

Modifying Templates from Documents

You can modify certain template items from documents in Word for Windows 6. When you change font formatting, margins, page orientation or size, or languages, select Default to save those settings to the document's template. When you create toolbars, keyboard assignments, or menus, select which template they should be saved to.

Related Topics

AutoText
Glossary
Macros
Margins
Page Size and Orientation
Paper Source
Sections
Styles

Text Color

You can assign a color to text that will appear on color monitors and documents printed on color printers.

Procedures

Text color is a character format and is applied as the text is being typed or after it is typed. To apply while typing, add the format, type the text, and remove the format. To apply to typed text, select the text and add the format.

1. Select Format | Font (Character in Word for Windows 2) or right-click the text in Word for Windows 6.

2. Select a color from the Color drop-down list box.

3. Select OK.

Hints

Remember that the text appears in color only if you use a color monitor or printer. If the printer is black-and-white, all colors except white print as black.

Related Topics

Character Formats
Printing

Text Files

A *text file* is a file that contains no formatting codes. Almost all programs can accept a text file. A text file is also known as an ANSI or *ASCII file* since it contains only characters that represent ANSI or ASCII codes. For a full explanation of saving files as text files and opening text files, see "Opening Files" and "Saving Files."

Thesaurus

The Thesaurus shows you words with meanings similar or opposite to those of words in your document (synonyms/antonyms). You can use the Thesaurus to add variety to the vocabulary in your documents.

Procedures

1. Put the insertion point in or beside the word to look up. To look up a phrase select the phrase.

2. Select Tools | Thesaurus or press SHIFT+F7. The word or phrase you are looking up appears in the Looked Up (Synonyms For in Word for Windows 2) text box. If the word does not appear in the Thesaurus dictionary, it appears in a Not Found text box.

3. Select the meaning for the word in the Meanings list box.

   Most words have more than one possible meaning. The meaning you select controls which synonyms appear. If the word being looked up does not appear in the dictionary, a list box called Alphabetical List displays words spelled like the looked up word.

   Select Related Words to see words that are related in meaning but not synonymous to your word, or select Antonyms to see words that are opposite in meaning.

4. Select an appropriate synonym in the Replace With Synonym list box (Synonyms in Word for Windows 2).

   You can select a word in this list box, or type it in the Replace with Synonym text box (Synonyms in Word for Windows 2) and select Look Up to look up the word. If you look up multiple words in a single

Problem Verbs

Some verbs cause repeated problems as they are commonly substituted incorrectly for other verbs or their irregular tenses are improperly formed. The following list shows some verbs that frequently cause problems, a definition of each verb, and the present, past, and past participle form of the verb.

Lay - to place

lay	lay	laid

Lie - to rest

lie	lay	lain

Raise - to lift

raise	raised	raised

Rise - to move up on its own

rise	rose	risen

Set - to place an object in a location

set	set	set

Sit - to rest on a chair or other surface

sit	sat	sat

See - to observe

see	saw	seen

Do - to take an action

do	did	done

Leave - to depart

leave	left	left

Let - to allow

let	let	let

Learn - to absorb knowledge

learn	learned	learned

Teach - to share knowledge with others

teach	taught	taught

Thesaurus session, the Looked Up (Synonyms For in Word for Windows 2) text box displays all the words looked up (the last six in Word for Windows 2).

5. When the correct word appears in the Replace with Synonym (Replace Within Word for Windows 2) text box, select Replace. This word replaces the selected word in the text.

Hints

If you are uncertain, check the spelling of a word before you look it up in the Thesaurus to prevent mistakes in meaning. Some of the more commonly misused verbs are described in the box "Problem Verbs." You can use the Thesaurus to find words close in meaning to these verbs and use the Grammar feature to find some of the misused verbs.

Foreign Languages

You can use a foreign language thesaurus file to look up synonyms and antonyms of a word in a foreign language. Contact Microsoft at the number included in your Word for Windows documentation and to ask about foreign language thesauruses.

Related Topics

Grammar Checking
Spelling

Time

See "Date and Time."

TIME Field

See "Fields."

TITLE Field

See "Fields."

TOA Field

See "Table of Authorities."

TOC Field

See "Table of Contents and Figures."

Toolbar Options

You can modify any of the toolbars that come with Word or design new toolbars for use with the Normal template or other templates.

Procedures

The following procedures explain how to modify or create toolbars in Word for Windows 2 and 6.

For Word for Windows 6

1. Display the toolbar you want to modify (if you are editing an existing toolbar).

2. Open the Customize dialog box and select the Toolbars tab. You can open this dialog box by:

   - Right-clicking a toolbar and selecting Customize to modify an open toolbar.

   - Selecting View | Toolbars, then Customize or New. When you select New, assign a toolbar name and select a template from the Make Toolbar Available To drop-down list box to set where it is saved. Then select OK.

   - Selecting Tools | Customize, and selecting the Toolbars tab to modify an open toolbar.

3. Select where you want to save this toolbar by selecting a template from the Save Changes In drop-down list box.

4. Select the category of buttons or features you want to use in the Categories list box.

   Depending on the option selected, the Buttons/Macros/Font/AutoText/Styles list box to the right displays buttons or other selections.

   Click a button or selection to see its description in the Description box at the bottom of the dialog box.

5. Drag a button or other option to the place on the toolbar you want it to appear.

When you drag a button to the toolbar, that button appears on the toolbar. When you select a command, macro, font, AutoText, or style, however, you need to select or create a button to use.

6. After dragging a non-button to the toolbar, highlight one of the buttons displayed under Button, then select Assign to use that button for that feature.

   When you select a text button which displays text rather than a picture, enter the text to appear on it in the Text Button Name text box.

   Select Edit to create a picture to appear on the button yourself. The button appears in the Picture box. You can select a color under Color and click a square in the Picture box, changing the square to that color. Use this method to draw your button picture, then select OK to use that button.

7. To remove a button, drag the button off the toolbar.

8. To separate buttons, drag them apart. Spaces are always the same width.

9. To rearrange buttons, drag one on top of another. The moved button takes that space, while the others move apart to make room for it.

10. When the toolbar looks the way you want it, select Close.

For Word for Windows 2

In Word for Windows 2, there can be only one toolbar in each template. When you want to create a new toolbar for a template, you need to modify the old toolbar to create the new one. The process of editing a toolbar is less graphically oriented than in Word for Windows 6.

1. Select Tools | Options.

2. Select the Toolbar icon from the Category box.

3. Select Commands or Macros to display what you want to assign to the toolbar buttons.

4. Select Global to save the toolbar with the NORMAL.DOT template, making it globally available, or select Template to save it with the current template, making it available for documents created with the template.

5. Select a button or space in the Tool to Change list box, which displays all of the buttons and spaces in the current toolbar. The new button or space which you add to the toolbar will take the place of that button or space.

T

6. Select a button from the Button list box to appear on the toolbar.

7. Select the command or macro to assign to the button from the Commands or Macros list box.

   When you want to convert the button selected in the Tools to Change list box to a space, you select [space] from this list box.

8. Select Change to add the new button and command or macro to the toolbar. Select Reset Tool to make the tool match the tool in that location in the toolbar saved with the Normal template. Select Reset All to return to the default toolbar.

9. Select OK.

Related Topics

Toolbars

Toolbars

Toolbars are sets of buttons that you can select to carry out a command or use Word's features. The advantage to toolbars is that they are fast and easy to use.

In Word for Windows 6, the toolbar feature is greatly expanded from the previous version. You can display several toolbars at once, as shown in Figure 4-63, and can create and modify any of them. You can also change where toolbars appear on the screen by dragging them. Some features work by opening a toolbar to make special commands available, such as headers and footnotes. In Word for Windows 2, only one toolbar can appear, and it always appears directly beneath the menu bar. You can create new toolbars for different templates, however, and switch between them.

Procedures

The following procedures explain how you can select buttons on toolbars, and control the display and location of toolbars.

Selecting Toolbar Buttons

■ Click the toolbar button with the mouse.

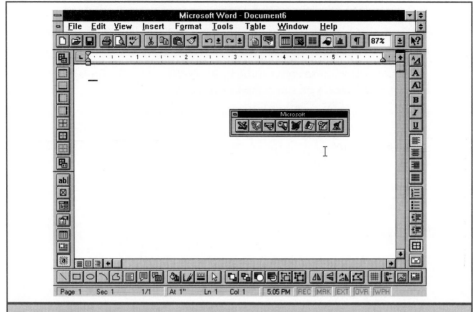

Figure 4-63.   *Display and move toolbars in Word for Windows 6*

In Word for Windows 6, keys can be assigned to the same features as buttons, as described in "Keyboard Options." In some cases, such as the Style box, pressing the key for a feature activates the toolbar element for the same feature. In Word for Windows 2, you cannot use the toolbar with the keyboard.

Setting Toolbar Display in Word for Windows 6

1. Select View | Toolbars or right-click a toolbar and select Toolbars.

2. Select or clear the check boxes in the Toolbars list box to select which toolbars are displayed.

TIP: To display or hide a toolbar, right-click a displayed toolbar and select the toolbar you want to display or hide from the shortcut menu.

3. Clear the Color Buttons check box to have Word display the buttons in shades of gray instead of in color.

4. Select Large Buttons to have Word use a larger button that can be more easily seen. You may need to customize your toolbars if you plan to use this feature so that you can see all the buttons on the toolbars.

5. Select Show ToolTips to have Word display a small box with the name of the button when you point the mouse at the button for a few seconds.

6. Select New to create a new toolbar file. The steps for actually adding buttons to the toolbar are described under "Toolbar Options."

7. Select Customize to edit the highlighted toolbar. The steps for editing a toolbar are described under "Toolbar Options."

8. Select OK.

Moving a Toolbar in Word for Windows 6

To move a toolbar, click an empty spot of the toolbar and drag it to the new location. A dotted gray line indicates where the toolbar appears when you release the mouse button. You can put toolbars at the top, bottom, right, or left edge of the screen, or you can display them within the document area, as you can with dialog boxes. See Figure 4-63 for all the positions where you can put a toolbar.

Hiding or Displaying a Toolbar in Word for Windows 2

Select View | Toolbar to toggle the display of the toolbar on or off.

"Hints

The buttons of the Word for Windows 2 default toolbar, what they do, and where to look for an explanation of the associated commands, are shown in Table 4-28. To find a complete listing of the several default toolbars in Word for Windows 6, see Appendix C.

Related Topics

Formatting Toolbar (Ribbon)
Ribbon
Toolbar Options

Button	Use	Topic
	Opens a new document using the Normal template	New Document
	Opens the Open dialog box	Opening Files
	Saves the current document to the same filename, or opens the Save As dialog box	Saving Files
	Cuts the selected text and copies it to the Clipboard	Clipboard
	Copies the selected text to the Clipboard	Clipboard
	Pastes the Clipboard's contents into the document	Clipboard
	Reverses the last action taken	Undoing and Redoing Actions
	Creates a numbered list from the selected paragraphs	Lists
	Creates a bulleted list from the selected paragraphs	Lists
	Moves the indent of the selected paragraph one tab stop to the left	Indents
	Moves the indent of the selected paragraph one tab stop to the right	Indents
	Inserts a table with the number of rows and columns you specify	Tables
	Formats the active section with the number of columns you specify	Columns
	Inserts a frame containing any selected objects	Frames
	Starts the Microsoft Draw program	Drawing on a Document

Table 4-28.   *Word for Windows 2 Default Toolbar Buttons*

	Starts the Microsoft Graph program	Graph
	Creates an envelope	Envelopes
	Checks the spelling of the document or selected text	Spelling
	Prints the document	Printing
	Changes view to Page Layout, showing the entire page	Viewing Documents
	Changes view to Normal, at 100% magnification	Viewing Documents
	Displays the full width of the document, in the current view	Viewing Documents

Table 4-28.   *Word for Windows 2 Default Toolbar Buttons (continued)*

Tools|AutoCorrect (Word for Windows 6)

See "AutoCorrect."

Tools|Bullets and Numbering (Word for Windows 2)

See "Lists" and "Outlines."

Tools|Calculate (Word for Windows 2)

See "Math Calculations."

Tools|Compare Versions (Word for Windows 2)

See "Comparing Versions."

Tools|Create Envelope (Word for Windows 2)

See "Envelopes."

Tools|Customize (Word for Windows 6)

See "Toolbar Options," "Keyboard Options," or "Menu Options."

Tools|Envelopes and Labels (Word for Windows 6)

See "Envelopes" and "Mail Merge."

Tools|Grammar

See "Grammar Checking" or "Grammar Options."

Tools|Hyphenation

See "Hyphenation."

Tools|Language (Word for Windows 6)

See "Foreign Language Support."

Tools|Macro

See "Macros."

Tools|Mail Merge (Word for Windows 6)

See "Mail Merge."

Tools|Options

This command is used to set default options for many Word features. See "AutoFormat," "Comparing Versions," "Compatibility Options," "Edit Options," "File Location Options," "General Options," "Grammar Options," "Keyboard Options," "Menu Options," "Print Options," "Save Options," "Spelling Options," "Toolbar Options," "User Info Options," "View Options," or "WIN.INI Options."

Tools|Protect Document (Word for Windows 6)

See "Locking and Protecting Documents."

Tools|Record Macro (Word for Windows 2)

See "Macros."

Tools|Repaginate Now (Word for Windows 2)

See "Pagination."

Tools|Revision Marks (Word for Windows 2)

See "Comparing Versions."

Tools|Revisions (Word for Windows 6)

See "Comparing Versions."

Tools|Sorting (Word for Windows 2)

See "Sorting."

Tools|Spelling

See "Spelling."

Tools|Thesaurus

See "Thesaurus."

Tools|Word Count (Word for Windows 6)

See "Word Count."

TrueType Fonts

See "Fonts."

Type Style

See "Fonts."

Underline

Underlining is a character format that produces text with a line underneath. You can use underlined text to provide emphasis. You can underline words with a single line, double line, or dotted line; or you can underline characters only with a single line.

Procedures

You can apply the Underline style as text is being typed or after it is typed. Apply the Underline style while typing by adding the format, typing the text, and then removing the format. Apply it to typed text by selecting the text and then adding the style.

Adding and Removing Underlining with the Dialog Box

1. Select Format | Font (Character in Word for Windows 2) or right-click the text in Word for Windows 6 and select Font.

2. Select a type of underlining from the Underline drop-down list box. To apply underlining, choose Single, Words Only, or Double. In Word for Windows 6, you can also choose Dotted. Select None to remove underlining.

3. Select OK.

Adding and Removing Underlining with the Mouse

■ Select the Underline button, shown here in the margin, in the Formatting toolbar to add or remove the Single Underline format.

The underlining added to the text in your document is the default underlining style. Unless you change the default underlining style, it is a single line under all the text.

Adding and Removing Underlining with Shortcut Keys

■ Press CTRL+SHIFT+U (CTRL+U in Word for Windows 2) to add or remove single underlining from the text.

■ Press CTRL+SHIFT+D (CTRL+D in Word for Windows 2) to add or remove double underlining from the text.

■ Press CTRL+W to add or remove underlining from words only in the text.

Hints

Another procedure for removing underlining from text is to select the text and press CTRL+SPACEBAR. This removes all character formatting from the selected text.

Related Topics

Character Formats
Fonts

Undoing and Redoing Actions

You can easily undo most actions you take in Word. After undoing them, you can choose to redo them.

Procedures

You can undo actions by using the toolbar, menus, or shortcut keys. In Word for Windows 2, you can undo only the last action you took, but in Word for Windows 6, you can redo as many actions as Word has room to store.

Using the Toolbar

■ Click the Undo button on the Standard toolbar.

In Word for Windows 6, you can also select the down arrow next to this button, to display a list of actions, and drag across this list to undo more than the last action.

■ In Word for Windows 6, click the Redo button or display the list of actions and drag to select the ones you want to redo.

Using the Menus

■ Select Edit | Undo. The command changes to indicate the last action taken. For example, the command may change to Undo Typing or Undo Paste.

In Word for Windows 6, the Undo command indicates the last action taken. If you undo that action, it indicates the last action before the action that was undone. Each time you select Edit | Undo, you undo the next action. In Word for Windows 2, selecting this command a second time undoes the undoing, effectively redoing the action.

Using the Shortcut Keys

■ Press CTRL+Z.

In Word for Windows 6, pressing CTRL+Z undoes the last action before the last action is undone, as when you use the menu.

Hints

The Undo command undoes most actions in Word, excluding those that change basic settings or have an effect beyond the program, such as saving a file.

When you undo typing, Word removes all the text since the last command you executed. However, it does not move the insertion point.

In Word for Windows 6, actions must be undone or redone in a series. Therefore, if you want to undo a formatting change, but there are four other actions between that change and the most recent action, you must undo all five actions. To redo that same formatting change, you must redo all five actions.

In Word for Windows 2, you must select Undo immediately after carrying out an action. Undo undoes the last action you took. If you select Undo but did not execute a command, Undo will undo your typing, deleting it. You can undo Undo by immediately selecting Undo again.

Related Topics

Repeating Actions

Unlocking Documents

See "Saving Files," "Annotation," "Comparing Versions," "Locking and Protecting Documents," and "Forms."

Updating Links

See "Object Linking and Embedding."

Uppercase

See "Capitalization."

User Options

You can change the information about the user that you entered when you installed Word. Changing the user options will not, however, change the display in the title bar.

Procedures

1. Select Tools | Options.

2. Select the User Info tab or icon.

3. Enter your name in the Name text box.

4. Enter your initials in the Initials text box.

5. Enter your address in the Mailing Address text box.

6. Select OK.

Hints

In Word for Windows 6, the initials entered in the User Options are used to set the initials used in annotation marks or to distinguish among different authors while marking revisions. The mailing address is used as the default return address for creating envelopes and labels.

In Word for Windows 2, the settings in the User Info Options dialog box are used with the File Sharing options and are automatically used as the default return address when you use the Tools I Create Envelope command.

Related Topics

Comparing Versions
Envelopes

USERADDRESS Field

This field returns the user address from the User Info tab of the Tools I Options command. See "Fields."

USERINTIALS Field

This field returns the user initials from the User Info tab of the Tools I Options command. See "Fields."

USERNAME Field

This field returns the user name from the User Info tab of the Tools I Options command. See "Fields."

Vertical Lines

See "Borders and Shading."

View Options

You can change what appears when you view your document, by changing which nonprinting characters or screen elements are displayed.

V

Procedures

1. Select Tools | Options.

2. Select the View tab or icon.

3. Select from among the options described under "Options."

4. Select OK.

Options

The view options set what appears in the document as you are working on it. The available options depend on the current view. For example, a view option that only applies to normal view only appears when you select Tools | Options from the normal view. In Word for Windows 2, unavailable options are dimmed.

Show

The options under Show (Show Text With in Word for Windows 2) let you use some display features that can help you better edit your document.

In Word for Windows 6, display options that effect only some of the view modes are available only if you open this dialog box in that mode. For example, if an option affects only how text is displayed in page layout mode, you must be in the page layout view when you open the View Options dialog box or you will not see that option available.

DRAFT FONT (WORD FOR WINDOWS 6 ONLY)   Select the Draft Font check box to display all text using a draft font, character formatting as underlined and bold, and graphics as empty boxes in outline and normal views.

DRAWINGS (WORD FOR WINDOWS 6 ONLY)   Select this check box to have Word display objects created using the Draw feature in page layout view. Clearing this option lets your work with documents proceed more rapidly.

WRAP TO WINDOW (WORD FOR WINDOWS 6 ONLY)   Select this check box to have Word wrap text at the end of the window rather than the end of the line and so make sure that you can see all of the text as you edit. This option effects only the display in the normal and outline views. When this option is in effect, the Status bar does not display the Line and At measurements which indicate the insertion point's location.

OBJECT ANCHORS (WORD FOR WINDOWS 6 ONLY)   Select the Object Anchors check box to have Word display a small anchor in the paragraph a frame is anchored to while in the page layout view, as shown here:

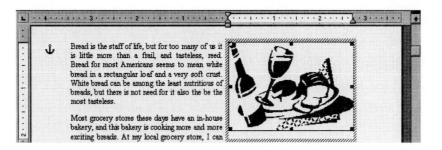

TABLE GRIDLINES (WORD FROM WINDOWS 2 ONLY)   Select the Table Gridlines check box to have Word display dotted lines indicating the edges of cells in tables. When this check box is cleared, you must select Table | Gridlines to display these lines.

TEXT BOUNDARIES   Select the Text Boundaries check box to have Word display dotted lines indicating text boundaries at margins and around objects and frames in the page layout view.

PICTURE PLACEHOLDERS   Select the Picture Placeholders check box to have Word display boxes in place of graphics inserted in your document, enabling the document to scroll and update the screen more quickly. This option affects the page layout, normal, and outline views.

FIELD CODES   Select the Field Codes check box to display field codes instead of field results in the page layout, outline, and normal views. You can temporarily change the display using the View | Field Codes command.

BOOKMARKS (WORD FOR WINDOWS 6 ONLY)   Select the Bookmarks check box to display bookmarks in the document, enclosed in square gray brackets, in the page layout, outline, and normal views.

LINE BREAKS AND FONTS AS PRINTED (WORD FOR WINDOWS 2 ONLY)
Select the Line Breaks and Fonts as Printed check box to display fonts and line breaks as they will print, even when Word uses a substitute font because the selected font is not available. When this command is cleared, Word displays the document as formatted, including even fonts or graphics that cannot print.

FIELD SHADING (WORD FOR WINDOWS 6 ONLY)   You can select when nonprinting shading is applied to field results in your document. You can choose Never, Always, or When Selected, which is the default option, to never shade field results, to always do so, or to shade results only when part or all of the field is selected. This command affects the page layout, outline, and normal views.

Window

The selections under Window let you set what elements appear in your document and application windows.

HORIZONTAL SCROLL BAR Clear the Horizontal Scroll Bar check box to remove the horizontal scroll bar from the bottom of your document windows in all views.

VERTICAL SCROLL BAR Clear the Vertical Scroll Bar check box to remove the vertical horizontal scroll bar on the right side of your document windows in all views.

STATUS BAR Clear the Status Bar check box to remove the status bar from the bottom of your application window in all views.

STYLE AREA WIDTH Enter a measurement to open the style area at the left edge of your document window. The style area displays style names for paragraphs formatted with styles in the outline and normal views.

VERTICAL RULER (WORD FOR WINDOWS 6 ONLY) Clear the Vertical Ruler check box to hide the vertical ruler that appears in the page layout view and print preview.

Nonprinting Characters

Use this check box to set the nonprinting character that are displayed by default. Select Show/Hide in the Standard toolbar to toggle between showing all nonprinting characters or the default characters only.

TAB CHARACTERS Select the Tab Characters check box to show tabs in text. Tab characters are right-pointing arrows.

SPACES Select the Spaces check box to display spaces as small round dots in the document. Hard spaces are indicated with the degree symbol.

PARAGRAPH MARKS Select the Paragraph Marks check box to show paragraph marks in the text. Paragraph marks look like backward capital P's with two straight lines.

OPTIONAL HYPHENS Select the Optional Hyphens check box to show hard and optional hyphens. Optional hyphens appear in words, indicating where the word should be hyphenated when necessary and look like normal hyphens.

Hard hyphens stop Word from hyphenating a word in that position and are indicated by long hyphens.

HIDDEN TEXT   Select the Hidden Text check box to show text formatted as Hidden. Hidden text does not print, even when this check box is selected.

ALL   Select the All check box to show all nonprinting characters. In Word for Windows 2, the other check boxes under Nonprinting Characters are selected. In Word for Windows 6, the other check boxes are not selected, although Word displays all nonprinting characters as if the check boxes were selected.

Related Topics

Fields
Frames
Styles
Tables
Viewing Documents

View|Annotations

See "Annotation."

View|Draft (Word for Windows 2)

See "Viewing Documents."

View|Field Codes (Word for Windows 2)

See "Fields."

View|Footnotes

See "Footnotes and Endnotes."

View|Full Screen (Word for Windows 6)

See "Viewing Documents."

View|Header and Footer

See "Headers and Footers."

View|Master Document (Word for Windows 6)

See "Master Documents."

View|Normal

See "Viewing Documents."

View|Outline

See "Outlines."

View|Page Layout

See "Viewing Documents."

View|Ribbon (Word for Windows 2)

The ribbon, a Word for Windows 2 feature, is the equivalent of the Formatting toolbar in Word for Windows 6. See "Ribbon."

View | Ruler

See "Ruler."

View | Toolbars

See "Toolbars."

View | Zoom

See "Viewing Documents."

Viewing Documents

Word offers several views of documents. Each view provides another method of both viewing and working with the document.

Procedures

Switching Views

You can switch to using the menus by selecting the view you want to use from the View menu.

- Select View | Normal. The normal view is the default document view. Columns of text appear after each other, instead of on the same page, and breaks are indicated by lines across the screen.

   You can also select the Normal View button in Word for Windows 6, which appears next to the horizontal scroll bar, to switch to the normal view. In Word for Windows 2, select the next-to-last toolbar button to switch to the normal view and show the document at full size.

- Select View | Draft (Word for Windows 2 only). In draft mode, a variant of the normal view, all text is displayed in the same font, with character formatting represented by underlining. Graphics appear as empty frames.

■ Select View | Full Screen (Word for Windows 6 only). The full screen view removes all Word and other elements from the screen and displays the document using the entire area. You can use shortcut keys and menus or toolbars to format in this view. To return to the previous view, press ESC or click the Full Screen button on the Full screen toolbar.

■ Select View | Master Document (Word for Windows 6 only). In the master document view, you can see the overall organization of your master document on a single screen. See "Master Documents" for an explanation of how to work with master documents in this view.

■ Select View | Page Layout. In page layout view, Word displays your document the way it will print. In Word for Windows 6, you can also select the Page Layout View button to switch to this view. In Word for Windows 2, select Zoom Whole Page to switch to this view and reduce the display zoom value so you can see the entire page in the window at once.

■ Select View | Outline. In the outline view, you can manipulate the document by showing headings only or showing only headings of certain levels. In this view you can easily promote and demote outline items and reorganize the headings and text in the outline.

   In this view in Word for Windows 6, the horizontal ruler is hidden and the Outline toolbar is displayed. You can also switch to this view in Word for Windows 6 by selecting the Outline View button.

■ Select File | Print Preview. Print preview lets you see your document to review it before printing. If you are looking at a document in the outline view, the print preview displays the document in nonoutline mode.

Zooming Your Document

You can change the magnification of your document in all views (normal and page layout views only in Word for Windows 2).

1. Select View | Zoom.

TIP: You can also activate the Zoom drop-down list box in the Standard toolbar and select an option or type a percentage before pressing ENTER or clicking on another location.

2. Select a zoom option to size your document. You can choose a percentage of the document, and the screen will display the document at that size.

Select Percent (Custom in Word for Windows 2) and enter a specific percentage, to have the document displayed at that percentage.

You can also have Word calculate the zoom percentage by indicating what part of the document you want to view. Select Page Width, Whole Page, or Many Pages and set the number of pages you want to see in the window. The last two selections are available only for the page layout view.

3. Select OK.

Working in Print Preview View in Word for Windows 6

In Word for Windows 6, unlike in Word for Windows 2, you can actually edit your document in print preview, using most of the features available in normal text editing. This includes using keys and the scroll bar and the mouse to move through your document. To edit the document, click the Magnifier button on the Print Preview toolbar and click the now normal mouse pointer on the text you want to edit. When you are finished editing the document, click the Magnifier button again to return the mouse pointer to a magnifying glass.

You can also use the Print Preview toolbar to change the amount of document displayed, to add rulers, or to shrink the document to fit on one page. The Print Preview toolbar buttons are shown and listed in Table 4-29. You can change the margins and indents using the ruler just as you can for the page layout view. See "Ruler" for more information on making these types of changes.

Working in Print Preview in Word for Windows 2

Unlike in Word for Windows 6, you cannot actually edit text in print preview in Word for Windows 2.

1. Select File | Print Preview.

2. Select the Two Page button to display two pages at once. To switch back to a single page, select One Page.

3. Press PGUP or PGDN to move to the previous or following page.

4. Change the margins by selecting Margins, which displays margin lines with their black handles for dragging. With the mouse, drag the margin line by its handles and click outside the page. With the keyboard, press

V

Button	Name	Purpose
	Print	Prints the document using the default print settings
	Magnifier	Toggles being able to edit the document on and off
	One Page	Displays one full page at a time
	Multiple Pages	Displays the number of pages you select at a time
34%	Zoom Control	Lets you set a zoom percentage
	View Ruler	Toggles the horizontal and vertical rulers on and off
	Shrink to Fit	Reformats the document to eliminate a last page with little text
	Full Screen	Displays the document on the full screen without other elements
Close	Close	Returns to the previous display
	Help	Turns on the help feature

Table 4-29. *Print Preview Toolbar Options (Word for Windows 6)*

TAB so the margin line disappears and a cross appears in place of the handle. Use the arrow keys to move the line. Then press ENTER twice.

5. Select Cancel to return to your document or Print to begin printing your document.

Splitting Windows into Panes

1. Select Split from the Window menu (Split from the document's Control menu in Word for Windows 2)and a line with arrows appears.

TIP: You can also drag the split box, at the top of the vertical scroll bar, to where you want the document split. You cannot split a document in the print preview view.

2. Use UP ARROW or DOWN ARROW to move the line where you want the document split.

3. Press ENTER.

The document window is now split into two panes. This is like having two windows looking at the same landscape because the document is the same in both panes. The advantage to panes is that you can view two different parts of your document at the same time. For example, you can view the introduction to your document and the conclusion at the same time to make sure that all issues raised in the introduction are resolved in the conclusion.

Hints

Before sure to preview every document before you print it. Although the page layout view is a good way to check the appearance of your document, you may not have a correct screen font, or you may have difficulty displaying the page correctly. In print preview, Word displays the document graphically, so that even if you do not have the appropriate size of screen font, the text takes the correct amount of room on the page.

Related Topics

Master Documents
Outlines
View Options
Windows

Watermarks

Using Word for Windows 6, you can create watermarks: designs or text that appear on each page. Watermarks were originally markings included in some papers to identify the maker or the user of the paper.

Procedures

1. Select View | Header and Footer.

2. Click the Drawing button on the Standard toolbar to open the Drawing toolbar.

3. You can create your own watermark or import a graphic to use as a watermark.

■ Draw or enter the drawing or text using the features described under "Drawing on a Document."

■ Create a text box. Then select Insert | Picture to import a graphic.

4. Select all elements of the watermark and select the Send Behind text button on the Drawing toolbar.

5. Select Close on the Header and Footer toolbar or select View | Header and Footer again.

The watermark will appear on every page that the header or footer appears on.

Hints

When you use a graphic or text as a watermark, try to make it pale—for instance, a light-colored graphic or light-colored text—so that it does not compete with the actual document text and make it difficult to read. Watermarks provide an easy way to add a border graphic to all pages of a document.

Related Topics

Drawing on a Document
Headers and Footers
Graphics

Widows and Orphans

Widows and orphans are single lines of paragraphs that appear at the top or bottom of pages while the rest of the paragraph appears on another page. Word offers a feature that lets you prevent widows and orphans. See "Pagination."

WIN.INI Options (Word for Windows 2)

WIN.INI is the Windows file that contains the default setting for Windows and many other Windows applications, including Word. You can edit the WIN.INI file from Word.

Procedures

1. Select Tools | Options.

2. Select the WIN.INI file from the Category box.

3. Select the portion of the file you want to edit from the Applications drop-down list box.

4. To remove a startup option that is a line of the WIN.INI file, highlight it in the Startup Options list box and select Delete.

5. To add a startup option, enter the option in the Option text box and the setting itself in the Setting text box. Then select Set.

6. When you are done, select Close.

Hints

To find out what options and settings are available and the format you need to use, see Appendix B, "Modifying WIN.INI," in your Word for Windows 2 documentation.

You can change the settings for many of Word's default options by modifying the WIN.INI file.

W-Z

Window|Arrange All

See "Windows."

Window|List of Open Windows

See "Windows."

Window|New Window

See "Windows."

Window|Split (Word for Windows 6)

See "Viewing Documents."

Windows

You can move quickly between document windows or create or arrange the currently open document windows by using the Window menu.

Procedures

You can work with document windows several ways. You can open a second window to look at the same document two different ways. You can select which document window you want to work with. You can also have Word arrange your open document windows to see all of the documents you are working with.

Opening a Second Window for a Document

You can open multiple windows for the same document to compare text in different parts of a long document. You can also use separate windows to look at the same document in different views.

■ Select Window | New Window.

TIP: Changes made in one window for a document are reflected in all windows for that document.

Moving to Another Document Window

You can move between document windows quickly.

■ Select Window and then the number of the window to which you want to move.

■ Press CTRL+F6 or SHIFT+CTRL+F6 to move forward or backward through the active document windows, in the order they appear on the Window menu.

■ Click on any visible part of the document window.

Arranging Open Document Windows

You can arrange open document windows so you can see into each document.

■ Select <u>W</u>indow | <u>A</u>rrange All.

Word arranges the windows so that each one can be completely seen, as Figure 4-63 shows.

Wizards

Wizards are special Word for Windows 6 features that can help you create a new document. Wizards ask you questions, which you respond to. Word uses your answers to create the document. Although wizards are normally used when creating a document, Word also has a special wizard that can help you create a table.

W-Z

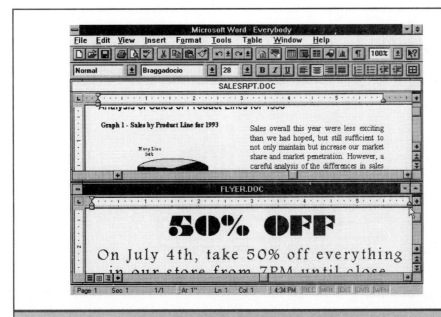

Figure 4-63. *Arranged windows in Word for Windows*

Procedures

1. Select File | New.

2. Select a wizard from the Template list box.

3. Select OK.

4. Respond to the questions of the wizard, using standard dialog box elements. Select Back or Next to move between the different dialog boxes setting options.

5. Select Finish in the last dialog box.

WordArt

WordArt is a separate program that can be started in Word to enable you to create graphic images with text. Figure 4-64 shows a document that has the unusual word affects created with WordArt.

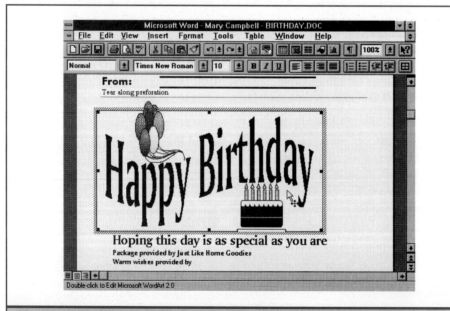

Figure 4-64.   *Enhanced text created with WordArt*

Procedures

WordArt has been enhanced in Word for Windows 6, although many of the basic features are available in Word for Windows 2.

In Word for Windows 6

1. Select Insert | Object.

2. Select Microsoft WordArt 2.0. Then select OK. Word now displays a new toolbar and the Enter Your Text Here dialog box.

TIP: Don't click in the document, because doing so closes WordArt.

3. Type your text in the box in the Enter Your Text Here dialog box. Select Insert Symbol to insert a special character. When you are finished, enter Update Display.

4. Select the effects, using the toolbar, as shown in Table 4-30. Several of these effects are also available as commands since WordArt has modified the menu.

5. Click on your document to exit WordArt.

You can edit your WordArt by double-clicking the existing WordArt, right-clicking it, and selecting Edit, or selecting Edit | WordArt Object | Edit. The toolbar and menu change just like they did in step 2. At this point, you can edit the text and the effects. You can also edit your WordArt by right-clicking it and selecting Open or selecting Edit | WordArt Object | Open. When you edit WordArt by opening it, the WordArt options display in a dialog box. When you select OK, you finish editing the WordArt and return to editing your document.

In Word for Windows 2

1. Select Insert | Object.

2. Select WordArt. Then select OK.

3. Enter the text in the box at the top.

Button	Purpose
— Plain Text ▾	Lets you select a shape for the text to fill
Arial ▾	Lets you select a font to use for the text
Best Fit ▾	Lets you select a font size
B	Boldfaces the text
I	Italicizes the text
Ee	Makes all letters the same height
◁A	Flips the text on its side
A	Stretches the text to fill the space you created
≡	Lets you select an alignment for the text
AV ↔	Lets you adjust the spacing between letters
C	Lets you rotate the text
⊘	Lets you set a color or pattern to fill the text
◻	Lets you choose a method of shadowing your text
≡	Lets you set a border for your WordArt box

Table 4-30.   *WordArt 2.0 Toolbar Buttons*

4. Select a font from the Font drop-down list box and a font size from the Size drop-down list box.

5. Select a shape for the text from the Style drop-down list box.

6. Select a fill for the text in the Fill drop-down list box.

7. Select an alignment from the Align drop-down list box.

8. Select Shado<u>w</u>, Color <u>B</u>ackground, or Stretch <u>V</u>ertical to format the text.

9. Select OK.

Word Count

In Word for Windows 6, you can easily find out how many pages, words, characters, paragraphs, or lines are in your document. This feature is especially useful if you are writing for a publication with limited space, which can use only so many words or lines of text.

Procedures

1. Select <u>T</u>ools | <u>W</u>ord Count.

2. Select the Include <u>F</u>ootnote and Endnote check box to have Word count these when it counts words, lines, paragraphs, pages, and characters in your document.

3. Select Close.

Related Topics

Summary Info

WordBasic

Word Basic is a programming language that you can use to create macros in Word. Chapter 7 has more information on how macros use WordBasic.

WordPerfect

WordPerfect is another word processing application. Word can open WordPerfect files in Word format and save Word files in a WordPerfect format for use with WordPerfect. Word supports WordPerfect format for WordPerfect Releases 4.1, 4.2, 5.0, and 5.1.

W-Z

See "Opening Files" and "Saving Files" for a full explanation of how to open WordPerfect files or save files in a WordPerfect format.

WordStar

WordStar is another word processing application. Word can open WordStar files in Word format and save files in a WordStar format for use with WordStar. Word supports WordStar format for WordStar Releases 3.3, 3.45, 4.0, 5.0, and 5.5.

See "Opening Files" and "Saving Files" for a full explanation of how to open WordStar files or save files in a WordStar format.

Workgroup Features

Several of Word's features make working on a network easier. See "Master Documents," "Electronic Mail," "Annotation," "Comparing Versions," and "Forms" for information on those features.

Worksheet

Spreadsheet applications create documents, called worksheets, that are arranged like Word's tables. Worksheets can carry out calculations using cell entries. Word can open Lotus 1-2-3 and Excel worksheet files. These worksheets appear in Word as tables in Word for Windows 6. You can use fields to create spreadsheet-like tables that perform limited math calculations.

See "Opening Files" and "Math Calculations" for more information on opening worksheet files and performing math calculations in a table.

XE Fields

This field marks an index entry. See "Index."

Zoom

See "Viewing Documents."

THE COMPLETE

REFERENCE

PART THREE

Special Features

CHAPTER 5

Exchanging Data with Other Applications

Word documents are not limited to being created and used with Word alone. Not only can you share your Word data with other applications, but you can take data that you have worked with in other applications—for instance, eye-catching graphics and complex spreadsheets—and incorporate them into your Word documents.

Word takes advantage of Windows Object Linking and Embedding (OLE) and Dynamic Data Exchange (DDE) capabilities. The OLE and DDE technology lets Windows applications share data with one another, even if those applications cannot otherwise use one another's data files. Often, the initial problems you may have with OLE and DDE as you first start using these features occur because you are working with two applications at once.

Besides using the DDE and OLE features of Windows, you can share data among applications by *inserting* files into Word documents. This applies to files containing text, spreadsheets, and graphics. Word can also share data with some applications by opening their files and saving them in different formats.

NOTE: *This chapter assumes that you have read the "Object Linking and Embedding" section in Chapter 4, and are comfortable using terms and ideas introduced there, since that section introduces you to the basics of linking and embedding objects. If you have not, please return to Chapter 4, and read the section.*

Why Use Embedding and Linking?

Data sharing among Windows applications means the data is still available to you, even if it is created and stored in an application other than Word. You can use your Excel data in your Word documents, and you can put Word documents into Excel worksheets. Rather than having Word read Excel files, Word works with Windows and other Windows applications to establish a two-way communication that sends data between applications.

This two-way communication allows one Windows application to request data from another application, and have the other application fill the request by sending the data. The data sent to another application can have its appearance set by the requesting application or by the application where the data appears. Because this two-way communication link remains in place, you can make changes in the original data, and the changes will also be made where the data appears.

Embedding and linking have an advantage over strictly copying data from one application to another. Copying adds the data to a document, but there is no updating after the copy operation. Linking, on the other hand, not only provides the contents of the data, but as the original data changes, so does the linked copy in the document. Embedding puts the original data in the document. When you want to change the embedded data, you edit it using the application which created it.

The difference between embedding and linking is where or how the data is stored in the new location.

Embedded objects are placed in a file in the new application. For example, when you embed an Excel worksheet in a Word document, as illustrated in Figure 5-1, the Excel worksheet is *stored with the Word document.* However, when you edit the worksheet data in the Word document, you will be using Excel, not Word. Word tells Windows to open Excel, and the Excel data to put in a worksheet. You can see in Figure 5-1 how the worksheet does not have the filename that you normally see for Excel worksheet files. Excel in this case is telling Word how the worksheet data appears in the Word document, so when you want to change the data's appearance within the document, you use Excel.

Linked objects show data from another application that is *stored in the original application's data files.* This data is not stored with the application that contains the link. For example, when you link an Excel worksheet into a Word document, as in Figure 5-2, the Excel worksheet is in its own file. When you edit the Excel worksheet, you will use Excel, not Word. You can start Excel from Word or you can start Excel separately. When you modify the worksheet, this link makes sure that the Word document contains the latest version of the Excel worksheet. When you tell Word you want to edit the linked data, Word tells Windows to open Excel with the selected worksheet. Although the Excel worksheet data is

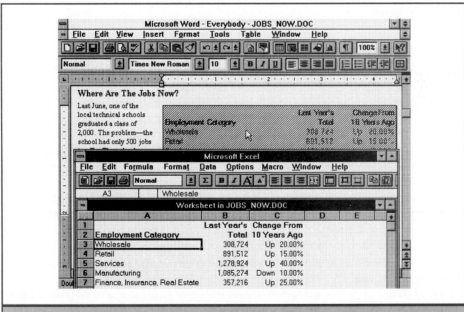

Figure 5-1.   *An Excel worksheet embedded in a Word document*

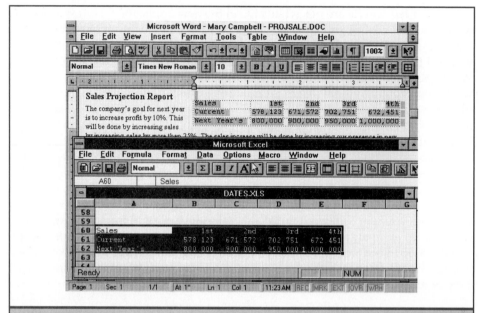

Figure 5-2.   *An Excel worksheet linked into a Word document*

displayed in the Word document, it is stored in an Excel worksheet file. You can see in Figure 5-2 that the Excel worksheet has a standard filename. With linked data, you can either have the application tell Word how the linked data appears in the Word document, or let Word format the linked data depending on the type of link. In our example, the linked data uses the Rich Text format, so Excel initially tells Word how the data appears, but you can still use Word features to change the data's appearance within Word. The linked Excel data appears shaded, because it is edited by starting Excel from within Word.

With either linked or embedded data, you are using another application within your Word document, to include spreadsheet and database data and capabilities (for example) in your Word documents. For the two examples above to work, you need to have Excel installed. Embedding and linking adds the *capabilities* of the other applications you already have installed on your system, not the applications' software.

Word data can be embedded or linked into other applications, as well. Figure 5-3 shows a Word document as a linked object in an Access report. (This report also includes an embedded WordArt object.) Access uses this linked object to give itself word processing capabilities.

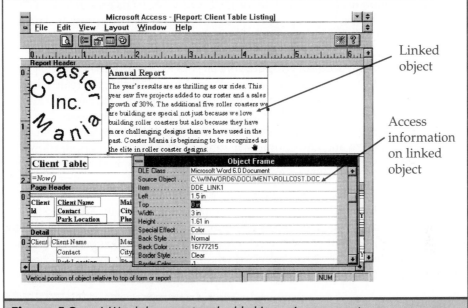

Figure 5-3.   *A Word document embedded in an Access report*

TIP: If you want several Word documents to use data from one file, or to use data from a single file in two or more locations in a Word document, create a link to the file containing the desired data. If you only need to insert the data in one location, you can either embed or link the data.

Understanding Windows DDE and OLE

Object Linking and Embedding (OLE) and Dynamic Data Exchange (DDE) are the technologies Windows uses to share data between applications. DDE and OLE provide gateways for data to pass among applications. Windows 3.0 has DDE and some OLE capabilities, depending on the applications. Windows 3.1 has both DDE and OLE. For applications to use DDE and OLE, they must be able to support these technologies. Windows cannot provide DDE and OLE capabilities to applications that are not created to use them.

An application may provide data for DDE and OLE, or receive data for DDE and OLE, or both. The technical term for an application that can provide data is a *server application*, while an application that can accept data is a *client application*. Word is both, but not all other applications are. For example, you can use the Windows Paintbrush accessory application, as well as the supplementary applications that come with Word, such as WordArt and Graph, to create DDE and OLE objects in your Word documents; but these applications cannot contain DDE and OLE objects. The supplementary applications can only create embedded objects, because they cannot store the objects they create as separate files. To see if linking and embedding will work with a particular application, you can consult its documentation, or just try linking and embedding with the application and see if it works.

To share data between applications, you do not need to remember whether you are using OLE or DDE. You only need to remember that you are using Windows to share the data among applications. Word handles communication to Windows and placement of the correct information in your document. You only need to select the data to share, tell Word where you want the data, and whether you want it linked or embedded.

TIP: When you want to use data from another application that does not support DDE and OLE, you can still do it, as long as you can copy the data to the Clipboard and then copy it from the Clipboard to Word. The disadvantage with this method is that if you change the data in the other application, you must then repeat the copying process to get the new results into your Word document.

Working with Embedded and Linked Objects in Word

If you have not yet used embedded and linked objects in other applications, you will want to know something of how these objects work when you add them to your Word documents. The basic steps are described in the box "Embedding and Linking Data."

The data you want to embed or link must come from an application that supports embedding or linking. For example, you cannot select a .WK1 file for embedding or linking, because 1-2-3 Release 2.*x* does not support OLE or DDE. When you embed or link data using the Clipboard, the Edit I Paste Special command can tell you if the application for the source of the data supports object linking and embedding. When the source of the data is from an application that does *not* support linking, Paste Link is not available. When the source of the data is an application that does *not* support embedding, the word *Object* will not be included in any of the formats available for adding the data.

When you actually link or embed the data into your Word document, a field is inserted. This field inserts the linked or embedded data into your Word document. If you show field codes, instead of their results, you will see the fields used for linking or embedding, rather than the linked or embedded data. The fields used to link or embed data are the LINK, EMBED, or INCLUDE fields.

What Happens to Data When You Embed or Link It

When you bring data from other Windows applications into Word, the fonts do not change. Windows applications share fonts, so the fonts your system has in Word are the same fonts you have in Excel, Access, or other Windows applications.

Some formats of linked data can have their text altered, using the same Word features that you use on text stored in a normal Word document. Embedded data, and some other formats of linked data, appear in Word documents as a picture. The formats available for linked objects include both linked objects and bitmapped or picture formats. You cannot use Word features to change the appearance of the text in the object when the object is an embedded object or a picture format of a linked object. You can however, use the same Word features that you use to work with pictures.

The Format | Picture command can enlarge or reduce the size of the data, as well as crop it. The Insert | Frame and Format | Frame commands can set the location of the object. For example, the picture in Figure 5-4 is acquired via a link to a graphics file. The graphic is in a text box, which allows it to appear behind the document text, as shown in Figure 5-4. This graphic is sized and cropped using the Format | Picture command. The embedded Excel worksheet in the lower-right has a frame around it to make placement easier. The picture was created with CorelDRAW!, using a trumpet clip-art image from Presentation Graphics. CorelDRAW! was used because it lets you draw lines and subsequently modify them, so you can create the naturally flowing bands of color in the flag. CorelDRAW! has more features for altering the look of text than does WordArt; CorelDRAW! also has 18,000 pieces of clip art, 750 fonts, and more graphic alterations than are offered by Paintbrush or Word's Draw feature.

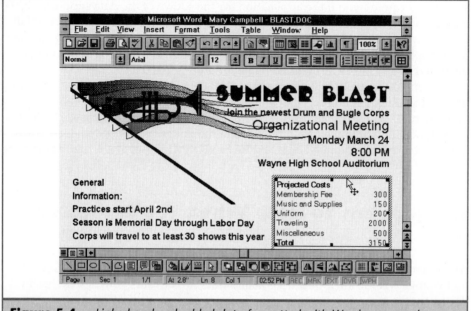

Figure 5-4. *Linked and embedded data formatted with Word commands*

TIP: If you frequently use embedded and linked objects, you will want to invest in more memory (RAM) for your computer. The additional memory improves the performance of Word and other applications when working with embedded and linked objects.

Embedded or linked objects remain embedded or linked until you unlink the object by pressing CTRL+SHIFT+F9, or delete all of the embedded data, or delete the field code for the embedded or linked data. A linked object can also be converted to the link's contents by selecting Edit I Links, then the link, and the Break Link command button (Cancel Link in Word for Windows 2), then Yes. When you do this, the link to the original file is broken, and the linked object is converted into text or a picture.

Updating Data from Embedded and Linked Objects

The primary advantage of linked and embedded objects is that when you change the data used by the embedded or linked object, the data that appears in

Embedding and Linking Data

Here is a summary of how to create linked and embedded objects. For the complete procedures, see "Object Linking and Embedding" in Chapter 4.

Linking and Embedding Data with the Clipboard

1. Copy the data you want to link/embed to the Clipboard, starting from within Word or another server application.

2. Open the document that will receive the linked/embedded data in the client application, and move to where you want the data positioned.

3. Select Edit | Paste Special, and choose the appropriate options to specify how you want the data embedded/linked, as well as the version of Word you are using.

   - To embed the data in Word for Windows 6, select the Paste option button and then the Object option in the As list box (usually the first one). If none of the As options include the word *Object*, the data cannot be embedded.

   - To link the data and have the data's appearance set by its creating application in Word for Windows 6, select the Paste Link option button and then the Object option in the As list box.

   - To link the data in Word for Windows 6 and have the data's application (server application) initially set the data's appearance, but allow you to change it with Word, select the Paste Link option button and then Rich Text Format in the As list box.

   - To link the data and have Word for Windows 6 set the data's appearance, select the Paste Link option button and Unformatted Text in the As list box.

   - To link the data and display it as a Word 6.0 picture or as a bitmapped image, select the Paste Link option button and then Picture or Bitmap in the As list box.

   - In Word for Windows 2, choose the format you want for the data and select Paste or Paste Link. When Data Type is Object and you select Paste, you create an embedded object. When you select one of the options and the Paste Link button, you create a link. Paste Link is not available when the selected data type cannot be linked. Selecting Paste when a data type other than the Object option is selected copies the Clipboard data without creating an embedded object or a link to the data.

4. Select OK.

Linking and Embedding Existing Objects with Insert|Object

1. Move the insertion point to where you want the object to start.

2. Select Insert | Object and the Create From File tab.

3. Select the file using the File Name text box, the Directories list box, and the Drives drop-down list box, just as if you are opening a file.

4. Select the Link to File check box if you want the data linked to the Word file, or clear the check box if you want the file's contents embedded into the current document.

5. Select OK to add the object to the document.

Linking and Embedding New Objects with Insert|Object

1. Move the insertion point to where you want the object to start.

2. Select Insert | Object.

3. From the Object Type list box, select the application for the type of data you want to add, and select OK.

4. Create the data you want to appear as the embedded object, using the server application you have selected.

5. Leave the server application by selecting Exit from the File menu, OK from the dialog box, or by clicking another part of the Word document.

the Word document changes. Word handles updating the embedded and linked data for you.

Data embedded in Word is updated when you edit the data in the source application and then return to Word. When you exit from the source application, you will often see a prompt for updating the object in the document. Select Yes to update, and the data in the Word document is updated to match the changes you have made. Selecting No cancels the changes you have made while working in the other application. Since the Word document contains the original (not updated) data, Word does not have to verify that the data is up-to-date.

You can set when linked data is updated by specifying how it is to be updated. Most links are automatically updated. When you add linked objects with Edit | Paste Special and Insert | Object, Word sets the links to be updated automatically. You can use the Edit | Links command to set the link to only be updated manually, or to not be updated until you indicate otherwise. When you select the Manual option button from the Links dialog box, the linked is updated only when you tell Word to do so, and not when other links are automatically updated. Selecting the Locked check box freezes the locked data while still keeping the link available. Locked links cannot be updated until you select the Edit | Links command again and clear the Locked check box.

Word updates linked data at the following times:

■ When you tell Word to update the data, by selecting Edit | Links, then the links to update, and then Update Now. You can also do this by moving to a linked object or selecting several linked objects and pressing F9. Or you can select Update Link from the linked object's shortcut menu in Word for Windows 6.

■ When you open a document containing automatically updated links. You may see a prompt; select Yes, and the links are updated.

■ When you print a document containing linked objects. In Word for Windows 6, this assumes the Update Links check box is selected on the Print tab in the dialog box that the Tools | Options command displays, or when you select Options from the Print dialog box that the File | Print command displays. In Word for Windows 2, this assumes the Updated Fields check box is selected for the Print category of the Tools | Options command, or when you select Options from the Print dialog box that the File | Print command displays.

When Word and Windows update linked data, in the background they open the source application, open the file containing the original version of the linked data, update the copy in Word, then close the source application and its data files. Since the linked data is replaced with an updated version, if you have made changes to the contents of a linked section, those changes are replaced. This is not necessarily true for formatting or picture settings you have made, however. Most linked objects keep the formatting you apply to the data in Word. If you want the formatting updated as well as the data, remove the * mergeformat statement that is part of the linked data's field code.

Word continues to update linked data until one of the following occurs:

■ You tell Word you want to manually update links, by selecting Edit | Links, then the link, then Manual, and OK.

■ You break the link by selecting Edit | Links, then the link, then Break Link, and then Yes to confirm that you want to break the link. This is the same as selecting the link and pressing CTRL+SHIFT+F9.

■ You delete the link by deleting either the linked data or the field code.

■ You lock the link by selecting Edit | Links, then the link, then the Locked check box, and OK.

TIP: *Make sure that your computer's clock is correct. Word uses the computer's clock to determine whether linked files need to be updated. Also, if you have several versions of a file, having the correct time and date makes it easier to determine which file version you want to use. In Word for Windows 6, you can see the time in the status bar. In Word for Windows 2, you will need to check the clock's time using the Window's Clock accessory, or by opening the Control Panel from the Main Program Group, and selecting Date/Time.*

Changing the Data Shown in a Link

You can change the part of the linked item that appears in your Word document. One way is to change the field, but Word makes it easier with the Edit | Links command. This command opens the Links dialog box that lists the links in the current document and lets you change the section of the linked data.

When you select a link and the Change Source button, you can select the part of the file you want to show in the linked object, by changing the contents in the Item text box. When this text box is empty, the entire file will appear as the linked data. The format of the Item text box entry depends on the source of the data. For example, to select part of an Excel worksheet, you supply the range of rows and columns. Therefore, R1C1:R50C6 in the Item text box selects rows 1 through 50 and columns 1 through 6.

Using this command changes the field code that represents the linked data. Although you can make the same changes directly in the field, using Word's dialog box prevents you from accidentally typing something that will corrupt the link.

Switching Between Embedded and Linked Objects

An object that is linked can be switched to be embedded, and vice versa. However, this switch does not involve just selecting the object and telling Word that you want it to be embedded into the document or linked to a file. Rather, you are transferring the data in the object to another source and using the new version to create a new link or embedded object. With an object that can only be embedded (such as those created with the supplementary applications Graph, Equation Editor, and WordArt), you cannot convert it to a linked object because these applications do not save their results in a file.

If you want to transfer embedded data into linked data, edit the embedded data and copy it to a new file in the source application. For example, if you have an embedded Excel worksheet that you want to include in multiple Word documents, you can edit the Excel data, select it, and copy it to a new worksheet. Save the new worksheet and use the new version to link the data in all documents where you want to work with it—including the document that contained the original embedded object. After creating the new data file, delete the embedded object and create a link to the new data file.

If you want to transfer linked data into embedded data, edit the linked data and copy to the Clipboard the part you want to embed. For example, if you have a linked Excel worksheet in one Word document that you no longer want to be available to other documents, you can make an embedded object with the data. First, edit the Excel worksheet, select the part you want to embed in your document, and copy it the Clipboard. Next, switch to the document, delete the linked data (since you still have the data in a file, you will not lose it), and add the Clipboard data as an embedded object. Once you add the embedded object, try editing it. If it is now an embedded object, you can delete the file that the link used, assuming you no longer want the file.

Fields Used for Embedded and Linked Data

Word has several fields that you will see when you embed and link fields. Embedded data is represented by the EMBED field and linked data by the LINK field. The EMBED and LINK fields are used even when the source of the data is a Word document. These fields are just like the fields that Chapter 4 describes under "Fields." You can edit these fields directly, or you can use the Edit | Links command to change settings which will change the fields. Usually, you will only see these field codes and let Word change them for you.

NOTE: You may also see the DDE and DDEAuto fields that Word supports. These fields appear when you are using Windows 3.0, which did not support OLE. The DDE and DDEAuto fields use the same three pieces of information for application, filename, and location, as described below for the LINK field.

In the EMBED field:

- After EMBED is the *ClassName* that describes the application you use to modify the embedded data. This might be ExcelWorksheet for an Excel worksheet, or Equation.2 for the Word for Windows 6 Equation Editor.

- After the *ClassName*, the \s switch may appear when you want the embedded object to remain the same size when you finish working on it, instead of letting the embedded object become larger or smaller as its data changes.

- The * mergeformat switch tells Word that any formatting changes you make to the embedded object should stay with the embedded object when you edit the embedded data. This includes the picture scaling and cropping set with Format I Picture. Format I Drawing Object has no effect on these objects, since they are objects rather than drawings.

In the LINK field:

- After LINK is the *ClassName*, as described just above for the EMBED field.

- After *ClassName* is the file containing the linked data.

- Next comes *PlaceReference* for the part of the file to show, unless you are including the entire document in a link. *PlaceReference* is the same entry you see in the Item text box when you change a link's source with the Edit I Links command.

- Next is the \a switch if the linked data is automatically updated. When this switch is omitted, the link is manually updated.

- Other switches may include the \b for bitmap, \p for graphic or picture, \r for Rich Text format, and \t for unformatted text that indicates the format of the linked data in the Word document. Linked and embedded objects often use the \p switch since they appear in the document as a picture. You can also include the \d switch to omit keeping the graphic image of the linked data in the file; this makes the file smaller.

- This field, like EMBED, can use the * mergeformat switch to keep the formatting when the linked data is updated.

Figure 5-5 shows several embedded and linked objects, and the same document showing the field codes instead. Word also has INCLUDE, INCLUDETEXT, and INCLUDEPICTURE fields that include text and graphics from other files. These linked objects are not the same type as the ones discussed so far; these fields are handled solely by Word, as described under "Linked/Inserted Files" later in this chapter.

Word Documents as Embedded and Linked Data

Word documents can be embedded or linked into other documents. Several applications can take Word data that you put on the Clipboard and copy it or paste it into their own data files as embedded or linked data. You must use the other application's commands to import the Word data.

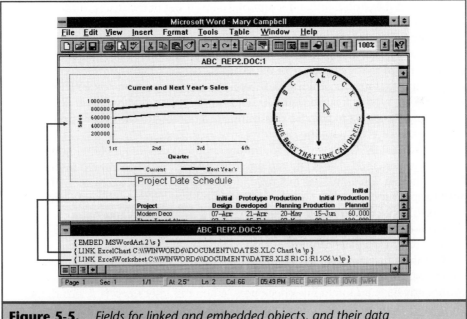

Figure 5-5. *Fields for linked and embedded objects, and their data*

When you use a Word document as the source file for a linked object in another Word document or a client application's document, you can change which part of the Word document is shown in the linked object. A link to a Word document creates, in the source file, a bookmark of DDE_LINK*n*, where *n* is the next sequential number. To change what part of the Word document appears in the link, assign the DDE_Link bookmark to a different part of the document. When you embed a Word document in another file, the embedded object shows all of the embedded data, not just a part.

Working with Files in Other Formats

Word can work with files that are stored in the format of another application. When you open one of these files, Word can convert the file into Word's own format. When you save the file, depending on the original format, Word can save the data in a format designed for another application. You can also insert files when you want to add a file's contents into your documents.

A file can be copied into a document, so anything in the inserted file comes into the Word document, and later changes you make to the original file do not get incorporated into the Word document.

Another possibility is to insert/link the file to the document. Then if the file changes, those changes appear in the Word document. It's important to understand that this file linking is different from the Windows OLE/DDE linking. This type of inserted/linked file is entirely handled by Word. Rather than using Windows to create a communication link with the other application, Word works directly with the file.

The advantage to the second method is that you do not need the other application installed. The disadvantage is that Word must be able to insert the type of the file you want. For example, if you have a data file created with the application VaporWare (not a real product name), and VaporWare can use DDE/OLE, you can link and embed its data. If VaporWare cannot use DDE/OLE, however, the only way you can insert the VaporWare file is if Word has text or graphics file converters that handle this type of file.

Graphics files are inserted into to Word files using the Insert | Picture command and other files are added with the Insert | File command. Both commands have a Link to File check box. When this check box is selected, the Word document is linked to the inserted file, so as the file changes, the version that appears in the document changes. After selecting the command, select the file and select OK.

Linked/Inserted Files

Once you insert linked files, they are treated just like the data you link using Windows's OLE and DDE. Linked/inserted Word documents can be automatically or manually updated; other types of linked/inserted files can only be manually updated. Just like OLE and DDE linked data, you can change the settings for the links (except for how the link is updated) using the Edit | Links command.

Linked/inserted files are represented by different fields than links created through Windows. As with Windows links, you normally do not enter the fields, but let Word add them for you. Depending on the file contents and version of Word, you will see the following fields:

File Type	Field
Graphics in Word for Windows 2	IMPORT
Graphics in Word for Windows 6	INCLUDEPICTURE
Nongraphics files in Word for Windows 2	INCLUDE
Nongraphics files in Word for Windows 6	INCLUDETEXT

After any of the above-listed fields you will see

- ■ The filename to insert.

- ■ After the filename for INCLUDE and INCLUDETEXT is any bookmark name or description of the part of the file you want inserted. This is just like the item selection with the Edit | Links command when you are changing a link.

- ■ INCLUDETEXT and INCLUDEPICTURE can also use \c and a converter name to specify the converter to use with the picture. Omitting this switch lets Word use the default converter based on the extension.

- ■ INCLUDEPICTURE can also use the same \d switch that the LINK field uses to omit storing a graphics image of the picture in the document, so only the link is stored.

- ■ INCLUDETEXT can include \l to prevent Word from updating fields from the inserted file, so they are only updated when you update them in the file you are inserting.

Converting Files

When you take a document that is not in a Word for Windows format and bring it into a Word for Windows document, or when you take a Word for Windows document and save it in a format designed for another application, Word *converts* the file.

File conversion does not usually have perfect results; to write a perfect conversion program would require the programmer to consider every possible combination of features. When the conversion program overlooks some feature combination, the conversion process cannot provide the results you want. Also, how you want a feature of the document converted when the document is imported into Word may depend on what you plan to do with the data in Word.

For example, depending on the other application, you may get different fonts, or very different text formatting from what you expected. This process also affects how a Word document appears when you save it in a format designed for another application.

Conversion is usually limited to the features both applications share in common. For example, when you save a Word for Windows document in Word for DOS format, you lose expanded or condensed character spacing, because Word for DOS cannot change this setting.

In Word for Windows 6, conversion can be altered with Compatibility options; these are on the Compatibility tab in the dialog box that the Tools | Options command displays. Compatibility options include the fonts Word uses. For example, when you bring a WordPerfect document into Word for Windows, you can have Word replace the document's fonts with the TrueType fonts you have installed in Windows. These options are further described under "Compatibility Options" in Chapter 4.

TIP: The converter for the file type must be installed. If it is not, run the Word Setup program and install it.

You can also edit the document converter, using the EditConversionOptions macro that is part of the CONVERT.DOT template. To use this macro, open the CONVERT.DOT template; then use the Tools | Macro command, run this macro and follow the dialog boxes for setting the options.

You can convert multiple documents at once using the BatchConverter macro that is part of the CONVERT.DOT template. To use this macro, open the CONVERT.DOT template; then use the Tools | Macro command, run the BatchConverter macro, and follow the dialog boxes for selecting the files to convert.

If you want to bring a Word document into an application with which Word is not compatible, find out in what other formats the other application can save its data. Often, applications can save their data in more than one format, and one of these may be one that Word will accept.

> *TIP: When you import a document from a spreadsheet or database program such as Excel, 1-2-3, Quattro Pro, or dBASE, the data often appears in a table. You can use Word's table features to change the table's appearance, and formatting features to improve the appearance of the data in the table's cells.*

ANSI versus ASCII

You need to know the difference between ASCII and ANSI codes when converting documents between Windows applications and non-Windows applications. Your computer remembers every character by using a code. Word for Windows uses ANSI characters, but most programs that are not intended to run under Windows use ASCII characters. When you are using solely characters from the first half of either the ANSI or ASCII character set (characters, numbers, and common punctuation symbols), it doesn't matter which character set you are using, because the first half of these character sets are the same. The characters in the second half of the ASCII or ANSI character set, however, are different. When you are working with a document that uses these characters, make sure that you are using the correct set; you want to prevent, for instance, a £ (ANSI 163) symbol from appearing as a ú (ASCII 163).

When you save a text file, Word has various format options that save text in an ASCII versus ANSI format. Text Only and Text Only with Line Breaks are text file formats that use the ANSI character set. MS-DOS Text Only and MS-DOS Text Only with Line Breaks are text file formats that use the ASCII character set.

Looking in the Clipboard

When you copy data to switch it between applications, you use the Clipboard. You may want to view the Clipboard data to ensure that the data converts properly. You may also want to view how the data looks using different formats, before you paste it into the client application and select a format. You can look at the Clipboard's contents using the Clipboard Viewer application. This application opens when you select Clipboard Viewer in the Main program group of the Program Manager.

What you see in the Clipboard Viewer window is a picture of the current contents of the Clipboard; you cannot change the contents from this window. But you can change how you look at the Clipboard data. Clipboard data can appear in more than one format, depending on the data's source. For example, a Word document can appear as Text, Picture, or OEM Text (OEM stands for original equipment manufacturer).

Clipboard data is often in more than one format because the format you use when you paste it in another location depends on the application used to create the other location. For example, if you are copying the Word document data shown in Figure 5-6 to another Word document, you would expect it to be copied as text. When you copy it to Paintbrush, you would expect it to be copied as a picture of the text. When you copy it to Access or Excel, you can select whether the data is copied in a Microsoft Word 6.0 Document Object, or Picture, or Text format.

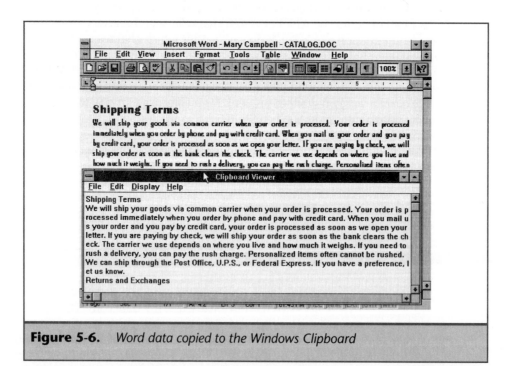

Figure 5-6. *Word data copied to the Windows Clipboard*

File Associations

When you install Word for Windows, Windows is informed that .DOC files are used with Word for Windows. What this means is that you can start Word with methods other than starting the Word for Windows program item. So if you open a .DOC file, Windows knows to open Word for Windows with the document. If you open a .DOC file from the File Manager, Windows opens Word and the document you have selected. You can also add Word documents as program items to a program group window. Selecting any one of the program items shown just below will open the document in Word, as well as the Word program if it is not already open.

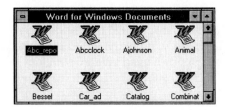

CHAPTER 6

Desktop Publishing in Word

When you first started using a word processor you probably felt lucky being able to type error free documents. After mastering the basics, though, you need to begin thinking about the most effective way to present your message. Most readers are bombarded daily with messages from many different sources. In order to get your reader's attention, your message must have an edge. This means you need to start focusing on document design more. You can then think of your task as publishing a document rather than just typing it. The term *desktop publishing* was coined because word processing programs like Word now let you perform tasks with the equipment on your desktop, that once could only be accomplished by a professional printer.

You can use Word's desktop publishing features for a wide variety of tasks. You can create forms such as invoices or purchase orders with a company logo and shading to make it easy to read and fill out. You can create interesting and attractive reports that include graphics and charts. And you can use different fonts, graphics, and text arrangement features to create flyers, business cards, and other mailers easily.

In this chapter you are introduced to some key desktop publishing terms and concepts. You will need these terms and ideas when you get involved with professional printers and other desktop publishers. Examples of many of the most popular types of documents created with desktop publishing features are presented, along with an explanation of the procedures involved in creating them, and some of the considerations involved in designing them.

How You Can Use Desktop Publishing

You may think that desktop publishing is something for professional graphics designers, using advanced computer systems. However, much of the work that you do with Word probably falls within the range of desktop publishing. As you use different fonts and font styles, add borders and shading, and include drawing objects and clip art in your documents, you are actually using desktop publishing features. Even creating a sales report with charts and an opening graphic uses desktop publishing skills you probably never knew you had.

The big difference between "desktop publishing" and what you have done with Word is the time spent planning the visual design of the documents. Desktop publishers start a document by considering its design, while you probably just start typing and think about design later. By integrating the process of designing a document with the process of writing it, you too can become a desktop publisher.

Basic Steps in Desktop Publishing

The following are some general steps in desktop publishing which will make creating visually interesting documents easier for you. You will find that these steps mirror the steps you already take to create the text of your document. They don't need to take much time, but even a few minutes of thought spent on design can create significant improvement in your document.

1. Consider your audience. Make sure you know who you are sending this document to and what you want to tell them. Just as you would create different text for an invitation to a child's birthday party and your company's reception, you should also create different designs.

2. Consider your message. Take a minute to make sure you know all the information that needs to appear in the document, so that you don't forget important text. If the document you are creating is primarily text, such as a report or paper, you probably want to finish creating the document, then start designing a format, since you will then know what kind of elements you need to include.

3. Sketch out your general design. Just grab a blank piece of paper and sketch out where you expect things to go, such as graphics, lines, or other elements. This gives you a quick idea of what you want to do, and how it might look. Remember, this sketch isn't a rough draft, but it will guide you.

4. Apply the formatting you want to use, such as character formats, borders or shading, paragraph and page formats.

5. Preview it. Always look the document over. If you display multiple pages, or small pages you will get a better idea of the graphic impact of the document than if you view each page full size on the screen. Use Print Preview to make sure you are viewing the document as it will print. You may need to go back and move figures, or adjust some formatting if you don't like how it looks.

   A good idea is to actually print out a preview copy of your document after previewing it on screen. Because of the difference in resolution between the screen and a printer, some graphic effects will look very different.

6. Print it. You can either print the document yourself, or take it to a service bureau and professional printer to have them print it using professional quality printing equipment.

Learning About Design

The hardest step for a new desktop publisher is to figure out how to make documents look good. Very few people who want to create nice documents have professional training in graphic design or layout, so figuring out where to get started is very difficult.

The first step in learning how to do graphic design is to remember that while you haven't created expertly laid out documents yet, you've been reading them for years. Thousands of professionally trained graphic designers and publishers spend millions of dollars every year to present you with potential learning experiences.

Start by looking at the documents around you with a more careful eye. When you receive business cards, flyers or brochures, make your own judgment. Do you like them? Do you know why? Try to break down the elements in a publication to see what it is about it that you like. When you create a similar document, keep those ideas in mind. If you find documents you really like, keep them as examples of good graphic design. When you need to create a similar document, imitate the one you liked.

You should also invest in a good book on graphic design or desktop publishing if you are going to be doing a great deal of it. The best book will have plenty of examples, perhaps even before and after examples showing you how a document was improved.

Remember to trust your own taste and judgment. There are no final answers in publishing or graphic design. Your own taste and judgment is the final arbiter that decides if the document's design works, or doesn't. Educate your judgment with books, and by looking out for effective documents that you can find elsewhere, but your judgment still has to make the final call.

Specialized Terms and Ideas

When you step into the arena of desktop publishing, you are going to quickly find many new terms and ideas. How much of this you need to know depends on what you use Word to do. If you are creating a flyer for a school bake sale, your requirements are going to be less rigorous than if your boss just handed you the task of creating a regular newsletter for your clients.

Some of the terms explained below were originally used in professional printing, back when printing used metal type in trays. You may never have a need for them; desktop publishing has revolutionized how printing is done and some terms just aren't used anymore. However, if you need to print your material professionally, your printer may use these terms:

■ *Art* In desktop publishing, this refers to all non-text material, including words which have been manipulated with WordArt or another package.

■ *Bleed* This is text or art that extends to the very edge of the page, so that it can be seen on the side. This is very hard to do with most desktop systems, because most standard printers can't print right up to the edge.

■ *Camera-ready material* Camera-ready material is material that is ready to print. If you are photocopying your document, this means your final printout, but if you are planning to use a professional printer, you may need to find out about creating "negatives."

■ *Clip Art* Clip art is a saved graphic image that you can use in Word. Packages of several images can be purchased from many different suppliers. Word itself comes with more than forty images, but you may find the need or desire for different types of images. You can purchase these through the mail, or from a local computer or software store. Many of the graphic images used in this book can be gotten from Yesterday's Art. These images, like most clip art, are sold with the right to use them anywhere—as part of your logo, in a company report, or in your church newsletter—as long as the purchaser is the one using them.

■ *Copy-fitting* Copy-fitting is the process of adjusting the amount of text you have and the space you have to put it in. You need to make sure that the whole message is included in your publication, but you also want to keep to a readable layout. You may need to change your layout, or adjust the text.

■ *Graphics Packages* Graphics packages are programs designed to create and manipulate graphic images. Most come with a selection of fonts and clip art, or previously saved graphic images.

While there are many graphics packages available, a common one is CorelDRAW!. You can see an example of CorelDRAW!'s work in the form in Figure 6-7. CorelDRAW! was used to create the company's logo. While Draw and WordArt have some of the abilities of a graphics package, if you intend to do a lot of work with art and graphics, you will probably want to invest in a high-end product such as CorelDRAW!. CorelDRAW! 4 also comes with 750 fonts and 18,000 images.

■ *Gutter* A gutter is the space between text, either the space between text on two facing pages, the space between columns, or the space between text and the bound edge of the document.

■ *Imagesetter* An imagesetter is a printer with more features and much higher resolution than you have in your office or home. Imagesetters can cost up to $100,000, so only service bureaus and professional publishers usually have one.

■ *Kerning* Kerning is the trick of removing or adding space between characters. Some pairs of characters look better if they are slightly closer together. You can let Word do automatic kerning or kern letters manually. Kerning is most important in high-quality publications.

See "Spacing Characters" in Chapter 4 to learn more about kerning.

■ *Offset printing* Offset printing is what many of us think of as "real" printing. Offset printing uses a system in which a film or metal plate of your document is created. The image from the plate or film directs where the image is printed on paper.

■ *Optical Center* The optical center of a page is where the reader's eyes naturally and immediately go to. The optical center is usually located at the horizontal center of the page approximately 3/5 of the way up, assuming your document is arranged in a rectangle. Use this idea in your layout plan.

■ *Pica/Point/Em/En* Publishers use an entirely different set of measurements than the rest of us. These measurements may be used when you submit ads to newspapers or magazines, or when talking to a printer. A point, which you've already encountered in learning about font sizes, is .0138 of an inch. A pica is twelve points.

   An em or en are horizontal measurements based on the height of the text around them. An em is the same height as the font (such as 6 point) while an en is half of an em. These are used to described certain spaces and dashes which use these measurements. See the "Rules for Using Specialized Characters" box for an explanation of these dashes and what they are used for.

■ *Print Shop* A company with the ability to print your document using advanced printing techniques, which is usually useful for printing runs in the hundreds and up. Make sure you talk to your print shop so you know what you need to provide them with. Many print shops use offset printing.

■ *Raster Images (bitmapped)* Raster or bitmapped images are composed of many little dots. Raster image files are usually larger than vector files, and, in Word, cannot be manipulated with the Draw feature. However, bitmapped images are often easier to obtain, since scanners save images as bitmapped, and can be accepted by more programs.

■ *Resolution (dpi)* Resolution indicates how many dots per inch (dpi) are used to create your document. The higher the resolution, the less your document's text and graphics will suffer from jagged edges, which look unprofessional. Most laser printers can print text at about 300 dpi, which is fine for most purposes. For creating documents such as a slick annual report for your corporation, consider printing your document at higher dpi to create a better look. Consult a service bureau about doing this.

■ *Rules* Rules are lines used to separate text, like those created with borders or between columns.

■ *Screens* Screens are blocks of a color or shade of black. You can use a light block with regular text, or a dark block with reversed text to create emphasis. Screens are often used as headings.

■ *Serif and Sans Serif Fonts* Serif fonts have little lines (serifs) at the corners and ends of characters; sans serif fonts don't. As a rule, use serif fonts for body text, and sans serif fonts for headings, since they are harder to read in long sections of text. Serif fonts usually have a more traditional feel, while sans serif fonts are more "techy." The types of fonts you use can have a great effect on how your document is perceived by the reader.

■ *Service Bureau* A company which can print out your document using a high-quality imagesetter, making it ready for printing by an offset printer. Most service bureaus can also do your desktop publishing, or provide training or equipment and software.

■ *Vector Images (algorithm)* Vector images are images composed of objects which are represented by mathematical formulas or algorithms. They are easier to edit in many ways, and, in Word, can be manipulated using Draw. Vector image files are usually smaller than comparable raster image files. When you size your graphic, these images will maintain a fine line with very little jaggedness.

NOTE: *Many of the graphics used in this chapter were provided by AJ Graphics (1-800-782-7321).*

Rules for Using Specialized Characters

There are some characters which were used in printing, but not in everyday typing, until the advent of computer desktop publishing. While these characters are available, few people know when or how to use them. You may have already encountered some of these characters, while others may be new to you.

Many of these special characters can be inserted by selecting Insert | Symbols and selecting them from the Special Characters tab.

- *Smart/Curly Quotes*   Many people are still using the straight inches mark (") rather than actual quote marks (") because the inches mark is entered from the keyboard and the quote marks involve extra steps. In Word for Windows 6, you do not have to worry about this, since Word's AutoCorrect feature will automatically convert these quotes as you type, assuming you've turned the feature on.

- *Hyphen*   The hyphen is the minus sign on the keyboard, and is commonly used as both a hyphen and a dash. Hyphens should be used between non-inclusive numbers (i.e. your phone number) or between compound words. Hyphens are the shortest of the dashes.

- *Em dash*   The em dash, also called the dash, is used when there is a break in the line of thought in a sentence. Em dashes are the longest of the hyphen-like characters.

- *En dash*   The en dash, which is half the length of an em dash, but longer than a hyphen, is used to combine numbers which are inclusive, as in 2-6 PM.

- *Ligatures*   Ligatures are two letters combined into one. These letters are no longer used in English, but are still appropriate when writing Old English or foreign words, since they represent a sound that the letter alone does not. You can approximate ligatures by radically changing the kerning between the two letters. Œ and æ are included in the ANSI character set, however, and can be entered as characters using the Insert | Symbol command.

- *Ellipsis*   An ellipsis is the three dots used to indicate missing text in quotes, or faltering conversation. An ellipsis is not actually three periods; it is a single character all of its own, which you can enter using the Insert | Symbols command.

Rules for Using Specialized Characters (*cont.*)

■ *Em and en space*   Em and en spaces are spaces of a set width. There are no set rules for when you should use these special spaces. You would use the differing spaces when you felt they were appropriate to create attractive documents.

■ *Copyright/Registered Trademark symbols*   The copyright symbol is a C in a circle, while an R in a circle is the registered symbol, and TM is the trademark symbol (©, ®, ™). These are all special characters which can be inserted using Insert | Symbol.

Creating Sample Documents

In the following section, you will see samples of several different kinds of documents you may want to create and an explanation of how they were created. Use these as a guide for creating your own, or as the start of developing your own ideas. The general steps used to create the sample documents are explained, as well as some of the considerations that went into the design.

Business Cards

You can create your own business cards using paper that can be divided into standard sized business cards. Creating your own business cards is useful because you only print the ones that you need, making the cost cheaper than if you went to a professional printer and had a thousand made up. You also have more control over how the cards look, and can quickly make changes for new numbers, names or other information.

Figure 6-1 shows the business card for Howard Robinson of Robinson and Nichols, a law firm.

Designing Business Cards

Business cards create a strong impression about yourself and your company. Make sure that your business cards give other people a good impression.

The primary factor to consider in designing a business card is size. You have very little space, and you have very definite information that must be on the card. Therefore, you must allocate space on the card carefully.

Robinson and Nichols, LPA

Howard Robinson
Senior Partner

123 East 12th Street   **216/555-5671**
Cleveland, OH 44114   **Fax 216/555-2233**

Figure 6-1.   *Howard Robinson's business card*

Keep your art simple, and relatively small. Rarely is there ever a good reason for a graphic to dominate a business card. Often stylized text which is both visually interesting and conveys information is the best choice. Simple line art or geometric designs are the best art because they print clearly. Complicated designs will seem blurry and hard to read since they are so small on the card. The sample card in Figure 6-1 uses a simple logo at the top, without much detail.

Everyone should find your card easy to read, so don't reduce your font size too much. Fonts smaller than 10 points are going to be very hard to read, and should be avoided. On the sample card, the address is 10 points, while Howard Robinson's name is 14 and his title is 12. The larger point sizes provide emphasis for the more important information.

Note that only one font is used on this card, Bookman Old Style. Generally, you shouldn't use multiple fonts on a business card, because too many fonts will make the card look very busy. Stick to one font in slightly different sizes, or use, sparingly, font styles such as italics. Remember that a business card is seen as a single image, and that image must look coordinated and professional.

Creating Business Cards

To create a business card follow these steps:

1. Select Word for Windows 6's Tools | Envelopes and Labels command. In the Envelopes and Labels dialog box:

   a.   Select the Labels tab.

b. Select Options, and choose the label layout you want to use. The labels provided are standard formats that many different companies use to set up their sheets of labels. For business cards, you probably want Avery 5371 - Business Card, but check the package of paper you are using to make sure. After choosing the setup, select OK.

c. Select New Document to create a new, unnamed, document which contains a table. Each cell of the table is the precise size of the business cards on the form you are using. If you selected Avery 5371, there are ten cells arranged in two columns.

Each cell of this table matches the location of one business card on the paper; you can create ten individual cards, or you can copy one card to each of the cells.

Usually, this feature is used with the Mail Merge feature to create mailing labels or other sets of labels. See "Mail Merge" in Chapter 4 to learn how to create a new document with these features.

2. Insert or draw any graphic images you want to use. Because a table is used to divide the page into the business cards, you cannot insert a frame around the graphic image. You have three choices:

■ Use an imported graphic that you do not want to put text beside. Figure 6-1 uses this option.

■ Split the cell, and add an imported graphic to one cell and the text to the other.

■ Draw the graphic using Word Draw features, then send it behind the text. You can either make the text avoid appearing over this drawing object, or use it as a watermark like a background figure. Do not make this graphic a picture, or you will have the same problems as with an imported graphic.

See "Drawing on a Document" or "Graphics" in Chapter 4 for more information on working with graphic images in Word, or "Tables" for more information on working with tables.

3. Add the text. You can include text formatting as usual.

4. Copy the business card to each of the other cells in the table, to print the ten business cards available on the sheet.

Letterheads

Figure 6-2 shows the letterhead for Kensington Designs, which was created as a template in Word. By creating a letterhead as a template, you can simply open a document using that template, and the letterhead is right there.

Designing Letterheads

Letterheads were originally just the name and address of the sender, appearing at the top of the page, usually centered. Now, you can add a lot more to your letterhead. Your clients will see more of your letterhead than they will of any other single document you put out. Therefore you should be very careful about your letterhead design, because it will do a lot to set the image of your company in other people's minds.

When you design letterhead, remember that while it is supposed to convey information and an image of your company, it is not supposed to overwhelm the actual message, which is the letter, proposal or other document. It's supposed to function as a frame; attractive, but not the center of attention.

You can create a letterhead without graphics which appears only at the top of the page. This is a traditional format which is good for companies with a conservative image, such as accounting firms and banks. Companies that need to project a more creative and up-to-date impression can use letterhead that is less traditional, using graphics, unfamiliar fonts or unique placement of information.

The sample letterhead in Figure 6-2 is for an interior design company, a company that wants to convey a sense of style and a creative image. The company name and slogan are at the top, in a font chosen to convey the image of being creative. The company name is large enough to catch attention. The graphic was chosen because it is simple enough not to steal the reader's attention, but suitable for the company. These graphics are fairly large for a letterhead, and are appropriate for a creative service firm, but probably not for a professional company.

Splitting the information, that is, putting the company name at the top and address at the bottom, is easily done and conveys a contemporary image. In this letterhead, it helps to balance the page, since the company name and slogan are so "heavy." You will want to consider the comparative weight of text and graphics on a page when designing a letterhead.

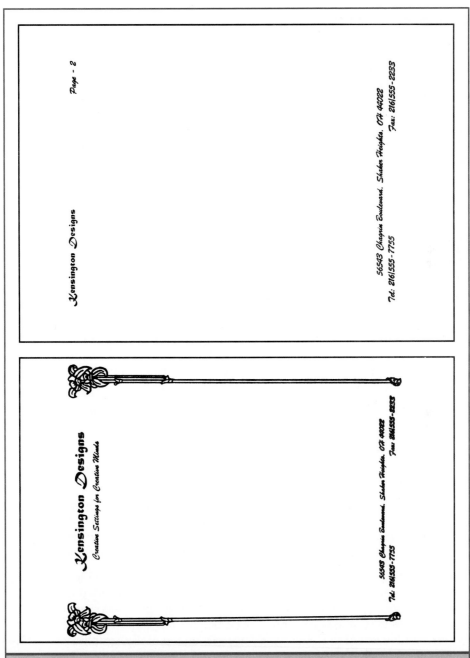

Figure 6-2. *Kensington Designs letterhead*

Creating Letterheads

To create a letterhead template, follow these steps:

1. Open a new template file.

See "Templates" in Chapter 4 to learn more about templates and how they work.

2. Select View | Header and Footer. You want to create your letterhead as a header or footer so that it appears on every page.

See "Headers and Footers" in Chapter 4 for more information on creating headers and footers.

3. Change the Header and Footer options to use a different header and footer for the first page than the rest of the document. In Word for Windows 6, select File | Page Setup, the Layout tab, and Different First Page check box, and OK. In Word for Windows 2, you select the Different First Page check box then the First Header or First Footer in the Header/Footer list box to edit when you select OK.

4. Add the graphics and text of the letterhead to the header or footer.

   In Figure 6-2, the company name and slogan appear in the header and the address and phone information appears in the footer. You can include these elements of the letterhead in either. The split design balances the graphic elements of the page nicely.

   You can add graphics to a header or footer which can appear either in the header or footer area, or elsewhere on the page. An interesting effect for some letterheads is to add the company name as a WordArt image, and arrange it down one side of the page, rather than across the top.

   In Figure 6-2, a graphic from AJ Graphics was added to the header. The graphic is in a bitmapped format, so it had to be inserted in a text box created with the Draw feature. After the graphic was sized to fit across the entire page, Draw's Send Behind Text button was selected, so that the text of the letter would appear "on top of" the graphic.

See "Graphics" and "Drawing on a Document" to learn how to work with imported graphic images. See "Watermarks" for more detailed steps on inserting a graphic image in a header or footer.

5. Close the Header and Footer view so that you return to the document.

6. Insert a hard page break.

7. Select View | Header and Footer again. You will not want the letterhead on the first page to appear on all the pages of the letter or document. Instead, you should create a simpler header and footer for subsequent pages, so that more information can be included on them.

8. Create the header and footer for the remaining pages.

    Usually, graphic images are not repeated on the remaining pages. Instead, you might create a second page letterhead like that shown in Figure 6-2.

    The address and telephone number are the only information that appears in the footer of the subsequent pages. You do not want to divide the document into sections to have different headers and footers in each section. While dividing a document into sections is one solution, it will not work well as you edit the document and the page breaks within the document move.

TIP: See "Sections" in Chapter 4 for an explanation of what sections are and how they work. See "Headers and Footers" to learn about creating headers and footers.

9. Close the Header and Footer view.

10. Save the document as a template.

Brochures

Figure 6-3 shows a brochure (mailer) created in Word using columns and frames. Brochures are normally designed around a standard sized paper, which is then folded. Legal paper (8 1/3 by 14 inches) can be folded four ways, while 8 1/2-by-11 inch paper is normally folded 3 ways.

Rodwell Landscapers

Rodwell Landscapers is an internationally recognized landscape design and maintenance company, based in Cleveland. We are best known for designing and maintaining unique landscaping projects.

"Rodwell Landscapers design has introduced our daughter, blind from birth, to nature in a safe, pleasant garden."

Richard and Ann Lewis

"I travel a lot, but Rodwell Landscapers is always at home, keeping my yard looking marvelous."

Sarah Jones

"Rodwell Landscapers helped me design a beautiful yard. When I sold my house, the realtor said the yard alone was worth $3,000 of the selling price."

Jay Samuels

Do You Need a Landscaper?

You may think that your small yard doesn't need a landscaper, just a neighborhood kid to mow it once a month. Think again! Landscapers offer more than mowing or trimming. A professional landscaper, like *Rodwell Landscapers*, is a plant and lawn expert with experience in landscape design, plant maintenance and improvement, and environmentally approved fertilizing, chemical weeding and waste removal.

Rodwell Landscapers can provide a variety of services that can help you:

- Save the time you now spend on lawn and garden maintenance.

- Design a garden and lawn that will look good all year round.

- Dispose of leaves, tree and bush trimmings, old mulch and garden chemicals such as fertilizers and herbicides.

Rodwell Landscapers
33445 Derbyshire Rd.
Cleveland Hts. OH 44118

Rodwell Landscapers

"Landscaping for Everyone

Why Rodwell Landscapers?

Rodwell Landscapers isn't just any landscaper. We have been in business in this area for over 35 years. Sarah Rodwell, our founding president, was a respected horticulturist with a master's degree in her field, and a record of creating and maintaining gardens in great homes and institutions around the world. We have continued in her tradition of extensive training, scientific plant maintenance, and skilled design.

Unlike many landscapers, we don't depend on unskilled summer help. Each of our associates is skilled in many different aspects of plant care, and undergoes continual training and skill checks. Our employees switch between different jobs and positions as the seasons change, matching their skills to the current work needed in our customers' gardens and lawns.

216/555-3434

Who Comes First?

Despite our extensive academic and professional credentials, we're not here to tell you what your garden should look like. We're here to help you design and maintain the lawn or garden you want, whatever it is.

Are you looking for a landscape design to complement your home, a garden for cut flowers, or a working herb garden? Do you want a durable lawn for kids to play on, a vegetable garden to feed them, or a garden meant to introduce a blind child to nature through textures and smells? We've designed them all.

Are you looking for a landscaper who will do the yearly chores of mulching, fertilizing, or pruning? Or do you want a landscaper to come every week and make suggestions on how you can keep your lawn and garden looking like a magazine cover? We can and have done it all.

Figure 6-3.   *Rodwell Landscapers mailing brochure*

Designing a Brochure

A brochure like the example shown in Figure 6-3 is one of the more difficult documents to design. You are working with very limited space, and a very confined layout.

Try to think about someone reading a brochure. They will either read the front or the back, then open it up and read the inside. You have to make both the front and the back interesting enough to get them to open it. The inside three panels have to work together to create an attractive look.

Consider your front and back panels as individual pages, since that is how a reader will view them. The front panel should usually include a title and enough text to get someone to open the brochure. This is a good location for catchy graphics, which will grab someone's eye before they throw the brochure out.

The back panel should also be attractive and catchy. A selection of endorsements or effective quotes is a good way to catch a reader's interest.

When you format the inside, make sure that all three panels work well together. The inside of a brochure is usually primarily text, but you will want to make sure that there is plenty of white space and graphics to keep the interest of readers. Lines of tightly-packed text with no relief provided by white space and graphics make the text hard to follow, and present an unpleasant appearance that turns readers away.

Creating a Brochure

Follow these steps to create a similar brochure:

1. Use the File | Setup command. You need to change the page orientation to landscape to create a brochure. In the sample brochure, the page alignment was changed to justified so that the text would stretch from the top to the bottom margin, even though the text didn't quite fill the space.

2. Use the Format | Columns command to evenly divide the page into three newspaper style columns.

See "Columns" in Chapter 4 for more information about creating columns.

3. Enter the text of the document. If you typed the text first, you just have to worry about fitting the text to the size of the panels in the brochure.

You can use styles to format headings in your brochure to keep them consistent. For example, in this document, the three headings on the inside of the brochure are formatted with a SectionHead style.

The return address on the center panel of the outside page was included as a WordArt object rather than as text. WordArt makes it easy to rotate sections of text.

See "WordArt" in Chapter 4 for more instructions on using the WordArt program.

4. Insert or create the graphic images. You want to add the graphic images after the text so that you don't add more graphic images than there is room on the page. If the image is important, you can delete text to make room for it, but why play around with your message if you don't have to.

In Figure 6-3, the graphic images are included in frames so that they can appear alongside the text, as you can see on the first panel of the inside page.

Flyers or Announcements

Figure 6-4 shows a flyer created in Word for the Cleveland Wine Festival. Flyers are basically small posters which you can post for people to read, or mail. While you can make flyers of any size, creating them in a standard size like 8 1/2 by 11 makes it easy and inexpensive to have them copied or printed.

Designing a Flyer

The difficulty with flyers, as with posters, is that they depend more than most documents on their layout or graphic design. Flyers usually need to catch someone's attention immediately, since they are probably only seen in passing. You will see many ineffective flyers created by people who simply threw the text and graphics on the page, and printed.

It is even more important with flyers than with other documents that you take the time to consider the effect of the fonts and graphics that you are using on your intended audience.

Remember to consider how your flyer will be seen. If it's to be posted, make very certain that the text is large enough to be read from a distance. If it's going

Fifth Annual
Cleveland Wine Festival

- Taste award-winning Ohio wines.
- Visit with Ohio wine makers.
- Buy wine at the Oeno-Auction.
- Learn more about making and tasting wines of all kinds.

The Cleveland Wine Festival is the only festival of its kind in Northeastern Ohio. Sponsored by the Oeno-cultural Club of Cleveland, it is meant for those who enjoy drinking wine or creating it non-professionally. The Wine Festival is a fun and interesting educational experience for those who feel you really can't know enough about good wines.

xxxxxxxxxxxxxxxxxxxxxxxxxxxxxxxxxxxxxxxxx

Registration Form

Name: Address:

Number Attending:

Adults $12 Children $5 (Under 21 cannot drink)   Tel: 216/555-1293
Send to: Oeno-Cultural Club of Cleveland, 212 E. 18th St., Cleveland, OH 44118

Figure 6-4.   *Flyer for the Cleveland Wine Festival*

to be distributed by hand, you can afford to use a smaller font. Never include so much text on a flyer that it's like reading a book, because readers will just drop the document off in the nearest waste can.

Designing flyers is a great test of your personal sense of style. Since they can be used for so many different purposes, you will need to determine which elements are most important based on your needs. Don't be afraid to spend a fair amount of time on a flyer. Once you find the art and text you want, spend some time playing with different fonts and placement until it looks right.

A flyer is a good place to use large, complicated graphics, like the cluster of grapes in Figure 6-4. In a smaller document, the fine lines in this graphic might blur or disappear, but in a document like this flyer, it's perfect. This old-style line drawing was chosen over other possible selections because it fits the style of the event, which is meant to be fun, but elegant. The same decision went into the font, which is meant to convey an elegant but "artsy" feeling.

Creating a Flyer

Flyers are remarkably easy to create. There are only two steps to actually putting a flyer together:

1. Enter and format the text.

2. Insert or create the graphics.

Greeting Cards

You can create a greeting card for your business or personal use, like the one shown in Figure 6-5. Use Word to create individualized cards for friends or family, or to create effective low-cost cards for your company.

Designing a Greeting Card

Greeting cards can differ according to why you are creating them. The elements of design and format you choose can vary greatly. However, the format of a standard greeting card is very simple. You will have a panel or graphic, and an inside message, or more rarely another graphic.

The greeting card in Figure 6-5 is an 8 1/2- by 5 1/2-inch sheet folded, with a message or graphic on the front outside flap and a message or signature on the inside. This size is useful because it uses a standard paper, and a fairly standard envelope, A-2.

Choose your graphic according to the feeling you are trying to convey. In this case, a traditional winter scene has been chosen, suitable for a traditional company. Any message in a greeting card should be kept very short and fairly

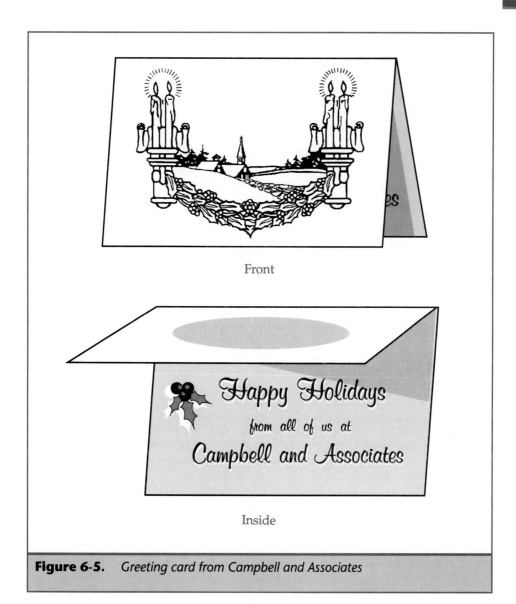

Front

Inside

Figure 6-5. *Greeting card from Campbell and Associates*

generic, unless you are making the card for only one person. Keep it short because there isn't a lot of space on a greeting card. Choose a font that reflects the same mood as the outside message, in this case a traditional feeling exemplified by this calligraphic-type font.

Creating a Greeting Card

To create a greeting card follow these steps:

1. Use the File | Page Setup command to set landscape orientation.

2. Change the top margin to 4.5 inches.

   If you fold the page in half with a horizontal crease, the fold is at 4.25 inches. You've added .25 inch to the top margin to allow for a margin from the fold. Adjust this measurement depending on the size of paper you are using.

See "Page Size and Orientation" in Chapter 4 for details on changing page orientation. See "Margins" for information on changing margins.

3. Use Format | Columns to create two equal-sized columns.

4. Insert or create your outside message or art on the first page.

   The outside message on the greeting card in Figure 6-5 is the graphic with the candles. You could also use WordArt to create a message, or just use a nice font to include a message.

5. On the second page, enter the message that will appear on the inside.

   In the greeting card in Figure 6-5, this is the "Happy Holidays" message. Not all greeting cards need to have an inside message. For example, a thank you card created in this way might have "Thank You" on the outside flap, with space left on the inside flap for a message.

Unless you have a two-sided printer or copier, you will need to print twice on the same sheet of paper. The second time, you want to reverse the page from left to right to get the inside and outside art in the correct locations. To envision this, imagine you are holding the paper with the outside message at the bottom. The inside message should appear on the back of that page, at the top, upside down.

Cards created in this way fit into A-2 sized envelopes. You should be able to get these envelopes in a paper that matches what the cards are printed on at most paper supply stores.

Reports

You may not think of creating a report as a graphic design feature, but it can be. Most reports have a purpose beyond simply making data available; they involve trying to persuade a boss or group of people to decide to do something. You are going to want to make that report as persuasive as possible. Careful graphic design will help you make your point. Figure 6-6 shows a multiple page view of a report created in Word, showing how the careful use of graphic design can help your report look better.

Designing a Report

Designing a report depends less on the use of graphics, and more on the layout and formatting of text, unlike the previous example documents. Reports are not the place to show off all the new desktop publishing tricks you have learned, since this will detract from the message of the text. The point in designing a report is to keep it simple, and make it easier to read and enjoy.

Figure 6-6.   *Thumbnail sketch of a report*

In the sample report the design elements are kept to a minimum. The cover page is very simple; it includes the title, a copy of the company's logo, and the authors' names. This page means to attract with simplicity, a style that seems to reinforce the streamlined appearance of the logo.

The text of the report is formatted into two columns because two columns are easier for most people to read. The lines are shorter and the gutter between columns allows for a fair amount of white space to break up the page. Despite the added white space, the text actually takes fewer pages when you use columns.

The header and footer are kept simple, serving as frames for the text. They include a double line, the report's title, and the page number. When the reader opens this document, which is meant to be printed double-sided and bound, the lines will frame the text.

A watermark of the company's logo is repeated on every odd-numbered page to provide a visual continuity to this report. Since there are so few graphics in this report, the watermark adds a graphic element that would otherwise be lacking.

One problem with using the watermark graphic is that it looks odd if your charts or other graphics overlay it. Graphs in this report either appear on the page without the watermark, or are carefully placed away from the watermark.

Choose the fonts for your headings and text carefully. You want to select fonts that do not stand out, but that reinforce your document's impression. A technical paper might use a sans serif font primarily, since sans serif fonts often convey a feeling of technology. However, they are hard to read for long stretches of text. Using them in headings, when the body text is in a serif font, contrasts the headings to the body text further, and introduces a similar feel without making the document difficult to read.

Creating a Report

To create a similar report follow these steps:

1. Use File | Page Setup to make Word use a different header and footer for odd and even pages, and the first page. In Word for Windows 2, you make this change with the View | Header/Footer command.

For more information on headers and footers see "Headers and Footers" in Chapter 4.

2. Enter the cover page information on the first page, inserting the graphic into a frame.

3. Enter an odd page section break at the end of the first page, so that the actual text of this report will appear on the next odd page.

For more information on sections and how they work, see "Sections" in Chapter 4.

4. Create a header on the first odd page using a border line across the top, and a watermark, which, in this case, is the company's logo.

   The watermark is included in the odd page's header within a text box added with the Draw feature. It is then sent behind the text so that it never overwrites the text.

For more information on inserting a watermark, see "Watermarks" in Chapter 4.

5. Create an even paged footer using a border line and text.

6. Format the second section with two columns.

For more information on creating columns, see "Columns" in Chapter 4.

7. Add graphics or charts to the text. The charts used in this report were created using Word's Graph program.

See "Graph" in Chapter 4 to learn about creating charts with this supplementary program.

8. Use styles to format headings in the text.

See "Styles" in Chapter 4 for an explanation of how styles work in Word.

Forms

Figure 6-7 is an invoice form created using Word for Windows 6. A form is any type of document meant to be filled in by hand or on a computer.

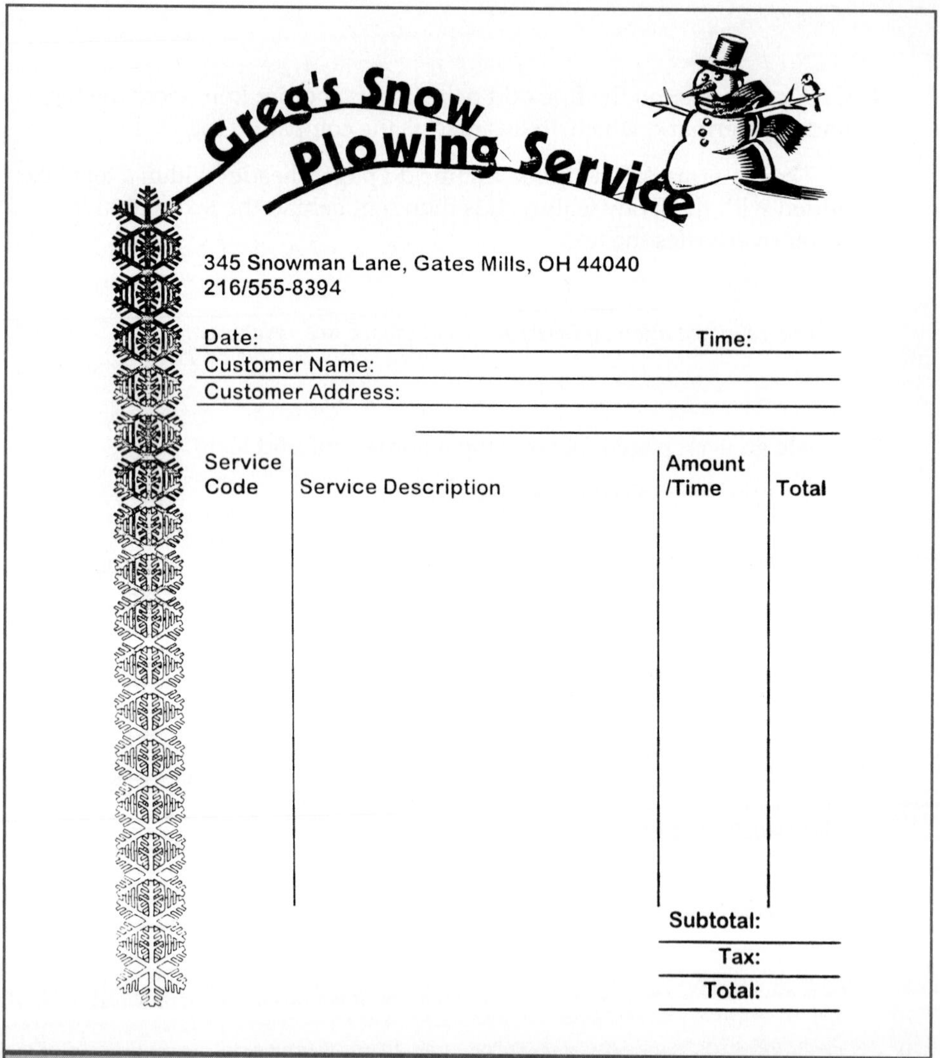

Greg's Snow Plowing Service

345 Snowman Lane, Gates Mills, OH 44040
216/555-8394

Date: Time:
Customer Name:
Customer Address:

Service Code	Service Description	Amount /Time	Total
		Subtotal:	
		Tax:	
		Total:	

Figure 6-7.   *An invoice for Greg's Snow Plowing Service*

Designing a Form

A primary consideration in designing a form is how it will be filled out. The example form was designed to be filled out by hand, so it needs to allow plenty of space for people to write in.

Another important consideration is that information has to be arranged in an easy to follow fashion, and those places that need to be filled out have to be marked carefully so that users don't miss a piece of information.

Since the sample form in Figure 6-7 is handed back to customers, it also needs to serve as advertisement for Greg's Snow Plowing Service. The comparatively large amount of space dedicated to the graphic is meant to help Greg's company advertise. Almost anybody who sees this form will take a second look.

The information is arranged in tables, making alignment of the different pieces of text easy. The comparatively large font size makes the form easier to read, even if it is filled out by customers standing out in the snow after having their driveway plowed.

The row heights are set to 20 points. Again, this is in consideration of how the form is likely to be used. Since it is going to be filled in by hand, the rows are high to let anyone's handwriting fit. Since it is probably not going to be filled out at a desk, but rather on a clipboard outside, these rows are even higher than usual. A form meant to be used in an office would probably have rows only 14 or 15 points high.

The alternating rows of gray and white are used to make it easier to follow a single line across the form. It is very easy while filling out a form to skip down a line, making the form much harder to figure out later. This light shading not only makes it easier to follow single lines across the form but also provides further graphic interest.

Creating a Form

To create a form like the sample invoice, follow these steps:

1. Insert the art, then use the Draw feature to send it to the back.

   This piece of art does not need to be inserted into a text box because it is a vector format file rather than a raster or bitmapped piece. To create a form like this, you want to insert your art first because the art limits the text area of the document. If your art is meant to appear as a watermark, or as part of a heading in the document, it may not need to be inserted first.

See "Graphics" and "Drawing on a Document" in Chapter 4 for information on working with imported graphics.

This particular graphic was created using the CorelDRAW! graphics package, and saved in the .CGM format. The snowman and snowflake are pieces of clip art that come with that package. The text was formatted with the "Align with Line" format to make it match the drawn lines. The snowflake was inserted in two places in two different colors, then blended, creating those intervening snowflakes. Being able to create graphics like this is why you may want to purchase a graphics package.

2. Adjust your margins so that the text area is limited to inside the art.

See "Margins" in Chapter 4 for information on adjusting margins.

3. Add any text that won't appear in a table, such as the address in this form.

4. Add the tables you are going to use to create the form. In this document, there are two tables, one for the customer information, and the second for the invoice data.

See "Tables" in Chapter 4 for further information on creating tables.

5. Enter the form's text.

6. Use the Format | Borders and Shading command to add lines and screen to your tables. In this form, every other row in the invoice area is formatted with 20% shading. This makes it easier to follow text across the lines when the text is written in. The row height is 20 points, which is fairly high, to make it easy for someone to write in information.

Newsletters

Creating a newsletter, for a social group, business or charity, is the first step many people take into the realm of desktop publishing. Many different groups use newsletters to keep their members aware of current information, and if you have access to a computer and some skill in using it, you are very likely to be corralled into serving as the editor.

The sample newsletter shown in Figure 6-8 was created using Word for Windows 6. While you could not create the same uneven column effect in Word for Windows 2, there are no other features involved in the newsletter that could not be done with Word for Windows 2.

Designing a Newsletter

Designing a newsletter can be difficult. You first need to know what kind of information is to go into it. You will have a different type of newsletter if you can expect two or three four-page articles every issue, or two pages of short snippets of information.

When you create the newsletter design, remember that you want to create a flexible design that can be used without significant change for many issues. Readers will feel more comfortable with your newsletter if they know what it's going to look like, and where to find regular features. A familiar layout also lets the publishing group, and editor, look more professional.

TIP: You can save the first page of your newsletter as a template, to make it easier to recreate, or simply save individual elements, such as the masthead, as AutoText items to make creating them easier.

Start with your masthead or flag, which is the title and other publishing information for the newsletter. This appears in every single issue, and sets the tone for your group and the publication. Make sure that the masthead contains all the necessary information, such as the group your newsletter is for, the date the newsletter is published, and any other information you deem necessary.

The masthead should be fairly large, just as the masthead of your local newspaper is large. As a quick rule of thumb, make your total masthead use a little less than a quarter of the page. Font sizes of 24 to 36 points are appropriate for the title, depending on the font, and how you've laid your masthead out. While having mastheads at the top of the first page isn't required, it is traditional, and makes sure that readers know from the beginning what it is they are reading.

Choose the column structure of your newsletter. Two columns is traditional and easily formatted. Three columns also conveys an attractive and balanced look to the page. Uneven columns, like those used in the sample, are less traditional, but can be effective. Selecting the column structure is a personal choice, without any particularly strong arguments in favor of one direction. Do,

West Side Gardener
Serving Gardeners West of the Cuyahoga

Vol. 1, Issue 27   September 12, 1994

Winter Preparations

Sandra Jorgson

While it's only the beginning of September, and most of us are worrying about getting children to school and keeping the yard raked, it is none too early to start planning for the winter. The Almanac is predicting an early winter this year, and, since it's right a lot more often than the Weather Bureau, I recommend that you start planning right away.

The first step to getting gardens ready for winter is a final weeding. Don't leave this step out. Your final weeding is a headstart on getting ready for next year, since this prevents those weeds from spreading seeds that will be ready to germinate in the spring.

Turn over any beds you'll be leaving empty, or beds you'll be planting bulbs in for the spring. Turning empty beds over now will help make them easier to work in the spring, and you'll need to aerate the soil for those bulbs to lie in all winter.

Mulch all beds. Mulch will help keep the root systems of shrubs and other plants from freezing, especially those bulbs. Mulching empty beds will help enrich the soil in this off season, preparing it for the spring growth.

Bring in all your plants that won't last the season outside, such as ferns. You can also bring in those plants that you want to have as houseplants in this season, even if they are hardy enough to survive the season, such as herb plants you plan to use. A greenhouse is the best choice for these winter houseplants.

Put fencing around small shrubs and trees and wrap the trunks of small trees. This protection is against the cold, and against deer, who will kill these plants while grazing through the winter. Deer will eat virtually everything.

Congratulations to Norma Dryer. Norma entered her garden in the "Primerica Garden and Landscaping Competition" and took first place. Norma's home is surrounded by herb and cut-flower gardens, and has a shrubbery walk in her backyard.

Our next monthly meeting will be October 10 at 2:30 at Stan Hywet Hall in Akron. The gardeners of Stan Hywet Hall will take us on a guided tour of the extensive gardens, and share some of their expertise. We will have tea in Stan Hywet Hall itself at 3:00 and the guided tours will start at 3:30. The actual business meeting will begin at 6:30.

Dawn Fox, forty year member of the West Side Gardening Society, passed away on September 3. Her family is asking for memorial donations to the Society for the Blind, Dawn's favorite charity.

Figure 6-8.   *A newsletter for the West Side Gardening Club*

however, stay away from single column newsletters. Long stretches of text like that leave little room for graphic development and are actually harder to read than columns. Also, with columns you can fit more text in the same amount of space.

Make sure you use standard styles for article titles, author bylines and other regular text features. This helps make your newsletter look more consistent, and will speed up the layout time.

To the extent feasible, avoid jumping stories across pages. The "Continued on page 4." message frustrates readers, and makes them more likely to just stop reading at that point. Also, this tends to leave short ends of stories all gathered on the back page of your newsletter. Since the reader is as likely to see the back of the newsletter as the front when it is picked up, this may help decrease readership.

Limit the use of rules, or lines, in your newsletter. Used indiscriminately, they can confuse rather than help the reader separate individual stories and determine where sections fall.

Never go gung-ho on the fonts in your newsletter. Many first-time publishers will use a different font for every element in their newsletter. Instead of looking professional, the newsletter ends up looking messy. As a rule of thumb, don't use more than three fonts on a single page.

Also, make sure that your fonts all go together. The following illustration shows how poorly selected fonts detract from the message in your document. You should contrast text that you want to stand out, such as headings and the masthead, but not enough so that it looks like two different people designed the elements of the newsletter.

WEST SIDE GARDENER

SERVING GARDENERS WEST OF THE CUYAHOGA

Vol. 1, Issue 27	September 12, 1994
Winter Preparations	*Congratulations* to Norma Dryer. Norma entered her garden in the "Primerica Garden and Landscaping Competi-
Sandra Jorgson	
While it's only the beginning of September, and most of us are worrying about getting children	

Creating a Newsletter

In Word for Windows 6, you have a shortcut for creating a newsletter, the Newsletter Wizard. The Wizard can guide you through several steps for creating a newsletter. Newsletters created this way are quite functional and attractive, and take advantage of the time and experience of the professional graphic designers who put the designs together. However, the sample newsletter shown in Figure 6-6 was created without this tool.

Follow these steps to create a newsletter:

1. Design and insert your masthead. As explained above, your masthead is vital to the effect of your document. Usually, a masthead extends across the whole page of a newsletter, and the text is divided into columns. A useful thing to do is to create your masthead, than save it as an AutoText entry so you never have to create it from scratch again.

See "AutoText" in Chapter 4 for more information on saving your masthead as an AutoText entry.

2. Enter your text. You are likely to receive articles for your newsletter on disk, in which case you can use the File | Insert command to bring them into the newsletter. You can also type your own articles or short bits of information, such as those in the second column of the sample newsletter. This is also the stage in which you should proofread or edit the text you have been given. It helps to edit text you receive on disk before inserting it. However, you may find after bringing it into your newsletter that you need to edit it again so that it uses less space.

See "Inserting Files" in Chapter 4 for an explanation of inserting text from other files into a Word document. You may also need to convert the file, in which case, see "Opening Files" in Chapter 4 for information on file conversion.

3. Format your text. You should save the formatting to apply to various elements as styles, to speed up the formatting stage, and to keep your document consistent. For example, in the sample newsletter, the article title and author byline are saved as paragraph styles. The format applied to "Congratulations" is saved as a character style, to be used for emphasizing text.

See "Styles" in Chapter 4 for more information on creating and using styles. Character styles are a new feature in Word for Window 6.

4. Insert or create any art you want to use. You will want to use a fair amount of art in a newsletter, because it helps to make the newsletter more interesting to readers. You will want to edit and format the text first, so that you can select your clip art based on the room that you have

available after the text is inserted and to make sure that it is appropriately placed.

5. Adjust the text and art. You probably need to adjust how the document is formatted to make everything fit comfortably. You can size or move the art to fit the text more accurately. You may also want to remove a word or line of text in an article to make it fit better in the space you allotted for it. Little things, like a single extra line, or lines with just a single word, may need to be corrected to make your newsletter look its best.

CHAPTER 7

Adding Sophistication to Merge and Macro Features

This chapter is for the user who wants to take macro and merge features beyond the basics presented in Chapter 4. It is important that you have mastered the basics presented there; however, here you will add to your knowledge of those features. You will also learn how to plan your macros and establish strategies for merge operations.

This chapter takes a look at several considerations involved in creating more sophisticated macros and merges. The information here is not comprehensive, but is designed to get you started with these topics, which are complex enough to merit several books, not just this one—the Microsoft

Developer's Documentation on macros alone spans two volumes. After absorbing the highlights presented here, you can decide if you would like to order the Microsoft Word Developer's Kit to get all the details.

What you will learn in this chapter are the important first steps in creating more sophisticated macros and merges. You will see how to extend macros beyond Word's basic macro recorder functions, by examining some of the WordBasic commands that allow you to add logic to menu selections. You will also learn how to take full advantage of the Word fields available to you while you are performing a merge operation. The emphasis in this chapter is on Word for Windows 6 examples, but you will find that most of the capabilities discussed are also available with Word for Windows 2.

Although macros and merges are completely different functions in Word, the advanced features covered in this chapter are typically used by the same group of users. The same users who are eager to work with advanced merge features are likely to also be willing to explore sophisticated macro capabilities.

Macros

Macros are sets of WordBasic instructions that tell Word how to complete a task. WordBasic, like its predecessor, QBasic, is a programming language; it has the commands you would find in other versions of Basic, plus additional commands tailored to completing Word tasks. Word has hundreds of different functions and commands, allowing you to create or modify existing Word commands, create dialog boxes and process a user's input, and perform tasks usually handled by the menus.

Using the Macro Recorder

You have probably already experimented with Word's macro recorder, described in Chapter 4, "Macros." Using the macro recorder, you can create a macro while you perform a task. As you work, the recorder creates WordBasic commands that duplicate the task you are executing.

In summary, the process of recording a macro is started with the Tools | Macro command (Tools | Record Macro in Word for Windows 2). You supply a name or description for the macro, as well as assign the macro to a toolbar button, menu command, or key combination. (In Word for Windows 2 you can only assign a macro to a key combination at the time you record the macro, but you can later assign it a toolbar button or menu command.) These steps are all spelled out for you in Chapter 4, "Macros."

Using the Macro Toolbar to Edit and Test a Macro

To change how a macro works, you edit it by selecting Tools | Macro, highlighting the macro name, and selecting Edit. While you are editing a macro, the Macro toolbar is displayed. This toolbar appears even when you are working in other windows in Word. This way, you can edit a macro, make changes, switch to a document window, and use the Macro toolbar to run the macro from the document window. The toolbar lets you run a macro from any document window. For example, suppose you have the Logo macro, shown in Figure 7-1, for adding a logo to a document. Let's say this macro is not perfect yet, and you want to test it and edit it using the Macro toolbar.

Before testing a macro, switch to where you plan to use it. For example, since you would run the macro in Figure 7-1 from a document, either open a new document or retrieve an existing one. The Macro toolbar continues to display in

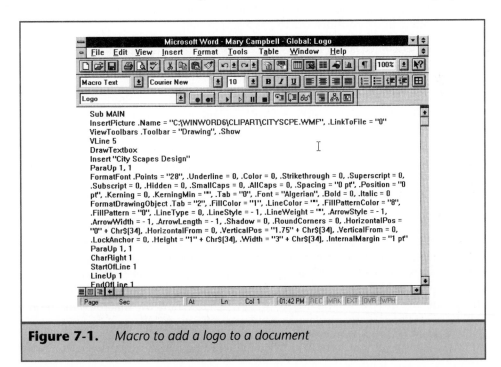

Figure 7-1. *Macro to add a logo to a document*

this document window so you can use the Macro toolbar to run the macro instead of the Tools | Macro command.

TIP: *If your macro will work on both new and existing documents, test it first on a new document. When it works correctly on the new document, test it on an existing one.*

Next, make sure the macro appears in the Active Macro button (the only drop-down list box in the Macro toolbar, at the far left end), and click the Start button. In Word for Windows 2, you can also select this button by pressing ALT+SHIFT and the underlined letter. Word will execute the macro until it reaches either the end of the macro or an error.

In a fast-running macro, it is difficult to see the actions the macro performs because they are happening so fast. The Macro toolbar has other options for running a macro more slowly:

- Instead of the Start button, you can click the Step button to run a macro one command at a time. You must click the Step button to perform each subsequent command in the macro.

- Or you can click the Step Subs button; this performs the macro one step at a time with subroutines treated as a single step.

- Another choice is to click the Trace button, which highlights the macro's commands as they are performed, one at a time.

If you freeze a macro while it is running, with the Stop, or Step, or Step Subs button, you can later continue the macro's execution at normal speed by clicking the Continue button.

When you use Step or Step Subs to examine a macro more closely, you may want to also use the Window | Arrange All button and show both the macro and the affected document in their own windows. In Figure 7-2 a macro is being executed using the Step button; you can see one of the steps highlighted as Word performs it.

You can see in Figure 7-1 that menu commands in a macro include many statements and settings. Rather than having to remember them, or copying them from another macro, you can perform the command and have Word install it in the macro for you, using buttons in the Macro toolbar. When you need to insert one command or several, move to the position where you want the commands inserted in the macro, and switch to where the macro commands will be performed, such as a document window. Then click Record Next Command in the toolbar to add one command to the macro, or Record to add

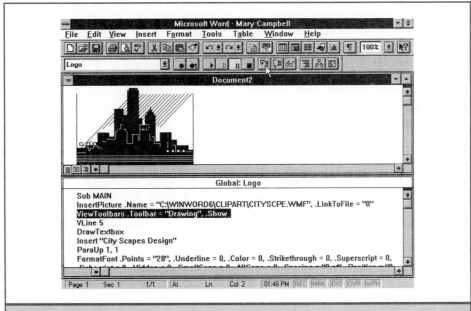

Figure 7-2. *Using Step to show the macro instruction being performed*

several; then perform the commands to record. If you have recorded several commands, click Record again when you have finished. When you return to the macro, the commands you performed will have been inserted at the proper location in the macro.

TIP: If you have a problem reading the macro text, select Tools | Options and select the Draft Font check box. In Word for Windows 6, you can change the character and paragraph formatting of macro text by modifying the Macro Text style. For example, you can change this style to use a different font and different tab stops when you look at and edit macros. Changing this style has no effect on how a macro performs.

Using the WordBasic Programming Language to Create Macros

If you stick with the recorder method, your macros will not be any more difficult to create than the one in the example just above. Using the recorder is easy to do, since there is no need to learn the syntax of the commands or even how to spell the command names. The recorder automatically enters the correct WordBasic command for you. The downside of this method is that you cannot add logic and conditions to your macro. To use these extras you need to enter the WordBasic instructions yourself.

The following sections cover some suggestions, guidelines, and basic instructions that you will need as you work with WordBasic, to enhance your ability to create successful macros.

Planning Macros Can Actually Save Time

You may feel that you are not making progress on your computer tasks unless you are actually at the keyboard making entries. This is not true: You may actually accomplish your task more quickly if you first spend some time planning how to attack it. Well-planned macros are likely to have fewer errors ("bugs") to fix. Preventing these problems usually takes less time than finding and fixing them.

The most important planning step is deciding exactly what you need to accomplish. Think this through in detail. Make sure that you consider who the macro's users will be. If you will be the only one to use your macro, you can assume more about when and where it will be used than if others will use it. If the macro is meant to be used by others, you will want to list your assumptions and have the macro verify that the user is entering the correct information, to ensure the macro is always successful. For example, if you assume that the macro will be used after a paragraph of text is selected, the macro should check for that circumstance and display a message if a paragraph has not yet been selected.

MAPPING OUT YOUR LOGIC   For planning the logic of your macro, a brief sketch of what you want to accomplish and the steps required to get there are sufficient. You can write the steps in phrases or, if you want to get fancier, use some of the tools of the programming trade, such as flowcharts or diagrams, to map out the logic.

Flowchart templates use symbols such as a diamond to represent condition checks, and a rectangle to show a formula or procedure. Writing down the logical processing you plan to accomplish is helpful even if your diagram or list is not neat. Its purpose is to help you consider all conditions. Figure 7-3 shows the design for a macro entered in a document.

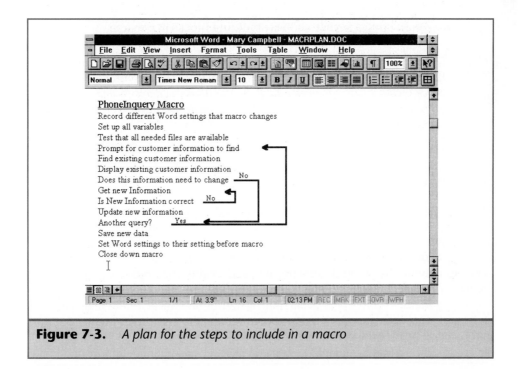

Figure 7-3.   *A plan for the steps to include in a macro*

The Building Blocks of Your Macro

No matter what project you attempt, you need to use the correct materials, and building a Word macro is no exception. Here are the components of the WordBasic language that you will use:

- A *statement* carries out a specific action.

- A *function* performs a computation or other action to provide information. Functions are predefined expressions where you provide the information a function works with and the function calculates the result.

- *Variables* are special storage locations for numeric or string values.

- *Expressions* perform computations. They are not predefined like functions and you are free to create whatever you need.

- You will use all of these components as you create *logical structures* to control the order in which macro instructions are executed.

Figure 7-4 illustrates several of these building blocks in a macro.

TIP: If you need help for a macro, don't forget the help that is available with F1. When you press F1 while working on a macro, you see the WordBasic Help, which includes descriptions for all of the WordBasic statements and functions you can use, as well as other topics that help guide you through creating your own macros.

Statements

Statements provide a way to duplicate the actions of Word commands within your macro. Most of the entries recorded by the macro recorder are statements. These statements are executed one after another, starting at the top and going to the bottom of the macro. Since you may not always want the statements to execute sequentially, some statements are used to alter the processing flow, to create a macro with a logical structure.

Most statements have *arguments* that further define the action to take. For statements that are equivalent to Word commands, the arguments are the options in the dialog box for the command. Arguments start with a period and are

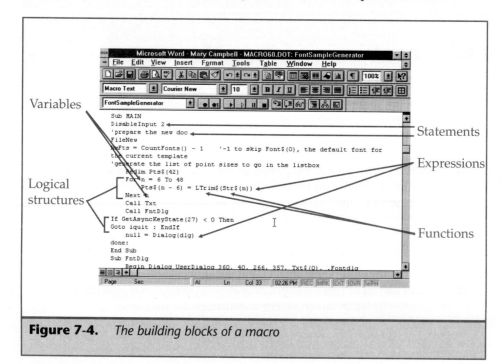

Figure 7-4. *The building blocks of a macro*

separated from one another by commas. For example, the following statement has four arguments:

```
EditFind .Find = "Mary", .Direction = 1, .MatchCase = 1,\
.WholeWord = 1
```

Notice that Mary is enclosed in quotes; this is because Mary is text and therefore considered a *string*. Strings are always enclosed in quotes. The backslash (\) at the end of the statement's first line is a line break and makes the line more readable by continuing the statement on the next line. This statement is long because of the arguments, but even short statements must have a paragraph mark at the end. In other words, they appear on a line by themselves.

It is easy to make mistakes when you first start writing macros with WordBasic. The box "Things to Watch Out for When Writing Macros" contains some mistakes you should avoid when creating your macros.

Things to Watch Out for When Writing Macros

Mistakes come easily when you are first writing macros using WordBasic. After you write a few, you will become more careful. Here is a list of some things that can cause problems. Watch out for them when you are writing your code:

- Quotation marks missing from string values

- A reserved word used as a variable name

- Two subroutines with the same name

- A statement that requires multiple reserved words, such as If...Then missing a reserved word

- A missing closing parenthesis in a function

- A dialog box option argument that does not have the initial period, or a missing comma separator when there are multiple arguments

- A misplaced comma separator or extra comma

- A misspelled statement or function name

- A data type that is incorrect for an argument

There are many different categories of Word statements in WordBasic. Every statement will be in one of these categories:

Application Control	Finding and Replacing
AutoCorrect	Footnotes, Endnotes, and
AutoText	Annotations
Basic File Input/Output	Forms
Bookmarks	Help
Borders and Frames	Macros
Branching and Control	Mail Merge
Bullets and Numbering	Moving the Insertion Point and
Character Formatting	Selecting
Customization	Object Linking and Embedding
Date and Time	Outlining and Master Documents
Definitions and Declarations	Paragraph Formatting
Dialog Box Definition and Control	Proofing
Disk Access and Management	Section and Document Formatting
Documents, Templates, and Add-Ins	Strings and Numbers
Drawing	Style Formatting
Dynamic Data Exchange	Tables
Editing	Tools
Environment	View
Fields	Windows

Functions

Functions return information about the current Word document or the actions of Word. They also convert one type of data to another type. Functions are distinguished from statements by the parentheses at the end. There are many statements with the same name as functions. The difference is that the statement sets a value, and the function checks its current setting. For example, the AppMinimize statement minimizes an application window, and the AppMinimize() function checks to see if an application window is minimized. Some functions, such as Files$(), contain a $ in their name. The $ indicates that the function returns a string. These parentheses distinguish them from statements. Functions are organized into the same categories as statements.

Data Values

Macro statements often contain data values, such as the name of a document, the number of copies, or the value to search for. Depending on the argument the value is supplying, it must be either a string or a number. If it is a string, it must be enclosed in quotation marks and cannot exceed 65,280 characters. A number can be a whole number, or it can include decimal digits. Its length cannot exceed 14 digits. Do not use a comma separator in numbers because WordBasic uses commas to separate different values or strings.

Variables

Variables are memory locations to which you assign a name and use to hold either numbers or strings. Variables add flexibility to macros that use data values in statements and functions, because you can use a new data value for a variable each time you use the macro. You can create string variables with names that have a $ at the end, such as MYDOC$ or THISMANY$. The $ lets Word know the variable contains a string (or text) as compared to a number.

Variable names are limited to 40 characters. Numbers and the underscore character are allowed, but the first character must be a letter. Never use any of WordBasic's reserved words as variable names; this includes the names of functions, statements, arguments, and operators.

You assign a value to a variable by following the variable name with an equal sign. The value is entered to the right of the equal sign. Remember to use the quotes for string values. The following are valid examples of variable assignments:

```
MyDoc$ = "Letter9"
Copies$ = 2
MyState$ = "Ohio"
```

Expressions

Expressions are either string or numeric formulas. Numeric formulas use the following operators: addition (+), subtraction (-), multiplication (*), division (/), and modular division (MOD). String expressions use only the concatenation operator to join strings (+). You can use variables or data values in expressions; for example:

```
Whole - 10
Some + More
```

Logical Structures

The commands you capture with the macro recorder represent a list of steps to execute sequentially. There is no way to skip or repeat steps. You can use Word statements and the other building blocks to create logical constructs like those you use daily to process data and make decisions. These include If...Then statements, loops, and subroutines.

When you use If...Then, a condition is tested and evaluated as true or false. Depending on the outcome, one of two paths are followed. For example, you may test to see if data is selected. If it is, the macro can proceed to process it. If data is not selected, the macro can display a message box asking the user to make a selection. There is no way to handle this type of situation with the recorder; you must use the If condition.

A While loop is an extension of the condition. It continues to execute a series of instructions while a condition is true. A second statement, Wend, marks the end of the statements to be repeated.

A subroutine is a self-contained unit of WordBasic code that carries out a specific task. You can call a subroutine from within a macro and then return to the next statement in the macro after executing the instructions in the subroutine. Subroutines offer organizational advantages, because you can remove many of the details from the main routine, making it easier to follow. You can use a single subroutine in a number of different macros, increasing your productivity.

Some Macro Examples

Word for Windows 6 contains a number of macro examples that are stored as part of the MACRO60.DOT template. If you do not have this file in your MACROS subdirectory, you can always go back to Setup and install the Wizards, Templates, and Letters option. Looking at these examples is a good way to see some of the WordBasic commands in action, as well as some common logic constructs that you can use when you create your own macros. Following are several examples of the most popular logical structures. If you have ever programmed with another language, these logical structures will be familiar to you, although the exact format of the logical structure varies by language.

Goto

The Goto logical structure, shown in the OrganizationChartMaker macro in Figure 7-5, changes the next direction that Word performs. The two Goto statements are after the Then in the If...Then logical structure. Combining If...Then with Goto means the Goto statements are only performed when the condition after IF is true. In this case, Word only goes to Bye when A equals 0, and only goes to DisplayDialog when A equals 1. Both Bye and DisplayDialog are labels identified elsewhere in the same subroutine.

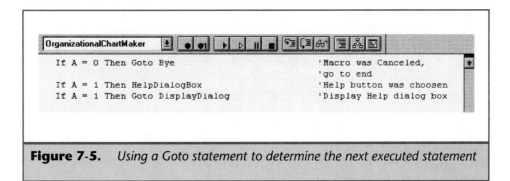

Figure 7-5.   *Using a Goto statement to determine the next executed statement*

With WordBasic's extensive subroutine and function features, you can create better-working macros using subroutines and functions rather than Goto statements. However, Goto is a fundamental element for changing the order in which Word performs the statements in a macro.

If...Then...Else

The If...Then...Else logical structure in Figure 7-6 determines which one of two sets of steps are performed. These statements are from the FontSampleGenerator macro in MACRO60.DOT. When you run this macro, Word prompts for the point size you want for the sample fonts. Since 48 is the largest size font that the FontSampleGenerator can generate, the If...Then...Else logical structure handles what happens when you enter a larger number.

The DlgText$() function returns the point size selected, and the Val() function converts the result of the DlgText$() function from a string to a value. Word uses the result of these two functions to compare to 48. When this value is more than 48, Word performs the three statements between Then and Else. When the value is 48 or less, the macro performs the Do_It subroutine and ends the If...Then...Else logical structure.

Select Case

The macro statements from the MindBender macro shown in Figure 7-7 use the Select Case statement to select the parameters used for the DlgValue( ) function. This function selects or clears dialog box controls such as check boxes and options.

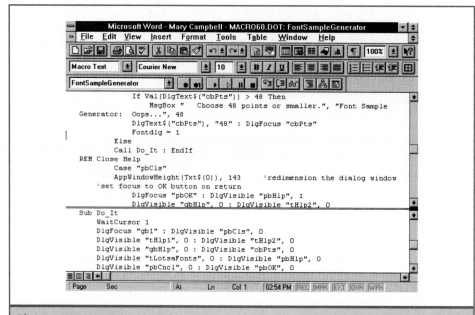

Figure 7-6.   *Using If...Then...Else to determine which statements are performed*

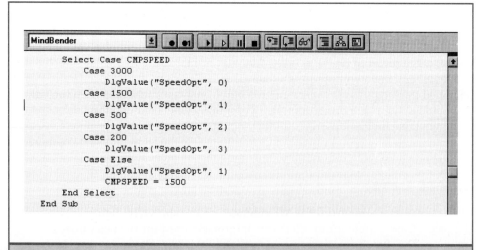

Figure 7-7.   *Using Select Case to select one of multiple choices*

The Select CaseSelect Case statement looks at the value of CMPSPEED. When it equals 3000, Word evaluates the statement below Case 3000...and so on down to the statement below Case 200. When it equals anything else, Word evaluates the statements below Case Else.

For...Next

The For...Next logical structure in Figure 7-8 performs a set of steps a specific number of times. These statements are from the FontSampleGenerator macro in MACRO60.DOT, which creates samples of each of the fonts you have installed. The (NmFts) equals the number of fonts you have installed on your system. This macro repeats the statements between For and Next for each of the installed fonts. The statements between For and Next use the value of X to select the font the macro is currently working with. When Word reaches the Next X statement, Word increases the value of X and repeats the statements until X equals the number of installed fonts.

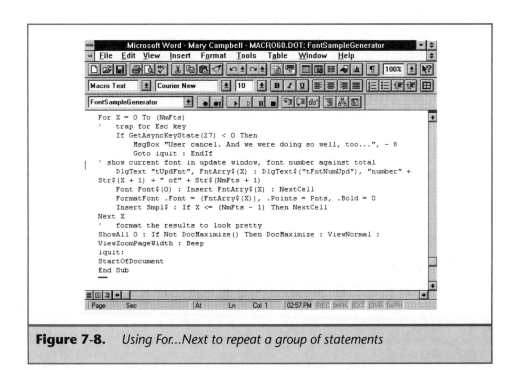

Figure 7-8. *Using For...Next to repeat a group of statements*

MsgBox

The statements that illustrate the If...Then...Else logical structure in Figure 7-6 also use the MsgBox statement. This MsgBox statement makes the macro tell you that you have entered a number that is too large. When Word executes this statement, Word displays the dialog box shown below. You can see how the text in the MsgBox statement is repeated in the dialog box. The exclamation mark appears next to the message because the MsgBox uses a Type (the third argument in the MsgBox command) of 48, which creates an attention symbol. In Windows 3.1, the attention symbol is an exclamation mark. Word executes the next macro statement when you select the OK button in the dialog box.

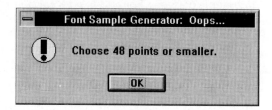

InputBox

When you run the MindBender macro and get a higher score than the current posted high score, the macro prompts you for your name, like this:

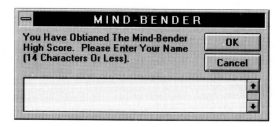

If you look at the MindBender macro, you'll find this statement:

```
name$ = InputBox$(HighScore$, UCase$(appName$) + " " +
HighScoreTitle$)
```

This statement uses the InputBox function to return the user's name. The macro uses the InputBox function rather than a dialog box, because only one piece of information is needed. The statement sets the value of Name to the entry you make in the dialog box. If the macro needs more information than you can get from the one input box, you would create a dialog box.

Subroutines

The section of the FontSampleGenerator macro shown in Figure 7-7 verifies whether you have entered a valid point size and then generates the list of fonts. When you enter a number below 48 in the dialog box that prompts for the point size to use in the generated samples, the Else part of If...Then...Else is true. The statement after Else,

Call Do_it : EndIf

starts the Do_it subroutine. When the Do_it subroutine is finished, Word performs the EndIf statement and continues with the next statement.

Remarks

A macro like those in Figures 7-5 through 7-8 needs some explanations, or *remarks,* to describe what it does; these remarks are the macro *documentation.* Documentation lets you or another user know what the macro does; it prevents a macro from becoming useless if you forget why you created it, or another user can't determine its role. Documentation also helps you understand the roles of the macro's statements when it is necessary to modify the macro. In Word macros, the lines that start with an ' (apostrophe) are the documentation comments or remarks.

NOTE: Remarks must be created by editing an existing macro, because Word does not create them for you when you record a macro.

The Word Dialog Editor

The Word Dialog Editor is a separate program that lets you create custom dialog boxes to use with your macros. A full installation of Word creates a Word Dialog

Editor program item. If this program item is not available you can return to the Word setup procedure to modify your installation.

The Dialog Editor is an advanced feature but it is useful if you want to create an interactive macro that accepts user input. Since the dialog boxes you can create have the look and feel of other Word dialog boxes, you can feel comfortable using them to define your needs. Although this section provides only a brief introduction to creating your own dialog boxes, you can learn more information about the Word Dialog Editor in the Microsoft Word Developer's Kit.

Creating a Dialog Box

Although you can create a dialog box by adding WordBasic commands directly to a macro, the Word Dialog Editor is the only practical approach. The Word Dialog Editor displays the dialog box to show you that it is what you want. As you make changes these modifications are also visible. When the dialog box is complete, you use the Clipboard to copy the dialog box from the Word Dialog Editor into your Word macro. The dialog box appears in a Word macro as the WordBasic commands that create the dialog box.

When you start the Word Dialog Editor application, you have an empty dialog box. You can alter the size of the dialog box and where it appears on the screen. Change the size by dragging a side of the dialog box, just like you would size a document or application window. Change a dialog box's placement by dragging the dialog box's title bar to a new location. Word records the changes you make as commands that will later become part of your Word macro.

A dialog box contains *items* such as text, text boxes, check boxes, list boxes, option buttons, and other buttons such as OK and Cancel. You add these items with the Item pull-down menu. After selecting Item and the type of item to add, you may be prompted for further clarification of the type of item to add. Each item has its own settings that you can change by double-clicking the item or by selecting the item and selecting Edit | Info. You can select an item by clicking it or pressing TAB until the item has an extra outline. The settings include the size and position of the item.

Figure 7-9 shows a dialog box created with the Word Dialog Editor. This dialog box is designed to be used in a macro that adds data to a table in Word. The table data is then used to create form letters. In this dialog box, several text boxes, a picture item (currently shows the filename ARTIST.WMF), check boxes, option buttons, etc. are displayed.

As you add items to the dialog box, they will not appear in their final form. For example, text items initially have text of "Text" and check boxes initially have text of "Check Box."The initial text is replaced by the text that you see in Figure 7-9. Most of the text includes an & in the text. This & indicates that the letter

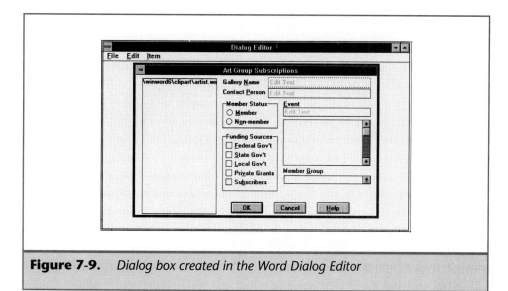

Figure 7-9. *Dialog box created in the Word Dialog Editor*

that follows is underlined. For example, the Gallery Name text item actually has the text Gallery &Name.

The items are then placed and sized by dragging the item or item's borders to the desired location in the dialog box. By double-clicking the item you can type numbers for the placement and size that will position and size the item in small increments. The dialog box title is added by selecting the Edit | Select Dialog and Edit | Info commands.

When the dialog box is complete, select the Edit | Select Dialog and Edit | Copy commands to copy the dialog box to the Clipboard. Next, switch to the macro-editing window and move the insertion point to where you want the macro statements that create the dialog box. Select Edit | Paste. The WordBasic instructions to create the dialog box are pasted from the Clipboard to the location of the insertion point in the macro code. Figure 7-10 shows the WordBasic statements Word pastes for the dialog box in Figure 7-9.

TIP: If you add items to a dialog box in a different order than you will use them, you might notice that pressing ALT and the underlined letter does not select the dialog box item. Make sure that Text statements for text items are before the dialog box item described by the text item. Selecting a text item actually selects the dialog box item described immediately after the Text statement. For example, a Text statement that displays Name in a dialog box must be the statement immediately before the TextBox statement to store the name. You may have to move some of the Text statements after copying a dialog box from the Word Dialog Editor.

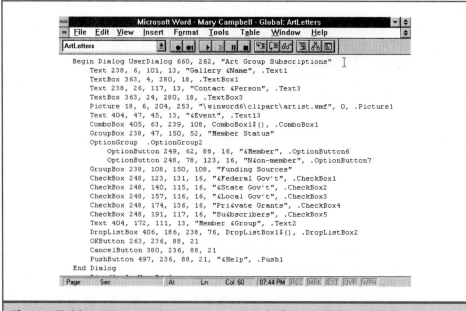

Figure 7-10.   *Macro statements created with the Word Dialog Editor*

At the end of each WordBasic statement that creates an item in the dialog box is an *identifier* that starts after the period. This identifier is the text that other WordBasic statements use to set the value of an item. Other statements can use this identifier to return the value of the item when the macro user makes an entry. For example, a macro can have a statement that sets the identifier "TextBox$1" to "Letters." Assuming TextBox$1 is for a text box, this text box will initially contain the string "Letters." When the user finishes with the dialog box, TextBox$1 contains either "Letters" or what the user typed as a replacement. After the macro's user finishes with the dialog box, another statement can use the identifier to determine this text box's value. The identifier names can be set by you or the Word Dialog Editor. When you double-click an item in the Word Dialog Editor, one of the settings is .Field. *.Field* sets the identifier of the item. Once the WordBasic statements for a dialog box are in a Word macro, you can rename an identifier by changing the existing identifier in the WordBasic statement that creates that dialog box item.

Besides the statements that set up a dialog box like the ones shown in Figure 7-10, the macro must also have other statements to use the dialog box. For instance, in the dialog box shown in Figure 7-11, the text that appears in the drop-down list boxes and list boxes must be added. This text is added to the macro before the Begin Dialog statement that creates the dialog box. To add "Art

for a Day" that you see in Figure 7-11, the macro has the statement
**ComboBox1$(0) = "Art for a Day"**. In this example, ComboBox1$ is the array
variable containing the items that the list box displays.

The macro in Figure 7-10 also includes two other required statements to use
the dialog box. Below the macro statements you see in Figure 7-10 are the
following statements:

> Dim dlg As UserDialog
> Dialog dlg

The first statement tells Word that you are working with a user defined dialog
box. The second statement activates the dialog box. After the Dim statement that
describes the dialog box name (dlg in this case) is a Dialog statement or function.
It is the Dialog statement or function that tells Word to take the statements like
the ones in Figure 7-10 and display a dialog box like the one in Figure 7-11. If
you are using the dialog box to return one value, use the Dialog() function.
Otherwise, use the Dialog statement. After these two statements shown above
are the macro statements to perform when the user finishes using the dialog box.

*TIP: If you need to modify a dialog box you already have in a macro, select the
statements from the Begin Dialog to End Dialog statements. Copy them to the
Clipboard then paste them to the Word Dialog Editor. The dialog box defined by
the copied statements appears in the dialog box in the Word Dialog Editor.*

Where Macros Are Stored

In Word, macros are always stored in a template, just like styles. When you create
or record the macro, it is stored automatically in the NORMAL.DOT template.
When a macro is stored in NORMAL.DOT, it is available no matter which
document you are working in. If you want to store the macro in another
template, you will need to select that template when you record the macro.

In Word for Windows 6, select the template to contain the macro from the
Macros Available In drop-down list box, *before* selecting Record and performing
the steps of the macro. The Macros Available In list box displays only attached
templates, so you may also have to attach the template to the current document,
using File | Templates (File | Template in Word for Windows 2), before you start
to record the macro.

In Word for Windows 2, you can specify the template for storing the macro only
when more than one template is in use. After you select OK in the Record Macro

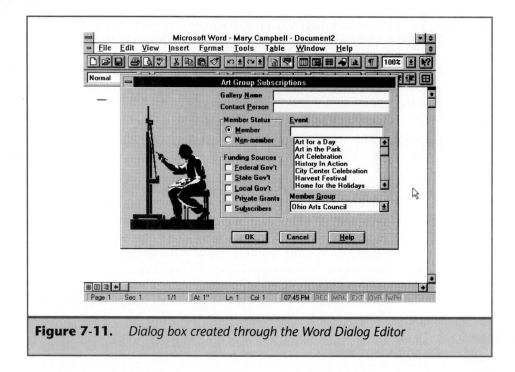

Figure 7-11. *Dialog box created through the Word Dialog Editor*

dialog box, Word will display a dialog box in which you select the template (the active one or NORMAL.DOT) that will contain the macro you are recording.

Making a Macro Available to All Documents

As stated just above, macros in NORMAL.DOT are "global"—they are automatically available in all documents. You can arrange for other macros, too, to be global. When you want to edit global macros in a template besides NORMAL.DOT, you must be working in a document that uses that template; open the template with File | Open, or make the other template globally available with the File | Template command.

Priority of Macros with the Same Names

If all of your macros are stored in NORMAL.DOT, you will not have name conflicts, because Word does not let you create macros with the same name in a particular template. You can, however, have the same macro name in two *different* templates. If you do this, the macros will be assigned the following execution priority whenever both templates are active:

1. Macros in the template attached to the active document

2. Macros in NORMAL.DOT

3. Macros in other global templates, in alphabetical sequence of template names from A to Z

Copying and Moving Macros Among Templates

To transfer a macro from one template to another in Word for Windows 6, use the Organizer, described under "Organize" in Chapter 4, which lets you copy macros from one template to another. In Word for Windows 2, you need to edit the macro, copy its statements to the Clipboard, open the template to which you want to add the macro, create a new macro, and paste in the Clipboard's contents.

Automatic Macros

You can create macros with special names that will execute automatically when a certain condition occurs in the templates to which they are attached. What makes these macros special is their names, which determine when they start executing. Automatic macro names and the conditions that trigger their execution are listed in the following table:

Automatic Macro Name	Executed
AutoExec	When you start Word
AutoOpen	When you open a file
AutoNew	When you create a new document
AutoClose	When you close a document
AutoExit	When you exit Word

NOTE: All automatic macros function globally if stored in NORMAL.DOT. If stored in another template, all automatic macros except AutoExec function only on the document that uses the other template.

What to Do When Your Macros Don't Work

If all your macros work correctly the first time you use them, you will be very lucky. Unfortunately, this kind of luck is highly unlikely. Nearly everyone who creates more than a few macros or programs gets stumped occasionally by a mysterious problem of one sort or another. Though it is may be obvious that the task isn't being completed correctly, the actual cause of the problem can be difficult to identify. I have personally found the following strategies to be helpful when wrestling with stubborn bugs in macros or programs:

■ Work on something else for a while—you will come back to the problem with a fresh perspective.

■ Explain the problem to a coworker or friend. Even if none if you is an expert, frequently the process of simply explaining what is supposed to be happening will turn on the light that illuminates the problem.

■ Add message boxes to your macro temporarily, to help you track your progress, using the MsgBox statement. Remove them when you've fixed the bug.

■ On the Macro toolbar, use the Trace button to have Word highlight the macro instructions as they are performed. Or use the Step button and step through the instructions one by one as slowly as you like.

■ If you have subroutines, use the Step Subs button to have Word walk through the main routine a step at a time and perform a subroutine without interruption as if it is one statement.

■ Use the Show Variables button to display variable values while the macro is paused or stopped, so you can track the values currently in the variables.

■ Use the Rem statement to treat an instruction as a remark. Selecting the Add/Remove REM button adds a REM to the beginning of the selected statements. Select it again to remove the REM so Word performs the statement in the macro.

■ Test your code one section at a time, by saving the entire macro file under a new name and deleting everything except what you want to test.

■ Limit the amount of data you are testing with. First try simple data that is unlikely to "break" your code. You can then progress to real-life data, and then potential-problem data.

Mail Merge

Merging is easier than ever in Word for Windows 6. A new wizardlike feature, the Mail Merge Helper dialog box, makes it easy to create exactly what you need in your first attempt. But beware: The Mail Merge Helper looks so inviting that you may be tempted to start making selections without thinking through the full process of your merge.

If you have never performed a merge operation, be sure to review the fundamentals in "Mail Merge" in Chapter 4. If you are a Word for Windows 2 user, look under "Print Merge." Although the more advanced topics here in this chapter are based on Word for Windows 6, you will still find a number of them applicable if you are using Word for Windows 2. The following text describes how to setup mail merge documents. Once they are set up, they need to be merged when you want the variable data inserted into the document. The steps for merging the document are described under "Mail Merge" and "Print Merge" in Chapter 4.

Putting Together a Long-Term Merge Strategy

Although you can create a new data source for every merge you perform, the creation of this data source file is the most time-consuming part of the merge operation. It's a good idea to take some additional time when you first created your data source, to ensure that it is suited for future merge needs as well as current ones.

For example, if you are creating mailing labels for clients, you may think that you do not need to have phone numbers in the data source. Although it may save a few seconds not to have to enter them on each record, these numbers would be useful if you later need to create a customer contact list. If you have left them out of the data source records, you will later have to look up and add a phone number for each client, spending minutes rather than seconds on each record.

As you extend the scope of your merge goals to a longer time frame, have other users who work with the data review the contents of a planned data source. Explain the merge concept, and ask if they can think of any other information that would be useful to add.

Merge Documents Other Than Form Letters

Certainly form letters are the most typical product of a merge operation, but Word can easily create other types of merge documents. Word will automatically adjust the page layout, depending on the type of document you select when creating your main document.

Envelopes

In a merge to print envelopes, Word will help you set up layout and print options specific to envelopes. You specify the envelope size, and the font used for the return and sending addresses. You can even print a POSTNET delivery point bar code.

The steps for creating an envelope-type merge operation start with setting up the main document. You can create a new data source for the envelopes, but you will likely be using an existing one, such as the one you use for form letters. Here are the steps:

1. Select Tools | Mail Merge.

2. Under Main Document, select Create.

3. Select Envelopes.

4. Select Active Window or New Main Document.

TIP: Active Window becomes Change Document Type if the current document is already a main document.

5. In the Mail Merge Helper, select Get Data, and then either open or create the data source. To open an existing source, select Open Data Source and specify the name of the data source file. To create one select Create Data Source, create the list of field names to use, and then enter the data, as follows:

   a. To add field names to the list, type them in the Field Name text box and select Add Field Name. To remove field names from the list, highlight them in the Field Names in Header Row list box and select Remove Field Name.

   b. When you are finished creating field names, select OK, assign the file name, and select OK again.

c. Select Edit Data Source to add data to the data source. Word opens a Data Form dialog box that prompts you to fill in the data for each field in the table.

d. Enter the data records using the Data Form dialog box. After entering the data for each data record, select Add New. When you are finished entering them, select OK.

6. When Word prompts you, select Set Up Main Document. (Word will prompt you after you select a data source or finish entering data in the new data source.) The Envelope Options dialog box appears, which has two tabs: Envelope Options and Printing Options.

7. Select the Envelope Options tab, if necessary. On this tab, specify the following options about what Word will print on your envelopes:

TIP: The options under the If Mailed in the USA heading are dimmed out because they are not currently available. You can enter the bar code options in the next dialog box, but not here.

■ Select the size of envelope from the Envelope Size list box. If the size you want is not listed, select Custom Size, enter the height and width of the envelopes, and select OK.

■ To set the font for the addresses, select Font under Delivery Address or Font under Return address.

■ To set the location of the addresses, enter measurements in the From Left or From Top text boxes under Delivery Address, or the From Left or From Top text boxes under Return Address. The Default is Auto, which changes depending on the envelope selected.

8. Select the Printing Options tab and specify any of the following options for how your envelopes will be printed:

■ One of the icons under Feeding Method to designate how your printer will be fed the envelopes.

■ Face Up or Face Down to designate whether envelopes will be sent into the printer with the printing side up or down.

■ Clockwise Rotation if you want to reverse which edge of your envelope is fed into the printer first.

■ One of the options in the Feed From list box to specify where your printer will get the envelopes. The available sources depend on the printer you have selected.

9. Select OK when you have set all the needed envelope and printing options.

10. Using the Envelope Address dialog box options, enter the merge fields and text to use as the delivery address:

   a. Enter the address in the Sample Envelope Address box.

   b. Insert merge fields at the insertion point's location by selecting the Insert Merge Field button, and then the field name to insert.

   c. Add a postal bar code by selecting Insert Postal Bar Code. In this dialog box, choose the field containing the zip code in the Merge Field with ZIP Code drop-down list box, and the field containing the street address in the Merge Field with Street Address drop-down list box. Word will then include the delivery point postal bar code at the top of the address. This code can help your mail reach its destination faster. When you are finished with the Insert Postal Bar Code dialog box, select OK.

TIP: Select the FIM-A Courtesy Reply Mail check box to include a facing identification mark on your documents. This mark is often used with courtesy reply mail and can get you a discount from the Postal Service.

11. When you are finished creating the address, select OK.

Using the options you have specified, Word sets up the main document, which appears behind the Mail Merge Helper dialog box. If you select Edit under Main Document and this document, or Close, Word removes the Mail Merge Helper dialog box so the document looks like Figure 7-12.

NOTE: You will see "Zip code not valid" where the bar code should appear because you have not entered any real zip codes in this document; you have entered just the merge field for zip codes. This message will be replaced by the actual bar code when you start the merge.

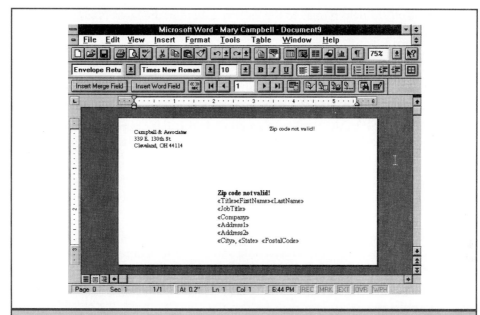

Figure 7-12.   *A main document for merging to envelopes*

Mailing Labels

You can easily create mailing labels with the Mail Merge feature, using a variety of standard label formats. Once you define the format of a label and the type of label stock you want to use, the merge operation automatically arranges labels across and down the page. Follow these steps:

1. Select Tools | Mail Merge.

2. Under Main Document, select Create.

3. Select Mailing Labels.

4. Select Active Window or New Main Document.

5. In the Mail Merge Helper, select Get Data, and then either open or create the data source. To open an existing source, select Open Data Source and specify the name of the data source file. Or select Create Data Source, create the list of field names to use, and then enter the data, as follows:

a. To Add field names to the list, type them in the Field Name text box and select Add Field Name. To remove field names from the list, highlight them in the Field Names in Header Row list box and select Remove Field Name.

b. When you are finished creating field names, select OK, assign the file name, and select OK again.

c. Select Edit Data Source to add data to the data source. Word opens a Data Form dialog box that prompts you to fill in the data for each field in the table.

d. Enter the data records using the Data Form dialog box. After entering the data for each data record, select Add New. When you are finished entering them, select OK.

6. When Word prompts you, select Set Up Main Document. (Word will prompt you after you select a data source or finish entering data in the new data source.)

7. The Label Options dialog box appears, where you choose options for your labels:

a. Specify your printer: Dot Matrix or Laser. This determines which label formats are available. When you select Laser, specify the source of the labels in the Tray list box.

b. From the Label Products list box, choose which set of label formats you need to select. These may include Avery Standard, Avery Pan-European, and Other, depending on what type of printer you have selected and when you purchased Word for Windows 6.

c. In the Product Number list box, choose the labels you are using. These selections are standard label layouts. For example, Avery's 5160 label format is used by many companies, so these labels can be used interchangeably. Your labels will be marked with the equivalent standard size, no matter who manufactured them.

d. If needed, select Details to open another dialog box and set other label options, such as the margins inside and outside the label boundaries. You can use the Details options to create custom labels.

8. When all label options are specified, select OK, and Word displays the Create Label dialog box.

a. Enter the address in the Sample Label box.

b. Insert merge fields at the insertion point's location, by selecting the Insert Merge Field button, then the field name to insert.

c. Add a postal bar code by selecting Insert Postal Bar Code. In this dialog box, choose the field containing the zip code in the Merge Field with Zip Code drop-down list box, and the field containing the street address in the Merge Field with Street Address drop-down list box. Word will then include the delivery point postal bar code at the top of the address. This code can help your mail reach its destination faster. When you are finished with the Insert Postal Bar Code dialog box, select OK.

TIP: Select the FIM-A Courtesy Reply Mail check box to include a facing identification mark on your documents. This mark is often used with courtesy reply mail and can get you a discount from the Postal Service.

9. Select OK after entering the label text.

Using the options you have specified, Word sets up the main document, which appears behind the Mail Merge Helper dialog box. If you select Edit under Main Document and this document, or Close, Word removes the Mail Merge Helper dialog box so the document looks like Figure 7-13.

Catalogs

The Catalog option for the main document of a mail merge is like the Form Letter option, in that the document itself is not formatted in any way. In contrast to form letters, however, catalogs are not designed to create a series of individual documents; rather, they draw information from the data source together into one document. Each copy of the main document, instead of being separated by section breaks, is part of the same section, creating a single document.

Since the only difference between form letters and catalogs is the final product of the merge, the steps to creating a catalog are identical to those of creating a form letter main document, except that you select Catalog from the Create list box under Main Document in the Mail Merge Helper. See "Mail Merge" in Chapter 4 for the steps to create a form letter merge.

The Catalog main document type is useful for creating documents such as product catalogs and lists, in which you want all of the information extracted from the data source and stored together.

Combine the Catalog main document type with the Query Options, and select exactly the records you need to create lists of specific clients that you may want to call back or send correspondence to. For example, the merged document shown in Figure 7-14 was created using a very large database. The

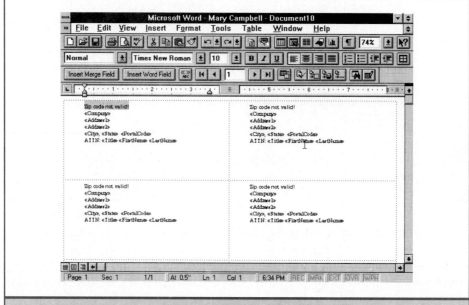

Figure 7-13.   *A main document for merging to mailing labels*

merge operation document selected only those customers who had not placed an order since 1993, and extracted only the information necessary for a salesperson to contact these companies. The main document used for this merge is shown in Figure 7-15; you can see that it is very much like one you might create for a form letter.

REMINDER: Query options are set by selecting Query Options from the Mail Merge Helper dialog box.

Utilizing the Full Potential of Word Fields

By now you are probably a pro at inserting merge fields from the data source into your main document. Now you will want to explore the Word fields that are supported in both Word for Windows 2 and 6, to ensure that you are utilizing these fields, too. In this section you will have an opportunity to take a closer look

ABC Company		216\762-1212	
Contact:	Jane Nichols	*Last Order In:*	5\2\93

XYZ Company		216\762-4541	
Contact:	Sam Jones	*Last Order In:*	11/4/94

Maple Street Supply		216\790-7309	
Contact:	Jeffrey Fein	*Last Order In:*	12\1\94

Sam's Supply		216\983-4920	
Contact:	Susan Knettel	*Last Order In:*	10\3\93

Rimber & Associates		217\931-3985	
Contact:	George Forester	*Last Order In:*	9\6\93

March Inc.		216\783-3920	
Contact:	Kristin Estep	*Last Order In:*	9\4\93

Otlowski Company		216\392-9304	
Contact:	Darren Horan	*Last Order In:*	10/16/93

Elegil & Associates		216\943-9203	
Contact:	Isabella Wade	*Last Order In:*	9\28\93

Manzuk Supply		216\839-2034	
Contact:	Tobias Walters	*Last Order In:*	10\8\93

Matthew Company		217\983-3924	
Contact:	Elise Knapp	*Last Order In:*	11/16/93

Figure 7-14.   *A document created by merging to a Catalog main document*

at these fields, as well as explore some situations where they might be just what you need.

TIP: See "Mail Merge" (Word for Windows 6) and "Print Merge" (Word for Windows 2) in Chapter 4 for explanations of merging and the fundamentals of inserting and using Word fields.

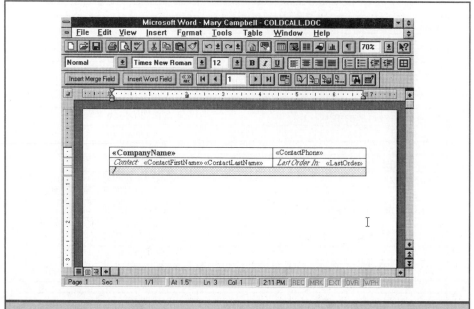

Figure 7-15.   *A main document for merging to a Catalog*

Displaying Field Codes

How you edit merge fields depends on how they are displayed, so it is important to know about their display. You can choose to either display or hide field codes.

- When you hide field codes, merge field codes are displayed between chevrons << >>, and you'll see only the name of the field that will be inserted. All other fields, such as those explained in the following sections, simply do not appear.

- When you display field codes, the fields appear in curly brackets. They begin with a field code, followed by the arguments or switches that create settings for the field. To display field codes, select Tools | Options and the View tab (View icon in Word for Windows 2), and turn on the Field Codes check box option.

TIP: See "Fields" and "View Options" in Chapter 4 for more details on displaying field codes.

ASK

Use the ASK field when your main document requires information that needs to change for each merge, but that cannot be saved in a data source.

When you merge a document containing an ASK field, a dialog box is displayed for this field, showing a prompt you have assigned. Users enter the response in the dialog box and select OK, and that text that is assigned to a bookmark. You can then use that data in an IF field to determine what happens next with the merge, or insert it into a document using another field.

A good use for ASK fields is to make a form letter seem less of a form. For example, form letters are often used by salespeople to contact clients about new offers or products. However, sales figures often improve when clients believe the letter is personally written to them. Using ASK, various names and other information can be inserted into these letters. Instead of using the title and last name of the client in the salutation and body of a letter, you use an ASK field to prompt for the correct way to refer to this person. Each salesperson can customize letters by using a nickname or other familiar term of address for clients with whom this is appropriate.

An ASK field for this purpose might read as follows:

```
{ASK Nickname "What is {MERGEFIELD FirstName}
{MERGEFIELD LastName}'s nickname, if you use one?"
\d {MERGEFIELD Title} {MERGEFIELD LastName}}
```

When the merge process encounters this ASK field, it prompts the user for the nickname of the client and assigns that nickname to the Nickname bookmark. Notice that the embedded merge fields in the prompt let the user know which client is being discussed. The default, when the user selects OK without entering a nickname, is to use the title and last name.

When you select ASK from the list box that appears when you click the Insert Word Field button in the Mail Merge toolbar, a dialog box appears where you can insert the bookmark name, prompt, default text, and whether you want to be prompted for this text only once for the entire merge.

TIP: If you want to insert a merge field into a prompt used by an ASK field, add the ASK field as described above. Then edit the ASK field code and insert the merge field code. For example, after inserting the merge field into an ASK field code, your document may contain the code {ASK Numb_Encl "How many copies do you want to send to {MERGEFIELD Name}?" \D "1"}.

To insert the text assigned to this bookmark, you type the bookmark in the main document, and press CTRL+F9 to place field code brackets around it.

FILLIN

The FILLIN field is similar to the ASK field because it prompts the user for input. However, where the ASK field assigns the text requested by a prompt to a bookmark, the FILLIN field inserts that text as the field result. Since it is not assigned a bookmark, the response text can only be used once in the merge document.

For example, Misty Rivers Boating uses the same response letter to all people who call and request a pamphlet about boating trips, and that letter is saved as read-only to prevent it from being altered. The information gathered by phone about the client goes into a data source, but each response letter must be personalized for the person who took the call. In the read-only main document, the code

{FILLIN "Who took these calls?" \d Misty Travel Boating \o}

appears for the signature line. The \o switch means the user (the company employee) is only prompted the first time that the document is merged, and all remaining documents in the merge use the same text entered initially. The \d switch provides the default text, to be used when no name is provided.

In Word for Windows 2, the FILLIN feature is used not only in merges, but in filling in on-line forms, since Word for Windows 2 does not have the form fields that are available in Word for Windows 6. In Word for Windows 2 you enter the FILLIN fields everywhere in the on-line form where you plan to enter data, and save the form as a template. After opening a new document from that template, the user selects the entire form and presses F9 to update the fields. Word then moves from field to field in the form, requesting the correct input. An automatic macro could also be used to start the updating process.

IF

Sometimes it seems that for every rule there are ten exceptions. Dealing with all the exceptions is made easier by the IF...THEN...ELSE merge field. Without this field you would have to select subsets of records and perform separate merges with altered main document files. With the IF field, however, you can test for any condition in merge fields and provide text depending on the situation. You can also use other fields, such as INCLUDE, to place text from a file into the merge document, depending on the condition test.

You can choose a variety of comparison operators for use in the If dialog box:

=	Equal
<>	Not equal
<	Less than
<=	Less than or equal to
>	Greater than
>+	Greater than or equal to
=""	Is blank
<>""	Is not blank

You can create simple or complex conditions within the IF statement. You can compare a merge field to a string or value, or the contents of another merge field. The entire expression is displayed within brackets, and the comparison is enclosed within a second set of brackets. Any strings are enclosed in quotation marks. Consider the following examples:

```
{IF {MERGEFIELD State} = "CA" "We received your insurance
application but regret to inform you that we no longer write new
business in California." "We received your insurance application
and have referred it to out underwriting department for
evaluation. We will notify you within 10 days if we feel that you
are a good risk."}
```

```
{IF {MERGEFIELD Thisyear} <= {MERGEFIELD Lastyear} "Your sales
performance is lower than last year. We would like to help you
improve your sales performance and income and have enrolled you
in the seminar, Doubling Your Sales Potential on Friday October
10 at 9 a.m.. You will receive more information in the next few
weeks." "Economic times have caused our overall sales to decrease
significantly. Since you have been able to exceed your sales level
from last year you should feel proud of your accomplishment."}
```

You can join conditions with "and" or "or." When conditions are joined with "and," all conditions must be met. To create an IF statement that requires a second condition, place another IF statement where you would normally enter text for the THEN, which is the text to use when the first IF statement is true. To create an IF statement in which text is used when *either* of two conditions is true, create a second IF statement where you would normally place the ELSE text, which is used when the IF statement is false. An IF statement requiring that *both* conditions be met might look like the following:

```
{IF {MERGEFIELD State} = "MD" {IF {MERGEFIELD City} = "Towson"
"We are having an open house in our Towson location we would
like you to attend from 8 a.m. to 5 p.m. on Tuesday, August 14."
""} ""}
```

Next Record

The NEXT field lets you use data from several records in one copy of the main document. When Word encounters the field in your Word document, it immediately advances to the next data record and uses that record for filling in the remainder of the main document.

Word for Windows 2 used the NEXT field for creating lists. For example, you could use merge fields to create a directory listing, and then copy that listing as many times as you needed, adding the NEXT field in front of each copy. In this way you could create a single document, your directory, with data from several records.

In Word for Windows 6, there is not much reason to use the NEXT field because you can get a similar effect by creating a Catalog main document, as described above.

Next Record If

The NEXTIF field combines the features of the NEXT and IF fields. In response to NEXTIF, Word tests the condition just as if it were evaluating an IF field. However, instead of entering text depending on the result of this evaluation, Word does nothing if the evaluation is false, and moves to the next data record if it is true.

As with NEXT, you can use NEXTIF in Word for Windows 2 to create lists. The advantage here is that you can choose which lists you want to use by testing against some criteria. For example, you could create a list of your first 25 customers who ordered over $50,000 of goods last year.

In Word for Windows 6, of course, the Catalog main document type does much the same thing as NEXTIF, without the complications of repeatedly entering the field and copying the merge fields and text in your main document. You can combine this Catalog main document with query options, to select which data records are used in the final document for merging.

MERGEREC and MERGESEQ

The MERGEREC field inserts the number of the current data record into your final merged document. The MERGESEQ field inserts the number of the current data record as a subset of the total data records. You can use these fields in other fields to control the merge or to label your documents.

MERGESEQ inserts a number that is different from what MERGEREC inserts only if you are using only some of the data records in the data source. If you were to open the data source and count down the records, the number MERGEREC inserts is always the number of the data record. MERGESEQ inserts the number of the data record in the list of records used in this merge. In a merge that only includes data records from a specific zip code, for example, MERGEREC will leave gaps in the numbers of the records used, as in 1, 4, 7, 10, 14, 16, 20, 30, 39, 40, and so on. MERGESEQ, on the other hand, would use one run of numbers, for instance, from 1 to 10.

Set Bookmark

A bookmark is used as a variable within a merge document. You can place a value in a bookmark once and then use it throughout your merge document by placing the bookmark field within your document. For example, you might set the term of a loan to 30 years, and refer to the loan term in three locations within the main document. You would have a statement like this:

```
{SET Loanterm "30 years"}
```

When you need this value within the main document, you use the bookmark name. (Enter the bookmark name and press CTRL+F9 to add the brackets around the name.)

Skip Record If

The SKIPIF field is used to skip records in your document, based on Word's evaluation of a comparative statement you include in this field. When SKIPIF is encountered in a merge, Word evaluates the statement. If it is false, Word ignores this field. If the statement is true, Word skips the current data record. SKIPIF is different from NEXTIF because the copy of the main document created for this data record is completely erased and a new copy is started for the next data record.

You can use the SKIPIF field to help restrict your merge. For example, if you include the field

{SKIPIF zipcode <> 44302}

Word will only merge data records with a zip code field not equal to 44302.

You will use this field more in Word for Windows 2 than 6. You are unlikely to need this field in Word for Windows 6 because you can set up the criteria for using and skipping fields using the Query Options, rather than by directly entering the fields to use. In addition, Query Options give you more choices for combining various rules and criteria in selecting the records to use.

Solving Merge Problems

Merge problems can be frustrating to solve, because there are several components involved in the merge operation. If you are having difficulty with a merge, check out the following sections; your problem may be here, and you can try the suggested solutions.

Printed Data Is Not Correct

If you find an address in your merged documents where you expect to see a name, the problem is in your data source file. If you used a table for the data entries, you may have placed the first and last name in the same column, putting the address in the last name column by mistake. This problem occurs most frequently with delimited data, where it is easy to forget to put in an extra delimiter when a field is empty.

The Field Names Print Instead of the Data

This problem occurs often for first-time users, since it is easy to accidentally type the field name you want rather than have Word insert it. The only way to insert fields is to have Word do it; you cannot type the field name even if you enclose what you type in curly braces or << and >>. You will need to return to the main document and replace the field names with field codes that insert the field names.

Blank Lines Appear in the Merged File

The display of blank lines that represent a missing field can be turned on and off. To change the setting, select the Merge button in the Mail Merge Helper dialog box. Then check to be sure the Don't Print Blank Lines When Data Fields Are Empty option button is selected.

Labels or Envelopes Have Entries in the Wrong Location

You have probably chosen the wrong size for your labels or envelopes. Edit the document to have the setting you want.

You Get an Out of Memory Message

The first thing to do in this situation is try closing other applications and other unneeded Word windows. By reducing the operations that are using your computer's memory, you may free up enough to continue the merge. If the problem persists, you can use the Query Options to select a subset of the data records and try the merge again. The last option is to check and see if you are using TrueType fonts. If so, try switching to built-in printer fonts, which require less memory.

Merge Does Not Produce All the Documents You Expect

Look in the Mail Merge Helper, and check to see if the message "Query Options have been set" is displayed under Merge Data with the Document. If it is, you have defined a selection criteria or specified that the records will be sorted. If you are not getting all of the records you expect, there is likely to be a mistake in the selection criteria. Select Query Options, and to make sure your criteria are correct.

CHAPTER 8

Using Word in a Workgroup Environment

Word has the features you need whether you are working by yourself to complete a memo or collaborating with a group of people to produce a project report. In addition to typing text and formatting, which work the same on individual or collaborative projects, other Word for Windows features are designed especially for group projects.

Word provides complete support for network activities when your group is linked through a local area network (LAN). For example, you can place shared documents on the file server to allow group members to review and modify appropriate sections of the document.

749

You can also interface directly with Microsoft Mail and other compatible electronic mail (e-mail) systems, to route documents to each member of your workgroup.

Even when the various users are not on the same network, Word provides support for group efforts. Features that support large documents, such as master and subdocuments, annotations, and document revisions, can expedite shared contributions on a project even without the benefits of network connections. The ability to annotate documents and mark revisions lets you elicit the contributions of many group members and track the contributions of each. Microsoft Mail Remote extends document routing capabilities to employees who are traveling, and to clients that are not on the network.

This chapter's overview of these group-environment issues focuses on the support available in Word for Windows 6. For details on Word group features available in Word for Windows 2 and the procedures for their use, consult the sections of Chapter 4 that describe the relevant commands.

Workgroup Options

A *workgroup* is simply a group of people that work together to complete a project. Thanks to the advantages of technology, workgroup members do not need to be in the same physical department or office to work together effectively. Individual workgroup participants can be selected for the set of skills they bring to the project—regardless of their location.

Workgroup members who work in the same office often have face-to-face meetings about a project before creating the Word documents they will ultimately share. With Word's workgroup features, they may be able to reduce the number of these meetings before completing all the work involved, because of the ease with which they can share their work in progress. Workgroup users may work in different locations and discuss the project by phone, before going off to do their own part of the project. Notes can then be placed in the documents shared by these users, reducing the need to schedule meetings to discuss the project. This can be especially helpful when all of the participants are not in the same time zone. Sometimes the shared information in Word is the sole communication between workgroup members. They may be geographically dispersed and, because of time zone or working schedule differences, may need to rely on Word for sharing all the information that passes between them.

Workgroup members can share in the creation of information in Word documents, or data can be placed in templates by one individual and used by the others. Shared templates are a practical way to share forms for proposals, budget data, purchase orders, and in other areas where consistency is important.

Some Workgroup Scenarios

Each of the following scenarios describes workgroup activities in which the features of Word for Windows 6 make the task of completing collaborative projects easier.

John works for a large manufacturing company and is collaborating with individuals in several departments on a competitive bid for a large government contract. All the workgroup members are connected by the same LAN, although they are members of three different Microsoft Mail post offices, as shown in Figure 8-1. After a meeting on the project and a discussion of the tight time schedule for the project, the four team members divided up the proposal into several segments that needed to be written. John agreed to create a master document on the network file server to provide the introductory information in the proposal. Each team member, including John, will write a separate section. John creates an outline for the proposal and has Word create a subdocument for each level 1 heading in the outline. This lets each person work on a subdocument

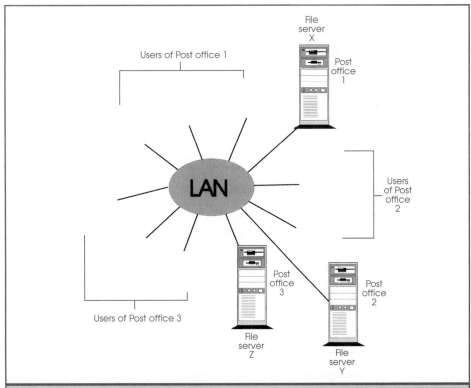

Figure 8-1. *A local workgroup can access Word documents on the network as well as route Microsoft Mail messages*

component, and still allows John to access the master document to review all of the subdocuments—all of which use the same formatting and styles John has placed in the master document. When the subdocuments are complete, John will work with the master document in Normal view, making the final formatting and reorganizing changes. Workgroup members can also route messages to one another using Microsoft Mail, even though they use different post offices. Microsoft Mail allows you to establish a global address list with entries in address books for both local and remote Microsoft Mail users. With the efficient use of Word, the company is able to meet the deadline for the project.

A large publishing company needs to update a best-selling book within a short time frame, without compromising the quality of the final product. The author is asked to use revision marks within Word to the mark changes in each chapter. This file is zipped to achieve a compressed format and is then routed electronically to a technical reviewer who has Microsoft Mail Remote. The technical reviewer checks the accuracy of the chapter, with special attention paid to the updated material—using as guidance the revision marks noting changes—before routing the document to the publisher's copy editor. The copy editor checks the material for grammatical accuracy. Figure 8-2 provides an overview of the connections. By focusing special attention on the manuscript revisions, the publisher is able to meet a tight deadline. The revision marks also make it easy to track changes throughout the process and to consult with the author before finalizing each chapter.

Several consultants who live in different cities are pooling their talents to provide training for a Fortune 500 company on the use of Microsoft Access. They develop their training materials with Word for Windows 6 and share document files in process, with revision marks, eventually developing the final version of the training materials. Once the training sessions start, each consultant works with several instructors to complete the training in a timely manner. They have developed a template for the instructors' billings; a second template is used for client-reimbursable travel and living expenses during the training. Despite the remote locations of the consultants, with the help of Word they are able to present a consistent, professional image in both the delivered material and the billing data. Because their client has Word for Windows and Microsoft Mail installed on a network, all concerned parties are able to utilize Microsoft Mail Remote to maintain communication with instructors during the on-site teaching.

Network Options

Most of what users do with Word on a network is no different from what users do with Word on a stand alone PC. Documents are created and revised in the

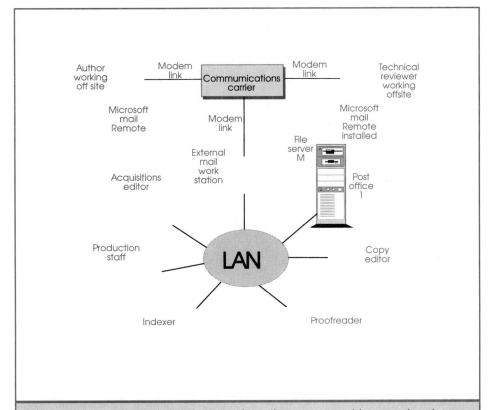

Figure 8-2.   *Off-site users of Microsoft Mail Remote are able to send and route documents to the publishing company's staff on the LAN*

same way. The differences are the way Word is installed, and the fact that documents are often stored on the network file server rather than the hard disks built into individual PCs. The central storage capability makes sharing documents easier.

NOTE: Whether or not you are a network user, you will be able to use the Word commands discussed throughout this book. The rest of this section, "Network Options," however, focuses on some of the tasks and features of special interest to users on a network.

Installing Word on a Network

Word must be installed on the network file server before it can be installed on network workstations, and a license must exist for each Word user. Installation of Word on the file server is typically performed by the network administrator, because this individual must have full privileges for the directories into which Word will be installed. The administrator will want to insure that the following conditions are met before attempting the installation:

- Windows 3.1 must be installed on the file server.

- Network users sharing Windows and Word for Windows or other Microsoft applications must be logged off.

- The administrator must have create, write, read, and erase privileges for directories such as WINWORD and MSAPPS that will be used for the installation.

- There must be at least 7MB of space in the WINWORD directory (or in whatever location will store the Word files). Shared files that are normally stored in MSAPPS require another 9.5MB of storage space.

Follow these steps when you are ready to set up Word on the file server:

1. Start Windows, and make sure no other applications are active.

2. Place the Setup disk in drive A.

3. In Program Manager, choose File | Run, and then type **a:setup /a** and press ENTER. This tells Word that you have placed the setup disk in drive A and want to perform an administrator's installation.

4. Complete the installation, following instructions on the screen.

5. Use the appropriate network commands to set the directories used for setup to read-only.

Installing Word on Network Workstations

Once the network administrator installs Word on the file server, Word can be installed on other network workstations. Depending on how your company handles such matters, either a user or the network administrator can install Word on the workstations. The actual installation is done by someone working at the workstation, no matter who that person is. Each workstation must have a license.

There are four different installation options; from the server, you choose Typical, Laptop, Custom/Complete, or Workstation installation. If the Workstation option is chosen, the workstation user will access Word from the file server, rather than copy program files to the workstation hard disk.

If additional control is desired, the network administrator can create a script that will control the options selected during setup, as described in the following section. For a large number of users, scripts provide the control needed to insure consistent application features for groups of users.

Creating Scripts to Automate Setup for Network Users

If you are responsible for the installation of Word on network workstations, you need to insure that the software is set up properly. Since you want to insure a consistent installation for groups of users, you want them to set up Word in the same way. Physically traveling from workstation to workstation and setting up each copy yourself is one way to ensure this consistency, but there is a faster way: Word for Windows 6 provides a script-writing feature that lets you provide a set of detailed setup instructions for each user. You can then instruct network users to set up their Word software at the workstation using the command **setup /q**, which causes the setup program to run with your specifications. Figure 8-3 illustrates the process for automating setup for all users.

Defining Setup Instructions

Word provides a file named SETUP.STF in the Word directory after you have completed a network installation for Word. In the event that you make mistakes and need to access the original file again, it's best to rename the original file to something like SETUP.OLD. You will also want to make a copy of this file; for this copy you can use the original filename SETUP.STF, once you have a copy of the original with a different name.

Since the entries in SETUP.STF are arranged in a tabular fashion, you might want to use a spreadsheet program such as Excel or Quattro Pro to make your changes, although you can use Word if you prefer. Figure 8-4 shows some of the entries in SETUP.STF in an Excel spreadsheet. The file has entries in over 800 lines, so you can only see a small portion of it at a time.

Once you have retrieved the working copy of the SETUP file, follow these steps to revise the current settings:

1. Locate the entries in column 3 that refer to the type of installation. If you are using a spreadsheet, these entries will begin around row 37. If you are not using a spreadsheet, look down the Object ID field and find number 15, Typical. The default is to have "yes" in the column to the left, creating a typical setup.

2. In column 2, titled "Install During Batch Mode," next to the type of installation that you want, type a **yes**.

   If you typed a yes in column 2 (Complete/Custom Installation), continue with step 4. Otherwise, you are now finished defining setup instructions.

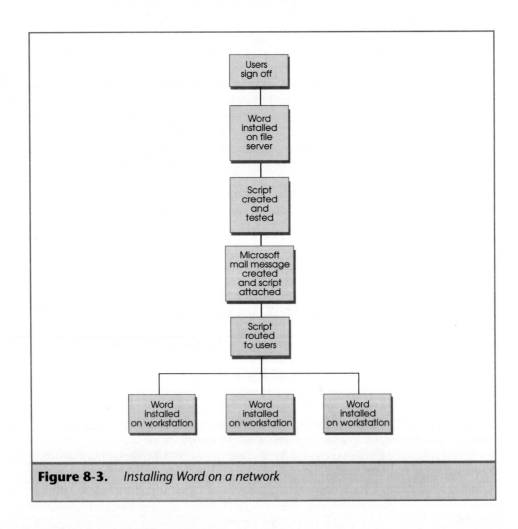

Figure 8-3.   *Installing Word on a network*

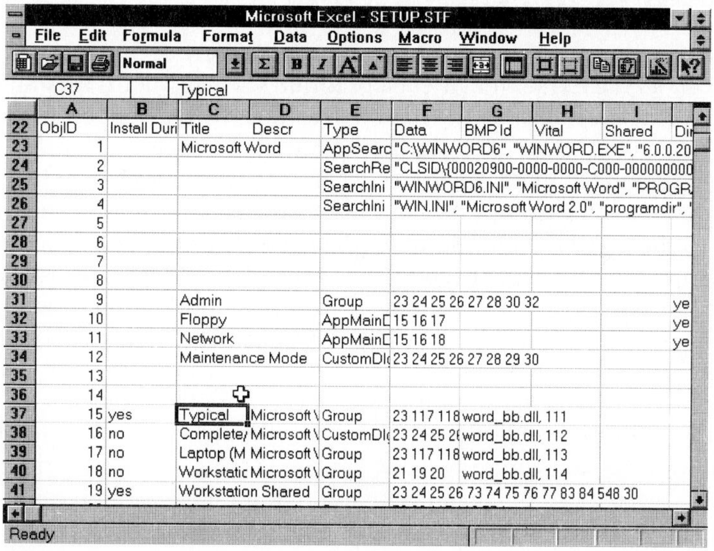

Figure 8-4.   *A section of the .STF file for creating installation scripts for network users*

3. Move down in column 3 to row 46 (or Object ID 25). This is the location where you will begin to see the individual components of Word, such as Applets, Equation Editor, and Spelling. Type **yes** in column 2 for all the features you want installed.

NOTE: Column 11 (DestDir) contains %1 for the destination directory. You can change this entry to specify a particular location.

4. Save the new setup data, using a text format, as SETUP.STF. You can also use a new name for the table, if you want, but you will have to provide workstation users a new SETUP.EXE file since the .STF and .EXE files must have matching names.

WARNING: Be extremely careful not to make changes to other areas of the .STF files.

Distributing the Final Scripts

You can distribute your newly created script and a copy of the setup program via shared access to the file server, or via a program such as Microsoft Mail that routes data to network users or to remote locations with Microsoft Mail Remote attached. Attach the script file to a Microsoft Mail message by choosing Insert Object after typing the message. Select Package for the Object Type.

If you have created groups for your Microsoft Mail post office, you may be able to send the script file to a group. If you have different setup configurations for the groups, you will want to create several .STF files. You will also need to copy SETUP.EXE to a file with the name you selected for the .STF file. Using the same name as the group makes it easy to keep track of each group's matching setup files.

You can send a message and script file to users at other post offices, as long as your mail is addressed correctly. Any other location where you can send Microsoft Mail message can receive the attached scripts: other post offices, other networks connected through gateways, and remote sites can all receive a Microsoft Mail message with an attached script.

Using the Scripts to Set Up Word

Before distributing the scripts to users so they can set up their copies of Word, you will want to test the installation on a workstation, to ensure that the setup works smoothly and is error free. You can then distribute the scripts to users, along with the instructions for what to enter.

You will want to provide users the *exact* entries they need to make to set up Word on their system. The three setup switches used are

/t to specify a new script
/u to indicate the user name, to prevent the user from being prompted
/q to run setup without user interaction

For example, if you renamed SETUP.STF and SETUP.EXE to ACCNTG.STF and ACCTNG.EXE on the file server N, the following entry will prompt the user for a username:

N:\WINWORD\ACCTNG.EXE /T ACCTNG.STF /Q

If you were setting up an entry for Sam Storm and did not want Sam to be prompted for his username, the entry would be:

N:\WINWORD\ACCTNG.EXE /T ACCTNG.STF /N "Sam Storm" /Q

Note the required quotes around the username.

Routing Documents to Network Users

You can use Microsoft Mail to route a document to a group of users, either to one user after another or to all at once. When the setting for Mail as Attachment, under the General tab in Tools | Options is checked, Word uses the current document as an attachment to your e-mail transmission. Otherwise, when you select Send from Word's File menu, Word assumes the current document should be an e-mail message.

E-mail has become very popular, because it eliminates the telephone tag games that often occur when busy people are trying to communicate. If e-mail seems a little impersonal to you, consider spicing up your messages with *emoters*; a few examples are shown in the box "Adding Emotional Impact to Your E-mail Messages."

Adding Emotional Impact to Your E-mail Messages

With increased use of e-mail in corporations, symbols have been invented for adding to the end of e-mail messages, to give a personal touch to these messages. The word, *emoters*, was coined to refer to these symbols. It is a bit easier to interpret these emoters if you turn your head to the side as you look at them. Here are a few to get you started, but feel free to create your own:

Emoter	Meaning
:-)	Smiley face
:-(	Frowning face
;-)	Winking face
(:-&	Angry face
|-)	Sleepyhead
=:-)	Punk rocker
=|:-)>	Uncle Sam
:-X	Kissey face
@>—>—	A rose

After creating and saving a Word document for routing, follow these steps to add a routing slip for sending the document to multiple users:

1. Choose Add Routing Slip from the File menu.

2. Click the Address button, and then select the names of all the users to whom you want to route the document.

3. Choose Add, and select OK.

4. Select the desired routing method: One After Another or All at Once.

5. Select the Route button to send the document.

Users will be able to review the document and then use annotations, revision marks, or normal editing features to make their changes. The first two methods are preferred because they maintain the integrity of the original document. Recipients use the Send command on the File menu in Microsoft Mail when they are ready to send the document back.

Using Word's Protection Features

When you are working on a network, you will have access to all the file-protection features of the network. In addition, Word's file-locking capability prevents conflicting changes from being made to a document, yet allows more than one user to read a document at the same time. When you open a file on a network drive, other users who attempt to open the same file will be informed that it is in use. You also have the option of selecting the Read-only check box in the Open dialog box, which will allow other users to open the document as read-only. If you open a document as read-only and decide you want to save your changes, you will need to choose File | Save As and specify a different filename.

Word's Support of Local and Remote Workgroup Activities

Some Word features are available whether you are working with a group of local network users or with individuals to whom you mail or hand-deliver documents. These features make it easy to solicit the input of all group members and to have each member involved in the final product. For example, you can turn on Word's revision marks feature so that each user's changes to a shared document will be marked, as described under "Comparing Documents" in Chapter 4. With the annotations feature, the user can make comments without altering the document. To work more efficiently with long documents, you will want to consider the use of Word's master document feature.

Several of Word's features are mentioned in this section's overview of features that support workgroups. You will find detailed explanations of these features in Chapter 4. You will also want to look at Chapter 4 for features supported only in Word for Windows 2, or that work differently in Word for Windows 2.

Revision Marks

Revision marks allow each user in a group to review a document and make alterations. Both newly added text and text to be deleted will be marked in the document, with underlines or other marks, distinct from the other text. The project leader or other individual who is in charge of the report can then elect to accept revision marks or to delete them.

To begin recording revision marks in an existing document, follow these steps:

The following steps are specific to Word 6. However, you can perform the same action in Word 2, using slightly different commands. See "Comparing Versions" in Chapter 4 for an explanation of the procedures.

1. Select File | Open and open the document you want to revise.

2. Select Tools | Revisions.

3. Select Mark Revisions While Editing under Document Revisions.

4. Select OK.

Another way to turn on the mark revisions feature is to double-click MRK in the status bar . Word for Windows 6 displays to each reviewer's revisions in a different color, which makes it easer to determine whose revisions you are reading when you have circulated the document to several people for their input.

TIP: If someone makes revisions without turning on the revision marks feature, you can still identify changes that were made by using the document compare feature. To use this feature, select the Compare Versions button in the Revisions dialog box.

You can accept or reject revisions all at once, or you can use the Review Revisions feature to look at each revision and make an individual decision. Figure 8-5 shows a document with this dialog box active (choose Tools | Revisions and select Review). Word can distinguish eight different reviewers with the use of different colors before it begins reusing the colors again. In Figure 8-5, you cannot see that the underlined text is shown in a different color, but the color difference is visible on your monitor. All of Elizabeth Reinhardt's revisions will be displayed in blue.

See "Revision Marks" in Chapter 4 for additional information on using the revision marks feature. You can also protect revisions and annotations, as discussed in "Annotation" in Chapter 4.

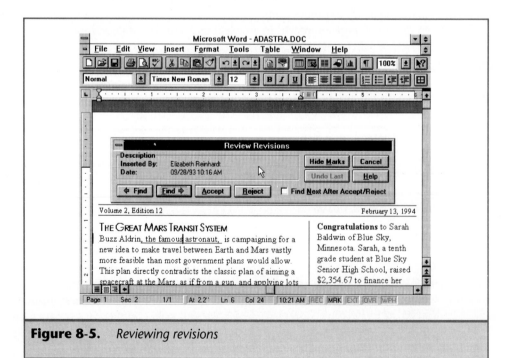

Figure 8-5.   *Reviewing revisions*

Master Documents and Subdocuments

If you need to work with long documents, the Word for Windows *master document* feature offers excellent organizing capabilities. A master document is nothing more than a sequence of *subdocuments* that divide the long document into manageable segments. The special Master Document view gives you an outline-style overview of the document, or you can use Normal view to show the detail in the subdocuments. You can also work in an individual subdocument.

Master documents let you move quickly from one section of a long document to another. It is also easy to restructure the document by moving the various subdocument sections to new locations within the master document. You can create a master document as large as 32 MB, with as many as 80 subdocuments.

You will also find that it is much easier to create references from master documents. Indexes, tables of authorities, and cross-references are all maintained in the master document for the entire document. It is also easier to keep track of all the subdocuments; since you create them directly from headings within the master document, you do not have to scan the file server looking for all the pieces.

Creating a New Master Document

Creating a new master document is easy. All you need to do is open a new document in Word and follow these steps:

1. Select Master Document in the View menu.

2. Type the master document using headings in place of each subdocument you will want to insert. You can create all the subdocuments at once if they use the same heading level in the master document and you select this level first.

3. Select the first heading that is to become a subdocument, and all the entries between it and the last heading to become a subdocument.

REMINDER: All headings in this selection must be at the same level.

4. Select the Create Subdocument button from the Master Document toolbar; it looks like this:

In Figure 8-6, the master document GREENER.DOC, you can see the subdocument icons beside the History and Advantages headings.

5. Select Save <u>A</u>s from the <u>F</u>ile menu, and enter the filename for the master document.

Working in Master and Subdocuments

You can work in either the master document or subdocuments. Most often, you will work in each subdocument to complete it. You might then return to working in the master document for tasks such as reorganization. Normally the work of setting up and finalizing the master document's organization is the responsibility of one individual, even though the subdocuments might be divided among the members of the workgroup.

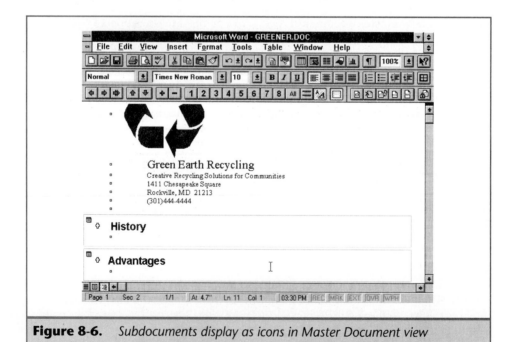

Figure 8-6.   *Subdocuments display as icons in Master Document view*

To work in a subdocument, use the File | Open command just as you would with any other document. Make any editing changes you want, and print the subdocument as needed.

If you decide you need to rename or move a subdocument, do so after opening the master document. Use the Master Document view for reorganizing the structure or opening a subdocument. Use the Normal view when you want to make detailed changes within subdocuments. Double-click the icon for the subdocument you need to rename, choose Save As from the File menu, type a new name, and close the subdocument. To move the subdocument to a new position in the master document, click its icon and drag it to a new location.

To move passages of text or graphics among subdocuments, you will need to have the master document open in Normal view. You can then proceed to make changes just as you would in any other document.

WARNING: Never rename or delete subdocuments using DOS or Windows commands. Because of the links from the subdocuments to the master document, this approach will cause problems the next time you attempt to open the master document. Subdocument naming and deletion must always be accomplished from within the master document.

Special File-Locking Features for Network Users

If you are sharing a master document with other network users, you will want to utilize the new file-locking features in Word for Windows 6. Although anyone can unlock any subdocument for use, Word automatically opens subdocuments for read-write access only by their creator, and restricts other users to read-only access. The Unlock Document button on the Master Document toolbar allows you to unlock other documents that you must update. You also have the option of adding a password or other file-protection capabilities.

See "Master Documents" in Chapter 4.

Annotating Documents

Earlier in this chapter you read about how multiple users can revise a document and keep track of changes, using revision marks. When you need to enter comments about a document without actually making any changes to it, use Word's *annotations* feature. You can attach annotations to any selected text, perhaps to note that a passage is unclear, to suggest a specific revision, or to indicate disagreement with a particular point. Each annotation is numbered and shows the initials of the person who created it.

Annotations are a better choice than revision marks when you are seeking the comments of others, whereas revision marks might be more appropriate when a group has joint responsibilities for the creation of a report or proposal.

To annotate a document follow these steps:

1. Move to the location in the document where you want to insert an annotation.

TIP: *In Word for Windows 6, if you select a section of text before inserting an annotation, that text will automatically be selected when someone views or goes to that annotation. This helps the reader of the annotations to easily refer to the text about which you are commenting.*

2. Select Insert | Annotation to insert the annotation mark and open the Annotations pane.

3. Type the text of your comment, as shown in Figure 8-7.

4. Close the Annotations pane, by clicking Close or pressing ALT+SHIFT+C.

   If you prefer, you can switch back to the document window without closing the Annotations pane by clicking on the document text or pressing F6. To return again to the open Annotations pane, click on it, or press F6, or use Insert | Annotation again.

5. When you are done making annotations, save the annotated document; if appropriate, you can then route it to another user for additional review and comments.

When you want to review all the annotations in a document or focus on the input of a single reviewer, select View | Annotations. The default choice is All Reviewers, but you can specify the name of a specific reviewer if you want. Select the Close button when you are finished reviewing the annotations. Another way to review annotations is to use the Go To option in the Edit menu to locate an annotation. Select Annotation and the reviewer's name if you are looking for a particular reviewer's comment, and select Next until you locate the comment you are looking for.

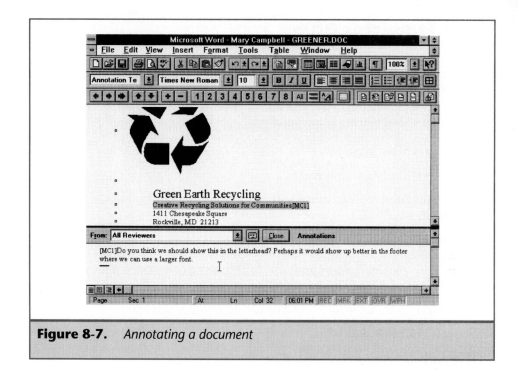

Figure 8-7.   *Annotating a document*

Chapter 4 provides specific information on topics such as creating and reviewing audio annotations, editing annotations, deleting annotations, and printing annotations (see "Annotation"). If you have circulated several copies of a document and want to merge annotations and revisions, see also "Comparing Versions" in Chapter 4 for more information.

Templates

A *template* is a model for the creation of documents; use a template when you want to have consistent-looking documents when they are created by several members of a workgroup. Templates can provide preset formats, graphics, styles, macros, customized settings, and AutoText or glossary entries. Word provides templates for many common types of documents, but you can create your own or modify existing ones to improve productivity as well as consistency.

What Templates Offer

In most manufacturing operations, a mold or template is used to create parts that are needed to complete the items being produced. Using the mold insures uniformity and is much faster than fashioning each piece by hand. The same is true for documents created with Word templates. Some of the specific things you can set up in a template are listed here:

- Document margins
- A specialized header or footer
- A customized toolbar, containing buttons needed for the tasks in this document
- Macros
- A letter closing, or letterhead with a logo
- Columns with graphics in specific locations
- Custom styles for level 1 and 2 headings, or other elements
- Special keyboard settings
- AutoText entries available to all users

Using or Modifying Existing Word Templates

Every time you open a new document without selecting a specific template, the document will automatically use Word's NORMAL.DOT template. If you create macros and styles while using this template they will be available in all documents using the template. This general-purpose template can be used to create a short report or menu, but you may find that some of the specialized templates have special settings or features which make creating documents with special requirements easier.

To use an existing template, select File | New, select the Document option button, and then choose a template from the Template box and select OK. If the template uses a Word wizard, a series of dialog boxes will prompt you for the information needed to complete the document. Otherwise, the template will be available for entries directly in the document editing window. You can make your entries and save the document under any name you wish.

You might find a Word template that comes close to meeting your needs but wish you could change a few features. This is easy to do. Just retrieve the template file (.DOT file), make your changes, and save the template again. If you want to keep the original template available, be sure to save the modified one with the File | Save As command and specify a new name. Follow these steps to retrieve and modify an existing template:

1. Choose Open from the File menu.

2. Select List Files of Type, and select the .DOT files from the list box.

3. From the Directories list box, choose the directory for the templates.

    In the default Word for Windows 6 installation, the templates are in WINWORD6\TEMPLATE on the drive where you installed Word. If you changed the location for the templates, you will need to revise the directory name accordingly.

4. Select the name of the template from the File Name list box.

5. Make your modifications to the template, adding formatting, creating macros, adding text, or otherwise customizing the template.

6. Select File | Save As and type a new name for the file before pressing ENTER.

Figure 8-8 shows the LETTER1.DOT template provided by Word, saved as SMITH.DOT and with modifications made to the company name and address, as well as the letter closing. Making this change in the template will save time for Mr. Smith's secretary, who will then not need to make these modifications when using the template to create future letters. Some templates have macros attached to them that create dialog boxes and step the user through needed responses. Others, such as LETTER1.DOT in Figure 8-8, require the user to select each variable item and type new text to replace it.

NOTE: The Options dialog box, opened by selecting Tools | Options allows you to select the Locations tab to specify a location for both User Templates and Workgroup Templates.

Creating Your Own Word Templates

You may have a newsletter heading or a proposal outline that you feel would make a good template. To create a template from the current document, all you need to do is select File | Save As, type a filename, and select Document Template in the Save File As Type text box. Select OK, and Word will save the document in the correct directory with a .DOT extension.

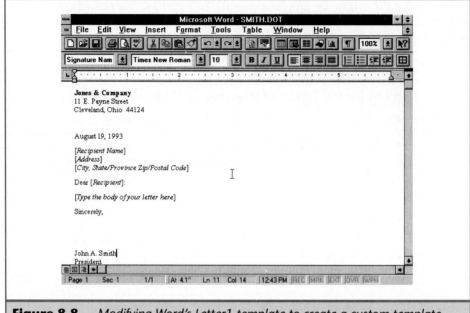

Figure 8-8.   *Modifying Word's Letter1 template to create a custom template*

Routing Documents with Microsoft Mail

You can route documents among network users and remote users who have a copy of Microsoft Mail Remote installed on their machines. For more information on routing a document with Microsoft Mail, see the discussion under "Network Options" earlier in this chapter.

THE
COMPLETE

REFERENCE

PART **FOUR**

Appendices

APPENDIX A

Installing Word for Windows 6

Installing Word for Windows 6 is a very easy process. The Microsoft Word 6.0 Setup program takes care of most of the questions that might come up when installing Word. However, Setup does offer several variations that let you customize how Word is installed on your system.

While you need to make a best guess on how to install Word on your system, how Word is installed can be changed. You can later restart Word to reinstall updated sections, to install features you did not originally install or to remove features.

Hardware Requirements

Before you can install Word for Windows, you need to make sure that you can use it on your computer. Word's minimum requirements are given in the table below. While you need at least the minimum requirements, there is no restriction about having more than the minimum. The better your computer and its resources, the better Word will run for you.

Microprocessor	An 80286 or higher compatible chip
Disks	A 1.2 MB or higher floppy disk drive and a hard drive
Operating software	DOS 3.1 and Windows 3.1
RAM	4 MB
Monitor	EGA

You do not actually need a mouse or a printer to run Word. However, a mouse makes working with Word for Windows much easier. If you do not have a printer you cannot, of course, easily print your documents.

Hard Disk Space Requirements

You can customize which aspects and features of Word you want to install to make the maximum use of the disk space you have available. If you have no reason to use a feature, simply do not install it, and save that hard disk space for other purposes.

Word	5396 KB
Applets	2585 KB
Graph	837 KB
Equation Editor	594 KB
WordArt	1154 KB
Proofing Tools	2699 KB
Spelling	336 KB
Hyphenation	72 KB
Thesaurus	755 KB
Grammar	1536 KB
Converters, Filters, and Data Access	7651 KB

Text Converters	2193 KB
Graphic Filters	1137 KB
Data Access (ODBC)	4620 KB
Online Help, Examples, and Demos	4837 KB
Examples and Demos	1376 KB
Word Help	1964 KB
WordBasic Help	1036 KB
Help for WordPerfect Users	164 KB
PSS Help	48 KB
Word Readme Help	104 KB
Wizards, Templates, and Letters	3584 KB
Templates and Wizards	2692 KB
Letters	332 KB
Macro Template	560 KB
Tools	1160 KB
Macro Tools	104 KB
MS Info	40 KB
Setup	1016 KB
Clip art	1080 KB

Installing Word for Windows 6

1. In the Windows Program Manager, select File | Run.

2. Enter **a:\setup** and select OK. (If you are using a different drive, substitute the correct designation.)

3. Microsoft Word 6.0 Setup prompts you to close all other applications before selecting OK. You need to close other applications because Setup restarts Windows later, and because Setup changes settings that may be in use by other applications. To close other applications, switch to the other application by pressing CTRL+ESC and selecting it or pressing ALT+TAB until you move to it. Close the application as you would normally. When you are done, only the Program Manager and Setup should be open.

4. Enter your name and your company's name and select OK.

5. Setup displays your serial number. Before selecting OK, copy it down somewhere that makes it easy to retrieve later (for example, inside your User's Manual).

6. Setup asks you to confirm the directory Word is installed into, C:\WINWORD. Select OK to use this directory.

   To use another directory, select Change Directory, then select a directory, and then select OK. If you select a nonexistent directory, Word asks if you want to create it. Select Yes, then OK.

7. Setup offers you three choices for installing Word.

   ■ *Typical*   Takes 15 MBs of hard disk space and includes the more commonly used Word features.

   ■ *Complete/Custom*   Takes up to 28 MBs of hard disk space and lets you install any features you select.

   ■ *Laptop* (Minimum)   Takes 6 MBs of hard disk space and includes only Word, the spelling checker, and the Readme Help file.

   If you do not select Complete/Custom, skip to step 9.

8. After selecting Complete/Custom, you can choose the features to install. Select or clear feature check boxes in the Options list box. When you are finished, select Continue.

   You can include some features by highlighting the check box, selecting Change Option, then selecting or clearing check boxes for the specific features and selecting OK.

   TIP: See "Hard Disk Space Requirements" earlier in this appendix for a complete list of how much hard disk space each option uses.

9. Choose the program group in the Program Manager that the Word for Windows' program icons will appear in by: selecting one from the Existing Groups list box, or typing a name for a new one in the Program Group text box. Then select Continue.

   By default, Setup installs these icons in the Microsoft Office program group, creating it if necessary.

10. Word asks if you want to provide help on features each time you press keys used in WordPerfect. Select Yes if you do want this set up. No is the default.

11. Exchange disks when Setup prompts you to.

12. When Setup is done, it prompts you to close all other applications before it restarts Windows. Select Continue. Setup restarts Windows to make the default setting changes in Windows active.

Updating Word

You can restart Setup in order to change which features are installed. You can also update features if Microsoft sends you update disks, install features you did not originally install, or remove features you've found you never use.

To use Setup again:

1. Select the Word Setup program item, or start Setup using File | Run from the Program Manager. The Setup application file should be in the directory that contains the Word for Windows application file.

2. Select the option that matches what you need to do with Word.

   ■ *Add/Remove* Opens the dialog box for selecting Word components. Select the options you want to install, or clear those you want to remove, and select Continue.

   ■ *Install Again* Reinstalls Word using the same settings you used originally. Replaces files that were accidentally deleted or altered.

   ■ *Remove All* Uninstalls Word, deleting all files and changing the Windows default settings back. Setup asks you to confirm that you want to do this.

APPENDIX B

Switching from WordPerfect to Word for Windows

WordPerfect is one of the most widely used word processors. If you have been using WordPerfect 5.1 or 6 for DOS and are ungrading to Word for Windows you will find many differences. This appendix outlines some of the major differences and also provides a feature conversion list to make it easy to locate the Word command that you can use to complete a familiar WordPerfect task.

One of the major differences between WordPerfect and Word is that Word does not have a Reveal Codes screen. WordPerfect is a *text-based* word processor, which means that if you look at a WordPerfect file, it is basically a long string of words, interspersed with codes. Codes indicate exactly where different formats are supposed to be turned on and off. You can basically think of codes as special-purpose characters, and work with them that way in the Reveal Codes screen.

> *TIP: Word for Windows provides some special help for WordPerfect users to make the transition easier. You can choose WordPerfect Help from the Help menu when you need assistance.*

Word is a *paragraph-based* word processor. You never see codes for formatting because formatting is not applied as part of the text. In a sense, the text of your Word document is saved in once place, and the map indicating where all of the formats are applied is stored in another. You never directly move or change the "codes" that apply formatting. For an old WordPerfect user, this is confusing because you cannot simply open Reveal Codes and see where all the formatting is applied. However, it does mean that you do not have to worry, in the same way, about where your insertion point is when you change a formatting setting. For example, if you want to change margins for your entire document, you don't need to go back to the beginning of your document, delete the old margins code, and insert a new one. Instead, you just change the setting, and Word knows to apply it to the entire document.

Codes are selected somewhat differently in Word for Windows than in WordPerfect. In WordPerfect, the primary method of accessing commands is to use the function keys. In Word for Windows, like most other Windows applications, you use the menu bar and the toolbars. Also, though Word offers all the same features as WordPerfect, you may have difficulty finding them since many have different names. The following chart indicates the equivalent Word commands for most WordPerfect features.

> *TIP: If you are very familiar with the WordPerfect function keys and don't want to have to change, consider creating a new keyboard which assigns the equivalent commands to those keys. This is one way in which Word is more flexible than WordPerfect.*

WP Feature	WP Key	Word Menu Command
Block	ALT+F4	Select text by pressing SHIFT and the movement keys or dragging across it
Bold	F6	Format | Font | Font | Font Style | Bold
Cancel	F1	ESC
Center	SHIFT+F6	Format | Paragraph | Indents and Spacing | Alignment | Center

WP Feature	WP Key	Word Menu Command
Columns/Table	ALT+F7	Format	Columns or Table	Insert Table
Copy	CTRL+F4	Edit	Copy and Edit	Paste or drag selected text while holding the CTRL key
Date/Outline	SHIFT+F5	View	Outline or Insert	Date and Time
End Field	F9	Data sources are set up differently in Word, there is no equivalent command because there is no end field code
Exit	F7	File	Exit
Flush Right	ALT+F6	Format	Paragraph	Alignment	Right
Font	CTRL+F8	Format	Font	Font	Font
Footnotes	CTRL+F7	Insert	Footnote
Format	SHIFT+F8	Any of the options on the Format toolbar and File	Page Setup
Graphics	ALT+F9	Insert	Picture
Help	F3	F1
Indent Left & Right	SHIFT+F4	Format	Paragraph	Indents and Spacing	Left and Right
Indent Right	F4	Format	Paragraph	Indents and Spacing	Right
List	F5	File	Find File
Macro	ALT+F10	Tools	Macro
Macro Define	CTRL+F10	Tools	Macro	Record
Margin Release	SHIFT+TAB	Format	Paragraphs	Indents and Spacing	Right
Mark Text	ALT+F5	Edit	Index and Tables	*select a tab*	Mark Text
Merge Codes	SHIFT+F9	Tools	Mail Merge
Merge/Sort	CTRL+F9	Tools	Mail Merge or Table	Sort Text or Table
Move	CTRL+F4	Edit	Cut and Edit	Paste or drag selected text

WP Feature	WP Key	Word Menu Command
Print	SHIFT+F7	File	Print
Replace	ALT+F2	Edit	Replace
Retrieve	SHIFT+F10	File	Open, Insert	File or Insert	Database
Reveal Codes	ALT+F3	Since Word does not use codes, there is no equivalent
Save	F10	File	Save or Save As
Screen	CTRL+F3	Any option on the View menu
Search Backwards	SHIFT+F2	Edit	Find
Search Forward	F2	Edit	Find
Setup	SHIFT+F1	Tools	Customize or Tools	Options
Shell	CTRL+F1	CTRL+ESC for the Task Manager or ALT+TAB to move to another application
Spell	CTRL+F2	Tools	Spelling
Style	ALT+F8	Format	Style
Switch	SHIFT+F3	Window	and a number for the correct window
Tab Align	CTRL+F6	Format	Tabs
Text In/Out	CTRL+F5	Insert	File or File	Open and File	Save or Save As
Thesaurus	ALT+F1	Tools	Thesaurus
Underline	F8	Format	Font	Font	Underline

APPENDIX C

Word for Windows 6 Buttons

Word for Windows 6 offers many different toolbars that serve as shortcuts for creating your documents. You will find it easy to become confused about why you should use a specific toolbar, or what that toolbar offers. Tables C-1 through C-18 list all of the available toolbar buttons, including those which do not appear on any of the default toolbars, but which can be used to create your own toolbars.

Button	Button Name	Purpose
	New	Opens a new document using the Normal template
	Open	Displays the Open dialog box for opening files
	Save	Saves files or displays the Save dialog box
	Print	Prints the document with the default settings
	Print Preview	Switches to Print Preview
	Spelling	Checks the spelling in the document
	Cut	Deletes the selected text after copying it to the Clipboard
	Copy	Copies the selected text to the Clipboard
	Paste	Copies the Clipboard's contents into the document
	Format Painter	Copies the format of the selected text to the next selected text
	Undo	Lets you select the actions to undo
	Redo	Lets you select the actions to redo
	AutoFormat	Automatically formats your document
	Insert AutoText	Inserts an AutoText entry for the name in the document
	Insert Table	Inserts a table with the specified rows and columns

Table C-1. *Standard Toolbar*

Button	Button Name	Purpose
	Insert Microsoft Excel Worksheet	Inserts a worksheet created by Excel as a table
	Columns	Reformats the current section as a specified number of equal-width columns
	Drawing	Displays the Drawing toolbar
	Insert Chart	Opens the Graph application so you can create and embed a chart
	Show/Hide	Toggles between displaying or hiding nonprinting characters
100%	Zoom Control	Sets the magnification used to display the document
	Help	Provides help on a feature when you select a button or command, or tells you the current formatting for text you select

Table C-1.   *Standard Toolbar* (continued)

Button	Button Name	Purpose
Normal	Style	Lets you select a style to apply to the selected text
Times New Roman	Font	Lets you select a font to apply to the selected text
10	Font Size	Lets you select or enter a font size to apply to the selected text
B	Bold	Boldfaces the selected text

Table C-2.   *Formatting Toolbar*

Button	Button Name	Purpose
I	Italic	Italicizes the selected text
U	Underline	Underlines the selected text
(align left)	Align Left	Aligns the selected paragraphs with the left margin
(center)	Center	Centers the selected paragraphs between the margins
(align right)	Align Right	Aligns the selected paragraphs with the right margin
(justify)	Justify	Aligns the selected paragraphs with the left and right margins
(numbering)	Numbering	Makes the selected paragraphs a numbered list
(bullets)	Bullets	Makes the selected paragraphs a bulleted list
(decrease indent)	Decrease Indent	Moves the left indent of the selected paragraphs one tab stop to the left
(increase indent)	Increase Indent	Moves the left indent of the selected paragraphs one tab stop to the right
(borders)	Borders	Displays the Borders toolbar

Table C-2.   *Formatting Toolbar* (continued)

Button	Button Name	Purpose
¾ pt	Line Style	Lets you select the style of line to apply
(top border)	Top Border	Toggles a top border for the selection on and off

Table C-3.   *Borders Toolbar*

Button	Button Name	Purpose
	Bottom Border	Toggles a bottom border for the selection on and off
	Left Border	Toggles a border on the left of the selection on and off
	Right Border	Toggles a border on the right of the selection on and off
	Inside Border	Toggles a border between cells or paragraphs on and off
	Outside Border	Toggles a border outside the table, selected cells, or paragraphs on and off
	No Border	Removes all borders
☐ Clear	Shading	Lets you select a shading to apply to the selected paragraphs or cells

Table C-3. *Borders Toolbar (continued)*

Button	Button Name	Purpose
	Data Form	Lets you update a delimited list or table using a Data Form dialog box
	Manage Fields	Lets you add or delete a field from a database
	Add New Record	Adds a new record to the database
	Delete Record	Removes a record from the database
	Sort Ascending	Sorts from A to Z or 1 to 9

Table C-4. *Database Toolbar*

Button	Button Name	Purpose
	Sort Descending	Sorts from Z to A or 9 to 1
	Insert Database	Inserts data from another file into the current document
	Update Fields	Updates all fields in the current document
	Find Record	Finds a record containing specified data
	Mail Merge Main Document	Switches to the main document the current document is assigned to

Table C-4.   *Database Toolbar* (continued)

Button	Button Name	Purpose
	Line	Creates a line drawing object
	Rectangle	Creates a rectangle drawing object
	Ellipse	Creates an ellipse (oval or circle) drawing object
	Arc	Creates an arc drawing object
	Freeform	Creates a freeform drawing object
	Text Box	Creates a text box drawing object
	Callout	Creates a callout drawing object

Table C-5.   *Drawing Toolbar*

Button	Button Name	Purpose
	Format Callout	Formats a callout drawing object
	Fill Color	Sets the fill color of a drawing object
	Line Color	Sets the color of a drawing object's lines
	Line Style	Sets the style of a drawing object's lines
	Select Drawing Objects	Changes the mouse pointer so you can select drawing objects
	Bring to Front	Places the selected object over other objects
	Send to Back	Places the selected object behind other objects
	Bring in Front of Text	Places the selected object over the document text
	Send Behind Text	Places the selected object behind the document text
	Group	Groups the selected objects into one object
	Ungroup	Breaks the selected objects back into their component objects
	Flip Horizontal	Flips the right and left of the selected object
	Flip Vertical	Flips the top and bottom of the selected object
	Rotate Right	Rotates the selected object so it's right becomes it's bottom
	Reshape	Lets you reshape a freeform object

Table C-5. *Drawing Toolbar* (continued)

Button	Button Name	Purpose
	Snap to Grid	Lets you set a grid for aligning objects
	Align Drawing Objects	Aligns the selected objects
	Create Picture	Opens a window and lets you create a picture
	Insert Frame	Inserts a frame

Table C-5.   *Drawing Toolbar* (continued)

Button	Button Name	Purpose
	Text Form Field	Inserts a Text form field
	Check Box Form Field	Inserts a Check Box form field
	Drop-Down Form Field	Inserts a Drop-Down form field
	Form Field Options	Lets you set the options for the selected form field
	Insert Table	Inserts a table with the specified rows and columns
	Insert Frame	Inserts an empty frame or frames the selected data

Table C-6.   *Forms Toolbar*

Button	Button Name	Purpose
	Form Field Shading	Toggles between shading and not shading the form fields
	Protect Form	Protects the document against changes

Table C-6.   *Forms Toolbar (continued)*

Button	Button Name	Purpose
	Microsoft Excel	Starts or switches to Microsoft Excel
	Microsoft PowerPoint	Starts or switches to Microsoft PowerPoint
	Microsoft Mail	Starts or switches to Microsoft Mail
	Microsoft Access	Starts or switches to Microsoft Access
	Microsoft FoxPro	Starts or switches to Microsoft FoxPro
	Microsoft Project	Starts or switches to Microsoft Project
	Microsoft Schedule+	Starts or switches to Microsoft Schedule+
	Microsoft Publisher	Starts or switches to Microsoft Publisher

Table C-7.   *Microsoft Toolbar*

Button	Button Name	Purpose
	New	Opens a new document using the Normal template
	Open	Displays the Open dialog box for opening files
	Save	Saves files or displays the Save dialog box
	Cut	Deletes the selected text after copying it to the Clipboard
	Copy	Copies the selected text to the Clipboard
	Paste	Copies the Clipboard's contents into the document
	Undo	Lets you select the actions to undo
	Numbering	Makes the selected paragraphs a numbered list
	Bullets	Makes the selected paragraphs a bulleted list
	Decrease Indent	Moves the left indent of the selected paragraphs one tab stop to the left
	Increase Indent	Moves the left indent of the selected paragraphs one tab stop to the right
	Insert Table	Inserts a table with the specified rows and columns
	Columns	Reformats the current section as the specified number of equal-width columns
	Insert Frame	Inserts a frame
	Drawing	Displays the Drawing toolbar

Table C-8.   *Word for Windows 2 Toolbar (in Word for Windows 6.0)*

Button	Button Name	Purpose
	Insert Chart	Opens the Graph application so you can create and embed a chart
	Create Envelope	Sets up an envelope for the current document
	Spelling	Checks the spelling in the document
	Print	Prints the document with the default settings
	One Page	Changes the view to Page Layout, showing the entire page
	Zoom 100%	Displays the document at full size
	Zoom Page Width	Zooms the document so you can see both sides of the page

Table C-8. *Word for Windows 2 Toolbar (in Word for Windows 6.0)* (continued)

Button	Button Name	Purpose
	Promote	Makes the selected heading one level higher
	Demote	Makes the selected heading one level lower
	Demote to Body Text	Makes the selected heading body text
	Move Up	Moves the selected heading up in the outline
	Move Down	Moves the selected heading down in the outline

Table C-9. *Outline Toolbar*

Button	Button Name	Purpose
+	Expand	Shows lower level headings and body text under the current heading
−	Collapse	Hides lower level headings and body text under the current heading
1	Show Heading 1	Shows only level one headings in the document
2	Show Heading 2	Shows through second level headings in the document
3	Show Heading 3	Shows through third level headings in the document
4	Show Heading 4	Shows through fourth level headings in the document
5	Show Heading 5	Shows through fifth level headings in the document
6	Show Heading 6	Shows through sixth level headings in the document
7	Show Heading 7	Shows through seventh level headings in the document
8	Show Heading 8	Shows through eighth level headings in the document
All	All	Shows all headings in the outline
≡	Show First Line Only	Toggles between showing all body text and only the first line
AA	Show Formatting	Toggles between showing formatting or using a draft font
▤	Master Document View	Opens the Master Document toolbar

Table C-9.   *Outline Toolbar* (continued)

Button	Button Name	Purpose
	Print	Prints the document with the default settings
	Magnifier	Toggles the mouse between zoom in/out and normal mode
	One Page	Zooms the document to show the entire page
	Multiple Pages	Zooms the document to show the specified number of pages
34%	Zoom Control	Sets the magnification used to display the document
	View Ruler	Shows or hides the vertical and horizontal rulers
	Shrink to Fit	Changes formatting slightly to use one less page
	Full Screen	Displays the document using the full screen
Close	Close	Returns to the previous view
	Help	Provides help on a feature when you select a button or command, or tells you the current formatting for text you select

Table C-10. *Print Preview Toolbar*

Button	Button Name	Purpose
	Switch Between Header and Footer	Moves between the current header and footer
	Show Previous	Shows the header or footer of the previous section

Table C-11. *Header and Footer Toolbar*

Button	Button Name	Purpose
	Show Next	Shows the header or footer of the next section
	Same as Previous	Links the current header or footer to the previous section's header and footer
	Page Numbers	Inserts a field which displays the page number
	Date	Inserts a field which displays the current date
	Time	Inserts a field which displays the current time
	Page Setup	Opens the Page Setup dialog box
	Show/Hide Document Text	Hides or displays document text
Close	Close	Returns to the document text

Table C-11.   *Header and Footer Toolbar* (continued)

Button	Button Name	Purpose
Insert Merge Field	Insert Merge Field	Lets you select a merge field to insert
Insert Word Field	Insert Word Field	Lets you select a Word field to insert
« » ABC	View Merged Data	Toggles between showing codes and data from the data source

Table C-12.   *Mail Merge Toolbar*

Button	Button Name	Purpose
	First Record	Displays the first record
	Previous Record	Displays the previous record
	Go to Record	Lets you enter the record to display
	Next Record	Displays the next record
	Last Record	Displays the last record
	Mail Merge Helper	Opens the Mail Merge Helper dialog box
	Check for Errors	Runs the merge, checking for errors and creating no output
	Merge to New Document	Runs the merge, storing the merged document in a new document
	Merge to Printer	Runs the merge, sending the merged document to the printer
	Mail Merge	Opens the Merge dialog box letting you set merge options
	Find Record	Finds a record in the data source that contains the specified data
	Edit Data Source	Displays the Data Form dialog box for editing the data source

Table C-12. *Mail Merge Toolbar* (continued)

Button	Button Name	Purpose
	Create Subdocument	Makes the selected headings into a subdocument
	Remove Subdocument	Makes the selected subdocument part of the main document
	Insert Subdocument	Opens a file and inserts it as a subdocument
	Merge Subdocument	Combines the selected subdocuments into a single subdocument
	Split Subdocument	Splits the current subdocument into two documents at the insertion point location
	Lock Document	Locks or unlocks the document for editing

Table C-13. *Master Document Toolbar*

Button	Button Name	Purpose
Logo	Active Macro	Selects which macro is the active macro that is controlled by the buttons on the Macro toolbar
	Record	Records the commands you select and adds them to the macro
	Record Next Command	Records the next command you select and adds it to the macro

Table C-14. *Macro Toolbar*

Button	Button Name	Purpose
▶	Start	Runs the macro
▷	Trace	Runs the macro and highlights each statement as the statement is performed
‖	Continue	Continues macro execution
■	Stop	Halts macro execution
	Step	Goes through the macro one statement at a time
	Step Subs	Goes through the macro one subroutine at a time
	Show Variables	Shows the variables in a macro when you are running a macro so you can see their current value
	Add/Remove REM	Adds and removes REM from the selected lines to convert statements into remarks
	Macro	Displays the Macro dialog box that the Tools I Macro command displays
	Dialog Editor	Starts the Dialog Editor application to create a dialog box the macro uses

Table C-14.   *Macro Toolbar (continued)*

The following buttons can be used to create new toolbars, but do not actually appear in any of the default toolbars. These are buttons you will see when you select Tools I Customize and the Toolbars tab.

Button	Button Name	Purpose
	Close	Closes the current document
	Find File	Finds a file on your system
	Send Mail	Sends an electronic mail message
	Routing Slip	Adds an electronic mail routing slip to your document
	Repeat	Repeats your last action
	Find	Finds text or formatting in your document
	Zoom Control	Lets you select the zoom for your document
	View Field Codes	Toggles between showing field codes or results
	Insert Footnote	Inserts a footnote reference at the insertion point
	WordArt	Starts WordArt
	Equation	Starts the Equation Editor
	Insert Sound Object	Inserts a sound stored in a file or that you create by recording
	Pen Annotation	Inserts a text annotation at the current location
	Double Underline	Double underlines the selected text
	Word Underline	Underlines text but not spaces

Table C-15.   *Miscellaneous Buttons*

Button	Button Name	Purpose
ABC	Strikethrough	Applies strikethrough to the selected text
ABC	Small Caps	Makes the selected text small capitals
A	All Caps	Makes the selected text all capitals
=	Single Space	Single spaces the selected paragraphs
=	1.5 Space	One and a half spaces the selected paragraphs
=	Double Space	Double spaces the selected paragraphs
A≡	Drop Cap	Makes the first letter of the paragraph a dropped capital
x^2	Superscript	Superscripts the selected text
x_2	Subscript	Subscripts the selected text
	Compare Versions	Compares the current document to a previous version
	Review Revisions	Lets you accept or reject revisions made to your document
	Insert Cells	Adds cells to a table
	Insert Rows	Adds rows to a table
	Insert Columns	Adds columns to a table

Table C-15.   *Miscellaneous Buttons* (continued)

Button	Button Name	Purpose
	Delete Cells	Removes cells from a table
	Delete Rows	Removes rows from a table
	Delete Columns	Removes columns from a table
	Table Gridlines	Toggles displaying table gridlines on and off
	Table AutoFormat	Applies a standard format to the table
	AutoSum	Inserts a formula field that sums a row or column
	New Window	Opens a new window for the current document
	Arrange All	Arranges all open documents so you can see all of them
	Open Subdocument	Opens a subdocument from a master document
	Split Window	Splits the window into two panes
	Disassemble Picture	Splits a metafile into its component drawing objects
	Rounded Rectangle	Creates a rounded rectangle drawing object
	Send Backward	Puts the selected object behind the object just behind it
	Bring Forward	Puts the selected object on top of the object above it

Table C-15.   *Miscellaneous Buttons* (continued)

Button	Button Name	Purpose
	Reset Picture Boundary	Eliminates white space in a picture
	Rotate Left	Rotates the selected object so its left becomes its bottom

Table C-15. *Miscellaneous Buttons* (continued)

The following are some buttons which are not assigned any particular task. When creating your own toolbars you can assign any task to these buttons.

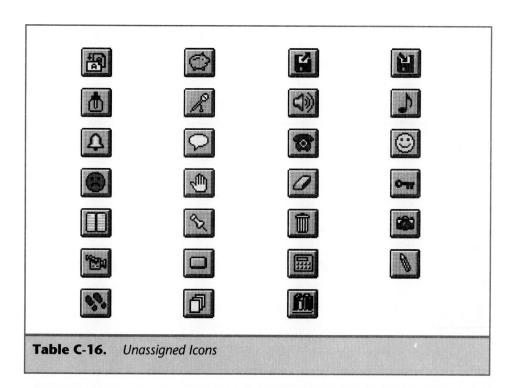

Table C-16. *Unassigned Icons*

Word's secondary applications use toolbars for their features. In the Equation Editor, the toolbar buttons have no names, but insert different mathematical symbols and templates. In WordArt, the toolbar buttons format how the text appears.

Button	Inserts
≤ ≠ ≈	Relational symbols such as "not equals" or "approximately"
⅄ a͟b ∵	Spaces and ellipses
ẋ ȧ ä	Embellishments such as primes and arrows
± • ⊗	Draws mathematical operators such as • and division signs
→ ⇔ ↓	Arrows
∴ ∀ ∃	Logical symbols
∉ ∩ ⊂	Set theory symbols
∂ ∞ ℓ	Miscellaneous symbols such as infinity and the degree symbol
λ ω θ	Lowercase Greek letter
Λ Ω ⊕	Uppercase Greek letter
(ⁱⁱ) [ⁱⁱ]	Templates to put entries inside parentheses, braces, and brackets
⅜ √⎕	Templates for fractions and radicals
▦ ⎕	Templates to include superscript and/or subscript slots

Table C-17.   *Equation Editor Toolbar*

Button	Inserts
$\Sigma_{\square}^{\square}$ $\Sigma_{\square}^{\square}$	Templates for summation with possible superscript and subscript slots
$\int_{\square}^{\square}$ $\oint_{\square}^{\square}$	Templates for integrals with possible superscript and subscript slots
☐ ☐	Templates for underbar and overbar slots
→ ←	Templates for underarrow and overarrow slots
☐̇ ☐̇	Templates for products and set theory expressions
▫▫▫ ▦	Templates for matrices

Table C-17. *Equation Editor Toolbar (continued)*

Button		Purpose
— Plain Text	⬇	Lets you select a shape for the text to fill
Arial	⬇	Lets you select a font to use for the text
Best Fit	⬇	Lets you select a font size
B		Boldfaces the text
I		Italicizes the text
Ee		Makes all letters the same height

Table C-18. *WordArt 2.0 Toolbar Buttons*

Button	Purpose
	Flips the text on its side.
	Stretches the text to fill the space you created
	Selects an alignment for the text
	Lets you adjust the spacing between letters
	Lets you rotate the text
	Lets you set a color or pattern to fill the text
	Lets you choose a method of shadowing your text
	Lets you set a border for your WordArt box

Table C-18.   *WordArt 2.0 Toolbar Buttons* (continued)

APPENDIX D

Templates

Templates are molds for creating documents. Templates were made part of Word for Windows to allow you to create frequently used documents quickly. Templates give you a head start by providing a defined appearance. Some may even have some text already in them. You are, of course, free to add your own text and change any of the formatting that you want; the changes you make will affect the document, but will not alter the template from which it was created.

There are 40 different templates in Word for Windows 6 and 18 in Word for Windows 2. Some of these templates function as wizards and guide you through the needed entries.

The default template used for new documents is NORMAL.DOT if you do not select another one. The NORMAL.DOT template does not offer much in the way of formatting with only the basics in margins and character appearance and does not contain any text. It does offer some attached macros, styles, toolbars, and AutoText entries. In this appendix, you will have an opportunity to learn about each of the other templates offered by Word. You will learn which text is already stored in the template and the formatting which is part of the template.

Creating a Document from a Template

To use a template for a document, you merely select the template from the list of available ones when you open a new document.

1. Select File | New, opening the New dialog box.

   The Template list box lists all of the templates you can use for your new document. As you highlight the templates, a description appears in the bottom of the dialog box.

2. Select a template from the Template list box (Use Template in Word for Windows 2).

3. Select OK.

At this point, Word opens a new document using the template you have selected. This template provides the styles, macros, toolbars, and AutoText entries initially available in a document. If the template you select is a wizard, the template has macros that display dialog boxes. You can use the dialog boxes displayed by the wizard to control exactly how the document is created. When the macros finish executing, the wizard is finished and the newly created document is active on your screen. Most wizards set the template of the document the wizard creates to NORMAL.DOT when completed so you have all of the toolbar, macro, styles, and AutoText entries as most of your documents.

If you later change your mind about the template you want the document to use, you can change it. In Word for Windows 6, follow these steps:

1. Select File | Templates.

2. Select Attach to select a new template file.

3. Select a template file and OK.

4. Select OK.

Follow these steps if you are using Word for Windows 2:

1. Select File | Template.

2. Select a new template file from the Attach Document To drop-down list box.

3. Select OK.

A Look at Each of the Templates

Word for Windows 6 includes all of the templates listed in this section. For each template listed below there is a description of why you would use it and some of the styles and macros it offers.

TIP: *If you want help using the wizards, you can select help in the last Wizards dialog box. The help information you will see depends on the selected wizard.*

Agenda Wizard

This template is a wizard that creates an agenda for a meeting. Figure D-1 shows a document created with this wizard. Some of the customizing you can do through this wizard includes:

- Selecting the style of the agenda
- Inserting the date and time of the meeting
- Inserting the title and location of the meeting
- Setting headings for sections of the agenda
- Inserting names for people performing various duties at the meeting
- Setting a table of topics, who is responsible, and expected length
- Adding a form for recording minutes

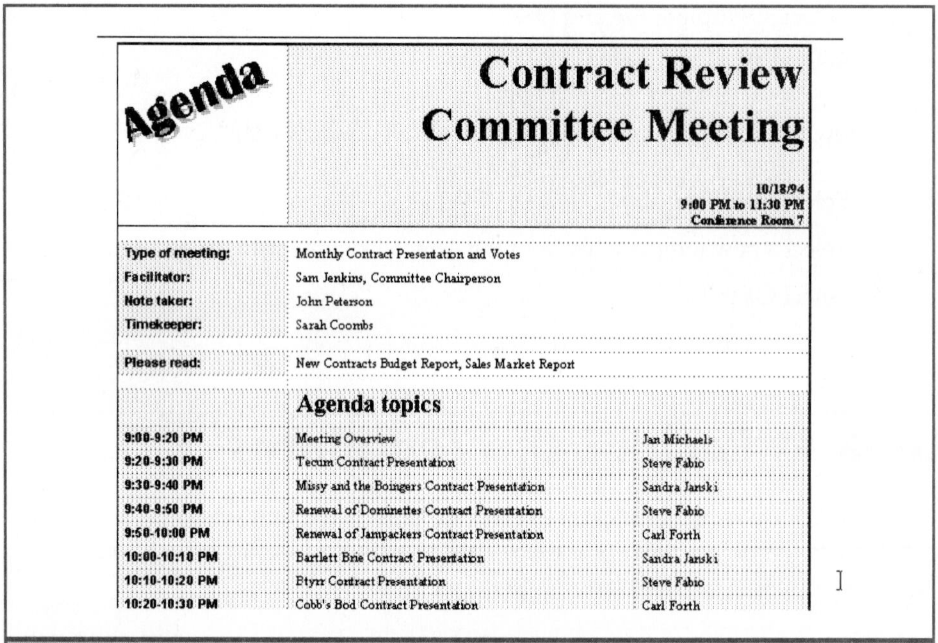

Agenda

Contract Review Committee Meeting

10/18/94
9:00 PM to 11:30 PM
Conference Room 7

Type of meeting:	Monthly Contract Presentation and Votes
Facilitator:	Sam Jenkins, Committee Chairperson
Note taker:	John Peterson
Timekeeper:	Sarah Coombs
Please read:	New Contracts Budget Report, Sales Market Report

Agenda topics

9:00-9:20 PM	Meeting Overview	Jan Michaels
9:20-9:30 PM	Tecum Contract Presentation	Steve Fabio
9:30-9:40 PM	Missy and the Boingers Contract Presentation	Sandra Janski
9:40-9:50 PM	Renewal of Dominettes Contract Presentation	Steve Fabio
9:50-10:00 PM	Renewal of Jampackers Contract Presentation	Carl Forth
10:00-10:10 PM	Bartlett Brie Contract Presentation	Sandra Janski
10:10-10:20 PM	Btyrr Contract Presentation	Steve Fabio
10:20-10:30 PM	Cobb's Bod Contract Presentation	Carl Forth

Figure D-1. *A meeting Agenda created with the Agenda Wizard*

Award Wizard

This template is a wizard that creates awards that you can use for anything from the employee of the month or top sales performer to the top average on your bowling team or the winner of the spelling bee at your son's school. Some of the customization options include:

- Selecting the style of text and border
- Selecting the orientation and whether the paper has its own border
- Inserting the recipient and title of award
- Inserting signatories and presenters
- Inserting date and reason for award

Brochur1 Template

This template is used to create a folded brochure. The brochure can be printed on one sheet and folded in thirds. Figure D-2 shows one side of a brochure created with this template. Most of the style names match the style names in the Normal template although several of their settings have changed. When you use the template, here are some things to keep in mind:

- The normal text will use the Body Text, Body Text Indent, or Body Text Keep (to keep the text with the next paragraph) styles. Headings use the same Heading 1 through Heading 9 styles that the Normal template has.

- Divide the document into three columns, assuming you will fold the paper into thirds. The first three columns appear on one side of the paper and the other three appear on the back. The column that appears in the front will be in the third column.

- You can purchase specialty paper just for brochures which is scored where the paper is folded. This paper may have designs where your brochure has empty space. Check your local paper suppliers for some of the different paper options available.

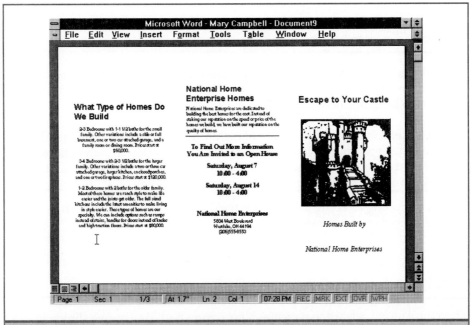

Figure D-2.   *A brochure created using the Brochur1 template*

TIP: *When you select the template from the Style Gallery, you can see an example of the styles available in the template by selecting* Example *under* Preview. *If you want to insert the sample into the document to see how it uses the styles available through the template, open a document using the template, select* Edit | AutoText, *select Gallery Example from the* Name *list box, and* Insert.

Calendar Wizard

This template is a wizard that creates monthly calendars. Some of the customization options include:

- Selecting the style of the calendar and placement of the days and months
- Selecting whether you want to include a picture (Word inserts CITYSCPE.WMF but you can change it to another picture)
- Selecting a portrait or landscape orientation for the calendar
- Setting the starting and ending month and year for the calendar so each month has its own page

Directr1 Template

This template is used to create directories. Most of the style names match those in the Normal template, although several of their settings have changed. When you use the template, here are some things to keep in mind:

- Each entry uses a combination of Name, Job Description, Company Name, and Address styles. Name boldfaces the text, Job Description italicizes and indents the text, Address shows the text using all capital letters, and Address includes the text without special formatting.
- Use Section Heading for dividing the directory into sections such as letters, states, or division.

Fax Wizard

This template is a wizard that creates a fax cover sheet like the one shown in Figure D-3. Some of the changes you can make while using the wizard include:

■ Setting page orientation

■ Selecting the style of text and placement of fax cover sheet items

■ Inserting your name, company, address, and phone numbers

Once you create the fax sheet you only need to enter the addressee's information, the number of pages, and any comments. This document is a form so you will notice that you can move to the check boxes in the form and press the SPACEBAR to select the ones you want.

Faxcovr1 and Faxcovr2 Templates

These templates create fax cover sheets using a classic or contemporary style. These are the same templates that the Fax Wizard uses when you select a classic

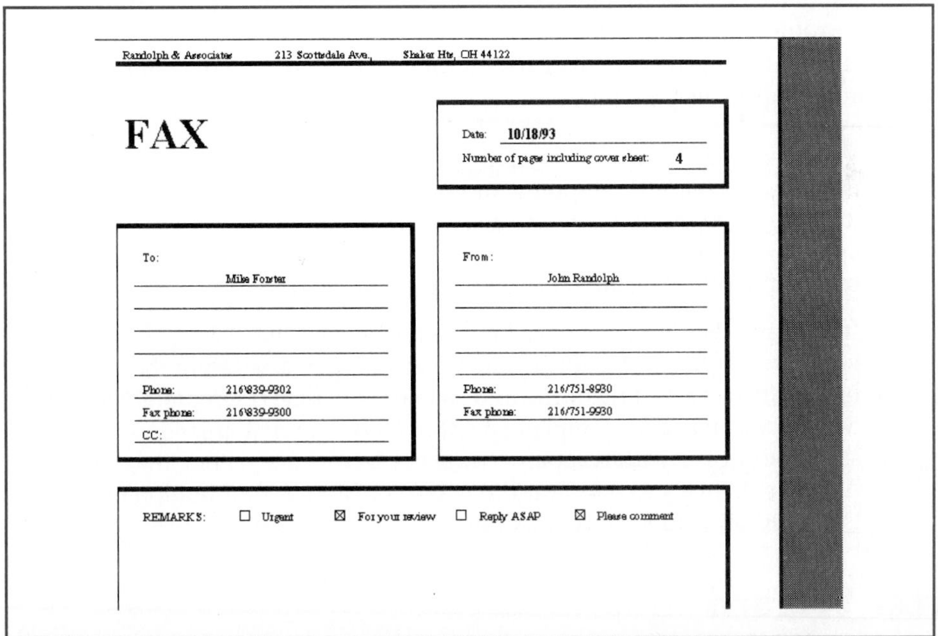

Figure D-3. *A fax cover letter created using the Fax Wizard*

or contemporary style for the appearance. When you use the template, here are some things to keep in mind:

■ When you open a document using this template, the document has text enclosed in brackets ([ ]), prompting you to supply information in that spot.

■ To replace the text prompts, use the Edit | Find command with \[*\] in the Find What text box and the Use Pattern Matching check box selected. This selects each segment of text surrounded by brackets and their surrounding brackets. When you type the replacement, the text and brackets disappear.

■ You can alter the fax cover sheet so it automatically contains the information that remains the same every time you fax. Then change the prompts for other information into form fields. Next, protect the document for forms. You can then save the document and make the document read-only with Windows' File Manager. Every time you need to create another fax cover sheet, you can open the document, fill in the form fields that change every time, and, if you want, save it to another document.

Invoice Template

This template creates an invoice form. It will do many of the basic computations such as multiplying the amount of each item ordered by its price and adding the amounts for all items for the invoice's subtotal. When you use the template, here are some things to keep in mind:

■ When you open a document using this template, the invoice has fields already set up for the shipping and ordering information as well as the items ordered. All you have to do is move to each form field and enter the appropriate information. When you are finished, print the invoice just like printing another document and save it if you want.

■ If you are planning to use this invoice form, open the INVOICE.DOT template, unprotect the form, make changes such as altering the company information, protect the form, and save the document template. Then the next time you use the template, it will include the customized version with such specifics as your company name in place of the generic information. Another change you may want to make is to add a computation for sales tax based on your locality's tax rate.

Letter Wizard

This template is a wizard that creates various types of letters. Some of the customization options include:

- Selecting one of several standard business letters that you can modify to fit your own purposes. (These letters are stored in the files in the LETTERS directory.)

- Setting up a document to use a layout appropriate for a standard business or personal letter.

- Selecting whether the letter uses stationery. (You may want to select Yes if you are going to add graphics to print as a letterhead.)

- Providing the addressee's address.

- Using the address.

- Selecting the font and indentation style.

- Creating an envelope or mailing label for the letter.

- Adding the date, page number, account or document identification, the writer's initials, typist's initials, CC for copies, number of enclosures, and whether any attachments are included.

Letter1, Letter2, and Letter3 Templates

These templates create letters using a classic, contemporary, or typewriter style. These are the same templates that the Letter Wizard uses when you select a classic, contemporary, or typewriter style for the letter's appearance. When you use the template, here are some things to keep in mind:

- When you open a document using this template, the document has text enclosed in brackets ([ ]), prompting you to supply information in that spot.

- To replace the text prompts, use the Edit | Find command with \[*\] in the Find What text box and the Use Pattern Matching check box selected. This selects each segment of text surrounded by brackets and its surrounding brackets. When you type the replacement, the text and brackets disappear.

- You can alter the form letter so it contains the information that remains the same every time, such as the return address and your name. After you save the modified version of LETTER1.DOT, LETTER2.DOT, or LETTER3.DOT, the next letter you create with the modified template will already contain the correct return address and name.

Manual Template

This template is for creating manuals with a table of contents, body text, and index. Most of the style names match those in the Normal template, although several of their settings have changed. When you use the template, here are some things to keep in mind:

- Use the styles such as Heading 1 through Heading 9 to automatically include the headings in the table of contents.

- The normal text will use the Body Text, Body Text Indent, or Body Text Keep (to keep the text with the next paragraph) styles.

Manuscr1 and Manuscr3 Templates

These templates create manuscripts using a classic or typewriter style. When you use the template, here are some things to keep in mind:

- The normal text will use the Body Text, Body Text Indent, or Body Text Keep (to keep the text with the next paragraph) styles.

- Most of the other styles you use when you create a document with either template have the same names as when you are creating the document from the Normal template, but they have a different appearance.

Memo Wizard

This template is a wizard that creates an interoffice memo. Some of the customization options include:

- Adding a title to the memo

- Using a separate page for the distribution list

- Inserting items in the memo's heading such as To, From, Date, CC, Subject, and Priority

- Inserting other text such as writer's initials, typist's initials, number of enclosures, and whether any attachments are included

- Inserting text for header including a title, date, and page number and text for a footer including the date, page number, and the word Confidential

- Setting the style of text and placement of items

Memo1, Memo2, and Memo3 Templates

These templates create memos using a classic, contemporary, or typewriter style. These are the same templates that the Memo Wizard uses when you select a classic, contemporary, or typewriter style for the memo's appearance. When you use the template, here are some things to keep in mind:

- When you open a document using this template, the document has text enclosed in brackets ([ ]), prompting you to supply information in that spot.

- When you work with the Memo Wizard, you will see more prompts than you see in the documents created by selecting File | New and the Memo1, Memo2, or Memo3 template. These prompts include the typist's initials, the author's initials, the number of enclosures, and an attachment notice. If you want these in your memo that you create by using one of these templates, you will have to type them yourself. This also applies to entering a header and footer.

- To replace the text prompts, use the Edit | Find command with \[*\] in the Find What text box and the Use Pattern Matching check box selected. This selects each segment of text surrounded by brackets and their surrounding brackets. When you type the replacement, the text and brackets disappear.

- You can alter the Memo1, Memo2, and Memo3 templates to change the [Names] prompt after From to your name since this is probably the same every time. After you save the modified version of MEMO1.DOT, MEMO2.DOT, or MEMO3.DOT, the next memo you create with the modified template will already contain the correct author.

Newslttr Wizard

This template is a wizard that creates newsletters like the one shown in Figure D-4. Some of the customization options include:

- Setting the character style and lines added to the newsletter

- Selecting the number of columns in the newsletter

- Inserting the newsletter name

- Setting whether the newsletter is printed on one or both sides of the paper

- Setting the number of pages in the newsletter

- Selecting whether the newsletter includes a table of contents, dropped capitals, the date, and volume and issue numbers

Figure D-4. *A newsletter created with the Newslttr Wizard*

Normal Template

This template is the default template. It includes many styles to fit varying tasks. These named styles include:

- Normal style, which is used for paragraphs unless you select another one.

- Styles for headers, footers, endnotes, and footnotes.

- Styles named Heading 1 through Heading 9 that automatically label headings in a document for outline levels and entries for a table of contents. The styles named TOC 1 through TOC 9 set the format of the entries in the table of contents. If a document has an index, Index 1 through Index 9 sets the format of index entries.

- Three styles for lists: List through List 5, List Bullet through List Bullet 5, and List Number through List Number 5. If you have list text you want indented the same amount use List Continue through List Continue 5. The five levels of the lists indicate how much the text is indented; the higher numbers are indented more.

- Named styles for addresses, including Closing and Signature.

- Other styles for title pages, such as Title and Subtitle.

- The Macro Text style, which sets the appearance of macros when you open a macro editing window.

 TIP: Try out the appearance of different templates using the Style Gallery available with the Format | Style Gallery command. When Document is selected under Preview, the Style Gallery shows the current document using the same styles as another template. Since each template can assign different appearance features to the same style name, you can easily try out another template.

Pleading Wizard

This template is a wizard that creates pleadings that are legal documents submitted to a court. Some of the customization options include:

- Setting the font, line spacing, and margins

- Adding a line on the sides of the pages

- Adding page numbers and line numbers

- Adding the attorney's name and address as well as setting its position

- Adding the name of the court

Present1 Template

This template is for creating presentations. It has many of the same style names as the Normal template, although the font size of many of the named styles are larger than their Normal template counterparts. Also, more styles center their text rather than use the left alignment that most Normal styles use.

Presrel1, Presrel2, and Presrel3 Templates

These templates create press releases using a classic, contemporary, or typewriter style. When you use the template, the following are some things to keep in mind:

■ When you open a document using this template, the document has text enclosed in brackets ([ ]), prompting you to supply information in that spot.

■ To replace the text prompts, use the Edit | Find command with \[*\] in the Find What text box and the Use Pattern Matching check box selected. This selects each segment of text surrounded by brackets and their surrounding brackets. When you type the replacement, the text and brackets disappear.

Purchord Template

This template creates a purchase order form. This form performs many of the basic computations such as multiplying the amount of each item ordered by its price and adding the amounts for all items for the subtotal. When you use the template, here are some things to keep in mind:

■ When you open a document using this template, the document is already set up as a form with fields for the shipping and ordering information as well as the items you are ordering. For each field, move to the field and type the information. When you are finished, print the invoice just like printing another document and save it if you want.

■ If you are planning to use this purchase order frequently, open the PURCHORD.DOT template, unprotect the form, make changes (such as to the company information), protect the form, and save the document template. Then the next time you use the template, the purchase order will include the customized information with such specifics as your company name.

Report1, Report2, and Report3 Templates

These templates create reports using a classic, contemporary, or typewriter style similar to the classic, contemporary, and typewriter styles that other templates use. The documents are initially empty but you can see the difference between these templates and the Normal template when you start assigning the text to different styles available in the template.

Resume Wizard

This template is a wizard that creates resumes like the one shown in Figure D-5. Some of the customization options include:

■ Creating a resume based on chronological experience, function, professional credentials, or for an entry level position

■ Adding the name, address, and phone number

■ Adding headings for objective, education, awards, interests, hobbies, languages, work experience, volunteer experience, hobbies, and references

■ Adding headings for extracurricular activities, summer jobs, summary of qualifications, community activities, professional memberships, accreditations and licenses, patents and publications, civil service grades, and security clearance

■ Arranging headings

■ Creating a cover letter by starting the Letter Wizard with Resume cover letter selected as the letter you want to create

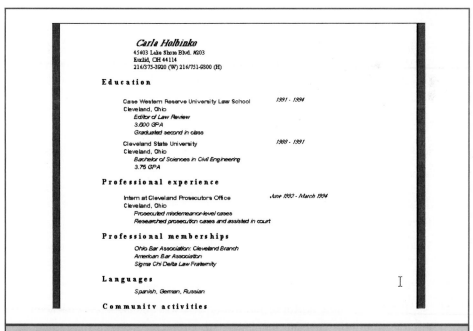

Figure D-5. *A resume created with the Resume Wizard*

Resume1, Resume2, and Resume4 Templates

These templates are for creating a resume using a classic, contemporary, or typewriter style. These are the same templates that the Resume Wizard uses when you select a classic, contemporary, or typewriter style for the appearance. When you use the template, here are some things to keep in mind:

- When you open a document using this template, the document has text enclosed in brackets ([ ]), prompting you to supply information in that spot.

- To replace the text prompts, use the Edit | Find command with \[*\] in the Find What text box and the Use Pattern Matching check box selected. This selects each segment of text surrounded by brackets and their surrounding brackets. When you type the replacement, the text and brackets disappear.

- The templates do not offer all of the choices you have when you use the Resume Wizard. For example, the Resume Wizard has more choices for sections within a resume and lets you change the order of the sections. When you want to have the most options, use the Resume Wizard instead.

Table Wizard

This template is a wizard that creates a table like the one shown in Figure D-6. The Table Wizard can also be started by selecting Wizard from the Insert Table dialog box that the Table | Insert Table command displays. Some of the customization options include:

- Selecting the line style for the table

- Selecting whether you have one or more rows used as table headings

- Selecting the number of columns

- Aligning the table headings and table entries

- Repeating table headings

- Adding table headings based on a regular series such as months, quarters, or years

- Setting the orientation of the table to portrait or landscape

- Displaying the Table AutoFormat dialog box so you can select character and paragraph formatting styles for the table

Sales	1994				1993				1992			
in millions	Q1	Q2	Q3	Q4	Q1	Q2	Q3	Q4	Q1	Q2	Q3	Q4
Division A	23	24.3	24.1	23.8	24.5	24.3	24.6	24.3	24.5	24.3	24.6	24.7
Division B	10	10.3	10.5	11	11.3	11.4	11.6	11.5	11.8	12	12.2	11.8
Division C	14.3	14.3	14.2	14.3	14.2	14.1	14.3	14.4	13.9	14.1	14.1	14.2
Total	47.3	48.9	48.8	49.1	50	49.8	50.5	50.2	50.2	50.4	50.9	50.7

Figure D-6. *A table created with the Table Wizard*

Thesis1 Template

This template is for creating a thesis. Most of the style names match those in the Normal template although several of their settings have changed. The difference between this template and the Normal template is the settings match the most common settings for theses. Use this template in place of Normal when you are creating a thesis.

Weektime Template

This template creates a weekly timesheet form which calculates total regular and overtime hours. When you use the template, here are some things to keep in mind:

■ When you open a document using this template, the document is a form. Thus, you can move from field to field, supplying the appropriate information. When you are finished, print the invoice just as you would any other document and save it if you want.

■ If you are planning to frequently use this form, open the WEEKTIME.DOT form, unprotect the form, make changes (such as to the company information), protect the form, and save the document template. Then the next time you use the template, it will show the customized version with such specifics as your company name in place of the generic information.

Altering a Template

Several of the templates mentioned in this chapter can be customized to fit your needs. For example, the Faxcovr1 and Faxcovr2 templates can be modified to include your name, address, and phone number. You can modify templates to assign different formatting to the styles a template provides. To change a template, follow these steps:

1. Select File | Open.

2. Select Document Templates (*.dot) under List Files of Type.

3. Select the template file to open and OK.

NOTE: Remember that the template files mentioned above are in the \TEMPLATE directory in the directory containing your Word program files.

4. Make the changes you want.

   If you modify the styles in a template, the modified style only changes documents you create afterwards. Documents that you created before using the template do not adopt the latest modifications.

5. Select File | Save to save the changes you have made to the template.

Creating Your Own Templates

You can create your own templates for specialized documents that you use repeatedly. To create a template, follow these steps:

1. Select File | New.

2. From the Template list box, select the template you want to use as the basis for the template you are creating. The template you are creating will have the same styles, toolbars, macros, and AutoText entries as the template you select in this step.

3. Select the Template option button and OK.

4. Make the changes you want, such as:

   ■ Using Format | Style to create new styles, modify existing ones, and delete the ones you do not want.

   ■ Adding text to the document template that you want to be in every document created with the template. For example, if you want every document created with the template to have the same header, add the header to the template.

   ■ Using the File | Summary Info command and typing the description for the title in order to have a description of the template appear when you highlight it in the New File dialog box.

5. Select File | Save to save the changes you have made to the template.

   You will want to save the template file in the \TEMPLATE directory in the directory containing your Word program files or in whatever directory you have put these files.

6. Type the name for the template and select OK.

Index

B

D

G

I

J

K

L

M

U

V